HANDBOOK OF NEUROPSYCHOLOGY

HANDBOOK OF NEUROPSYCHOLOGY

Series Editors

FRANÇOIS BOLLER

Department of Neurology, University of Pittsburgh, Pittsburgh, PA, U.S.A.,
and Centre Paul Broca, Paris, France

and

JORDAN GRAFMAN

Medical Neurology Branch, NINCDS, Bethesda, MD, U.S.A.

ELSEVIER

Amsterdam – New York – Oxford

HANDBOOK OF NEUROPSYCHOLOGY

Section Editors

H. GOODGLASS
A.R. DAMASIO

VOLUME 2

1990

ELSEVIER

Amsterdam – New York – Oxford

Preface

In recent years there has been an enormous increase in interest in disorders of higher cortical functions and in brain-behavior relationships. The Handbook of Neuropsychology, the second volume of which we now present, has been planned as a reference source that will provide for the first time comprehensive and current coverage of both experimental and clinical aspects of neuropsychology. To this end the chapter authors have produced in-depth reviews that go beyond a summary of their results and points of view. Each chapter is up-to-date, covering the latest developments in methodology and theory. Discussion of bedside evaluations, laboratory techniques and theoretical models are all to be found in the Handbook. In addition, the editors have attempted to make the Handbook as coherent as possible by encouraging minimal overlap in topic matter.

The first part of the second volume (Topic Editor: Professor H. Goodglass) encompasses aphasia and related disorders: it is the continuation of section 3 of the first volume. It includes chapters on clinical–anatomical (including imaging) and electrophysiological correlates of language and aphasia, and on recovery and therapy of aphasia. Related topics include aphasia in polyglots and in left-handers, artistry after unilateral brain lesions, nonverbal conceptual impairment in aphasia and sign language aphasia. The section ends with three chapters which are only indirectly related to language: one chapter is on disorders of body awareness, one on motor control and one on apraxia.

The second part of this volume (Section Four – Topic Editor: Professor A. Damasio) addresses the topic of disorders of visual behavior. The section covers both experimental issues, in animals and man, and issues of diagnosis. Special emphasis is given to the remarkable analyses of anatomy and function in the field of vision research in the past decade. The chapters address disorders of recognition, visuospatial analysis, imagery, blindsight and stereopsis, and they also address visual neglect and constructional apraxia.

The third volume will include a section (Topic Editor: Professor L. Squire) which will deal with memory and its disorders. Specific topics will include clinical assessment, the role of specific brain regions and etiologies in memory and its disorders, as well as specific syndromes such as post-traumatic amnesia, transient global amnesia, and functional amnesia. This section will conclude with chapters on rehabilitation and pharmacological treatment of memory disorders. Section Six (Topic Editor: Professor G. Gainotti) will cover emotional behavior and its disorders. It will include a review of theories of emotion, of the anatomical and neurochemical bases of emotion, lateralization of emotion, as well as of specific disorders of emotion and emotional arousal.

Volume Four will include a section (Topic Editor: Professor R. Nebes) which will deal with the neurobehavioral sequelae of congenital and surgically induced lesions of the corpus callosum and hemispherectomy in animals and humans. Section Eight (Topic Editor: Professor S. Corkin) will address issues related to aging and dementia. It will cover the neuropsychology of aging in animals and humans; clinical and pathological correlates of dementia; and modern clinical and experimental techniques such as PET and NMR spectroscopy. Also included will be chapters on psychiatric symptoms in dementia, sleep studies of demented patients, statistical considerations, and issues related to pharmacological therapy of dementia. Section Nine will be concerned with cognitive models. We are in an advanced stage of planning an additional section dealing with Developmental Neuropsychology.

The Handbook is expected to be an essential reference source for clinicians such as neurologists, psychiatrists and psychologists, as well as for all scientists engaged in research in the neurosciences.

Many people have contributed to the successful preparation of the Handbook. We again wish to particularly thank the Topic Editors, who have spent long hours both in the planning stage and in the actual compiling of the various sections. Ms. Annette Grechen in Pittsburgh and the editorial staff of Elsevier in Amsterdam continue to provide invaluable technical assistance.

F. BOLLER
J. GRAFMAN

List of contributors

Alexander M.P.   Braintree Hospital, 250 Pond Street, Braintree, MA 02184, U.S.A.

Basso A.   Neuropsychology Center and Second Clinic for Nervous Diseases, University of Milan, Via Francesco Sforza, 35, 20122 Milano, Italy

Bellugi U.   The Salk Institute for Biological Studies, P.O. Box 85800, San Diego, CA 92138, U.S.A.

Benton A.L.   Department of Neurology, University of Iowa, College of Medicine, Iowa City, IA 52242, U.S.A.

Bizzi E.   Department of Brain and Cognitive Sciences, Massachusetts Institute of Technology, 77 Massachusetts Avenue, Cambridge, MA 02139, U.S.A.

Cameron P.A.   Department of Neurological Sciences, Department of Speech and Hearing Sciences, University of Washington Medical School, Seattle, WA 98195, U.S.A.

Colby C.L.   Laboratory of Sensorimotor Research, National Eye Institute, Building 10, Room 10-C-101, National Institutes of Health, Bethesda, MD 20892, U.S.A.

Damasio A.R.   Department of Neurology, University of Iowa Hospitals and Clinics, Iowa City, IA 52242, U.S.A.

Damasio H.   Department of Neurology, University of Iowa Hospitals and Clinics, Iowa City, IA 52242, U.S.A.

Denes G.   Department of Neurology, University of Padova, Via Giustiniani 5, 35128 Padova, Italy

List of contributors

De Renzi E.   Clinica Neurologica, Via del Pozzo 71, 41000 Modena, Italy

Desimone R.   Laboratory of Neuropsychology, National Institute of Mental Health, Building 9, Room 1N107, Bethesda, MD 20892, U.S.A.

Farah M.J.   Department of Psychology, Carnegie-Mellon University, Pittsburgh, PA 15213, U.S.A.

Gardner H.   Psychology Service (116B), Veterans Administration Medical Center, 150 South Huntington Avenue, Boston, MA 02130, U.S.A.

Goldberg M.E.   Laboratory of Sensorimotor Research, National Eye Institute, Building 10, Room 10-C-101, National Institutes of Health, Bethesda, MD 20892, U.S.A.

Holland A.L.   Departments of Otolaryngology, Psychiatry and Communication, University of Pittsburgh, 4th Floor Eye and Ear Institute, 203 Lothrop Street, Pittsburgh, PA 15213, U.S.A.

Joanette Y.   Laboratoire Théophile-Alajouanine, CHCN, 4565, Chemin de la Reine-Marie, Montréal, Quebec, Canada H3W 1W5

Kaplan J.A.   Aphasia Research Center, Department of Neurology, Boston University, School of Medicine, Boston V.A. Medical Center, 150 South Huntington Avenue, Boston, MA 02130, U.S.A.

Klima E.S.   University of California, San Diego, Department of Linguistics, La Jolla, CA 92093, U.S.A.

Mateer C.A.   Department of Neurological Surgery RI-20 and Department of Neurological Sciences, University of Washington Medical School, Seattle, WA 98195, U.S.A.

Mesulam M.-M.   Department of Neurology, Harvard Medical School and Division of Neuroscience and Behavioral Neurology, Dana Research Institute, Beth Israel Hospital, 330 Brookline Avenue, Boston, MA 02215, U.S.A.

Mussa-Ivaldi F.A.   Department of Brain and Cognitive Sciences, Massachusetts Institute of Technology, 77 Massachusetts Avenue, Cambridge, MA 02139, U.S.A.

Newcombe F.   Neuropsychology Unit, University Department of Clinical Neurology, The Radcliffe Infirmary, Woodstock Road, Oxford OX2 6HE, U.K.

Paradis M.   Department of Linguistics, McGill University, 1001 Sherbrooke St. West, Montreal H3A 1G5, Canada

Poizner H.   The Salk Institute for Biological Studies, P.O. Box 85800, San Diego, CA 92138, U.S.A.

Ratcliff G.   Harmarville Rehabilitation Center, P.O. Box 11460, Guys Run Road, Pittsburgh, PA 15238, U.S.A.

Rizzo M.   Division of Behavioral Neurology and Cognitive Neuroscience, Department of Neurology, The University of Iowa College of Medicine, Iowa City, IA 52242, U.S.A.

Tranel D.   Department of Neurology, Division of Behavioral Neurology and Cognitive Sciences, University of Iowa Hospitals & Clinics, Iowa City, IA 52242, U.S.A.

Ungerleider L.G.   Laboratory of Neuropsychology, National Institute of Mental Health, Building 9, Room 1N107, Bethesda, MD 20892, U.S.A.

Vignolo L.A.   Clinica Neurologica dell'Università (II Divisione di Neurologia), Spedali Civili, Brescia 25125, Italy

Weintraub S.   Department of Neurology, Harvard Medical School, and Division of Neuroscience and Behavioral Neurology, Dana Research Institute, Beth Israel Hospital, 330 Brookline Avenue, Boston, MA 02215, U.S.A.

Weiskrantz L.   Department of Experimental Psychology, University of Oxford, South Parks Road, Oxford OX1 3UD, U.K.

Acknowledgements

The editors and publisher gratefully acknowledge Sandoz Ltd, Basle, Switzerland, CIBA-Geigy, Summit, NJ, U.S.A., Fondation IPSEN, Paris, France, and Farmitalia Carlo Erba, Milan, Italy, for partially supporting the publication of this volume.

Contents

Contents

Section 4: Disorders of Visual Behavior (Damasio)

Section 3

(Part 2)

Language, Aphasia and Related Disorders

editor

H. Goodglass

© 1989 Elsevier Science Publishers B.V. (Biomedical Division)
Handbook of Neuropsychology, Vol. 2
F. Boller and J. Grafman (Eds)

CHAPTER 1

Neuroimaging contributions to the understanding of aphasia

Hanna Damasio

Department of Neurology, University of Iowa College of Medicine, Iowa City, IA, U.S.A.

Introduction

The understanding of the relationship between brain structure and language function has, until recently, depended on only two methods: (1) the lesion method, which establishes a connection between the presence of damage in a given anatomical locus and a set of neuropsychological disturbances; and (2) the electrical stimulation of direct recording from exposed cerebral cortex during surgical procedures for the treatment of seizures. Although neither approach is ideal, both have remained effective ways of gathering knowledge about brain and language processing, since it is manifestly impossible to gather equivalent information in experimental animals. The lesion method, in particular, has recently emerged as a most vigorous way of advancing this field of study for multifold reasons. Firstly, whereas early studies with the lesion method relied on simplified psychological models, current studies are taking advantage of developments in the cognitive sciences which include theoretical and practical advances in linguistics, computational modelling and experimental techniques. Secondly, developments in experimental neuroanatomy, neurophysiology and neuropathology now permit a richer conceptualization of neural structure and function and a more comprehensive understanding of the effects of localized brain damage. Thirdly, the advent of new imaging technologies has led, in just a decade

and a half, to the establishment of techniques that permit fine anatomical descriptions of normal and abnormal brain. In short, the technical requirements for the proper application of the lesion method are now more satisfactory, the theoretical background for the formulation of hypotheses testable by the lesion method has become more sophisticated, and the knowledge necessary for the appropriate interpretation of findings has increased noticeably.

Until 1973, autopsy specimens were the prime material for the anatomical investigation of acquired language disturbances. Some early neuroradiological methods provided modest structural information and were used, on rare instances, to advance the anatomical understanding of the aphasias. For instance, the study by Benson and Patten (1967) on the localization of the aphasias using radionuclide brain scanning helped support the observation that most nonfluent aphasic patients had damage in the anterior perisylvian region, while patients with fluent aphasias had damage in and about the posterior perisylvian region. Nonetheless, the anatomical resolution of radionuclide scans was poor, and amounted to nothing but a pointer to large brain regions defined by vague anatomical landmarks such as the sylvian fissure and the central sulcus, as seen in lateral templates of the hemispheres. In the early seventies, however, modern neuroimaging techniques began to revolutionize the study of patients with language disorders. The first step was the advent of X-ray computerized tomography (CT) of the brain in 1973. CT allowed us to look at multiple and parallel brain 'slices' in a living subject, obtained at the time the deficit appeared, or at any other required epoch. Even if by today's standards we can look with amusement at the resolution of those early images, there is no doubt that they fostered a tremendous leap forward in the investigation of behavioral/brain relationships. The first study to make use of the new technology was by Naeser and Hayward (1978) and many others followed (e.g. Kertesz et al., 1979; Mazzocchi and Vignolo, 1979; Damasio et al., 1979), not the least important of which helped settle the historical dispute between Dejerine and Pierre Marie regarding the lesion localization in Broca's aphasic patient Leborgne (Castaigne et al., 1980). In the confrontation, Dejerine had defended Broca's interpretation and maintained that the lesion causing Leborgne's aphasia was in Broca's area and did not extend into the posterior temporal region, while Marie contended that the lesion was not only in Broca's area but would have to extend into the basal ganglia and posterior language areas. The CT study allowed Castaigne and his co-workers to slice 'non-invasively' this precious brain (which had since disappeared and later resurfaced), and to conclude that, somehow, both Dejerine and Pierre Marie were right: the lesion did, in fact, involve the left basal ganglia as Pierre Marie wanted but did not involve Wernicke's area in the posterior regions of the superior temporal gyrus, as Dejerine had stated.

The past decade and a half has improved the quality of CT to the point that its resolution is about 1 mm in the cross-section plane. There is no doubt that, with certain types of pathology, the correlation between CT images and autopsy charting of brain structure is almost flawless (see Case 9 in Damasio and Damasio, 1983), and CT becomes a superb instrument for the gathering of fine anatomical information. One problem that plagued CT has remained and will persist because of inherent technical problems in the delivery of X-

rays: in the transverse incidence images must be obtained at angles quite different from the near horizontal angle of classical neuroanatomy as seen, for instance, in Dejerine's brain sections. More often than not CT is obtained in an angle of cut parallel to a plane with a caudal angulation of about 15° to 20° in relation to the standard anatomical horizontal plane (although the incidence can vary from a caudal 30° to a 10° angulation in relation to the inferior orbital meatal line). This fact poses grave problems in the interpretation of the radiological images because CT images are deceptively similar to classical anatomical sections and yet quite different in their real anatomical content. In order to read these images correctly we must make use of appropriate atlases (DeArmond et al., 1976; Matsui and Hirano, 1978; Gado et al., 1979; Palacios et al., 1980) and of some form of procedure for the transfer of anatomical information (Hayward et al., 1977; Damasio, H., 1978; Naeser and Hayward, 1978; Kertesz et al., 1979; Mazzocchi and Vignolo, 1979; Luzzatti et al., 1979; Damasio, H., 1983, 1989; Poeck et al., 1984; Basso et al., 1985).

Magnetic resonance imaging (MRI) became available almost one decade later. Some current MR scanners, when properly used, can depict anatomical details even better than CT. For instance, MR permits clear-cut separation of gray and white matter. On the other hand, MR is not a standard technique and the appropriateness of the images for the anatomical analysis depends greatly on the pathology and on the magnetic pulse sequences used in a given study. Also, the comparison of MR images obtained with different pulse sequences requires special care and the comparison of the typical transverse MR and CT images demands special methodology because MR images are usually obtained in a more horizontal plane than CT, parallel to the inferior orbitomeatal line, or, on occasion, even with a rostral tilt in relation to this line.

Emission tomography (ET) is likely to become the principal source of information in future neurophysiological studies of higher brain function. It is available in two forms: positron emission tomography (PET) or single photon emission computerized tomography (SPECT). These procedures have made their impact as research tools and not as diagnostic methods. While anatomical detailing has so far been poor, the images provide information about the functional status of brain regions (see Raichle, 1987).

The contribution of ET to the lesion method has been small given its limited anatomical resolution. Some attempts have been made to overcome those difficulties, however. Fox et al. (1985) have developed a localization method based on stereotactic information, and we have developed a method to reconcile ET images and either CT or MR information obtained in the same subject (described below).

Methodology

Most of the progress reported in this chapter comes from studies which used the lesion method approach. While the behavioral aspects of the lesion method depend on the performance of neuropsychological experiments and on neuropsychological measurements with standardized testing instruments, the neural aspects of the lesion method depend on the availability of (1) fine-quality imaging techniques, and (2) standard methods of analysis of images in such a way that good-quality neuroanatomical descriptions can be generated. This section deals with the methodology required for appropriate analysis of images and is illustrated by procedures developed in the Department of Neurology's Neuroimaging Laboratory, at The University of Iowa.

Analysis of CT and MR images

Because of the variability of angles of incidence of CT, the first step in the development of our method, was to prepare different sets of templates, each with a different angulation in relation to the inferior orbitomeatal line. We prepared five sets within the range 0° to 90° (Damasio, H., 1987b).

These template systems were based on sections of actual brains prepared by us, counterchecked with information available in standard atlases (DeArmond et al., 1976; Hanaway et al., 1977; Matsui and Hirano, 1978; Palacios et al., 1980). For instance, for the typical 15° angulation, photographs of the lateral and mesial views of one brain were obtained. On these images we marked the major cytoarchitectonic areas conforming to the classic cytoarchitectonic maps of Brodman (1909) as well as to the more recent maps of Sarkissow (Sarkissow et al., 1955), Braak (1978) and Sanides (1970). The incidence and level of the CT cuts were also marked on the lateral and mesial surfaces of the brain, using the method described by Matsui and Hirano (1978) (Fig. 1). The brain was then cut at the levels drawn in the photograph, and the upper surfaces of the sections so obtained were used to chart a series of templates. The cytoarchitectonic areas were marked in those templates using as guidelines the pictures of the lateral and

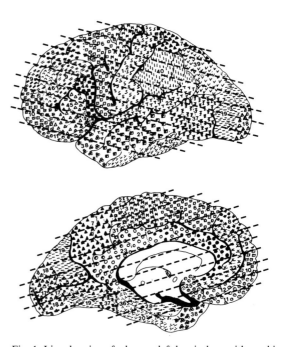

Fig. 1. Line drawing of a human left hemisphere with markings of cytoarchitectonic areas. Broken lines indicate incidence of sections obtained in this brain (15° caudal angulation in relation to the inferior orbitomeatal line).

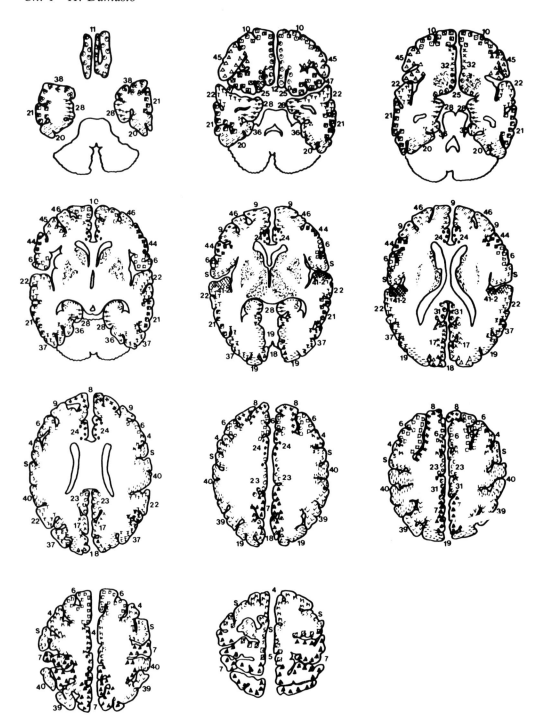

Fig. 2. Line drawing of each of the sections obtained from the brain depicted in Fig. 1.

mesial surface of the brain previously obtained (Fig. 2). In order to obtain template systems with markings of vascular territories these were also plotted on the same brain photographs, based on current knowledge of vascular anatomy (Waddington, 1974; Lazorthes et al., 1976; Salamon and Huang, 1976). The vascular territories were marked on the different sets of templates following the procedure described above for the cytoarchitectonic markings (Damasio, H., 1983, 1987).

The standard procedure for the analysis of CT and MR images in our laboratory is as follows:

(a) A technician collects all the film transparencies obtained in a given case and masks the subject identification in all of them, substituting a numerical entry code on the basis of which imaging data are stored in both computer and hard-copy files. These steps ensure that the anatomical investigators are blind to the neurological and behavioral data collected in the same subject.

(b) Working at a light table dedicated to charting, the investigators then proceed to: (1) in the case of CT, determine the angle of incidence at which tomographic cuts were obtained on the basis of a pilot scan and of the relative position of anatomical, cerebral and bone landmarks; (2) in the case of MR, make the same determination on the basis of a midsagittal pilot cut; MR images do not show bone landmarks but their resolution is such that actual anatomical structures, e.g., sulci, gyri and visually recognizable gray matter structures, can be clearly identified; (3) choose the set of best-fitting templates on the basis of the above determination; (4) chart the lesion on the templates, at every level at which it occurs, using an x/y plotting approach (Figs. 3 and 4)*; (5) superimpose over the template an appropriate 'in-register' transparency which contains anatomical cells

representing neural 'areas of interest' in both gray and white matter structures (each of those cells is limited by a linear boundary and has a letter and number code on the basis of which it can be anatomically identified (Fig. 5); (6) assign the area of damage charted in the template to the cells which encompass the abnormal images; (7) estimate amount of involvement within target cells (coded as *0* when less than 25% involvement of the total area is noted; *1* if the involvement is between 25% and 75%; and *2* if more than 75% of the total area is damaged); (8) determine the vascular territory in which the lesion occurred, using the appropriate vascular transparency (Fig. 6); (9) file the results of the above analysis as a hard-copy visual record and a computerized record, keyed to the codes mentioned above.

Some cerebral areas pose special localization problems and require the use of additional sets of cuts, generally coronal, and the appropriate charting of the cuts.

Procedures involving emission tomography

The anatomical localization of regional changes in cerebral blood flow or metabolism, on the basis of PET or SPECT images, follows similar principles but is made more difficult because of the lack of invariant landmarks in those images and the limited amount of resolution, which yields little recognizable anatomical detail.

At the Division of Nuclear Medicine of the Department of Radiology, emission tomography studies are currently performed in a dedicated SPECT system (Tomomatic-64, by Medimatic, Inc., of Denmark) which combines the technology of computerized tomography with the classic radioxenon cerebral blood flow clearance. The application of tomography permits the assessment of rCBF in anatomically defined brain regions, and helps minimize the measurement problems posed by surface probe devices, such as interhemispheric crosstalk, poor sensitivity and resolution at depth, and signal contamination from the external carotid circulation. In our studies we are not concerned

---

* Note that in this chapter CT, transverse MR and SPECT cuts are always oriented in such a way that the right hemisphere is on the right and the left hemisphere on the left, as if we are looking at the brain from above. The MR coronal cuts show the right hemisphere on the left and the left hemisphere on the right, as if facing the patient.

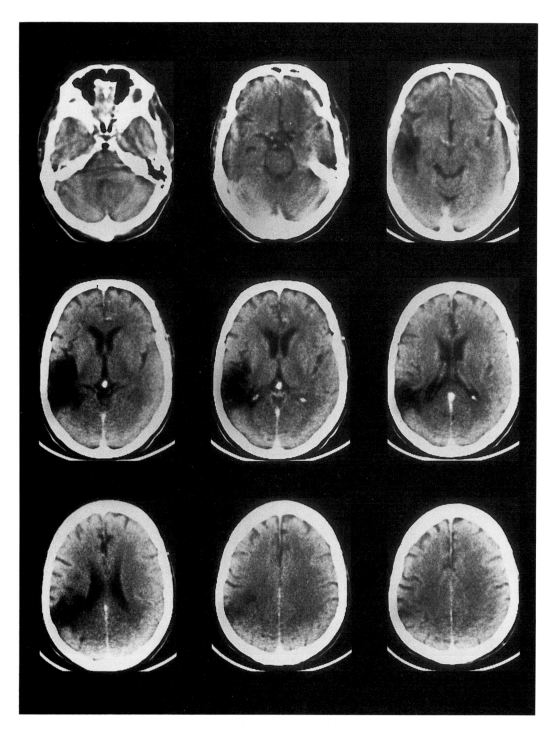

Fig. 3. CT of a 56-year-old man with Wernicke's aphasia due to a left temporal lobe infarct. CT obtained 1 month post-onset.

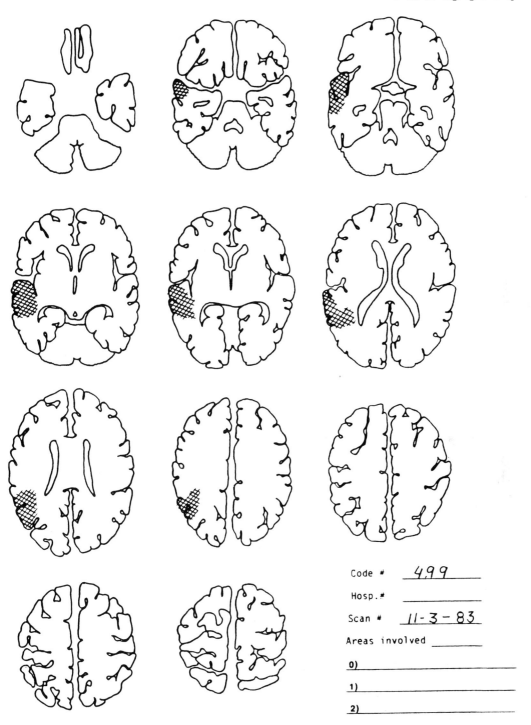

Code #   _499_

Hosp. # _____

Scan #   _11-3-83_

Areas involved _____

0) _____

1) _____

2) _____

Fig. 4. Plotting of the lesion seen in Fig. 3, in its best-fitting template system.

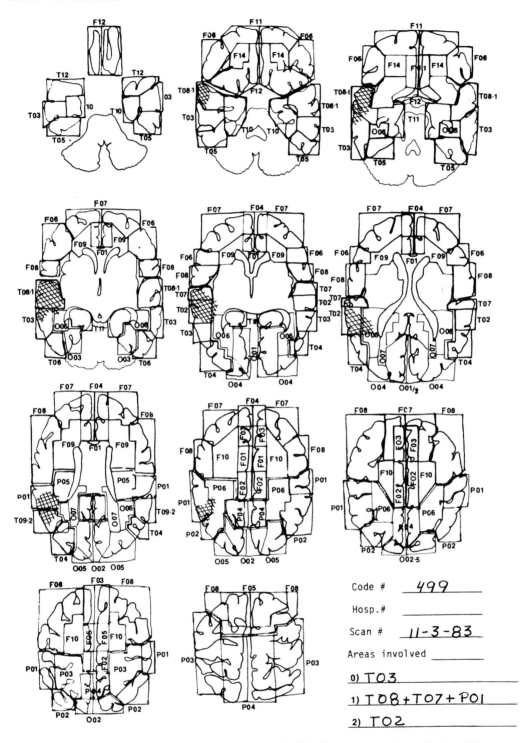

Code #   _499_

Hosp. #   _____

Scan #   _11-3-83_

Areas involved _____

0) TO3

1) TO8 + TO7 + PO1

2) TO2

Fig. 5. Same template system as in Fig. 4. The superimposed grid indicates the boundaries of cells which contain areas of interest. The cells provide a means of recording the position and grade of involvement of different areas. TO2 = posterior superior temporal gyrus; posterior area 22: TO3 = anterior middle temporal gyrus; area 21: TO7 = primary auditory cortices; areas 41/42: TO8 = anterior superior temporal gyrus; anterior area 22: PO1 = supramarginal gyrus; area 40.

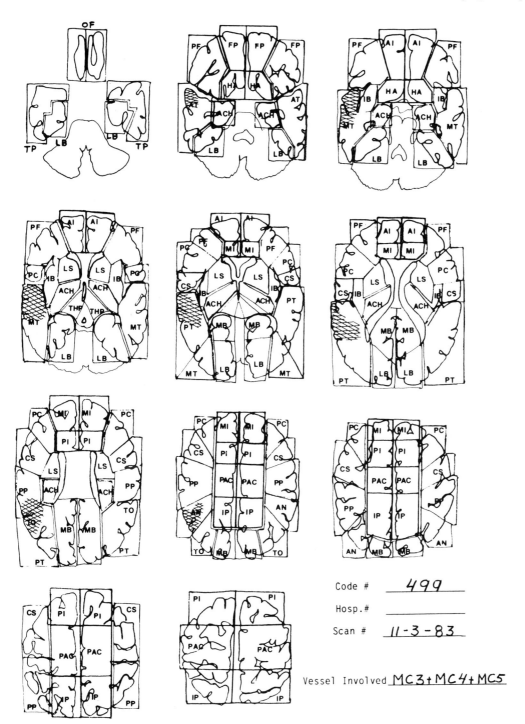

Code # 499

Hosp.#

Scan # 11-3-83

Vessel Involved MC3+MC4+MC5

Fig. 6. Same template as in Fig. 4 with a superimposed grid delineating different vascular territories. MC3 = posterior parietal; angular; temporo-occipital: MC4 = temporo-polar; anterior temporal: MC5 = middle temporal; posterior temporal.

with the validity of the actual measurements of cerebral blood flow but rather with the use of differential increases or decreases of radio signal in a given brain region, in subjects assessed under the same circumstances.

Patients are studied in supine position. The patient couch is equipped with a sliding mechanism that permits precise positioning of the head inside the imaging chamber. A set of five simultaneous brain images are obtained at 1, 3, 5, 7 and 9 cm above the orbito-meatal (OM) line. SPECT images are obtained under two conditions: at rest (baseline study) and during the performance of a cognitive task (activation study).

In the baseline study patients are studied in a resting supine position with their eyes open. The examination room is quiet and dimly lit, and an attendant is present throughout the study to minimize patient anxiety. Using the guide marks of the SPECT system, the patient's head is positioned so that the inferior orbito-meatal line is parallel to the plane of the tomographic images. Small radio-opaque markers are then affixed to the skin surface, indicating the level of the OM line. Fig. 7A (colour plate) shows a resting SPECT image of a 20-year-old right-handed man, with partial complex seizures since the age of 7. This image represents the habitual normal resting-state image.

The activation study is obtained about 24 hours later. The patient is positioned as described previously. Particular attention is devoted to duplicating the head position exactly, using the radio-opaque markers as a guideline. In the instance of language studies, the patient listens through earphones to a list of 240 audio-taped English words (all open-class lexical items), spoken by a male voice, at a rate of one word every 2.5 seconds. The test procedure is as follows: (1) before the study is started a target sound is given to the subject (the sound *ate* as in abdic*ate* or fr*eight*; (b) randomly interspersed in the list of 240 words are 78 words which rhyme with the target sound; (c) the subject is asked to listen to the incoming words and detect those that rhyme with the target sound; (d) whenever such a rhyme is

detected the subject is asked to wiggle the toes of the left foot (this task is a modification of a procedure first used by Knopman et al. (1982) for lateral-probe cerebral blood flow studies).

Prior to starting the actual activation, a trial run of twenty words is given to ensure full comprehension of the task and proper adjustment of sound level. Once this is achieved, the patient is connected to the radio-tracer source and the task is started one minute before the initiation of data collection. The task is continued throughout the entire length of the procedure (5 minutes).

A record of the actual motor response to individual words is kept to allow for investigation of accuracy of performance.

Fig. 7B shows the activation SPECT study obtained in the same young man as in Fig. 7A. The comparison of these two images shows that the general level of radio signal is higher during activation than at rest. More remarkable, however, is the asymmetry in the level of radio signal in two distinct areas in the left hemisphere, one in the frontal region and one in the temporal region, the latter just behind the symmetrically increased activity in the auditory region. The determination of the magnitude of change in radio signal is achieved by visual identification of the area under consideration. Once the area is identified it is delineated by a square of 3×3 pixels. A computer program chooses the point of maximum radio signal and delineates an area including this point plus all areas with a value of 80% or more of the highest value found. It then picks up a symmetrical area in the opposite hemisphere. The computer program is set to compare the values of these areas in relation to the resting state as well as the right to the left in both study conditions. The results are obtained in raw and normalized values, and as percentage of difference between the two studies as well as percentage of lateralization of increase of radio signal in the activation study. The same procedure is applied to the visual cortex, which in our paradigm should be equally activated in the two studies (the lights are on in both conditions and the subject keeps the eyes open). The values obtained

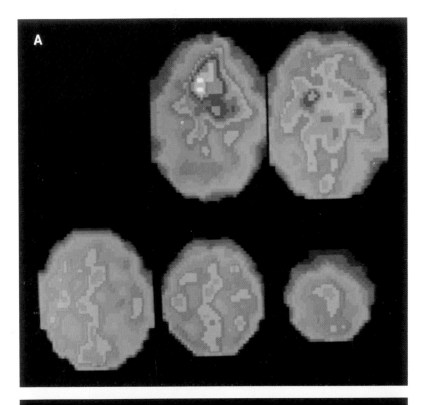

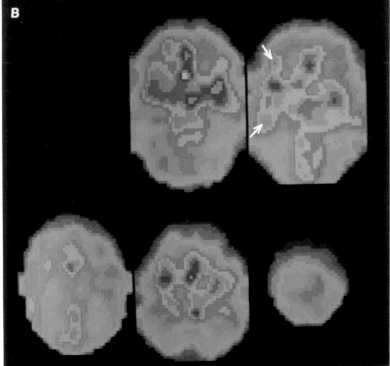

Fig. 7. (A) SPECT of a 20-year-old right-handed, non-aphasic man, obtained at rest. (B) SPECT of the same subject, obtained during a language activation task. Note the two areas in the left hemisphere (identified by arrows) with increased radio signal when compared to the resting state and when compared to the right hemisphere.

for the visual cortex serve as a reference term for the activation values, which, to be meaningful, must be greater.

Analysis of emission tomography images

Following the activation task, a right lateral skull X-ray is obtained after two additional radiopaque markers have been placed on the nose and forehead of the patient exactly 10 cm from each other. The latter two marks are used to determine the magnification factor in the X-ray image. This lateral skull X-ray is used as the reconciliation ground for two types of information: (a) the lines of incidence of CT/MR cuts and the location of 'areas of interest' in those cuts; (b) the lines of incidence of SPET cuts and the location of 'areas of activation' as seen in the SPET images. The anatomical localization of the latter is thus achieved by topographic transposition of these areas to the CT/MR cuts (Fig. 8). As an alternative method Talairach's stereotactic procedure (Talairach and Szikla, 1967) may also be used (Fig. 9).

Sources of error

The pitfalls of the lesion method are related to a variety of sources of error on both sides of the brain/behavior equation. In this section we will address only those that relate to the gathering and analysis of neural data. Assuming that the techniques for obtaining images are sound, the principal challenges faced by investigators in this area are: (1) the appropriate choice of neuropsychological

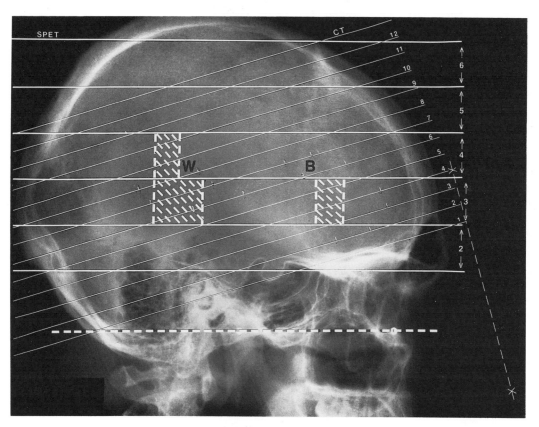

Fig. 8. Lateral skull of the patient referred to in Fig. 7 obtained at the time of SPECT. Note the white markings on the CT lines (tilted) demarcating the boundaries of Broca's area (B) and Wernicke's area (W). The hatched regions between the SPECT lines indicate the areas of increased radio signal.

specimens; (2) the appropriate timing of the CT or MR procedure; (3) the gathering of sufficient images for adequate anatomical analysis; (4) the generation of correct anatomical descriptions; and (5) the correct interpretation of group data.

The choice of inappropriate neuropathological specimens

A major methodological problem lies with the choice of pathology, especially when group studies are considered. An infarction, an intraparenchymal hemorrhage or tumors such as a meningeoma or a glioma behave neuropathologically in entirely different ways. Cerebral infarctions cause actual destruction of brain parenchyma. In the chronic phase the infarcted area is replaced by scar tissue and by CSF, which are, in turn, well

delineated as areas of decreased density in CT, and in MR as a dark area in T_1 weighted images, and as a bright signal region in T_2 weighted images. In the chronic state these images map with great precision the actual area of macroscopic brain destruction. (At this stage in the development of imaging techniques it is not possible to assess the potential microscopic damage that occurs in the area immediately surrounding an infarction and which clearly varies from case to case, depending on numerous physiopathological factors.) An equivalent fine correspondence only occurs with one other type of neuropathology: herpes simplex encephalitis. In fact, resolved herpes simplex encephalitis provides excellent anatomical studies due to a variety of factors. First, the virus has a particular affinity for a limited set of brain struc-

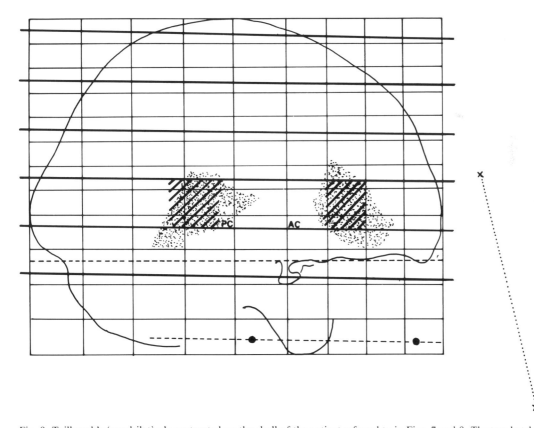

Fig. 9. Taillerach's 'quadrilatère' constructed on the skull of the patient referred to in Figs. 7 and 8. The two hatched areas correspond to the regions of increased radio signal seen in the left hemisphere in Fig. 7B. They coincide with the projection of Broca's (B) and Wernicke's (W) areas.

tures mostly within the limbic system. Secondly, it destroys those areas quite completely, by a mechanism of vascular collapse not unlike that of infarction. Both CT and MR produce extremely neat images of the areas actually involved.

In practically all other instances of pathology the precise anatomical definition of a lesion is more problematic and so is the functional impact of the lesion itself. For instance, the region of low or high density seen on the CT of a glioma corresponds not only to areas of tumor but also to edema and even functionally competent brain tissue. This is to say that, even when we look at a region where there is a definite abnormal signal, this does not mean automatically that the brain parenchyma is destroyed in that area, or that the area is functionally inoperative. Nor can we be sure that an area with no apparent abnormality is free of tumor. Gliomas infiltrate brain tissue by dislocating neurons and often not destroying them. It is for this reason that they may grow for long periods of time in complete clinical silence. Meningeomas, because they originate in the meningeal membranes external to the nervous tissue proper, impinge on brain by pressure as the tumor grows and compresses the cerebral surface. They generally cause dysfunction in this indirect manner (although in some cases the tumor may derive its blood supply from the surrounding brain parenchyma and damage it too). CT or MR images show large areas of abnormal signal although real dysfunction may be confined to a small pool of neurons.

There is one exception to the use of tumor material, and that is the use of subjects in whom the tumors have been excised and a cerebral ablation performed. Provided the disease process is stable, those cases are quite appropriate if the investigation establishes a relationship between the anatomical site of the ablation and the neuropsychological profile obtained *after* the ablation took place. In short, any correlation obtained at the time the tumor was present is invalid but the situation changes after it has been removed and a circumscribed ablation performed. The same comments apply, to a large extent, to ablations performed for the treatment of seizures.

Intracerebral hemorrhages behave in a mixed fashion, both by destroying neural tissue, as non-hemorrhagic infarctions do, and by occupying space among displaced neurons, as tumors do. For this reason, during the acute phase, neither CT nor MR provides a real picture of the areas of abnormality. In the area of abnormal signal some neurons are destroyed; others are simply moved about. It is only after the resolution of the local hematoma that we may actually estimate the amount and location of brain tissue destruction. In short, it seems obvious that when the purpose of a study is to establish a relationship between behavioral dysfunction and the site of brain destruction, the material of choice is stroke. Hemorrhages, provided they are studied in the chronic stage, may provide useful information. However, the use of tumors of any kind is unacceptable. Naturally, no groups of subjects should be formed involving different types of pathology.

Timing CT and MR data collection
The timing of data collection in CT and MR is of the essence, especially in relation to subjects with cerebrovascular disease, by far the most frequent and appropriate type of subject. Both CT and MR may fail to show *any* abnormality if obtained immediately after the occurrence of a stroke. With fourth-generation CT scanners most images will be positive after 24 hours but this is certainly not the case in older scanners. Numerous CT scans obtained less than 24 hours post-onset of stroke are negative. Positive CT images obtained in the first week post-onset may show areas of abnormality that are far larger than the region of actual structural damage because of confounding factors such as edema. Furthermore, when CT is obtained in the 2nd or 3rd week after the onset of a stroke, without i.v. infusion of a contrast-enhancement substance, the images will be negative in a fair number of cases (Fig. 10A), even after a previous CT obtained days after the onset may have shown an area of decreased density. In contrast-enhanced

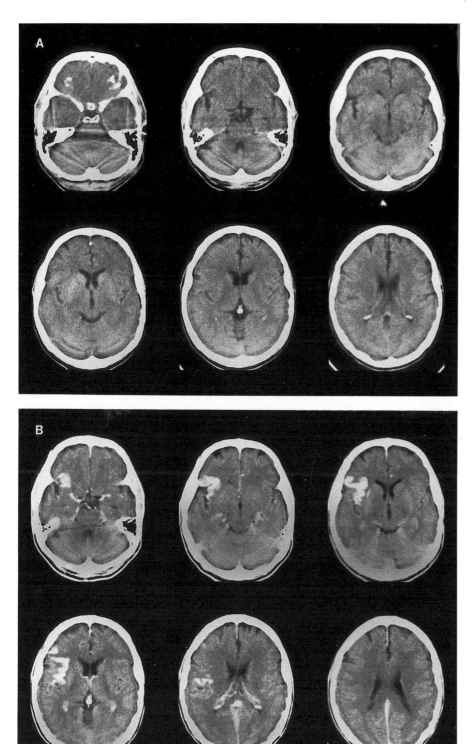

Fig. 10. (A) CT of a 63-year-old woman with sudden onset of nonfluent aphasia. CT obtained 13 days post-onset without the previous injection of contrast material. Note that no abnormal area can be seen. (B) CT of the same patient, obtained the same day, after injection of contrast material. Note the region of cortical enhancement in the left frontal operculum and in the insula.

CT images, otherwise silent areas of infarction appear as areas of increased density (primarily due to seepage of contrast substance through the walls of newly formed vessels in the affected region; Fig. 10B).

In the chronic stage (i.e. three months post-onset and beyond) most CTs of infarctions will be unequivocally positive. However, even then, when strokes are small and located close to a major sulcus or to the wall of a ventricle, the chronic CT may suggest a misleading image of focal 'atrophy' with sulcal enlargement, or ventricular dilatation (Fig. 11). If no previous images are available for comparison with those obtained in the chronic stage, the correct interpretation and the establish-

ment of an adequate behavioral/anatomical correlation may not be possible. Similar problems befall MR when images obtained with only one pulse sequence are studied. For instance, it is known that T_1 weighted images obtained with an inversion recovery pulse sequence (IR) provide maximal anatomical detail. However, infarctions with this pulse sequence appear as dark areas, in precisely the same range of grays used to depict the ventricular system or any region filled with cerebrospinal fluid such as the cerebral sulci and fissures. If an infarct is small and close to one of these structures it may not be readily distinguishable. T_2 weighted images obtained with spin echo pulse sequences (SE) will show the damaged area

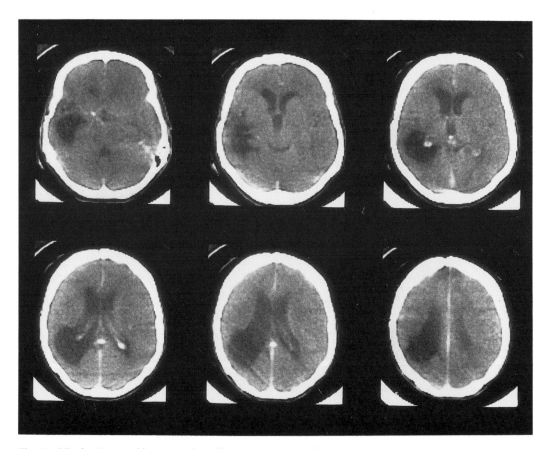

Fig. 11. CT of a 57-year-old woman who suffered a subarachnoid hemorrhage seven years before this scan. After surgery for her ruptured aneurysm she developed jargonaphasia. The left lateral ventricle is enlarged, especially in the temporal and posterior portions. However, no clear area of abnormal density can be seen outside the region of ventricular enlargement.

as a region of intense bright signal, more easily distinguishable from the bright signals generated by white and even gray matter.

At this point, it should be emphasized that any meaningful relationship between a given anatomical image and a particular neuropsychological pattern, depends on a reasonable closeness between the epoch at which the image and neuropsychological data were obtained. For instance, during the acute period there is often edema and distortion of brain structures and it is not possible to define precisely the amount and location of brain tissue that is actually destroyed. When such images are related to observations obtained during the chronic state the interpretation is, of necessity, quite erroneous. Naturally, the same applies to the inverse situation, i.e., relating the results of acute neuropsychological observation obtained in the acute state with anatomy derived from chronic images.

Our impression is that both the anatomical and the neuropsychological data crucial to the understanding of brain-behavior relationships should be obtained in the chronic phase. However, data obtained during the acute or periacute period are not useless. Provided such early anatomical and neuropsychological observations coincide, they can be interpreted and used as guidelines. However, they should not be mixed with data gathered in the chronic phase.

The generation of incorrect anatomical descriptions

A major source of error in the lesion method is the incorrect description of the anatomy affected by a brain lesion, either because insufficient data were gathered for adequate analysis or because the interpretation of images is incorrect. This is the reason why we developed the different template systems described above and why we use them to guide us in the detailed analysis of CT and MR images. The first step for a correct analysis is to read both CT and MR images with *all* cuts available, including the lower cuts especially. The lower cuts need to be carefully studied in order to determine

the incidence in which that particular CT has been obtained. This is crucial for the correct localization of a lesion which may only be seen in high-lying cuts. The following example illustrates the importance of these two steps.

The CT in Fig. 12 was obtained in a patient who suddenly developed a profound weakness of the left arm. The neurological examination confirmed that he had a flaccid monoparesis of the left arm, that the reflexes in that extremity were slightly more active than in the normal right arm, and that there were no other areas of weakness on either side. A CT was obtained and it showed the lesion depicted it the last five cuts of Fig. 12. The lesion is predominantly supraventricular, with only the lower limit at the level of the highest cut that courses through the body of the lateral ventricle. To analyse this CT, with only the cuts in which the lesion can be seen, several template systems could be used. For instance, a posterior fossa incidence would seem completely appropriate (Fig. 13) as would a more horizontal incidence, at approximately 10° angulation to the orbitomeatal line (see Fig. 14). The results of these two plottings, however, would be read in completely different ways. In the former, one would assume the lesion to be located in the parietal lobe, while in the latter the lesion would be in the posterior frontal region. However, if, instead of using only the upper cut of the CT, attention had been paid to the lower cuts, in which bony landmarks can be found demarcating the anterior, middle and posterior fossae structures, *only* the 10° angulation template system could have been chosen, and a proper localization would have been obtained. This is the only template system that shows the right proportion of frontal lobe, temporal lobe and cerebellum seen at those lower levels.

Some cerebral areas pose particular problems. The occipital areas are a case in point. To investigate such impairments as abnormal facial recognition or abnormal detection of spatial relationships, it is important to state whether a given lesion is above or below the calcarine fissure. However, the position of the calcarine fissure is

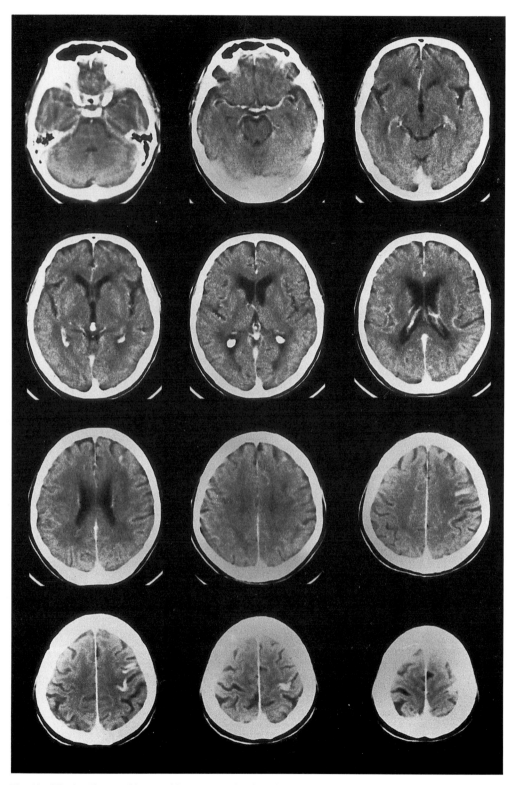

Fig. 12. CT of a 70-year-old man with monoparesis of the left arm. Note the area of cortical enhancement in the left hemisphere in the top four cuts (two bottom rows).

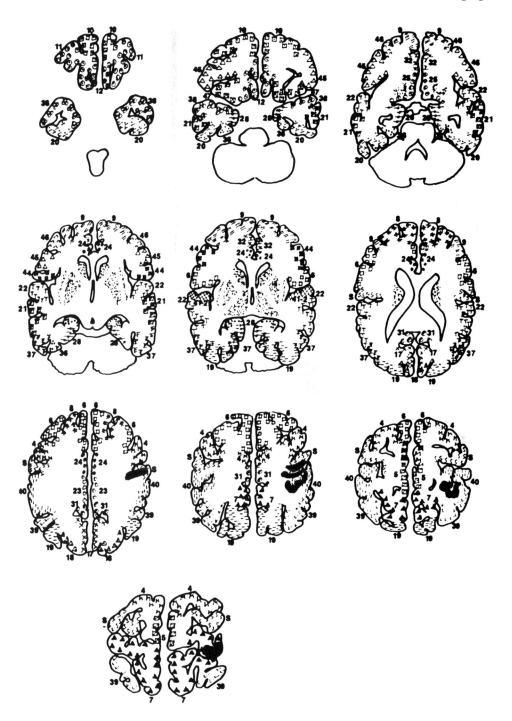

Fig. 13. Template system obtained with posterior fossa angulation. Note that the highest five cuts of this template system seem perfectly adequate to chart the lesion seen in Fig. 12. If such a template is chosen the lesion would be plotted in the parietal lobe, in the post-rolandic and anterior supramarginal gyrus.

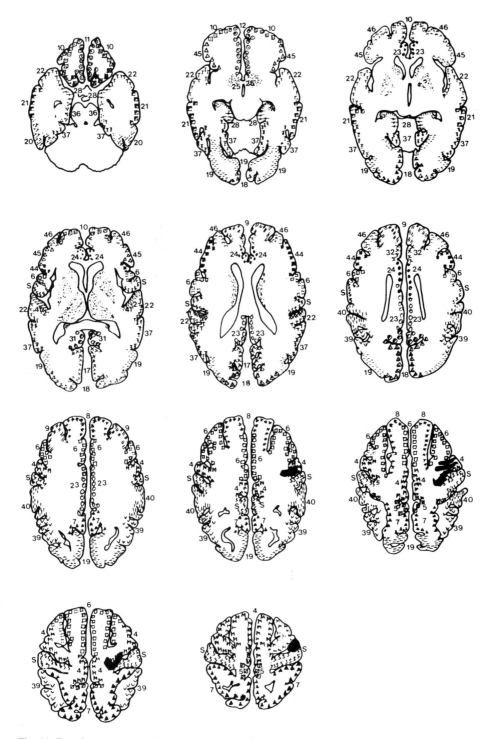

Fig. 14. Template system obtained with a 10° caudal angulation in relation to the inferior orbitomeatal line. This template system fits not only the higher cuts of the CT of Fig. 12 but also the lower ones. In this system the lesion is appropriately plotted in the posterior frontal lobe (motor region).

not only variable from person to person but, in the same subject, it varies from one hemisphere to the other. Furthermore, in transverse cuts, CT or MR, it is not possible to recognize the calcarine fissure. With the advent of MR this problem can be solved by studying coronal cuts through the occipital lobe. As can be seen in Fig. 15 the calcarine fissure is easily identified, permitting the correct localization of lesions in relation to this fissure.

For the lesion method to be practised properly, cerebrovascular disease, cerebral ablations and herpes simplex encephalitis constitute the ideal material. Neuropsychological and neuroimaging data should be obtained contemporaneously and, if possible, in a chronic and disease-stable state. Analysis of images should be performed carefully and rigorously, not by mere visual inspection, always taking into account transparencies of the whole brain, and supplementing the traditional transverse views, whenever possible, with coronal incidences.

Neuroimaging findings in the classical aphasia syndromes

It is widely acknowledged that most classifications of biological phenomena are as much a help as they are a hindrance. The classification of aphasias is no exception and most available systems have been criticized either for their inappropriate theoretical basis or for their practical imperfections. Perhaps the major problem with classifications, especially syndrome classifications, lies with their use in research projects, because exemplars of syndromes are hardly ever entirely comparable in terms of their constituent symptoms and signs. On the other hand, it is certainly justifiable to use syndromes for clinical purposes and as a shorthand to improve communication between investigators and clinicians. In this chapter, we retain a classical and widely used syndromatic classification as an entry key to the systematization of neuroimaging findings in the aphasias. In the future it may be possible to establish new sets of relationships between linguistic defects and brain structure that may well

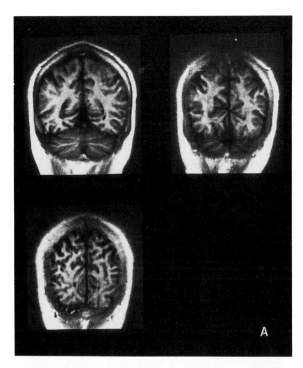

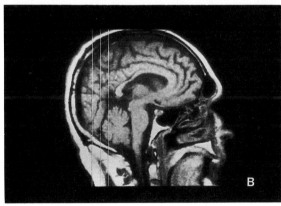

Fig. 15. (A) Coronal MRI cuts, T_1 weighted images, obtained at the points marked on B. Note the common trunk of the calcarine fissure and parieto-occipital sulcus, in the first cut on each side of the midline. In the second cut the emergence of the calcarine fissure (inferior sulcus) and the parieto-occipital sulcus (superior sulcus) form a typical V pattern, with the vertices of the two Vs facing each other. On the third cut the two sulci are separated with the calcarine fissure occupying the lower position and the parieto-occipital sulcus moving upwards. (B) Midsagittal MRI pilot scan of a normal subject, showing the level at which the three coronal cuts of section A were taken. Note that the parieto-occipital sulcus, the calcarine fissure and their anterior junction are clearly visible.

bypass such syndromatic classifications. That is indeed the approach we are currently taking in our research. However, we believe it is premature to forego syndrome tags if we are to describe effectively the currently available knowledge regarding the anatomical correlates of the aphasias. The operational definition of each of the syndromes indicated below conforms to the time-honored aphasia categories used by the Boston Aphasia Research Center (see Geschwind, 1971; Goodglass and Kaplan, 1982). For the same reason, our reference to the manifestations of language impairment largely conforms to classical and widespread neuropsychological concepts rather than to current cognitive science concepts.

Wernicke's aphasia

More than a decade of neuroimaging studies indicates that the typical presentation of Wernicke's aphasia is consistently associated with lesions in the dominant posterior temporal region. Fine anatomical analysis reveals that these lesions involve the auditory association cortices contained in the part of Brodman's field 22 located posteriorly to the primary auditory cortices (areas 41 and 42). In our experience lesions that do not extensively involve the posterior aspect of area 22 are not associated with Wernicke's aphasia. However, the damage is rarely confined to this locus. For instance, the primary auditory cortices are often damaged too. The lesions that involve Wernicke's area can also extend into the inferior parietal lobule, and involve the angular gyrus (area 39) or the supramarginal gyrus (area 40). In some cases the lesions remain limited to the temporal lobe and invade, instead, the cortices located in the lateral temporal surface, including areas 20, 21 and the lateral aspect of 37. In addition to these cortical fields the subjacent white matter is almost inevitably damaged, to a greater or lesser extent. So far we have insufficient evidence to assign functional meaning to different degrees and directions of white matter extension, except to note that greater depth involvement almost invariably means

greater severity and lesser recovery of aphasia symptoms.

It is interesting to note that, in essence, this anatomical account is consonant with Wernicke's original description in 1886. Furthermore, the

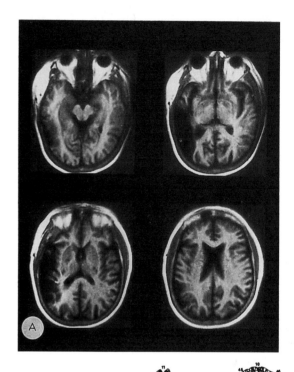

Fig. 16. (A) Chronic MRI (T_1 weighted, transverse cuts) of a 63-year-old woman with Wernicke's aphasia. Note lesion damage in left temporal lobe. (B) Template of MRI shown in A.

anatomical descriptions added through the years are really quite convergent and this applies to the contemporary investigators (Naeser and Hayward, 1978; Kertesz et al., 1979; Mazzocchi and Vignolo, 1979; Damasio, H., 1981; Selnes et al., 1983, 1984, 1985; Knopman et al., 1984a).

Figs. 16 and 17 show the MR images of a 63-year-old right-handed woman who, 5 months

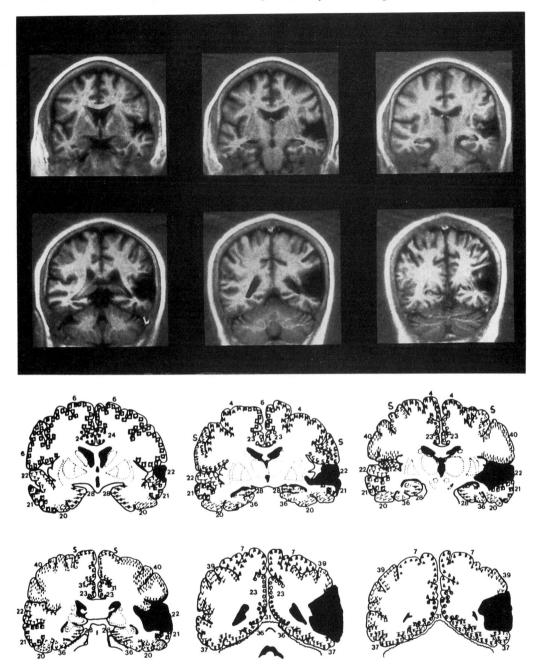

Fig. 17. Chronic MRI (T$_1$ weighted, coronal cuts) and template of the same patient seen in Fig. 16. Compare with the transverse cuts.

earlier, developed Wernicke's aphasia. The images show partial destruction of the primary auditory cortices and complete destruction of the posterior sector of area 22 in the superior temporal gyrus (Wernicke's area), as well as extension into the posterior region of the middle and inferior temporal gyri (area 37 and, in part, areas 20 and 21). However, the inferior parietal lobule is preserved (areas 39 and 40). At the time of this scan the patient was already improving but was still aphasic.

Her auditory comprehension for complex material was still severely impaired. Sentence repetition was also clearly defective and she continued to produce some paraphasic errors. The relationship between this constellation of deficits and her lesion is in concordance with the findings of Rubens and collaborators (Selnes et al., 1983, 1985).

Some patients with Wernicke's aphasia recover only to a limited extent, as exemplified by the case of a 64-year-old right-handed man who, 4 years

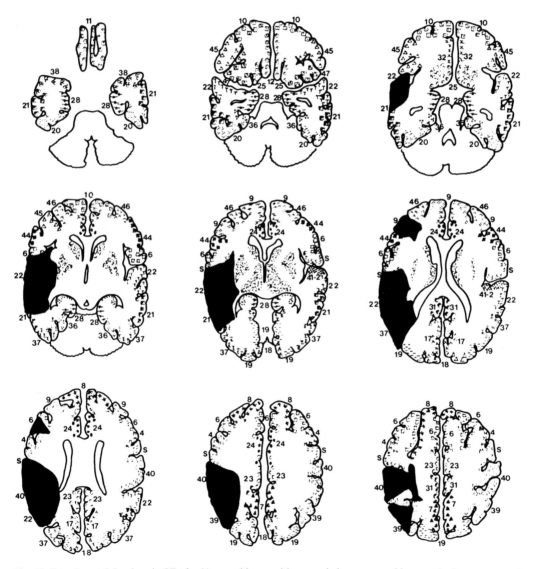

Fig. 18. Templates of the chronic CT of a 64-year-old man with semantic jargon caused by a stroke four years previously. Note that the lesion involves most of the left temporal lobe and extends into the supramarginal and angular gyrus.

after his stroke, still had severe Wernicke's aphasia producing mainly semantic jargon. The template of his chronic CT can be seen in Fig. 18. In comparison to the previous example note that the lesion is more extensive, not only involving most of the left temporal lobe but spreading into the inferior parietal lobule, which is almost entirely damaged.

Conduction aphasia

Conduction aphasia has not been as free of controversy as Wernicke's regarding both the nature of the syndrome and its anatomical substrate. Konorski et al. (1961), and later Geschwind (1965), established the syndrome's individuality but it was only in 1973 that Benson and co-workers provided some evidence that the anatomy was equally special. This they did in a post-mortem study of three individuals with conduction aphasia (Benson et al., 1973). Several investigators have since confirmed the anatomical individuality of the syndrome (Naeser and Hayward, 1978; Kertesz et al., 1979; Damasio and Damasio, 1980; Rubens and Selnes, 1986) and, in so doing, expanded the original description.

There are probably three different anatomical loci whose damage is associated with this symptom complex. They are: (1) the supramarginal gyrus and its subjacent white matter where a large sector of the arcuate fasciculus courses; (2) the auditory cortices, especially the primary region (areas 41, 42); and (3) the insular cortex. In our experience patients with conduction aphasia tend to have damage either in (1) alone or in (2) and (3), i.e., the lesions are centered either in the supramarginal gyrus and subjacent white matter, or in the primary auditory cortex and insula. Curiously, either type of lesion is quite destructive to the white matter connectional systems subsumed under the concept of 'arcuate fasciculus', as it is now known that this projection system not only uses the high route initially described by Dejerine (1901, 1906), in the depth of the parietal operculum, but also has an inferior component coursing under the insula.

In fact the whole system is a vast sheath of white matter of which the classical arcuate fasciculus is only the superior aspect (for evidence from non-human primates see Galaburda and Pandya, 1983). Lesions in auditory cortex and insula, without involvement of the parietal lobe, have been associated with conduction aphasia (Damasio and Damasio, 1980), and recently even involvement of the insula alone has been noted to cause the typical presentation (Rubens and Selnes 1986).

The images in Fig. 19 are from a typical case of conduction aphasia in a 40-year-old right-handed patient. This CT was obtained 7 years post-onset. The thin cuts and coronal reconstruction show that most of the supramarginal gyrus (area 40) and the underlying white matter are missing. The angular gyrus was not involved and the primary auditory cortices (areas 41, 42) as well as the posterior portion of the superior temporal gyrus (area 22) remain intact. Seven years after onset the patient continues to have defective repetition of sentences.

In this case damage clearly falls in the anterior portion of the inferior parietal lobule and involves both cortex and the arcuate fasciculus. However, even a smaller and subcortical lesion in this region can cause a similar syndrome acutely, as was noted in a 25-year-old right-handed man. One year later, however, this patient had returned to normal and had no detectable deficits on formal language testing. His lesion, as seen in the chronic MRI (Fig. 20), was limited to a small area in the white matter underlying the supramarginal gyrus (area 40), with possible extension into the cortex of the very superior region of the inferior/superior parietal junction.

Broca's aphasia

There has been a continual historical controversy regarding the anatomical correlates of Broca's aphasia. The dissent can be traced to the famous debate between Dejerine and Pierre Marie at the Paris Société de Médicine in 1908. In a way, the discussion between Dejerine and Marie was resolved by the study of Castaigne et al. (1980), as

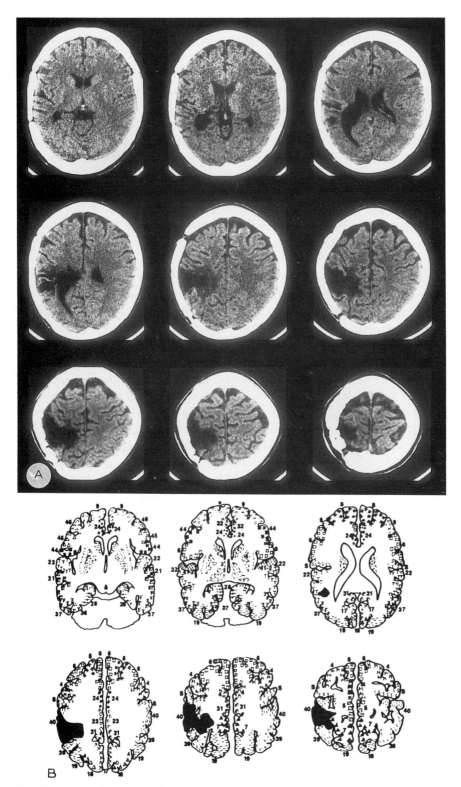

Fig. 19. (A) Chronic thin cut CT of a 40-year-old woman with conduction aphasia due to a lesion in the left parietal lobe. Lesion involves the supramarginal gyrus and subjacent white matter but spares the temporal lobe altogether. (B) Template of CT in A.

discussed before. More recent investigations of cases of Broca's aphasia with CT have led Mohr and collaborators (1978) to point out that infarctions confined to the inferior frontal gyrus cause only a brief period of mutism which gives way to effortful speech but generally without significant linguistic defects. In other words, such lesions do not appear to cause aphasia proper. These investigators also showed that a more severe disturbance which does conform to the traditional notion of Broca aphasia requires considerably larger areas of damage involving most of the frontal operculum and the insula. In general, subsequent studies have confirmed those findings (Naeser and Hayward, 1978; Kertesz et al., 1979; Damasio, H., et al., 1979; Damasio, H., 1981).

In 1981 Tonkonogy and Goodglass called attention to two patients with circumscribed frontal lesions, one involving the frontal operculum and the other the rolandic operculum. They noted that the patient with damage in the frontal operculum had transient linguistic difficulties, while the other, with damage only in the lower rolandic region, showed dysarthria, dysprosody and only mild word-finding difficulty, without disturbances of phonemic, lexical or syntactical processing. Two years later Schiff et al. (1983) published a larger series of cases and called attention to this type of presentation, under the general term of aphemia, noting its common association with small, subcortical lesions immediately subjacent to the lateral frontal cortices.

There is no question that the distinction between transient, albeit marked, Broca's aphasias which evolve fairly rapidly into nearly normal language production and true aphasias with major and persistent linguistic defects is honored by a neuroanatomical distinction.

An example of the former is that of a 47-year-old right-handed woman, whose MRI, obtained 7

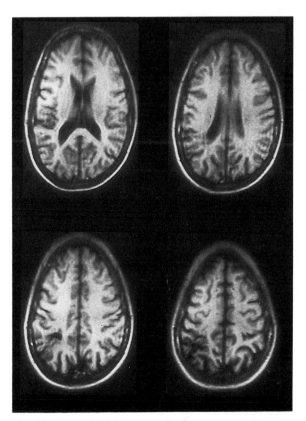

Fig. 20. Chronic MRI (T$_1$ weighted) of a 25-year-old man with conduction aphasia. Lesion is in the white matter underneath the supramarginal gyrus.

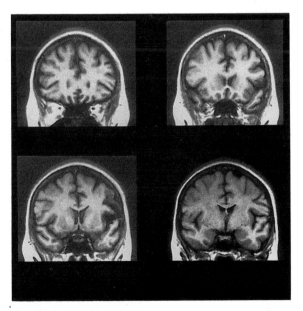

Fig. 21. Chronic MRI (T$_1$ weighted) of a 47-year-old woman who developed Broca's aphasia at the time of a stroke 7 years earlier. Note the region of decreased signal in the left frontal lobe (cut 3).

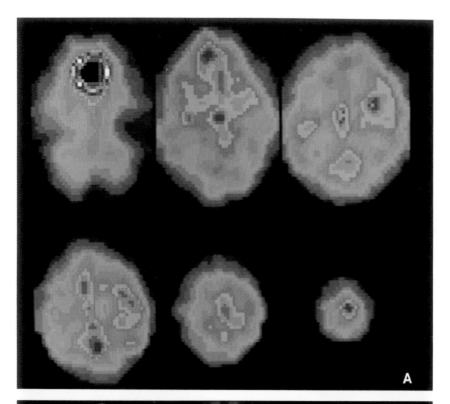

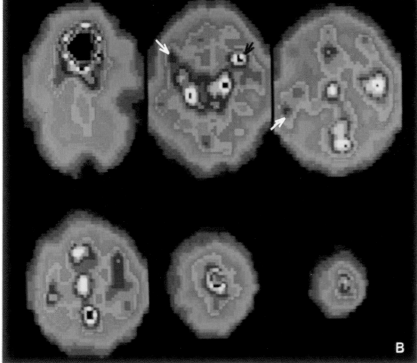

Fig. 22. (A) SPECT of the patient referred to in Fig. 21 (resting study). Note the general asymmetry in radio signal, indicative of reduced cerebral blood flow in left hemisphere. (B) SPECT obtained during language activation in the same patient. Note the general increase in radio signal as well as the clearer delineation of the left frontal area with low radio signal, corresponding to the region of the infarct. In the second cut of Section B there are two discrete regions of increased radio signal in the left hemisphere, one anterior (white arrow) and one posterior, which become clearer in the next cut (white arrow). In cut number 2 there is also an area of increased signal in the right frontal region, symmetrically placed in relation to the one seen on the left.

years post-onset, is seen in Fig. 21. It shows an area of abnormal signal involving only the highest portion of the frontal operculum (area 44) and extending further upward into the immediately adjacent area 6. This location and extension of damage was exactly as seen with CT during the acute stage.

SPECT obtained at the time of MRI shows a significant asymmetry in radio signal between the hemispheres, at rest. The left hemisphere is generally lower than the right and furthermore shows lower values in the frontal region. During language activation, however, the amount of radio signal increases and brings both hemispheres to similar levels. The area of abnormally low values in the frontal lobe, which corresponds to the area of infarct, becomes much better defined. Of interest is the fact that, as expected, both auditory regions show marked increase in radio signal, but

on the left this area of change expanded more posteriorly than on the right, probably indicating increase of activity in Wernicke's region. The most interesting feature, however, is the change seen in the frontal lobes. Just below the area of abnormally low signal in the left hemisphere, the area of infarct, we can see a well delineated region of increased radio signal and, in the right hemisphere, in a symmetrically placed region, an area of increased radio signal (Fig. 22 (colour plate)). The plotting of these areas can be seen in Fig. 23, where it is evident that the areas of increased signal are in the region of the frontal operculum immediately below the area of infarction, and in Wernicke's area.

Fig. 24, on the other hand, shows the chronic MR of a 40-year-old right-handed man, who presented acutely with a severe Broca's aphasia

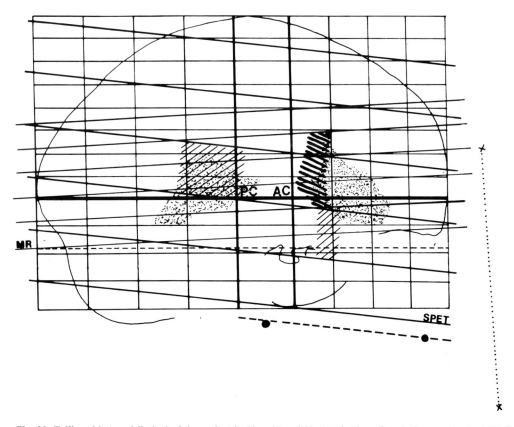

Fig. 23. Taillerach's 'quadrilatère' of the patient in Figs. 21 and 22: (a) plotting of the lesion seen in the MRI (heavy hatched area), (b) areas of increased radio signal as seen in the activation SPECT (thin hatched areas), (c) projection of Broca's and Wernicke's areas (stippled zones).

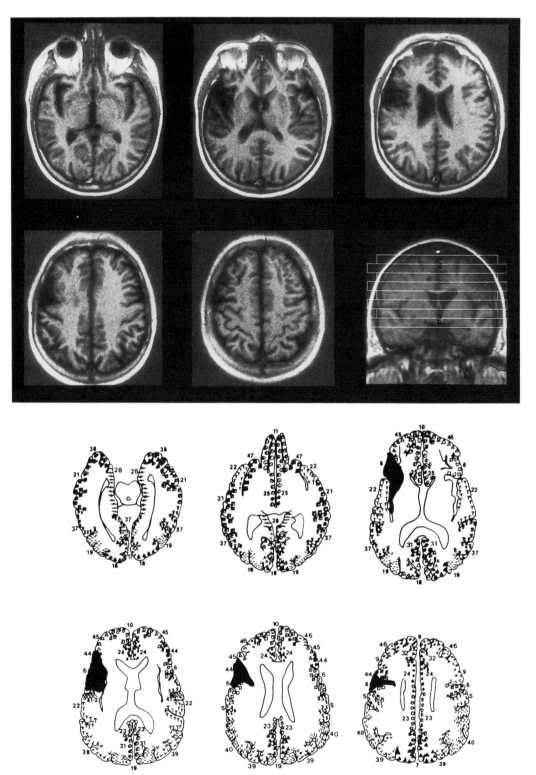

Fig. 24. Chronic MRI (T$_1$ weighted) and template of a 40-year-old man with Broca's aphasia and a left frontal lobe lesion. The coronal pilot (right lower corner) shows the levels of scan cuts.

and who, in spite of remarkable recovery, must still be classified as a Broca aphasic 2 years later. As can be seen in the transverse cuts his lesion involves the posterior and superior region of the inferior frontal gyrus (area 44), which seems completely destroyed. The lesion also extends into immediately adjacent premotor cortex (area 6). Furthermore, the lesion involves the white matter under these cortical regions and extends to the cortex and lateral white matter of the insula. The region of the basal ganglia is spared, however.

Global aphasia

In addition to severe defects of speech production and auditory comprehension, patients with global aphasia generally have a dense right hemiplegia. The traditional concept is that the correlates of global aphasia encompass (1) the anterior language region, as in Broca's aphasia, (2) the basal ganglia, (3) the insula and auditory cortices, as in conduction aphasia, and (4) the posterior language-related cortices (posterior area 22, area 37, and areas 40 and 39), as in Wernicke's aphasia. Such damage can only be the consequence of a large infarct in the region supplied by the middle cerebral artery (Naeser and Hayward, 1978; Kertesz et al., 1979; Damasio, H., 1981).

Global aphasics with such lesions are severely aphasic from the outset and show little or no improvement. This is no surprise given that most language-related structures in the left hemisphere have been destroyed and that subcortical language-related structures have perished too. A good example of such a presentation can be seen in Figs. 25 and 26. However, with the advent of CT, we have come to realize that some patients with similar impairments at the onset of their aphasias have an entirely different set of anatomical correlates and often a different type of out-come as well (Damasio, H., 1981; Vignolo et al., 1986; Tranel et al., 1987). Furthermore, they do *not* have hemiplegia or at least do not have lasting motor defects. Most such patients have in fact two lesions, one in the frontal lobe and another in the temporoparietal region. The damage spares a wide area of motor and language-related structures. Fig. 27 shows such an example.

Another group of patients presenting with global aphasia show only dominant frontal lobe damage with extension into insula and basal ganglia but leaving temporal and parietal regions entirely intact (Fig. 28). In the chronic stage some of these patients become severe Broca aphasics rather than global aphasics (Mohr et al., 1978).

A large subcortical infarct in the region of the basal ganglia may also present as global aphasia. That was the case in a 74-year-old right-handed woman, who suddenly became globally aphasic with a right hemiparesis. MRI revealed an infarct that had damaged the caudate and lenticular nucleus in the left hemisphere as well as the internal capsule in its entirety. The lesion extended to the extreme capsule but did not seem to reach the cortex of the insula. Both frontal lobe and temporoparietal lobe structures were intact (Fig. 29).

The transcortical aphasias

The anatomical correlate of transcortical sensory aphasia have only been fully appreciated with the advent of CT (Kertesz et al., 1979; Damasio, H., 1981). In patients with this type of fluent aphasia the primary auditory cortices (areas 41, 42) as well as most or all of Wernicke's area (posterior area 22) are spared. The damage lies in areas 37 and 39, extending, on occasion, anteriorly into the middle temporal gyrus (area 21), or postero-inferiorly into part of areas 18 and 19 (Damasio, H., 1981). Similar localization of lesions has been described by Kertesz and collaborators (Kertesz et al., 1982). Transcortical sensory aphasia can also be seen with purely subcortical lesions located in the white matter underlying the above cortices, as exemplified in Fig. 30, where one can see both the CT and the post-mortem specimen.

The anatomical correlates of transcortical motor aphasia (TMA) include two distinct locations. The first is in the subcortical white matter, immediately anterior to the left frontal horn. From a vascular

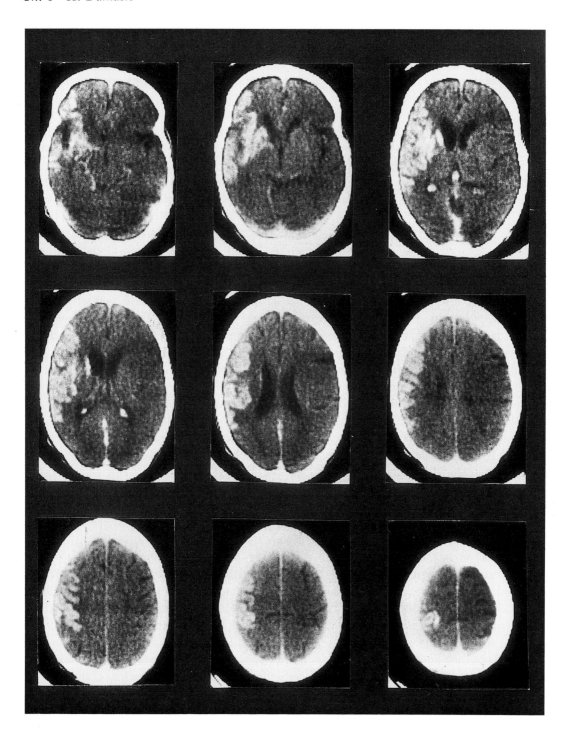

Fig. 25. CT of a 56-year-old patient showing contrast enhancement in the left frontal lobe, insula, temporal lobe and inferior parietal lobule as well as basal ganglia. This is the typical image of a large middle cerebral artery infarct producing global aphasia.

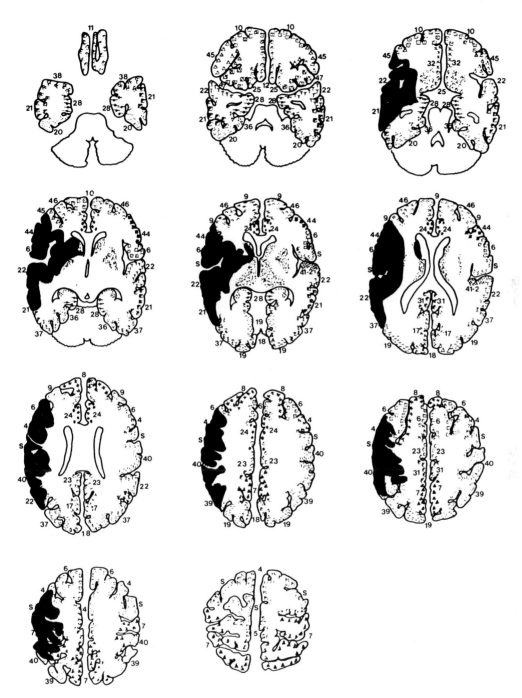

Fig. 26. Template of the CT shown in Fig. 25.

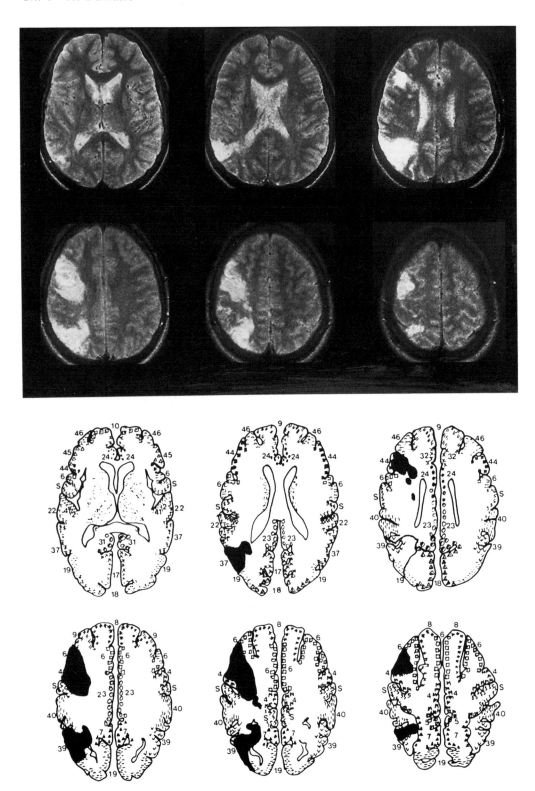

Fig. 27. Chronic MRI (T$_2$ weighted, transverse) and template of a 41-year-old man with global aphasia *without* hemiplegia. The anterior lesion damages only the most superior portion of the frontal operculum and extends into superior motor and premotor regions. The posterior lesion occupies the caudal portion of the inferior parietal lobule (angular gyrus).

standpoint this region is part of the anterior watershed area and can be damaged in isolation (i.e. when no cortical territory is involved), or in combination with a cortical territory. An example of damage to this area can be found in Fig. 31. A small infarction strategically placed in this position disrupts major projections between key mesial frontal lobe areas (supplementary motor area and anterior cingulate), and lateral premotor cortices in the frontal operculum, including Broca's area. It also interrupts projections from the mesial cortices to the head of the caudate on the left. Furthermore, it interrupts connections from the right supplementary motor area and cingulate, which

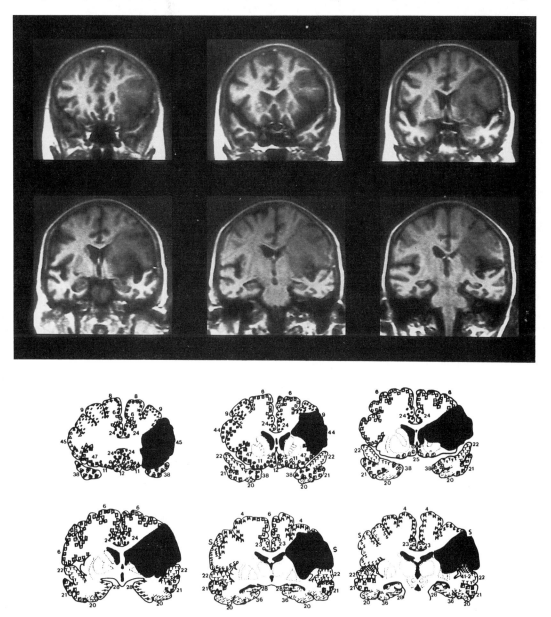

Fig. 28. MRI (T$_1$ weighted, coronal) and template of a 65-year-old woman with global aphasia during the acute stage. The infarct involves the frontal operculum, the underlying white matter, the basal ganglia and the insula, but the temporal lobe is entirely spared.

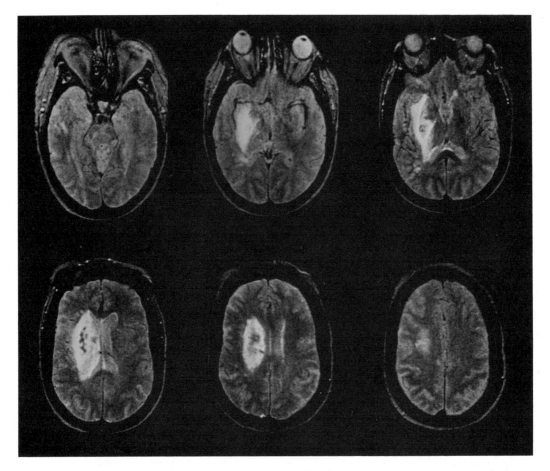

Fig. 29. Periacute MRI (T$_2$ weighted) of a 74-year-old woman with global aphasia caused by a large left basal ganglia lesion. The damage involves the caudate nucleus, all of the lenticular nucleus, all of the internal capsule, and extends laterally towards the insula. However, the lower portion of the head of the caudate and the thalamus are spared, as can be seen in the second and third cuts in the upper row.

traverse the anterior callosum and course anteriorly to the frontal horn.

The second critical locus noted in patients with TMA encompasses cortical and subcortical white matter in prefrontal and premotor regions surrounding the frontal operculum (areas 46, 10, 9, 8 and 6). Occasionally there is partial involvement of the frontal operculum proper (areas 44 or 45) (Damasio, H., 1981). An example of such a case is seen in Fig. 32.

Some patients with manifestations of TMA, but clinically and anatomical distinctive features, have been considered under the umbrella of TMA. For instance, in 1975 Rubens called attention to patients with poor speech output and preserved repetition, who had damage in the mesial frontal cortex which includes the supplementary motor area. Several studies have reported compatible findings (Alexander and Schmitt, 1980; Jonas, 1981; Környey, 1975; Masdeu et al., 1978; Naeser and Hayward, 1978). However, our view is that most patients with infarcts in the supplementary motor region and anterior cingulate can be clinically distinguished from TMA patients. They have mutism initially, followed by slow, aspontaneous speech, which is largely intact from the linguistic standpoint, and they have normal repetition. Furthermore, unlike most patients with TMA, those patients do not only have paucity of spontaneous speech but have, rather, a general akinesia. Most never produce paraphasias nor do they have

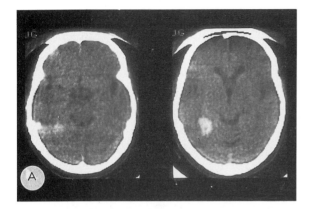

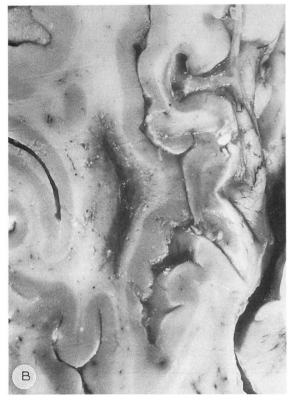

Fig. 30. (A) CT of a 76-year-old woman with an intercerebral hemorrhage producing transcortical sensory aphasia. The hematoma is located in the depth of the left posterior temporal lobe. (B) Post-mortem section showing the resolving hematoma in the white matter of the posterior temporal lobe.

agrammatism. Finally, their auditory comprehension and naming are normal. We believe the disturbance of these patients is more one of motor production and affect than of linguistic formulation (Damasio and Kassell, 1978; Damasio, H., 1981; Ross et al., 1986; Damasio and Van Hoesen, 1980, 1983). Freedman et al. (1984) have described this same location. In their study, the three patients had lesions in the territory of the anterior cerebral artery, and in one of them the lesion involved the supplementary motor area. This patient was said to have 'virtually no language disturbance other than difficulty in speech initiation.' It is perhaps preferable to maintain the designation of mutism for these patients and to consider them separately from the TM aphasias. It is also important to note that this syndrome occurs only when SMA and/or anterior cingulate immediately below are damaged. If the lesion is placed in the mesial frontal lobe but outside this critical area mutism does not occur (Ross et al., 1986).

When a combination of the lesions described for TMA and TSA occurs in the same patient a virtual 'isolation of the speech areas' ensues. This is a rare but possible phenomenon, an outcome of severe hypotensive episodes in which the watershed areas are irrevocably damaged. It should be noted that while that approximates, for the left hemisphere, the type of lesion described by Geschwind et al. in 1968, the extent of such lesions is still smaller than those found in a well known case of isolation of speech area caused by carbon monoxide poisoning. Another possible and related presentation was described by Assal et al. (1983), a patient with extensive infarcts in the territory of both the anterior and the posterior cerebral arteries.

Aphasias with basal ganglia and thalamic lesions

The advent of CT also brought the discovery that damage to the dominant basal ganglia, without concomitant cortical damage, could cause aphasia (Damasio, A., et al., 1982; Naeser et al., 1982; Brunner et al., 1982; Damasio, H., et al., 1984; Fromm et al., 1985). Patients had radiological

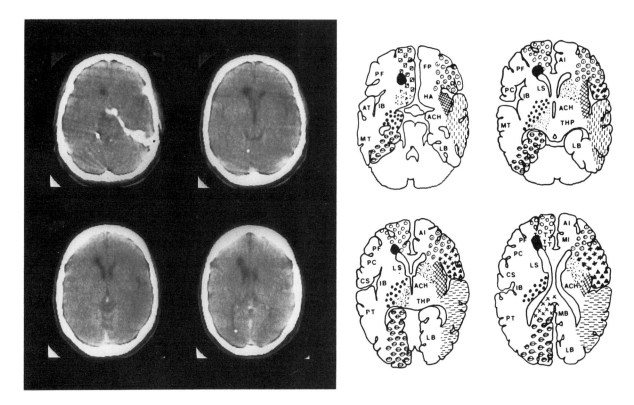

Fig. 31. CT and vascular template of a 47-year-old woman with transcortical motor aphasia. Note the small area of decreased density adjacent to the anterior horn of the left lateral ventricle in the anterior watershed area.

evidence of infarction in the head of the caudate nucleus and in the putamen on the left side.

An intriguing aspect of the aphasias seen in those patients was the association of elements normally found in Broca-type aphasics with elements noted in Wernicke-type aphasics. The patients did not fit the global category either, as such a conjunction of deficits might suggest. Furthermore, they showed a tendency to good recovery and were, in the majority of cases, rather young individuals. Because these aphasias did not easily fit any of the Boston diagnostic categories, they became known as 'atypical'.

In all cases the infarcts involved variable amounts of the caudate nucleus (the anterior portion or head), and of the putamen, as well as the anterior limb of the internal capsule between these two gray matter structures. The vascular supply af-

fected in those infarcts was that of the lateral lenticulo-striate arteries. When the infarct was more anteriorly and inferiorly placed, in the territory of Heubner's artery, involving the inferior aspect of the head of the caudate at the level at which it blends with the lenticular nucleus, no language disturbance was noted. The same could be said for infarcts placed laterally, damaging anterior insula, subjacent white matter and lateral aspect of the lenticular nucleus, in which case dysarthria and dysprosodia might be noted but no aphasia. When the infarct was more posterior and superior, involving posterior lenticular nucleus and corona radiata, or posterior limb of internal capsule, no aphasia ensued. When it was placed in the right hemisphere, the appropriate motor deficits would be seen but no language disturbance would appear either. Fig. 33 shows an example of a patient with an infarction of the head of the caudate, anterior limb of the internal capsule and part of the putamen who presented with one of these 'atypical aphasias.'

Of special interest is the fact that aphasia has also been observed in children with lesions in the left basal ganglia (Aran et al., 1983) and even in a left-handed child with a right hemisphere lesion (Ferro et al., 1982).

Barat et al. (1981) were able to carry out a post-mortem study in such a case and they could demonstrate the intactness of the cortical regions in the left hemisphere while the caudate, lenticular nucleus and the internal capsule were destroyed. Those cases we have followed over an extended period of time, with repeated CTs (Damasio, H., et al. 1984) and, more recently, with MRI continue to show no evidence of cortical lesion (see Fig. 33).

That disorders of speech and language may follow thalamic hemorrhages (e.g. Mohr et al., 1975; Cappa and Vignolo, 1979; Alexander and LoVerme, 1980) and thalamic tumors (e.g. Arseni, 1958; Cheek and Taveras, 1966) has been known for many years. Some patients also have severe attentional disturbances which makes it difficult to analyse in detail what is a true linguistic deficit and what is the result of the disturbances of attentional processes. Furthermore, as mentioned in the section on sources of error, it is difficult, if not impossible, to have a precise idea about which structures are impaired in these cases. A better understanding of the language deficits encountered with thalamic lesions only came recently with the ability of CT scanners to detect small, localized infarctions in the thalamus (Cohen et al., 1980; Archer et al., 1981; Graff-Radford and Damasio, 1984;

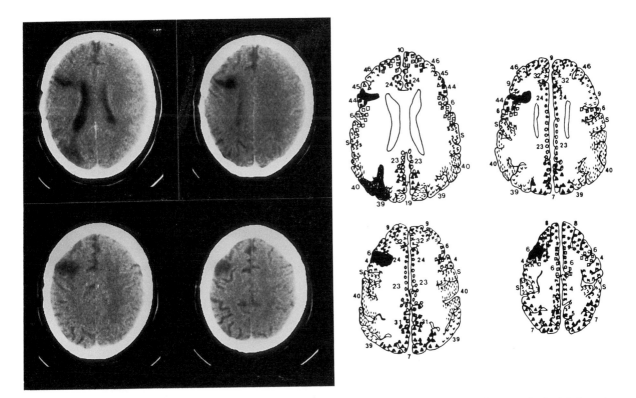

Fig. 32. Chronic CT and template of a 41-year-old man with transcortical motor aphasia. The area of damage in the left frontal lobe touches on the most superior portion of area 44 and extends upward into premotor cortex (area 6). There is a second area of infarct in the left parieto-occipital region which did not cause aphasia.

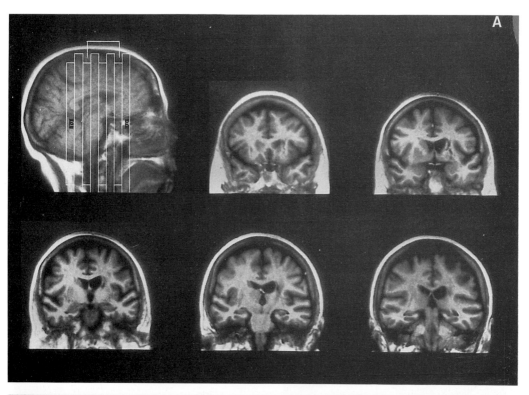

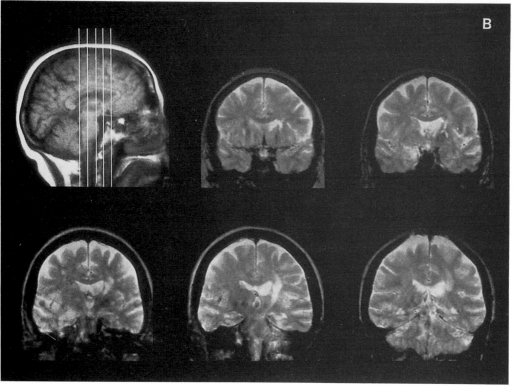

Graff-Radford et al., 1985a,b).

From these studies it became clear that lesions in the anterior nuclei of the left thalamus (VL and AV predominantly) cause language deficits which share several of the characteristics of the transcortical aphasias. These infarcts are located in the territory of the tuberothalamic artery. Infarcts located in other regions of the left thalamus or in the right thalamus may cause sensory or motor disturbances but not aphasia.

Conclusion

The classical account of the relationship between brain and language can be traced back to the studies of Broca (1861) and Wernicke (1874), continues in the work of Dejerine (1906) and Liepmann (1914), and culminates with the presentation of Geschwind's views during the 1960s. The advent of neuroimaging has contributed to modify that account.

The components of the Geschwind model of brain and language were as follows:

(a) Two major non-contiguous centers: the anterior, Broca's area, located in the posterolateral and orbital aspects of the frontal operculum; the posterior, Wernicke's area, located in the posterolateral aspect of the left superior temporal gyrus.

(b) A large connectional pathway joining these centers, the arcuate fasciculus, coursing in the depth of the supramarginal gyrus and the insula.

(c) The two primary auditory cortices and their interhemispheric connecting pathways.

(d) The lower third of the motor and somatosensory cortices in the Rolandic region.

(e) The left angular gyrus and its linkage to the limbic temporal lobe.

With the availability of neuroimaging, new cortical and subcortical areas as well as new white matter pathways have been added as language-relevant regions. Prominent among the additions are:

(a) the left caudate nucleus;

(b) anterolateral nuclei of the left thalamus;

(c) some mesial left frontal cortices, such as the supplementary motor area and the anterior cingulate.

The anatomical definition of the classical 'centers' has also changed. The 'anterior language center' has suffered considerable expansion. Some left lateral frontal cortices surrounding areas 44 and 45 such as the lower portion of lateral area 6, as well as part of areas 8, 9, 10 and 46, are now included in this anterior language region. The same applies to the posterior language region, which now extends not only into cytoarchitectonic area 39, already linked to visually mediated language, but also into areas 40 and 37.

Neuroimaging has been instrumental in establishing that right hemispheric damage can impair the processing of some linguistic and para-linguistic stimuli (Ross, 1981; Gardner et al., 1983). More recently, the study of recovered aphasics with dynamic imaging techniques has shown that the nondominant hemisphere does participate prominently in language-related processing after left language areas have been damaged (Damasio, H., et al., 1986; Knopman et al., 1984b). In short, neuroimaging has helped show that the nondominant hemisphere has a far more interesting function than the traditionally assigned role of motor effector and sensory receptor.

As viewed with the new technologies the list of neuroanatomical units associated with language processing has thus been greatly expanded. No less important, however, is the fact that the units are now conceptualized in a radically different way. The units are not mere independent centers linked by cable pathways. They are, rather, richly interconnected functional regions which form overlap-

---

Fig. 33. Chronic MRI of a patient with left basal ganglia infarct and aphasia. Note that in both the T_1 weighted (A) and the T_2 weighted images (B) the head of the caudate is damaged and the anterior horn of the lateral ventricle has dilated into the region previously occupied by the caudate. There is also damage to the lenticular nucleus and to the anterior limb of the internal capsule. There is no damage in the cerebral cortex.

ping networks. Each region, inasmuch as it can be viewed as relatively independent, contributes to the maintenance and operation of distributed records of linguistic and nonlinguistic information.

Acknowledgements

I want to thank Drs. P. Eslinger and D. Tranel for making available the neuropsychological data used in the description of the patients; Dr. Cornell, Dr. Yuh and Dr. Rezai, for CT, MR and SPECT transparencies on which our anatomical interpretations were based; and P. Reiman for the photography of all images used in this chapter. I also want to thank B. Redeker for her help in the preparation of the manuscript.

This work was supported by NINCDS Grant PO1 NS19632.

References

Alexander MP, Schmitt MA: The aphasia syndrome of stroke in the left anterior cerebral artery territory. *Arch. Neurol. (Chicago): 37,* 97 – 100, 1980.

Alexander MP, LoVerme SR Jr.: Aphasia after left hemispheric intracerebral hemorrhage. *Neurology: 30,* 1193 – 1202, 1980.

Aran DM, Rose DF, Rekate HL, Whitaker HA: Acquired capsular/striatal aphasia in childhood. *Arch. Neurol. (Chicago): 40,* 614 – 617, 1983.

Archer CR, Ilinsky IA, Goldfader PR, Smith KR: Aphasia in thalamic stroke: CT stereotactic localization. *J. Comput. Assist. Tomogr.: 5,* 427 – 432, 1981.

Arseni C: Tumors of the basal ganglia. *AMA Arch Neurol. Psychiatry: 80,* 18 – 26, 1958.

Assal G, Regli F, Thuillard F, Steck A, Deruaz J-P, Perentes E: Syndrome d'isolement de la zône du langage. *Rev. Neurol. (Paris): 139,* 6 – 7, 417 – 424, 1983.

Barat M, Mazaux JM, Bioulac B, Giroire JM, Vital C, Arne L: Troubles du langage de type aphasique et lésions putamino-caudées. *Rev. Neurol. (Paris): 137,* 343 – 356, 1981.

Basso A, Lecours AR, Moraschíni S, Vanier M: Anatomo-clinical correlations of the aphasias as defined through computerized tomography: exceptions. *Brain Lang.: 26,* 201 – 229, 1985.

Benson DF: Positron emission tomography in aphasia. *Semin. Neurol.: 4,* 169 – 173, 1984.

Benson DF, Patten DH: The use of radioactive isotopes in the localization of aphasia-producing lesions. *Cortex: 3,* 258 – 271, 1967.

Benson DF, Sheremata WA, Bouchard R, Segarra JM, Price DL, Geschwind N: Conduction aphasia: a clinicopathological study. *Arch. Neurol. (Chicago): 28,* 339 – 346, 1973.

Braak H: The pigment architecture of the human temporal lobe. *Anat. Embryol.: 154,* 213 – 240, 1978.

Broca P: Remarques sur le siège de la faculté de langage articulé, suivie d'une observation d'aphémie (perte de la parole). *Bull. Soc. Anat. 36,* 330 – 357, 1861.

Brodman K: *Vergleichende Lokalisation-Lehre der Grosshirninde in ihren Prinzipion dargestellt auf Grund des Zewllenbanes.* Leipzig: J.A. Barth, 1909.

Brunner RJ, Kornhuber HH, Seemuller E, Suger G, Wallesch CW: Basal ganglia participation in language pathology. *Brain Lang.: 16,* 281 – 299, 1982.

Cappa SF, Vignolo LA: 'Transcortical' features of aphasia following left thalamic hemorrhage. *Cortex: 15,* 121 – 130, 1979.

Castaigne P, Lhermitte F, Signoret JL, Abelante R: Description et étude scannographique du cerveau de Leborgne (la découverte de Broca). *Rev. Neurol. (Paris): 136,* 563 – 583, 1980.

Cheek WR, Taveras J: Thalamic tumors. *J. Neurosurg.: 24,* 505 – 513, 1966.

Cohen JA, Gelfer CE, Sweet RD: Thalamic infarction producing aphasia. *Mt Sinai J. Med. (NY): 47,* 398 – 404, 1980.

Damasio A, Damasio H: The anatomical basis of pure alexia. *Neurology: 33,* 1573 – 1583, 1983.

Damasio A, Kassell NR: Transcortical motor aphasia in relation to lesions of the supplementary motor area. *Neurology: 28,* 396, 1978.

Damasio A, Van Hoesen G: Structure and function of the supplementary motor area. *Neurology: 30,* 359, 1980.

Damasio A, Van Hoesen G: Emotional disturbances associated with focal lesions of the limbic frontal lobe. In Heilman K, Satz P (Editors), *Neuropsychology of Human Emotion: Recent Advances,* The Guilford Press, pp. 85 – 110, 1983.

Damasio A, Damasio H, Rizzo M, Varney N, Gersh F: Aphasia with lesions in the basal ganglia and internal capsule. *Arch. Neurol. (Chicago): 39,* 15 – 20, 1982.

Damasio H: *Localization Method for CT and MR Images of the Brain.* The University of Iowa, 1978.

Damasio H: Cerebral localization of the aphasias. In Saino MT (Editor), *Acquired Aphasia,* New York: Academic Press, 1981.

Damasio H: A computed tomographic guide to the identification of cerebral vascular territories. *Arch. Neurol. (Chicago): 40,* 138 – 142, 1983.

Damasio H: Vascular territories defined by computerized tomography. In Wood JH (Editor), *Cerebral Blood Flow: Physiologic and Clinical Aspects.* New York: McGraw-Hill, 1987.

Damasio H, Damasio AR: The anatomical basis of conduction aphasia. *Brain: 103,* 337 – 350, 1980.

Damasio, H, Damasio A. *Neuroanatomy and Neuropsychological Disorders: Neuroimaging Procedures and Problems.* New York: Oxford University Press, 1989.

Damasio H, Damasio A, Hamsher K, Varney N: CT scan correlates of aphasia and allied disorders. *Neurology: 29,* 572, 1979.

Damasio H, Eslinger P, Adams HP: Aphasia following basal ganglia lesions: new evidence. *Semin. Neurol.: 4,* 151 – 161, 1984.

Damasio H, Rezai K, Eslinger P, Kirchner P, VanGilder J:

SPET patterns of activation in intact and focally damaged components of a language related network. *Neurology: 36*, 316, 1986.

DeArmond SJ, Fusco MM, Dewey MM: *Structure of the Human Brain*. London and New York: Oxford University Press, 1976.

Déjérine J: L'aphasie sensorielle et l'aphasie motrice. *Presse Méd.: 14*, 437 – 439, 453 – 457, 1906.

Déjérine J: *Anatomie des Centres Nerveux*. Paris: Reuff, 1901.

Ferro JM, Martins IP, Pinto F, Castro-Caldas A: Aphasia following right striato-insular infarction in a left-handed child: a clinicoradiological study. *Dev. Med. Child Neurol.: 24*, 173 – 182, 1982.

Fox PT, Perlmutter JS, Raichle ME: A stereotactic method of anatomical localization for positron emission tomography. *J. Comput. Assist. Tomogr.: 9*, 141 – 153, 1985.

Freedman M, Alexander MP, Naeser MA: Anatomic basis of transcortical motor aphasia. *Neurology: 40*, 409 – 417, 1984.

Fromm D, Holland AL, Swindell CS, Reinmuth OM: Various consequences of subcortical stroke. *Arch. Neurol. (Chicago): 42*, 943 – 950, 1985.

Gado M, Hanaway J, Frank R: Functional anatomy of the cerebral cortex by computed tomography. *J. Comput. Axial Tomogr.: 3*, 1 – 19, 1979.

Galaburda AM, Pandya DN: The intrinsic architectonic and connectional organization of the superior temporal region of the rhesus monkey. *J. Comp. Neurol.: 221*, 169 – 184, 1983.

Gardner H, Brownell HH, Wapner W, Michelow D: Missing the point: the role of the right hemisphere in the processing of complex linguistic materials. In Periman E (Editor), *Cognitive Process and the Right Hemisphere* New York: Academic Press, 1983.

Geschwind N: Disconnexion syndromes in animals and man. *Brain: 88*, 237 – 294, 585 – 644, 1965.

Geschwind N, Quadfasel FA, Segarra JM: Isolation of the speech area. *Neuropsychologia: 6*, 327 – 340, 1968.

Geschwind N: Aphasia. *N. Engl. J. Med.: 284*, 654 – 656, 1971.

Goldstein K: *Language and Language Disturbances*. New York: Grune and Stratton, 1948.

Goodglass H, Kaplan E: *The Assessment of Aphasia and Related Disorders*. Philadelphia: Lea & Febiger, 1982.

Graff-Radford N, Damasio A: Disturbances of speech and language associated with thalamic dysfunction. *Semin. Neurol.: 4*, 162 – 168, 1984.

Graff-Radford N, Schelper RL, Ilinsky I, Damasio H: Computed tomography and post mortem study of a nonhemorrhagic thalamic infarction. *Arch. Neurol. (Chicago): 42*, 761 – 763, 1985a.

Graff-Radford N, Damasio H, Yamada T, Eslinger P, Damasio A: Nonhemorrhagic thalamic infarctions: clinical, neurophysiological and electrophysiological findings in four anatomical groups defined by CT. *Brain: 108*, 485 – 516, 1985b.

Hanaway J, Scott WR, Strother CM: *Atlas of the Human Brain and the Orbit for Computed Tomography*. St. Louis, MO: Warren H. Green, Inc., 1977.

Hayward RW, Naeser MA, Zatz LM: Cranial computed tomography in aphasia. *Radiology: 123*, 653 – 660, 1977.

Jonas S: The supplementary motor region and speech emission.

J. Commun. Disord.: 14, 349 – 373, 1981.

Kertesz A, Lesk D, McCabe P: Isotope localization of infarcts in aphasia. *Arch. Neurol. (Chicago): 34*, 590 – 601, 1977.

Kertesz A, Harlock W, Coates R: Computer tomographic localization, lesion size, and prognosis in aphasia and nonverbal impairment. *Brain Lang.: 8*, 34 – 50, 1979.

Kertesz A, Sheppard A, MacKenzie R: Localization in transcortical sensory aphasia. *Arch. Neurol. (Chicago): 39*, 475 – 478, 1982.

Knopman DS, Rubens AB, Klassen AC, Meyer MW: Regional cerebral blood flow correlates of auditory processing. *Arch. Neurol.: 39*, 487 – 493, 1982.

Knopman DS, Selnes OA, Niccum N, Rubens AB: Recovery of naming in aphasia: relationship to fluency, comprehension and CT findings. *Neurology: 34*, 1461 – 1470, 1984a.

Knopman DS, Rubens AB, Selnes OA, Klassen AC, Meyer MW: Mechanisms of recovery from aphasia: evidence from serial Xenon 133 cerebral blood flow studies. *Ann. Neurol.: 15*, 530 – 535, 1984b.

Konorski J, Kozniewska H, Stepien L: Analysis of symptoms and cerebral localization of audio-verbal aphasia. *Proc. VII Int. Congr. Neurol.: 2*, 234 – 236, 1961.

Környey E: Aphasie transcorticale et ècholalie: le problème de l'initiative de la parole. *Rev. Neurol. (Paris): 131*, 347 – 363, 1975.

Lazorthes G, Gouaze A, Salamon G: *Vascularisation et Circulation de l'Encephale*. Paris: Masson, 1976.

Lichtheim L: On aphasia. *Brain: 7*, 433 – 484, 1885.

Liepmann H, Pappenheim M: Über einem Fall von sogenannter Leitungsaphasie mit anatomischem Befund. *Z. Neurol. Psychiatr.: 27*, 1 – 41, 1914.

Luzzatti C, Scotti G, Gattoni A: Further suggestions for cerebral CT-localization. *Cortex: 15*, 483 – 490, 1979.

Masdeu JC, Schoene WC, Funkenstein H: Aphasia following infarction of the left supplementary motor area: a clinicopathologic study. *Neurology: 28*, 1220 – 1223, 1978.

Matsui T, Hirano A: *An Atlas of the Human Brain for Computerized Tomography*. Tokyo: Igaku-Shoin Ltd., 1978.

Mazzocchi F, Vignolo LA: Localization of lesions of aphasia: clinical CT scan correlations in stroke patients. *Cortex: 15*, 627 – 654, 1979.

Mohr JP, Watters WC, Duncan GW: Thalamic hemorrhage and aphasia. *Brain Lang.: 2*, 3 – 17, 1975.

Mohr JP, Pessin MS, Finkelstein S, Funkenstein HH, Duncan GW, Davis KR: Broca's aphasia: pathologic and clinical. *Neurology: 28*, 311 – 324, 1978.

Naeser MA, Hayward RW: Lesion localization in aphasia with cranial compound tomography and the Boston Diagnostic Aphasia Exam. *Neurology: 28*, 545 – 551, 1978.

Naeser MA, Alexander MP, Helm-Estabrooks N, Levine HL, Laughlin SA, Geschwind N: Aphasia with predominantly subcortical lesion sites. *Arch. Neurol. (Chicago): 39*, 2 – 14, 1982.

Palacios E, Fine M, Henghton VM: *Multiplanar Anatomy of the Head and Neck: For Computed Tomography*. New York: John Wiley and Sons, 1980.

Poeck K, De Bleser R, Von Keyserlingk DG: Computed tomograph localization of standard aphasic syndromes. *Adv. Neurol.: 42*, 71 – 89, 1984.

Raichle M: Positron Emission Tomography. In Mountcastle V (Editor), *Handbook of Physiology,* 1987.

Ross M, Damasio H, Eslinger P: The role of the supplementary motor area (SMA) and anterior cingulate (AC) in the generation of movement. *Neurology: 36 (Suppl. 1),* 346, 1986.

Ross ED: The aprosodias. Functional-anatomical organization of the affective components of language in the right hemisphere. *Arch. Neurol. (Chicago): 38,* 561 – 564, 1981.

Rubens AB: Aphasia with infarction in the territory of the anterior cerebral artery. *Cortex: 11,* 239 – 250, 1975.

Rubens A, Selnes O: Aphasia with insular cortex infarction. In *Academy of Aphasia,* 1986.

Sanides F: Functional architecture of motor and sensory cortices in primates in the light of a new concept of neocortex evolution. In Noback CR, Montagna W (Editors), *The Primate Brain.* New York: Appleton, pp. 137 – 208, 1970.

Salamon G, Huang YP: *Radiologic Anatomy of the Brain.* Berlin: Springer Verlag, 1976.

Sarkissow SA, Filimonoft IN, Konowa EP, et al: *Atlas of the Cytoarchitectonics of the Human Cerebral Cortex.* Moscow: Medgiz, 1955.

Schiff HB, Alexander MP, Naeser MA, Galaburda AM: Aphemia: clinico-anatomic correlations. *Arch. Neurol. (Chicago): 40,* 720 – 727, 1983.

Selnes OA, Knopman DS, Niccum N, Rubens AB, Larson D: Computed tomographic scan correlates of auditory comprehension deficits in aphasia: a prospective recovery study. *Arch. Neurol. (Chicago): 13,* 558 – 566, 1983.

Selnes OA, Niccum N, Knopman DS, Rubens AB: Recovery of single word comprehension: CT-scan correlates. *Brain Lang.: 21,* 72 – 84, 1984.

Selnes OA, Knopman DS, Niccum N, Rubens AB: The critical role of Wernicke's area in sentence repetition. *Arch. Neurol. (Chicago): 17,* 549 – 557, 1985.

Talairach J, Szikla G. *Atlas d'anatomie stéréotaxique du télencéphale.* Paris: Masson et Cie, 1967.

Tranel D, Biller J, Damasio H, Adams H, Cornell S: Global aphasia without hemiparesis. *Arch. Neurol. (Chicago): 44,* 304 – 308, 1987.

Tonkonogy J, Goodglass H: Language function, foot of the third frontal gyrus, and rolandic operculum. *Arch. Neurol. (Chicago): 38,* 486 – 490, 1981.

Vignolo LA, Boccardi E, Caverni L: Unexpected CT-scan findings in global aphasia. *Cortex 22,* 55 – 69, 1986.

Waddington MM: *Atlas of Cerebral Angiography With Anatomic Correlation.* Boston: Little, Brown & Co., 1974.

Wernicke C: *Der aphasische Symptomen-Komplex* Breslau: Cohn and Weigert, 1874.

Wernicke C: Einige neuere Arbeiten über Aphasie. *Fortschr. Med.: 4,* 377 – 463, 1886.

CHAPTER 2

Clinical-anatomical correlations of aphasia following predominantly subcortical lesions

Michael P. Alexander

Aphasia Program, Braintree Hospital, 250 Pond St., Braintree, MA 02184, and Department of Neurology, Boston University School of Medicine, Boston, U.S.A.

Introduction

For 125 years the focus of clinical and investigational interest in aphasia has been the cerebral cortex. All textbooks have come to show a lateral drawing of the brain, marked with a 'B', a 'W', and often an 'SM' or an 'A'. Discussions of the various aphasia syndromes often started and ended with analysis of the extent of cortical involvement. Cortical regions have been given eponymous designations based on their presumed role in the clinical profile of the aphasic syndromes. But even from the first clinical-anatomical reports in aphasia, there has been recognition, sometimes explicit and sometimes only implicit, that lesions in subcortical structures are essential to aphasic syndromes. It has been amply rediscovered that the first case of Broca, with a lesion in Broca's cortical area, also had a very large subcortical lesion extension (Signoret et al., 1984). Marie came to argue that lesion in a particular zone of the capsular-striatal region, which has been called the 'quadrilateral space of Marie', was instrumental in the limitation of speech output in some cases of aphasia, although not critical in the language *processing* functions (Marie, 1906).

Isolated investigators returned to the question of subcortical pathways over the next decades. Déjerine (1906) observed that lesions of the subcortical white matter deep to motor cortex were as likely as lesions in the cortex itself to produce dysarthria even without aphasia. Bonhoeffer (1914) observed that a combination of lesions, including ones in the deep frontal white matter and in the anterior corpus callosum, would produce a language output disturbance as severe as a classical Broca's lesion. Liepmann (1905) observed that patients with right hemiparesis and aphasia were much more likely to be apraxic than patients with right hemiparesis alone. This observation has been interpreted in numerous ways, but for the purposes here it is enough to note that cases with lesion extending up along the paraventricular white matter are associated with left limb apraxia and lesions restricted to the deep capsular region are not. Kleist (1934) asserted that even the classical lesion of Broca's area only produced Broca's aphasia if it included the deep white matter efferent projections.

Despite these observations, the thrust of aphasia-anatomy research has focused on cortical structures. In the last 10 years, an entirely new class of observations about the role of subcortical structures in aphasia has emerged as a benefit of new techniques of neuroradiology, first CT and now MRI and PET. This chapter will review modern notions about the role of subcortical structures in speech and language disorders.

What is meant by subcortical?

We will review distinct cerebral regions as well as the evidence that lesions in those regions will result in any disturbance to speech or language functions. There are subcortical nuclear structures: the *putamen* and the *caudate* (together, the striatum) and the *thalamus* have been the most intensively analysed. There is the *cortex of the insula,* which is, of course, hardly 'subcortical'. Because it is buried beneath the visible surface of the brain and because on tomographic projections of the brain it seems to be lying deep to surface cortex, there has been some tendency to include the insula in discussions of subcortical structures so it is worth reviewing, if only to extract it, Orpheus-like, from the subcortical world.

There are the various layers of white matter structures (Nauta and Feirtag, 1986). The white matter deep to the cortex (*subcortical white matter, SCWM*), the deeper white matter lying adjacent to the lateral ventricle (*paraventricular, PVWM)* or wrapping around the frontal horn of the lateral ventricle (*periventricular, PVWM)* are readily differentiated. The paraventricular white matter can be subdivided along the anterior-posterior axis into geographically distinct regions; anterior lateral, anterior superior, middle superior and posterior superior *paraventricular white matter.* Our attempts to capture a coherent terminology for these regions have led to some changes in the labels since our first report in 1982 (Naeser et al., 1982).

There are deep efferent and afferent pathways and the structural bottlenecks through which they pass. There is a white matter area deep to frontal operculum but lateral to the internal capsule which we have designated the *frontal isthmus (FI).* In a similar vein there is a white matter area situated between the lateral thalamus and the temporal lobe which Nielsen (1946) designated the *temporal isthmus (TI).* Finally, there are the capsules. The *anterior limb of the internal capsule (ALIC)* is the one which seems the most involved with language function; the *genu of the internal capsule (GIC)* may have special significance for speech function.

Some of these structures are amenable to subdivision and will be subdivided in the text, but they are the basic building blocks for notions of subcortical structures in aphasia. The schematic Figs. 1 – 6 outline the usual location of these regions in the projections of CT methodology.

What types of material are appropriate for analysis?

There are assumptions made in the analysis which follows of the available lesion studies. These as-

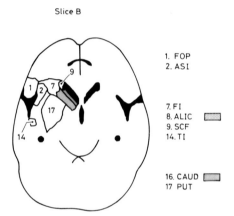

Fig. 1. Schematic representation of critical cortical and subcortical regions at the level of lower Broca's area; abbreviations are expanded in Table 1.

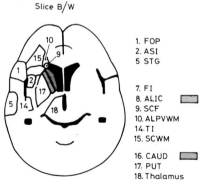

Fig. 2. Schematic representation of critical cortical and subcortical regions at the level of upper Broca's area and anterior Wernicke's area; abbreviations are expanded in Table 1.

sumptions need to be made explicit for the reader to judge the validity of the conclusions.

First, acute vascular lesions are the pathology of preference in building clinical-pathological correlations. With acute lesions there is no question of gradual compensation for lesions of insidious onset such as tumors or degenerative diseases. With discrete vascular lesions there is no question of differentiating the effects of infiltration of brain from actual destruction of brain as there is with tumors, and there is no question of differentiating the lesion effect from mass effects as there is in tumors, abscesses and early intracerebral hemorrhages.

With single vascular lesions there is less problem specifying the target lesion-behavior effect than there is in those diseases which are, by their very nature, multifocal such as degenerative disorders, trauma or multiple sclerosis. These observations do not eliminate the very likely possibility that all brain diseases follow some robust rules of brain-behavior relationships; they merely aver that the most appropriate substrate for establishing the gross level of lesion-aphasia correlations is with single, acute-onset destructive lesions. To be sure, the other etiologies probably follow, at least approximately, the same rules − after all, deep tem-

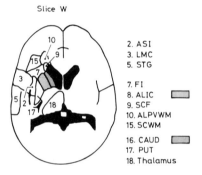

Fig. 3. Schematic representation of critical cortical and subcortical regions at the level of posterior Wernicke's area; abbreviations are expanded in Table 1.

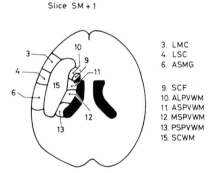

Fig. 5. Schematic representation of critical cortical and subcortical regions at the level of the upper body of the lateral ventricle; abbreviations are expanded in Table 1.

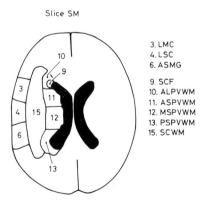

Fig. 4. Schematic representation of critical cortical and subcortical regions at the level of the body of the lateral ventricle; abbreviations are expanded in Table 1.

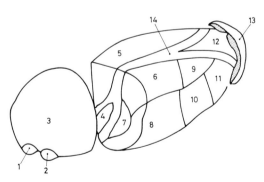

Fig. 6. Schematic representation of the thalamus (modified from Brodal, 1981). Perspective is oblique from the rear of the thalamus; the reticular nucleus has been peeled away except for the anterior-most portion in this schematic. Areas are: 1, medial geniculate; 2, lateral geniculate; 3, pulvinar; 4, centromedian; 5, dorsomedial; 6, posterolateral; 7, ventroposteromedial; 8, ventroposterolateral; 9, dorsolateral; 10, ventrolateral; 11, ventroanterior; 12, anterior; 13, reticular; 14, intralaminar region (specific nuclei not indicated).

TABLE 1

Abbreviations used in the figures and text

1. FOP: frontal operculum including pars opercularis and pars triangularis
2. ASI: anterior, superior insular cortex
3. LMC: lower motor cortex
4. LSC: lower sensory cortex
5. STG: superior temporal cortex including Wernicke's area
6. ASMG: anterior supramarginal cortex
7. FI: frontal isthmus
8. ALIC: anterior limb internal capsule
9. SCF: subcallosal fasciculus
10. ALPVWM: anterolateral periventricular white matter
11. ASPVWM: anterior third of superior paraventricular white matter
12. MSPVWM: middle third of superior paraventricular white matter
13. PSPVWM: posterior third of superior paraventricular white matter
14. TI: temporal isthmus
15. SCWM: subcortical white matter
16. CAUD: caudate
17. PUT: putamen, probably including the globus pallidus on the lower sections
18. Thalamus, individual nuclei represented in Fig. 6

poral glioblastomas are more likely to present with a Wernicke's aphasia than with prosopagnosia – but the other etiologies probably have some of their own rules which do not apply to the stroke rules.

Second, if they are not included in the acute phase, intracerebral hemorrhages may also be a valuable substrate for study of aphasia-lesion relationships because they are single lesions, because late scans can identify the area of tissue destruction rather than the mass lesion alone, and because they do not follow vascular territories so they can cause lesion configurations not available for study from ischemic stroke alone.

Third, strokes do not produce a single aphasia-lesion profile which remains unchanged over all subsequent time; it is essential that even cases of stroke be studied at appropriate times after onset. Research from various sources (Mazzocchi and Vignolo, 1979; Basso et al., 1985; Alexander et al., 1987a) over recent years has suggested a three-

epoch time-frame for models of aphasia investigations. The **acute phase** lasts until 2 (or perhaps 3) weeks after onset. During this interval there are remote effects of the lesion and recovery may be very rapid. This phase is an important part of the clinical profile of any lesion, but it is not usually considered the robust anatomical relationship. The **lesion phase** lasts for several weeks, perhaps up to 3 – 4 months after onset. During this interval the main effect on clinical presentation is the lesion. This is the period of greatest interest for brain-behavior relationships. The **late phase** begins at a few months after onset and goes on for the remainder of the patient's life or until a second neurological event occurs. During this interval the various contributors to recovery play a role in the clinical presentation. It is even probable that some very interesting **lesion phase** relationships go away altogether during the **late phase**; this would certainly make **late phase** studies with negative results somewhat dubious. The **late phase** may be exactly the same as the **lesion phase**; recovery or even improvement do not always occur. There may be some phenomena which are primarily **late phase** events such as most classical agrammatism (Zurif et al., 1972) and most deep dyslexia (Coltheart, 1980). They are not uninteresting or theoretically unimportant, but they are not necessarily the clinical-*anatomical* relationships of greatest importance. A full analysis of lesion-behavior relationships should probably try to capture all three phases, but in any case the phase needs to be specified as well as the behavior and the anatomy.

Lesions of subcortical nuclear structures

There is little evidence that lesions limited to the striatum produce lasting aphasia. There are numerous sources for this assertion. The literature on lacunar infarction does not include documented cases of aphasia after small lesions in the striatum (Fisher, 1982). The larger, but still 'small', lesions reported by several investigators as associated with aphasia have always included significant damage to adjacent white matter structures (Naeser et al.,

1982; Damasio et al., 1982; Cappa et al., 1983). In some of these reports, arguments are made that for a particular case the critical lesion is in the striatum, but the published scan will not clearly confirm that assertion or will clearly demonstrate lesion in adjacent structures as well. For instance, Cappa et al. (1983) discuss the role of the head of the caudate for their case 2 – 3, but the single section of CT published shows lesion in the paraventricular white matter at the margins of the frontal horn and does not even unequivocally show the head of the caudate nucleus, which is the focus of the presumed clinical-anatomical correlations. Other case material which claims to demonstrate a relationship between subcortical nuclear structures and aphasia is difficult to interpret for the very same reasons (Brunner et al., 1982; Wallesch et al., 1983; Puel et al., 1984).

In two reports Wallesch and coworkers (Brunner et al., 1982; Wallesch et al., 1983) have concluded that lesions in the basal ganglia result in a profile of transcortical motor aphasia. In the first report, patients were selected many months post-onset and the clinical testing does not really establish a clear profile of impairment, as all patients with restricted basal ganglia lesions are clumped together. In the second report, 7 cases are described and 3 are said to have basically transcortical motor aphasia with good recovery. The detailed evaluations were done within the first 10 days after onset. The first case is described as having had an infarct of the lateral putamen (although he was also apparently hemiparetic, so the lesion must have extended into white matter in the posterior limb of the internal capsule or the paraventricular white matter as well). The other two had lesions of the 'pallidum'. The second two cases are particularly instructive. Both are said to have transcortical motor aphasia, but one is dysarthric and the other is not. Their scores on a standardized test, expressed in percentiles, were: auditory comprehension – case 2, 90th; case 3, 5th; repetition – case 2, 100th; case 3, 30th: naming – case 2, 95th; case 3, 6th. The scores on the Token Test were 88% correct and 12% correct, respectively. No CT figures were

published. All three were apparently not aphasic after a few months. I do not believe that these three cases make an adequate argument that lesions restricted to the striatum or the pallidum result in any particular profile of aphasia. Reduction in speech output, in parallel with bradykinesia in other activities, would not constitute transcortical motor aphasia.

Puel and coworkers (Puel et al., 1984) have also described a role for lesions in subcortical nuclear structures in aphasia syndromes. In several patients with anomalous language profiles, they have concluded that lesions in striatum and thalamus interact with white matter lesion to produce peculiar constellations of signs. They have been unable, however, to attribute any robust rules of correlation to any single striatal or thalamic lesion profile.

Puel et al. also suggest that the work of Metter and colleagues using the [18]FDG PET methodology should be interpreted to conclude that the caudate and the thalamus play a special role in the aphasia syndromes. The observation has been made by Metter and coworkers (Metter et al., 1984) that all cases of aphasia have resting hypometabolism of the caudate and the thalamus, whatever the structural lesion revealed by CT or MRI. Puel et al. go further to assert that many of the aphasic signs in traditional aphasic disorders as well as in subcortical cases are due to damage to cortical-caudate or cortical-thalamic *connections*. In this argument, the combination of structural damage to subcortical nuclear structures combined with disconnections produces the atypical profiles of subcortical aphasia.

The report of Puel et al. is not satisfactory for conclusions about clinical-anatomical relationships. First, no information is provided about the time post-onset when the patients are being tested; it is apparently in the **acute phase.** Of the 25 cases reviewed 15 were intracerebral hemorrhages. As reviewed above, these cases *may* be suitable for clinical-anatomical studies, but not in the **acute phase** when there are uncomputable mass effects. The CT schematics presented are excellent, but only one level is presented per patient. The author's notion of the responsible lesion is obvious by the level they select to publish, but it is clear that the level selected is not the entire lesion. For instance, the published CT would not account for the hemiparesis or hemisensory deficit in most of these cases. If another level of CT would have to be shown to correlate with the elemental findings, perhaps the same is true of the language findings. Their first case, for example, has persistent hemiparesis and dysarthria without aphasia after an intracerebral hemorrhage. The published CT shows lesion in the external capsule, the posterior putamen and perhaps just edging into the posterior limb of the internal capsule. It is not certain that the published schematic accounts for the hemiparesis (posterior limb lesion perhaps?). How can we be sure that it accounts for the dysarthria any better? Without clarifying the interval in which testing occurred, without waiting for acute lesion effects to clear in cases of hemorrhage and without publishing the entire CT lesion, it is difficult to assess the role of any specific structures.

The work of Metter et al. does not lead to the conclusion that the caudate or the thalamus have a special role in aphasia syndromes; in fact, I don't think that Metter claims that it does. In the several reports of Metter's group (Metter et al., 1981, 1983, 1984, 1986), the hypometabolism of caudate and thalamus are prominent no matter what the clinical profile of aphasia. Studies of stroke, not selected for aphasia, have shown similar results even in the absence of aphasia. The contralateral cerebellum is also hypometabolic after aphasia-producing lesions (Kushner et al., 1984), but it is improbable that the cerebellum is going to be recruited as the brain structure of importance in subcortical aphasia. One of the key observations of Metter's group is from a single case study (Metter et al., 1985). The patient had lacunar lesions of the right striatum and the left internal capsule; PET demonstrated hypometabolism of the left frontal region. Postmortem confirmed the lacunar lesions and discounted any cortical pathology in the hypometabolic region. What can we conclude from this constellation of in vivo structural (CT),

in vivo physiological (PET) and postmortem microstructural observations? That the striatum is not a major projection to the lateral frontal lobe (including Broca's area)? That the anterior limb of the internal capsule actually carries the most significant connections for dorsolateral frontal areas? That the anterior limb of internal capsule is the critical region for anterior aphasia profiles after subcortical lesions? For the moment probably none of those are reasonable conclusions: the patient was not aphasic despite the hypometabolism of Broca's area!!

The only claim that Metter's group has made has come from retrospective correlation studies of individual elements of the aphasics' deficits with hypometabolism of cortical and basal ganglia regions (Metter et al., 1986). Hypometabolism in the caudate seems to correlate with speech impairments; hypometabolism of the thalamus seems to correlate with verbal memory deficits. Even these highly probable results need confirmation with a prospective series of cases with better control of time post-onset, which in the Metter work varies from weeks to over 10 years.

Isolated, and strictly unilateral, left lesions of the striatum may result in deficits in speech production. Transient periods of reduced output or longer latencies in production may also result. This is, I believe, the finding reported as 'transcortical motor aphasia' after pallidal lesions by Wallesch (Wallesch et al., 1983). Van Buren (1966) demonstrated that electrical stimulation in and near to the head of the caudate produced speech arrest – a loss of intent or 'impulse' to speak. The effect was similar to behavior after stimulation in the supplementary motor area. This work may be testimony to the importance of left caudate and supplementary motor area projections for speech initiation but also for the importance of the deep paraventricular white matter at the upper, outer angle of the frontal horn of the lateral ventricle (see discussion below).

Diseases which affect the striatum bilaterally (Parkinson's disease, Huntington's disease, and probably some cases of lacunar state) produce disturbances primarily in the rate and the volume of speech (Nakaro et al., 1973; Darley et al., 1975). Unilateral left striatal injury may contribute disturbances in rate or volume. The most common observation in our work has been of hypophonia after large left putaminal lesions, but the confounding effect of coincident damage to the ALIC, the frontal isthmus, the subcallosal fasciculus or the anterolateral periventricular white matter has not always been clear. We have reviewed above some of the conflicting anatomical conclusions in previous reports.

Isolated lesions of the anterior or lateral thalamus may result in a recognizable, albeit impermanent, aphasic profile. Review of the literature of 'thalamic' aphasia requires very careful attention to the etiology. The early modern reports were exclusively cases of intracerebral hemorrhage (Ciemens, 1970; Mohr et al., 1975; Cappa and Vignolo, 1979; Alexander and LoVerme, 1980). Case studies described an atypical aphasia with some superficial resemblance to transcortical aphasias; in some cases transcortical sensory aphasia – fluent, jargonaphasic output with impaired auditory comprehension but preserved repetition, and in others transcortical motor or mixed transcortical aphasia – reduced spontaneous output and prolonged latencies in responses. But every report also noted one or more of a number of quasi-aphasic elements: a generally underaroused state, variability and fatigability of performance, hypophonia which often worsened over the course of any single utterance, and production of bizarre elements in spontaneous output and in confrontation naming. The outcome was generally good. Subsequent larger studies have not consistently differentiated between the clinical profiles of putaminal intracerebral hemorrhage and thalamic intracerebral hemorrhage. The reports of Puel et al. (1984) and Alexander and LoVerme (1980) can both be interpreted to conclude that the variability, the progressive hypophonia, much of the bizarre element in output and the generally preserved repetition are all primarily features of acute deep intracerebral hemorrhage without

powerful specific association with any thalamic or putaminal region. Cases of thalamic hemorrhage have evolved to relatively stable deficit profiles of mild (see below) anomia and of amnesia; the residual language disorder presumably reflects the specific deficit pattern.

Cases of infarction of the thalamus have been reported with CT confirmation of lesion site (McFarling et al., 1982; Gorelick et al., 1984; Graff-Radford et al., 1984, 1985); these reports allow better definition of thalamic-aphasia syndromes. Large lesions of the left anterolateral thalamus have been most consistently associated with persistent aphasia (see Fig. 6 for orientation to thalamic nuclei). This is not the anatomical relationship that might have been expected from a knowledge of the anatomical projections of the association nuclei of the thalamus. Van Buren and coworkers (Van Buren, 1975) had demonstrated that when cases with large lesions of the temporal lobe came to postmortem, there would be significant neuronal loss in the ipsilateral posterior thalamic nuclei. These are the nuclei – posterolateral and pulvinar – which are known to have extensive projections to the language association areas of cerebral cortex (Peters, 1979). Ojemann and coworkers (Ojemann and Whitaker, 1978) had demonstrated that electrical stimulation of the anterior-superior pulvinar (Ojemann et al., 1968) and also of the ventrolateral nucleus (Ojemann and Ward, 1971) of the thalamus would result in speech arrest, word-finding failure or verbal memory deficits depending upon the timing and the strength of the current.

Ojemann has suggested that the VL nucleus of the thalamus has a 'specific alerting function' for language. Lesions result in a failure to recruit or activate cortical language zones in a timely manner for language operations that are, in fact, largely preserved. This deficit in activation would account for the transcortical qualities of the 'thalamic aphasia' commented on by most investigators in cases of hemorrhage (Cappa and Vignolo, 1979; Alexander and LoVerme, 1980) or infarction (McFarling et al., 1982; Gorelick et al., 1984). The

VL nucleus projects to the motor system of the cerebral cortex. Several reports have also noted hypophonia following lesions in the ventrolateral thalamus (Gorelick et al., 1984). This finding, too, may be due to the close connections of the ventrolateral thalamus to the pallidum and to the motor cortex. That the connections of lateral thalamus to cortex may be the critical factor in the disturbances seen after these cases is supported by observations in cases with infarctions in the territory of the left anterior choroidal artery (DeCroix et al., 1986). Large infarcts in this territory produced either dysarthria or an aphasia described as 'thalamic', that is, with 'loss of verbal fluency, difficulty in organizing speech, rare semantic paraphasias' but with intact comprehension and repetition. According to Percheron (1977), the anterior choroidal artery does not participate in the circulation of the thalamus although infarcts in its territory at least abut immediately on the lateral margin of the thalamus, and may actually involve the lateral thalamic structures (Graff-Radford et al., 1985). Review of the published CT scans of two of the cases of thalamic infarction with aphasia (McFarling et al., 1982, case 1; Gorelick et al., 1984) raises the possibility that these lesions were actually in the anterior choroidal circulations. It is uncertain what combinations of thalamocortical projections and thalamic attentional systems are damaged with these lesions placed at the lateral margin of the thalamus.

In addition to these findings with lateral thalamic infarcts, *language* deficits have been reported with lesions in the more anterior portions of the thalamus. The exact constellation of nuclei involved in the production of aphasic signs is not established with certainty. The number of potentially important structures is very great and the anatomical separation and definition by CT and probably by MRI is not great, so most conclusions are inferential.

Graff-Radford et al. described an aphasia profile after unilateral left thalamic infarction in the territory of the polar or paramedian arteries (Graff-Radford et al., 1984). This lesion involves the dorsomedian nucleus, the anterior nucleus, perhaps a portion of the centromedian nucleus and the intralaminar region of the thalamus. The implications for memory function are obvious, and, in fact, the patients with substantial aphasia have had significant amnesia. It is possible that the semantic deficit in anterior lesions is similar to that in the more laterally situated thalamic lesions (Gorelick et al., 1984). Katz et al. (1987) have described a patient with paramedian territory lesion but also with considerable involvement of the ventrolateral nucleus; there was severe anomia as the sole manifestation of aphasia.

In conclusion, the language disorder in cases of lateral thalamic, anterior thalamic or both regions simultaneously has been primarily a deficit at the semantic level; word-finding problems, semantic substitutions and impaired confrontation naming. There are usually abundant additional cognitive and attentional deficits, particularly in the cases with anterior or both lesions. Puel et al. (1984) described a dissociation between relatively good confrontation naming and quite impaired spontaneous word retrieval in conversation. The patients also had considerable difficulty with formulation of language, manifested as disorganized and incomplete narratives. These patients are also often somewhat inattentive and slow in responding, perseverative in content, unconcerned about their communication difficulties, and unmotivated to struggle to communicate better; these deficits combine to produce a failure of sustained communication which is much more severe than the isolated deficit at the level of semantics would have predicted.

It is likely that each element of this profile has its own morbid anatomy, but the exact relationships are not known with precision. It is probable that the memory deficit is due to lesions in either or both the DM nucleus and the mamillothalamic tract in the intralaminar region, that the motivation deficits are due to lesions in the DM nucleus and its prefrontal projections, that the language formulation deficits are due to damage to ventrolateral nucleus or its frontal projections and that the attentional/intentional deficits are due to lesions in the intralaminar alerting pathways or to the reticular nucleus or both. If there is a specific anatomy of the semantic deficit separable from those deficits, it has been difficult to establish. The likeliest lesion is one in the anterior or ventrolateral nuclei.

It also remains uncertain which isolated lesions of the left thalamus result in *permanent* aphasia. We have followed cases of infarction and of hemorrhage, and within months all significant evidence of language disorder cleared; other cognitive deficits, particularly memory disorder, have not cleared. One of the cases in the report of Alexander and LoVerme (1980) showed *complete* resolution of all language deficits within 3 months of a large posterior thalamic hemorrhage; subsequent postmortem study demonstrated *complete* destruction of the pulvinar and the posterior half of the thalamus and its replacement with a hemosiderin-stained cavity.

Clarification of the role of specific thalamic regions in aphasia will likely improve with better-resolution imaging, and better attention to the investigational constraints of the lesions. Intracerebral hemorrhage cases are only appropriate for lesion-behavior correlations in the **lesion phase** when imaging documents resolution of the mass effects, midline shifts, intraventricular blood, and all of the other complicating features of the intracerebral hemorrhage. There may well be a specific neurobehavioral syndrome of acute deep intracerebral hemorrhage as described by Mohr et al. (1975), Alexander and LoVerme (1980) and Puel et al. (1984); this is not a very specific *anatomical-functional* relationship. Cases of thalamic infarction are more appropriate for brain-behavior studies; in these cases the investigational constraint is the presence of other cognitive deficits which compromise unequivocal identification of the language deficit as opposed to the initiation deficit or the formulation deficit or the amnesic problem. PET, even with the limitations described above, may also be interesting in the thalamic infarct cases. If small lesions of the thalamus disrupt major cortical projection systems, there may well be very specific profiles of cortical hypometabolism which cannot possibly be accounted for by structural cortical lesion. Thus, different profiles of cortical hypometabolism *may* distinguish more effectively between the thalamic lesions resulting in aphasia and those which do not (Baron et al., 1986).

Lesions in the white matter pathways

It is probably most convincing to begin with a brief review of some of the more empirically defensible correlations between white matter lesions and specific deficits. Lesions in the descending motor pathways result in hemiparesis. Lesions in motor cortex could presumably result in hemiparesis, but, even in the cases of large middle cerebral territory infarction, few lesions ascend higher than the area for arm. Persistent hemiparesis is almost always due to lesion in the descending motor pathways. In a gross dissection study Ross placed the descending pyramidal system adjacent to the waist of the lateral ventricle (Ross, 1980). In the terminology introduced at the beginning of this review, these pathways would lie in the posterior part of the middle 1/3 of the superior paraventricular white matter (Fig. 4). The motor pathways then descend into the middle part of the posterior limb of the internal capsule before becoming the middle portion of the cerebral peduncles. In cases of subcortical lesions, any accompanying hemiparesis is caused by lesions in these descending pathways.

Dysarthria is another motor disturbance which is probably the result of a reasonably straightforward pathway effect. Lesions in the region of the genu and posterior portion of the ALIC (Figs. 1–3) have commonly been associated with dysarthria (Fisher, 1982). There is not adequate clinical evidence to unequivocally account for this effect or to characterize the dysarthria profile. Lecours and Lhermitte (1976) described an isolated dysarthric syndrome in their report of 'pure phonetic disintegration' due to cortical lesion in motor cortex (Fig.

4). They emphasized the dystonic quality of the impaired motor control of speech. Tonkonogy and Goodglass (1981) described a similar case. We have also described the effects of small lesions limited to lower motor cortex *or* to the descending pathways (Schiff et al., 1983). Aram et al. (1983) have described a similar dysarthric profile in a child after a discrete paraventricular lesion, presumably involving the descending pathways. These cases suggest that involvement of the system of descending corticobulbar structures in the left hemisphere produces a slow dysarthria with labored transition from phoneme to phoneme, even within a single word, which results in substantial abnormalities in prosody. There is hardly sufficient clinical evidence, however, to consider this assertion proven. Moreover, with the purely subcortical lesion cases there is often coincident injury to the adjacent striatum or to the anterior limb of internal capsule. In this latter structure course the descending pathways from motor association cortex to pons and contralateral cerebellum and the ascending pathways from thalamus to motor association cortex. The variability of lesion in these structures may account for the variability in disturbances of rate and volume which accompany the primarily articulatory deficits. It also seems to be the case that some right-handed patients do not show persistent dysarthria after damage to this system; there is apparently more redundancy in this functional system in some patients than there is in others. In any case, the specifics of the interaction of lesions in corticobulbar structures with those in extrapyramidal structures have yet to be worked out.

Lesions in paraventricular white matter

Anterolateral periventricular white matter is the area adjacent to and surrounding the frontal horn of the lateral ventricle (Figs. 1 – 3). In an earlier report, we had labelled this area the anterior, superior periventricular white matter (Alexander et al., 1987a), but the present terminology is less ambiguous. Lesions restricted to this area are not

common, but they have been reported (Alexander et al., 1987a). The clinical syndrome associated with lesions in this area is transient muteness, followed by a more prolonged reduction in spontaneous output. These patients may have word-finding deficits and semantic substitutions, but the major difficulty is in initiation of output. The same profile is seen with written language. If the patients are examined in a manner which allows short directed responses, they will not seem aphasic at all. Only when they are asked open-ended questions which require that they initiate a lengthier response will the reduction in output be obvious. Tasks such as word-list generation will emphasize their problem in initiation as well.

This lesion is situated to damage at least two structures which may be involved in initiation: the supplementary motor area and the subcallosal fasciculus. Botez and Barbeau (1971) observed that the supplementary motor area in the posterior portion of the medial face of the superior frontal gyrus was positioned to be the most cephalad representation of the limbic system with important ascending projections from thalamus and from adjacent cingulate. Lesions in the medial frontal region including the supplementary motor area may result in fairly restricted deficits in spontaneous output with reduced initiation. Efferent pathways from the supplementary motor area pass to the motor association cortex including the frontal operculum (Jürgens, 1984; Damasio and Van Hoesen, 1980). It is probable that the anterolateral periventricular white matter lesion disrupts this pathway and thus impairs the facilitating effect of supplementary motor area limbic input on spontaneous output. Even lesions in the white matter deep to the middle frontal gyrus may involve the radiations of this system toward motor association cortex and result in similar initiation deficits. Second, the lesion immediately adjacent to the frontal horn may damage the subcallosal fasciculus which is the short pathway of radiation of cingulate to caudate input (Yakovlev and Locke, 1961; Naeser et al., 1989). This is another avenue by which limbic facilitation (cingulate) may drive the motor systems for spontaneous output. All cases in the neurological literature which propose that striatal or head of caudate lesions alone can result in transcortical motor aphasia must be inspected for lesion in this area. The effect of small lesions in the anterolateral periventricular white matter is not long-lived. Within a few weeks, it may be difficult to confirm that there is any residual defect. This may lead to negative results which are correct but overlook the main lesion effect.

In our earliest report (Naeser et al., 1982), we simply referred to the entire region above the internal capsule and putamen as superior extension. It has come to be apparent that there are plausible subdivisions of this region (Alexander et al., 1987a), and the present terminology will reflect that (Figs. 4 and 5). Lesions of the *anterior 1/3 of the superior paraventricular white matter* adjacent to the lateral ventricle will result in a profile, similar to that described just above, of reduced spontaneous language output, but there may also be dysarthria, hemiparesis and left limb apraxia depending upon the exact anterior-posterior distribution of the paraventricular white matter lesion. The pathological anatomy of dysarthria and hemiparesis after damage to the *middle 1/3 of the superior paraventricular white matter* is reviewed above. That left limb apraxia is a common accompaniment of this lesion was demonstrated by Kertesz and Ferro (1984) and by Alexander et al. (1986). The lesion may disrupt one or both of two well-established pathways. First, *intra*hemispheric bidirectional connections between the parietal lobe and the motor association cortex which are the likely anatomical substrate for learned motor activities (Heilman et al., 1982) and, second, *inter*hemispheric pathways through the body of the corpus callosum which are the probable substrate for the control of the left limb in learned motor activity, at least in response to verbal stimuli. This is reviewed in greater detail below.

Lesions in the *posterior 1/3 of the superior paraventricular white matter* (Figs. 4 and 5) do not have an important functional effect on language,

but they are associated with an illuminating pathway effect. In a patient with complete section of the corpus callosum, Sparks and Geschwind (1968) demonstrated that auditory stimuli presented to the left ear were detected normally when presented alone, but completely suppressed when presented simultaneously (dichotically) with stimuli to the right ear. This phenomenon seemed unequivocally an effect of damage to a major white matter pathway normally crossing the corpus callosum from right to left. Sparks et al. (1970) later demonstrated that among aphasics with unilateral left damage there were many who demonstrated suppression of right ear stimuli, some who did not suppress either ear, and a minority who suppressed the left ear. They suggested that the last condition − unexpected or 'paradoxical' suppression of stimuli to the ear ipsilateral to the left hemisphere lesion − was due to damage to the very same pathway as in the callosal section case, but in the aphasic patients the pathway was damaged within the deep left hemisphere after the pathway exited the callosum proper. Rubens et al. (1978) and Damasio and Damasio (1979) subsequently demonstrated the CT anatomy of this effect. The callosal auditory pathways are in the posterior 1/3 of the superior paraventricular white matter; left hemisphere lesions in that region are associated with the suppression of the left ear stimulus.

The exact location of the auditory pathways in the callosum has recently been demonstrated (Alexander, 1988). This pathway is only of direct significance to clinical phenomena if the left hemisphere *intra*hemispheric pathways from thalamus to temporal lobe are damaged; then there are no alternative pathways for auditory-verbal processing. This effect would be the auditory-verbal equivalent of the impaired reading comprehension which occurs after simultaneous damage to the left occipital lobe and the callosal splenial fibers carrying visual information from the right hemisphere (Damasio and Damasio, 1983). The extent to which the callosal auditory pathways are preserved with unilateral left temporal lesions may also play a role in recovery from incomplete lesions of Wernicke's area. There is, as yet, no empirical evidence to be recruited in support of either of these anatomically likely statements.

In our first report (Naeser et al., 1982), we referred to lesions which extended posteriorly from the putamen as simply posterior extension. Inspection of cases has suggested that the critical area of damage with posterior extension was the white matter convergence at the posterior, inferior temporal lobe. This had been labelled the *temporal isthmus* by Neilsen (1946). The exact arrangement of ascending and descending and association tracts within the temporal isthmus is not known (Figs. 1 and 2). The anterior half of the temporal isthmus is known to carry the ascending connections of the medial geniculate nucleus to the auditory cortex. The posterior half of the temporal isthmus is the posterior coursing visual radiations from lateral geniculate nucleus. It is also likely that some connections from the posterior thalamic nuclei, at least the pulvinar and posterolateral nucleus (Fig. 6) to the temporoparieto-occipital association areas pass through the temporal isthmus (Peters, 1979). We have reported in two different groups of patients that infarcts which damage the anterior half of the temporal isthmus are associated with significant deficits in auditory comprehension (Naeser et al., 1982; Alexander et al., 1987a). These were cases with primarily capsular-putaminal infarcts but the extent of nuclear injury did not predict the comprehension deficits. Relatively minor posterior extension of the lesion caudally from the posterior putamen across the temporal isthmus and the posterior part of the posterior limb of internal capsule were more convincingly associated with comprehension deficits.

In the cases of cerebral infarction, the lesion has primarily been anterior to the temporal isthmus and the profile has been similar to classical Wernicke's aphasia. In retrospect, this lesion may account for some confusing results reported in our first study of aphasia after deep intracerebral hemorrhage (Alexander and LoVerme, 1980). We

reported a persistent Wernicke's aphasia associated with hemiplegia in 3 of 15 cases after deep intracerebral hemorrhage; two had primarily posterior putaminal intracerebral hemorrhage and one had a lateral thalamic intracerebral hemorrhage. While standing as further evidence that the thalamic and putaminal portions of the lesions per se were not critical in the clinical profiles, the cases probably should have told us that it was the injury to the temporal isthmus that was the cause of comprehension deficits. It may also be that pressure effects on the thalamic pathways to the temporal isthmus are the cause of the early, but rapidly clearing, comprehension problems often described in thalamic intracerebral hemorrhage aphasia.

Damage to the more posterior portions of the temporal isthmus may result in a different profile. There are very few well-described cases to analyse, but the literature on transcortical sensory aphasia suggests that the anatomical feature which distinguishes transcortical sensory aphasia from Wernicke's aphasia is the sparing of the direct auditory connections in transcortical sensory aphasia despite involvement of the association connections (Damasio, 1981). Patients with cortical lesions and transcortical sensory aphasia (Damasio, 1981) have had injury to the posterior portions of the middle and inferior temporal gyri and the temporoparieto-occipital junction (areas 37, 39 and 19) with sparing of the auditory cortex and the proximate Wernicke's area (areas 41, 42 and 22). Another group of patients with transcortical sensory aphasia have had infarcts in the territory of the posterior cerebral artery (Kertesz et al., 1982). In addition to the usual lesion in the occipital lobe and in the inferior temporo-occipital junction after posterior cerebral artery infarction, these cases of posterior cerebral artery transcortical sensory aphasia have involved the white matter confluence deep to the inferior temporal gyrus at the level of the posterior temporal isthmus. This suggests that the simultaneous damage to the left visual and auditory association regions (while the direct geniculo-temporal connections are preserved) is the substrate for transcortical sensory aphasia.

We have recently described the same type of aphasia with posterior cerebral artery territory lesions but only when they included the lateral thalamic nuclei as well (Hiltbrunner et al., 1989). This, again, suggests that damage to connections in the posterior temporal paraventricular white matter including the posterior elements of the temporal isthmus may play a role in the generation of deficits in the semantic aspects of language. This disturbance may be accompanied by preservation of more anterior temporal isthmus and thus preserved phonemic aspects of language, including unwittingly preserved repetition. This combination is the classical profile of transcortical sensory aphasia. If both systems of connections or their cortical terminations are damaged a very profound Wernicke's aphasia would be expected. The precise subcortical profile that accomplishes this effect has not been described.

This postulated anatomy suggests another possible mechanism for the aphasia of thalamic lesions: direct damage to the lateral thalamic region may injure the association projections from thalamus to temporoparieto-occipital junction. It is likely that in any specific case of thalamic infarction or hemorrhage, the aphasia profile depends upon the extent of direct injury to or pressure effects on specific auditory-verbal pathways and specific association pathways.

Combinations of lesions in the paraventricular white matter

Three caveats at the outset of this section. First, the discussion to follow will suggest a brain that is little more than a series of modules working in parallel and series. The actual effects of combined lesions are surely more complicated than simple arithmetical ones. Second, very few naturally occurring lesions will involve just paraventricular white matter. The majority of the cases in our experience and in the neurological literature are infarctions in the territory of the lenticulostriate arteries. There is almost invariably simultaneous injury to the striatum or at least the head of the caudate and the anterior part of the putamen. The earlier discussion summarized the evidence that striatal lesions alone do not result in aphasia. Even if that conclusion is correct, it does not follow that the striatal injury does not contribute to the clinical profile when it occurs simultaneously with a complex combined paraventricular white matter lesion, as Damasio et al. (1982) suggested. Third, the discussion is meant to be a summary of known and suspected effects of combinations of lesions only in the paraventricular white matter. There may also be important consequences of combinations of specific cortical lesions with specific paraventricular white matter lesions.

One example of the effects of combined lesions was suggested above for simultaneous temporal isthmus and posterior third of superior paraventricular white matter lesions (Figs. 1, 2, 4 and 5). One (temporal isthmus) produces a moderate deficit in auditory comprehension but considerable recovery often occurs. The other (posterior third of superior paraventricular white matter) has no important clinical effect. The two together produce a more substantial deficit in comprehension and reduced prospects for recovery. This combination effect is plausible but unproven.

A second example of the effects of combined lesions has also been reported by our group from the Boston VAMC. This example has been seen in cases with simultaneous injury to the *frontal isthmus* which we referred to as simply anterior extension in the earlier report (Figs. 1–3), the anterolateral periventricular white matter (Figs. 1–4) and the anterior third and middle third of the superior paraventricular white matter (Figs. 4 and 5) (Naeser et al., 1982; Alexander et al., 1987a). These patients had a persistent aphasia which was primarily nonfluent in structure: dysarthric, dysprosodic, marked initiation struggle, and shortened phrase length, but not typically agrammatic. This type of case would be similar to the hypothesis of Bonhoeffer (1914) that simultaneous lesions of the descending motor and motor association pathways and of the anterior callosal pathways would deprive Broca's area of a coherent output avenue and result in a severely reduced language output capacity.

The critical role of the deep paraventricular white matter area in the production of persistently nonfluent aphasia has been highlighted by other investigators and serves as a third example of the effects of combined lesions. Mohr et al. (1978) demonstrated conclusively that lesions in Broca's area did not produce Broca's aphasia unless they also involved much of the deep paraventricular white matter. It was not their conclusion, but Naeser and I have argued that the regions of critical interest in their cases of persistent Broca's aphasia were the anterolateral periventricular white matter and the anterior third and middle third of the superior paraventricular white matter (Naeser et al., 1989; Alexander et al., 1987b). Knopman et al. (1983) in a study of the pathological foundations of persistent nonfluency also highlighted the critical importance of the paraventricular white matter. One particular case in that report seems to argue persuasively for the importance of paraventricular white matter (case 84) although that is not the conclusion of the authors of that report.

Naeser and co-workers have extended the observations about the importance of the paraventricular white matter in an analysis of patients with severe disturbances in language output (Naeser et al., 1989). They subdivided cases into those with no speech output, those with limited stereotypes only and those with limited, agrammatical output. Analysis of the CT scans demonstrated a strong correlation between lesion in the paraventricular white matter and the exact profile of poor language output. Cases with stereotype only and those with no output all had lesion which involved two areas. First, there was lesion in the frontal isthmus (Figs. 1–3) but specifically in the most medial part of the frontal isthmus. Review of the neuroanatomy of that region suggested that the structure of greatest relevance to aphasia was the subcallosal fasciculus (Figs. 1–5) (Jürgens, 1984; Yakovlev and Locke, 1961). This deep white matter structure is the major bidirectional connection between limbic cortical areas (the supplementary

motor area and the anterior cingulate) and the caudate (discussed above). The white matter immediately adjacent to and above the subcallosal fasciculus includes the anterolateral periventricular white matter in which connections from supplementary motor area to and from dorsolateral frontal cortex (including Broca's area) travel. We suggested previously that these connections were usually involved in transcortical motor aphasia (Freedman et al., 1984). Naeser et al. (1989) reported that the lesion in subcallosal fasciculus had to occur in combination with a second lesion in the middle third of the superior paraventricular white matter for speech to be reduced to stereotypic or no-output levels. Most other reports do not define the language deficit as strictly as this study did or have used a lesion composite technique of CT analysis which may miss the necessary *combinations* of lesions. An additional problem, one that is distressingly common in research in this field, is the publication of very selected CT levels, leaving readers unable to inspect the entire lesion.

In our recent reports (Naeser et al., 1982; Alexander et al., 1987a), we described six cases with very extensive lesions through the entire paraventricular white matter, including the temporal isthmus. All six cases had severe global aphasia. In most cases there was some involvement of cortical structures, but the exact region varied from case to case; in no single case did the area of cortical involvement account for more than a fraction of the clinical profile. The cumulative effects of the combined lesions seem evident.

Lesions in the subcortical white matter

Déjerine, Marie and Kleist are three of the many early investigators who observed or suggested that lesions in the immediately subcortical white matter could produce clinical effects very similar to direct damage to the cortex. The implication of those reports was that efferent and/or afferent pathways were most susceptible to damage in regions with highly consolidated fiber tracts immediately before their termination or origination. The clinical syndromes of aphemia (deficit limited to speech output; Schiff et al., 1983) pure word deafness (deficit limited to auditory comprehension; Auerbach et al., 1981) and pure alexia (deficit limited to reading comprehension; Greenblatt, 1976) have been described after lesions in the immediately subcortical regions.

Other deficits have been more tenuously attributed to specific pathways in the deeper but not paraventricular subcortical white matter. (See Figs. 2–5 for representation of the region considered SCWM for this review). Three will be considered here: (1) the repetition defect of conduction aphasia, (2) agraphia, (3) ideomotor apraxia, particularly left limb apraxia.

This is not the context for a larger consideration of the neurology of conduction aphasia. Suffice it to say that one of the consistent elements in the diagnosis of conduction aphasia is the production of phonemic substitutions in spontaneous speech, but particularly in repetition and/or oral reading. The traditional focus for the lesion in this syndrome has been the inferior parietal lobule (Green and Howes, 1975; Benson et al., 1973; Kertesz et al., 1979). Depending on the size of the lesion, the accompanying signs could show considerable variation. The same syndrome has also been described with small lesions directly in the superior temporal cortex, i.e., Wernicke's area. Damasio and Damasio (1980) have also reported that lesions in the posterior insula which involve the external and/or extreme capsules may also result in the same aphasia profile. What do the regions have in common, and how do these observations pertain to subcortical cases?

Alexander et al. (1987b) demonstrated that lesions involving lower motor cortex (Figs. 3–5) and frontal operculum (Figs. 1 and 2) or lesions deep to the sensorimotor cortices are both associated with phonemic substitutions. Combined with the observations of Damasio and Damasio (1980), we suggested that lesions which disrupt the interconnections of Wernicke's area and the frontal operculum to which Wernicke's area projects were the substrate of phonemic substitutions. The

interconnections run in the subcortical white matter deep to posterior insula, deep to supramarginal gyrus in the inferior parietal lobule, and deep to the lower sensory and motor cortex before terminating in the operculum. The exact lesion configuration determines whether the overall syndrome is conduction aphasia, Wernicke's aphasia, one of the subtypes of Broca's area aphasia or one of the subtypes of subcortical aphasia. But most importantly for this summary of subcortical syndromes, we have shown that the profiles of subcortical aphasia described here are not artifacts of insular damage. If there is a syndrome produced by insular damage, it may be due to damage to the white matter immediately deep to the insula, and the syndrome is conduction aphasia with abundant phonemic substitutions. Primarily subcortical lesions may extend laterally to involve the subcortical white matter structures. The combined lesions may result in a profile which is not classical conduction aphasia, but which includes the phonemic substitution features of conduction aphasia.

Pure agraphia is another hoary chestnut of neurology which cannot be properly reviewed in this context, but there is one anatomical point of relevance to the larger issue of subcortical cases. The few cases of isolated agraphia have not had a specific anatomy, but one location often suggested as critical for writing with little relevance to any other aspect of language is the superior parietal lobule (Kinsbourne and Rosenfield, 1974; Rosait and DeBastiani, 1979; Auerbach and Alexander, 1981). This area, more or less representing Brodmann's area 7, is a multimodal association region into which both visual and tactile-kinesthetic sensory systems map. Mountcastle et al. (1975) have demonstrated with single-cell recordings that neuronal columns in this region are oriented to particular parts of external space. One major projection of this area is forward to the motor association cortex. Haaxma and Kuypers (1975) demonstrated in monkeys that discrete disconnection of these two areas by a white matter lesion could result in difficulty with controlling the direction of forepaw movements under visual guidance. A similar behavior in humans has been called optic atax-ia or impaired visually guided movement; this disorder has been attributed to lesions in the superior parietal lobule (Vighetto and Perenin, 1981; Damasio and Benton, 1979). It has been accompanied by agraphia without any other disturbance in language.

Tanridag and Kirshner (1986) have also demonstrated that lesions in the posterior limb of the internal capsule may result in severe agraphia. The three cases in that report were not altogether satisfactory for conclusions about anatomical mechanisms, but the posterior paraventricular white matter above the posterior limb of internal capsule probably carries the bulk of the thalamic projections to the superior parietal lobule. We believe that one contributor to the significant agraphia present in cases of subcortical aphasia may be due to disruption of the ascending thalamo-parietal connections and/or of the intrahemispheric parietal-frontal connections in either the deep superior paraventricular white matter, particularly for those cases with lesion extent above the level of the corpus callosum, or the subcortical white matter in the parietal lobe.

Apraxia, dare I have another disclaimer, is also too complex an operation to be reviewed here, other than for one particular anatomical point. Although many traditional accounts attributed limb apraxia to disruption of subcortical connections in the arcuate fasciculus, there are few studies which have been designed to specify the pathological anatomy for ideomotor apraxia of specific body parts. Tognola and Vignolo (1981) and Alexander et al. (1986, 1987b) have all demonstrated the importance of damage to both the frontal operculum and the lower motor cortex for significant and lasting buccofacial apraxia. Heilman and coworkers (1982), Kertesz and Ferro (1984) and Alexander et al. (1986) have demonstrated that damage to the deep superior paraventricular white matter is the most important lesion in the production of significant and lasting left limb apraxia. In fact, the studies may be interpreted to demonstrate that the paraventricular white matter is a key re-

gion for bilateral limb apraxias. The critical connections between the parietal/spatial-kinesthetic regions and the motor association regions may well run in the deep paraventricular white matter. Subcortical lesions with anterior and middle superior paraventricular white matter damage may disrupt all or some of three important motor systems: the descending pyramidal pathways, resulting in a right hemiparesis: the *intra*hemispheric frontal-parietal connections producing bilateral limb apraxia; and the midcallosal *inter*hemispheric connections producing left limb apraxia. The intersection of all of these systems is in the superior paraventricular white matter.

Synthesis of findings and hypotheses

The foregoing summary of the clinical observations of subcortical lesion sites and aphasic signs suggests some general conclusions about the pathological anatomy of aphasia. These general conclusions depend upon two assertions.

First, it is likely that the classical syndromes are not the most useful independent variables for aphasia research whatever their value in clinical diagnosis. The classical syndromes do not describe deficits that are reduced to the basic operations of language. For instance, consider Broca's aphasia. The syndrome consists of *impaired articulatory agility, reduced prosodic line, shortened phrase length* (to single words or telegraphic tabulations at worst), *impairments in usage of grammatical form* (to frank agrammatism at worst), *word-finding difficulties, paraphasic* substitutions (both *phonemic* and *semantic*), *struggle to initiate* output, and a profile of *impaired comprehension* which parallels the agrammatic production defect, that is, impaired comprehension of specifically grammatical or syntactical operations (Goodglass and Kaplan, 1983). There are then nine separate aphasic signs which define the full syndrome. Each of these signs may have its own pathological anatomy; Broca's aphasia is only the clinical 'site' where they *all* come together. Does this make the syndrome the most biologically basic process for study or should the individual behaviors, reduced to their most coherent operational definition, be the targets of study? This chapter has been constructed with as little reference to the classical syndromes as possible because the individual signs and their individual anatomies seem the more profitable foci for improving understanding.

The second assertion has to do with identifying an operational basis for approaching the study of the individual signs and their anatomies. Mesulam (1981) has analysed the disorders of attention in a manner which offers a useful lesson for the analysis of many cognitive functions. He reviewed the large and often contradictory literature on directed attention. He demonstrated that the apparently disparate brain regions implicated in this function were actually related by known anatomical connections. He argued that the best concept for understanding the anatomy of directed attention was that of a geographically widespread but functionally highly connected system, with different parts of the system contributing different necessary elements of the function. The different parts of the system might themselves also be integrated into other, different functional systems. Thus, damage to any part of the system for directed attention would result in impairments in attention, although these impairments would likely be different depending upon exactly which part was damaged. Depending upon the part damaged, however, the other signs accompanying the disturbance in attention might vary dramatically. It is the *totality* of the accompanying signs that defines the differences between the *syndromes* of the inferior parietal, deep medial frontal, thalamic or other areas in which lesions result in disturbed attention.

This review will conclude by summarizing the functional anatomical systems for some elements of speech and language which are suggested by analysis of subcortical lesion cases, with due consideration for the classical notions of cortical localization. These systems are only suggestions at the present time. Much more study of the complex action of lesions of the brain on function is required

to define accurately the biologically relevant working systems of language and related cognitive activities.

1. The system for speech and language initiation includes:

   (a) the supplementary motor area (and perhaps the anterior cingulate); this medial frontal region is the termination of ascending systems which are involved in the initiation and maintenance of language output, particularly in response to internal stimuli;

   (b) the efferents from this region dispersed through the *anterolateral periventricular white matter* primarily at the lateral angle of the frontal horn to

   (c) the dorsolateral convexity of the frontal lobe and

   (d) the striatum (via the *subcallosal fasciculus*).

2. The system for speech output:

   (a) originates in the lower frontal operculum, but requires the contribution of the lower motor cortex as well.

   (b) These motor regions distribute descending pathways which travel in the *anterior third portion of the middle of the paraventricular white matter* to the *genu of internal capsule* and to the *posterior portion of the ALIC.*

   (c) The extrapyramidal structures – *putamen* and caudate and their cortical connections – may contribute to the qualities of rate and volume in the spoken output and probably to the initiation of output as well as a result of the limbic inputs to striatum.

3. The system for organizing output at the phonemic level includes:

   (a) the frontal operculum and lower motor cortex and probably their output in *the anterior third and middle third of the paraventricular white matter,*

   (b) Wernicke's area, and

   (c) the *subcortical white matter connections* (between 3a and 3b) *in the subinsular white matter and the arcuate fasciculus* deep to inferior parietal lobule and sensory-motor cortex.

   (d) There may be other connections to the cortex of insula and supramarginal gyrus involved in this system.

4. The system for auditory comprehension includes:

    (a) the auditory-cortex,

    (b) Wernicke's area,

    (c) the callosal connections in the *posterior superior paraventricular white matter* between auditory association cortices of the two hemispheres,

    (d) the temporoparietal association cortex,

    (e) the ascending thalamic projections *in the temporal isthmus* to the primary cortex and to the auditory association cortices,

    (f) perhaps the *lateral nuclei of the thalamus* as well.

5. The system for ideomotor praxis includes:

    (a) the parietal spatial/kinesthetic association cortex,

    (b) the motor association and primary motor areas, and

    (c) their intrahemispheric connections in the length of the *superior paraventricular white matter*

    (d) For the specific problem of praxis in the left arm, the interhemispheric connections in the *middle third of the superior paraventricular white matter* are involved.

6. There is some evidence for a system of semantic function which involves the anterior and lateral thalamus, the temporoparieto-occipital junction association cortex and their connections in the posterior temporal isthmus and the posterior paraventricular white matter. There is currently inadequate information to do more than suggest such a system.

7. It is not the role of this review to discuss alexia, but a similar system could be constructed for alexia (Damasio and Damasio, 1983).

That coherent syndromes emerge in this welter of functional systems is clear from the long history of aphasia. That many patients do not happen to distribute lesions in exactly the manner necessary to produce a recognized syndrome should not be surprising. That many patients can have similar syndromes without having precisely the same lesion profiles should not be astounding. Finally, that there are patients who have lesion-behavior profiles at variance with these systems is an unassailable observation from excellent sources (Basso et al., 1985), but there may be separate neurobiological rules which delineate the nature of these exceptions. Defining the biology of exceptions is important, but a different problem from establishing the principles of the commonplace.

Acknowledgement

This work was supported in part by USPHS Grant NS 06209.

References

Alexander MP, Warren RL: Localization of callosal auditory pathways: a CT case study. *Neurology: 38*, 802 – 804, 1988.

Alexander MP, Baker E, Naeser MA, et al: The anatomical basis of ideomotor apraxia. *Neurology: 36 (Suppl 1)*, 319, 1986.

Alexander MP, LoVerme SR: Aphasia after left hemispheric intracerebral hemorrhage. *Neurology: 30*, 1193 – 1202, 1980.

Alexander MP, Naeser MA, Palumbo CL: Correlations of subcortical CT lesion sites and aphasia profiles. *Brain: 110*, 961 – 991, 1987a.

Alexander MP, Naeser, MA, Palumbo CL: *Clinical CT correlations of subsyndromes of Broca's aphasia.* Paper presented at 39th Annual Meeting of the American Academy of Neurology, New York, 9 April, 1987b.

Aram DM, Rose DF, Rekate HL, et al: Acquired capsular/striatal aphasia in childhood. *Arch. Neurol. (Chicago): 40*, 614 – 617, 1983.

Auerbach SH, Alexander MP: Pure agraphia and unilateral optic ataxia associated with a left superior parietal lobule lesion. *J. Neurol. Neurosurg. Psychiatry: 44*, 430 – 432, 1983.

Auerbach SH, Allard T, Naeser M, et al: Pure word deafness: Analysis of a case with bilateral lesions and a defect at the prephonemic level. *Brain: 105*, 271 – 300, 1982.

Baron, JC, D'Antona RD, Pantano P, et al: Effects of thalamic stroke on energy metabolism of the cerebral cortex. *Brain: 109*, 1243 – 1259, 1986.

Basso A, Lecours AR, Moraschini S, et al: Anatomical correlations of the aphasias as defined through computerized tomography: exceptions. *Brain Lang.: 26*, 201 – 229, 1985.

Benson DF, Sheremata WA, Bouchard R, et al: Conduction aphasia: a clinicopathological study. *Arch. Neurol. (Chicago): 28*, 339 – 346, 1973.

Bonhoeffer K: *Monatschrift. Psychiat. Neurol.: 35*, 113, 1914.

Botez MI, Barbeau A: Role of subcortical structures and particularly the thalamus in the mechanisms of speech and language. *Int. J. Neurol.: 8,* 300 – 320, 1971.

Brodal A. Neurological Anatomy. New York: Oxford University Press, 1981.

Brunner RJ, Kornhuber HH, Seemuller E, et al: Basal ganglia participation in language pathology. *Brain Lang.: 16,* 281 – 299, 1982.

Cappa SF, Cavalotti G, Guidotti M, et al: Subcortical aphasia: two clinical-CT scan correlation studies. *Cortex: 19,* 227 – 241, 1983.

Cappa SF, Vignolo A: 'Transcortical' features of aphasia following left thalamic hemorrhage. *Cortex: 15,* 121 – 130, 1979.

Ciemens VA: Localized thalamic hemorrhage: a cause of aphasia. *Neurology: 20,* 776 – 782, 1970.

Coltheart M: Deep dyslexia: a review of the syndrome. In Coltheart M, Patterson K, Marshall JC (Editors), *Deep Dyslexia.* London: Routledge and Kegan Paul, 1980.

Damasio AR, Benton AL: Impairment of hand movement under visual guidance. *Neurology: 29,* 170 – 178, 1979.

Damasio AR, Damasio H, Rizzo M, et al: Aphasia with nonhemorrhagic lesions in the basal ganglia and the internal capsule. *Arch. Neurol. (Chicago): 39,* 15 – 20, 1982.

Damasio AR, Van Hoesen G: Structure and function of the supplementary motor area. *Neurology: 30,* 359, 1980.

Damasio H: Cerebral localization of the aphasias. In Sarno MT (Editor), *Acquired Aphasia.* New York: Academic Press, 1981.

Damasio H, Damasio AR: 'Paradoxic' ear extinction in dichotic listening: possible anatomic significance. *Neurology: 29,* 644 – 653, 1979.

Damasio H, Damasio AR: The anatomical basis of conduction aphasia. *Brain: 103,* 337 – 350, 1980.

Darley FL, Aronson AE, Brown JR: *Motor Speech Disorders.* Philadelphia: WB Saunders Co., pp. 204 – 210, 1975.

DeCroix JP, Graveleau Ph, Masson M, Cambier J: Infarction in the territory of the anterior choroidal artery: a clinical and computed tomographic study of 16 cases. *Brain: 109,* 1071 – 1085, 1986.

Déjerine J: L'aphasie motrice. Sa localisation et sa physiologie pathologique. *Presse Med.: 14,* 453 – 457, 1906.

Fisher CM: Capsular infarct: the underlying vascular lesions. *Arch. Neurol. (Chicago): 36,* 65 – 73, 1979.

Fisher CM: Lacunar strokes and infarcts: a review. *Neurology: 32,* 871 – 876, 1982.

Freedman M, Alexander MP, Naeser MA: Anatomic basis of transcortical motor aphasia. *Neurology: 40,* 409 – 417, 1984.

Goodglass H, Kaplan E: *The Assessment of Aphasia and Related Disorders.* Philadelphia: Lea and Febiger, 1983.

Gorelick PB, Hier DB, Benevento L, et al: Aphasia after left thalamic infarction. *Arch. Neurol. (Chicago): 41,* 1296 – 1298, 1984.

Graff-Radford N, Damasio H, Yamada T, et al: Nonhemorrhagic thalamic infarctions: Clinical, neurophysiological and electrophysiological findings in four anatomical groups defined by CT. *Brain: 108,* 485 – 516, 1985.

Graff-Radford NR, Eslinger PJ, Damasio AR, et al: Nonhemorrhagic infarction of the thalamus: Behavioral, anatomic and physiologic correlates. *Neurology: 34,* 14 – 23, 1984.

Graff-Radford N, Schelper RL, Ilinsky I, et al: Computed

tomography and post mortem study of a nonhemorrhagic thalamic infarction. *Arch. Neurol. (Chicago): 42,* 761 – 763, 1985.

Green E, Howes DH: The nature of conduction aphasia: a study of anatomic and clinical features and of underlying mechanisms. *Studies in Neurolinguistics, Vol. 3.* New York: Academic Press, pp. 123 – 156, 1977.

Greenblatt S: Subangular alexia without agraphia or hemianopia. *Brain Lang.: 3,* 229 – 245, 1976.

Haaxma R, Kuypers HCJM: Intrahemispheric cortical connections and visual guidance of hand and finger movements in the rhesus monkey. *Brain: 98,* 239 – 260, 1975.

Heilman KM, Rothi LJ, Valenstein E: Two forms of ideomotor apraxia. *Neurology: 32,* 342 – 346, 1982.

Hiltbrunner B, Alexander MP, Fischer R: Anatomical basis of transcortical sensory aphasia. *Arch. Neurol.:* in press, 1989.

Jürgens U: The efferent and afferent connections of the supplementary motor area. *Brain Res.: 300,* 63 – 81, 1984.

Katz DI, Alexander MP, Mandell A (1987) Dementia syndrome after bilateral mesencephalic-diencephalic stroke. *Arch. Neurol. (Chicago): 1987,* in press.

Kertesz A, Harlock W, Coates R: Computer tomographic localisation, lesion size, and prognosis in aphasia and nonverbal impairment. *Brain Lang.: 8,* 34 – 50, 1979.

Kertesz A, Ferro JM: Lesion site and extent in ideomotor apraxia. *Brain: 107,* 921 – 933, 1984.

Kertesz A, Sheppard A, MacKenzie R: Localization in transcortical sensory aphasia. *Arch. Neurol. (Chicago): 39,* 475 – 478, 1982.

Kinsbourne M, Rosenfeld DB: Agraphia selective for written spelling: an experimental case study. *Brain Lang.: 1,* 215 – 226, 1974.

Kleist K: *Gehirnpathologie.* Leipzig: Barth, 1934.

Knopman DS, Selnes OA, Niccum ND, et al: A longitudinal study of speech fluency in aphasia: CT correlates of recovery and persistent nonfluency. *Neurology: 33,* 1170 – 1178, 1983.

Kushner M, Alavi A, Reivich M, et al: Contralateral cerebellar hypometabolism following cerebral insult: a positron emission tomography study. *Ann. Neurol.: 15,* 425 – 434, 1984.

Lecours AR, Lhermitte F: The 'pure form' of the phonetic disintegration syndrome (pure anarthria): Anatomo-clinical report of a historical case. *Brain Lang.: 3,* 88 – 113, 1976.

Liepmann H (1905): cited by Geschwind N: Disconnexion syndromes in animals and man. *Brain: 88,* 237 – 294 and 585 – 644, 1965.

Marie P: Révision de la question de l'aphaisie: que faut-il penser des aphasies sous-corticales (aphasies pures?). *Sem. Méd.: 42,* 493 – 500, 1906.

Mazzocchi F, Vignolo LA: Localisation of lesions in aphasia: clinical CT scan correlations in stroke patients. *Cortex: 15,* 627 – 654, 1979.

McFarling D, Rothi LJ, Heilman KM: Transcortical aphasia from ischaemic infarcts of the thalamus: A report of two cases. *J. Neurol. Neurosurg. Psychiatry: 45,* 107 – 112, 1982.

Mesulam MM: A cortical network for directed attention and unilateral neglect. *Ann. Neurol.: 10,* 309 – 325, 1981.

Metter EJ, Jackson C, Keysler D, et al: Left hemisphere intracerebral hemorrhage studied by (F-18)-flourdeoxyglucose PET. *Neurology: 36,* 1155 – 1162, 1986.

Metter EJ, Mazziotta JC, Itabaski HH, et al: Comparison of

glucose metabolism, X-ray, CT and post mortem data in a patient with multiple cerebral infarcts. *Neurology: 35,* 1695 – 1701, 1985.

Metter EJ, Riege WH, Hanson WR, et al: Correlations of glucose metabolism and structural damage to language function in aphasia. *Brain Lang.: 21,* 187 – 207, 1984.

Metter EJ, Riege WH, Hanson WR, et al: Comparison of metabolic rates, language, and memory in subcortical aphasias. *Brain Lang.: 19,* 33 – 47, 1983.

Metter EJ, Wasterlain CG, Kuhl DE, et al: [18]FDG Positron Emission Computed Tomography in a Study of Aphasia. *Ann. Neurol.: 10,* 173 – 183, 1981.

Mohr JP, Pessin MS, Finkelstein S, et al. Broca's Aphasia: Pathologic and Clinical. *Neurology: 28,* 311 – 324, 1978.

Mohr JP, Watters WC, Duncan GW: Thalamic hemorrhage and aphasia. *Brain Lang.: 2,* 3 – 17, 1975.

Mountcastle VB, Lynch JC, Georgepoulus A: Posterior parietal association cortex of the monkey: command functions for operations within extrapersonal space. *J. Neurophysiol.: 38,* 871 – 908, 1975.

Naeser MA, Alexander MP, Helm-Estabrooks N, et al: Aphasia with predominantly subcortical lesion sites. *Arch. Neurol. (Chicago): 39,* 2 – 14, 1982.

Naeser MA, Palumbo CL, Helm-Estabrooks N, et al: Severe non-fluency in aphasia. Role of the medial subcallosal fasciculus and other white matter pathways in recovery of spontaneous speech. *Brain: 112,* 1 – 38, 1989.

Nakano KK, Zubeixh H, Tyler HR: Speech defects of parkinsonian patients. *Neurology: 23,* 865 – 870, 1973.

Nauta WJH, Feirtag M: *Fundamental Neuroanatomy.* New York: WH Freeman & Co., p. 304, 1986.

Nielson JM: *Agnosia, Apraxia, and Aphasia: Their Value in Cerebral Localization.* New York: Hafner Publishing Co., Inc., pp. 119 – 120, 1946.

Ojemann GA: Subcortical language mechanisms. In Whitaker H (Editor), *Neurolinguistics, Vol. 1.* New York: Academic Press, pp. 103 – 138, 1976.

Ojemann GA, Fedio P, Van Buren JM: Anomia from pulvinar and subcortical parietal stimulation. *Brain: 91,* 99 – 116, 1968.

Ojemann GA, Ward AA: Speech representation in the ventrolateral thalamus. *Brain: 94,* 669 – 680, 1971.

Ojemann GA, Whitaker HA: Language localization and variability. *Brain Lang.: 6,* 239 – 260, 1978.

Percheron G: Les artères du thalamus humain: Les artères choroïdiennes. *Rev. Neurol.: 133,* 547 – 558, 1977.

Peters A: Thalamic input to the cerebral cortex. *Trends Neurosci.: 2,* 183 – 185, 1979.

Puel M, Demonet JF, Cardebat D, et al: Aphasies sous-corticales: étude neurolinguistique avec scanner X de 25 cas. *Rev. Neurol.: 140,* 695 – 710, 1984.

Rosait G, DeBastiani P: Pure agraphia: a discrete form of aphasia. *J. Neurol. Neurosurg. Psychiatry: 42,* 266 – 269, 1979.

Ross ED: Localization of the pyramidal tract in the internal capsule by whole brain dissection. *Neurology: 30,* 59 – 64, 1980.

Rubens A, Johnson MG, Speaks C: Location of lesions responsible for the 'paradoxical ipsilateral ear effect' with dichotic listening tests in patients with aphasia due to stroke. *Neurology: 28,* 3996, 1978.

Schiff HB, Alexander MP, Naeser MA, Galaburda AM: Aphemia: clinico-anatomical correlations. *Arch. Neurol.: 40,* 720 – 727, 1983.

Signoret JL, Castaigne P, Lhermitte F, et al: Rediscovery of Leborgne's brain: anatomical description with CT scan. *Brain. Lang.: 22,* 303 – 319, 1984.

Sparks R, Geschwind N: Dichotic listening in man after section of the neocortical commissures. *Cortex: 4,* 3 – 16, 1968.

Sparks R, Goodglass H, Nickel B: Ipsilateral versus contralateral extinction in dichotic listening resulting from hemisphere lesions. *Cortex: 6,* 249 – 260, 1970.

Tanridag O, Kirshner HS: Aphasia and agraphia in lesions of the posterior internal capsule and putamen. *Neurology: 35,* 1797 – 1801, 1986.

Tognola G, Vignolo LA: Brain lesions associated with oral apraxia in stroke patients: a clinico-neuroradiological investigation with CT scan. *Neuropsychology: 18,* 257 – 271, 1980.

Tonkonogy J, Goodglass H: Language function, foot of the third frontal gyrus, and rolandic operculum. *Arch. Neurol.: 38,* 486 – 490, 1981.

Van Buren JM: Evidence regarding a more precise localisation of the posterior frontal-caudate arrest response in man. *J. Neurosurg.: 24,* 416 – 418, 1966.

Van Buren JM: The question of thalamic participation in speech mechanisms. *Brain Lang.: 2,* 31 – 44, 1975.

Vighetto A, Perenin MT: Ataxie optique. *Rev. Neurol.: 137,* 357 – 372, 1981.

Wallesch CW, Henriksen L, Kornhuber HH, et al: Observations on regional cerebral blood flow in cortical and subcortical structures during language production in normal man. *Brain Lang.: 25,* 224 – 233, 1985.

Wallesch CW, Kornhuber HH, Brunner RJ, et al.: Lesions of the basal ganglia, thalamus and deep white matter: differential effects on language functions. *Brain Lang.: 20,* 286 – 304, 1983.

Yakovlev PI, Locke S: Limbic nuclei of thalamus and connections of limbic cortex. *Arch. Neurol.: 5,* 364 – 400, 1961.

Zurif EB, Caramazza A, Myerson R: Grammatical judgements of agrammatic aphasics. *Neuropsychologia: 10,* 405 – 427, 1972.

© 1989 Elsevier Science Publishers B.V. (Biomedical Division)
Handbook of Neuropsychology, Vol. 2
F. Boller and J. Grafman (Eds)

CHAPTER 3

Therapy of aphasia

Anna Basso

Neuropsychology Center and Second Clinic for Nervous Diseases University of Milan, via F. Sforza, 35, 20122 Milan, Italy

Introduction

Aphasia rehabilitation is a relatively new discipline. Until World War II aphasia in elderly stroke patients was viewed as a natural state and only occasional reports of retraining post-stroke aphasic patients had been published. After World War II several army hospitals in the United States started programs for the rehabilitation of post-traumatic patients, and at approximately the same time rehabilitation medicine became a medical speciality and speech pathology a health profession (Sarno, 1981). Moreover, Wepman (1951) drew attention to the large population of untreated civilians who could benefit from therapy, and some programs at the Veterans Administration Hospital originally devised for traumatic aphasic patients continued to function for civilians, as in Minneapolis with Hildred Schuell.

Today the major cause of aphasia is vascular disease. A number of recent clinical studies provide some data on the incidence of cerebrovascular accidents (Howard et al., 1963; Adams, 1965; Brust et al., 1976). According to Brust et al. (1976), there are about 84 000 new aphasic patients in the United States each year. A large proportion of those who do not die within 6 months will need long-term rehabilitation. Traffic accidents also provide a substantial number of patients requiring specialized rehabilitation. Encephalitis, anoxia and space-occupying lesions are yet other causes of aphasic disturbances, although they concern a much smaller number of cases.

Aphasia is not a static state; it is susceptible to improvement, both spontaneous and due to rehabilitation. As a consequence, aphasia rehabilitation has become an important problem. Unfortunately, both *aphasia* and *rehabilitation* are difficult to define. A widely accepted definition of aphasia is that it is 'loss or impairment of language caused by brain damage' (Benson, 1979, p. 5). This definition, however, does not say much about characteristics of the loss; whether, for instance, language is impaired in all of its functions, or whether there is a selective loss of one or more processes (such as reading or comprehension); whether aphasia is a single condition, or takes several forms that may selectively impair one linguistic component (phonology, syntax, semantics), leaving the others relatively unimpaired. Even more ambiguous is the word *rehabilitation,* which is supposed to indicate all the different approaches intended to improve impaired function. The only thing common to all aphasia rehabilitation approaches is that patient and therapist try to communicate with each other. The content of communication and what the therapist does in order to elicit a response from the patient vary from place to place and from speech pathologist to speech pathologist.

A conceptual framework of the nature of aphasia is needed to construct a sound rehabilitation approach, systematically evaluate it and use the results to refine one's understanding of the aphasic disorder and of recovery. If the framework is minimally specified, there will be space for different approaches; if it is highly specified the approach should be exactly the same for similar patients. What therapeutic intervention is used should be based on the particular definition of aphasia, and, in fact, for many of the interpretations of aphasia given there are one or more intervention procedures that are apparently associated with that interpretation.

In this chapter I will first review some conceptualizations of the nature of aphasia and indicate one or more therapeutic approaches that can find their rationale in those conceptualizations. I will then try to regroup the various rehabilitation approaches into some broader categories, though it must be remembered that whatever taxonomy one proposes, there will be some overlap between the different categories. As Sarno (1980, p. 61) aptly puts it, 'it is not possible to classify therapeutic method in any logical way'.

The major global approaches to rehabilitation – the classical or stimulation approach, the Programmed Instruction approach, the pragmatic approach and the cognitive approach – will be briefly described. In the following section only a few illustrative examples of specific methods will be given. While all intervention strategies may be classified, more or less correctly, in one or another of these broad categories, it is in fact not possible to mention the hundreds of specific interventions to be found in the literature, some of which have been described only briefly and in reference to a single case. Finally the relationship between recovery and intervention strategy will be dealt with briefly, as will some practical questions.

Concepts of aphasia and related intervention strategies

Aphasia was considered by Finkelnburg (1870) to be only one aspect of a more general disorder. One of the patients he had observed could not make the sign of the cross when asked to do so, although she could imitate it exactly. Another one was unable to count money, since he confused the values of the coins, and still another one, an official, confused the signs of rank. On these and other similar observations Finkelnburg based his belief that there was more than disruption of language in aphasia and that *asymbolia* would be a more correct term for those patients who have partial or total inability to use acquired signs.

Following Finkelnburg, other clinicians (Goldstein, 1948; Bay, 1964; Luria, 1966; Wepman, 1976) have also opposed the linguistic orientation of aphasia, considering aphasia to be a more general disorder. Some support for this interpretation of aphasia has come from studies of gestural ability, which is generally found to be impaired in aphasia – a circumstance which suggests a common underlying symbolic incompetence. Artificial language techniques involving gestures (Glass et al., 1973; Gardner et al., 1976; Schlanger and Freiman, 1979) and more structured sign languages such as Amerind and American Sign Language (ASL) (Skelly et al., 1975; Bonvillian and Friedman, 1978; Kirshner and Webb, 1981) have been used in aphasia therapy.

There is probably a logical link between the interpretation of aphasia as a more general symbolic disorder and the proposal of teaching aphasics the use of artificial languages. However, it is unclear what kind of link. If aphasia is considered not to be a general symbolic disorder but a specific linguistic disorder it seems rational and coherent to enable patients to use another language which is supposed to be intact. If, on the other hand, there is a global disorder, it still seems reasonable to try to develop an easier code. So it is difficult to understand what the rationale of such a rehabilitation procedure is: whether to use gestures because they are unimpaired, or to use them because they are easier although impaired.

A second interpretation of aphasia that seems to have had widespread acceptance among speech therapists can be traced back to Jackson (1958). Jackson drew attention to the dissociation of the automatic and voluntary in use of language, the voluntary uses of language being the more profoundly altered. Aphasia is, thus, viewed as a reduction in the availability of language rather than a loss of language. This dissociation can be most clearly demonstrated at the semantic level, where it has repeatedly been shown that aphasics tend to use the more frequent words proportionately more frequently than normal speakers but that they do on occasion have access to infrequently used words. The potential vocabulary is not restricted but the aphasic patient has difficulty gaining access to it. This interpretation of aphasia as impaired access to a well-preserved language has influenced aphasia rehabilitation. According to Vignolo (1964), one of the main principles of aphasia therapy is the recruitment of automatic abilities to enable the patient to recover more voluntary uses of language. Weigl's (1961) deblocking technique, also, can be considered an example of automatic language facilitating voluntary use. Finally, Wepman's (1976) thought-stimulation therapy also tends to switch the patient's attention from language to the content of information, thus facilitating use of language that may arise incidentally.

In 1974 Kimura and Archibald advanced the hypothesis that speech disturbances and apraxia were different manifestations of an impairment of control of motor sequencing. The analogy between practic and language dominance convinced some authors that the same anatomical structures were utilized because praxis and speech were only two different expressions of the same basic mechanism (Mateer and Kimura, 1977; Ojemann and Mateer, 1979; Ojemann, 1982; Kimura, 1982). The most decisive evidence against this view was in case reports demonstrating that one hemisphere is dominant for praxis and the other for speech. Despite the fact that this interpretation of aphasia has not been widely accepted, some therapeutic suggestions based on the idea that left hemisphere dominance of praxis and speech is not just fortuitous can be found. Buzzard (quoted by Goodglass and Quadfasel, 1954) was convinced that better use of the left hand would result in amelioration of the aphasic disturbances. 'The idea is, as I have said, in the failure from disease of Broca's convolution, to develop by afferent impulses the corresponding convolution in the right cerebral hemisphere'. A century later, Johnson (1983) considered that the primary goal in treatment of transcortical motor aphasia is improvement of motor processing which is functionally interrelated with language.

Aphasia has been referred to as a disorder of communication, thus stressing one, probably the most important, function of language. Communication is a process of interaction between two or more people who exchange messages. Language is one tool a person has at his disposal to communicate but it is not the only one. Messages are also exchanged by gestures, mimicry, gaze, etc. A rehabilitation approach based on the idea that aphasia is more than a linguistic disorder and is better explained as a disorder of communication is PACE (Promoting Aphasics' Communicative Effectiveness; Davis and Wilcox, 1981), which will be discussed below.

A central disorder of language, as aphasia has been defined, would be explainable by the breakdown of one single mechanism. The centrality of aphasia is illustrated by word-finding difficulties, a pervasive disorder in aphasia that is the same no matter which sensory channel is used to present the stimulus object (Goodglass et al., 1978). Rehabilitation will consequently be concentrated on the central disorder, without considering the different aspect that the same breakdown may have in different language modalities. Schuell's (Schuell et al., 1964) rehabilitation technique, for example, emphasizes the use of auditory stimulation for all patients concerned.

The last ten years or so have witnessed an increase of interest in cognitive neuropsychology and information-processing models. The basic assumption common to all these models is the modularity assumption. It is supposed that any system is organized in such a way that one component can be disrupted without disruption of other components. In line with the modularity hypothesis, the models presuppose that different impairments follow disruption of different modules, thus explaining the observed variety of different patterns of impaired and retained abilities. It is not the notion that aphasia is a language disorder that is disputed by cognitive neuropsychologists, but the idea that language is a monolithic function. The subcomponents of language must be analysed and for each aphasic patient the specific pattern of impairments must be identified. The therapeutic intervention based on the models of cognitive neuropsychology will be highly detailed and directed only towards the impaired subcomponents and not towards such general function as comprehension or production. Examples of such an approach will be given later.

These are but some interpretations of aphasia and I have tried to briefly exemplify how widely different aphasia rehabilitation techniques can loosely be linked to these interpretations.

The classical or stimulation approach

What is common to the methods grouped under the heading of classical or stimulation approach is that they are generally facilitatory rather than didactic. Both Wepman (1951) and Schuell (Schuell et al., 1964) clearly stated that it was not the role of the speech pathologist to teach but to stimulate. The term *stimulation* refers to what the therapist does in order to *facilitate* the patient's processing of language, either in comprehension or expression. Supporters of the stimulation approach consider aphasia to be essentially unitary in nature and due to a general depression of language knowledge. The variability of performance of individual patients has been considered to be proof against the interpretation of aphasia as a loss of language. If a patient can use language on some occasions, even if not on all, this is sufficient evidence that language knowledge may not be easily accessible but it is still there. Variability of performance has been demonstrated in confrontation naming (Howard et al., 1984) and for agrammatism it has been maintained (Gleason et al., 1975, p. 467) that in a facilitatory situation such as the Story Completion Test patients have 'a relatively large repertoire of constructions which

are accessible inconsistently and with difficulty, rather than being missing or lost'.

Wepman (1951) was one of the first to elaborate a therapeutic approach devised to stimulate language use in the patient. However, the therapist whose influence has been greatest is Schuell (Schuell et al., 1964), who developed a very detailed approach. According to Schuell there are not different forms of aphasia but only one, which may be rendered more complex by the presence of other non-aphasic disorders. Underlying aphasia there is an auditory processing impairment, and aphasia therapy is consequently based on adequate auditory stimulation, carefully controlled for length and complexity. Schuell's recommendations are still followed in clinical practice.

The stimulation approach in treatment can be either direct or indirect. In direct treatment exercises for specific language functions are devised. The patient's primary deficit should be identified and specific tasks which should improve the impaired process are proposed to the patient. The main difficulty lies in identifying the primary deficit. All too often this is done only by looking at test results and then training the function which appears from the results of the test to be the most impaired. In this case treatment is nothing but an expansion of the diagnostic procedures.

Indirect approaches are less formally structured and less directed towards specific language processes. An example of an indirect approach is Wepman's (1976) thought-centered therapy. The patient's attention is directed to the content he wants to express and away from the search for a specific word, for instance. A second example of an indirect approach is Chapey's (1981) divergent semantic therapy, which, like Wepman's thought-centered therapy, cannot be used for severely aphasic patients. Divergent language tasks are originally devised as a means of broadening the patient's capacity for word retrieval. In divergent semantic therapy, in order to exercise divergent language behavior, the patient is asked to generate a number of and a variety of responses to the same stimulus and not one single response, as in convergent therapy.

In French-speaking countries it is mostly Ducarne (1986) who has influenced aphasia therapy. Her approach can be likened to the stimulation approach but has a more pedagogic quality. The aphasic patient is seen as a person who was previously able to speak but who must relearn his language, and it is considered that he will achieve this goal by applying the same procedures used in learning a second language. There is a clear prevalence of production exercises over comprehension exercises, probably because the patient is asked to train largely by himself. The exercises are described in a fairly detailed way and differ for production and comprehension as well as for oral and written language. For very severe aphasics prelinguistic rehabilitation is suggested as a start, in order to enable the patient to understand the rehabilitation situation. Only then can aphasia therapy really start.

To summarize, all the different approaches that consider aphasia as a unitary process and have in common the idea that language must not be taught since it has not been lost, but stimulated, because it is difficult to get access to, go under the heading of the classical or stimulation/facilitation approach. Therapeutic techniques regrouped thus may have very little in common and much is left to the ingenuity of the speech pathologist.

Programmed instructions

In the sixties a group of investigations were devoted to the study of verbal and non-verbal learning of aphasic patients (Tikofsky and Reynolds, 1962, 1963; Edwards, 1965; Brookshire, 1969). These studies firmly established that learning is possible for most aphasics and that there are strategies they use even though less efficiently than normals.

The logical step that followed was to devise remedial procedures based on Programmed Instruction, which is an important application of the Operant Conditioning paradigm. Language rehabilitation is viewed as an education process, although aphasia rehabilitation differs from initial language acquisition in a number of ways. The basic assumption is that there is a behavior similar to the desired one in the patient's repertoire and that this behavior can be manipulated by using Operant Conditioning procedures. The behavior to be taught must be defined and a response related to that behavior must be identified in the repertoire of the person to be rehabilitated. Once the behavior to be taught and the program's starting point have been established, a series of carefully controlled steps, each of which is a closer approximation to the desired behavior, must be constructed on the basis of a structural analysis of the behavior to be attained. A verbal program is generally based on a psycholinguistic analysis of the content to be taught.

In other cases the behavior of the patient is not asked to change but it is elicited under different stimulus conditions, generally going from an easier one to a more demanding one. An example in aphasia therapy could be naming an object by first repeating what the therapist says, then in response to a phonemic cue and finally only after looking at the object. The first case in which the behavior is manipulated is called *shaping* and the second, in which the stimulus conditions are changed, is called *fading*.

Procedures based on programmed teaching techniques to instruct aphasics have been used by Sarno et al. (1970) and Holland (1970), among others. The paper by Sarno et al. (1970) is interesting because the effects of Programmed Instruction, clinical rehabilitation and no therapy were compared in a group of 31 severe aphasics at least three months post-stroke. The three groups were comparable for age, cultural level, severity of aphasia and time post-onset. All patients in the three groups showed a little improvement but no group responded significantly differently from the other. More favorable results are reported by Holland (1970), Holland and Sonderman (1974) and Smith (1974).

The advantages of such an approach are straightforward. It is possible to control the amount of information and the effect of therapy, and the patient is continuously stimulated to respond. Variability among therapists should not be a problem either as the program is clearly detailed and does not allow for variations. This, however, is also a drawback: the lack of flexibility of such programs does not take into account subtle differences among patients. A greater amount of individualization is required, and Holland (1970, p. 389) states 'it is probably more practical for the clinician to devote his time to experimental development of his own programmed materials, to understand thoroughly how behavioral principles can be applied to therapy, and to apply them to his own clients systematically, than it is for him to search through others' materials to find what someone else has programmed for aphasics'.

The most serious defect of Programmed Instruction is, in my opinion, the lack of interest in the content of the program. What seems to be important is how the program is organized and applied and not what its content is. Principles of Programmed Instruction have in fact been applied in aphasia therapy to totally different contents, such as learning to use verb tenses (Holland, 1970), to use a small vocabulary (Sarno et al., 1970), to use an artificial language (Glass et al., 1973; Gardner et al., 1976) or Melodic Intonation Therapy (Goldfarb, 1981).

In the late 1970s, approaches based on learning principles fell into some disrepute, partly because of some confusion between the content of the treatment and how the treatment was approached methodologically. In a strict sense, Programmed Instruction should refer to the principles of Operant Conditioning. Treatment was often based on rote-learning, and aphasia rehabilitation was viewed primarily as a re-learning program. A criterion level is established and when a patient has learnt responses to the stimuli presented, the stimuli are changed and the patient practises with these until he achieves the criterion level again. However, there are therapists who use some techniques and procedures of Programmed Instruction, such as collection of base-line data, fading and learning to criterion, without adhering to the principles of Operant Conditioning. In the literature on aphasia therapy, it is not always clear which of these two different uses of Programmed Instruction is referred to. While I personally do not agree with the idea that aphasia therapy should be based on the principles of Operant Conditioning, it is self-evident that if one wants to objectively record the patient's performance and the stimuli used, the procedures of Programmed Instruction are very useful tools.

An approach which uses the methodology of learning principles without sacrificing the importance of content and individualized programs is LOT (Language-Oriented Therapy; Shewan and Bandur, 1986). This views aphasia as both an impairment of the language system and a reduced efficiency in processing language. Because of the language system's impairment, the content of treatment is important and it is directed toward the impaired modalities at the level of impairment. According to Shewan and Bandur, the content of LOT is based on what is known about language, its organization and processing and for that reason it is called Language-Oriented Therapy. The methodology of application comes from Operant Conditioning but the same stimuli are not used over and over again until specific stimulus-response links are created. LOT is an example of how principles from different approaches can be unified in treatment of aphasia.

The pragmatic approach

This is not a totally new or different approach; rather, it is a development of the stimulation approach. The major difference between the two is the level at which language is considered. In the classical approach it is the syntactic level; the speech pathologist strives to obtain from the patient the intended words assembled in a syntactically correct order, and the level of the sentence is rarely exceeded either in comprehension or production.

Pragmatics, in contrast, refers to the use of language rather than its formal properties and it studies the relationship between language behavior and the contexts in which it is used. The linguistic context is what occurs before or follows a given linguistic unit. The extralinguistic context is more difficult to define; it consists of all the data common to speaker and hearer; it includes the situation, the participants' cultural and psychological backgrounds and their knowledge of the world. When a speaker constructs a sentence, he must take into account what he presupposes that the listener already knows, since comprehension is affected by knowledge.

There is a second important aspect that differentiates the classical and the pragmatic approaches. In the classical approach, the patient is frequently requested to describe a picture or retell a story. The utterances he uses are in most cases descriptive and affirmative and the speech pathologist's job consists of verifying whether they are true or false. There are, however, many utterances for which it does not make sense to verify their truth. If I say 'I promise I'll come' or 'I beg you to pardon me', I perform the act of promising or begging just by saying 'I promise' and 'I beg'; if, on the other hand, I say 'I am reading a book', I do not perform the act of reading just by saying it. When an action is performed just by saying it, it is called an illocutive act, but people also perform acts when they say 'I am reading a book'. The action performed can be an assertion, as in this case, or a request, or an order or something else. To understand a sentence one must also understand what speech act the sentence accomplishes. These and other aspects of language use were generally not considered in traditional therapy. Some of the previously neglected aspects of a successful linguistic intercourse to which speech pathologists working at the pragmatic level have directed attention are the following: to understand a text or discourse one must draw inferences, thus gaining new information not stated in the text; to correctly answer a question one must identify what part is the given and what the new which must be answered; and the problem of phrasing new information in a way which takes into account the listener's knowledge.

Pragmatics is, however, an ill-defined and extremely broad area and it is difficult to find a way of gaining meaningful information about patients' communicative ability. Some studies indicate that aphasics' communicative ability is greater than their language skills and that they can understand indirect speech acts (Wilcox et al., 1978; Kadzielawa et al., 1981; Foldi et al., 1983). At the moment, it seems unlikely that a single procedure will give relatively precise information of the patient's pragmatic competence, even though some attempts in this direction have been made. Holland's (1980) CADL, for instance, is a test battery specifically devised to ascertain the patient's communicative ability by some symbolic system, in contrast with more traditional language batteries in which a gestural answer is generally not considered a correct answer.

The best-known therapeutic method which has shifted the accent from language to communication in a broader sense is PACE (Davis and Wilcox, 1981). The principles of PACE are that therapist and patient participate equally in receiving and sending messages and that they exchange new information, using whatever communication channel is applicable. PACE is considered by its designers to be appropriate for all types of aphasia, at any level of severity. One criticism that can be applied to PACE is that it allows too much space to nonverbal communicative behavior, at the expense of a more linguistically based mode of communication. Language is a much more potent system and one that permits expression of much more than any other system. Aphasics should not be confined to a lower system of communication and should be helped to recover their full potential. However, PACE is not only based on gestural communication and it has the virtue of being clearly stated and usable by anyone.

In conclusion, the pragmatic approach is not a substitute for other techniques. It simply adds a new dimension to aphasia therapy, that of the use of language, which becomes once more a way of communicating new information and is no longer confined to informing the therapist whether or not the patient can retrieve a given word or use a syntactic structure. To use a fashionable word, language must be ecological.

The cognitive approach

During the last ten years or so more psychologists have become interested in analysing impaired cognitive processes and it has been claimed that rehabilitation techniques can benefit from models of cognitive processes. Cognitive models provide hypotheses about the components of a cognitive function and about how they interact with one another. The assumption of modularity is common to all models, that is, that any cognitive function is the result of the interaction and collaboration of different sub-components. The latter represent different aspects of the function and may be disrupted separately. The overall pattern of performance in a patient must be carefully analysed by a number of different tests supposed to require integrity of the same processing component. If the patient fails in all the tests, one can conclude that that component is impaired. When the specific locus of impairment is known, it is possible to design a more rational treatment, although knowing what is impaired does not automatically tell us how to rehabilitate it.

According to cognitive neuropsychology, the classical aphasia syndromes are not a good starting point for planning therapy because the various symptoms (for instance non-fluency, effortful articulation, reduction and simplification of syntax) do not necessarily co-occur (see, for example, Schwartz, 1984; Caramazza, 1984). In classical taxonomy, the notion of syndrome is used in a weak sense; the various deficits co-occur in a statistically significant number of cases following damage to a specific area of the brain and not because they depend on a single underlying mechanism. Moreover, the same symptoms can arise for different reasons, and in rehabilitation it is not the symptom that should be considered but the underlying cause.

The major novelty of cognitive neuropsychology in aphasia rehabilitation is not that it offers models

of normal language processing. The selection/combination dichotomy proposed by Jakobson (1964) and Chomsky's (1965) competence/performance dichotomy have both influenced aphasia rehabilitation. Weigl's (1961) deblocking technique is an example of a therapeutic approach based on the assumption that competence is preserved and that only performance is impaired in the aphasic patient. However, these models are extremely general and in fact do not help in understanding a patient's behavior. Cognitive neuropsychology models are much more detailed, at least for such functions as reading and writing, and can thus rationally limit aphasia therapy. It is now possible to find in the literature a description of a few individual patients rehabilitated according to principles of cognitive neuropsychology (Beauvois and Dérouesné, 1982; Hatfield, 1983; de Partz, 1986; Byng and Coltheart, 1986).

Of more interest to the clinical speech pathologist are the studies on word-finding difficulties, facilitation and remediation. Almost all patients have some degree of difficulty in finding a word or a name for something. In a series of carefully controlled studies, Howard et al. (1984, 1985a,b) confronted the problem of anomia. On the basis of the observed day-to-day variability in responses in a confrontation naming task (although the overall scores remained more constant) and the facilitatory effect of phonemic cueing, the authors come to the conclusion that the impairment in word-finding is one of access. Moreover, comparing the effects of two therapy methods, they found a small but significant advantage with the technique that required the patient to process the meaning of the picture to be named rather than the phonological treatment. These conclusions should obviously be considered when planning therapy for anomia.

In conclusion I am convinced − and it cannot be otherwise − that a better knowledge of the underlying impairment is essential for planning rational intervention approaches. A cognitive approach to aphasia rehabilitation, however, is not the solution for all existing problems. First of all, as I pointed out before, even if we know exactly what is wrong with a patient, we still do not know what to do to remedy it. At best, cognitive neuropsychology tells us what to reeducate, but not how to do it. Moreover, cognitive neuropsychology is founded on a specific assumption, that of modularity, which seems sensible but has not been proved and in the long run may prove to be wrong. On the other hand, if the assumption is correct, the various models might still be wrong. This, too, is more hypothetical than real, as existing models, even if not exactly the same, have much in common and thus mutually reinforce one another.

My last feeling against the cognitive approach is that, in a sense, in adopting it we are again taking a step backwards, ignoring the pragmatic level of language in aphasia therapy.

Specific techniques of remediation

In the literature there are literally hundreds of techniques of remediation of specific problems or of groups of patients. Many of them I do not know. In the following pages I will briefly indicate some of the disorders considered and some of the techniques used, and mention some specific methods.

Reading and writing. The existence of 'pure alexia' has not been disputed since Dejerine's (1892) first description. The existence of 'pure agraphia' has been debated much more. That probably explains why specific techniques for remediation of alexia but not for agraphia were common in the facilitation approach long before cognitive neuropsychology's models for reading and writing. The reading disorder was considered to be more 'agnosic' than 'aphasic' in nature and consequently rehabilitation was based on the use of different sensory inputs. The patient was instructed to follow – with his finger or eyes – the contour of the letters, thus rendering possible their recognition. In recent years, other reading and writing disturbances have been described meticulously (surface dyslexia and dysgraphia, deep dyslexia and dysgraphia and phonological dyslexia and

dysgraphia) and some examples of rehabilitation procedures based on principles of cognitive neuropsychology have been described (Hatfield, 1983; de Partz, 1986; Carlomagno, 1989).

Articulation. Effortful articulation has generally been considered a peculiar aspect of global and Broca's aphasia. However, the nature of the disorder – whether articulatory or linguistic – has been much debated, and the term apraxia of speech has recently been introduced by the Mayo Clinic Group (Johns and LaPointe, 1976). It emphasizes dissociation between a relatively good performance in automatic production and a relatively poor purposive speech performance.

No matter what the nature of the disorder is, speech pathologists have proposed a method that has been widely used in different countries with subtle differences. Basically it consists of first teaching the patient the articulatory positions of isolated phonemes and then to assemble them into words and phrases with the help of visual control. A detailed description of the method can be found in Ducarne de Ribaucourt (1986).

Agrammatism. Agrammatism has also been the object of much debate and many studies. A treatment program has been described by Helm-Estabrooks et al. (1981). It is based upon the hierarchy of syntactic difficulty shown by agrammatic patients (Gleason et al., 1975) and uses the story-completion format. A different approach based on a linguistic analysis of the defect is briefly described by Hatfield and Shewell (1983). Wiegel-Crump (1976) treated agrammatism by having the patients repeat a sentence in a picture-description task up to ten times, or until two correct repetitions. Therapy designed to achieve accessibility to mapping relations between semantics and syntax and to acquire the concept of predicate-argument assignment has proven efficacious in an agrammatic patient whose single word output had remained unchanged for some years (Jones, 1986).

Luria's research and aphasia rehabilitation scheme have not been mentioned in this chapter. It is in fact almost impossible to summarize his intervention techniques, as each deficit calls for its own peculiar rehabilitative program. It is, however, possible to sketch Luria's suggestions for rehabilitation of expressive agrammatism (Luria, 1970; pp. 447–452). The central problem in rehabilitation of agrammatism is to restore the use of predicative statements, as these patients can only name individual objects, while the predicative function of language is severely impaired. Accordingly, they must first be led to conscious awareness of the basic grammatical rules of normal speech and then to substitute external aids for the missing inner schemata. The agrammatic patient must be brought to sense the incompleteness of his one-word statements and learn to use elementary diagrams, first to specify the number of words he must use in a sentence and then to fix the relationship between the words. At each step of the program the patient must practise using the external aid until the procedure becomes essentially automatic.

Beyn and Shokhor-Trotskaya (1966) suggested that *prevention* of agrammatism is possible at an early stage after onset of aphasia. Only words bearing a predicative, verbal character and expressing complete ideas (*here, take*) must be introduced, excluding all substantive words. Later on nouns of generalized denotation can be introduced. In this way the program advances from the sentence to the word, thus preventing the emergence of agrammatism.

Auditory comprehension.   This label covers widely different things and different methods of remediation. Auditory Comprehension Training (ACT; Marshall, 1981) can be considered a stimulation approach but it differs in that it aims at improving only comprehension disorders by helping the patient to process meaningful linguistic units. Recently Naeser et al. (1986) have proposed a three-level program to improve comprehension of sentences. At the first level the patient is trained to discriminate CVC word pairs (i.e., fill/sill); at the second level, to identify a prerecorded target word in a fixed frame sentence; and finally at level three to identify the same words in more complex sentences. At each level the patient points to the correct printed response. Understanding the meaning of the word will probably help the patient at level 3, but at levels 1 and 2 he may very well respond correctly without understanding the meaning of the word, just by acoustic discrimination. Gielewsky (1983) proposes a retraining program specifically requiring the patient to perform acoustic analysis and auditory training.

Gestures and signs.   Non-oral strategies have been repeatedly employed for treatment of aphasia in patients with severe aphasia (for a review, see Peterson and Kirshner, 1981). In 1973 Glass et al. trained seven adult aphasics with an artificial language adapted from Premack (1971), with varying degrees of success. The Visual Communication System (VIC; Gardner et al., 1976) uses ideographic forms to denote meaningful units, and in the Visual Action Therapy (VAT; Helm-Estabrooks et al., 1982) patients learn to produce gestures in association with objects. Pantomime therapy has also been claimed to improve pantomime performance (Schlanger and Freiman, 1979) and Amerind and American Sign Language have been proposed as alternative means of communication for severe aphasics. Despite the success reported in these studies, alternative non-vocal modes of communication are not widely used. A general problem in these techniques is the transfer of learned gestures to spontaneous communication situations.

Right hemisphere.   With two patients, aphasia therapy to directly enhance right hemisphere competence for language has been attempted. Buffery and Barton (1982) stimulated the right hemisphere of their patient with three concomitant inputs. Three different words were presented through the left visual field, the left ear and the left hand while the left hemisphere was receiving neutral stimuli. The patient had to find the odd word among the three presented. Code (1983) used a similar technique. Both studies report a certain amount of improvement but these techniques are still at the experimental stage. A much better known and more widely used technique based on some capacity of the right hemisphere is Melodic Intonation

Therapy (Sparks and Holland, 1976), which exploits right hemisphere dominance for music. The prosodic patterns of spoken utterances are converted into intonation patterns using only a few notes. They are initially intoned by therapist and patient. The therapist gradually withdraws his support and the patient can eventually intone without aid. MIT has proven useful for patients with severe output limitations and relatively preserved comprehension.

Communication aids. This approach follows from a rather pessimistic view of recovery and refers to the use of external devices which can act as substitutes for speech or writing. Bruce (cited in Howard and Patterson, 1989) used a microcomputer which produced auditory letter sounds when letter keys were pressed. Four of five patients able to trace the first letter of a wanted word could self-cue with the computer and were better at naming with the microcomputer than without it. Blissymbols have also been employed in aphasia rehabilitation (Bailey, 1983). However, except in the case of a severe dysarthric problem that may be associated, the usefulness of such communication aids in aphasia therapy seems limited.

Recovery

Recovery from aphasia will be adequately covered in another chapter. Here I only want to hint at the relationship between the choice of an intervention strategy and what one thinks about recovery. Basically two positions can be identified: the first holds that total or partial recovery is possible and the second that it is not possible to restore what has been lost.

The stimulation approach, based on the theory that aphasia is not a loss but a reduction in accessibility of language, is a good example of aphasia therapy trying to restore normal language, i.e., language that is not qualitatively different from that used before the onset of aphasia. If, on the other hand, one holds the idea that the impaired function will remain so, one will not try to restore the function to its previous level but simply try to minimize the consequences of the impairment. This can be done at three levels: at level one by supplying the patient with an external aid such as Blissymbols, or manipulating the patient's environment; at the second level, one can try to get the patient to use alternative modes of communication, such as Amerind or pantomime; finally, one may still hold that the impaired function will not recover but be convinced that the same result can be obtained in different ways by changing algorithms. Reeducation of alexia by tracing the contour of the letters with a finger is one example. A second example is the reeducation of agraphia by Hatfield (1983) in three deep dysgraphics. Being unable to spell such words as *in, been, on,* they were taught to write a homophonic content word (inn, bean, etc.) and then correct it.

To sum up, when choosing a treatment strategy the speech pathologist must not only take a position about what aphasia is and carefully analyse the impaired cognitive processes, but he also has to anticipate the possible outcome and adapt his intervention to it.

Some practical questions

I will now very briefly consider some practical questions of importance in rehabilitation. The first question is which patients to reeducate and which not. There is no precise answer to this. It depends on prognostic factors. However, only the presence of a cluster of negative factors can justify withdrawing therapy. Darley (1982, p. 59) states 'The preponderance of data from all studies would compel one to believe that no *single* factor that negatively influences recovery appears to be so uniformly potent as to justify one's automatically excluding a patient from at least a trial of therapy on the basis of its existence'.

When to begin is a second important question. While 'the sooner the better' is the view generally held, some clinicians suggest that direct treatment be delayed a few weeks after onset (Wepman, 1972; Duffy, 1972). However, I am not aware of any experimental data in favor of either position.

We (Basso et al., 1979) did not find that the numbers of patients improved or unchanged in oral expression were significantly different in three groups: patients first seen less than two months post-onset, those seen between two and six months post-onset, and those seen after more than six months. Time post-onset being a negative factor for recovery, a smaller number of patients improved in groups of patients seen later but the difference between reeducated and non-reeducated was not very large. This result can be interpreted to indicate that all patients, no matter at what time post-onset they are first seen, are equally potentially good candidates for treatment, at least concerning oral expression. Wertz et al. (1986) also did not find any detrimental effects of delayed therapy. There is no advantage, however, in postponing rehabilitation after the general medical situation allows it to start, and early initiation of treatment appears advisable.

Once treatment has been initiated the speech pathologist has to decide for how long it must be continued to attain the maximum possible gains. In many cases the decision is determined by the available facilities, as apparently was the case in the Lincoln et al. (1984, p. 1199) study. 'Our results therefore seem applicable to the treatment regimens of the majority of aphasic stroke patients in this country. There is some evidence that, for the small number of patients who can cope with more intensive and prolonged treatment, speech therapy is beneficial. However, *very few speech therapy departments at present are staffed to offer this level of treatment*' (emphasis added). Nevertheless, duration of therapy seems to be an important factor in recovery. In all the randomized controlled studies in which no significant effect of therapy was found (Meikle et al., 1979; David et al., 1982; Lincoln et al., 1984; but see Wertz et al., 1986), treatment was not carried out for a long period, in contrast to the duration of treatment in studies in which a significant difference between treated and untreated patients was found (Basso et al., 1975, 1979; Marshall et al., 1982). We investigated the effects of length of treatment on im-

provement of oral comprehension and expression, comparing three groups of patients first examined at least two months post-onset: non-rehabilitated, rehabilitated for less than three months and rehabilitated for at least six months (Basso, 1987). Duration of rehabilitation had a significant effect on improvement of expression but not of comprehension. Other studies have also found that comprehension recovers more quickly and to a greater extent than other language modalities in non-rehabilitated patients. In conclusion, it seems probable that duration of treatment is an important factor and that aphasia rehabilitation should continue for several months to give treatment its best chance. Treatment can be interrupted when no improvement is seen after a period of at least 2 – 3 months. However, with a different therapeutic approach amelioration cannot be ruled out.

I am not aware of any study that specifically confronted the problem of intensity of treatment. It seems logical, however, that sessions should not be infrequent. A good rule of thumb is to schedule individual therapy sessions daily.

The importance of the patient's family in the rehabilitation process has often been emphasized. Considering the rehabilitation process from a restricted and technical point of view, the involvement of the family in the treatment program will partly depend on the therapeutic approach adopted, for example whether drilling is considered important. If, on the contrary, it is felt that language must be evoked in specific circumstances, the speech pathologist can rely less on the help of the family. From a less restricted and technical point of view, however, the family must always be involved as they may be of much help to the patient and therapist. A prerequisite for any treatment, for instance, is the patient's motivation and this must by no means be taken for granted. Some patients are not willing to collaborate because of anosognosia or for other reasons. As long as the patient is not motivated, treatment cannot really be undertaken, and the role of the family in helping the therapist motivate the patient is indisputable.

Finally, rehabilitation cannot start without a previous adequate neuropsychological screening that will permit individuation of the primary deficit and subsequent recording of possible gains. The choice of a test is directly influenced by one's overall concept of the nature of aphasia, and by what one hopes to accomplish. Assessment can aim at arriving at a diagnosis and at establishing a rehabilitation program or evaluating progress. Clinicians can construct their own batteries, but it requires a lot of time and energy to construct a standardized, reliable and valid test, and probably it is not worth it unless one wants to carefully investigate some specific and unusual deficit. To adopt an already existing aphasia examination, however, is not a neutral action. It also means the adoption of the author's position, as batteries reflect the author's theoretical position about the nature of aphasia and his choice of a model of language.

Nor is interpretation of test results straightforward. Many of the comprehensive tests provide their own interpretations of the test results, especially those devised for diagnostic purposes. In other cases, interpretation is open. The test user may simply determine scores for the different subtests and train the most impaired performances, or he may look for a common explanatory factor. Having once identified the lowest scores, he can see, for instance, whether a common underlying disorder might explain all of them, or, vice versa, whether all subtests that require a common ability are equally impaired or preserved. In this case, he will treat them together with the same exercises.

Conclusions

In 1982 Beauvois and Dérouesné complained about the fact that researchers were not interested in rehabilitation, except perhaps to assess its effectiveness. Since then things have changed, mainly due to the contributions of cognitive neuropsychologists. Many research papers in the field of rehabilitation (see, for example, Howard, 1986; Byng and Coltheart, 1986) and some studies aimed at evaluating the effects of treatment (Meikle et al., 1979; David et al., 1982; Lincoln et al., 1982, 1984) have appeared, but a significant difference in recovery in favor of rehabilitated patients has not been found and one gets the impression that clinical speech pathologists are now asked to justify their methods. This is certainly correct and badly needed in aphasia therapy but it must also be recognized that research and clinical application are not exactly the same.

As in all disciplines, in speech language therapy there is a time for research and a time for application. From a theoretical point of view research should precede application and, at least theoretically, it is easy to differentiate the two moments. What are the tasks of the researcher in the aphasia rehabilitation field? If he starts from observation of the patient, he must hypothesize a sufficiently detailed interpretative model of the observed impairment to be verifiable, define a therapeutic program, and apply it to the patients in such a way as to be able to demonstrate that it really was the treatment program that was effective, instead of spontaneous recovery or aspecific improvement. If, on the contrary, he starts from an abstract model of a given function he must find a patient with demonstrable impairment in one or more loci of the model, define a therapy program and apply it as before. Results should then be made known; if positive, in order to enable other similar patients to be treated in the same way and, if negative, in order to stimulate different ideas.

The clinical speech pathologist is confronted with different tasks: he should have a good theoretical and practical knowledge acquired during the years of his training and he should know the different therapeutic approaches, their limits and their possible efficacy. His task is to apply what he has learnt, to learn from his clinical experience and provide treatment for all patients who request it. It is not his task to demonstrate that what he does is effective. It would be the same as asking the general practitioner to demonstrate each time he prescribes a drug that the drug is effective.

In practice things are not so clear. It is very difficult, for instance, to demonstrate the efficacy of a therapeutic procedure and even more difficult to interpret a null result. If the proposed procedure is relatively general and has been applied to a group of patients who appear statistically to have improved more than the control group, all the problems relative to comparison of two groups arise (see Howard, 1986): groups may not be homogeneous, a general treatment may be applied differently to different patients by different therapists, spontaneous recovery may have occurred and so on. If, however, the procedure is highly detailed, the patient has been carefully described and the trial correctly planned, there are still other problems. Identical patients will hardly ever be found, the procedure cannot be exhaustively described and the therapist himself is an important variable. The clinical speech pathologist who wants to use the new procedure will eventually have to adapt it to his patients. Moreover, interpretative models of language and aphasia change with the growth of our knowledge. In clinical rehabilitation we therefore must be content with a reasonable certainty of the positive effects of a therapeutic procedure and apply it critically.

Aphasia rehabilitation has always taken advantage of new knowledge as it appears. It was started on a large scale only approximately 40 years ago, with its only theoretical basis the pedagogic principles of teaching a second language. Patients were asked, for instance, to recognize, imitate and retrieve single words. Later it was recognized that lexicon was not the same as language and patients were asked to comprehend and produce sentences. Now it is known that to satisfactorily use language it is not enough to understand and produce a sentence, and the level of pragmatics has entered into aphasia rehabilitation.

In parallel, cognitive psychologists have developed very detailed models in some areas for language functioning. Aphasic patients have consequently been studied more in depth and when it has been possible to identify the malfunctioning of one (or more) subcomponent(s), treatment has been specific.

The practical success of aphasia therapy is, however, still limited, as shown by the many studies on efficacy of therapy. This relative lack of success is counterbalanced by lively research and the ever-growing belief that aphasia rehabilitation must in the end be founded on a sound theoretical basis.

To close on an optimistic note I will quote Benson's (1979, p. 191) own concluding statement: 'Many aphasics benefit from aphasia therapy and almost every aphasic deserves consideration for therapy'.

References

Adams GF: Prospects for patients with strokes with special reference to the hypertensive hemiplegic. *Br. Med. J.:* 2, 253 – 259, 1965.

Bailey S: Blissymbolics and aphasia therapy: a case study. In Code C, Mueller D (Editors), *Aphasia Therapy*. London: Edward Arnold, Ch. 16, pp. 178 – 186, 1983.

Basso A: Approaches to neuropsychological rehabilitation: language disorders. In Meier M, Diller L, Benton A (Editors), *Neuropsychological Rehabilitation*. London: Churchill Livingstone, Ch. 14, pp. 284 – 314, 1987.

Basso A, Faglioni P, Vignolo LA: Étude controlée de la rééducation du langage dans l'aphasie: comparaison entre aphasiques traités et non-traités. *Rev. Neurol. (Paris):* 131, 607 – 614, 1975.

Basso A, Capitani E, Vignolo LA: Influence of rehabilitation on language skills in aphasic patients: a controlled study. *Arch. Neurol. (Chicago):* 36, 190 – 196, 1979.

Bay E: Present concepts of aphasia. *Geriatrics:* 19, 319 – 331, 1964.

Beauvois MF, Dérouesné J: Recherche en neuropsychologie cognitive et rééducation: quels rapports? In Seron X, Laterre C (Editors), *Rééduquer le Cerveau*. Brusells; P Mardaga, Ch. 11, pp. 163 – 189, 1982.

Benson F: *Aphasia, Alexia and Agraphia*. New York: Churchill Livingstone, 1979.

Beyn ES, Shokhor-Trotskaya MK: The preventive method of speech rehabilitation in aphasia. *Cortex:* 2, 96 – 108, 1966.

Bonvillian J, Friedman R: Language development in another mode. The acquisition of signs by a brain-damaged adult. *Sign Lang. Stud.:* 19, 111 – 120, 1978.

Brookshire RH: Probability learning by aphasic subjects. *J. Speech Hear. Res.:* 12, 857 – 864, 1969.

Brust JCM, Shafer SQ, Richter RW, Bruun B: Aphasia in acute stroke. *Stroke:* 7, 167 – 174, 1976.

Buffery A, Burton A: Information processing and redevelopment: towards a science of neuropsychological rehabilitation. In Burton A (Editor), *The Pathology and Psychology of Cognition*. London: Methuen, Ch. 10, pp. 253 – 292,

1982.

Byng S, Coltheart M: Aphasia therapy research: methodological requirements and illustrative results. In Hjelmquist E, Nilsson L-G (Editors), *Communication and Handicap. Aspects of Psychological Compensation and Technical Aids.* Amsterdam: North-Holland, 1986.

Caramazza A: The logic of neuropsychological research and the problem of patient classification in aphasia. *Brain Lang.: 21,* 9 – 20, 1984.

Carlomagno S: Writing rehabilitation in brain damaged adult patients: a cognitive approach. In Seron X, Deloche G (Editors), *Cognitive Approaches in Neuropsychological Rehabilitation.* Hillsdale NJ: Lawrence Erlbaum, in press, 1989.

Chapey R: Divergent semantic intervention. In Chapey R (Editor), *Language Intervention Strategies in Adult Aphasia.* Baltimore MD: Williams and Wilkins, Ch. 7, pp. 155 – 167, 1981.

Chomsky N: *Aspects of the Theory of Syntax.* Cambridge: MIT Press, 1965.

Code C: Hemispheric specialization retraining: possibilities and problem. In Code C, Mueller D (Editors), *Aphasia Therapy.* London: Edward Arnold, Ch. 4, pp. 42 – 69, 1983.

Darley FL: The treatment of aphasia. In De Monfort Supple M (Editor), *Language Disability – Congenital and Acquired.* Dublin: Boole Press, pp. 56 – 70, 1982.

David R, Enderby P, Bainton D: Treatment of acquired aphasia: speech therapists and volunteers compared. *J. Neurol. Neurosurg. Psychiatry: 45,* 957 – 961, 1982.

Davis GA, Wilcox MJ: Incorporating parameters of natural conversation in aphasia treatment. In Chapey R (Editor), *Language Intervention Strategies in Adult Aphasia.* Baltimore, MD: Williams and Wilkins, Ch. 8, pp. 169 – 193, 1981.

Déjérine J: Contribution à l'étude anatomo-pathologique et clinique des différentes variétés de cécité verbale. *Mém. Soc. Biol.: 4,* 61 – 90, 1892.

De Partz MP: Reeducation of a deep dyslexia patient: rationale of the method and results. *Cognitive Neuropsychol.: 3,* 149 – 177, 1986.

Ducarne de Ribaucourt B: *Rééducation Sémiologique de l'Aphasie.* Paris: Masson, 1986.

Duffy RJ: Aphasia in adults. In Weston AJ (Editor), *Communicative Disorders: An Appraisal.* Springfield IL: Charles C Thomas, 1972.

Edwards A: Automated training for a 'matching-to-sample' task in aphasia. *J. Speech Hear. Res.: 8,* 39 – 42, 1965.

Finkelnburg DC: Niederrheinische Gesellschaft, Sitzung von 21 März 1870 in Bonn. *Berl. Klin. Wochenschr.: VII,* 449 – 450, 460 – 462, 1870.

Foldi NS, Cicone M, Gardner H: Pragmatic aspects of communication in brain-damaged patients. In Segalowitz SJ (Editor), *Language Functions and Brain Organization.* New York: Academic Press, Ch. 3, pp. 51 – 86, 1983.

Gardner H, Zurif E, Berry T, Baker E: Visual communication in aphasia. *Neuropsychologia: 14,* 275 – 292, 1976.

Gielewsky EJ: Acoustic analysis and auditory retraining in the remediation of sensory aphasia. In Code C, Mueller D (Editors), *Aphasia Therapy.* London: Edward Arnold, Ch. 12, pp. 138 – 145, 1983.

Glass A, Gazzaniga M, Premack D: Artificial language training in global aphasics. *Neuropsychologia: 11,* 95 – 103, 1973.

Gleason JB, Goodglass H, Green E, Ackerman N, Hyde M: The retrieval of sintax in Broca's aphasia. *Brain Lang.: 24,* 451 – 471, 1975.

Goldfarb R: Operant conditioning and programmed instruction in aphasia rehabilitation. In Chapey R (Editor), *Language Intervention Strategies in Adult Aphasia.* Baltimore, MD: Williams and Wilkins, Ch. 12, pp. 249 – 263, 1981.

Goldstein K: *Language and Language Disturbances.* New York: Grune and Stratton, 1948.

Goodglass H, Quadfasel FA: Language laterality in left-handed aphasics. *Brain: 77,* 521 – 548, 1954.

Goodglass H, Barton MI, Kaplan E: Sensory modality and object-naming in aphasia. *J. Speech Hear. Res.: 11,* 488 – 496, 1978.

Hatfield FM: Aspects of acquired dysgraphia and implications for re-education. In Code C, Mueller D (Editors), *Aphasia Therapy.* London: Edward Arnold, Ch. 14, pp. 157 – 169, 1983.

Hatfield FM, Shewell C: Some applications of linguistics to aphasia therapy. In Code C, Mueller D (Editors), *Aphasia Therapy.* London: Edward Arnold, Ch. 5, pp. 61 – 75, 1983.

Helm-Estabrooks N, Fitzpatrick P, Barresi B: Response of an agrammatic patient to a syntax stimulation program for aphasia. *J. Speech Hear. Disord.: 46,* 422 – 427, 1981.

Helm-Estabrooks N, Fitzpatrick P, Barresi B: Visual action therapy for global aphasia. *J. Speech Hear. Disord.: 47,* 385 – 389, 1982.

Holland AL: Case studies in aphasia rehabilitation using programmed instruction. *J. Speech Hear. Disord.: 35,* 377 – 390, 1970.

Holland AL: *Communicative Abilities in Daily Living.* Baltimore, MD: University Park Press, 1980.

Holland A, Sonderman J: Effects of program based on the Token Test for teaching comprehension skills to aphasics. *J. Speech Hear. Res.: 17,* 589 – 598, 1974.

Howard D: Beyond randomised controlled trials: the case for effective case studies of the effects of treatment in aphasia. *Br. J. Disord. Commun.: 21,* 89 – 102, 1986.

Howard D, Patterson KE: Methodological issues in neuropsychological therapy. In Seron X, Deloche G (Editors), *Cognitive Approaches in Neuropsychological Rehabilitation.* Hillsdale, NJ: Lawrence Erlbaum, in press, 1989.

Howard D, Patterson KE, Franklin S, Morton J, Orchard-Lisle VM: Variability and consistency in picture naming by aphasic patients. In Rose FC (Editor), *Advances in Neurology, Vol. 42. Progress in Aphasiology.* New York: Raven Press, pp. 263 – 276, 1984.

Howard D, Patterson KE, Franklin S, Orchard-Lisle VM, Morton J: The facilitation of picture naming in aphasia. *Cognitive Neuropsychol.: 2,* 49 – 80, 1985a.

Howard D, Patterson KE, Franklin S, Orchard-Lisle VM, Morton J: Treatment of word retrieval deficits in aphasia: a comparison of two therapy methods. *Brain: 108,* 817 – 829, 1985b.

Howard FA, Cohen P, Heckler RB, Locke S, Newcombe T, Tyler HR: Survival following stroke. *J. Am. Med. Assoc.: 183,* 921 – 925, 1963.

Jakobson R: Towards a linguistic typology of aphasia improvements. In De Reuck AUS, O'Connor M (Editors), *Disorders of Language*. London: Churchill, pp. 21 – 46, 1964.

Jackson JH: *Selected Writings of John Hughlings Jackson*. New York: Basic Books, 1958.

Johns DF, LaPointe LL: Neurogenic disorders of output processing: apraxia of speech. In Whitaker H, Whitaker HA (Editors), *Studies in Neurolinguistics, Vol. 1*. New York: Academic Press, Ch. 5, pp. 161 – 199, 1976.

Johnson MG: Treatment of transcortical motor aphasia. In Perkins WH (Editor), *Language Handicaps in Adults*. New York: Thieme Stratton pp. 87 – 95, 1983.

Jones EV: Building the foundations for sentence production in a non-fluent aphasic. *Br. J. Disord. Commun.: 21,* 63 – 82, 1986.

Kadzielawa D, Dabrowska A, Nowakowska MT, Seniow J: Literal and conveyed meaning as interpreted by aphasics and non-aphasics. *Pol. Psychol. Bull.: 21,* 57 – 62, 1981.

Kimura D: Left hemisphere control of oral and brachial movements and their relation to communication. *Philos. Trans. R. Soc. London Ser. B: 298,* 135 – 149, 1982.

Kimura D, Archibald J: Motor functions of the left hemisphere. *Brain: 97,* 337 – 350, 1974.

Kirshner H, Webb W: Selective involvement of the auditory verbal modality in an acquired communication disorder. Benefit from sign language therapy. *Brain Lang.: 16,* 161 – 170, 1981.

Lincoln NB, Pickersgill MJ, Hankey AI, Hilton CR: An evaluation of operant training and speech therapy in the language rehabilitation of moderate aphasics. *Behav. Psychother.: 10,* 162 – 178, 1982.

Lincoln NB, McGuirck E, Mulley GP, Lendrem W, Jones AC, Mitchell JRA: Effectiveness of speech therapy for aphasic stroke patients. *Lancet: i,* 1197 – 1200, 1984.

Luria AR: *Higher Cortical Functions in Man*. New York: Basic Books, 1966.

Luria AR: *Traumatic Aphasia*. The Hague: Mouton, 1970.

Marshall RC: Heightening auditory comprehension for aphasic patients. In Chapey R (Editor), *Language Intervention Strategies in Adult Aphasia*. Baltimore, MD: Williams and Wilkins, Ch. 15, pp. 297 – 328, 1981.

Marshall RC, Tompkins CA, Phillips DS: Improvement in treated aphasia: examination of selected prognostic factors. *Folia Phoniatr.: 34,* 305 – 315, 1982.

Mateer C, Kimura D: Impairment of non-verbal oral movements in aphasia. *Brain Lang.: 4,* 262 – 276, 1977.

Meikle M, Wechsler E, Tupper AM, Benenson N, Butler J, Mulhal D, Stern G: Comparative trial of volunteer and professional treatments of dysphasia after stroke. *Br. Med. J.: 2,* 87 – 89, 1979.

Naeser MA, Haas G, Mazursky PG, Laughlin S: Sentence level auditory comprehension treatment program for aphasic adults. *Arch. Phys. Med. Rehabil.: 67,* 393 – 399, 1986.

Ojemann GA: Interrelationships in the localization of language, memory and motor mechanisms in human cortex and thalamus. In Thompson RA, Green JR (Editors), *New Perspectives in Cerebral Localization*. New York: Raven Press, pp. 157 – 175, 1982.

Ojemann GA, Mateer G: Human language cortex: localization of memory, syntax and sequential motor phoneme identifica-

tion systems. *Science: 205,* 1401 – 1403, 1979.

Peterson LN, Kirshner HS: Gestural impairment and gestural ability in aphasia. A review. *Brain Lang.: 14,* 333 – 348, 1981.

Premack D: Language in chimpanzee. *Science: 172,* 808 – 822, 1971.

Sarno MT: Aphasia rehabilitation. In Sarno MT, Hook O (Editors), *Aphasia. Assessment and Treatment*. Stockholm: Almqvist and Wiksell, pp. 61 – 76, 1980.

Sarno MT: Recovery and rehabilitation in aphasia. In Sarno MT (Editor), *Acquired Aphasia*. New York: Academic Press, Ch. 17, pp. 485 – 529, 1981.

Sarno MT, Silverman M, Sands E: Speech therapy and language recovery in severe aphasia. *J. Speech Hear. Res.: 13,* 607 – 623, 1970.

Schlanger P, Freiman R: Pantomime therapy with aphasics. *Aphasia Apraxia Agnosia: 1,* 34 – 39, 1979.

Schuell H, Jenkins J, Jimenez-Pabòn E: *Aphasia in Adults*. New York: Harper and Row, 1964.

Schwartz MF: What the classical aphasia categories can't do for us, and why. *Brain Lang.: 21,* 3 – 8, 1984.

Shewan CM, Bandur DL: *Treatment of Aphasia. A Language-Oriented Approach*. London: Taylor and Francis, 1986.

Skelly M, Schinsky L, Smith R, Donaldson R, Griffin J: American Indian sign: a gestural communication system for the speechless. *Arch. Phys. Med. Rehabil.: 56,* 156 – 160, 1975.

Smith M: Operant conditioning of syntax in aphasia. *Neuropsychologia: 12,* 403 – 405, 1974.

Sparks R, Holland A: Method: melodic intonation therapy for aphasia. *J. Speech Hear. Disord.: 41,* 287 – 297, 1976.

Tikofsky R, Reynolds G: Preliminary study: non-verbal learning and aphasia. *J. Speech Hear. Res.: 5,* 133 – 143, 1962.

Tikofsky R, Reynolds G: Further studies on non-verbal learning and aphasia. *J. Speech Hear. Res.: 6,* 329 – 337, 1963.

Vignolo LA: Evolution of aphasia and language rehabilitation: a retrospective exploratory study. *Cortex: 1,* 344 – 367, 1964.

Weigl E: The phenomenon of temporary deblocking in aphasia. *Z. Phonet. Kommun. Forsch.: 14,* 337 – 364, 1961.

Wepman J: *Recovery from Aphasia*. Chicago: Ronald Press, 1951.

Wepman JM: Aphasia therapy: a new look. *J. Speech Hear. Disord.: 37,* 203 – 214, 1972.

Wepman J: Aphasia: language without thought or thought without language. *Am. Speech Hear. Assoc. Rep.: 18,* 131 – 136, 1976.

Wertz RT, Weiss DG, Aten JL, Brookshire RH, Garcia-Bunuel L, Holland AL, Kurtzke JF, LaPointe LL, Milianti FJ, Brannegan R, Greenbaum H, Marshall RC, Vogel D, Carter J, Barnes NS, Goodman R: Comparison of clinic, home, and deferred language treatment for aphasia. A Veterans Administration cooperative study. *Arch. Neurol. (Chicago): 43,* 653 – 658, 1986.

Wiegel-Crump C: Agrammatism and aphasia. In Lebrun Y, Hoops R (Editors), *Recovery in Aphasics*. Amsterdam: Swets and Zeitlinger, pp. 243 – 253, 1976.

Wilcox MJ, Davis GA, Leonard LD: Aphasics' comprehension of contextually conveyed meaning. *Brain Lang.: 6,* 362 – 377, 1978.

© 1989 Elsevier Science Publishers B.V. (Biomedical Division)
Handbook of Neuropsychology, Vol. 2
F. Boller and J. Grafman (Eds)

CHAPTER 4

Recovery in aphasia

Audrey L. Holland

Departments of Otolaryngology, Psychiatry and Communication, University of Pittsburgh, Pittsburgh, PA, U.S.A.

Introduction

Far from being a static condition, aphasia is a dynamic problem reflecting change over time, particularly during the first year after its having been incurred. In addition to the simple passage of time, recovery from aphasia is also influenced by a number of variables that have both discrete and interactive effects. The purpose of this chapter is to examine the physiological and demographic variables that affect the degree of recovery an adult aphasic patient is likely to achieve, and the theories that purport to explain it. The implicit goal is to sensitize readers to the notion that it is always appropriate to question where in the time course of the disorder an individual called 'aphasic' might be, and how additional factors might affect the time course. We shall focus here on stroke, because stroke provides the largest data base for aphasia studies, and because stroke is the most likely condition to cause aphasia. It is also true that other cognitive and behavioral deficits that follow stroke, such as visuospatial deficits and hemispatial neglect associated with right hemisphere stroke, are also dynamic and likely to change over time. Their time course has been far less well-studied, however, and it is unclear what, if any, features of recovery from left hemisphere-engendered aphasia also apply to them. However, recovery from language disorders in right hemisphere stroke will also be briefly discussed.

Time course

Virtually all studies of recovery from aphasia show that maximal improvement occurs in the first three months following stroke (Demeurisse et al., 1980; Pickersgill and Lincoln, 1983; Kertesz and McCabe, 1977; Vignolo, 1964; Culton, 1969; Sarno and Levita, 1971; Wade et al., 1986). This is the so-called 'spontaneous recovery' period. Some writers extend this period to include the first six months post-stroke (Butfield and Zangwill, 1946; Porch, 1971), and others, such as Sarno and Levita (1971), suggest that individuals with global aphasia begin the process later than do patients with other forms of aphasia, and show its effects from six to twelve months post-stroke. Regardless of the putative endpoint of the process, the shape of the spontaneous recovery curve is negatively accelerated, with the greatest amount of improvement seen soon after stroke, and diminishing effects progressively discernible over time. Our own work (Holland et al., in press; Pashek and Holland, 1988) has led us to believe that the slope of the spontaneous recovery curve is steeper than is generally assumed, with most of the spontaneous recovery occurring by two months post-stroke, or even earlier.

Some aphasic patients continue to improve, both with and in the absence of aggressive aphasia rehabilitation over much longer periods of time. Sometimes this phenomenon is dramatic, as was the case with a former aphasic patient of mine, who suddenly regained the ability to read at his pretraumatic level, two years after the termination of therapy, three years after his aphasia began. This type of change is neither well studied nor well understood. Spontaneous recovery is not limited to speech and language change alone, of course. Improvements in accompanying sensory and motor deficits and cognitive behaviors also occur. And, particularly late in the spontaneous recovery process, individual adaptations to particular disabilities are often difficult to distinguish from actual physical restitution.

Variables that influence extent of spontaneous recovery

A number of variables are thought to influence the extent of spontaneous recovery. These include type and severity of stroke, age, gender, premorbid abilities, type of aphasia, handedness, psychological state, history of previous stroke, and general health. Some of these factors have clear and relatively well-demonstrated influence on spontaneous recovery; others have more tenuous relationships to the process. Finally, these variables often interact to affect recovery. We shall examine each in turn.

Type of stroke

Although the slope of the spontaneous recovery curve does not appear to differ as a function of type of stroke, persons who have had brain hemorrhages appear to begin the process somewhat later than do patients who have incurred ischemic infarction, and probably achieve a higher degree of spontaneous functional restitution (Rubens, 1977; Holland et al., in press), provided they survive the hemorrhage itself. This better recovery probably relates to the destruction of brain tissue in ischemic infarction, and its relative sparing in hemorrhage, a feature of recovery mechanisms to be discussed later in this chapter.

Severity of stroke

It seems logical to assume that the severity of the stroke that produced the aphasia should negatively affect spontaneous recovery. And to the extent that size of lesion (volume) (Knopman et al., 1983, 1984), presence of associated motor and sensory deficits (Wade et al., 1986) and length of hospitalization (Holland et al., 1987) reflect severity, this conclusion is correct. However, stroke severity is intertwined with many other factors, as we shall see later in this chapter. These interactive effects considerably complicate the relatively simplistic conclusion that severity of stroke affects the amount of spontaneous recovery one finds in aphasic individuals.

Age

It is a relatively commonplace observation that children who acquire aphasia show greater recovery than one might expect from adults who have incurred a similar degree of aphasia (Lenneberg, 1967; Woods and Carey, 1979). The literature does not, however, show much agreement concerning the relationship between age and spontaneous recovery once adulthood is achieved. Some researchers (Sands et al., 1969; Vignolo, 1964) have demonstrated poorer recovery to be associated with advancing age. Others, such as Sarno and Levita (1971), Basso et al. (1979) and Kertesz and McCabe (1977), suggest that age is not a strong deterrent for recovery. Our own research on the relationship between spontaneous recovery and aging (Holland and Bartlett, 1985) showed an unequivocal age effect at three months post-stroke, with older patients (i.e., those over age 70) not only having more severe and difficult-to-manage forms of aphasia, but showing less spontaneous recovery than those under age 60. This poorer spontaneous recovery for the older patients anticipates their problems at one year post-stroke, when we again compared them to the group under age 60. Not only had they made fewer and smaller gains than the younger group by that point, but substantially more older patients had incurred second strokes, begun to develop signs of multi-infarct dementia, or had died in the 9 months subsequent to our spontaneous recovery follow-up.

Gender

There have been some suggestions in the literature that females show a more heterogeneous pattern of speech representation than do males (McGlone, 1977). Thus, males might be expected to show poorer spontaneous recovery than females. The few studies that have investigated recovery as it relates to gender have produced equivocal results. Basso et al. (1982) demonstrated that females recovered better than males in auditory verbal comprehension. Pizzamiglio et al. (1985) found no initial sex differences in severity of aphasia; however, females with global aphasia showed significantly greater improvement than males in language comprehension. In our own study of spontaneous recovery in an unselected stroke sample referred to previously, our few gender differences favored males over females, in agreement with Marquardsen (1969). Thus, it is difficult to argue enthusiastically in favor of clear-cut gender differences in recovery from aphasia.

Premorbid characteristics

Almost every textbook on aphasia rehabilitation points out the importance of premorbid patient characteristics as they affect prognosis about recovery from aphasia. Yet there is virtually no evidence except the anecdotal to suggest that factors such as intelligence (provided it was pretraumatically within the normal range), socioeconomic status, occupation, etc., have much effect upon treatment for aphasia, much less upon its spontaneous recovery.

Type of aphasia

Even if one does not agree with the neurolinguistic distinctions that constitute classical aphasic syndromes, there is little doubt that component linguistic behaviors change during the process of spontaneous recovery. These changes are usually referred to as evolution of aphasia, and there are a number of aspects of change in language behavior that are well-supported by the literature. Virtually all studies agree that the severity of aphasia lessens over time, and that the path of syndrome evolution is toward those forms with less debilitating linguistic consequences. For example, the changes observed by Kertesz and McCabe led them to conclude that anomic aphasia was the common endpoint for evolution of aphasic symptoms (1977). Such evolution can occur for all types of initial presentations, except for the initially anomic patient, where change in this least severe aphasia would necessarily be simply further lessening in severity. We have documented an impressive evolution, over the first two weeks post-stroke from an initial global aphasia to a mild anomia (Holland et al., 1985). Changes in aphasic symptomatology can occur throughout the spontaneous recovery period, but our research, when we began to follow an unselected sample of stroke patients very soon (within 48 hours) after stroke, suggests strongly that much of the evolution occurs in the first two weeks post-stroke. Kohlmeyer (1976) suggests that if globally aphasic patients have not changed ,by this point, there is little likelihood of subsequent evolution. This was not the case in our sample, where some globally aphasic patients evolved at 4 weeks post-stroke. Nevertheless, individuals with global aphasia appear to have poorer language recovery if the condition persists into the second month post-stroke.

While some patients evolve through more than one type of aphasia, there is a predictable pattern to these changes. In essence, patients who initially show fluent aphasic syndromes evolve to milder fluent patterns; patients with non-fluent aphasias evolve non-fluently. Global aphasic patients may take either route. This evolutionary model was proposed by Gloning and Quatember in 1964. However, they failed to provide data to support it at that time. Subsequent research, including our own, has largely substantiated the model.

Observing changes in classical syndromes of aphasia is but one way to discuss the influence of presenting symptomatology on the recovery process. It is also possible to look at changes in the component behaviors themselves. A number of investigators (Kertesz and McCabe, 1977; Lomas and Kertesz, 1978) have shown that auditory comprehension is the behavior most likely to improve over time. Rubens and his co-workers have shown that improvement in the ability to comprehend sentences is related to both size and site of lesion (Knopman et al., 1983), while other components such as naming are probably less related to site and more to size of lesion (Knopman et al., 1984), and still others, such as single-word comprehension, are likely to improve, regardless of the lesion's site or size (Knopman et al., 1984). Studies such as these suggest that understanding spontaneous restitution of language function should be a ripe field of inquiry for researchers whose goal is to isolate and to understand the component behaviors as well as the subsystems that underlie language processing.

Handedness

Handedness as it is discussed here will relate to right- and left-handers who have aphasia as the result of damage to the left hemisphere, or left-handers who have had right-hemisphere strokes. Aphasia found in right-handers who have incurred lesions in the right hemisphere will be covered later in this chapter. There is some evidence to suggest that the relative incidence of aphasia is higher in left-handed patients who have suffered strokes (Subirana, 1958; Brown and Simonson, 1957; Zangwill, 1980). However, both Smith (1971), studying recovery from stroke, and Luria (1970), studying the head-injured, report better recovery among left-handed aphasic patients. To the best of my knowledge, no studies have investigated whether particular forms of aphasia predominate among left-handed individuals. Our own experience suggests that there is little difference in the severity and forms of aphasia as a function of handedness, and that handedness does not appear to exert a particularly strong influence on amount of spontaneous recovery.

Psychological state

Robinson and his co-workers have studied depression following stroke, and have concluded that it interacts negatively with spontaneous recovery (Robinson et al., 1983, 1984; Robinson and Price, 1982). Depression appears to be particularly associated with left-hemisphere frontal lesions, and therefore non-fluent aphasias. The Robinson group postulates a neurochemical basis for post-stroke depression. Whether or not this is the case, depression is a deterrent to active participation in treatment programs.

Previous strokes

It is generally thought that previous strokes, involving either hemisphere, negatively affect spontaneous recovery. Yarnell et al. (1976) correlated CT scan findings to recovery from aphasia, and found that both multiple lesions to the same hemisphere and bilateral lesions were related to poorer recovery. Gloning et al. (1976) showed poor results for patients with bilateral lesions. In many instances, these previous lesions were so-called 'silent lesions' whose effects were made manifest only at the time of the stroke in question.

General health

Schuell's factor analysis of performance on an extensive aphasia test led her to describe five groups of aphasic patients with differing prognosis for recovery (1964). One of her groups comprised aphasic individuals who had a potpourri of associated medical deficits, and overall they manifested subsequent poorer recovery from aphasia than did all but her globally aphasic group. Studies of recovery from stroke generally support this conclusion. Freed and Wainapel (1983) list prior stroke among their negative indicators for recovery; Delisa et al. (1982) associate unfavorable outcome with concomitant disease and bilateral brain damage, among other conditions.

Interactions among the foregoing variables

None of the above variables exists in vacuo, making it imperative to understand the interactions among them if we are to comprehend the spontaneous recovery process in aphasia. We know, for example, that Wernicke's and global aphasias are disproportionately frequent among the aging aphasic population (Obler et al., 1978; Harasymiew et al., 1981; Holland and Bartlett, 1985); that severity of stroke and type of aphasia are interrelated; and that more males than females incur stroke. General health factors probably interact with all of the others. It is therefore important to conduct research on recovery using the tools of multivariate analyses to gain a clearer picture of interactions that affect spontaneous recovery. Holland et al. (in press) have used logistic regression to investigate language recovery in a prospective study of both right- and left-hemisphere stroke patients. The data from 50 patients concerning side of lesion, sex, race, type of stroke, presence of hemiplegia, history of previous stroke, length of hospitalization and age were used to build a multiple linear logistic regression model of recovery. Although the sample size was small, and we were looking only at recovery of language function using the model, we were able to fit our data very well into our model. Short length of hospital stay and young age were significantly related to the likelihood of recovery, whereas being male and having had an ischemic infarction which

resulted in hemiplegia had a modest relationship to recovery. Other variables were noncontributory. Using our model, we were able to state log odds for recovery for patients in this study. For example, the odds of recovery for a male patient relative to a female patient with the same demographic and clinical characteristics were 10.4 to 1. This type of multivariate approach is a promising way to deal with the interactions among the variables that affect recovery from aphasia.

Language disorders following right-hemisphere stroke

'Crossed aphasia' is defined as aphasia occurring in right-handers following insult to the right cerebral hemisphere. A number of such cases have been described in the literature (Boller, 1973; Carr et al., 1981; Assal et al., 1981; Basso et al., 1986). Different recovery patterns have not been reported for such patients. Basso et al. (1986) report classical aphasic syndromes in their crossed aphasia sample. However, few other studies clearly differentiate so-called 'crossed aphasia' from the more typical speech and language problems associated with right-hemisphere strokes, such as aprosodia, digressiveness, tangentiality, failure to appreciate context, etc. These problems are well described and summarized by Myers (1984).

Fromm et al. (1987) reported language deficits in 14 of the 37 consecutive right-hemisphere patients they studied from ictus to 3 months post-stroke. No quantitative differences occurred in their performances on the Western Aphasia Battery, and, using that test's classification taxonomy, at discharge from the hospital thirteen of the fourteen could be categorized as having classical aphasic syndromes (and therefore, crossed aphasia). Fromm et al. argued that the striking qualitative differences between these right-hemisphere-damaged right-handers and their left-brain-damaged aphasic counterparts make the diagnosis of crossed aphasia untenable for them despite the WAB classification. It is important to note that the right-hemisphere language problems appeared to follow a timetable for spontaneous recovery similar to that for language problems following left-hemisphere stroke. Nevertheless, this work calls into question the concept of 'crossed aphasia' generally, suggesting instead that more careful examination of some of these reported patients would have indicated language disorders typical of right-hemisphere language problems instead.

Implications for treatment and research

Brookshire (1983) surveyed the frequency with which these and a number of other variables are reported in aphasia research published over a period of approximately 10 years in four major scientific journals. Although most research lists age of subjects, time post-onset was reported in only 60% of the articles, etiology in 49%, lesion lateralization in 53%, gender in 48%, and so on. It should be clear from the preceding that these variables contribute to the recovery process, probably affect the validity of data and must be accounted for if we are to understand the dynamic problem that is aphasia. The clinician perforce is probably more attuned to these factors as they apply to individual aphasic patients. Nevertheless, where the individual stands in relationship to the recovery process when he or she is either being treated or serving as a subject in a research study should be a matter of serious concern to neurolinguistic science.

Mechanisms of recovery

With varying degrees of sophistication, most of the mechanisms that are thought to affect recovery of function following lesioning in experimental animals have been invoked to explain recovery from aphasia. Some spontaneous recovery seems to derive from reversals of physiological changes that initially accompanied the stroke itself. Rubens (1977) has enumerated these changes to include lessening of edema, re-establishment of pretraumatic neurotransmitter activity, reabsorption of

the hemorrhagic mass in the case of intracerebral hemorrhage, and recovery from diaschisis, or the remote effects of lesions to specific brain areas. Other mechanisms, probably occurring later in the recovery period, that have been postulated to explain spontaneous recovery have been succinctly summarized by Johnson and Almli (1978) as follows: (1) substitution, implying a redundancy or multiple representation in the central nervous system which permits a secondary neural system to take over the functions of a primary one; (2) vicariation or equipotentiality, in which nonspecialized brain areas assume the function; (3) regeneration, or new growth in damaged neurons; (4) collateral sprouting, or new growth in areas adjacent to damaged tissue; (5) denervation sensitivity, or increased sensitivity to transmitter substances by neurons which have lost innervation as the result of the brain damage; and (6) behavioral strategy change, where both internal and external environmental cues are utilized to maintain function. Fazzini et al. (1987) have recently organized the available facts regarding recovery from aphasia, analysed a number of the above explanatory mechanisms and developed from it a falsifiable theory of recovery. However, it is clear that at present we have only an incomplete picture of the process of recovery of function. In fact, we do not understand the process of recovery of function following brain damage of simple behaviors in organisms less complex than humans. And given the universally recognized adaptive capacities of the central nervous system, we cannot rule out the possibility that after the earliest, trauma-related reversals, there is no further spontaneous recovery of higher cortical functions at all. What one observes as aphasia in the aftermath of stroke, then, might simply be the adaptive workings of a now imperfect nervous system. Therefore much more work remains to be done if we are to understand recovery following brain damage of one of a human being's most complex behaviors.

Laurence and Stein (1978, page 401) summarize the situation as follows:

' . . . we cannot claim to have "solved" the riddle of recovery, any more than we have "solved" the riddle of the brain. In fact, our knowledge of recovery will only parallel our knowledge of the normal operations of the brain, and in our opinion, most of the ambiguity, confusion and apparent conflict within the field of recovery is due to a lack of a comprehensive, explicit, and consistent approach to the entire range of nervous system operations and effects.'

Conclusions

In this chapter, an attempt has been made to describe the natural language changes that occur following the development of aphasia in adults. The variables that appear to interact with the recovery process have been described and some attempts to explain interactions among those variables have been made. In addition, a brief look at explanatory mechanisms has been attempted. It is important to point out that some of the features which affect recovery have been left untouched, notably the effects of direct manipulation of both environment and language itself on the recovery process. This is because therapy for aphasia is covered in another chapter, and to have included it here was unnecessary. It is clear that there is much to be learned about the nature of recovery from aphasia. Nevertheless, if we are to understand it fully, the complexity of the phenomenon must be acknowledged.

Acknowledgement

The author acknowledges the diligent help of Susan Jackson in the preparation of this chapter.

References

Assal G, Perentes G, Deruaz JP: Crossed aphasia in a right handed patient. *Arch. Neurol. (Chicago): 38,* 455 – 458, 1981.

Basso A, Capitani E, Vignolo AL: Influence of rehabilitation on language skills in aphasic patients. *Arch. Neurol. (Chicago): 36,* 190 – 196, 1979.

Basso A, Capitani E, Moraschini, S: Sex differences in the recovery of aphasia. *Cortex: 18,* 469 – 475, 1982.

Basso A, Capitani E, Laiacona M, Zanobio ME: Crossed aphasia: one or more syndromes? Referred to in Fazzini M, Bachman D, Albert M: Recovery in aphasia. *J. Neuro-*

linguist.: 1987.

Boller F: Destruction of Wernicke's area without language disturbance: a fresh look at crossed aphasia. *Neuropsychologia: 11,* 243 – 246, 1973.

Brookshire RH: Subject description and generality of results in experiments with aphasic adults. *J. Speech Hear. Disord.: 48,* 342 – 346, 1983.

Brown JR, Simonson J: A clinical study of 100 aphasic patients. *Neurology (Minneap): 7,* 777 – 783, 1957.

Butfield E, Zangwill OL: Re-education in aphasia: a review of 70 cases. *J. Neurol. Neurosurg. Psychiatry: 9,* 75 – 79, 1946.

Carr MS, Jacobson T, Boller F: Crossed aphasia: analysis of four cases. *Brain Lang.: 14,* 190 – 202, 1981.

Culton G: Spontaneous recovery from aphasia. *J. Speech Hear. Disord.: 12,* 825 – 832, 1969.

Delisa JA, Miller RM, Melnick RR, Mikulic MA: Stroke rehabilitation: Part 1. Cognitive deficits and prediction of outcome. *Am. Fam. Physician: November issue,* 207 – 214, 1982.

Demeurisse G, Demol O, Derouck M, deBeuckelaer R, Coekaerts MJ, Capon A: Quantitative study of the rate of recovery from aphasia due to ischemic stroke. *Stroke: 11,* 455 – 460, 1980.

Fazzini M, Bachman D, Albert M: Recovery in aphasia. *J. Neurolinguistics:* 1987.

Freed MM, Wainapel SF: Predictions of stroke outcome. *Am. Fam. Physician: November issue,* 119 – 123, 1983.

Fromm D, Swindell CS, Holland AL: *Language difficulties following right hemisphere stroke: evidence from the Western Aphasia Battery.* Paper presented at the 15th Annual Meeting, International Neuropsychological Society. Washington, DC, 1987.

Gloning K, Quatember R: Some classification of aphasic disturbances with special reference to rehabilitation. *Int. J. Neurol.: 4,* 296 – 302, 1964.

Gloning K, Trappl R, Heiss WD, Quatember R: Prognosis and speech therapy in aphasia. In Lebrun Y, Hoops R (Editors), *Recovery in Aphasia.* Englewood Cliffs, NJ: Humanities Press, pp. 57 – 64, 1976.

Harasymiew SJ, Halper A, Sutherland B: Sex, age, and aphasia type. *Brain Lang.: 12,* 190 – 198, 1981.

Holland AL, Bartlett C: Some differential effects of age on stroke-produced aphasia. In Ulatowska HK (Editor), *The Aging Brain: Communication in the Elderly.* San Diego: College Hill Press, Ch. 10, pp. 141 – 155, 1985.

Holland AL, Fromm D, Greenhouse JB, Swindell CS: Predictors of language restitution following stroke: a multivariate analysis. *J. Speech Hear. Res.:* in press.

Holland AL, Miller J, Reinmuth OM, Bartlett C, Fromm D, Pashek G, Stein D, Swindell C: Rapid recovery from aphasia: a detailed language analysis. *Brain Lang.: 24,* 153 – 176, 1985.

Johnson D, Almli CR: Age, brain damage, and performance. In Finger S (Editor), *Recovery from Brain Damage.* New York: Plenum Press, Ch. 6, pp. 115 – 134, 1978.

Kertesz A, McCabe P: Recovery patterns and prognosis in aphasia. *Brain: 100,* 1 – 18, 1977.

Knopman DS, Selnes OA, Niccum N, Rubens AB, Yock D, Larson D: A longitudinal study of speech fluency in aphasia: CT correlates of recovery. *Neurology: 33,* 1170 – 1178, 1983.

Knopman DS, Selnes OA, Niccum N, Rubens AB: Recovery of naming in aphasia: relationship to fluency, comprehension, and CT findings. *Neurology: 34,* 161 – 170, 1984.

Kohlmeyer K: Aphasia due to focal disorders of cerebral circulation: some aspects of localization and of spontaneous recovery. In Lebrun Y, Hoops R (Editors), *Recovery in Aphasics.* Amsterdam: Swets and Zeitlinger, pp. 79 – 95, 1976.

Laurence S, Stein DG: Recovery after brain damage and the concept of localization of function. In Finger S (Editor), *Recovery from Brain Damage.* New York: Plenum Press, Ch. 14, pp. 369 – 409, 1978.

Lenneberg EH: *Biological Foundations of Language.* New York: John Wiley and Sons, 1967.

Lomas J, Kertesz A: Patterns of spontaneous recovery in aphasic groups: a study of adult stroke patients. *Cortex: 5,* 388 – 401, 1978.

Luria AR: *Traumatic Aphasia.* The Hague: Mouton, 1970.

Marquardsen J: The natural history of cerebrovascular disease. A retrospective study of 769 patients. *Acta Neurol. Scand.: 45(38),* 1 – 192, 1969.

McGlone J: Sex differences in the cerebral organization of verbal functions in patients with unilateral brain lesions. *Brain: 100,* 775 – 793, 1977.

Myers PS: Right hemisphere impairment. In Holland AL (Editor), *Language Disorders in Adults.* San Diego: College Hill Press, Ch. 6, pp. 177 – 208, 1984.

Obler LK, Albert ML, Goodglass H, Benson D: Aging and aphasia type. *Brain Lang.: 6,* 318 – 322, 1978.

Pashek GV, Holland AL: Evolution of aphasia in the first year post onset. *Cortex: 24,* 411 – 423, 1988.

Pickersgill MN, Lincoln NB: Prognostic indicators and the pattern of recovery of communication in aphasic stroke patients. *J. Neurol. Neurosurg. Psychiatry: 46,* 130 – 139, 1983.

Pizzamiglio L, Mammucari A, Razzano C: Evidence for sex differences in brain organization in recovery in aphasia. *Brain Lang.: 25,* 213 – 223, 1985.

Porch BE: *A comparison of unilateral and bilateral PICA profiles on brain-damaged adults.* Paper presented at the 47th Annual Convention, American Speech and Hearing Association. Chicago, 1971.

Robinson RG, Price TR: Post-stroke depressive disorders: a follow-up study of 103 patients. *Stroke: 13,* 635 – 641, 1982.

Robinson RG, Starr LB, Kubos KL, Price TR: A two year longitudinal study of post stroke mood disorders: findings during the initial evaluation. *Stroke: 14,* 736 – 741, 1983.

Robinson RG, Starr LB, Price TR: A two year longitudinal study of mood disorders following stroke. *Br. J. Psychiatry: 144,* 256 – 262, 1984.

Rubens AB: The role of changes within the central nervous system during recovery of aphasia. In Sullivan M, Kommers MS (Editors), *Rationale for Adult Aphasia Therapy.* Lincoln, NE: University of Nebraska Press, pp. 28 – 43, 1977.

Sands E, Sarno MT, Shankweiler D: Long term assessment of language function in aphasia due to stroke. *Arch. Phys. Med. Rehabil.: 50,* 202 – 207, 1969.

Sarno MT, Levita E: Natural courses of recovery in severe aphasia. *Arch. Phys. Med. Rehabil.: 52,* 175 – 178, 1971.

Schuell H: *Aphasia in Adults: Diagnosis, Prognosis and Treatment.* New York: Harper and Row, 1964.

Smith A: Objective indices of severity of chronic aphasia in stroke patients. *J. Speech Hear. Disord.: 36,* 167 – 207, 1971.

Subirana A: The prognosis in aphasia in relation to cerebral dominance and aphasia. *Brain: 81,* 415 – 425, 1958.

Vignolo A: Evolution of aphasia and language rehabilitation: a retrospecitve exploratory study. *Cortex: 1,* 344 – 367, 1964.

Wade DT, Hewer RL, David RM, Enderby PM: Aphasia after stroke: natural history and associated deficits. *J. Neurol. Neurosurg. Psychiatry: 49,* 11 – 16, 1986.

Woods BT, Carey S: Language deficits after apparent clinical recovery from childhood aphasia. *Ann. Neurol.: 6,* 405 – 409, 1979.

Yarnell P, Monroe P, Sobel L: Aphasia outcome in stroke: a clinical neuroradiological correlation. *Stroke: 7,* 516 – 522, 1976.

Zangwill OL: *Cerebral Dominance and its Relation to Psychological Function.* Edinburgh: Oliver and Boyd, 1980.

© 1989 Elsevier Science Publishers B.V. (Biomedical Division)
Handbook of Neuropsychology, Vol. 2
F. Boller and J. Grafman (Eds)

CHAPTER 5

Electrophysiological correlates of language: stimulation mapping and evoked potential studies

Catherine A. Mateer and Paul A. Cameron

Department of Speech and Hearing Sciences and Department of Neurological Surgery, University of Washington, Seattle, WA, U.S.A.

Introduction

The electrochemical nature of neuronal activity provides a variety of opportunities to study brain functioning. Electrophysiology is as old as the knowledge of electrical currents. It was Galvani's chance observation of a twitching frog leg that led him to the discovery that electricity could be generated by the contact of two dissimilar metals. Studies in which electrical current has either been applied to the brain or recorded from the brain provided much of our knowledge about brain-behavior relationships. While this is particularly true for basic motor and sensory systems, it is also the case for a variety of emotional, behavioral and cognitive systems, including language. The lack of a true system of 'language' in most laboratory animals has limited the use of electrophysiological studies of language, but many opportunities to collect electrophysiological data in a variety of control and patient populations have yielded valuable information about the neural bases of this important aspect of human behavior.

Behavioral studies of language in control subjects and in patients with brain damage have led to theories about the localization of language processes in the brain. Electrophysiological studies in combination with behavioral observations are helpful in evaluating and expanding these theories. The discrete spatial and temporal characteristics of brain function revealed in electrophysiological studies can provide a tighter link in our understanding of language processes and neuroanatomy. This chapter describes two different electrophysiologically based techniques used in the study of language – cortical stimulation procedures and studies of event-related potentials.

Electrical stimulation studies

History and basic principles of cortical stimulation

Focal application of a small electrical current has been known to alter cortical function in animals and man (Cushing, 1909). Focal electrical stimulation in men was first introduced by Penfield and his colleagues at the Montreal Neurological Institute in association with surgical methods for cortical resection of epileptic foci under local anesthesia. Stimulation mapping was used to identify functional areas of the cortex, including cortical areas important to language and other cognitive processes (Penfield and Jasper, 1954; Penfield and Perot, 1963; Penfield and Roberts, 1959). Performance on such tasks as naming and counting is commonly disrupted in association with stimulation at discrete cortical sites on the dominant, usually left, cortex. Identification of sensorimotor cortex and of cortex important to language by the stimulation-mapping procedure allows these areas to be spared during resection, greatly increasing the margin of safety associated with cortical resection. Continued experience with stimulation mapping of cortical function has identified minimal, if any, additional risk to surgical patients specific to cortical stimulation (Ojemann, 1983). Individual variability in the exact localization of functional sites necessitates careful mapping in each patient (Ojemann, 1979).

Application of an alternating electrical current to cortical tissue has a variety of excitatory and inhibitory effects both locally and at a distance from the stimulation site (Ranck, 1975). With few exceptions, the stimulation sites associated with motor and sensory responses are located in areas one might predict for them on the basis of classic neuroanatomical organization. In contrast, in the quiet patient, who is not engaged in task-specific behavior, stimulation of the cortex outside these areas usually has no observable or reported effects. These areas of the cortex are said to be silent. If, however, the patient is engaged in a specific task, for example, a measure of spoken language such as naming, application of the current to one or more sites in the silent region may disrupt performance on the ongoing task. If care is taken so that the level of stimulation used is below that generating afterdischarges, recovery of normal function resumes the instant the current is removed. This disruptive effect of stimulation on behavior has been modeled as a reversible temporary lesion similar to the transient disruptive effect on isolated function seen in focal seizures. The exact nature and extent of functional neuronal disruption caused by the stimulating current is not well documented; empirically, the effects of stimulation at a particular site on behavior are often both repeatable and quite different from the repeated effects of stimulation at sites only a few millimeters away (Ojemann and Whitaker, 1978a). Stimulation effects are thus modeled as temporary lesions localized in both space and time.

Advantages and limitations of the technique

The stimulation-mapping technique has a number of advantages and disadvantages in the study of intrahemispheric functional localization. In many respects the theoretical basis underlying observations based on the stimulation-mapping technique is similar to that underlying studies based on spontaneously occurring lesions. One major advantage over spontaneous lesion studies, however, is the very small size of the involved cortical area disrupted during stimulation. This provides a much greater degree of spatial resolution for evaluating functional cortical localization. A second advantage is the sudden onset and immediate reversibility of the effect. It is unlikely that observations attained in stimulation-mapping studies are as affected by recovery of function and compensatory reorganization as are observations made in studies based on spontaneous brain lesions.

A third advantage of the stimulation-mapping technique is that stimulation effects on multiple behaviors can be assessed at multiple cortical sites in an individual patient. The resultant pattern of changes not only provides evidence for the involvement of particular areas in aspects of cognitive function, but can provide valuable insights into the relative dependence and/or independence of different language-related functions. Spontaneous lesions involving a much broader area usually result in a wider variety of symptoms and are thus far more likely to mask these important interrelationships. Dissociation of functions by their disruption at different sites, as well as association of functions by their mutual disruption at common sites, is critical to a better understanding of neurolinguistic organization. Indeed, the double dissociations of stimulus-related disruption of separate language functions provide the bases for our development of a model of brain organization of language that is different in several respects from those derived from lesion data.

The major limitations of the stimulation-mapping technique include the population available for investigation and the testing constraints. The patient population which provides most of the opportunities for cortical mapping is generally undergoing surgical treatment of medically intractable epilepsy. Patients undergoing this neurosurgical procedure obviously have neurological abnormalities which predate the clinical procedures. Aside from sodium amytal determination for language lateralization and the data regarding probable conditions for interhemispheric reorganization (Rasmussen and Milner, 1977; Mateer and Dodrill, 1983), the effects of the disease process on cerebral organization in general and functional interhemispheric localization in particular are essentially unknown. Preliminary data (Ojemann and Whitaker, 1978a) do not support a correspondence between the extent of epileptic cortex as determined by electrocorticography and language localization as identified by stimulation mapping, suggesting that the disease process may have little effect on the intrahemispheric localization of language; however, further observations of this nature are necessary.

A second limitation of the stimulation-mapping technique relates to the nature of test procedures. Since the technique is used in the unusual and sometimes changing environment of the operating room, repeated measures of baseline performance must be incorporated into the test design. Electrical stimulation can be continuously applied to the brain for only brief periods; 15 seconds is an upper limit. Thus test items must be of a level of difficulty and length such that each item can be completed within the limits of stimulation duration. The difficulty level must be set so that baseline control nonstimulation errors are near zero and yet the tasks are demanding enough to engage various levels of linguistic or cognitive involvement. Language measures designed for more leisurely testing of patients with brain lesions, such as paragraph reading or open-ended picture description, cannot be used in stimulation mapping.

General methods

The specific data discussed in this section were derived from cortical stimulation studies carried out in the Department of Neurological Surgery at the University of Washington in Seattle. All the studies were conducted during awake craniotomies for the resection of medically intractable epileptic foci, carried out under local xylocaine or bupivocaine anesthesia. In most cases the epileptic focus was in the anterior temporal lobe and the surgical exposure included superior portions of the lateral temporal lobe, inferior posterior portions of the frontal lobe, and the inferior parietal lobe adjacent to the Sylvian fissure. Preoperative assessment of these patients includes administration of the Neuropsychological Battery for Epilepsy (Dodrill, 1978), and an assessment of language lateralization by intracarotid amytol (WADA) testing. Almost all patients come to surgery with a history of pharmacological intervention for the seizure disorder. The patients were almost always on one or more of phenytoin, carbamazepine or valproate, and occasionally on primadone or phenobarbital. However, these pharmacological agents would not be expected to have differential effects on stimulation and nonstimulation trials, the type of effects sought in these studies.

The strategy of these intraoperative stimulation mapping studies has been to obtain multiple samples of a number of different tasks at multiple cortical sites in an individual patient. Whether language-related tasks or visuospatial tasks are tested depends on the side of operation and the known language lateralization. Frequent samples of task performance on which no stimulation occurs are pseudorandomly interspersed with stimulation trials. Obtaining multiple samples of a particular task at a particular site allows for statistical evaluation of whether the changes evoked with stimulation are different from control conditions. There are usually a number of stimulation conditions for a given task at a given cortical site, commonly three, and a number of nonstimulation control trials, commonly 70 to 80. A binomial single-sample test for which the control performance serves as the estimate of error probability is utilized for the statistical assessment (Siegel, 1955). A site is related to a given task only when the binominal probability is 0.05 or less that stimulation-evoked errors on that task at that site occur by chance.

The strategy of looking at multiple tasks at a given cortical site was developed in an effort to identify the role of a particular cortical site by the presence or absence of interactions on these different tasks. The larger the number of sites that can be sampled for each task, the more detailed the mapping. However, there are definite time limitations on stimulation mapping in the operating room. Thus, there is always a trade-off between the number of samples, the number of tasks, and the number of cortical sites where stimulation effects on various tasks can be assessed. So only the appropriate and relevant tasks should be selected for stimulation.

Stimulation studies are carried out after electrocorticographic identification of the epileptic focus and identification of sensori-motor cortex by cortical stimulation. The primary goal of these studies is to identify for the surgeon the relationship of particular tasks to the epileptic focus. The surgeon would like to know that changes in a task are not evoked from the site of the proposed resection but rather from some other area in a particular patient. Thus, the sites selected for stimulation generally encompass the posterior margins of the identified epileptic focus and sites in the nonepileptic cortex in the posterior temporal, inferior parietal, and posterior frontal cortex. These sites are identified by small, sterile, numbered tickets. The threshold current for afterdischarge is identified for each site. The stimulations during mapping are at a single current level just below the lowest of these thresholds. Trains of 60 Hz, 2.5 ms total duration biphasic square-wave pulses from a constant current stimulator are delivered through bipolar silver ball electrodes, 5 mm apart. With these stimulation parameters the threshold for afterdischarge varies considerably from patient to patient. The currents range from 3 to 8 mA (between peaks of the biphasic pulse). However, the afterdischarge threshold is very stable for repeated stimulation of a particular site, and usually varies only moderately, several mA, between sites outside the rolandic cortex in a given patient. The patients are unaware of when current is applied. Stimulation is applied at the onset of a trial or segment of a trial and is maintained for the duration of the task, typically 4 – 12 s depending on the task being tested. Patient's responses and markers indicating both trial and stimulation onset and offset are recorded on audio tape and, when appropriate, videotape for subsequent analysis.

Language and language-related measures

Three language tests measuring five different language functions have been used in these stimulation-mapping studies. One test measures naming, reading of simple sentences and short-term verbal memory. This test consists of a series of consecutive trials presented visually as slides. The first segment of each trial is a slide of an object whose name is a common word with a carrier phrase 'this is a _____' printed above it. The second segment of each trial is a slide with an 8 – 10-word sentence which the patient is to read aloud. The verb in the second clause of each sentence is left blank, and is to be completed by the patient. The sentences are constructed so they must be completed with one of a small number of inflected verb forms. The third segment of each trial is a slide with the word 'recall' printed on it. This acts as a cue for the patient to state aloud the name of the object pictured on the first slide of this trial, a name retained across the distraction produced by reading the sentences. Stimulation occurs during the naming segment on some trials, the reading segment on some trials, and the recall segment on still other trials. Control trials are pseudorandomly interspersed with stimulation trials. The sequence of site and test conditions is so arranged that no site is stimulated consecutively and stimulation at each site on each condition is distributed throughout the test period. Performance on this test is analysed for stimulation effects on naming and reading, and for effects of stimulation at the time of input (naming), storage (reading) or retrieval (recall) on short-term verbal memory. Trials with errors in naming are excluded from analysis of memory performance to ensure that the information to be remembered has been adequately perceived.

A second test of language-related function assesses the ability to mimic single or sequential orofacial movements. The patient is shown a series of slides each with three simple oral-facial postures such as protrusion of the tongue or pursing of the lips. One series of slides shows the same posture repeated three times; the second series shows three different postures. Stimulation occurs on a randomly selected half of each series. The patient's facial movements are recorded onto videotape together with markers identifying onset, offset and location of stimulation. These tapes are initially evaluated without knowledge of whether stimulation has occurred or not. Note that there is no memory component to this task; it is only a measure of motor mimicry.

The final language test measures the ability to identify phonemes embedded in a carrier phrase. A stop consonant, /p, b, t, d, k or g/, is embedded in the nonsense disyllable /ae ___ ma/ on pre-recorded tapes in a live voice. Each syllable is presented in a two-second period followed by a two-second quiet period during which the patient is to report which consonant was heard. Stimulation occurs only during the two seconds when the disyllable with its embedded stop consonant is presented and not during the two-second quiet period when the subject is supposed to respond, to avoid any confounding effects of stimulation on speech output. For all tests, markers indicating that stimulation has or has not occurred are recorded on a separate channel so off-line scoring can be done blindly as to the presence or absence of stimulation.

Patterns of language breakdown with cortical stimulation

Arrests of speech

A fairly common response to language tasks at one or more sites in an individual patient is what is termed arrest. During an arrest, the patient appears to remain alert with eyes open and may open his/her mouth in an apparent attempt to speak but there is no real articulatory movement and no audible vocalization. A correct response often appears immediately upon removal of the stimulating current. Arrest responses appear to be tied critically to speech motor control systems, but cannot be further analysed in terms of their possible linguistic role. On all of the brain 'maps' used to illustrate patterns of speech/language alteration, these arrest sites are marked. In the sample under discussion they were broadly distributed in the left lateral cortex, but were always located within one gyrus of the sylvian fissure. Stimulation of a small area in the left posterior inferior frontal cortex (Broca's area) almost invariably produces speech arrest. If the arrest is associated with evoked nonverbal oral movement it suggests stimulation of the motor strip; stimulation there is not usually applied repeatedly as seizures can easily result.

Naming errors

Naming is the language task most extensively studied with cortical stimulation mapping. Penfield and his colleagues (Penfield and Jasper, 1954; Penfield and Roberts, 1959) were the first to report naming data from cortical stimulation. In our studies, naming errors are divided into three types: (1) total speech arrest – during stimulation the patient is unable to produce the carrier phrase or name the object, (2) anomia – during stimulation the patient is able to produce the carrier phrase but is unable to name the object, and (3) misnaming – during stimulation the patient is able to produce the carrier phrase but incorrectly names the object.

Naming errors have been demonstrated with stimulation of a very broad area of the lateral dominant cortex (Ojemann and Whitaker, 1978a; Ojemann, 1979; Ojemann and Mateer, 1979; Van Buren et al., 1978). Some of the individual sites where naming changes have been evoked extend well beyond the traditional limits of the lateral cortical language areas, but most are located in the immediate peri-sylvian cortex. Fig. 1 designates all sites associated with naming errors in 14 patients.

There have been a few studies involving cortical stimulation-mapping and naming in multiple languages (Ojemann and Whitaker, 1978b; Mateer and Rapport, 1982). In all cases, there have been some dissociated sites implicated in each language, cortical sites where stimulation altered naming in one language but not in the other. This dissociation of cortical sites involving different languages is consistent with dissociated recovery of different languages seen in cases of polyglot aphasia (Paradis, 1977). One striking feature of the stimulation-mapping in two languages is that naming in the language in which the patient was least competent can be altered from a greater number of cortical sites. It has been hypothesized that larger areas of cortex must be used for object naming in the language of greater unfamiliarity and/or less automaticity.

Reading errors
The relationship between errors of naming and errors on the reading task. One of the reasons for developing the reading task was to evaluate more complex aspects of linguistic production in order to sensitize our measure of language function. The distribution and overlap of naming and reading errors is also shown diagrammatically in Fig. 1. In the 14 patients whose results on the reading task were presented in the previous section, 26 sites were associated with evoked naming errors. Of these sites, 88% were also associated with significant alterations in at least one error category on the reading task. Of the 53 total sites associated with evoked changes in reading, 28 (63%) were not associated with naming errors. Thus, whereas most sites associated with naming errors were also associated with reading errors, many sites are associated only with what appears to be the more sensitive reading task. Two of the three sites involved with naming only were located in the posterior portion of the middle temporal gyrus. These findings are strikingly consistent with the lesion data. Although naming deficits are ubiquitous with almost all aphasic types and usually overlap to some extent with other kinds of linguistic disruption, anomic patients in whom the naming deficit is prominent and often isolated have been reported to have restricted lesions in this same region involving the posterior mid-temporal gyrus (Mazzocchi and Vignola, 1979).

Analysis of types of evoked reading error. Reading tasks provide for much more varied language performance than a naming task, and stimulation of the dominant cortex during the reading of simple sentences has demonstrated striking patterns of linguistic alteration. Categorization of the myriad of possible changes in reading during both control and stimulation trials is a critical feature of the analysis. Therefore, we devised a method to analyse and code error responses that was applied to each response. The major error categories associated with stimulation-related alteration include speech arrest, grammatical errors, semantic errors and articulatory (phonetic or phonemic) errors. Each individual error in any part of a sentence was categorized. Errors from nonstimulation trials were compared to errors from stimulation trials. Only errors not seen on nonstimulation

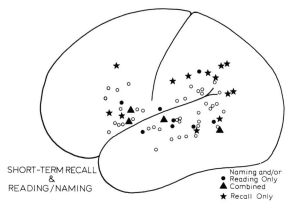

SHORT-TERM RECALL
&
READING/NAMING

Naming and/or
● Reading Only
▲ Combined
★ Recall Only

Fig. 1. Overlap of naming and reading sites in a series of 14 patients undergoing cortical stimulation.

trials were considered as potentially stimulation-related. In order for a given site to be said to be associated with a certain type of change attributable to stimulation, two of three trials with stimulation at the site had to show a particular error category. Sites could be identified with more than one error type. Reliability within and between two trained judges ranged from 80 to 100% on each of the four decision levels, namely identification of errors, coding of errors, identification of sites associated with change, and identification of category of change at those sites. Fig. 2 illustrates naming and reading error sites in a single patient (J.M.) The figure legend details the type of stimulation-related area.

The reading data presented here were based on 14 native English-speaking monolingual adult patients (10 females, 4 males), mean age 28.1 years (18 – 46 years) (Mateer, 1982). Mean preoperative Verbal IQ was 102.3 (90 – 126). All patients were right-handed and determined as being left hemisphere dominant for language by the WADA procedure. The stimulation items each consisted of two clauses: a dependent clause followed by an independent clause, with the verb missing in the se-

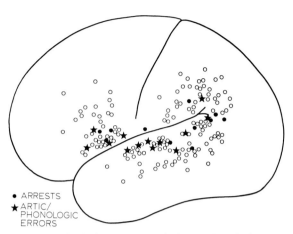

● ARRESTS
★ ARTIC/
  PHONOLOGIC
  ERRORS

Fig. 3. Stimulation-related articulatory/phonologic errors (*n* = 14 subjects).

cond clause. The patient read the entire sentence filling in the grammatically and semantically correct inflected verb form, for example: 'If my son is late for class again, he _____ principal'.

Articulatory/phonologic errors

A total of thirteen sites were statistically associated with articulatory or phonologic errors (Fig. 3). By definition these errors were divided into literal paraphasias (productions which had 50% or more of the target word; i.e., tencil/pencil) and neologisms (productions which displayed acceptable phonologic form but contained less than 50% of the phones of the target word). Some neologisms were seen in the context of extensive semantic and grammatic breakdown ('If next winzer is worth and sucks . . .'). Other neologisms were seen as isolated speech sound selection errors in the context of otherwise accurate productions ('If it is sunny next bedevali'). In some cases a patient started a sentence correctly with neologisms appearing only when content words were required, suggesting a possible semantic basis for the disturbance. Sites associated with articulatory/phonologic errors were distributed broadly in peri-sylvian cortex.

Grammatical errors

Fifteen sites, including sites in nine of the 14 pa-

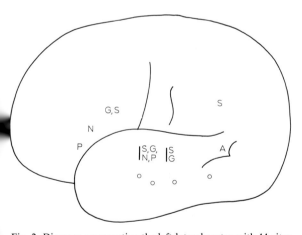

Fig. 2. Diagram representing the left lateral cortex with 11 sites stimulated during a cortical mapping study (3 frontal, 1 parietal and 7 temporal sites). Open circles represent sites not associated with evoked language change. Remaining sites were statistically associated with one or more errors as follows: A, arrests: N, naming errors; P, phonologic/articulatory errors; G, grammatical errors; S, semantic errors.

tients, were associated with grammatical errors upon stimulation (Fig. 4). Grammatical errors associated with stimulation were widely distributed throughout superior temporal, parietal and frontal regions of the lateral cortex. Disruptions of grammar with stimulation of sites in the mid superior temporal lobe and parieto-temporal region were very similar to the paragrammatical deficit seen in aphasic patients with posterior lesions. These aphasic patients often misuse function words and demonstrate errors in verb forms, though all parts of grammar are represented. An example of a grammatical error made during electrical stimulation of the posterior temporal lobe is 'She will be visit the mountain'.

Grammatical errors elicited from frontal lobe sites were of particular interest given the association of agrammatism with frontal lobe lesions (Goodglass, 1976). Although the early lesion literature had suggested that the telegraphic agrammatic style of patients with nonfluent Broca's aphasia was the result of motor programming deficits or an effort to economize speech output, the stimulation data support an independent grammatical deficit. Grammatical errors occurred with stimulation in the absence of any articulatory alteration. An observed feature of agrammatism associated with frontal lesions has included replacement of unstressed grammatical words with stressed items. Below are examples of responses given by one patient in association with stimulation at a frontal lobe site:

TARGET

If my son is late.
If you are serious.

RESPONSE

If my son will getting late.
If you gonna serious.

The responses were on separate trials; articulation was unaffected and all nongrammatical words were accurate. The patient did not demonstrate grammatical errors on nonstimulation trials. These stimulation-evoked errors are strikingly similar to errors seen in aphasia with paragrammatic or agrammatic features.

Semantic errors

Sixteen sites were associated with semantic errors (see Fig. 5). Semantic errors were, like grammatical errors, distributed widely in frontal, temporal and parietal regions. Semantic errors include productions marked by inappropriate meaning, (e.g., 'Should the soap be too salty, you can add in salt water'), as well as productions marked by categorical substitutions (soldier/sailor, mother/sister) or failures to complete the verb stem on the fill-in portion of the sentence, although clearly in-

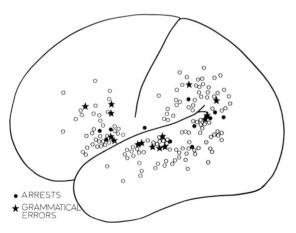

Fig. 4. Stimulation-related grammatical errors.

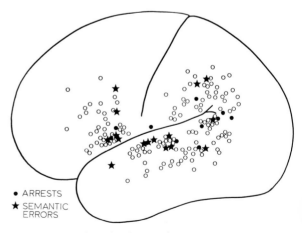

Fig. 5. Stimulation-related semantic errors.

dicating adequate grammatical inflection by appropriate use of auxiliaries.

Overlap and independence of stimulation-evoked errors

One of the unique capabilities of the stimulation-mapping technique is the very focal, restricted nature of the cortical disruption. It thus provides a unique way of assessing the detailed organization of functional language sites. Detailed functional analysis of other cortical systems for vision, audition and sensori-motor control have revealed exquisitely fine 'mosaics' or 'columns' of functional capacity in tightly structured cortical neuron systems. We wanted to look in this way at the relative independence and interdependence of language function at different cortical sites. Two additional maps were constructed. In one (Fig. 6), only those sites at which a single error type was observed were illustrated. In the other (Fig. 7), those sites at which more than one language function was altered (multiple error types) were il-

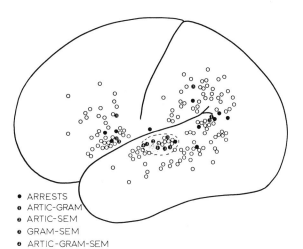

- ARRESTS
- ARTIC-GRAM
- ARTIC-SEM
- GRAM-SEM
- ARTIC-GRAM-SEM

Fig. 7. Sites associated with multiple error types. Note the heavy representation of 'integrative' multiple error types in the mid-superior temporal gyrus.

lustrated and the nature of the overlap was indicated.

There were 16 sites which were associated with one and only one category of error (Fig. 6). Eight of these were associated with phonologic (articulatory) errors. These are, in all cases, located within one gyrus of the peri-sylvian fissure, though they included frontal (4), temporal (3) and parietal (1) sites. Five sites were associated only with semantic errors. Four of these were located at the furthest 'corners' of the sample area with sites in mid-frontal, anterior temporal, posterior middle temporal and mid-parietal locations. In each of the four cases, these sites were two or more gyruses distal to the sylvian fissure. At only three sites were grammatical errors seen in isolation. These were all supra-sylvian (2 mid-frontal sites and 1 parietal site) and again located more than one gyrus distal to the peri-sylvian core.

Overall the pattern of cortical organization revealed in this analysis suggested that the motoric execution of speech as reflected in speech sound selection and production (articulatory/phonologic errors) was highly dependent on the peri-sylvian core. Both the traditional anterior 'motor' area and the posterior peri-sylvian areas were critically involved. Aspects of reading relating to more

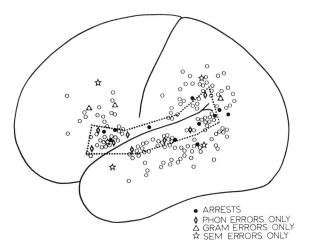

- ARRESTS
- PHON ERRORS ONLY
- GRAM ERRORS ONLY
- SEM ERRORS ONLY

Fig. 6. All stimulated sites in 14 patients are diagrammed. Only those sites at which a single kind of error was associated with stimulation are specially identified. Phonologic errors extend from premotor cortex and along superior temporal cortex to inferior parietal cortex, all within the peri-sylvian core. Sites associated only with grammatical or semantic errors in all cases but one fall outside this peri-sylvian core.

linguistically based aspects of language including grammatical and semantic selection, without any associated articulatory component, occupy more distal sites. The concentric 'ring-like' appearance of the distributions (see shaded area of Fig. 6) is highly reminiscent of the concentric field features associated with the primary, secondary and teriary association fields of other major cortical motor and sensory systems.

In Fig. 7, the possible multifunctional nature of cortical language sites is evaluated by plotting the nature of overlap at the 13 sites where stimulation resulted in more than one type of linguistic error. Sites marked by (3) represent sites where both semantic and grammatical aspects of sentence reading were altered. These nine sites account for 69% of the multifunctional sites. Though again broadly distributed, seven of the nine sites (77%) were within one gyrus of the peri-sylvian region. In comparison to Fig. 6, this suggests that while isolated linguistic capacity for grammar or semantic usage may have a more distal lateral distribution, integration of these functions may occur more centrally in left lateral cortex.

Articulatory function was altered at only two sites in conjunction with grammatical alteration (sites marked by (1)), and at only one site in conjunction with semantic alteration (site marked by 2)). Finally, just one site, located in the mid-superior temporal region, was associated with errors of all three types (articulatory, grammatic and semantic) (site marked by (4)). It was striking to us that although the general distribution of all three types of error looks roughly equivalent (Figs. 3, 4 and 5), the detailed functional specificity of cortical sites was substantial. Articulatory changes rarely (two sites only) overlapped with semantic errors, suggesting that these linguistic systems are highly independent and mediated by small, distinct cortical networks. The model of a mosaic pattern of cortical cells for functional language components may represent the best fit for these data.

Another observation supported by these data (Fig. 7) is the critical function of the middle superior temporal region. This region often ap-

pears 'silent' on the traditional maps of language cortex derived from the stimulation studies of Penfield (Penfield and Roberts, 1959), but appears highly active in these studies (Fig. 7, shaded area). A striking feature of sites here is that they all represent integrative, multiple function sites (see comparison to Fig. 6) and in almost all cases have important grammatical and semantic functions which would not be revealed in measures of straight naming behavior of the type used by Penfield and his colleagues. Although maps of traditional Broca's and Wernicke's areas also suggest a limited function of this mid-superior temporal region, those diagrams are typically based on more 'pure' forms of aphasia. The great majority of spontaneous lesions giving rise to aphasia involve this region (Mazzocchi and Vignolo, 1979), and our own data would argue strongly for recognition of its importance in linguistic integration.

Individual variability in evoked alterations of sentence reading

As seen with naming errors, there is a substantial degree of individual variability in the distribution of sites associated with stimulation evoked alteration in reading. Fig. 8 represents the percentage of patients in whom sites located in 1 of 16 designated

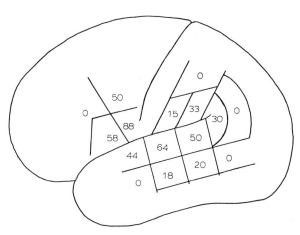

Fig. 8. Individual variability in cortical regions important for reading. Numbers indicate the percentage of sites in each demarcated region which were associated with reading errors.

areas were associated with significant reading disruption, errors in one or more categories relative to baseline performance. As can be seen from Fig. 8, the areas most often involved in reading disruptions include, in order of frequency; the inferior posterior frontal zone (88%), the middle superior temporal gyrus zone (64%) and the inferior anterior frontal zone (58%), followed by the posterior mid-frontal and the posterior superior temporal gyrus zones (50% each). Only 0 – 44% of the patients demonstrated significant reading disruptions with stimulation of the other surrounding zones.

Short-term verbal memory

Short-term verbal memory (STVM) deficits are a persistent problem for patients with aphasia, suggesting that the dominant cortex plays a role in memory (Butters et al., 1970; Albert, 1976). Milner (1967) found that resection of the dominant temporal cortex increased the verbal memory deficit almost as much as extension of the resection further into hippocampus. Selective loss of immediate and short-term verbal memory after small left parietal lesions has been reported (Warrington and Shallice, 1969; Warrington et al., 1971; Saffran and Marin, 1975). Early observations made with the stimulation-mapping technique noted different effects of stimulation during input to or retrieval from STVM at different cortical sites. Fedio and Van Buren (1974) reported STVM changes with left but not right cortical stimulation.

Separation of input, storage or retrieval as parts of STVM can be obtained with a single-term memory task paradigm. Ojemann and Mateer (Ojemann, 1978a,b, 1983; Ojemann and Mateer, 1979) have used a visually presented single-term memory test during stimulation-mapping. Object naming was the input memory. The name of the object was stored for a few seconds during a verbal distraction, reading or counting. Output of the name of the object from STVM was then cued by the word 'recall.' Stimulation at a given cortical site was applied during either input storage or out-

put on different trials of the memory task.

The locations of sites associated with STVM change in eight patients were usually at some distance from but surrounding the peri-sylvian cortex in high-to-mid-frontal, mid-temporal and especially parietal cortex (Fig. 1). These memory-related sites are often adjacent to but generally separate from the sites where stimulation alters language, as identified by changes in naming or reading (Ojemann, 1979). Two-thirds of the sites which evoked changes in memory failed to evoke any kind of language change. Memory sites have consistently been characterized by this largely separate cortical representation across several series of patients (Ojemann, 1979, 1983; Ojemann and Mateer, 1979).

Data from a study by Ojemann (1983) suggested different roles for the frontal, temporal and parietal cortex for STVM, based on whether memory changes were evoked by stimulation during the input, storage or retrieval phases of the task. During the input or storage phase of the memory stimulation of 27% of the frontal sites, 62% of the temporal sites and 64% of the parietal sites were associated with recall errors. This represented a significantly greater role for temporal-parietal cortex relative to frontal cortex in memory input and storage. In contrast, frontal sites were significantly more often associated with errors in recall when stimulated during the recall or output phase of the task than were parietal or temporal sites.

Oral movement sequencing and phonemic identification

Insight into motor mechanisms supporting speech/language function was obtained by mapping the effects of cortical stimulation on the ability to mimic repeated single and sequential movements (Ojemann and Mateer, 1979; Mateer, 1983a). These studies were prompted by the observations of Mateer and Kimura (1976) that the ability to mimic sequential facial movements is altered in both fluent and nonfluent aphasic patients compared to either normal subjects or those with brain damage not associated with aphasia.

Using the imitation task previously described, Ojemann and Mateer (1979) found that repetition of the same movement was disrupted with stimulation of sites only in a small region of the posterior, inferior frontal cortex just anterior to the face motor cortex. This region of disruption corresponds roughly to, but is smaller than, the traditional motor speech area. Fig. 9 is based on data from eight patients (Mateer, 1983a). Six sites of disruption are indicated by filled triangles. In all cases, these sites were also associated with arrests on naming and reading, suggesting that these sites represent part of the cortical pathway for oral-facial movement which is critical for speech. It is not part of the face motor cortex per se since no oral or facial movements were evoked.

Sequences of oral movements were disrupted over a broader area from sites throughout the extent of peri-sylvian cortex in the frontal, temporal and parietal lobes. Seventeen sites, marked by filled circles in Fig. 9, were associated with alterations of sequenced oral movement. Oral motor sequencing involves a larger area of cortex than repetition of the same movement, involving a broader range

of peri-sylvian cortex outside the classical sensorimotor cortex, including portions of frontal, parietal and superior temporal cortex surrounding rolandic and motor speech areas.

Disruption of consonant identification was also evoked from a broad range of peri-sylvian cortex. The task used was a taped live voice presentation of stop consonants /p, b, t, d, k and g/, embedded in the carrier phrase /ae _____ ma/. Stimulation occurred during the two-second presentation of the phase. There was a high overlap between sites associated with disrupted phoneme identification and disrupted sequencing of oral movements. In the patient sample presented in Fig. 9, 14 of the 17 sites (82%) associated with disruption of sequential oral movements were also associated with disruption of phoneme identification. The overlap is significant at the 0.01 level. These sites are represented by large Ps. These changes localized a sequential motor-phoneme identification system in language cortex, a common region for speech production and comprehension.

We hypothesized that these areas of peri-sylvian cortex which are involved in both the production of movement sequences and the perception of phonemes provide the neural bases for much of the basic production and perception of speech. There are several indications of the importance of this region of cortex to language. In one sample, naming or reading changes were evoked in 71% of the motor/perception sites, representing 60% of the sites with naming and reading changes in these patients (Ojemann, 1983). In addition, the peri-sylvian region is clearly implicated when one looks at sites which alter articulatory/phonologic aspects in the reading task (Fig. 6). The extent of lesions that give rise to a permanent motor aphasia as identified by Mohr (1976) encompasses the same peri-sylvian areas of the cortex where these sites are located, again suggesting that this is a crucial area for the generation of language. Damage to this area is hypothesized to account for production and comprehension deficits associated with most aphasias.

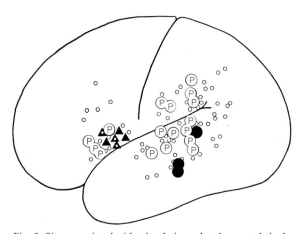

Fig. 9. Sites associated with stimulation-related repeated single oral movement errors (triangles), sequential oral movement errors (filled circles) and errors in phoneme identification (Ps or squares).

Variability in language organization relative to gender and Verbal IQ

The degree of variability in the localization of cortical sites related to language change is great for all three linguistic behaviors, naming, reading and memory. With the multiple linguistic function test, most patients, although not quite all, do show some kind of language change with stimulation in the traditional language zones, the inferior posterior frontal cortex and the middle to superior temporal gyrus. This suggests that the overall areas related to language functions may be relatively uniform, but with individual variability of sites related to specific language function. Such observations are consistent with the data from spontaneous lesions. Aphasias resulting from what appear to be similar cortical lesions may have quite variable linguistic characteristics (Mazzocchi and Vignolo, 1979). Variability in the behavioral correlates of cortical areas is not surprising in view of the high variability in both gross morphological structure (Rubens et al., 1976) and cytoarchitechtonic patterns (Galaburda et al., 1978) in human cortex. The morphological structure of this language area is quite different from person to person. Rubens et al. (1976) noted individual variability in the gyral pattern at the end of the sylvian fissure in the dominant hemisphere. Stensass et al. (1974) examined the total area and surface area of visual cortex in 25 normal brains. They found there were variances of 300% in estimated total area and variances of 400% in surface area.

Individual variability of cortical organization for language functions by the stimulation-mapping technique was not unexpected. We attempted to use it to further explore what may be important underlying correlates of cortical organization of language functions. Not all individuals use language with the same degree of facility, and across groups of individuals a variety of investigative techniques yield different patterns of neurolinguistic organization. Evidence that at least some of the individual variability is not an artifact of the stimulation-mapping technique or choice of anatomical landmarks comes from the correlations that are present between the pattern of naming change in individual patients and independent measures. We correlated two independent patient characteristics, the patient's gender and their preoperative Verbal IQ with patterns of stimulation related to naming changes. We used gender as a correlate because there are data suggesting differential pattern of aphasias in males and females following anterior versus posterior left hemisphere spontaneous lesions (Kimura, 1980). Verbal IQ was selected as an independent measure of verbal facility.

Gender-related distribution of sites on the lateral cortex involved in naming varied significantly for a series of eight males and ten females (Mateer et al., 1982). Naming changes were evoked from more sites in men than in women. Overall, naming errors were evoked from 63% of the total sites sampled in males (32 of 51) but only from 38% of the total sites in females (16 of 68) ($0.025 < p < 0.05$). When the lateral cortex was divided into eight zones (Fig. 10) the percentage of sites in a zone related to naming changes was significantly higher for males in two of the zones, an anterior frontal zone (80% of males versus 22% of females, $p < 0.05$) and a posterior parietal zone (males 57%, females 0%, $p < 0.05$). Proportionally, males were also at least twice as likely to

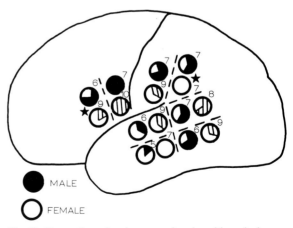

Fig. 10. Proportion of males versus females with evoked naming errors in eight cortical regions.

demonstrate evoked naming errors with stimulation of an anterior parietal zone and two middle temporal gyrus zones, though these differences did not reach significance. Males appeared to use a broader overall area of left cortex for naming. That is, it appears that larger areas of lateral frontal and parietal cortex are involved in naming processes in males than in females. Thus, gender may to some degree determine not only interhemispheric patterns of language organization, but the extent and pattern of intrahemispheric representation of language.

Verbal IQ was also correlated with patterns of stimulation-evoked naming change (Polen, Mateer and Ojemann, unpublished observation; Whitaker and Ojemann, 1977). A series of 21 patients ranging in preoperative IQ from 69 to 115 was divided into two groups on the basis of Verbal IQ. Of 10 patients with Verbal IQ at or below 96, seven demonstrated naming changes with stimulation in the posterior parietal region, while only one of 10 patients with Verbal IQ greater than 96 demonstrated evoked changes in naming stimulation in that area ($p < 0.025$). Patients with Verbal IQ above 96 were more likely to show naming changes from superior temporal gyrus stimulation than those with lower IQs (seven out of ten versus four out of eight), though this difference does not reach statistical significance. We have hypothesized that parietal representation of naming in patients with low Verbal IQs does not necessarily suggest that naming is represented more broadly in these patients. Rather, it suggests that the presence of language functions in the parietal lobe may constitute a less than optimal arrangement. Thus, the poor language function in some patients may reflect a less advantageous pattern of cortical language organization.

Stimulation effects in the nondominant hemisphere

Stimulation mapping of the nondominant hemisphere, as established by preoperative amytal testing, does not generally alter language-related tasks, outside the motor cortex (Fried et al., 1982; Mateer, 1983b; Ojemann, 1983). Stimulation of the face motor cortex alters mimicry of single movements, with some arrests of speech. However, there is no disturbance of phoneme identification with stimulation such as that seen with stimulation of the dominant hemisphere. There are changes in mimicry of sequential orofacial movements with stimulation of the motor cortex, but not with stimulation outside the motor cortex. Short-term verbal memory, naming and reading changes are likewise rarely evoked from the nondominant cortex.

Stimulation of the nondominant cortex does alter various visual spatial tasks. We have previously described discrete nondominant cortical localization of evoked changes in a variety of spatial tasks: perception of and memory for faces and angles, and the identification of facial emotional expressions (Fried et al., 1982; Mateer, 1983b,c; Ojemann, 1983). In general, these studies have demonstrated a strong dissociation of cortical sites involved in separate functions across individual patients. Contrary to the notion of diffuse functional organization in the nondominant cortex, visospatial functions in the right hemisphere appear to be as discretely localized as verbal functions in the left dominant hemisphere.

Event-related potential studies

Event-related potentials (ERPs) are changes in the electrical activity of the nervous system that are time-locked to specifiable events. ERPs are temporally associated with physical stimuli or psychological processes which are more or less directly linked to observable events. When ERPs are recorded in response to sensory stimuli they are called evoked potentials (EPs). EPs consist of a series of upward and downward deflections, peaks or waves, which are characterized by polarity, latency, amplitude, waveshape and distribution (see Spehlmann, 1985, for a more detailed description of EP characteristics). ERPs are classified as exogenous or endogenous evoked potentials.

The spatiotemporal configuration of exogenous potentials is determined by the integrity and organization of the sensory receptors and pathways involved and by the physical parameters of the stimuli. Exogenous potentials are not sensitive to variables in the psychological state of the individual receiving the stimuli. The auditory brainstem evoked potential is a good example of an exogenous potential. Brainstem evoked potentials are sensitive and effective in assessing hearing deficiencies due to impairments of sound conduction to the cochlea, as wel as cochlear and retrocochlear disorders (Davis, 1976).

Endogenous potentials, in contrast, are primarily affected by psychological variables. Endogenous potentials are associated with perceptual, cognitive and motor processes in the brain. They may be triggered by external stimulus events, but their waveform and timing are determined by the particular cognitive processes which are activated by the stimulus event and not by the stimulus modality or its physical properties. The contingent negative variation, a slow potential shift which arises during periods of expectancy or response preparation (Donchin et al., 1978), and the P300 wave, which is correlated with certain decision processes and the auditory oddball paradigm (McCarthy and Donchin, 1981), are examples of endogenous potentials.

Fig. 11 illustrates the different classes of ERPs in the auditory modality. During the first 10 ms after the onset of the stimulus are a series of up to seven waves, labeled I to VII, which have positive polarity at the vertex. These waves represent the far fields of evoked neuronal activity in the auditory pathways of the brainstem. Waves I – V represent conduction from the acoustic nerve to the upper midbrain, waves I – III represent conduction through lower brainstem, and waves III – V represent conduction through the upper brainstem. These brainstem evoked potentials are exogenous potentials which are sensitive to stimulus parameters, including intensity, rise time and stimulus rate (Pratt and Sohmer, 1976; Hyde et al., 1976; Hecox et al., 1976). However, they do

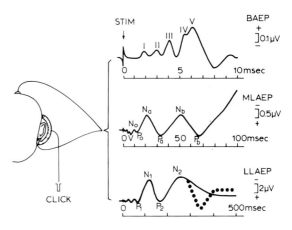

Fig. 11. Auditory evoked potentials are characterized by latencies as indicated on the abscissa. The upper panel illustrates the brainstem auditory evoked potential (BAEP), the middle panel illustrates the middle latency auditory evoked potential (MLAEP), and the lower panel illustrates the late latency auditory evoked potential (LLAEP). The dotted line signifies ERP components, which may vary as a function of information-processing demands.

not change appreciably with changes in sleep (Amadeo and Shagass, 1973) or during induced narcosis (Starr and Archer, 1975).

Ten to 50 ms after the stimulus onset are a series of waves called middle latency auditory evoked potentials (MLAEPs), named N_a, P_o, N_a, P_a, P_b. These waves probably represent a combination of evoked neural activity outside the classical auditory pathway and reflect myogenetic activity (Picton et al., 1974). MLAEPs are often obscured by scalp and neck muscle responses. Changes of attention, light sleep and mild sedation do not affect the shape or threshold of MLAEP (Mendel et al., 1975).

Fifty to 250 ms after stimulus onset are a series of waves called vertex potentials, named P_1, N_1, P_2 and N_2. These waves are termed vertex potentials because they are largest at the vertex of the scalp (Hillyard and Picton, 1979). The latencies of vertex potentials are somewhat inconsistent, P_1 at $50 - 70$ ms, N_1 at $100 - 150$ ms, P_2 at $170 - 200$ ms and N_2 at $200 - 250$ ms. Unlike the earlier evoked potentials, vertex potentials vary in amplitude and latency as a function of alertness level, arousal, selective attention, stimulus rate and stimulus duration. Finally, the P3 or P300 wave is a positive peak with a maximum at the vertex which occurs between 250 and 600 ms after the stimulus onset. A P300 may be elicited in an oddball paradigm in which a target stimulus (e.g., a high tone) is presented in a larger set of stimuli on no more than 20% of presentations. It may also be elicited by instructing the subject to guess the next stimulus or count or pay attention to brief presentations of stimuli which occur irregularly or infrequently within a series of stimuli. The P300 is an endogenous potential which occurs only when the stimulus conveys certain kinds of information that require a decision from the subject. It is sensitive to the subject's alertness level and state of arousal.

Methodological considerations and lateral asymmetries

Excellent guidelines for satisfactorily performing EP asymmetry experiments have been provided in Donchin et al. (1977a,b). In asymmetry experiments, as with EP studies in general, it is necessary that the determination of any difference in activity between channels can be made unambiguously; a common reference is therefore desirable. Obviously the ideal reference should be located where it is unlikely to be affected by the variables manipulated in the experiment, and asymmetrical reference sites should be avoided since these may be differentially affected by manipulations intended to alter the lateral distribution of EPs. The use of mastoids or earlobes as a reference is undesirable since they may be within the potential field generated by the EPs. Given these circumstances a reference placed away from the head is most appropriate.

A variety of cognitive tasks have been employed in studying possible EP correlates of asymmetrical processing. However, many of these investigations have paid little attention to the behavioral literature concerning the nature or strength of perceptual asymmetries related to the tasks in question. It makes sense to choose tasks which

have been previously validated by behavioral and clinical techniques when considering tasks for EP studies of cerebral asymmetry. The monitoring of the subjects' performance is essential to check on the relative difficulty of the tasks employed. The task should not be too hard or too simple, resulting in floor or ceiling effects which could confound the relative asymmetries in the EPs. Finally, the use of subject populations which are as homogeneous as possible with respect to cerebral lateralization and the controlling of factors which are known to be related to cerebral lateralization are important (e.g., handedness).

Event-related potentials and language processes

Studies in control subjects
In the last 15 years a vast number of studies have examined the electrophysiological correlates of language while recording from the scalp in non-neurologically impaired subjects (see Hillyard and Woods, 1979; Neville, 1980; Molfese, 1983; Kutas, 1987, for reviews of the literature). Pragmatics, semantics, sentence processing and phonology are the areas of language processing which have received most attention in the ERP literature.

A large number of these investigations attempted to determine whether ERPs would reflect differences between processing of language and non-language stimuli (Cohn, 1971; Morrell and Salamy, 1971; Molfese et al., 1975; Neville, 1974; Friedman et al., 1975; Galambos et al., 1975; Hillyard and Woods, 1979) and whether there were lateral asymmetries to clicks and speech stimuli when electrodes were placed over the right and left side of the head (Buchsbaum and Fedio, 1969, 1970; Wood et al., 1971; Neville, 1974; Friedman et al., 1975; Kutas and Donchin, 1977; Wood, 1975). Results have often been conflicting; many studies comparing speech and non-speech stimuli failed to be replicated, as did a variety of the studies which focused on lateral asymmetries in ERPs evoked during language tasks (Molfese et al., 1975; Galin and Ellis, 1975; Brown et al., 1976; Chapman, 1979; Neville et al., 1977; Grabow et al., 1980). Many of these early attempts at replication failed for a variety of methodological reasons (for example, Grabow et al. (1980) apparently failed to replicate Morrell and Salamy (1971) because they used a different baseline measure).

One of the best-controlled ERP studies has been that of Wood et al. (1971). They compared ERPs to the syllable /ba/ when it was processed for fundamental frequency cues versus phonetic cues, and demonstrated left – right hemispheric processing differences. The left side ERP response changed significantly between the two conditions whereas the right side ERP did not. However, the magnitude of difference was very small. Attempts to replicate the study have met with mixed success. Wood (1975) obtained similar results in a follow-up study, but Smith et al. (1975) and Grabow et al. (1980) failed to replicate the study. While the results of the latter two studies differed from those of Wood et al. (1971), so did their methodologies. Despite failures to confirm asymmetrical effects, findings across studies suggested that manipulation of phonological variables resulted in changes in the $N_1 - P_2$ ERP components recorded from the vertex.

Studies have also demonstrated that as the stimuli change as a function of context, or pragmatics, so does the ERP change (Matsumiya et al., 1972; Teyler et al., 1973; Brown et al., 1973, 1976, 1980). The ERP changes were seen in the $N_1 - P_2$ components. Investigators have used the ERP technique to study semantic processing (Thatcher, 1976; Neville et al., 1986), responses to words versus non-words (Buchsbaum and Fedio, 1969, 1970; Matsumiya et al., 1972; Molfese, 1980; Rugg, 1984, 1985), generation of synonyms and antonyms (Thatcher, 1976) and appreciation of connotative meaning (Chapman, 1979; Chapman et al., 1977, 1978, 1980). More recently, investigators have used the ERP technique to assess language activity during reading and sentence-processing (Friedman et al., 1975; Kutas and Hillyard, 1980a,b,c, 1983; Kutas, 1987). These studies have demonstrated larger P300 amplitudes for the last word during reading tasks as compared

to the baseline P300 amplitude.

The ERP technique has added to our understanding of the neural bases of normal language processing. Most early electrophysiological studies have been concerned with ERP correlates of specific linguistic operations (e.g., semantics, pragmatics, phonology). Recently, many electrophysiological studies have turned attention to ERP generators (Halgren et al., 1980; Wood et al., 1984; Johnson, 1985) and variables which control the various exogenous components (e.g., P300 and attention; Johnson, 1984, Johnson and Donchin, 1978, 1980, 1985). Electrophysiological studies, including the use of ERP paradigms, will undoubtedly continue to clarify the nature of lateral asymmetries for normal language processing. However, despite advances in electrophysiological recording and data analysis, the technique has yet to reach the level of sophistication required to determine which neural structures are involved in language processing or to begin to understand how language is processed as a whole.

Clinical ERP studies

The clinical applicability of evoked potentials in demonstrating abnormal sensory system functioning, localizing brainstem, midbrain and cerebral lesions, and defining the distribution of many disease processes is well recognized. ERPs have begun to be widely used in the diagnostic workup for multiple sclerosis, nervous system tumors, CVAs, head trauma, mental retardation, brain death, and in the assessment of mental functions in aging and dementia (Chiappa and Ropper, 1982; Pfefferbaum et al., 1980, 1984a,b; Polich et al., 1985; Squires et al., 1979, 1980). More recently they have been incorporated into neurosurgical and surgical procedures. While historically ERPs have played a major role in diagnosis, they are increasingly being assessed for applicability in rehabilitative and functional contexts.

Electrophysiological studies and aphasia. Right and left hemispheric processing of linguistic information in aphasic patients has been a subject of considerable interest. As yet we have little understanding of the cognitive and information-processing capabilities of the cerebral hemispheres when one hemisphere is damaged. Standard EEG procedures have been employed to explore hemispheric asymmetries in aphasic patients with left hemisphere damage. Hemisphere alpha suppression has been demonstrated in normal subjects over the hemisphere primarily involved in information processing (Moore and Haynes, 1980). Moore (1984) went on to demonstrate decreased alpha activity in the right hemisphere for both fluent and nonfluent aphasic patients when contrasted with normal non-neurologically impaired control group. Moore attributed this finding to 'contralateral compensation' whereby the right hemisphere was postulated to be processing information normally handled by the left hemisphere.

Event-related potentials have also been used to investigate cerebral hemisphere processing strategies when one hemisphere is damaged. Little information is currently available regarding the relationship between ERPs and the abnormal processing of language in aphasic patients. The few published studies have been concerned primarily with indicators of recovery, comparisons of levels of severity and localization of lesions (Neville et al., 1979; Harmony and Alvarez, 1981; Duffy, 1982; Wood et al., 1984). Many of these studies have yielded inconclusive and inconsistent results. One problem may be the frequent use of stimuli which had no relationship to language to elicit ERPs. Although most of the investigators used left and right electrode placements, only a few studies used tasks which could be expected to differentially activate left and right hemisphere functions. Failure to use such tasks limits any conclusions one might make concerning hemispheric involvement in the various measures.

The application of electrophysiological techniques to aphasia provides great potential for further research; however, better-controlled studies are needed. For example, theories regarding the degree to which the right hemisphere takes over language functions to the exclusion of the left hemisphere may be too simplistic. There is likely to be a wide range of right hemisphere involvement for different language functions across aphasic subjects. The degree of right hemisphere activation will surely be related to the severity and nature of the aphasic disorder (Selinger, 1984). Better tests which differentially activate right and left hemisphere functions are needed. The use of larger sample sizes and more varied patient groups would allow previous conclusions to be generalized to a broader population of aphasic patients with a broader range of impairment. Given the individual variability of language organization and language breakdown, careful analysis of each patient's language capabilities is essential. Future research projects could thereby more rigorously examine the relationship between language capabilities and ERP responses. Finally, more frequent use could be made of longitudinal designs. Longitudinal designs could contribute information to the field of aphasiology in terms of assisting in prognosis, predicting recovery curves and rehabilitation potential, and developing rehabilitation techniques.

Electrophysiology and normal speech perception. Since the mid 1980s, the averaged evoked potential to auditory stimuli has been used as a tool for determining and describing neurological mechanisms underlying auditory perceptual functions. Studies of hemispheric asymmetry using late components have provided support for specialized processing of speech stimuli in the left hemisphere (Morrell and Salamy, 1971; Molfese, 1980; Wood et al., 1971). Several of these authors have also used ERP studies to study how the cortex may be specialized for extracting linguistic features from acoustic signals.

In both human infants and adults, EPs recorded from the scalp have been shown to differ with speech sounds according to acoustic features believed to underlie speech perception. EPs to /da/ and /ba/ manifest an initial positivity which peaks approximately 150 ms after stimulus onset, while the initial peak to /ta/ occurs at 220 ms. This latency difference in EP morphology has been hypothesized to reflect the delay in voice onset time (VOT) which characterizes voiceless as compared to voiced phonemes. The responses change little in morphology or topography, though the components peak at progressively shorter latencies in the developing and mature human (Kurtzberg et al., 1986).

Despite promising results, a major drawback of such analyses, particularly when they involve late cortical components, is the significant attenuation and dispersion of the signal inherent in scalp recording. Direct recording from the cortical surface affords much better resolution and localization of the signal origin.

Event-related potentials recorded directly from human cortex

Recently, we have recorded cortical potentials to computer-generated speech stimuli directly from human cortex (Mateer et al., 1987; Cameron et al., 1987). These data have been obtained from patients undergoing craniotomies under local anesthesia or strip electrode recording, two procedures used in the diagnosis and treatment of medically intractable epilepsy.

Two stimuli signalling the phonetic categories /ba/ and /pa/ were synthesized by means of a computer-controlled parallel resonance synthesizer. The two stimuli only differed in voice-onset-time (0 ms for /ba/ and 55 ms for /pa/). Prior to EP recording, the patients had demonstrated a clear ability to perceive the signals categorically in a categorical perception paradigm. Two patients had strip electrodes placed on the cortical surface of each hemisphere as part of preoperative work-up for a medically intractable seizure disorder. The electrodes were placed over the lateral and inferior surface of the temporal lobes. Sodium amytal tests in all patients confirmed left hemisphere dominance for speech/language functions.

In one study, sixteen channels of EEG signals were derived from cortical strip electrodes using a

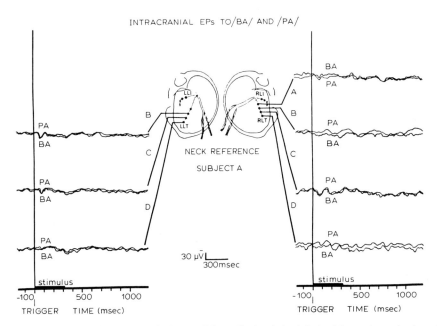

Fig. 12. Diagram illustrates evoked potentials to /ba/ and /pa/ derived from electrode sites along a strip placed along the cortical surface under the dura (LLT = left lateral cortex, LLI = left lateral/inferior temporal cortex, RLT = right lateral cortex; RLI = right lateral/inferior temporal cortex). EPs from the left electrodes are characterized by better-formed, higher-amplitude waves than from the right electrodes. There is also a consistently shorter N$_1$ latency to /ba/ (0 ms VOT) than the /pa/ (0 ms VOT). Subject A.

linked neck reference (Mateer et al., 1987). Each strip consisted of a row of four 7 mm stainless-steel discs embedded in silastic with an interelectrode distance of 15 mm. The subject, wearing headphones, lay on a bed in a darkened room with eyes focused on a point on the ceiling, and was instructed to listen and count the target stimuli. Fifty /ba/ and 50 /pa/ tokens were randomly presented in a single run with an interstimulus interval of three seconds. A total of three runs comprising 150 samples of each token were presented.

We asked: (1) is there a differential response to the speech sounds from the right and left hemisphere?; (2) if so, do the EP latencies or morphologies differ at different cortical sites within each hemisphere?; and (3) do EP latencies or morphologies vary systematically between the two different sounds (/ba/ and /pa/)?

Results from the two subjects are displayed in Fig. 12 (Subject A) and Fig. 13 (Subject B). First, ERPs were much more clearly seen from sites in the left hemisphere than from sites in the right hemisphere, and amplitudes of the ERPs recorded from left hemisphere were clearly larger than those

recorded from the right hemisphere. Second, responses were localized within the left hemisphere; ERPs were seen at one point along the strip, but not at a point only a few millimeters away. Third, in addition to amplitude differences, latency differences were noted between the two stimuli. The latency of the negative peak for /pa/ stimuli was consistently later than that for /ba/ by 5 – 40 ms. The explanation we have proposed for this latter finding is that the difference relates to the acoustic difference between the two signals. The shorter latency to /ba/, which is characterized by a shorter VOT, may relate a 'signature' in the wave representing cortical encoding of the acoustic difference between the stimuli. More recent studies comparing stimuli not only across but within designs suggest that the morphological differences in ERP wave forms correspond to the phonemic as opposed to the phonetic differences in the stimuli.

Very similar results have recently been recorded directly from the cortex in a series of four patients undergoing craniotomies for epilepsy (Cameron et al., 1987). Recordings from two patients undergoing right craniotomy failed to reveal speech-sound-

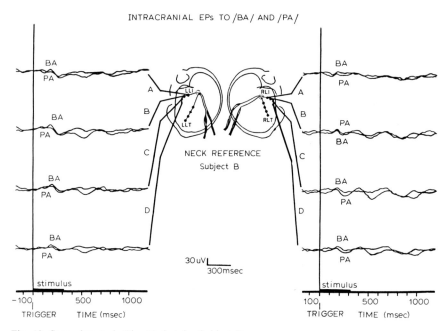

Fig. 13. Same data as in Fig. 12, but for Subject B.

related evoked potentials. Recording in the two patients undergoing left craniotomies revealed well-formed potentials. Two of their features are notable: (1) the N_1 latencies for /ba/ were always shorter by 5 – 40 ms, and (2) the evoked potentials were identified not only over left auditory cortex but over the left face motor and pre-motor cortex (Fig. 14). We have suggested that this is evidence that the face motor cortex plays an important role in the analysis of speech sounds.

In another series of studies, Ojemann and his associates have reported changes in ERPs during silent naming from the exposed dominant left hemisphere during awake craniotomy procedures (Fried et al., 1981; Ojemann and Fried, 1982). Patients engaged in two tasks utilizing the same stimuli, (1) name matching, which elicits silent object naming, and (2) line matching, which elicits spatial processing. Each task was given in separate blocks, and the patient was informed before each block of trials as to whether the task required silent naming or a spatial match. ERP changes were demonstrated for silent naming trials but not for spatial matching trials. These changes were only demonstrated at sites which were related to naming on subsequent stimulation mapping. Two basic changes in the ERPs were identified at these naming sites. The first change was a slow potential shift

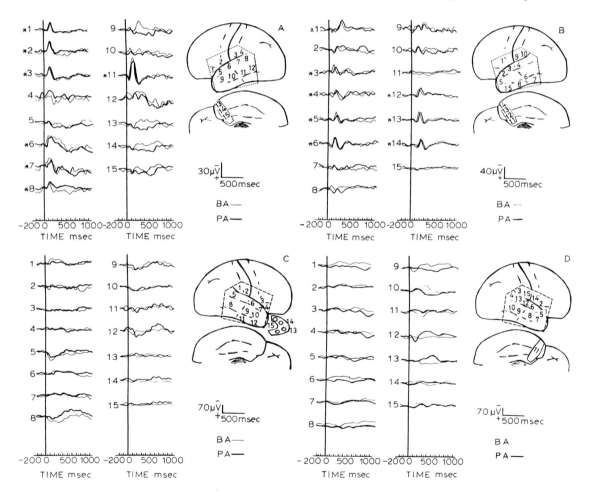

Fig. 14. (A and B) Evoked potentials obtained from direct left-sided cortical recording during craniotomy in 2 subjects. Potentials are indicated over both temporal and motor/premotor face areas. N_1 latencies to /ba/ (0 ms VOT) precede N_1 latencies to /pa/ (55 ms VOT). (C and D) Evoked potentials obtained from direct right-sided cortical recording during craniotomy in 2 subjects.

which lasted for approximately one second. The second change identified was a local desynchronization with flattening of the ERP and loss of rhythmic activity lasting for about one second. The first change was localized to posterior naming sites. The second change was localized to posterior temporal-parietal and frontal naming sites. Ten responses to spontaneous speech ('yes') were also averaged in the studies. ERP changes during speech were greatest at sites which demonstrated ERP changes for overt naming. These changes were seen earliest in time after speech onset at premotor sites, then at motor sites followed by posterior sites. These investigators drew two major conclusions. They argued that the data suggest focal cortical activation by language stimuli rather than activation of the cortex as a whole. They also suggested that the early potential shifts with spontaneous speech seen in premotor cortex indicate that premotor areas are involved in an earlier stage of language production than motor cortex. Although to postulate discrete localization of cortical language generators is premature, ERP data may have much to offer in this regard.

Summary of the model for cortical organization of language

In this chapter we have reviewed electrophysiologically derived data which have a bearing on the neural bases of language. The evidence from stimulation mapping suggested that language may be concentrically organized around the sylvian fissure in the left dominant cortex. A small inferior frontal region, approximately the posterior portion of the third frontal gyrus, immediately in front of the face motor cortex appears to be critical to voluntary orofacial motor functions, including basic speech production. Surrounding this area anteriorly, posteriorly and inferiorly in the perisylvian cortex of frontal, temporal and parietal lobe is a broad region with sites which subserve the selection and sequencing of orofacial movements and speech.

Surrounding this peri-sylvian area frontally and parieto-temporally are cortical areas related to short-term verbal memory which are largely separate from any other measured language functions. Frontal portions of this area are related to memory retrieval, and parieto-temporal portions of this are related to memory storage. At both the frontal and parieto-temporal interface between these systems are sites related to specialized language functions, naming, reading, grammar and semantics.

At the core of this region, in the cortex immediately surrounding the sylvian fissure are sites which appear to be involved in the phonemic decoding of speech sounds. Many sites stimulated in this region give rise to speech sound identification errors. Evoked potentials recorded from the left cortical surface have also consistently been found, not only at posterior temporal sites but also at face motor and premotor sites. These data suggest that it is not only classical auditory areas but also premotor and motor areas which are critically involved in speech sound decoding.

The data for the organization for language functions derived from both the electrical stimulation mapping and ERP studies indicate quite discrete functional localization within all cortices, including those areas commonly known as association cortex. The data would predict that the effects of brain damage are very dependent on the location of the injury, with increasing area of injury relating to greater impairment primarily because of the greater likelihood of damage to multiple yet discrete functional areas. Within a general framework, there appears to be considerable individual variability in the exact location of areas related to a particular task. To some degree, however, the individual patterns of localization appear to be related to other variables. In the case of naming, these variables include overall language ability and gender of individual. Finally, a strong suggestion emerges from this work that, even in adults, there is a considerable plasticity of cortical function in that, for all the tasks measured, there are multiple sites.

Data described in this chapter are somewhat different from yet not inconsistent with the major findings from clinical studies of aphasia. A few aphasias are characterized predominantly by one kind of linguistic disruption, agrammatic aphasia, anomic aphasia, conduction aphasia, and semantic jargonaphasia. These syndromes usually involve not only smaller lesions, but lesions that do not involve the immediate peri-sylvian cortex (Mazzocchi and Vignolo, 1979). In the context of results from stimulation mapping, they might be seen as disrupting aspects of language function which are more separately represented outside the peri-sylvian cortex. In contrast, most patients with persisting aphasia present with a broad array of expressive and receptive deficits involving multiple linguistic, memory and motoric deficits. Lesions underlying these more common aphasias typically involve large portions of the peri-sylvian cortex and/or its underlying connections (Mazzocchi and Vignolo, 1979; Mohr, 1976). This is the area of cortex that we have suggested, on the basis of stimulation-related disruption, is critical to oral motor sequencing, articulatory production and phonemic perception as well as to multiple aspects of linguistic function.

While the stimulation-mapping and ERP studies have generated several hypotheses about the organization of language functions, we are far from developing a comprehensive model of language processing in the brain. Advances in knowledge about the neural bases of language processing will critically depend on continued development of a broad range of interdisciplinary observations, techniques and theories.

Acknowledgements

Support of this project was provided by an NIH-NINCDS award to the principal author and by NIH Epilepsy Program Project (Neurological Surgery, P. Schwartzgroin (P.I.)). Additional support and preparation of the manuscript were provided by the Department of Speech and Hearing Sciences and Arlene Chaussee.

References

Albert M: Short-term memory and aphasia. *Brain Lang.: 3,* 28 – 33, 1976.

Amadeo M, Shagass C: Brief latency click evoked potentials during the awake and sleep in man. *Psychology: 10,* 244 – 250, 1973.

Benson FD: Fluency in aphasia: correlation with radioactive scan localization. *Cortex: 3,* 373 – 394, 1967.

Brown WS, Marsh JT, Smith JC: Contextual meaning effects on speech-evoked potentials. *Behav. Biol.: 9,* 755 – 761, 1973.

Brown WS, Marsh JT, Smith JC: Evoked potential waveform differences produced by the perception of different meanings of an ambiguous phrase. *Electroencephalog. Clin. Neurophysiol.: 41,* 113 – 123, 1976.

Brown WS, Lehmann D, Marsh JT: Linguistic meaning related differences in evoked potential topography: English, Swiss-German, and Imagined. *Brain Lang.: 11,* 340 – 353, 1980.

Buchsbaum M, Fedio P: Visual information and evoked responses from the left and right hemisphere. *Electroencephalogr. Clin. Neurophysiol.: 26,* 266 – 272, 1969.

Buchsbaum M, Fedio P: Hemispheric differences in evoked potentials to verbal and nonverbal stimuli in the left and right visual fields. *Physiol. Behav.: 5,* 207 – 210, 1970.

Butters N, Samuel I, Goodglass H, Brody B: Short-term visual and auditory memory disorders after parietal and frontal lobe damage. *Cortex: 6,* 440 – 459, 1970.

Cameron PA, Mateer CA, Polly D, Thompson P: Recording of auditory evoked potentials in man from the cortex. (Abstract) *J. Clin. Exp. Neuropsychol.: 9,* 49, 1987.

Chapman RM: Connotative meaning and averaged evoked potentials. In Begleifer H (Ed.), *Evoked Brain Potentials and Behavior.* New York: Plenum Press, 171 – 196, 1979.

Chapman RM, Bragdon HR, Chapman JA, McCrary JW: Semantic meaning of words and average evoked potentials. In Desmedt JE (Ed.), *Language and Hemispheric Specialization in Man: Cerebral Event-Related Potentials, Progress in Clinical Neurophysiology (Vol. 3).* Basel: Karger, pp. 36 – 47, 1977.

Chapman RM, McCrary JW, Chapman JA, Bragdon HR: Brain responses related to semantic meaning. *Brain Lang.: 5,* 195 – 205, 1978.

Chapman RM, McCrary JW, Chapman JA, Martin JK: Behavioral and neural analyses of connotative meaning: Word classes and relations scales. *Brain Lang.: 11,* 319 – 339, 1980.

Chiappa KH, Ropper AH: Evoked potentials in clinical medicine. *N. Engl. J. Med.: 306,* 1140 – 1150, 1982.

Cohn R: Differential cerebral processing of noise and verbal stimuli. *Science: 172,* 599 – 601, 1971.

Cushing H: A note upon the Faralic stimulation of the postcentral gyrus in conscious patients. *Brain: 32,* 44 – 54, 1909.

Davis H: Principles of electric response audiometry. *Ann. Otololaryngol.: 85,* Suppl. 28, 1976.

Dodrill C: A neuropsychological battery for epilepsy. *Epilepsia: 19,* 611 – 623, 1978.

Donchin E, Kutas, M, McCarthy G: Electrocortical indices of hemispherical utilization. In Hernad S, Doty R, Goldsteen L,

Jaynes J, Krauthamer G (Eds.), *Lateralization in the Nervous System*. New York: Academic Press, pp. 339 – 384, 1977a.

Donchin E, McCarthy G, Kutas M: Electroencephalographic investigations of hemispheric specialization. In Desmedt JE (Ed.), *Progress in Clinical Neurophysiology, Language and Hemispheric Specialization in Man: Event-Related Potentials (Vol. 3),* Basel: Karger, 1977b.

Donchin E, Ritter W, McCallum C: Cognitive psychophysiology: the endogenous components of the ERP. In Callaway E, Tenting P, Koshow S (Eds.), *Brain Event-Related Potentials in Man*. New York: Academic Press, pp. 349 – 441, 1978.

Duffy FH: Topographical display of evoked potentials: clinical applications of Brain Electrical Activity Mapping (BEAM). *Ann. N. Y. Acad. Sci.: 385,* 183 – 196, 1982.

Fedio P, Van Buren J: Memory deficits during electrical stimulation of speech cortex in conscious man. *Brain Lang.: 1,* 29 – 42, 1974.

Fried I, Ojemann GA, Fetz E: Language-related potentials specific to human language cortex. *Science: 212,* 353 – 356, 1981.

Fried I, Mateer CA, Ojemann G, Wohns R, Fedio P: Organization of visuospatial functions in human cortex: Evidence from electrical stimulation. *Brain: 105,* 349 – 371, 1982.

Friedman D, Simson R, Ritter W, Rapin I: Cortical evoked potentials elicited by real speech words and human sounds. *Electroencephalogr. Clin. Neurophysiol.: 38,* 13 – 19, 1975.

Galaburda A, Sanides F, Geschwind N: Human brain: cytoarchetectonic left-right asymmetries in the temporal speech region. *Arch. Neurol. (Chicago): 35,* 812 – 817, 1978.

Galambos R, Benson P, Smith TS, Schulman-Galambos C, Osier H: On hemispheric differences in evoked potentials to speech stimuli. *Electroencephalogr. Clin. Neurophysiol.: 39,* 279 – 283, 1975.

Galin D, Ellis R: Asymmetry in evoked potentials as an index of lateralized cognitive processes: Relation to EEG alpha asymmetry. *Neuropsychologia: 13,* 45 – 50, 1975.

Goodglass H: Agrammatism. In Whitaker H, Whitaker HA (Eds.), *Studies in Neurolinguistics, 1*. New York: Academic Press, pp. 237 – 260, 1976.

Grabow JD, Aronson AE, Rose DE, Greene KL: Summated potentials evoked by speech sounds for determining cerebral dominance for language. *Electroencephalogr. Clin. Neurophysiol.: 49,* 38 – 47, 1980.

Halgren E, Squires NK, Wilson CL, Rohrbaugh JW, Babb TL, Crandall PH: Endogenous potentials generated in the human hippocampol formation and amygdala by infrequent events. *Science: 210,* 803 – 805, 1980.

Harmony T, Alvarez A: Evoked responses after head trauma. *Act. Nerv. Sup.: 23,* 303 – 310, 1981.

Hecox K, Squires N, Galambos R: Brainstem auditory evoked responses in man. I. Effect of stimulus rise-fall time and duration. *J. Acoust. Soc. Am.: 60,* 1187 – 1192, 1976.

Hillyard SA, Picton TW: Event-related brain potentials and selective information processing in man. In Desmedt J (Ed.), *Progress in Clinical Neurophysiology, Vol. 6. Cognitive Components in Cerebral Event-Related Potentials and Selective Attention*. Basel: Karger, pp. 1 – 52, 1979.

Hillyard SA, Woods DL: Electrophysiological analysis of human brain function. In Gazzaniga MS (Ed.), *Handbook of Behavioral Neurobiology, Vol. 2*. New York: Plenum, pp. 345 – 378, 1979.

Hyde ML, Stephens SD, Thornton RR: Stimulus repetition rate and the early brainstem response. *Br. J. Audiol.: 10,* 41 – 50, 1976.

Johnson R Jr: P300: a model of variables controlling its amplitude. *Ann. N. Y. Acad. Sci.: 425,* 223 – 229, 1984.

Johnson R Jr, Donchin E: On how P300 amplitude varies with the utility of the eliciting stimuli. *Electroencephalogr. Clin. Neurophysiol.: 44,* 424 – 437, 1978.

Johnson R Jr, Donchin E: P300 and stimulus categorization: two plus one is not so different from one plus one. *Psychophysiology: 17,* 167 – 178, 1980.

Johnson R Jr, Donchin E: Second thoughts: multiple P300s elicited by a single stimulus. *Psychophysiology: 19,* 182 – 194, 1985.

Kimura D: Sex differences in intrahemispheric organization of speech. *Behav. Brain Sci.: 3,* 215 – 263, 1980.

Kurtzberg D, Stone CL Jr, Vaughan HG Jr: Cortical responses to speech sounds in infants. In Cracco RQ, Bodis-Wollner I (Eds.), *Evoked Potentials*. New York: Alan R. Liss, Inc., pp. 513 – 520, 1986.

Kutas M: Event-related brain potentials (ERSs) elicited during rapid serial visual presentation of congruous and incongruous sentences. *Electroencephalogr. Clin. Neurophysiol.: Suppl.,* (in press) 1987.

Kutas M, Donchin E: The effects of handedness, the responding hand and response force on the contralateral dominance of the readiness potential. In Desmedt J (Ed.), *Attention, Voluntary Contraction and Event-Related Cerebral Potentials. Progress in Clinical Neurophysiology. Vol. 1,* Basel: Karger, pp. 189 – 210, 1977.

Kutas M, Hillyard SD: Reading between the lines: event-related brain potentials during natural sentence processing. *Brain Lang.: 11,* 354 – 373, 1980a.

Kutas M, Hillyard SA: Reading senseless sentences: brian potentials reflect semantic incongruity. *Science: 207,* 203 – 205, 1980b.

Kutas M, Hillyard SA: Event-related brain potentials to semantically inappropriate and surprisingly large words. *Biol. Psychol.: 11,* 99 – 116, 1980c.

Kutas M, Hillyard SA: Event-related brain potentials to grammatical error and semantic anomalies. *Memory Cognition: 11,* 539 – 550, 1983.

Mateer CA: Cortical organization of language: evidence from electrical stimulation studies. *Univ. Wash. Paper Linguist.: 7,* 32 – 38, 1982.

Mateer CA: Motor and perceptual functions of the left hemisphere and their interaction. In Segalowitz SJ (Ed.), *Language Functions and Brain Organization*. New York: Academic Press, 1983a.

Mateer CA: Functional organization of the right nondominant cortex: evidence from electrical stimulation. *Can. J. Psychol.: 37,* 36 – 58, 1983b.

Mateer CA: Localization of language and visuospatial functions by electrical stimulation mapping. In Kertesz A (Ed.), *Localization in Neuropsychology*. New York: Academic Press, 1983c.

Mateer CA, Cameron PS, Polly D, Thompson P. Intracranial

evoked potentials of voice-onset-time: two case studies. In Johnson R (Ed.), *Current Research in Event-Related Brain Potentials,* in press 1987.

Mateer CA, Dodrill C: Neuropsychological and linguistic correlates of atypical language lateralization. *Human Neurobiol.: 2,* 135 – 142, 1983.

Mateer CA, Kimura D: Impairment of nonverbal oral movements in aphasia. *Brain Lang.: 4,* 262 – 276, 1976.

Mateer CA, Polen SB, Ojemann GA: Sexual variation in cortical localization of naming as determined by stimulation mapping. *Brain Behav. Sci.: 5,* 310 – 311, 1982.

Mateer CA, Rapport R: Organization of language cortex in two bilinguals. Paper presented at meetings of the American Neurosurgical Society, Washington, DC, 1982.

Matsumiya Y, Tagliasco V, Lombroso OT, Goodglass H: Auditory evoked response: meaningfulness of stimuli and interhemispheric asymmetry. *Science: 172,* 790 – 792, 1972.

Mazzocchi R, Vignolo LA: Localization of lesions in aphasia: clinical CT scan correlations in stroke patients. *Cortex: 15,* 627 – 654, 1979.

McCarthy M, Donchin E: A metric for thought: a comparison of P300 latency and reaction time. *Science: 211,* 72 – 80, 1981.

Mendel MI, Hosick EC, Windman T, Davis H, Hisk SK, Dinges DF. Audiometric comparison of the middle and late components of the adult auditory evoked potentials awake and asleep. *Electroencephalogr. Clin. Neurophysiol.: 38,* 27 – 33, 1975.

Milner B: Brain mechanisms suggested by studies of temporal lobes. In Milliken C, Darley F (Eds.), *Brain Mechanisms Underlying Speech and Language.* New York: Grune and Stratton, pp. 122 – 145, 1967.

Mohr J: Broca's area and Broca's aphasia. In Whitaker H, Whitaker HA (Eds.), *Studies in Neurolinguistics, 1.* Academic Press, New York, pp. 201 – 236, 1976.

Molfese DL: The phoneme and the engram: electrophysiological evidence for the acoustic invariant in stop consonants. *Brain Lang.: 9,* 372 – 376, 1980.

Molfese DL: Event related potentials and language processes. In Gaillard AWK, Ritter W (Eds.), *Tutorials in ERP Research: Endogenous Components.* Amsterdam: Elsevier, pp. 345 – 367, 1983.

Molfese DL, Freeman RB Jr, Polermo DS: The ontogency of brain lateralization of speech and nonspeech stimuli. *Brain Lang.: 2,* 356 – 368, 1975.

Moore WH Jr: The role of right hemispheric information processing strategies in language recovery in aphasia: an electroencephalographic investigation of hemispheric alpha asymmetries in normal and aphasic subjects. *Cortex: 20,* 193 – 205, 1984.

Moore WH Jr, Haynes WO: A study of alpha hemispheric asymmetries and their relationship to verbal and nonverbal abilities in males and females. *Brain Lang.: 9,* 338 – 349, 1980.

Morrell LK, Salamy JG: Hemispherical asymmetry of electrocortical responses to speech stimuli. *Science: 174,* 164 – 166, 1971.

Neville H: Electrographic correlates of lateral asymmetry in the processing of verbal and non-verbal stimuli. *J. Psycholinguist. Res.: 3,* 151 – 163, 1974.

Neville H: Event-related potentials in neuropsychological studies of language. *Brain Lang.: 11,* 300 – 318, 1980.

Neville H, Schulman-Galambos C, Galambos R: Evoked potential correlates of functional hemispheric specialization. Presented to the International Neuropsychology Society, Santa Fe, February 1977.

Neville H, Snyder E, Knight R, Galambos R: Event-related potentials in language and non-language tasks in patients with alexia with agraphia. In Lehmann D, Calloway E (Eds.), *Human Evoked Potentials.* New York: Plenum Press, pp. 269 – 283, 1979.

Neville H, Kutas M, Chesney G, Schmidt AL: Event-related brain potentials during initial encoding and recognition memory of congruous and incongruous words. *J. Memory Lang.: 25,* 75 – 92, 1986.

Ojemann GA: Organization of short-term verbal memory in language areas of human cortex: Evidence from electrical stimulation. *Brain Lang.: 5,* 331 – 348, 1978a.

Ojemann GA: Intrahemispheric localization of language and visuospatial function: evidence from stimulation mapping during craniotomies for epilepsy. In Akimoto H, Kazamatsuri H, Seino M, Ward A (Eds.), *Advances in Epileptology, Vol. 13.* New York: Raven Press, pp. 127 – 138, 1978b.

Ojemann GA: Individual variability in cortical localization of language. *J. Neurosurg.: 50,* 164 – 169, 1979.

Ojemann GA: Brain organization for language from the perspective of electrical stimulation mapping. *Behav. Brain Sci.: 2,* 189 – 230, 1983.

Ojemann GA, Fried I: Event related potential correlates of human language cortex measured during cortical resection for epilepsy. In Akimoto H, Kazamatsuri H, Seino M, Ward A (Eds.), *Advances in Epileptology: XIIIth Epilepsy International Symposium.* New York: Raven Press, pp. 385 – 388, 1982.

Ojemann GA, Mateer CA: Human language cortex: localization of memory, syntax, and sequential motor-phoneme identification systems. *Science: 250,* 1401 – 1403, 1979.

Ojemann GA, Whitaker HA: Language localization and variability. *Brain Lang.: 6,* 239 – 260, 1978a.

Ojemann GA, Whitaker HA: The bilingual brain. *Arch. Neurol. (Chicago): 35,* 409 – 412, 1978b.

Paradis M: Bilingualism and aphasia. In Whitaker H, Whitaker HA (Eds.), *Studies in Neurolinguistics, 3.* New York: Academic Press, pp. 65 – 122, 1979.

Penfield W, Jasper H: *Epilepsy and the Functional Anatomy of the Human Brain.* Boston: Little Brown, 1954.

Penfield W, Roberts L: *Speech and Brain Mechanisms.* Princeton NJ: Princeton University Press, 1959.

Penfield W, Perot P: The brain's record of auditory and visual experience: A final summary and discussion. *Brain: 86,* 595 – 696, 1963.

Pfefferbaum A, Ford JM, Roth WT, Kopell B: Age-related changes in auditory event-related potentials. *Electroencephalogr. Clin. Neurophysiol.: 49,* 266 – 276, 1980.

Pfefferbaum A, Ford JM, Wenegrat BG, Roth WT, Kopell BS: Clinical applications of P3: I. Normal aging. *Electroencephalogr. Clin. Neurophysiol.: 59,* 1 – 30, 1984a.

Pfefferbaum A, Wenegrat BG, Ford J, Roth WT, Kopell B: Clinical application of the P3 component of event-related potentials. II. Dementia, depression and schizophrenia. *Elec-*

troencephalogr. Clin. Neurophysiol.: 59, 104 – 124, 1984b.

Picton TW, Hillyard SA, Krausz HI, Galambos R: Human auditory evoked potentials. I: Evaluation of components. *Electroencephalogr. Clin. Neurophysiol.: 36,* 191 – 199, 1974.

Polich J, Howard L, Starr A: Effects of aging on the P300 component of the event-related potential from auditory stimuli: peak definition, variation and measurement. *J. Gerontol.: 40,* 721 – 726, 1985.

Pratt H, Sohmer H: Intensity and rate functions of cochlear and brainstem evoked responses to click stimuli in man. *Arch. Otolaryngol. Rhinol.-Laryngol.: 212,* 8592, 1976.

Ranck J Jr: Which elements are excited in electrical stimulation of mammalian central nervous system: a review. *Brain Res.: 98,* 417 – 440, 1975.

Rasmussen T, Milner B: The role of early left brain injury in determining lateralization of cerebral speech functions. *Ann. N. Y. Acad. Sci.: 299,* 355 – 369, 1977.

Rubens A, Mahowald M, Hutton J: Asymmetry of the lateral (Sylvian) fissures in man. *Neurology: 26,* 620 – 624, 1976.

Rugg MD: Event-related potentials and the phonological processing of words and nonwords. *Neuropsychologia: 22,* 435 – 444, 1984.

Rugg MD: The effects of semantic priming and word repetition on event-related potentials. *Psychophysiology: 22,* 642 – 647, 1985.

Saffran E, Marin O: Immediate memory for word lists and sentences in a patient with deficient auditory short-term memory. *Brain Lang.: 2,* 420 – 433, 1975.

Selinger M: Using cortical evoked potentials in aphasiology. In Brokshire RH (Ed.), *Clinical Aphasiology Conference Proceedings.* Minneapolis: BRK Publishers, pp. 34 – 39, 1984.

Siegel S: *Nonparametric Statistics for the Behavioral Sciences.* New York: McGraw-Hill, 1955.

Smith TS, Nielson B, Thistle AB: Question of asymmetries in auditory evoked potentials to speech stimuli. *J. Acoust. Soc. Am.: 58,* 557, 1975.

Spehlman R: *Evoked Potential Primer: Visual, Auditory and Somatosensory Evoked Potentials in Clinical Diagnosis.* Stoneham, MA: Butterworth, 1985.

Squires KC, Chippendale TJ, Wrege KS, Goodin DS, Starr A: Electrophysiological assessment of mental function in aging and dementia. In Poon LW (Ed.), *Aging in the 1980s: Selected Contemporary Issues in the Psychology of Aging.* DC: American Psychological Association, Washington, pp. 125 – 134, 1980.

Squires NK, Galbraith GC, Aine CL: Event-related potential assessment of sensory and cognitive deficits in the mentally retarded. In Lehmann D, Callaway E (Eds.), *Human Evoked Potentials: Application and Problems.* New York: Plenum Press, pp. 397 – 413, 1979.

Starr A, Archer L: Auditory brainstem response in neurological disease. *Arch. Neurol. (Chicago): 32,* 761 – 768, 1975.

Stensass S, Eddington D, Dobelle W: The topography and variability of the primary visual cortex in man. *J. Neurosurg.: 40,* 747 – 755, 1974.

Teyler TJ, Roemer RA, Harrison TF, Thompson RF: Human scalp-recorded evoked-potential correlates of linguistic stimuli. *Bull. Psychonomic Soc.: 1,* 333 – 334, 1973.

Thatcher RW: Electrophysiological correlates of animal and human memory. In Terry RD, Gershon S (Eds.), *Neurobiology of Aging.* New York: Raven Press, pp. 43 – 102, 1976.

Van Buren J, Fedio P, Frederick G: Mechanism and localization of speech in the parieto-temporal cortex. *Neurosurgery: 2,* 233 – 239, 1978.

Warrington E, Shallice T: The selective impairment of auditory verbal short-term memory. *Brain; 92,* 885 – 896, 1969.

Warrington E, Logue V, Pratt R: The anatomical localization of selective impairment of auditory verbal short-term memory. *Neuropsychologia: 9,* 377 – 387, 1971.

Whitaker H, Ojemann GA: Graded localization of naming from electrical stimulation mapping of left cerebral cortex. *Nature: 270,* 50 – 51, 1977.

Wood CC: Auditory and phonetic levels of processing in speech perception: neurophysiological and information-processing analysis. *J. Exp. Psychol.: Hum. Percept. and Performance: 104,* 3 – 20, 1975.

Wood CC, Goff WR, Day RS: Auditory evoked potentials during speech perception. *Science: 173,* 1248 – 1251, 1971.

Wood CC, McCarthy G, Squires NK, Vaughan HG, Woods DL, McCallam WC: Anatomical and physiological substrates of event-related potentials. *Ann. N. Y. Acad. Sci.: 425,* 681 – 721, 1984.

© 1989 Elsevier Science Publishers B.V. (Biomedical Division)
Handbook of Neuropsychology, Vol. 2
F. Boller and J. Grafman (Eds)

CHAPTER 6

Bilingual and polyglot aphasia

Michel Paradis

Department of Linguistics, McGill University, 1001 Sherbrooke St. West, Montreal H3A 1G5, Canada

Patterns of recovery

Aphasic patients who spoke two or more languages fluently before insult do not necessarily recover both or all of their languages at the same rate or to the same extent. A survey of the world literature on aphasia in bilinguals and polyglots (Paradis, 1977) has revealed six basic patterns of recovery: parallel, differential, successive, antagonistic, selective and mixed. Recovery is said to be parallel when both (or all) languages are similarly impaired and restored at the same rate; differential when impairment is of a different degree in each language relative to premorbid mastery; successive when one language does not begin to reappear until another has been maximally recovered; antagonistic when one language regresses as the other progresses; selective when patients do not regain the use of one or more of their languages; and mixed when patients systematically mix or blend features of their languages at any or all levels of linguistic structure (i.e., phonological, morphological, syntactic, lexical and semantic) inappropriately. These patterns are not mutually exclusive, either over time or between languages. For example, successive recovery may be followed by reciprocal antagonism; or two languages may be recovered in a parallel or antagonistic fashion while a third remains inaccessible or is recovered only much later.

In recent years, three additional patterns of recovery have been reported, namely, alternate antagonism (Paradis et al., 1982; Nilipour and Ashayery, 1989); differential aphasia (Albert and Obler, 1978; Silverberg and Gordon, 1979), and selective aphasia (Paradis and Goldblum, 1989). Alternate antagonism may be considered a variant of antagonistic recovery. It refers to the fact that, for alternating periods of time, patients have access to only one of their languages. In three of the four cases reported so far, the patient retained a comparable degree of comprehension in both languages at all times but suffered word-finding difficulties so severe as to be unable to utter a word in the temporarily unavailable language. In the fourth case, comprehension was also affected in the inaccessible language. Differential aphasia refers to different symptoms in each of the patient's languages so that the clinical picture is one of one type of aphasia (e.g., Broca's) in one language, and of another type (e.g., Wernicke's) in the other language. Selective aphasia refers to obvious impairments in one language without any measurable deficit in the other(s).

Studies on bilingual aphasia published between 1843 and 1975 are readily available (Paradis, 1983), and this literature has been extensively reviewed (Paradis, 1977; Albert and Obler, 1978). Therefore, in order to avoid unnecessary duplication, only studies published since then will be reviewed here in detail.

Recent cases of bilingual aphasia

Of 27 cases published over the past 10 years, 9 exhibited parallel recovery (2 of which became differential after speech therapy), 8 differential, 3

TABLE 1

Cases of bilingual and polyglot aphasia reported over the past decade

Author(s)	Age	Sex Handedness	Educational level	Occupation	Mother tongue(s)	Used until	Other languages	Age of acquisition	Context of acquisition	Used until	Etiology	Side of lesion	Type of symptoms	Pattern of recovery
Lebrun (1976)	68	M ?	?13	translator	Dutch	TI	German	?12	SL_1	TI	trauma	L	MI	D
							English	A	?	TI				
							Spanish	A	?	TI				
							French	A	?	TI				
Watamori and Sasanuma (1976)	65	M R	18	businessman	Japanese/English	TI	NA	NA	NA	NA	CVA	L	B	P
Wechsler (1976)	83	F R	1	various	?Russian/Yiddish	TI	English	5	SL_1,E	TI	CVA	R	NF	P
April and Tse (1977)	53	M R	12	laundry owner	Cantonese	TI	English	7	SL_1	TI	CVA	R	B	D
Voinescu et al. (1977)	71	M R	?16	accountant	Greek	TI(O)	Rumanian	C	SL_1,E	TI	CVA	L	WF	exp.: D
							Russian	C	SL_1,E	TI			PA	rec.: P
							German	C	SL_1,E	TI(O)			N	some M
Albert and Obler (1978) case 2	34	F R	E	?	Hungarian	?	English	10	E	TI	tumor	L	E(EN)	DA
							French	11	SL_2	16			R(HE)	
							Hebrew	16	SL_2,E	TI			MI(HU, FR)	
case 78	55	M R	E	factory ad- ministrator	Czech	?	German	?	?	?	CVA	L	WF,E,A	D
							English	?	?	TI				
							Yiddish	?	?	?				
							French	?	?	?				
							Hebrew	20	?	TI				
Galloway (1978)	47	M L/A	16	Engineer	Hungarian	17	Hebrew	3		17	CVA	L	E + R	D
							Polish	4	E	6				
							Rumanian	10	SL_1,E	12				
							Yiddish	10	E	12				
							English	12	SL_2,E	TI				
							German	12	SL_2,E	25				
T'sou (1978)	31	F R	12	stenotypist	Cantonese	TI	English	10	SL_2	TI	CVA	L	C	D
Watamori and Sasanuma (1978)	52	M R	15	security agent	Japanese	TI	English	?	?	TI	CVA	L	W	P
Reynolds et al. (1979)	40	M?R	?	?	Navajo	?TI	English	?	?	TI	G(th)	L	P,N	C
Silverberg and Gordon (1979)	26	F R	16	nurse	Spanish	TI	Hebrew	23	SL_2,E	TI	CVA	L	F(HE) NF(SP)	DA
case 2	54	M R	20	physician	Russian	TI	Hebrew	53	SL_2,E	TI	CVA	L	WFD	DA
Zangwill (1979)	59	M R	WE	civil servant	English	TI	French	?	?	TI	CVA	R	E	P
April and Han (1980)	73	M R	7	accountant	Cantonese	TI	English	20	?E	TI	CVA	R	B	P
Chiarello et al. (1982)	66	F R	10	factory worker	EFS	TI	ASL	7	F	TI	CVA	L	W	P
							W English	7	S	TI				
Paradis et al. (1982)	48	F R	15	nurse	French	TI	Arabic	10	SL_2	TI	trauma	L	WFD	AA
								20 +	E	TI				
case 2	23	M R	16	electronics engineer	French	TI	English	4	E	TI	AVM	L	WFD	AA
Rapport et al. (1983)	41	M R	16	businessman	Hokkien	TI	Mandarin	6	SL_1	TI	tumor	L	M	P
							English	?16	SL_1	TI				
case 2	45	F R	13		Hokkien	TI	English	6	SL_1	TI	H(FPA)	L	G	P
							Cantonese	?	?E	TI				
case 3	39	M R	?	fishmonger	Hokkien	TI	Mandarin	?	?	TI	TU	L	P,N	P
Byng et al. (1984)	15	M R	10	student	Nepalese	TI	English	10	SL_2	TI	trauma	B	SA	D
Perecman (1984)	80	M ?	?	?	German		French		SL_2			B	W	M
							English	18	?E	TI	TR			
Chary (1986)	21	M ?	16	student	Telegu	TI	English	?	?	TI	tumor	L	WFD, PA, PE	D
Wulfeck et al. (1986)	70	M R	?12	cook	Spanish	TI	English	6	SL_2	TI	CVA	L	B	S,D
Nilipour and Ashayery (1989)	49	M R	20	orthopedic surgeon	Farsi	TI	German	18	CL_1 + E	TI	TR	L	A	AA + S
							English	13	SL_2	TI				
Paradis and Goldblum (1989)	27	M R	14	accountant	Gujarati	TI	French	5	SL_1	TI	SR	R	WFD, A,PA	SA,A
					Malagasy	TI								

Note: Any entry preceded by ? = presumably, likely, given the context, though not explicitly mentioned by the author(s).
NA = not applicable. ? = unreported.

Handedness: A = ambidextrous; L = left; R = right; ? = unreported.

Educational level: Numbers = years of schooling; preceded by ? = estimated; E = educated; WE = well educated (as reported).

alternate antagonistic (one with successive recovery of a third language), one selective, one successive, and one mixed. Three cases are reported to exhibit differential aphasia, and one case of selective aphasia in a trilingual patient, followed by reciprocal antagonism (Table 1). It is clear that statistical inferences cannot be derived from such a small sample of selected cases. Three of the patterns have been described for the first time, namely, differential aphasia, selective aphasia and alternate antagonism. Paradoxical translation behavior has also been reported for the first time. These patterns will therefore be examined in some detail, as they raise important theoretical issues.

Parallel recoveries have been reported in the context of early as well as late second language acquisition, in patients of either sex ranging in age from 39 to 83, with varied symptomatology (5 nonfluent, 3 Wernicke, 1 global), subsequent to right as well as left hemisphere lesions, and between related (e.g., Hokkien and Mandarin) and unrelated (e.g., English and Japanese) languages.

Differential recovery in this sample also involved second languages acquired between childhood and adulthood (though mostly after the age of 7) in patients of both sexes, ranging in age from 15 to 71, with varied symptomatology (2 nonfluent, 3 mixed, 2 Wernicke, 1 conduction), all but one subsequent to left hemisphere lesion, and, for the most part, between unrelated languages (e.g., Cantonese/English, Telegu/English, Nepalese/English). Four of the cases are polyglots (from 4 to 7 languages).

Lebrun (1976) has described the case of a professional translator who, prior to insult, had full command of his five languages. However, after insult, one foreign language (English) was recovered preferentially. The author attributes his patient's preference for English over his Dutch mother tongue and his three other languages to affective factors: English could be considered the sacred language of the patient's religion. It was also the language of his employers.

In the case reported by Voinescu et al. (1977), comprehension was equally impaired in all four of the patient's languages, but the two languages used most during the past 20 years (not including the mother tongue) were less impaired for expression.

Galloway (1978) relates the case of a heptaglot who, after a stroke, was able to speak only English (learned at the age of 12) and could understand English, German and Hungarian (his mother tongue), and Yiddish, but not Hebrew, Polish or Rumanian. However, it should not be surprising that the patient did not recover Polish, a language he had spoken only between the ages of 4 and 6 and had not used for the past 40 years. The same may be said of Rumanian and Yiddish, which were only spoken for a very short period of time (2 years) some 35 years before the stroke. Hebrew

---

Mother tongue(s) and other language(s): ASL = American sign language; EFS = English finger spelling; W English = written English.
Used until: TI = time of insult; TI(O) = only occasionally until time of insult; Number = age until which language was spoken habitually.
Age of acquisition: A = adult; C = childhood; Number = age.
Contex of acquisition: E = environment; SL_1 = school as first language; SL_2 = school as foreign language.
Etiology: CVA = cerebral vascular accident (stroke); H = thalamic tumor hemorrhage; SR = surgical removal of a parasitic cyst; TR = trauma; TU = tumor.
Side of lesion: B = bilateral; L = left; R = right.
Type of symptoms: A = anomia, amnestic aphasia; AG = agrammatism; B = Broca's aphasia; C = conduction aphasia; E = expressive aphasia; F = fluent aphasia; G = global aphasia; MI = mixed aphasia (expressive and receptive); MO = motor aphasia; N = neologisms; NF = non-fluent aphasia; PA = paraphasias; PE = perseveration; R = receptive; SA = speech apraxia; W = Werknicke's aphasia; WF = word-finding difficulty. Languages: EN = English; FR = French; HE = Hebrew; HU = Hungarian; SP = Spanish.
Patterns of recovery: A = antagonistic; AA = alternate antagonism; C = selective; D = differential; DA = differential aphasia; M = mixed; P = parallel; S = successive; SA = selective aphasia; exp. = expression; rec. = reception.

had not been practised for the past 30 years either (even if it had been used extensively between the ages of 3 and 17). This patient can therefore hardly be considered a heptaglot at the time of insult, but rather a person who had been exposed to some languages for very short periods of time before the age of 12, and who could still understand and speak four of them. While the patient had not used Yiddish often during the 25 years prior to insult, its similarity to German would in itself explain the patient's better comprehension of Yiddish relative to Hebrew. What Galloway's patient exhibited, then, was a differential recovery between the four languages of which he had some knowledge at the time of the stroke, with the language used almost exclusively over the past 22 years being preferentially recovered. One could almost term this a parallel recovery, in the sense that the languages were recovered proportionately to their premorbid relative proficiencies.

In the case reported by Albert and Obler (1978), Hebrew, the language of the environment, learned after the age of 20, was recovered better than English, and better still than French, which necessitated Hebrew and English vocabulary. No information was given about the patient's German (his mother tongue) or Yiddish.

The patient described by T'sou (1978) exhibited fewer deficits in her native Chinese than in her second language (English), though it is assumed that she had equal control over both languages before insult. (Her work as a secretary was carried out entirely in English.)

In the case reported by April and Han (1980), performance in English was better preserved than in the patient's native Chinese, which was also his current home language and the language used in his business.

In Byng et al.'s (1984) patient, while comprehension was similar for both languages, language production was worse for the mother tongue (Nepalese) than for the second language (English). This discrepancy is attributed to the fact that the patient had received intensive speech therapy exclusively in English before assessment.

Chary's (1986) patient recovered English, the language of instruction at the college he was attending as a student, over Telegu, his mother tongue. Before insult, the patient would use both languages interchangeably for all speech functions but was more fluent in English than in Telegu for writing.

Reynolds et al. (1979) briefly relate a case of selective recovery. A 40-year-old patient could speak only Navajo after a thalamic hemorrhage, although he was fluent in both Navajo and English before.

Wulfeck et al. (1986) report the case of a Spanish/English bilingual patient who, immediately after his stroke, could produce only fragments of Spanish (his mother tongue), although he seemed to understand simple commands in both languages. After a few weeks during which his Spanish continued to improve, English fragments began to appear. Six months later, the patient's fluency in Spanish was slightly better than in English. The patient thus seems to have undergone a successive recovery, with the second language not having quite caught up with the first recovered language after six months.

The most characteristic feature of Perecman's (1984) patient was the prevalence of spontaneous translation and abundant mixing at the phonological, morphological, syntactic and lexical levels, even when he read aloud. The patient would integrate German words into English sentences and even read English sentences entirely in German.

Albert and Obler (1978) report the case of a 34-year-old right-handed polyglot woman who displayed a right homonymous hemianopia and Broca's aphasia in English and Wernicke's aphasia in Hebrew, following the removal of a left posterior temporal glioma. The patient was born in Hungary and spoke Hungarian exclusively for the first 10 years. She moved to England at the age of 10, then to France from 11 to 16, where she attended school in French. She went to Israel at age 16, where she learned Hebrew at school and in the army, spent one year in Italy between the ages of 19 and 20, went back to England for 3 years, then to Israel again for 9 years, and finally to the United

States at age 32. At home she spoke Hebrew, Hungarian and English. When tested 10 days post-operatively, her English was hesitant and effortful and the patient tended to speak in a telegraphic style, producing a moderate number of para-phasias, while her auditory comprehension was at the 75 – 85% level. Her Hebrew, by contrast, was fluent, though containing phonemic, semantic and neologistic paraphasias, often as a result of in-terference from Hungarian or English. Her com-prehension of Hebrew, quite poor at first (in the 20 – 30% range), improved to 50% after 2 weeks.

Silverberg and Gordon (1979) describe two cases of differential aphasia. The first patient was a 26-year-old right-handed nurse, born and raised in Chile. She had spoken Spanish exclusively until she learned to read and write English at school be-tween the ages of 12 and 18. Her first contact with Hebrew occurred when she emigrated to Israel at age 23. She studied Hebrew 5 hours a day, 6 days a week, for 3 months. During that period, she con-tinued to speak Spanish with her sister and friends. After she had begun to work as a nurse, 9 months after her arrival, she was in a Hebrew environment for 8 hours a day. She continued to speak Spanish with her roommate, her sister, fiancé and friends. Three days after her stroke, her spontaneous speech in Hebrew was fluent and contained numerous literal and verbal paraphasias, with several mispronunciations and inappropriate word substitutions. On the following day, her spon-taneous speech in Spanish was telegraphic and nonfluent, and exhibited word-finding difficulty. In an object-naming task, she was able to name 6 of 20 common items in Hebrew, but only 2 in Spanish. Her repetition was better in Hebrew than in Spanish. Comprehension deficits were similar in both languages. One month later, her Hebrew was considered to have completely recovered, while there were still some difficulties in Spanish.

The second patient described by Silverberg and Gordon was a 54-year-old right-handed physician, born in Russia, where he had lived in an entirely Russian-speaking environment. He learned Ger-man and English in school. His first exposure to

Hebrew came after his immigration to Israel one year before his stroke. In spite of an intensive course in Hebrew for 3½ months, his knowledge of Hebrew was very rudimentary. His ability was below average compared to others in his class. He continued to speak Russian with his wife and friends. He often required help in conversing with his Hebrew-speaking patients at the hospital. Dur-ing the first days after his stroke, he had global aphasia in Hebrew and only word-finding difficul-ty in Russian. His comprehension of Hebrew re-mained poor after 6 months, while responses in Russian were close to normal.

Paradis et al. (1982) report two cases of alternate antagonism (or 'seesaw recovery') with para-doxical translation behavior in two bilingual aphasic patients. The first patient was a 48-year-old right-handed pediatric nurse. Born in Morocco of French parents, she had spoken only French as a child. She acquired some spoken dialectal Arabic from the environment but had little occasion to use it and did not start to learn the language seriously until age 10 at a French school where classical Arabic was taught by means of a traditional grammar-translation method. At age 21 she took intensive courses in dialectal Arabic. For the 24 years preceding a moped accident, which resulted in a left hemisphere temporo-parietal contusion, the patient used dialectal Arabic in her daily work with the nurses and the mothers of her young pa-tients, and French with her sisters and the hospital doctors. The second patient was a 23-year-old right-handed male who spoke both French and English fluently. For him, French had always been, and still was, the language of the home. English had been acquired from the environment before school age. For the past 6 years, the patient had been using English at work. He underwent surgery for the removal of an arterovenous malfor-mation deep in the left parietal lobe.

Both patients alternately suffered word-finding difficulty so severe that they could not name the most common objects, describe pictures or speak spontaneously in one language, although they re-mained relatively fluent in the other. The first patient was observed to alternate languages every 24 hours on 4 consecutive days. The second patient could not speak to his unilingual wife for the first week, and his father had to act as an interpreter. For the second week, when French was accessible but not English, he could no longer communicate with the nurses on the ward. Comprehension and repetition remained equal in both languages at all times for both patients. At the same time, both patients could translate, without hesitation or inaccuracy, difficult sentences from their fluent language into the one in which they could not find words to speak spontaneously. Yet they could *not* translate the simplest sentence from the language they understood into the language that they could speak fluently at the time.

Nilipour and Ashayery (1989) report a case of alternate antagonism between two languages and successive recovery of a third in a Farsi-German-English trilingual aphasic patient. A 49-year-old right-handed Iranian orthopedic surgeon suffered left fronto-temporal trauma as a result of the explosion of his booby-trapped car. The patient was a native speaker of Farsi. He had spent 16 years in Germany between the ages of 18 and 34, where he had obtained his medical degree. In high school, he had learned English as a foreign language, had spent one year in England to do research in medical institutions, and had recently passed the Iran American Society English proficiency exam. Upon regaining consciousness after his accident, the patient was able to speak a few words of Farsi but after 16 days switched to German and from then on spoke only German for the next 3 weeks, even to his unilingual Farsi-speaking relatives. During that period, the patient did understand Farsi, but responded only in German. After 3 weeks he suddenly became aware of the incongruity of speaking German to his sister-in-law, who was pleading with him to speak Farsi, and from then on was able to speak Farsi again. All previous attempts to have him speak Farsi had failed. The patient then gradually lost his ability to express himself in German during the following week. He did not recover the use of English until 6 weeks

after the accident, when he began to gain control over the choice of language to be used for expression.

Paradis and Goldblum (1989) describe a case of selective crossed aphasia in one of a trilingual patient's languages. After surgical removal of a parasitic cyst in the right prerolandic area, an educated 27-year-old male exhibited obvious language deficits in one of his three languages with no measurable deficits in the other two. The patient spoke Gujarati, Malagasy and French fluently before the operation. Gujarati and Malagasy had been acquired in infancy. Gujarati was the language of his parents and relatives, and was spoken daily with them and with other members of the Indian community of Madagascar. He used Malagasy daily with the local population. All the patient's schooling had been in French, the only language in which he was literate. He used French daily at work. The patient was tested pre- and postoperatively in French and showed no deficit. However, after his family had complained that he had difficulties in Gujarati, the patient was tested in Gujarati and in Malagasy. Malagasy did not reveal any measurable impairment. There were, however, noticeable deficits in Gujarati. The patient stuttered considerably, had a significantly depressed verbal fluency score (6, as opposed to 33 in French), and exhibited naming difficulties as well as difficulties with the token test. Spontaneous speech was seriously hampered by his severe pseudostuttering (which was totally absent in his other two languages).

Since the acquisition history for Gujarati and Malagasy was identical, while French had been acquired in a different context, one would have predicted, on the basis of Lambert and Fillenbaum's (1959) hypothesis, that Gujarati and Malagasy should be equally affected, with French possibly differently so. But it was Gujarati that was selectively affected. However, after the patient had spent 8 months in Madagascar, his Gujarati had recovered satisfactorily but his Malagasy had deteriorated considerably. When the patient was tested one year later, his French still showed no impairment and his Gujarati was normal, but his Malagasy exhibited morphological and syntactic deficits in both comprehension and expression and, in Malagasy, he had considerable word-finding difficulty. Thus, over a period of 8 months, the patient had recovered Gujarati but had seen his Malagasy proportionately deteriorate, thus exhibiting an antagonistic recovery for these languages, but not for French, which had remained unimpaired throughout.

TABLE 2

Cases of bilingual acquired dyslexia and dysgraphia

Author(s)	Age	Sex	Handedness	Educational level	Occupation	Mother tongue(s)	Literature in	Script	Direction of script		Type of impairment	Etiology	Side of lesion	Associated deficits	Patterns of recovery
Sroka et al. (1973)	40	F	?	12	?	Slovak	Slovak	alphabet	L	R	AD	AVM	L	CA	P
							German	alphabet	L	R					
							Hebrew	semitic	R	L				HH	
Streifler and Hofman (1976)	47	F	?L	12	business-woman	Polish	Hebrew	semitic	R	L	MI	TR		AG	C
							Polish	alphabet	L	R	RW				
Wechsler (1977)	57	M	R	?	?	English	English	alphabet	L	R	?	CVA	L	HH	D
							French	alphabet	L	R					
Albert and Obler (1978) (case 79)	20	F	L	E	?	Hebrew	Hebrew	semitic	R	L	MI	TR	B	AG	D
							English	alphabet	L	R					
Karanth (1981)	57	M	R	16	superintendent Customs inspector	Kannada	Kannada	syllabic	L	R	LL	CVA	L	HH	D
							English	alphabet	L	R					
Assal and Buttet (1983)	54	M	R	13	piano teacher	Italian	Italian	alphabet	L	R	AG	CVA	L	HH	D
							French	alphabet	L	R					
							Music	mus.not.	L	R					
Byng et al. (1984)	15	M	R	10	student	Nepalese	Nepalese	syllabic	L	R	DD	TR	L	HP	P
							English	alphabet	L	R				SA	
Regard et al. (1985)	84		R		architect	German	German	alphabet	L	R	G:PA			HH	D
							French	alphabet	L	R	F:LL	TU	L	WF	
							Stenogr.	syllabic							
							Shorthand	ideogr.							

Note: Any entry preceded by ? = presumably; ? = unreported.
Handedness: L = left; R = right.
Educational level: Numbers = years of schooling; E = educated (as reported).
Literate in: Stenogr. = stenography.
Script: Alphabet = alphabetic (Roman alphabet); ideogr. = ideographic; mus.not. = musical notation; Semitic = using the Hebrew alphabet in which vowels are optionally marked as diacritics.
Direction of script: L R = from left to right; R L = from right to left.
Type of impairment: AD = agnosic dyslexia; AG = agraphia; DD = deep dyslexia; LL = letter by letter reading; MI = mirror image; PA = paralexia; RW = reading and writing.
Etiology: AVM = arterovenous malformation; CVA = cerebral vascular accident (stroke); TR = trauma; TU = tumor partial removal.
Side of lesion: B = bilateral; L = left.
Associated deficits: AG = agraphia; CA = color agnosia; HH = (right) homonymous hemianopia; HP = (right) hemiplegia; SA = speech apraxia; WF = word-finding difficulty.
Pattern of recovery: C = selective; D = differential; P = parallel.

Bilingual dyslexia and dysgraphia

Of the 8 cases of bilingual dyslexia and dysgraphia reviewed, 5 exhibited differential recovery, 2 parallel, and one selective. The main features of each case are summarized in Table 2.

Sroka et al. (1973) report a case of agnosic alexia (pure word blindness) in a 40-year-old female who could read Slovak (her mother tongue), as well as German and Hebrew, before insult. The patient displayed color agnosia and a complete inability to read either print or handwriting in any language, though she remained able to write fluently in all. She suffered a right homonymous hemianopia. An arterovenous malformation in the occipital region (angular gyrus) of the left posterior cerebral artery was revealed. The alexia receded gradually and simultaneously in both reading directions.

Streifler and Hofman (1976) describe a 47-year-old businesswoman who was in full command of both Polish and Hebrew writing systems before she incurred a brain concussion during an automobile accident. The patient had learned the Hebrew script at the age of 4 and had used Hebrew as her everyday language for the past 25 years. She is assumed to have been left-handed though she was taught to write with her right hand (her father was ambidextrous and her son left-handed). After insult, the patient showed a selective dyslexia for Hebrew. She wrote each letter in mirror image from left to right, and could only read Hebrew in mirror image, with each letter reversed. She had no such deficit in Polish.

Wechsler (1977) relates a case of dissociative dyslexia. The patient was a 57-year-old right-handed American male who suffered alexia subsequent to left occipital lobe infarction. The degree of reading difficulty is reported to have been quite different in each of the languages affected, being greatest in his native English and much less severe in French (learned in high school and college). There was no associated agraphia or aphasia.

Albert and Obler (1978) describe a female left-handed patient who was literate in Hebrew (her native language) and English (which she had ac-quired as an adolescent, presumably from school as the language of instruction, and from the environment). At the age of 20, two years after her return to Israel, she had a car accident. Bilateral frontal destruction was surgically removed. Three weeks after her accident, the patient wrote English from right to left (i.e., as in Hebrew), occasionally reversing individual letters, with further phonetic and visual confusions. She did not use Hebrew letters when writing English words, but did use some English letters when writing Hebrew words.

Karanth (1981) relates the case of a right-handed 57-year-old superintendent in a customs inspection office, who was literate in Kannada and English. Kannada is a Dravidian language written in the Devanagari syllabic script. After a few days of total blindness of sudden onset, the patient presented with a right homonymous hemianopia and an inability to read, though he could see words and letters clearly. In either language, he could identify letters only by tracing them with his finger. Subjectively, the patient found reading Kannada more difficult, and it took him more time than reading English. This was true throughout the successive recovery stages, in spite of the fact that the patient had learned Kannada before he had learned English and even though the grapheme-syllable correspondence is very close in the Devanagari script.

Assal and Buttet (1983) report a case of aphasia, subsequent to a posterior temporo-parietal lesion, in a bilingual piano teacher. Born in Italy, the patient had been living in France since the age of 29, and could speak, read and write French fluently. Following a total aphasia that lasted for 2 weeks, rapid progress was recorded equally in both languages. Speech functions recovered considerably, except for a severe agraphia, in the context of a well-preserved ability to write music. The patient thus presented a clear dissociation between his relatively well-preserved musical writing system and his ability to write verbal material. The authors suggest that characteristics inherent to musical writing as well as the great musical skill and frequent practice of the patient may account for his relatively well-preserved musical writing system in the context of a severe agraphia for verbal material. This dissociation between two writing systems is not unlike cases of dissociation between *Kana* and *Kanji, Kanji* and numbers, *hiragana* and *katakana*, reported in Japanese dyslexic patients (Paradis et al., 1985) and suggests a neurofunctional modular organization of cognitive skills (Paradis, 1987b).

Byng et al. (1984) describe a case of deep dyslexia in a 15-year-old right-handed male student who premorbidly could read English and Nepalese. Nepalese is written in the Devanagari syllabic script. As a consequence of a severe head injury resulting in a right-sided hemiplegia and a complete speech apraxia, the patient exhibited most of the important features of deep dyslexia, such as semantic and derivational errors. Writing was also impaired. His ability to read aloud Nepalese words was much worse than his ability to read aloud English words, because of a differential speech apraxia. However, language comprehension was similar for both languages.

Regard et al. (1985) describe an 87-year-old right-handed retired polyglot architect who was proficient in the use of stenography and abbreviated shorthand. Subsequent to a presumed stroke, the patient's reading of print and cursive handwriting was restricted to single letters in both German and French, while reading of stenography remained completely normal.

Factors of non-parallel recovery

Many factors have been proposed over the years to account for non-parallel recovery. As a consequence of his law of regression, which states that the oldest acquisitions of memory are the most resistant to morbid dissolution, Ribot (1881) predicted that the native language of a polyglot patient should be better recovered, irrespective of its relative degree of fluency at the time of insult. However, Pitres (1895) argued that the reason why the native language was often better recovered was not that it was the first to be acquired, but that it

was the most familiar to the patient at the time of the accident and that, when it was not, the second, more familiar language would be preferentially recovered. Freud (1891) had already maintained that degree of practice (together with age of acquisition) was a determinant of the recovery pattern in polyglot aphasics. Pick (1921) further suggested that the order of recovery went from the language that was most automatized to the language that was the least automatized at the time of insult. This idea was echoed by Bálind (1923), Dedic (1926), Leischner (1948), Ledinský and Mřaček (1958), Kainz (1960) and Quadfasel (1963).

Pötzl (1925) noticed that degree of severity seemed to influence the type of recovery: the more severe the aphasia, the greater the chance of non-parallel recovery. Minkowski (1936, 1963) even hypothesized that there probably exists in the brain a functional substratum common to all languages stored therein and that, since only a limited number of linguistic functions are available to the aphasic polyglot, in cases of severe aphasia the patient is restricted to the use of one language instead of two or more. Halpern (1949, 1950) concurred with this idea of a balance effect. The choice of language of recovery is assumed to be less free to the extent that the brain functions less well (Krapf, 1957), or to the extent that a patient may concentrate on one language in order to economize his resources (Charlton, 1964). Green (1986) likewise suggests that brain damage affects the availability of resources (i.e., the energy to activate or inhibit a system). The various patterns of recovery are seen as outcomes of a system with limited inhibitory resources.

Pötzl (1925) also noticed an apparent connection between damage to the left supramarginal gyrus and selective recovery. It was then assumed that this cortical area played the role of a switch mechanism allowing transition from one language to another (Kauders, 1929; Pötzl, 1930, 1932; Hoff and Pötzl, 1932a,b). Leischner (1948) reached a similar conclusion: damage to the supramarginal gyrus results in the switch being either immobilized in one position (in which case the patient has access to only one language), or loose (in which case the patient keeps switching involuntarily from one language to another).

Minkowski (1927, 1928, 1949, 1965) speculated that psychosexual and psychosocial components of affective and emotional factors are capable, through a powerful psycho-neuro-biological dynamic force, of playing a decisive role in the struggle for the selection of the particular language to be used, and that language may thus very well be paradoxical and ill-adapted to the communicative situation. Winterstein and Meier (1939), Krapf (1955, 1957, 1961), Gerstenbrand and Stepan (1956), Charlton (1964), Jakobson (1964) and Lebrun (1976) also attribute to psychological, emotional and sociolinguistic factors the recovery of some of their patients.

Because he noted that some patients recovered Standard German or French over their currently used and usually more fluent native dialect, Minkowski (1927) also proposed that a language which is written as well as spoken might be more easily recovered than a language that is spoken only. The ability to visualize the written word might facilitate the patient's access to the spoken word. Halpern (1941, 1949) even speculated that, in some cases, recovery of a language might be facilitated if it had been learned through the written form. Rapport et al. (1983) report that the language in which their patients were literate was consistently recovered first. In Paradis and Goldblum's (1989) trilingual patient, the only language that remained unimpaired at all times was the one in which the patient was literate. On the other hand, T'sou (1978) explains his conduction aphasia patient's more severe paraphasias in English than in Cantonese by the fact that the patient's ability to 'visualize' English words in their grapheme-phoneme correspondence spelling may have led to additional difficulties. Literacy (as well as type of writing system involved) may thus interact with type of aphasia, and may make one of the languages either more accessible or, on the contrary, more interfering, depending on the syndrome.

Goldstein (1948) observed that patient's selec-

tion of language is determined by which one appears to be best for their purpose – the most appropriate for helping them at any given moment to communicate by means of language. The language best available may depend on the subject matter discussed (Bálind, 1923), on the ethnic origin of the interlocutor (Herschmann and Pötzl, 1920), or on the habitual use of a specific language in a given situation (Krapf, 1955). Bay (1964) also maintained that the best-preserved language is the one which is most needed (see also Charlton, 1964). The language of the environment may be better recovered because of the quantity of stimulation received in that language (Lebrun, 1982). Lebrun has argued elsewhere (Lebrun, 1978; Lebrun and Paradis, 1984) that an equal degree of stimulation in each language is an important factor in the acquisition of balanced bilingualism. The same reasoning seems to apply here: languages will improve in proportion to the degree of stimulation. If only one language is stimulated by the environment and/or therapy, that language may well recover better or faster, or even be the only one to improve.

Lambert and Fillenbaum (1959) hypothesized that coordinate bilinguals (i.e., those who have acquired each language in a separate context) should have more neurologically separated neural structures underlying their languages than should compound bilinguals (i.e., those who have acquired both languages in the same context). From their hypothesis, it follows that aphasia would likely affect all the languages of compound bilinguals but should lead to more selective disturbances for coordinate bilinguals.

Other possible types of influence from the context of acquisition (besides less neurofunctional separate representation when the languages have been acquired in the same context) are the formal or informal exposure to the second language and the acquisition by ear or by eye. The first is consonant with Lamendella's (1977) distinction between acquisition and learning, the former involving limbic structures, the latter, cortical structures only. The use of a language that has been learned may result in the involvement of processing mechanisms different from those involved when a language that has been acquired is used (i.e., conscious, monitored processes vs. unconscious, automatic processes). Minimally, a formal learning context would involve cognitive processes different from those involved in natural acquisitional contexts. The acquisition by eye rather than by ear involves different modalities, hence different cortical areas. Both types of context (formal/informal; by ear/by eye) in turn may lead to the use of specific processing strategies and possibly qualitatively different aphasic symptoms (Silverberg and Gordon, 1979; Gordon and Weide, 1983).

Wulfeck et al. (1986) have identified at least two different strategies used by normal bilinguals to derive meaning from syntactic clues. While it is not yet clear what prompts individuals to adopt one strategy over another (e.g., reliance on word order vs. agreement vs. semantic clues), the strategy used may be reflected in the recovery pattern of aphasic patients. The use of a different strategy for each language or of the same strategy for both may result in different degrees of accuracy in grammaticality judgement and comprehension tasks.

However, none of the above factors accounts for all or even for most of the reported cases of non-parallel recovery. About as many patients have been reported as having clearly recovered their mother tongue first as patients having recovered it last. There were slightly fewer patients who first recovered the language most familiar to them than patients who recovered a less familiar language (in some cases, the least familiar language). While some patients recovered the language of their surroundings, which was neither their mother tongue nor their most fluent language, about as many did not recover the language of the environment even though it was both their mother tongue and most fluent language. Some patients preferentially recovered a language which was neither their mother tongue, nor their most fluent language, nor that of the surroundings. It is difficult to deal with the 'affective charge'

hypothesis because it could be argued that the charge is either positive or negative, and thus provides a post hoc explanation for most cases, whichever language is better recovered. If, for instance, Hebrew is selectively recovered in a Jew who emigrated to Israel shortly after World War II, it could be interpreted as the result of positive affect; if, on the other hand, German is recovered at the expense of Hebrew, then a strong negative affective charge could be invoked. Even so, there are some cases in which there would be no reason to ascribe any particular affective charge, either positive or negative, to either language (e.g., the case reported by Van Thal, 1960). In some cases, the language clearly the least useful to the patient was preferentially recovered (Halpern, 1950). Thus, progress in one language or the other seems to be determined by different factors at different times. No single principle nor a hierarchy of principles has emerged to explain the whole array of recovery patterns. Neither primacy, automaticity, habit strength, stimulation pre- or post-onset, appropriateness, need, affectivity, severity of the aphasia, type of bilingualism nor type of aphasia could account for the non-parallel recovery patterns observed.

Ovcharova et al. (1968) suggest that a difference in the recovery of two languages may result from differences in the structures of these languages. This may be interpreted to refer to language-specific effects or to the structural distance between any two languages involved. Both hypotheses have had proponents in recent years. The structural distance hypothesis is echoed by Critchley (1974), Lebrun (1976) and Galloway (1978).

There are, in fact, at least four reasons why two structurally different languages may appear to be differently affected, as opposed to two structurally similar languages. (1) They may be stored in different ways. The language substrate may be shared to a greater degree if the languages are linguistically comparable, whereas in cases in which the two languages had markedly different syntactic or phonological rule systems one would predict greater differential representation in the language area. This reasoning is compatible with a tripartite hypothesis of bilingual cerebral organization (see below). Rapport et al. (1983) report greater similarities between the recovery of Chinese dialects than between either dialect and English in their bidialectal Chinese-English bilinguals. (2) Two structurally different languages may have fewer strong associations, which, in terms of the subsystems hypothesis of bilingual cerebral organization (see below), translates as less related systems. (3) The characteristics of the writing system may affect not only the areas involved in the processing of reading and writing, but also possibly the storage and/or processing of the languages themselves, given the influence of the writing system on the conceptual organization of the language (in terms of cognitive strategies). In Japanese conversation, for instance, the close association between the meaning of a word and the written character (*kanji*) which represents it (to the point that speakers draw a *kanji* in the palm of their hand to distinguish between homophones) may influence the way language is organized, and differ from that of a Spanish speaker (T'sou, 1978). (4) In languages that are closely related, when only comprehension seems to have been recovered or seems less impaired, it may not be because comprehension in that language is better *recovered* but because it is better *understood* due to its resemblance to the other language. (Even a unilingual French speaker will understand more Italian than Vietnamese or Russian.)

Differential language-related thought patterns, type and direction of script, vowel characteristics and presence or absence of tones have been suggested as possible language-specific features influencing differential lateralization and consequently differential recovery (see Vaid and Genesee, 1980; Vaid, 1983, for a comprehensive review). If such language-specific effects exist, they are not related to bilingualism per se. Even if bilingualism (per se) had no effect whatsoever on lateralization of language functions, one should nevertheless expect differences in lateralization between languages whose specific characteristics

cause each to be lateralized differently from the other. Each language would be lateralized in this manner in unilingual speakers as well.

More recently, neuropsychologists have turned to differential lateralization of language functions in bilinguals as a possible explanation. More than two decades ago, Vildomec (1963) speculated that the nondominant hemisphere might be specialized to a certain degree for foreign languages. Gorlitzer von Mundy (1959) had interpreted the selective recovery of Slovenian in an illiterate 94-year-old ambidextrous Slovenian-German bilingual, subsequent to a left hemisphere embolism, as indicative of bilateral representation of Slovenian and unilateral (left) representation of German. Slovenian, his mother tongue, was assumed to have been symmetrically represented, while German, learned at the same time as the manipulation of firearms with the right hand, was assumed to have been represented in the left hemisphere only.

Clinical evidence in support of a greater participation of the right hemisphere in bilinguals than in unilinguals is at present nonexistent. In the vast majority of cases, aphasia in bilinguals or polyglots has occurred subsequent to left hemisphere lesions. Of the right hemisphere lesions reported, many are in left-handers, or in people who sustained injury to the left hemisphere in childhood. Still, the percentage of crossed aphasia among bilinguals is higher than the incidence in the general population would lead one to expect. But statistics based on published cases are misleading at best, and are probably false. Since most cases of aphasia resulting from left hemisphere damage are not reported, and since most cases of crossed aphasia (unilingual or bilingual) do get reported because of their exceptional character, the percentage of crossed aphasia thus obtained is not representative of the percentage one would find in an unselected population and cannot be compared with the incidence of crossed aphasia in the general population.

Only one group study reports results obtained from a random sample (Chary, 1986). Of 22 right-handed multilingual patients with unilateral lesions seen at a neurological clinic in Madras, three were diagnosed as exhibiting crossed aphasia. The incidence of crossed aphasia in this sample thus appears to be very high (13.6%). However, three circumstances must be considered: (1) the sample is very small, (2) the severity of the aphasia is not mentioned (and consequently could be very mild – a suspicion heightened by the author's own remark that measures used in previous cases of right hemisphere damage may not have been sensitive enough to detect aphasia – and would thus be consonant with Joanette et al.'s (1983) findings), and (3) the incidence in unilinguals, as measured by the same method, is 12.8%, which is also very high.

Another study to which many authors have referred as evidence in support of greater incidence of crossed aphasia in bilinguals is that of Nair and Virmani (1973). Unfortunately, no figures whatsoever can be derived from that study since the number of bilingual or multilingual patients with crossed aphasia is not mentioned. Only the overall number of crossed aphasic patients, combining unilinguals and bilinguals, is reported. The distribution of the 33 polyglot patients among right and left hemiplegics with language disorders in the sample is not provided by the authors.

Given that more than half the world's population speaks at least two languages (Grosjean, 1982) and that anyone with a high-school education or better is likely to have studied a minimum of one foreign language (at least, outside North America), it should not be surprising that 'a large proportion of the crossed aphasic patients [reported in the literature] are polyglots' (Henderson, 1983). The incidence of bilinguals in the reported crossed aphasia cases cannot be interpreted as evidence in favor of differential lateralization of language in bilinguals. It merely reflects the proportion of bilinguals in a random sample of the world's population. Authors reporting cases of crossed aphasia in bilingual patients sometimes point out themselves that the cases they describe are exceptional and that bilinguals generally do not exhibit differential lateralization (April, 1979).

Albert and Obler (1978) proposed the hypothesis that the learning of a second language in some way influences the subtle interactions between left and right hemispheres, and between cortical and subcortical structures, so that cerebral function is different for unilinguals and bilinguals. Differential recovery might thus result from different premorbid patterns of anatomical organization of the languages. Gordon and Weide (1983) argue that there is an explanation of differential asymmetries in experimental groups other than different cerebral organization; namely, different ways of processing linguistic information. In their view the cerebral organization of bilinguals is the same as that of unilinguals, but, by making use of different cognitive strategies, subjects may utilize different parts of the brain when they process linguistic information. In other words, rather than assuming that the same function (e.g., language processing) is differently represented in the bilingual brain, these authors suggest that in some bilingual individuals different functional operations are applied to a given task (e.g., the processing of a second as opposed to a first or only language).

The three cases of differential aphasia reported so far could possibly be interpreted in terms of differential recovery (i.e., a difference in degree rather than a difference in the nature of the impairment between the two languages), and/or differential mastery of the various components of each language (some speakers of foreign languages could indeed pass for Broca's or Wernicke's patients). Some of the deviant features noted in the patients' aphasic performance might have been a reflection of their premorbid grammars (including *type* of deviance) rather than the effects of pathology (Paradis, 1977; Green and Newman, 1985; Grosjean, 1989). In particular, Silverberg and Gordon's second case could easily be interpreted as a selective recovery of the patient's native Russian. His knowledge of Hebrew was minimal to begin with. It is therefore not too suprising that after his CVA the patient lost access to Hebrew, thus exhibiting the selective loss of one (little known) language. This is a relatively common pattern. In the case of the Spanish-speaking nurse, the differences in performance between the two languages might also be explained in part by differences in pre-morbid mastery (e.g., as evidenced by mispronunciations and use of inappropriate words) and by a differential recovery, with symptoms being more severe in Spanish (more word-finding difficulty in Spanish; Hebrew repetition was impaired, and Spanish more so; comprehension deficits were similar in both languages).

Brown (1980) suggests a microgenetic interpretation. If localization, or regional specification, is related to skill in language, which develops over time (Ojemann and Whitaker, 1978; Brown, 1980; Kinsbourne, 1981; Whitaker et al., 1981), an anterior lesion could be expected to disrupt expression in the first language more severely because the first language is more focally represented. A posterior lesion would lead to a more severe fluent aphasia in the first language, while a more diffusely represented (weaker) language would show the picture of a nonfluent aphasia, as it does in children (Brown, 1980). However, in the case of Silverberg and Gordon's first patient, it is in the patient's first language that a nonfluent aphasia was observed, and in her second language that a fluent aphasia was noted. Wechsler (1977) also proposes, as an explanation for dissociative alexia, that reading lateralizes in proportion to training. Hence, the most severely affected language should be the one that was read most fluently, because it would be the most lateralized.

Silverberg and Gordon (1979) propose that differential aphasia resulting from a single hemispheric lesion is related to the disruption of different basic cognitive functions that participate to varying degrees in the performance of the languages affected. This argument is further developed by Gordon and Weide (1983). Differences in performance are interpreted in terms of different processing strategies.

Models of the bilingual brain

Whatever the characteristics of the preferentially

recovered languages – whether it is the first acquired, the most often used, or the language of the hospital environment – an important question remains: how is it possible for only one language to recover and not the other, or how can one be better recovered than another? This question has given rise to three hypotheses. (1) Each language is represented in a different locus in the brain, and thus a circumscribed lesion may affect one and not the other, or not affect the other to the same extent; (2) there is an area in the brain that acts as a switch mechanism which allows the bilingual to switch from one language to another; a lesion in this area either blocks the switch in one position so the patient can speak only one language, or causes the switch to become loose and so the patient uncontrollably keeps switching back and forth between languages; or (3) the unrecovered language is not destroyed but inhibited.

The first hypothesis has been attributed to Scoresby-Jackson (1867), who merely suggested differential localization along the third frontal convolution as one of at least three possibilities. The second was proposed by Pötzl (1925) and was believed from Pötzl (1925, 1930) to Leischner (1948) to be located in the supramarginal gyrus. The third dates as far back as Pitres (1895), who proposed it in one of the three concluding remarks to his 1895 monograph, along what was to become Pitres's rule.

While authors from Pitres (1895) to Penfield (1965) have argued against separate centers specifically assigned to each of the languages of polyglot subjects, a growing number of contemporary researchers are prepared to consider various kinds of differential representation, including distinct anatomical localization. In fact, some of these authors feel that there are numerous reasons to believe that cerebral representation of language is not entirely the same in polyglots as in unilinguals (Lecours et al., 1984), and that it would be surprising if bilingualism had no effect on brain organization (Segalowitz, 1983). The two languages of a bilingual may not be subserved by exactly the same neuronal circuits; it may even be that they are differently lateralized (Lebrun, 1981). Some authors propose that the two languages of a bilingual are represented in partly different anatomical areas in the dominant hemisphere, with some overlap (Ojemann and Whitaker, 1978; Rapport et al., 1983). Another possible hypothesis is that languages are subserved by different circuits intricately interwoven in the same language areas, so that both are represented in the same area at the gross anatomical level, while still being independently subserved by different neural circuits at the microanatomical level (Paradis, 1977).

Soon after its proposal, the second hypothesis was confronted with two types of counter-evidence: selective and mixed recovery with no damage to the temporo-parietal area, and parieto-temporal lesions with no selective or mixed recovery. In fact, it may not be necessary to postulate an anatomically localized (or even a neurofunctional) switch mechanism at all. The capacity to switch is not specific to the bilingual speaker. The decision to encode a message in English or in Urdu is surely of the same order as the decision to produce an active, a passive or a cleft sentence in either language. There is no reason to believe that language switching should not depend on the same general neuropsychological mechanism of internal choice that governs the capacity to speak or to remain silent. Language switching does not even require any psychological skill peculiar to bilingualism, but rather a skill that is equally applicable in a large number of operations in which persons are asked to switch modes of response (Macnamara et al., 1968; Paradis, 1977, 1980). Delays, if any, involved in switching languages in experimental tasks are of the same order as those of orienting to any new task (Lewis, 1968; Dalrymple-Alford, 1985).

A number of hypotheses concerning the way in which the representation of two (or more) languages is organized in one brain may be considered. Paradis (1981) examined five of them. The extended system hypothesis, according to which languages are undifferentiated in their representation, and elements of the various languages are

processed as allo-elements; the dual system hypothesis, according to which each language is represented independently in separate circuits; the tripartite system hypothesis, according to which those items that are identical in both languages are represented in one single underlying neural substrate common to both languages, and those that are different each have their own separate representation; the context of acquisition hypothesis, according to which the languages acquired in different contexts are neurofunctionally more separately represented than those acquired in the same context; and the subsystem hypothesis, according to which bilinguals have two subsets of neural connections, one for each language, within the same cognitive system, namely, the language system. The latter is compatible with all patterns of recovery as well as with the bilingual's ability to mix languages at each level of linguistic structure. Parallel impairment can be interpreted as the result of damage to, or interference with, the linguistic system as a whole, and differential impairment as the result of damage to, or interference with, one of the subsystems. Each language, as a subsystem, is susceptible to selective pathological inhibition. Yet subjects with intact brains have the choice of alternately using elements of one or the other linguistic subsystem, or of simultaneously using elements of both. Frequency of code-switching and code-mixing may be an important factor in how the two languages are processed. Frequent mixing may have the effect of lowering interlanguage inhibition. It may also lead to the adoption of mixed or amalgamated strategies for sentence interpretation (i.e., using the same cues for both languages, irrespective of their respective validity: see Wulfeck et al., 1986, and below).

Green and Newman (1985) rightly point out that whichever of these hypotheses is adopted, the means of selection between items of each language still needs to be characterized. However, the means of selection need not differ from that used by unilinguals to, for example, pick a baby-talk word rather than a familiar register word or a formal register word, given the appropriate circumstances. If choosing to speak one language rather than another requires the speaker to specify a language 'tag', then a similar 'tag' is necessary for unilinguals to select items among their various registers, and within the selected one, among possible synonyms, as well as between active, passive or topicalized constructions (Paradis, 1980). The selection mechanism between languages need not be different from that within each language. In other words, the selection mechanism used by a bilingual need not differ from that used by a unilingual. A direct-access hypothesis (i.e., access without the necessity of an additional language tag) is definitely consonant with the facts of comprehension (Grosjean and Soares, 1986). In production, the same process of selection used by unilinguals suffices to account for the bilingual's choice of words, constructions, or pronunciation (accent), allowing them to choose to speak one language (unilingual mode), or to freely mix (bilingual mode), or to use syntactic structures of one when speaking the other, with or without the pronunciation of the other (for special effects).

The language tag, or awareness of language membership, is a product of metalinguistic competence. In on-line processing, language awareness is as unconscious and of the same nature as the process that allows a unilingual speaker to understand (or select) the appropriate word in a given context. The process of selection of a Russian word by a bilingual when speaking Russian is the same as the process that allows a Russian unilingual to select among the indefinite, almost unlimited, possibilities of encoding a given message. In order to name an object on confrontation, competing synonyms within the same language must be inhibited just as translation equivalents (and their synonyms) must be. There is therefore no need to postulate a language tag specific to bilinguals any more than a bilingual switch or a bilingual monitor. The patient quoted in epigraph in Paradis and Lecours (1983) as well as Nilipour and Ashayery's (1989) patient had both lost language awareness and did not realize that they were speaking an inappropriate language, even when responding to

questions asked in the other language. The first patient kept switching uncontrollably; the second patient consistently spoke one language only.

The mere fact that the various languages form subsystems is sufficient to account for their susceptibility to selective inhibition. Inhibition is neither necessarily global (i.e., affecting the whole system) nor total (i.e., not admitting of degree). During the microgenesis of an utterance (i.e., during the process of selection and successive unfolding, in milliseconds, from the concept to the acoustic realization of the words that encode them), first the irrelevant semantic fields, then the irrelevant items within the selective field, are inhibited. Other modules within each subsystem are similarly susceptible to selective dysfunction; e.g., specific aspects of semantics (Yamadori and Albert, 1975; Goodglass et al., 1986), syntax (Caplan et al., 1985), morphology (Kehoe and Whitaker, 1973) or phonology (Johns and Lapointe, 1976). As some aspects of one language may be selectively inhibited by pathology, so may some language(s).

Moreover, there is no need to postulate that comprehension and production are subserved by different and separable systems. The differences in performance observed so far are compatible with an interpretation in terms of different thresholds of activation. A double dissociation between comprehension and production would have to be demonstrated in order to unequivocally support the notion of two separate systems. So far, no cases of preserved production without comprehension (save for pure word deafness or rare cases of echolalia) have been reported. (Pure word deafness is a peripheral phenomenon which does not affect competence, since patients are able to understand what they read. Echolalia has the characteristics of a reflex reaction to an incoming stimulus and is unlikely to be the self-activation of a trace.)

Four interpretative models of the bilingual brain have been proposed recently. Obler's (1984) parsimony, potency, and attrition model, Perecman's (1984) microgenetic framework, Paradis's (1984) threshold of activation level hypothesis, and Green's (1986) notion of control, activation and resource. Most of these proposals are not incompatible with each other but are either complementary or terminological variants.

Obler's notions of potency and attrition can be seen in terms of the lowering and raising of the threshold level, respectively. The threshold level is governed by the available energy or resource and regulated by a control mechanism (Green, 1986).

What Paradis (1985) refers to as strength of a trace corresponds to Obler's (1984) notion of potency. The strength of a trace (i.e., its propensity to being activated, its threshold level) is a function of both the frequency of its activation and the recency of its last activation. Recall or retrieval of a linguistic item (i.e., self-activation of its neural substratum, or trace) requires a lower threshold of activation than recognition (i.e., activation by an impinging outside stimulus). Translated into Green's (1986) terms, more energy is necessary to produce a word (i.e., self-activate its trace) than to understand it (have its trace activated by the perceived stimulus). Control refers to the ability to deliberately focus on one word in one language by activating that word while at the same time inhibiting all competing words in both languages. Paradis et al. (1982) explain alternate antagonism in terms of an impaired mechanism of inhibition and disinhibition.

Both uncontrolled, compulsive translation (Veyrac, 1931; Weisenburg and McBride, 1935; Jakobson, 1964; Schulze, 1968; Perecman, 1984) and an inability to translate (Goldstein, 1948; Paradis et al., 1982) have been reported. Some patients have been observed to be unable to speak a language other than through translating into it from another language (Charcot, 1887; Kauders, 1929; Paradis et al., 1982). When this ability to translate into a language inaccessible for spontaneous use is accompanied by an inability to translate into a language that *is* accessible, it has been dubbed paradoxical. Paradis (1984) attempts to explain paradoxical translation behavior by assuming (1) that the skill of translation is independent of, and different from, skill in the use of two language systems, and (2) that translation, like any other

function, is subjected to a system of inhibition/disinhibition. Green (1986) emphasizes the control component of such a model. Translation into the language of spontaneous use (e.g., French) would be precluded when the other language (e.g., Arabic) could not suppress its own activity sufficiently. When French can suppress its own activity, Arabic would be free to translate.

One controversial point is whether bilinguals possess neural mechanisms of a nature different from those possessed by unilinguals. On the one hand, language organization is assumed to be qualitatively different in bilinguals, and various bilingual-specific mechanisms are involved in language processing (switch, monitor, tagging). On the other hand, it is assumed that no mechanism exists in bilinguals that is not already operative in unilinguals, and that cerebral organization in bilinguals does not qualitatively differ from that in unilinguals (subsystem hypothesis, direct access).

Another controversial point is whether both languages can be active at the same time in the brain of a healthy bilingual speaker, or whether one is inhibited while the other is activated. Seemingly contradictory evidence emerges from experimental studies (Altenberg and Cairns, 1983; Scarborough et al., 1984). Green and Newman (1985) adopt the viewpoint that a language system (or any part thereof) can be in one of three states: dormant, activated and selected. Green (1986) further emphasizes that the unselected language is nevertheless active. Likewise, in terms of Paradis's (1984) model of activation threshold levels, the unselected language is not *totally* inhibited. Its threshold of activation is simply raised high enough to prevent self-activation, but not so high as to preclude comprehension. More energy is necessary to self-activate a trace (i.e., voluntary evocation) than to activate it through an impinging external stimulus.

Involuntary mixing is seen quite rightly by Green (1986) as a failure to exercise full control over a [relatively] intact system. This lack of control over the selection of appropriate items is of the same nature as that prevailing in target misselection in unilinguals. It can indeed be assumed that when one language is selected, the other's threshold of activation is raised, not, however, to such an extent as to preclude comprehension. The unselected language is suppressed or inhibited only to the extent that its threshold of activation is raised sufficiently to hinder self-activation. In normals, the degree of inhibition (i.e., the threshold level) is likely to be a function of the frequency with which one mixes: the more habitual the mixing, the lower the threshold. Even in aphasics, the 'deactivated' language is thus never totally inhibited, except in severe cases of selective recovery without comprehension.

As long as comprehension through grammatical clues is possible, linguistic competence must be available in the patient's brain. Even when comprehension is inoperant for a period of time, the fact that it is eventually regained − without being relearned − shows that it was not destroyed. In some cases, the underlying competence (which is still definitely there) becomes inaccessible and performance in one language (or more) is thus differentially or totally inhibited. Both patients reported by Paradis et al. (1982) and the one reported by Nilipour and Ashayery (1989) recovered the use of their languages over periods of time so short as to exclude the possibility of relearning. In addition, recovery after total aphasia is not uncommon, in unilinguals and bilinguals alike.

Inability to use a language spontaneously is likely to indicate a lower state of activation (i.e., a higher threshold), but it does *not* follow, as Green and Newman (1985) would suggest, that comprehension in that language is impaired. Both patients reported by Paradis et al. (1982) retained comprehension of both languages at all times. It is a characteristic of some forms of anomia that patients cannot retrieve the words they seek, but are able to immediately recognize them when they are provided in a multiple choice (or even when only part of the word, such as initial consonant, is provided, or rythm, or rhyme).

Paradis (1984) reasons as follows. When a speaker uses one of his two languages, the other is automatically inhibited so as to avoid interference. The activation of a word in unilinguals involves not only the activation of the cerebral substrate that subserves it but also the concomitant inhibition of the underlying substrate of all the other semantic fields, then of all other words within the same field, until all words except the one that is selected are inhibited. It is not unreasonable to assume that the same principle applies to the use of two languages: Dutch is inhibited while French is in use, and particularly the Dutch translation equivalent of the item selected in French. This perspective complies with Obler's requirement of parsimony as it is compatible with selective, successive and antagonistic recovery patterns (as well as all others): the temporarily or permanently inaccessible language is not destroyed but inhibited, a solution proposed by Pitres (1895) almost a century ago, revived by Paradis (1984) and espoused by Green and Newman (1985) and Green (1986). The same principle applies at all levels of linguistic structure in unilinguals as well as polyglots.

However, two questions remain unanswered. What determines the particular type of recovery (i.e., why are the resources distributed the way they are, e.g., divided up between two languages in one case and pooled together to maximally activate only one in another case)? And then, in non-parallel recovery, what selects a particular language for preferential recovery over another (which was possibly more fluent premorbidly and/or more useful postmorbidly)? None of the models proposed so far addresses these specific issues.

The assessment of bilingual aphasia

Although cases of aphasia in bilinguals and polyglots reported since 1843 make important contributions to our understanding of the organization of several languages in the same brain, and form an indispensable basis for further research, few meaningful comparisons can be made between them and little can be established on the strength of their evidence alone. Respective degrees of postmorbid fluency and type of deviance in each language, as well as contexts of acquisition and use, are seldom reported in sufficient detail. Yet the need to assess linguistic capacities in both of a bilingual's languages should be obvious for a number of reasons. Assessment is essential for purposes of diagnosis, research and prescription for treatment.

When the language of the hospital environment is almost unavailable to the patient, it is important to determine whether the other language may serve as a means of communication. Only when both languages have been tested with a comparable instrument can one ascertain which language is better retained or less impaired. Conversely, some deficits may be observable in only one of the patient's languages, either because of the nature of structural features specific to it or because of differential recovery. These deficits may nevertheless be suggestive of the general locus and extent of cerebral damage and would go unnoticed if the better-preserved language happened to be that of the hospital environment and if the other language were not tested.

In both cases the results may help one to decide in which language the patient should receive speech therapy. In the first case, once it has been established that one language is definitely better preserved, decisions can be made with respect to the language community in which the patient may choose to live subsequently (e.g., back in the country of origin or in the country of immigration), and the language of therapy may be selected on the basis of the language of social reinsertion. In the second case, the language showing deficits would be treated.

For research purposes, the results obtained on a comprehensive test equivalent in each language allow one to correlate the patient's pattern of recovery with the various acquisitional, utilizational, neurological and pathological factors involved, and to compare such correlations with those obtained in other patients, with a view to ultimately identifying the influencing factor or hierarchy of interactive factors.

In order to remedy the lack of systematicity in reporting cases of aphasia in bilinguals and polyglots encountered so far, a test battery has been developed over the past 10 years and is now available in over 40 languages and 65 specific language pairs (Paradis, 1987a). This *Bilingual Aphasia Test* (BAT) uses a quadrimodal, linguistically multidimensional approach. It is quadrimodal in that it examines language performance in all four modalities – hearing, speaking, reading and writing. It is linguistically multidimensional in that, for each modality, language performance is investigated along three dimensions – linguistic level (phonological, morphological, syntactic, lexical, semantic), linguistic task (comprehension, repetition, judgment of acceptability, lexical access, propositionizing) and linguistic unit (word, sentence, paragraph). This approach allows one to detect task-specific or task-independent deficits of any aspect of linguistic structure, as well as task- or modality-specific (or -independent) deficits at the level of the paragraph, the sentence or the word, in each of the patient's languages.

The BAT consists of three parts. In Part A information about the patient's bilingual background (contexts of acquisition and use, relative degree of mastery and frequency of use) is collected. This information may be obtained from the patients themselves, or from relatives or friends. Patients considered 'bilingual' do not form a homogeneous population but are situated at different points on a multidimensional continuum that allows for differences in the type of organization of their grammars as well as degree of proficiency at each level of linguistic structure and in each language skill. It is only in the light of such information that post-morbid relative deficits can be interpreted. Part B is to be administered on successive days at the same time of day, under identical circumstances, in each of the patient's languages, by a native speaker. Because the scoring procedure is highly objective, the examiner need not be a trained professional. This test comprises 32 subtests (each with its individual score) which can be grouped to obtain a number of measures of specific abilities either by skill, by modality, or by linguistic level. Part C examines the patient's ability to recognize translation equivalents, to translate words and sentences, and to make grammaticality judgements about sentences that incorporate morphological and/or syntactic features of the other language.

The different versions of the various languages are not mere translations of each other, but are of equivalent linguistic complexity for each task. Thus, in the verbal auditory discrimination test, minimal pairs depend on the structure of each language. Likewise, in the syntactic comprehension test, constructions of equivalent complexity (rather than the *same* constructions) are selected. A passive sentence in one language may be equivalent in complexity to a topicalized object construction in another.

When assessing the equivalence of linguistic complexity between sentences in two different languages, it is important to allow for the degree of 'cue validity' or 'cue strength' (see Bates and Mac-Whinney, 1982; MacWhinney et al., 1984; Wulfeck et al., 1986), that is, the degree to which, independently in each language, a given aspect of the grammar (e.g., word order) can be relied upon to furnish useful information about underlying logical-semantic relations (theta-roles) such as 'agent' or 'benefactor'. Wulfeck et al. (1986), for instance, argue that the cue validity of word order is higher in English than in Spanish, even though the unmarked word order in both languages is the same (SVO), because in informal Spanish every logically possible combination of subject-verb-object ordering can be found. Even when there is an unmarked, preferred, 'canonical' word order, word order can range from being absolutely fixed to totally free. To (relatively) free word order, some languages add morphological cues (e.g., case marking, S-V agreement). In sentence interpretation tasks, these varied sources of information (syntactic, morphological and/or semantic) are available in the stimulus and must consequently be controlled in sentences which must be equivalent in different languages. Some of the cues may be differentially vulnerable in different clinical types of aphasia. Such effects must be taken into account before a diagnosis of differential recovery can be made.

Only further systematic investigations of many different language pairs, based on large numbers of successive unselected cases and using identical testing procedures, will help us solve the puzzle of differential recovery patterns. These investigations will eventually provide us with clues as to whether the various languages of a polyglot are stored and processed by the brain separately, each as an independent linguistic system, or together, as one linguistic system.

The effects of language therapy

A methodological monitoring of the effects of various types of therapy applied in different circumstances will eventually point to the optimal conditions for prescribing which type of therapy is best (and in which language) under specific circumstances. Among other things, it will establish whether therapy is necessary in both (or all) languages or whether it is sufficient in one, and if so, which one, and under what conditions.

At present it is not known whether recovery significantly differs following therapy in one language or in both, and whether it is influenced by etiology, initial severity and type of aphasia, structural distance between the languages, patient's age, premorbid intelligence, educational level or type of therapy. Indeed, therapy may have differential effects on the premorbidly dominant (vs. weaker) language and/or on the best (vs. the least well) recovered language. Therapeutic effects on one language may transfer to another language in proportion to the structural similarity between the languages, or therapeutic effects may transfer irrespective of structural distance. Moreover, effects of therapy may transfer in the context of some aphasic syndromes, have no effect in others, and have negative effects in still others.

Therapy in one language has been reported to partially block spontaneous recovery of other languages (Lebrun, 1976). Recovery may be comparable for both the treated and the untreated language or may be somewhat less effective for the untreated language with one type of aphasia, but more effective with another type of aphasia, as reported by Watamori and Sasanuma (1978). While Voinescu et al.'s (1977) case would lend support to such a hypothesis, Bychowski (1919) has reported a case in which therapy in one language had no effect on the other, even though the patient exhibited the same type of aphasia as Watamori and Sasanuma's patient and spoke two closely related languages (Polish and Russian). Minkowski (1927) has related a similar case. Other authors have reported (Fredman, 1975) or assumed (Peuser, 1974) positive effects of therapy on the untreated language, irrespective of aphasia type. But according to some, therapy in several languages will only hinder their recovery (Wald, 1961), and hence only one language should be rehabilitated (Wald, 1958).

Only the systematic and detailed reporting of effects of therapy as measured by the same standard instrument in large numbers of cases can bring us closer to answering such complex questions.

Conclusion

Several intriguing patterns of recovery in bi- and multilingual aphasics have been described in the literature over the past century as well as in recent years. Yet no fully satisfactory explanation has been proposed to date. All we can say so far with some degree of assurance is that languages are dissociable within the same speaker; that comprehension is dissociable from expression in one or both languages; that translation ability is dissociable from the ability to use the two languages involved; that different individuals undergo different patterns of recovery; that, at least in some cases, the inaccessible language is not destroyed but inhibited; and that both (or all) languages are vulnerable to left hemisphere damage, in the same proportion as unilinguals. A number of influencing factors have been suggested to account for the data, but none has been shown to apply to all cases

or even to most cases. Several reasons are responsible for this state of affairs. The complexity of the phenomenon itself precludes a ready explanation.

Firstly, there is a great deal of individual variability with respect to several types of characteristic. Bilinguals do not form a homogeneous population. Individuals stand on several points of a multi-dimensional continuum, with varying parameters in the domains of age and context of acquisition, contexts and patterns of use, degree of mastery, type of organization of their grammars and structural distance between their languages, among others. In addition, several neurological, pathological and experiential dimensions must be taken into account, such as site, size and etiology of the lesion, as well as age, sex, handedness, intelligence, cognitive style, education and literacy of the patient, and more.

Secondly, different cases have been evaluated with different measuring instruments. Sometimes even the two languages of the same patient have not been assessed to the same extent with a comparable battery. Most cases reported so far lack systematicity and comprehensiveness in the data they do report.

Now that a standard test is available in a large number of languages and language pairs, and that versions in new languages can readily be developed, it is hoped that sufficient data will be collected over the next few years to enable us to consider reasonable samples of patients sharing the same variables. If such samples can be obtained we may, at last, be able to deduce reasonable explanations for the various phenomena observed in bilingual and polyglot aphasic patients.

References

Albert ML, Obler K: *The Bilingual Brain.* New York: Academic Press, 1978.

Altenberg EP, Cairns HS: The effects of phonotactic constraints on lexical processing in bilingual and monolingual subjects. *J. Verbal Learn. Verbal Behav.:* 22, 174–188, 1983.

April RS: Concepts actuels sur l'organisation cérébrale à partir de quelques cas d'aphasie croisée chez les orientaux bilingues. *Rev. Neurol.: 135,* 375–378, 1979.

April RS, Han M: Crossed aphasia in a right-handed bilingual Chinese man. *Arch. Neurol. (Chicago): 37,* 342 – 345, 1980.

April RS, Tse PC: Crossed aphasia in a Chinese bilingual dextral. *Arch. Neurol. (Chicago): 34,* 766 – 770, 1977.

Assal G, Buttet J: Agraphie et conservation de l'écriture musicale chez un professeur de piano bilingue. *Rev. Neurol.: 139,* 569 – 574, 1983.

Bálind A: Bemerkungen zu einem Falle von polyglotter Aphasie. *Z. Gesamte Neurol. Psychiatrie: 83,* 277 – 283, 1923.

Bates E, MacWhinney B: Functional approaches to grammar. In Wanner E, Gleitman LR (Editors), *Language Acquisition: The State of the Art.* Cambridge: Cambridge University Press, pp. 173 – 218, 1982.

Bay E: General discussion. In De Reuck AVS, O'Connor M (Editors), *Disorders of Language.* London: Churchill, 1964.

Brown JW: Speaking with forked brain. *Contemp. Psychol: 25,* 564 – 565, 1980.

Bychowski Z: Über die Restitution der nach einem Schädelschuss verlorenen Umgangssprache bei einem Polyglotten. *Monatsschr. Psychiatrie Neurol.: 45,* 183 – 201, 1919.

Byng S, Coltheart M, Masterson J, Prior M, Riddoch J: Bilingual biscriptal deep dyslexia. *Q. J. Exp. Psychol.: 36A,* 417 – 433, 1984.

Caplan D, Baker C, Dehaut F: Syntactic determinants of sentence comprehension in aphasia. *Cognition: 21,* 117 – 175, 1985.

Charcot JM: *Oeuvres Complètes de J.M. Charcot.* Paris: A. Delahaye & E. Lacrossier, Vol. 3, 1887.

Charlton M: Aphasia in bilingual and polyglot patients: a neurological and psychological study. *J. Speech Hear. Disord.: 29,* 307 – 311, 1964.

Chary P: Aphasia in a multilingual society: a preliminary study. In Vaid J (Editor), *Language Processing in Bilinguals.* Hillsdale, NJ: Lawrence Erlbaum Associates, pp. 183 – 197, 1986.

Chiarello C, Knight R, Mandel M: Aphasia in a prelingually deaf woman. *Brain: 105,* 29 – 51, 1982.

Critchley M: Aphasia in polyglots and bilinguals. *Brain Lang.: 1,* 15 – 27, 1974.

Dalrymple-Alford EC: Language switching during bilingual reading. *Br. J. Psychol.: 76,* 111 – 122, 1985.

Dedić ST: Zur Aphasiefrage. *Z. Gesamte Neurol. Psychiatrie: 106,* 208 – 213, 1926.

Fredman M: The effect of therapy given in Hebrew on the home language of the bilingual or polyglot adult aphasic in Israel. *Br. J. Disord. Commun.: 10,* 61 – 69, 1975.

Freud S: Zur Auffassung der Aphasie. Wien: Deuticke, 1891.

Galloway L: Language impairment and recovery in polyglot aphasia: a case of a heptaglot. In Paradis M (Editor), *Aspects of Bilingualism.* Columbia: Hornbeam Press, pp. 139 – 148, 1978.

Gerstenbrand F, Stepan H: Polyglotte Reaktion nach Hirnschädigung; ein kasuistischer Beitrag. *Wien. Z. Nervenheilkunde: 13,* 167 – 172, 1956.

Goldstein K: *Language and Language Disturbances.* New York: Grune & Stratton, pp. 138 – 146, 1948.

Goodglass, H, Wingfield A, Hyde MR, Theurkauf JC: Category specific dissociations in naming and recognition by aphasic patients. *Cortex: 22,* 87 – 102, 1986.

Gordon HW, Weide R: La contribution de certaines fonctions cognitives au traitement du langage, à son acquisition et à l'apprentissage d'une langue seconde. *Langages: 72,* 45 – 56, 1983.

Gorlitzer von Mundy V: Ein 94 jähriger mit einem deutschen Sprachzentrum und mit warscheinlich 2 slowenischen Sprachzentren. *Wien. Med. Wochenschr.: 109,* 358, 1959.

Green DW: Control, activation, and resource: A framework and a model for the control of speech in bilinguals. *Brain Lang.: 27,* 210 – 223, 1986.

Green D, Newman S: Bilingualism and dysphasia: process and resource. In Newman S, Epstein R (Editors), *Current Perspectives in Dysphasia.* Edinburgh: Churchill Livingstone, 1985.

Grosjean F: *Life With Two Languages.* Cambridge, MA: Harvard University Press, 1982.

Grosjean F: Polyglot aphasics and language mixing: a comment on Perecman (1984). *Brain Lang.: 26,* 349 – 355, 1985.

Grosjean F: Neurolinguists, beware! The bilingual is not two monolinguals in one person. *Brain. Lang.: 36,* 3 – 15, 1989.

Grosjean F, Soares C: Processing mixed language: some preliminary findings. In Vaid J (Editor), *Language Processing in Bilinguals.* Hillsdale, NJ: Lawrence Erlbaum Associates, pp. 145 – 179, 1986.

Halpern L: Beitrag zur Restitution der Aphasie bei Polyglotten im Hinblick auf das Hebräische. *Schweiz. Arch. Neurol. Psychiatrie: 47,* 150 – 154, 1941.

Halpern L: La langue hébraïque dans la restitution de l'aphasie sensorielle chez les polyglottes. *Sem. Hôp. Paris: 58,* 2473 – 2476, 1949.

Halpern L: Observations on sensory aphasia and its restitution in a Hebrew polyglot. *Monatsschr. Psychiatrie Neurol.: 119,* 156 – 173, 1950.

Henderson VW: Speech fluency in crossed aphasia. *Brain: 106,* 837 – 857, 1983.

Herschmann H, Pötzl O: Bermerkungen über Aphasie der Polyglotten. *Neurol. Zentralbl.: 39,* 114 – 120, 1920.

Hoff H, Pötzl O: Schiefe Körperhaltung und schiefer Gang bei Kleinhirnerkrankung. *Jahrb. Psychiatrie Neurol.: 48,* 217 – 262, 1932a.

Hoff H, Pötzl O: Ueber die Aphasie eines zweisprechigen Linkshänders. *Wien. Med. Wochenschr.: 82,* 369 – 373, 1932b.

Jakobson R: General discussion. In De Reuck AVS, O'Connor M (Editors), *Disorders of Language.* CIBA Foundation Symposium, London, pp. 21 – 47, 1964.

Joanette Y, Lecours AR, Lepage Y, Lamoureux M: Language in right-handers with right-hemisphere lesions: a preliminary study including anatomical, genetic, and social factors. *Brain Lang.: 20,* 217 – 248, 1983.

Johns DF, Lapointe LL: Neurogenic disorders of output processing: Apraxia of speech. In Whitaker H, Whitaker HA (Editors), *Studies in Neurolinguistics, Vol. 1.* New York: Academic Press, 1976.

Kainz F: *Psychologie der Sprache;* Zweite, umgearbeitete Auflage, vol. 2. Stuttgart: F. Enke, 1960.

Karanth P: Pure alexia in a Kannada-English bilingual. *Cortex: 17,* 187 – 198, 1981.

Kauders O: Über polyglotte Reaktionen bei einer sensorischen

Aphasie. *Z. Gesamte Neurol. Psychiatrie: 122,* 651–666, 1929.

Kehoe WJ, Whitaker HA: Lexical structure disruption in aphasia: A case study. In Goodglass H, Blumstein S (Editors), *Psycholinguistics and Aphasia.* Baltimore: The Johns Hopkins University Press, pp. 267–279, 1973.

Kinsbourne M: Neuropsychological aspects of bilingualism. In Winitz H (Editor), *Native Language and Foreign Language Acquisition.* New York: New York Academy of Sciences (Annals, Vol. 379), pp. 50–58, 1981.

Krapf EE: Über das Sprachverhalten hirngeschädigter Polyglotten. *Wien. Z. Nervenheilkunde: 12,* 121–133, 1955.

Krapf EE: A propos des aphasies chez les polyglottes. *Encéphale: 46,* 623–629, 1957.

Krapf EE: Aphasia in polyglots. *Proc. VII Int. Congr. Neurol.,* Rome: vol. 1, pp. 741–742, 1961.

Lambert WE, Fillenbaum S: A pilot study of aphasia among bilinguals. *Can. J. Psychol.: 13,* 28–34, 1959.

Lamendella J: General principles of neurofunctional organization and their manifestation in primary and non-primary language acquisition. *Lang. Learn.: 27,* 155–196, 1977.

Lebrun Y: Recovery in polyglot aphasics. In Lebrun Y, Hoops R (Editors), *Recovery in Aphasics.* Amsterdam: Swetz & Zeitlinger, pp. 96–108, 1976.

Lebrun Y: Vroegtijdige meertaligheid. *Streven:* July issue, 887–899, 1978.

Lebrun Y: Bilingualism and the brain: a brief appraisal of Penfield's views. In Baetens Beardsmore H (Editor), *Elements of Bilingual Theory.* Brussels: Vrije Universiteit Brussel, pp. 66–75, 1981.

Lebrun Y: L'aphasie chez les polyglottes. *Linguistique: 18,* 129–144, 1982.

Lebrun Y, Paradis M: To be or not to be a bilingual? In Paradis M, Lebrun Y (Editors), *Early Bilingualism and Child Development.* Lisse: Swets & Zeitlinger, pp. 9–18, 1984.

Lecours AR, Branchereau L, Joanette Y: La zone du langage et l'aphasie: enseignement standard et cas particuliers. *META Translators' J.: 29,* 10–26, 1984.

Ledinský DR, Mřaček DR: Vliv proanění temporálního laloku dominantní hemisféry na řecové funkce u polyglota. *Česk. Neurol.: 21,* 207–210, 1958.

Leischner A: Über die Aphasie der Mehrsprachigen. *Arch. Psychiatrie Nervenkr.: 180,* 731–775, 1948.

Lewis G: Discussion following Jakobovits. Dimensionality of compound-coordinate bilingualism. *Lang. Learn.: Special issue No. 3,* 50–55, 1968.

Mcnamara J, Krauthamer M, Bolgar M: Language switching in bilinguals as a function of stimulus and response uncertainty. *J. Exp. Psychol.: 78,* 208–215, 1968.

MacWhinney B, Bates E, Kliegl R: Cue validity and sentence interpretation in English, German, and Italian. *J. Verbal Learn. Verbal Behav.: 23,* 127–150, 1984.

Minkowski M: Klinischer Beitrag zur Aphasie bei Polyglotten, speziell im Hinblick aufs Schweizerdeutsche. *Schweiz. Arch. Neurol. Psychiatrie: 21,* 43–72, 1927.

Minkowski M: Sur un cas d'aphasie chez un polyglotte. *Rev. Neurol.: 49,* 361–366, 1928.

Minkowski M: Sur des variétés particulières d'aphasie chez des polyglottes. *Schweiz. Med. Wochenschr.: 66,* 697–704, 1936.

Minkowski M: Sur un cas particulier d'aphasie avec des réactions polyglottes, de fabulation et d'autres troubles après un traumatisme cranio-cérébral. *C. R. Congr. Méd. Aliénistes Neurol. France, Clermont-Ferrand;* pp. 315–328, 1949.

Minkowski M: On aphasia in polyglots. In Halpern L (Editor), *Problems of Dynamic Neurology.* Jerusalem: Hebrew University, pp. 119–161, 1963.

Minkowski M: Considérations sur l'aphasie des polyglottes. *Rev. Neurol.: 112,* 486–495, 1965.

Nair K, Virmani V: Speech and language disturbances in hemiplegics. *Indian J. Med. Res.: 61,* 1395–1403, 1973.

Nilipour R, Ashayery H: Alternating antagonism between two languages with successive recovery of a third in a trilingual aphasic patient. *Brain Lang.: 36,* 23–48, 1989.

Obler LK: The neuropsychology of bilingualism. In Caplan D, Lecours AR, Smith A (Editors), *Biological Perspectives on Language.* Cambridge, MA: The MIT Press, pp. 194–210, 1984.

Ojemann GA, Whitaker HA: The bilingual brain. *Arch. Neurol. (Chicago): 35,* 409–412, 1978.

Ovcharova P, Raichev R, Geleva T: Afaziia u Poligloti. *Nevrol. Psikhiatr. Nevrokhir.: 7,* 183–190, 1968.

Paradis M: Bilingualism and aphasia. In Whitaker H, Whitaker HA (Editors), *Studies in Neurolinguistics, Vol. 3.* New York: Academic Press, pp. 65–121, 1977.

Paradis M: The language switch in bilinguals: psycholinguistic and neurolinguistic perspectives. *Z. Dialektol. Ling.: Beiheft 32,* 501–506, 1980.

Paradis M: Neurolinguistic organization of a bilingual's two languages. In Copeland JE, Davis PW (Editors), *The Seventh LACUS Forum.* Columbia, SC: Hornbeam Press, pp. 486–494, 1981.

Paradis M (Editor): *Readings on Aphasia in Bilinguals and Polyglots.* Montreal: Marcel Didier, 1983.

Paradis M: Aphasie et traduction. *META Translators' J.: 29,* 57–67, 1984.

Paradis M: On the representation of two languages in one brain. *Lang. Sci.: 7,* 1–39, 1985.

Paradis M: *The Assessment of Bilingual Aphasia.* Hillsdale, NJ: Lawrence Erlbaum Associates, 1987a.

Paradis M: The neurofunctional modularity of cognitive skills: Evidence from Japanese alexia and polyglot aphasia. In Keller E, Gopnik M (Editors), *Motor and Sensory Processes of Language.* Hillsdale, NJ: Lawrence Erlbaum Associates, 1987b.

Paradis M, Goldblum MC: Selective crossed aphasia followed by reciprocal antagonism in a trilingual patient. *Brain Lang.: 36,* 62–75, 1989.

Paradis M, Goldblum MC, Abidi R: Alternate antagonism with paradoxical translation behavior in two bilingual aphasic patients. *Brain Lang.: 15,* 55–69, 1982.

Paradis M, Hagiwara H, Hildebrandt N: *Neurolinguistic Aspects of the Japanese Writing System.* New York: Academic Press, 1985.

Paradis M, Lecours AR: Aphasia in bilinguals and polyglots. In Lecours AR, Lhermitte F, Bryans B et al., *Aphasiology.* London: Baillère Tindell, pp. 455–464, 1983.

Penfield W: Conditioning the uncommitted cortex for language learning. *Brain: 88,* 787 – 798, 1965.

Perecman E: Spontaneous translation and language mixing in a polyglot aphasic. *Brain Lang.: 23,* 43 – 63, 1984.

Peuser G: Vergleichende Aphasieforschung und Aphasie bei Polyglotten. *Folia Phoniatr.: 26,* 167 – 168, 1974.

Pick A: Zur Erklärung gewisser Ausnahmen von der sogenannten Ribotschen Regel. Abhandlungen aus der Neurologie, Psychiatrie, Psychologie und ihren Grenzgebieter (*Beiheft 13 zur Monatsschr. Psychiatrie Neurol.*): 151 – 167, 1921.

Pitres A: Etude sur l'aphasie chez les polyglottes. *Rev. Méd.: 15,* 873 – 899, 1895.

Pötzl O: Über die parietal bedingte Aphasie und ihren Einfluss auf das Sprechen mehrerer Sprachen. *Z. Gesamte Neurol. Psychiatrie: 96,* 100 – 124, 1925.

Pötzl O: Aphasie und Mehrsprachigkeit. *Z. Gesamte Neurol. Psychiatrie: 124,* 145 – 162, 1930.

Pötzl O: Zum gegenwärtigen Stand der Aphasielehre. *Wien. Med. Wochenschr.: 82,* 783 – 791, 1932.

Quadfasel FA: Discussion of clinical diagnosis and treatment of aphasia. In Osgood CE, Miron MS (Editors), *Approaches to the Study of Aphasia.* Chicago: University of Illinois Press, p. 36, 1963.

Rapport RL, Tan CT, Whitaker HA: Language function and dysfunction among Chinese and English speaking polyglots: Cortical stimulation, Wada testing, and clinical studies. *Brain Lang.: 18,* 342 – 366, 1983.

Regard M, Landis T, Hess K: Preserved stenography reading in a patient with pure alexia. *Arch. Neurol. (Chicago): 42,* 400 – 402, 1985.

Reynolds AF, Turner PT, Harris AB, Ojemann GA, Davis LE: Left thalamic hemorrhage with dysphasia: a report of five cases. *Brain Lang.: 7,* 62 – 73, 1979.

Ribot TH: *Les Maladies de la Mémoire.* Paris: Baillère, 2e édition, 1881.

Scarborough D, Gerard L, Cortese C: Independence of lexical access in bilingual word recognition. *J. Verbal Learning. Verbal Behav.: 23,* 84 – 99, 1984.

Schulze HA: Unterschiedliche Rückbildung einer sensorischer und einer ideokinetischen motorischen Aphasie bei einem Polyglotten. *Psychiatrie, Neurol. Med. Psychol.: 20,* 441 – 445, 1968.

Scoresby-Jackson RE: Case of aphasia with right hemiplegia. *Edinb. Med. J.: 12,* 696 – 706, 1867.

Segalowitz SJ: *Two Sides of the Brain.* Englewood Cliffs, NJ: Prentice Hall, 1983.

Silverberg R, Gordon HW: Differential aphasia in two bilingual individuals. *Neurology: 29,* 51 – 55, 1979.

Sroka H, Solsi P, Bornstein B: Alexia without agraphia with complete recovery. *Confin. Neurol.: 35,* 167 – 173, 1973.

Streifler M, Hofman S: Sinistrad mirror writing and reading after brain concussion in a bi-systemic (oriento-occidental) polyglot. *Cortex: 12,* 356 – 364, 1976.

T'sou BK: Some preliminary observations on aphasia in a Chinese bilingual. *Acta Psychol. Taiwanica: 20,* 57 – 64, 1978.

Vaid J: Bilingualism and brain lateralization. In Segalowitz S (Editor), *Language Functions and Brain Organization.* New York: Academic Press, pp. 315 – 339, 1983.

Vaid J, Genesee F: Neuropsychological approaches to bilingualism. *Can. J. Psychol.: 34,* 417 – 445, 1980.

Van Thal J: Polyglot aphasics. *Folia Phoniatr.: 12,* 123 – 128, 1960.

Veyrac G-J: Etude de l'aphasie chez les sujets polyglottes. Thèse pour le doctorat en médecine, Paris, 1931.

Vildomec V: *Multilingualism.* Leyden: Sythoff, 1963.

Voinescu I, Vish E, Sirian S, Maretsis M: Aphasia in a polyglot. *Brain Lang.: 4,* 165 – 176, 1977.

Wald I: Zagadnienie afazji poliglotow. *Postçpy Neurol. Neurochir. Psychiatrii: 4,* 183 – 211, 1958.

Wald I: Problema Afazii Poliglotov. Moskva: *Voprosy Kliniki i Patofiziologii Afazii,* pp. 140 – 176, 1961.

Watamori T, Sasanuma S: The recovery process of a bilingual aphasic. *J. Commun. Disord.: 9,* 157 – 166, 1976.

Watamori T, Sasanuma S: The recovery process of two English-Japanese bilingual aphasics. *Brain Lang.: 6,* 127 – 140, 1978.

Wechsler A: Crossed aphasia in an illiterate dextral. *Brain Lang.: 3,* 164 – 172, 1976.

Wechsler A: Dissociative alexia. *Arch. Neurol. (Chicago): 3,* 257, 1977.

Weisenburg TH, McBride KE: *Aphasia, a Clinical and Psychological Study.* New York: Commonwealth Fund, 1935.

Whitaker HA, Bub D, Leventer S: Neurolinguistic aspects of language acquisition and bilingualism. In Winitz H (Editor), *Native Language and Foreign Language Acquisition.* New York: New York Academy of Sciences (Annals, Vol. 379), pp. 59 – 74, 1981.

Winterstein O, Meier J: Schäderltrauma und Aphasie bei Mehrsprachigen. *Chirurg: 11,* 229 – 232, 1939.

Wulfeck B, Juarez L, Bates E, Kilborn K: Sentence interpretation strategies in healthy and aphasic bilingual adults. In Vaid J (Editor), *Language Processing in Bilinguals.* Hillsdale, NJ: Lawrence Erlbaum Associates, pp. 199 – 219, 1986.

Yamadori A, Albert ML: Word category aphasia. *Cortex: 9,* 112 – 125, 1973.

Zangwill OL: Two cases of crossed aphasia in dextrals. *Neuropsychologia: 17,* 167 – 172, 1979.

Handbook of Neuropsychology, Vol. 2
F. Boller and J. Grafman (Eds)

CHAPTER 7

Artistry after unilateral brain disease

Joan A. Kaplan and Howard Gardner

Aphasia Research Center, Department of Neurology, Boston University School of Medicine; Boston Veterans Administration Medical Center; and Harvard Project Zero, MA, U.S.A.

Introduction: a cognitive view of the arts

A certain view of the arts has gained wide currency. On this view the arts are seen as primarily the realm of the emotions. Those individuals who create artistic works have a special access to the life of the emotions. Particularly when they are inspired, such individuals can create masterpieces which have the potential to move members of an audience. For their part, audience members participate in the arts for relaxation and amusement. For them, as for the practicing artistic creator, involvement in the arts is primarily an emotional pursuit. Those works are most effective which produce the greatest emotional charge, changes or catharsis in members of an audience.

In reality, however, qualities outside the emotions are also crucial in any artistic activity. To participate in the arts, as a creator or a perceiver, one requires skills specific to a domain (such as understanding tonal structures, pitch patterns and rhythmic configurations in music); further, one must also be able to integrate these components into a composite whole. Any individual competent in the arts must display these abilities; and damage to the brain will necessarily impair these capacities in as yet only partly understood ways.

The philosopher Nelson Goodman has put forth a concept of the arts which takes into account these various component processes. Taking an avowedly cognitive approach, Goodman (1968, 1979) views involvement in the arts as the ability to process certain kinds of symbols and to integrate them into symbol systems. Symbols can take a multiplicity of forms: linguistic, pictorial, musical or otherwise. An individual who would be competent in the arts must be able to traffic in one or more symbol system; and it therefore makes sense to construe artistic competence as a kind of literacy. An artistic creator is an individual who is capable of arranging and organizing symbols in certain kinds of ways – of 'writing with symbols'; and a competent member of an audience is one who is capable of interpreting symbols and combinations of symbols – in short of 'reading symbols'.

No symbol is by itself artistic or non-artistic. A symbol or symbol system enters into the realm of the arts because of the kinds of information it conveys and the ways in which it operates. Take, for example, the symbol system of language. Language is in itself neither artistic nor non-artistic. If language is used in such a way that it can be readily translated, or reworded, or converted into another symbol system, it is not functioning aesthetically; if, on the other hand, the language operates in such a way as to call attention to itself, and if a translation could destroy the significance of the text, then it is likely to be operating in an aesthetic manner (Langer, 1942).

Address correspondence to: Howard Gardner, Psychology Service (116B), Veterans Administration Medical Center, 150 South Huntington Avenue, Boston, MA 02130, U.S.A.

Each symbol system has the potential to be employed artistically, to the extent that it exhibits certain features. According to the point of view which we have developed, a symbol system functions aesthetically to the extent that it exhibits at least some of the following characteristics: (1) it conveys certain moods and is thus *expressive*; (2) it exhibits a characteristic form of detailed texture, or *style*; (3) its component parts are so organized that they have an effective *composition* or sense of *balance*; (4) it conveys a number of meanings, or is at least open to *multiple interpretations*. Artistic symbols need not exhibit all of these properties at any one time; but to the extent that these properties are operative, chances are that one is dealing with an artistic symbol. Hence, literacy in the arts involves the ability to create – or to appreciate – those symbols which function expressively, exhibit a characteristic style, are organized in an effective composition and are susceptible to multiple 'readings'.

In addition to these features which cut across art forms, certain features prove unique to given art forms. In literature, there are features of rhyme, metaphor and narrative structure; in painting, there are aspects of color, form manipulation, perspective, and the like; in music, there are features of rhythm, pitch, harmony, timbre, etc. Sensitivity to an art form requires an ability to detect and to appreciate the functions of these various art-specific elements.

This cognitive viewpoint possesses various advantages to the investigator of artistic activity (see Gardner, 1981, 1982, 1983; Gardner et al., 1974; Winner, 1982). When the arts are considered as areas involving literacy, it is possible to study the ways in which individuals become, or fail to become, literate in one or more art form (and the ways in which such literacy can be compromised following damage to the brain). A focus on the cognitive aspect also frees one from having to tackle issues of value or merit which, while important, have proved particularly refractory to scientific investigation.

Finally, the cognitive approach also bypasses some of the most problematic aspects of the aforementioned 'received view' – that the arts function exclusively in the realm of emotions. There is no denial that arts often elicit or embody emotions. But instead of the artist being seen as a victim of emotional states, he is here construed as someone who can handle a symbolic system so as to convey certain kinds of expressive states. The competent audience member, in turn, knows how to 'read' these symbol systems for emotional meanings. Moreover, the emotional facets of the arts often function cognitively: the experiencing of an emotion can sometimes draw one's attention to the way in which a symbol is working or to a meaning that is being conveyed.

To the neuropsychologist, an investigation of the artistic process can be illuminating. Most neuropsychological investigations have focused on relatively mundane human activities, such as perception of forms or the ability to use language. The question arises as to whether the same kinds of neural mechanisms govern more specialized activities, such as the composing of a symphony, the reading of a novel, the completion of a painting or a ballet.

The arts can also provide a privileged way of investigating certain controversial issues in neuropsychology. For instance, there has been considerable discussion of the optimal way to characterize the two cerebral hemispheres. One favored approach speaks of the dominant hemisphere as being involved in language activities, the nondominant hemisphere as dedicated to non-linguistic activities. Rival characterizations have focused on the issue of rationality versus intuition, with the right hemisphere deemed the particular locus of intuitive capacities. The question thus arises: will the apprehension of poetry, for example, prove to be a 'left hemisphere function' (because one is dealing with language), or a right hemisphere function (because one is dealing with intuitive, or nonrational understanding)? Of course, it may ultimately turn out that both hemispheres participate in poetry, but in characteristic ways.

Conversely, the neuropsychological approach

can help to illuminate issues which have plagued students of the arts. Many have pondered the role played by language in musical composition or in painting a portrait. If it turns out that aphasic individuals are still able to compose, or to paint, at a pre-morbid level, it will have been shown that language is not necessary to these forms of artistic creation.

An examination of the neuropsychological literature

We turn now to a discussion of findings from the neuropsychological literature which bear on human competence in the artistic realm. We will focus on three art forms – music, drawing and literature. While these do not comprise the entire range of art, they are representative of the spectrum (and constitute almost all the studies which have in fact been carried out). These art forms also differ instructively in the extent to which they are language-like. Like ordinary language, the visual arts typically communicate denotational meanings: one can draw a picture of something, or even convey a narrative pictorially. In contrast, though it can be highly expressive, music is entirely non-denotational (except for the odd case of 'program music').

Of course the arts can be compared on other dimensions as well. When it comes to the temporal dimensions, music and language are more similar, though at times even the visual arts can function temporally, as with film.

Two other organizational principles govern our survey. We begin with the more traditional experimental studies, which typically use matched groups of patients and examine basic and, to some extent, particularistic artistic components. We then turn to case studies, which for the most part look at more holistic processes in individuals who were once practicing artists. Within each art form we will look at skills of production – as in the creative artist – and at skills of perception – as in the critic or audience member. When appropriate, and when data are available, we will also

touch upon the fate of analytic or reflective capacities in the brain-injured individual.

It is possible to outline an ideal neuropsychological study of the arts. In such a study one would look at each art form in terms of the four aesthetic components (style, expression, composition and multiple meanings) for the three artistic roles (production, perception and reflection). Moreover, one would then carry out comparisons across art forms, to determine whether production occurs in the same way in music as in drawing, or whether sensitivity to style in one art form predicts sensitivity to style in another art form (see Winner et al., 1986 for an example of this approach).

Unfortunately, the neuropsychology of the arts is at a very early stage and much of this hypothetical grid cannot yet be filled in. Nonetheless it is useful to keep such a grid in mind as we review what has been established about the neuropsychology of the arts.

Music

The many forms of musical competence found in a culture and the many avenues by which musical competence can be achieved, have prompted several researchers to put forth their accounts of the representation of musical capacities in the brain (see Benton, 1977; Gardner, 1981; Gates and Bradshaw, 1977; Judd, 1979; Marin, 1982; Zatorre, 1984). In general, these investigators highlight the central role played by the right hemisphere in the processing of music-specific components.

Initial work revealed the link between right temporal lobe damage and loss of tonal memory and sensitivity to timbre and to intensity (Milner, 1962). Further research emphasized these associations, but also suggested left hemisphere involvement in the processing of rhythm, a time-dependent sequencing task (Sidtis and Volpe, 1981; Zattore, 1979). Zatorre (1984), in his review, stressed the primary role of the right temporal lobe in the processing of unfamiliar melodic sequences, and the importance of the left hemisphere in the processing of familiar sequences.

Observations of patients with left hemisphere damage (or left hemisphere patients) and aphasia often reveal the striking preservation of musical production (specifically through singing). Clinical examinations document that these patients can correctly combine the musical components of melody and pitch in the service of free production (for examples, see Goodglass and Kaplan, 1972). The data point to a dissociation between the production of language and the production of music-specific components (i.e., of words and of pitches). We have observed that, just as melody aids aphasics' language production, language and lyrics often aid right hemisphere damaged patients' (or right hemisphere patients') production of melody.

These findings have also sparked the development of a promising form of aphasia therapy: Melodic Intonation Therapy (Sparks et al., 1974). This therapy exploits aphasics' preserved singing ability in order to facilitate speech reconstruction.

The fact that most individuals do not play musical instruments, and the difficulty of obtaining information on pre-morbid musical skills have doubtless made it difficult to study musical production to the fullest. There have, in contrast, been numerous studies of musical perception in untutored individuals.

In an effort to document perception of the denotative meanings of familiar musical pieces, Gardner et al. (1977) asked patients with right and left hemisphere brain disease to choose the picture (from four possibilities) which 'went with' a given selection of music. Half of the items required knowledge of the lyrics of the piece (e.g., a picture of a boat matched with the melody "Row, row, row your boat"). The other half were taken from pieces where knowledge of the lyrics was unimportant (e.g., the Wedding March), where subjects would only need to recognize the situations in which the piece is customarily played.

Results suggested that right hemisphere patients could extract meaning better than left hemisphere patients in cases of lyrical associations. On the non-lyrical, situationally based comparisons, left hemisphere patients outperformed those with right hemisphere damage. Thus, when knowledge of language is not intrinsic to the task, patients with left hemisphere disease prove more musically competent.

Pursuing the same line of investigation, Gardner et al. (1977) examined organic patients' perception of expression in simple musical fragments. Expression was manifested through the manipulation of musical components (including pitch, tempo, duration and contour). Subjects listened to fragments differing on these musical components. They then matched each item with one of two contrasting geometric patterns. The picture pairs were systematically varied to represent the expressive aspects of musical connotation in the fragments: for example, passages with ascending or descending contours were respectively paired with lines pointing up or down; continuous tones were matched with intact circles, and discontinuous ones with fragmented circles.

An instructive pattern of perceptual skills emerged. Right hemisphere patients achieved success when expression was manifested through temporal features (such as regularity/irregularity) which required that processing be linear; in contrast, they experienced difficulties when expression was represented by gestalt aspects that involved the processing of the entire fragment (such as continuity/discontinuity). Patients with left anterior damage showed the reverse pattern: they proved better at perceiving expressive associations when judging gestalt features than when relying on linear, temporal components.

A few studies have probed brain-damaged patients' reflective judgements and critiques of musical stimuli. To assess reflection on musical structure or composition, Shapiro et al. (1981) presented familiar non-lyrical pieces to subjects in either intact or altered forms and asked them to decide whether that form sounded 'right' or 'wrong'. Compositional errors were created by varying the pitch, tempo, rhythm or phrasing of the original tune.

In this task, left anterior patients displayed skillful detection of most error types, evincing slight difficulty when pieces were played at altered tempos, either rapidly or slowly. Left posterior subjects and subjects with lesions in the peri-sylvian regions showed a somewhat poorer performance than left anterior patients, especially when judging compositions with temporal shifts. However, for *all* types of compositional variation, right anterior patients evinced greater difficulty than any patient group, performing only at chance levels when detecting errors of rhythm or tempo.

In preliminary work, Jacobs, Brownell and Gardner devised a situation which also probed reflective attention to musical composition. Patients heard a musical segment and two possible completions; they were then asked to choose the completion that fit best with the beginning. In these composition judgements, the performance of left hemisphere patients was slightly below that of normal controls (77 vs. 91% correct). But both of these groups far surpassed right hemisphere patients who responded only at chance levels. These findings confirm data from other studies which also suggest the particular importance of the right hemisphere in compositional reflection (Brownell et al., 1982; Shapiro et al., 1981).

On other pairs of musical fragments, Jacobs et al. asked the same subjects to make judgements of musical expression, i.e., choose which of two fragments was more happy, sad, calm or excited. These judgements proved equally difficult for right and left hemisphere patients; both groups responded below the level of normal controls (92% correct) but above chance, with approximately 75% correct judgements.

The pattern of results from our various studies suggests that right hemisphere patients have a decreased capacity to create an internal representation (or auditory image) of specific melodic features and contours. Production, perception and reflection abilities are all affected by this deficit. Patients fail especially when asked to perceive or judge the compositional structure of a musical fragment. In contrast, left hemisphere patients exhibit difficulty chiefly when perceiving tempo.

The errors made by right hemisphere damaged patients highlight the specifically musical nature of their difficulty: in the absence of sensitivity to melodic aspects, the patient is thrown back on non-melodic, linguistic, cues to guide musical involvement and processing. In contrast, left hemisphere patients' processing of melodic features is not aided, but rather confounded, by these cues.

Case studies

A particularly rich view of the links between art and neuropsychology can be obtained through in-depth case studies of brain damaged persons with significant talent in a given domain. Through this method, a researcher can ascertain the consequences of damage on skills and processes directly involved in high level artistic practice, and compare pre- and post-illness works.

Competent musicians can display their skills in a variety of ways: as instrumental performers, singers, conductors or composers. Irrespective of specialization, certain generalizations can be made from case studies of those who have suffered unilateral brain damage. In general, research has shown that despite significant aphasic damage, trained musicians can often regain or retain competence in their field.

The study of these talented musicians opens an area inaccessible to traditional experiments with untrained subjects. That is, one can now assess the effect of brain damage on the ability to read and write music. Intuitively, it would seem likely that aphasic damage, especially in the form of verbal alexia, would go hand-in-hand with a similar 'alexia' for musical symbols. In fact, many examples from case literature cite the opposite phenomenon: preserved ability to read music in the face of Wernicke's aphasia and alexia (Judd et al., 1980, 1983; Soukes and Baruk, 1930) or impaired ability to read music but spared ability to process text (Dorgueille, cited in Benton, 1977).

In the following six cases, which are representative of a larger number in the literature, researchers highlight the issues central to our discussion, giving extensive information about premorbid skill and probing deficits relevant to artistic competence. The first three cases distinguish linguistic and musical reading ability in composers with left posterior damage. They are followed by the case of a conductor with severe global aphasia and apraxia but preserved musical perception and conducting ability. The final two detail the effects of right hemisphere damage on a performer and on a composer.

The case of Shebalin, a renowned Russian composer who suffered a stroke resulting in aphasia, supports recovery of musical skills apart from language (Luria et al., 1965). After recovering from his stroke, Shebalin reportedly returned to composition and teaching. Critics hailed his skills to be equal to premorbid levels.

More recently, an American choral composer, B.L., sustained occipital lobe damage; he presented aphasia and, most notably, complete alexia for language. However, like Shebalin, his compositional and critical capacities in music recovered and enabled him to continue to practice and compose (Judd et al., 1980, 1983). He managed the demands of his work by implementing various compensatory strategies. For example, his alexia made it difficult to set the text of a poem to music, for he could not encode and hold onto the lyrics. To bypass this hurdle, he hired someone to read the lyrics aloud to him repeatedly as he composed, essentially creating an on-line memory on which to call.

Though unable to decode visual symbols essential to language reading, B.L. also had unusually well-preserved music reading ability. He could readily recognize scores even without the capacity to name individual notes or the composition. To aid his recognition and compensate for any reading difficulties, B.L. used the knowledge of formal musical structures and patterns to make accurate inferences about the scores.

In contrast to these two men, when the French composer Ravel sustained left hemisphere damage due to a tumor, he was left a permanent Wernicke's aphasic (Alajouanine, 1948). His deficits clearly dissociate expressive and receptive abilities

in music. His capacity to perceive and appraise musical pieces remained intact; he noticed even minor flaws in performances. He also expressed continued joy in listening to music. However, he never again successfully composed or performed music. The source of his productive deficits is not certain. Quite probably, there were mechanical or symbol decoding difficulties similar to those of B.L. on top of some impairment of musical intelligence.

Basso and Capitani (1985) detail the effects of severe left hemisphere damage on N.S., an Italian musical conductor. He sustained global aphasia and ideomotor apraxia due to cortical and subcortical damage of the left posterior region. His extensive language impairments included a range of difficulties in repetition, reading, writing, and comprehension beyond the single word level. In addition, he presented apraxia in almost all forms: buccofacial, ideomotor and 'apraxia of use' (pantomimes).

N.S.'s musical competence, on the other hand, was relatively spared. To be sure, he could neither name nor write notes, pitches, scales or sequences. However, even with paralysis, his performance of scales and simple unfamiliar pieces on the piano was good and improved with practice (unlike his language functions). His ability to perceive and appraise music remained flawless. Most surprisingly, N.S. continued to conduct orchestral pieces and to communicate with members of the orchestra through gestures. The authors argue that this preservation of gestural skill in conducting was due not to the fact that these were overlearned or automatic gestures but rather because the source of gesture in conducting was musical (not linguistic) processing.

Right hemisphere damage in musicians can result in a loss of musical intelligence (amusia) and especially a discontinuation of musical production, an 'expressive' amusia (see Botez and Wertheim, 1959). McFarland and Fortin (1982) report expressive amusia in an accomplished organist following a right tempero-parietal infarct. The patient was not formally trained in music notation, hence the reading and writing of music could not be assessed. His hearing and language functions remained intact, and he was able to recite rhymes, sing a song and imitate rhythm. Still he could not translate these correct musical perceptions into musical performance of even familiar and simple pieces on the organ. He eventually discontinued any playing partly because he correctly recognized errors in his own performance.

A.A., a composer, suffered a stroke which affected both the right frontal parieto and temporal regions (Judd, Arslenian, Davidson and Locke, unpublished research). Again, following the stroke, his musical understanding was preserved, excepting only subtle perception deficits. He even authored a textbook of music, mastered two foreign languages, and continued to teach music.

However, A.A. did not continue to compose, completely lost interest in the creative process and, in general, felt uninspired. He reported problems "conceiving of a whole piece" and "conjuring up the appropriate atmosphere" for composition. He listened to music infrequently, reportedly because he felt a loss of associations previously connected with hearing musical performances.

These cases together reveal some consistent patterns in the representation of music in the brain. Injury to the left hemisphere, while severely inhibiting linguistic and praxic capacities, seems to preserve musical competence. Left hemisphere damage can result in impairment in the reading of either musical or linguistic notation but, frequently, one or the other is preserved. The high musical intelligence of talented individuals often compensates for difficulties with more language-based systems. This state of affairs helps the conductor or composer with aphasia to continue in his work and overcome even severe language and movement deficits. With the notable exception of Ravel, all aphasic musicians seem able to return to their profession with continued critical acclaim.

When musical competence is affected (frequently following right hemisphere damage), dissociations between expression and reception do occur. Productive capacities can be impaired after brain damage while perceptive and reflective ones are retained. Most significantly, however, after right hemisphere injury, the motivation to continue to create or perform seems particularly compromised.

Drawing

The bulk of research with a variety of subject populations demonstrates a high dissociation between graphic and linguistic capacity. In fact, with only one exception (Bay 1962, 1964), authorities agree that graphic competence can exist at a high level in the case of severe aphasia, even as it can be grossly impaired while language ability remains relatively preserved.

Right hemisphere patients present certain deficits specific to the graphic arts. For example, they exhibit special difficulty in detecting and depicting the third dimension (Marr, 1982). They also tend to neglect the left side of space in artistic renderings as well as in analyses of other visually presented materials. This unilateral neglect is not usually manifested in any comparable pattern by left hemisphere injured aphasics. In experimental designs, compensations for neglect, such as presenting stimulus items to the right visual fields, are incorporated.

A useful conceptualization of graphic competence brings to light each hemisphere's unique contribution to the graphic arts. As conceived by Kaplan (1980), left hemisphere function is necessary for providing the details of a graphic copy or original production, while the right hemisphere assumes a significant role in rendering the overall form or external structure of the chosen object. Hence, a person with left hemisphere damage would likely produce and perceive the frame of a drawing, though he might well fail to integrate details or internal components. Conversely, right hemisphere patients may depict figures rich in detail, but will miss or distort features of external structure.

In general, the quality of brain damaged patients' graphic production has been examined by scanning their reproductions of presented stimuli or their drawings of simple objects from memory. Researchers have focused primarily on compositional features: the ease with which pictures are produced, drawing accuracy, and placement on the page. These productive capacities are sometimes difficult to assess, given hemiparesis in certain aphasic patients, often affecting the dominant hand.

Jones-Gotman and Milner (1977) assessed both the fluency and the accuracy of brain damaged patients' production of graphic symbols. They asked subjects to draw prototypical members of a category, for example vegetables. Their study showed that the right hemisphere plays a significant role in the ease and accuracy with which multiple drawings of a category are produced. Patients with left anterior injury, in contrast to right brain damaged patients, produce many drawings with little difficulty.

The performances of right hemisphere patients reflect some of their graphic compositional deficits. When asked, for example, to "draw a vegetable", they produced bizarre 'nonsense' drawings with extraneous information included (such as a picture of a potato with a stem). In these renditions, each portion of the drawing denoted one type of vegetable; the integration of normally separate pieces, however, rendered the drawing uninterpretable. In contrast, drawings by aphasics prove to be quite recognizable. Interestingly, fluent aphasics frequently cannot name their accurately represented depiction of a given object (Grossman, 1980).

To assess compositional accuracy, Gainotti et al. (1983) asked subjects to draw specific simple objects from memory, after they had successfully named and copied the object. Aphasics, especially those with lexical impairment, displayed great difficulty in completing the task. Right hemisphere patients, on the other hand, performed at the level of non-brain damaged controls. It is possible that the activity of linguistic encoding aided right hemisphere patients on this graphic task, just as lyrics have sometimes aided their singing.

There is scant evidence concerning patients' competence in perceiving or appraising the aesthetic nature of symbols. Initial studies by Gardner (1975a) documented specific difficulty of right hemisphere patients in perceiving the styles of works of art. When asked to group together works produced by the same artist, right hemisphere patients tended to associate those pieces which depicted the same subject matter instead of those exhibiting the same artistic style. Aphasic patients demonstrated normal or even better-than-normal competence at the stylistic groupings. Their superior ability could have possibly been due to their diminished perception of, or interest in, the subject matter.

A preliminary study explored brain damaged patients' attention to, and reflections about, composition and expression in graphic productions (Jacobs and Gardner, in progress). On a composition task, subjects were shown two pictures and asked to choose which they thought had been 'completed correctly'. Both aphasics and normal controls performed with 90% accuracy, while right hemisphere patients responded only at chance levels. An expression task required judgements on which of two pictures was the more happy, sad, calm or excited. The performance of both aphasics and right hemisphere patients was similar and above chance (75% correct) but below that of normal controls (90%).

Just as the preserved musical capacity of aphasic patients inspired melodic intonation therapy, the excellent graphic capacities of many aphasic patients have suggested a therapeutic innovation. A visual communication system (VIC), in which graphic symbols stand for both substantive objects and for grammatical particles, has been devised and used with severe global aphasics. Initially, this system was used with simple index cards (Baker et al., 1975; Gardner et al., 1976) and, more recently, it has been implemented on a personal computer (Steele et al., 1986). These pilot studies indicate a surprising degree of preserved communicational skills in this hitherto hapless population; and, at least in selected cases, the 'deblocking' engendered by VIC seems to have aided the recovery of some spontaneous propositional speech.

In summary, studies probing production, perception and reflection in the graphic arts do suggest distinct competences for each hemisphere and a central integrating role for the right hemisphere. The processing of features of style and composition are most clearly guided by right hemisphere functions. Deficits of aphasics, though they exist, seem to be more amenable to rehabilitation or spontaneous recovery (Swindell et al., 1987). Surprisingly, sensitivity to expression in graphic art productions proved comparable in both patient groups. It could be that expressivity is represented differently in the brain, for example, more limbically, more diffusely or subcortically.

Case studies

The dissociation between artistic and linguistic capacity discerned in the case of music seems at least as dramatic in the graphic arts. Research on talented graphic artists reveals that this dissociation is even more pronounced when an individual has been trained in the field. In support of this phenomenon, Alajouanine (1948) reported the case of a French artist who became severely aphasic after suffering left hemisphere injury. After recovery, the painter returned to work without any change in his artistic technique or style. The artist himself was awed by his preserved graphic skill. He described the perplexing nature of his condition as a manifestation of the "two men in [him]", the "normal" painter and the "lost fool" (p. 238).

Though an artist may continue to create, at times, more subtle changes in his or her work may result from brain damage. Perception and production of the graphic symbols may not be completely lost but significantly altered. For instance, Z.B., a Bulgarian painter suffered severe aphasic damage and complete right sided paralysis (Zaimov et al., 1969). Though originally right handed, he taught himself to work with his left hand and thereby continued his drawing and painting. This shift presented little problem for Z.B.; he did, however,

develop a new painting style. His post-stroke works placed less emphasis on narrative depictions and incorporated dreamlike images non-existent in earlier work.

Specific brain damage can on occasion distinguish components which appear indissociable in normal artists. Such was the case in the investigation by Wapner et al. (1978) of a visually agnosic amateur artist. Though his language abilities remained intact, the artist was completely unable to recognize and name objects presented to him. When asked to copy objects or pictures placed in front of him, his best drawings resembled slavish photographic renditions. Frequently, the drawing would be perfect in parts, but he often lost his place and did not proceed with any sense of the figure's unity. In the end, each part would be preserved with considerable fidelity, but one had to puzzle out what the object was as a whole. Further, even after drawings were made, the subject could still not identify what he had just completed.

In contrast to this, when asked to render objects from memory, the aphasic patient would draw quite facilely, retrieving overlearned schemata which he had presumably used hundreds of times in the past. In rare cases where he could name a presented object, he would abandon the slavish approach and instead utilize this more schematic representation in his 'copies'.

These two methods can be viewed as separate mechanisms of graphic competence: (1) a faithful copying which relies on a direct translation into motor patterns of perceived shape; and (2) a more schematic style, exploiting details and structures of the object as they have become internally represented over many earlier drawing attempts. Presumably, the two mechanisms are so intertwined in intact individuals, that only in brain damaged persons can they become disentangled.

Only a few examples exist of right hemisphere patients who continued to paint at all after damage. The cases of two German expressionist painters highlight some of the deficits which can be expected in this condition (Jung, 1974, reported in Gardner and Winner, 1981). After partial recovery from right hemisphere strokes, both painters returned to work. Their productions initially demonstrated a neglect of the left side of space, irregular contours and misplaced or fuzzy details. With recovery, neglect receded; however, drawing style was fundamentally altered. In contrast to premorbid work, which was characterized by light and faithful realism, the output of these artists featured a bizarre, emotionally primitive style with rough lines and grotesque effects (Gardner, 1975b).

It seems apparent that unilateral left hemisphere damage and subsequent language deficits do not render production impossible for the graphic artist. Strikingly, language abilities are not a prerequisite for continued participation. Aphasic artists do not lose the capacity to render or perceive details of a production. And those artists described here frequently continued to work with only stylistic changes (which, in the case of Z.B., could have also been due to the forced shift in handedness after damage).

Our examples reveal that right hemisphere damage, even in highly trained artists, results in a neglect of the left side of space. More importantly, though, if the artist continues to work after injury, his work may exhibit distinct stylistic changes. Paintings most prominently include a heightened emotionality and more primitive emotional expressions.

Literature

It is commonly accepted that the basic (domain-specific) components of language, e.g., syntax and semantics, are strongly lateralized in the left hemisphere; thus, a significant left hemisphere lesion almost always produces some aphasia. However, the right hemisphere has been found to play a major role in language, as well. The right hemisphere can mediate the production of overlearned phrases, such as 'How are you?' (Taylor, 1932), the access of certain vocabulary and syntax (Gazzaniga, 1970; Zaidel, 1973, 1978), and the understanding of the connotation of words

(Brownell et al., 1986).

Though the literary arts are necessarily dependent on language, the production and perception of literature draw on skills far beyond those of basic language. In literature, one must be able to incorporate the aesthetic properties of symbols: multiple meanings in non-literal language, the compositional rules applied to narrative structure, stylistic and expressive features of prose and poetry. The examination of right and left brain damaged individuals helps illuminate each hemisphere's contribution to literary competence.

Predictions about competence in literature after unilateral brain disease could follow two different tacks. From one perspective, one could view an aphasic's basic problems with language as impediments to his apprehension of any artistic features of literature; and, correlatively, a right hemisphere patient's facility with the basic features of language as facilitating deeper literary understanding. On the other hand, one could claim that the ability to interpret context and pragmatic aspects of language would be preserved in aphasics: according to this view, those with right hemisphere damage might be consigned to a literal and concrete interpretation of literary work.

For obvious reasons, assessments of the ability of aphasics to produce either spoken or written literature has been limited. There have, however, been studies of brain damaged patients' perceptual and receptive capacities. One study of sensitivity to metaphor (Winner and Gardner, 1977) showed that aphasic patients had difficulty paraphrasing a linguistic metaphor like a 'heavy heart' or a 'loud tie'. However, they succeeded when the task was presented in a non-linguistic mode. In the latter format, the metaphor had to be matched with the most appropriate picture of a set of four. For 'heavy heart', one drawing represented the metaphoric interpretation (e.g., a man crying), another depicted a literal representation (e.g., a man carrying a large, heavy heart shaped object in a wheelbarrow), and the final two were, respectively, adjective and noun foils (e.g., a 500-pound weight and a simple red heart). Aphasics frequently chose the correct metaphoric depictions. That is, their performance proved comparable to that of non-brain damaged controls. Right brain damaged patients showed a different response pattern. In contrast to aphasics, right hemisphere patients more frequently chose responses depicting literal rather than metaphoric representations of stimuli.

Recent work has explored interpretations of another type of non-literal language, indirect requests (Foldi, 1987; Hirst et al., 1984; Weylman et al., 1986). Here subjects must again distinguish two levels of meaning: that of the speaker, and that of the sentence. In the Weylman et al. paradigm, subjects heard and commented upon short stories. In one story, for example, two brothers sit in the kitchen discussing their chores for the week. At the end of the story, one brother asks the other, 'Can you walk the dog?'.

When asked to choose the most appropriate response from a set of four verbally presented options, aphasic patients were likely to respond similarly to (though not so flawlessly as) age-matched controls. Both groups chose the correct response, 'Yes, I'll do it right away' as best. Aphasics could differentiate the speaker's intended meaning from the sentence's literal request for information. Their impairments in basic language were also revealed in this study. Their responses were more often correct if the request was phrased in conventional ways (as above) than if "can" was replaced by the more circuitous "is it possible for you to".

Right hemisphere patients exhibited difficulties in using context to infer meaning beyond the surface level. When the brother asked 'Can you walk the dog?' in the above context, a right hemisphere damaged patient was more likely than an aphasic or a normal control to regard the concrete, 'Yes, I've been allowed to for two years now' as the appropriate retort.

While, as these studies show, contextual information contributes importantly to the appreciation of literary elements, there are also key structural features which must be apprehended. It is possible to subject narrative discourse to a grammatical type of analysis, indicating the formal features which are obligatory or optional in a particular literary form. Thus, for example, in the case of humorous narratives like jokes, a punchline is expected, but only at a certain place in the narrative. A grammatical analysis of this type can give insight into patients' processing of narrative composition.

In a series of studies in our laboratory, it has been shown that right hemisphere patients have a flawed sense of the 'grammar' of jokes. To apprehend a joke appropriately, the subject must first note that the punch line represents a surprise; but then the surprise must somehow be melded to content in the 'body' of the joke in order to produce a coherent interpretation. We found that right hemisphere patients are sensitive to the surprise element but are unable to make the coherent interpretation of results. Thus they show a predilection for endings which feature humorous non-sequiturs rather than ones which cohere with the body of the joke (Bihrle et al., 1986; Brownell et al., 1983; Gardner et al., 1983; Gardner et al., 1975).

Other studies of narrative competence reinforce this general picture (Delis et al., 1983; Gardner et al., 1983; Joanette et al., 1986; Moya et al., 1986; Wapner et al., 1981). Right hemisphere patients retain the facts of a story but are unable to order events properly or to figure out the moral or central point of the narrative. They have difficulties in drawing inferences from a statement and show an extreme reluctance to abandon a line of inference, once it has been initiated (Brownell et al., 1986). They also show a peculiar insensitivity to the line between fact and fiction, often accepting bizarre elements in a narrative, or themselves confabulating events which could not possibly have happened to them.

In one study, Gardner and colleagues (1983) attempted to assess sensitivity to narrative forms in a direct fashion. They added bizarre, non-canonical elements into stimulus items and probed how different subject groups incorporated this erroneous information in narrative retellings. As a general rule, normal subjects challenged the bizarre pieces and refused to incorporate them; aphasics altered the false information so that in its new form the overall story context would remain uniform. But right hemisphere patients accepted the given information and included it in retellings, sometimes offering elaborate justifications for its inclusion during probings. Once again, to the extent that they can be assessed on such tasks, left hemisphere patients show little comparable difficulty in appreciating the line between the plausible and the bizarre.

In general, then, despite their overt linguistic competence, right hemisphere patients display an impoverished ability to handle complex narratives and figurative language. They show a tendency to take language literally, they fail to analyse speaker meaning apart from utterance meaning, and they have difficulty in integrating elements into a coherent and sensible whole. It is of course difficult to assess left hemisphere patients on some of these measures; but to the extent that it can be done, and particularly when these competences are tapped in non-linguistic forms, these patients show a surprising degree of preserved sensitivity to humor, narrative structure and figurative meanings.

It would be virtually incredible, however, to hear of an aphasic writer who continued to practice in the absence of a rapid recovery. In fact, few such cases exist, even when considering patients with marked recovery. Basic language skills as well as competence in integration and inferencing (i.e. the abilities of both hemispheres) are necessary for success as a writer or a literary critic. Perhaps as a result, extensive case work has not been attempted with writers or critics suffering from unilateral brain damage.

However, various case studies, though not well documented, point out that aphasic damage does have different effects on some writers than others. Baudelaire, for example, suffered such severe damage that not only was he never able to write again, but he could utter no word other than the French cré-nom. On the other hand, according to Plimpton (1977), William Carlos Williams suf-

fered an aphasia but after recovery did continue to produce poetry. In addition, after recovering from aphasia, some physicians have been able to document their experience and rehabilitation (Gardner, 1975b).

There is little direct evidence about the effect of right hemisphere injury on writing and compositional ability. There are occasional examples of professionals whose jobs include writing skills, such as historians or lawyers, who have been able to continue their practice even after sustaining significant injury (Lezak, 1979). However, Associate Justice William O. Douglas, once an active, articulate contributor to the Supreme Court, provides a contrast. After a major right hemisphere stroke, Douglas manifested bizarre changes in his language and personality (Woodward and Armstrong, 1979). His oral productions and his comprehension of court cases were reported to be incorrect and often irrelevant. Eventually, he was forced to resign but, even after his resignation, he continued to make failed attempts to hear cases and write opinions. His right hemisphere damage clearly left him unable to attend properly to the linguistic and conceptual demands of his position.

It seems that language and literature are so inextricably linked that even writers cannot escape. Recovery from aphasia or right hemisphere damage could possibly leave someone able to write and even compose, but the cases described here seem very much the exception rather than the rule.

Concluding note: the implications of artistic studies for communication in aphasia

The cognitive study of artistic abilities is a new area of exploration, and its application to neuropsychology has just begun. We have outlined a possible research strategy — as captured in our idealized grid. To the extent that researchers can fill in the grid, and to the extent that their findings prove consistent with one another, we may one day secure a cognitive neuropsychology of the arts.

Our brief overview of experimental and case

studies in three art forms has yielded some tentative conclusions. In all three art forms, unilateral injury to the right hemisphere results in a significant impairment of performance. This result occurs with normal subjects on simple artistic tasks, and it occurs as well with practicing artists engaged in their work. There are exceptions, to be sure, but in general the right hemisphere seems to play an important – indeed a crucial – role in various cognitive facets of the arts. We find deficits in perception, production and reflection, as well as hints of a more general lessening of interest in involvement in the arts.

Perhaps surprisingly, an individual can sustain significant injury to the left hemisphere, including a severe aphasia, and still remain competent in the arts. In fact, in the case of the visual and musical arts, such selective sparing of abilities is not uncommon. Of course, to the extent that the artistic capacity relies on natural language, impairments can be expected; yet it is often possible to circumvent or minimize the linguistic import and, in such cases, artistry can flourish despite an aphasia.

In addition to its intrinsic scientific interest, this finding has important therapeutic implications. We have seen that spared musical capacities in aphasic patients led to the selective launching of Melodic Intonation Therapy; and, by the same token, the spared graphic capacities of aphasic patients have facilitated the devising and the testing of an effective means of visual communication. In all likelihood, other kinds of therapy could also exploit the spared artistry in the aphasic patients in the service of communication.

A final point concerns the pragmatics of language in aphasic patients. While aphasia inevitably compromises the ability to carry out basic syntactic and semantic operations, it may well leave relatively intact various kinds of pragmatic capacities: sensitivity to non-literal language (as in metaphor or sarcasm); appreciation of narrative forms in stories and jokes; the capacities to draw inferences or to integrate disparate linguistic points; and the potential to employ paralinguistic channels, such as those involved in gesture or intonation. These pragmatic capacities ought to be carefully noted and exploited, because they may spell the difference between effective and ineffective communication in aphasic patients.

Acknowledgements

This research was supported by NIH Grants NS 11408 and 06209, the Research Service of the Veterans Administration and Harvard Project Zero. We are especially grateful to Nancy Lefkowitz, Director of Speech and Language Pathology, and other personnel of the Spaulding Rehabilitation Hospital for their help and support in the conduct of our work.

References

Alajouanine T: Aphasia and artistic realization. *Brain: 71,* 229 – 241, 1948.

Baker E, Berry T, Gardner H, Zurif E, Davis L, Veroff A: Can linguistic competence be dissociated from natural language functions? *Nature: 254,* 509 – 510, 1975.

Basso A, Capitani E: Spared musical abilities in a conductor with global aphasia and ideomotor apraxia. *J. Neurol. Neurosurg. Psychiatry: 48,* 407 – 412, 1985.

Bay E: Aphasia and non-verbal disorders of language. *Brain: 85,* 411 – 426, 1962.

Bay E: Present concepts of aphasia. *Geriatrics: 19,* 319 – 331, 1964.

Benton AL: The amusias. In Critchley M, Henson RA (Editors), *Music and The Brain.* London: Churchill Livingstone, Ch. 22, pp. 378 – 397, 1977.

Bihrle AM, Brownell HH, Powelson JA, Gardner H: Comprehension of humorous and non-homorous materials by left and right brain damaged patients. *Brain Cognition: 5,* 399 – 411, 1986.

Botez MI, Wertheim N: Expressive aphasia and amusia following right frontal lesion in a right handed man. *Brain: 82,* 186 – 201, 1959.

Brownell HH, Postlethwaite W, Seibold M, Gardner H: Sensitivity to musical key and pitch height in organic patients. Paper presented at the International Neuropsychological Society Meeting, Pittsburgh, February 1982.

Brownell HH, Michel D, Powelson J, Gardner H: Surprise but not coherence: sensitivity to verbal humor in right-hemisphere patients. *Brain Lang.: 18,* 20 – 27, 1983.

Brownell HH, Potter HH, Michelow D, Gardner H: Sensitivity to lexical denotation and connotation in brain-damaged patients: a double dissociation? *Brain Lang.: 22,* 253 – 265, 1984.

Brownell HH, Potter HH, Bihrle AM, Gardner H: Inference deficits in right brain-damaged patients. *Brain Lang.: 27,* 310 – 321, 1986.

Delis DC, Wapner W, Gardner H, Moses JA: The contribution of the right hemisphere to the organization of paragraphs. *Cortex: 19,* 43 – 50, 1983.

Foldi NS: Appreciation of pragmatic interpretations of indirect commands: comparison of right and left hemisphere brain-damaged patients. *Brain Lang.: 31,* 88 – 108, 1987.

Gainotti G, Silveri MC, Villa G, Caltagirone C: Drawing objects from memory in aphasia. *Brain: 106,* 613 – 622, 1983.

Gardner H: Artistry following aphasia. Paper presented at the Academy of Aphasia, Victoria, British Columbia, October 1975a.

Gardner H: *The shattered mind.* New York: Knopf, 1975b.

Gardner H: Artistry following damage to the human brain. In Ellis A (Editor), *Normality and Pathology in Cognitive Functions.* London: Academic Press, Ch. 10, pp. 299 – 323, 1981.

Gardner H: *Art, Mind, and Brain: A Cognitive Approach to Creativity.* New York: Basic Books, 1982.

Gardner H: *Frames of Mind.* New York: Basic Books, 1983.

Gardner H, Winner E: Artistry and aphasia. In Sarno MT (Editor), *Acquired Aphasia.* New York: Academic Press, Ch. 12, pp. 361 – 384, 1981.

Gardner H, Howard V, Perkins D: Symbol systems: philosophical, psychological, and educational investigation. In Olson D (Editor), *Media and Symbols: The Forms of Expression, Communication, and Education.* Chicago: University of Chicago Press, Ch. 2, pp. 27 – 56, 1974.

Gardner H, Ling K, Flamm L, Silverman J: Comprehension and appreciation of humor in brain-damaged patients. *Brain: 98,* 399 – 412, 1975.

Gardner H, Zurif EB, Berry T, Baker E: Visual communication in aphasia. *Neuropsychologia: 14,* 275 – 292, 1976.

Gardner H, Silverman J, Denes G, Semenza C, Rosenstiel A: Sensitivity to musical denotation and connotation in organic patients. *Cortex: 13,* 243 – 256, 1977.

Gardner H, Brownell HH, Wapner W, Michelow D: Missing the point: the role of the right hemisphere in the processing of complex linguistic materials. In Perecman E (Editor), *Cognitive Processing in the Right Hemisphere.* New York: Academic Press, Ch. 9, pp. 169 – 191, 1983.

Gates A, Bradshaw J: The role of the cerebral hemisphere in music. *Brain Lang.: 4,* 403 – 431, 1977.

Gazzaniga M: *The Bisected Brain.* New York: Appleton, 1970.

Goodglass H, Kaplan E: *Assessment of Aphasia.* Philadelphia: Lea and Febiger, 1972.

Goodman N: *Languages of Art.* Indianapolis: Bobbs-Merrill, 1968.

Goodman N: *Ways of Worldmaking.* Indianapolis: Hackett, 1979.

Grossman M: Figurative referential skills after brain damage. Paper presented at the International Neuropsychological Society, San Diego, February 1980.

Hirst W, LeDoux J, Stein S: Constraints on the processing of indirect speech acts: Evidence of aphasiology. *Brain Lang.: 23,* 26 – 33, 1984.

Jacobs J, Brownell HH, Gardner H: Sensitivity to composition and expression in music. Unpublished research.

Jacobs J, Gardner H: Expression and composition in visual art. Unpublished research.

Joanette Y, Goulet B, Ska B, Nespoulous J-L: Information content of narrative discourse in right brain-damaged right-handers. *Brain Lang.: 29,* 81 – 105, 1986.

Jones-Gotman M, Milner B: Design fluency: the invention of nonsense drawings after local cortical lesions. *Neuropsychologia: 15,* 653 – 674, 1977.

Judd T: Towards a neuromusicology: the effects of brain damage on music reading and musical creativity. Unpublished doctoral dissertation. Cornell University, 1979.

Judd T, Gardner H, Geshwind N: Alexia without agraphia in a composer. *Project Zero Technical Report No. 15,* 1980.

Judd T, Gardner H, Geshwind N: Alexia without agraphia in a composer. *Brain: 106,* 435 – 457, 1983.

Kaplan E: Presidential address, Internatioinal Neuropsychology Society, San Diego, February 1980.

Langer SK: *Philosophy in a New Key: A Study in the Symbolism of Reason, Rite, and Art.* Cambridge, MA: Harvard University Press, 1942.

Lezak MD: Behavioral concomitants of configurational disorganization in right hemisphere damaged patients. Unpublished paper, Portland, Oregon, 1979.

Luria AR, Tsvetkova LS, Futer DS: Aphasia in a composer. *J. Neurol. Sci.: 2,* 288 – 292, 1965.

Marin OSM: Neurological aspects of music perception and performance. In Deutsch D (Editor), *The Psychology of Music.* New York: Academic Press, 1982.

Marr D: *Vision: A Computational Investigation into the Human Representation and Processing of Visual Information.* San Francisco: WH Freeman, 1982.

McFarland HR, Fortin D: Amusia due to right temporoparietal infarct. *Arch. Neurol. (Chicago): 39,* 725 – 727, 1982.

Milner B: Laterality effects in audition. In Mountcastle VB (Editor), *Interhemispheric Relations and Cerebral Dominance.* Baltimore: Johns Hopkins University Press, Ch. 9, pp. 177 – 195, 1962.

Moya KL, Benowitz LI, Levine DN, Finklestein S: Covariant defects in visuospatial abilities and recall of verbal narrative after right hemisphere stroke. *Cortex: 22,* 381 – 397, 1986.

Plimpton G (Editor): *Writers at work, Vol. 3.* New York: Penguin, 1977.

Shapiro B, Grossman M, Gardner H: Selective musical processing deficits in brain damaged populations. *Neuropsychologia: 18,* 21 – 31, 1981.

Sidtis JJ, Volpe BT: Right hemisphere lateralization of complex pitch perception: a possible basis for amusia. Paper presented at the International Neuropsychological Society, February 1981.

Soukes A, Baruk H: Autopsie d'un case d'amusie (avec aphasie) chez un professeur de piano. *Rev. Neurol.: 1,* 545 – 556, 1930.

Sparks R, Helm N, Albert M: Aphasia rehabilitation resulting from melodic intonation therapy. *Cortex: 10,* 303 – 316, 1974.

Steele RD, Weinrich M, Wertz RT, Carlson GS: A microcomputer-based visual communication system for treating severe aphasia. Paper presented at the Academy of Aphasia. Nashville, October 1986.

Swindell CS, Holland AL, Fromm D, Greenhouse JB: Characteristics of recovery of drawing ability in left and right brain damaged patients. *Brain Cognition:* in press, 1987.

Taylor J (Editor); *Selected Writings of John Hughlings Jackson, Volumes 1 and 2.* London: Hodder and Stoughton, 1932.

Wapner W, Hamby S, Gardner H: The role of the right hemisphere in the organizatioin of complex linguistic materials. *Brain Lang.: 14,* 15 – 33, 1981.

Wapner W, Judd T, Gardner H: Visual agnosia in an artist. *Cortex: 14,* 343 – 364, 1978.

Weylman ST, Brownell HH, Gardner H: Comprehension of indirect requests by organic patients: sensitivity to contextual information and conventionality of form. Paper presented at the Academy of Aphasia, Nashville, October 1986.

Winner E: *Invented Worlds: An Introduction to the Psychology of Art.* Cambridge: Harvard University Press, 1982.

Winner E and Gardner H: The comprehension of metaphor in brain-damaged patients. *Brain: 100,* 719 – 727, 1977.

Winner E, Rosenblatt E, Windmueller G, Davidson L, Gardner H: Children's perception of 'aesthetic' properties of the arts: domain-specific or pan-artistic? *Br. J. Dev. Psychol.: 4,* 149 – 160, 1986.

Woodward R, Armstrong S: *The brethren.* New York: Simon and Schuster, 1979.

Zaidel E: Linguistic competence and related functions in the right hemisphere following cerebral commissurotomy and hemispherectomy. Unpublished doctoral dissertation, California Institute of Technology, 1973.

Zaidel E: Auditory language comprehension in the right hemisphere following cerebral commissurotomy and hemispherectomy: a comparison with child language and aphasia. In Caramazza A, Zurif EB (Editors), *Language Acquisition and Lanuage Breakdown: Parallels and Divergences.* Baltimore, MD: Johns Hopkins Press. Ch. 12, pp. 229 – 275, 1978.

Zaimov K, Kitov D, Kolev N: Aphasie chez un peintre. *Encephale: 68,* 377 – 417, 1969.

Zatorre RJ: Recognition of dichotic melodies by musicians and non-musicians. *Neuropsychologia: 17,* 607 – 617, 1979.

Zatorre RJ: Musical perception and cerebral function: a critical review. *Music Percept.: 2,* 196 – 221, 1984.

© 1989 Elsevier Science Publishers B.V. (Biomedical Division)
Handbook of Neuropsychology, Vol. 2
F. Boller and J. Grafman (Eds)

CHAPTER 8

Sign-language aphasia

Howard Poizner[1], Ursula Bellugi[1] and Edward S. Klima[2]

[1] The Salk Institute for Biological Studies, P.O. Box 85800, San Diego, CA 92138, and [2] University of California, San Diego, Department of Linguistics, La Jolla, CA 92093, U.S.A.

Language in a visuospatial modality

One of the most striking findings in the study of the relationship between the structure of the human brain and behavioral functioning is differential cerebral dominance. Abundant evidence indicates that language processing (at least for such core aspects of the grammar of a language as phonology, morphology, and syntax) is generally a left hemisphere function; on the other hand the processing of visuospatial relations is generally a right hemisphere function. This evidence was obtained with hearing subjects, whose language was a spoken one.

Sign languages raise an interesting question with respect to this dichotomy, for, unlike the case with spoken languages, in American Sign Language (ASL), as well as in the other sign languages so far investigated, the *linguistic* signal is *spatially* organized. Because ASL involves both complex grammatical structure and complex spatial relations, it exhibits properties for which each of the hemispheres of hearing people shows a differing specialization. Deaf people who have been deprived of auditory experience and who rely on a sign language for their principal mode of communication throughout their lives thus provide a privileged testing ground for investigating how the brain is organized for language, how that organization relates to language modality, and how modifiable that organization may be.

This chapter reviews the evidence on brain organization for sign language from analysis of sign language breakdown following localized lesions to the brains of deaf signers. Since the field is only newly emerging, we focus here on recent studies that directly compare the language capacities of left with right brain-lesioned signers. These studies may have important implications for our theoretical understanding of the neural mechanisms underlying the human linguistic capacity. In order to bring these issues into focus, a brief description of the linguistic structure of ASL is first presented.

ASL exhibits formal structuring at the same two levels as spoken language (lexicon and grammar). There is a sublexical level whereby signs are formed from limited sets of elements which are themselves meaningless (a set of hand configurations, a set of places of articulation, a set of movements), and a second level of structure whereby morphologically complex signs are formed and signs are assembled into sentences according to formal rules of syntax. ASL is a heavily inflected language, with sentence contexts requiring particular grammatical inflections. However, the ultimate form these structures assume in this visual-gestural language is deeply rooted in the modality in which it developed and reflects properties specially offered by the modality. The inflectional devices of ASL, for example, make structured use of space and movement, nesting the basic sign stem in spatial patterns and complex dynamic contours.

ASL displays a marked penchant for layered organization, which is a pervasive structural characteristic at all levels of structure (Bellugi, 1980; Poizner et al., 1986a). This layered organization is most pronounced in the structure of the lexical items and in the morphological processes. The inflectional and derivational processes are conveyed as an isolable, co-occurring layer of structure. But even in the syntax and discourse structure, where there is certainly also linear organization, layering is still pervasive. The isolability of this layer of structure is demonstrated by the highly accurate identification of ASL inflections when inflected signs are presented as dynamic point-light displays in which only movement is conveyed (Poizner et al., 1981).

But the most significant distinguishing aspect of sign languages, and one that is crucial for understanding brain organization for language, is the unique role of *space*. Spatial contrasts and spatial manipulations figure structurally at all linguistic levels. Four ways that space functions in ASL (see Fig. 1) are as follows. (a) *Lexical contrasts:* spatial locus with respect to the body (forehead, nose, chin, etc.) minimally differentiates lexical signs at their place of articulation. The structural description of lexical units consists of features specifying the sign's spatial relation with the body, in conjunction with the features specifying the handshape, the orientation of the hand, and the movement of the hand(s). (b) *Morphological contrasts:* grammatical inflections are differentiated by planes of signing space in which the hands move, as well as different geometric contours (lines, arcs or circles). (c) *Syntactic contrasts:* the manipulation of space also figures structurally at the syntactic and discourse levels. Nominals introduced into the discourse are assigned arbitrary reference points in a horizontal plane of signing space; signs with pronominal function are directed toward these points and in a large class of verb signs their movement between such points specifies grammatical relations (subject of, object of). Thus in ASL a grammatical function served in many spoken languages by case marking or by linear

ordering of words is fulfilled by spatial mechanisms (Klima and Bellugi, 1979). Fig. 1 presents highlights of the use of space at each of the linguistic levels. (d) *Spatial mapping:* as opposed to its syntactic use, space in ASL may also function in a topographic way; the space within which signs are articulated can be used to convey the layout of objects in 'actual' space. In such 'spatial mapping,' the spatial relation of the signs (the location where they are articulated in articulatory space) corresponds in a topographic manner to the spatial relations of the objects described.

At all levels, then, spatial-locational contrasts convey linguistic information. Thus processing linguistic structures in sign languages also involves processing visuospatial relations. But the processing of spatial relations has otherwise been found to show *right* hemisphere specialization. What then is the effect on the organization of the brain for language when spatial relations have grammatical function?

Brain organization for visuospatial language

Until recently, little has been known about brain organization for sign language. Two lines of experimentation have been used to address the issue, one using normal deaf signers, and the other, brain-damaged signers. Investigating the lateralization of sign language within the paradigms used for other visual material in normal subjects is complicated by the difficulty of capturing movement in the very brief exposure necessary to (initially) stimulate one hemisphere exclusively. Investigators have generally presented static line drawings or photographs of signs tachistoscopically to the visual hemifields (see Poizner and Battison, 1980; Ross, 1983; Kettrick and Hatfield, 1986, for reviews). In general, more right than left hemisphere involvement has been found (but see Neville and Bellugi, 1978). One study presented moving signs (Poizner et al., 1979) and found a shift from right dominance to a more balanced hemispheric involvement with a change from static to moving signs. This shift is consistent with

LEXICON

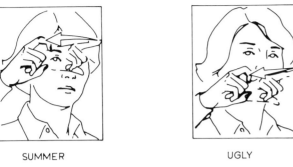

SUMMER   UGLY   DRY

Spatial Contrasts in the Lexicon

MORPHOLOGY

GIVE (uninflected)   GIVE [Index : to me]   GIVE [Habitual]   GIVE [Multiple]

GIVE [Allocative Determinant]   GIVE [Durational]   GIVE [Exhaustive]   GIVE [[Durational] Exhaustive]

Layered Structure of Inflectional Processes

SYNTAX

MOTHER   ₃₁FORCE₃ⱼ   ₃ⱼGIVE₃ₖ   DOX

Sentences with Verb Complement Structures

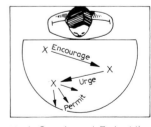

Verb Complement Embedding

Spatially Organized Syntax

Fig. 1. Linguistic spatial mechanisms in American Sign Language.

Kimura's (1979, 1982) position that the left hemisphere predominates in the analysis of skilled motor sequencing. In summary, however, greater right hemisphere involvement has been found in tachistoscopic presentations of *static* signs, probably reflecting the visuospatial preprocessing required of these static pictures.

New experiments using computer presentation of moving signs to the visual fields have in fact obtained significant left hemisphere dominance in normal signers. This left hemisphere dominance for moving ASL signs is emerging both for the identification of computer-synthesized signs (Poizner and Bellugi, 1984) and for signs that have been digitized and presented computergraphically (Neville, in preparation).

Kimura (1981) and Poizner et al. (1987) review the evidence from clinical studies. There have been fewer than 20 reported cases of effects of unilateral brain damage in deaf signers, including Battison (1979), Chiarello et al. (1982), Critchley (1938), Douglass and Richardson (1959), Kimura et al. (1982), Leischner (1943), Poizner et al. (1987) and Sarno et al. (1969). Unlike the tachistoscopic studies, these cases have repeatedly shown left hemisphere involvement. Not all of the cases were easily interpretable with respect to the possible breakdown of sign language, since systematic studies of the grammatical structure of sign languages have only recently become available (Bellugi, 1980; Klima and Bellugi, 1979; Lane and Grosjean, 1980; Liddell, 1984; Padden and Perlmutter, 1987).

Patterns of ASL impairments resulting from localized lesions in deaf signers can help illuminate the nature of neural organiation for language. Of course, the brains of deaf people did not evolve independently of those of hearing people, and language mechanisms have certainly evolved in part to meet the needs of spoken communication. The neural organization for a visual-gestural language in deaf signers may therefore be determined in part by the evolutionary history of language development in the oral-auditory transmission modality. To the extent that specializ-ed language structures developed for speech govern the representation and processing of ASL, neural mechanisms in deaf ASL signers will be similar to those found for hearing speakers. To the extent that the modality in which a language develops shapes the structure and processing of the language, modality-relevant neural structures may be implicated in its representation. The study of brain organization in deaf ASL signers may allow one to address such fundamental questions regarding neural mechanisms for language.

This review focuses on comparisons of the effects of left and right hemisphere lesions in deaf signers, on language, visuospatial and motoric functions. It is drawn from some studies recently completed at the Neurolinguistic Laboratory at the Salk Institute. The review addresses some of the following questions. Is sign language unilaterally represented to the same extent as spoken language or is it bilaterally represented in congenitally deaf signers to a degree not characteristic of speech in hearing people? Is the left or the right hemisphere dominant for sign language? When sign language breakdown occurs, will impairments be selective with respect to the structural components of the language? Because grammatical and spatial relations are so intimately interwoven in ASL, will the breakdown of sign language and visuospatial functions be linked or be independent?

The studies proceed along four lines of investigation (Poizner et al., 1987). (1) To begin to investigate sign aphasia, the Boston Diagnostic Aphasia Examination (BDAE; Goodglass and Kaplan, 1983) was adapted to ASL in order to see whether the pattern of impairment following brain damage in deaf signers is at all comparable to that found in brain-damaged hearing individuals. (2) A series of tests was also developed, directed toward assessing production and comprehension of particular grammatical structures of ASL. Specifically, the capacity to process sublexical structure, morphology and spatial syntax was tested. (3) To determine the relationship between apraxia and aphasia in users of a gestural language, the capacity for representational and nonrepresentational movements of the hands and arms was assessed. (4) Finally, an array of nonlanguage visuospatial tests that have been shown in hearing people to differentiate the effects of damage to the left as opposed to the right hemisphere was administered.

This chapter focuses on six deaf, brain-damaged signers, three with damage to the left cerebral hemisphere and three with damage to the right cerebral hemisphere. Deaf controls matched in age, age of onset of deafness, and language background were used throughout. Only subjects who were right-handed before their cerebral infarct and who had unilateral damage were selected. (Damage was assessed by CT scans whenever possible.) Subjects were typically prelingually deaf, had been signing throughout their lives, had deaf spouses, and were members of the deaf com-

munity. Fig. 2 presents a summary of the characteristics of the deaf signers.

Language in left-lesioned signers

The three patients with left hemisphere damage showed clear sign-language impairments, as indicated by their results on an aphasia examination, on tests for processing the structural levels of American Sign Language, and on a linguistic analysis of their signing. Furthermore, from the first results it appears that *differential* damage within the left hemisphere may lead to selective impairment of different structural layers of sign language. The rating scale profiles from the Boston Diagnostic Aphasia Examination for three patients with left hemisphere damage (Gail D.,

SUMMARY CHARACTERISTICS OF THREE LEFT LESIONED AND THREE RIGHT LESIONED DEAF SIGNERS

Patient	Age/Testing	Sex	Age/Onset Deafness	Handedness	Language Environment					Hemiplegia	Lesion
					Parents and Siblings	School	Spouse	Cultural Group	Primary Communication		
Left Hemisphere Damaged Signers											
PD	81	M	5 yrs.	R	Hearing	Residential, Deaf School	Deaf	Deaf	Sign	——	Left subcortical, deep to Broca's area extending posteriorly beneath parietal lobe
KL	67	F	6 mos.	R	Hearing	Residential Deaf School	Hard of Hearing	Deaf	Sign	Right Hemiplegic	Left parietal, supramarginal and angular gyri, extending subcortically into middle frontal gyrus
GD	38	F	Birth	R	Older Deaf Siblings	Residential Deaf School	Deaf	Deaf	Sign	Right Hemiplegic	Most of convexity of left frontal lobe; Broca's area damaged
Right Hemisphere Damaged Signer											
BI	76	F	Birth	R	Hearing	Residential Deaf School	Deaf	Deaf	Sign	Left Hemiplegic	Right Hemisphere
SM	71	F	Birth	R	Hearing	Residential Deaf School	Deaf	Deaf	Sign	Left Hemiplegic	Right temporoparietal area, most of territory of right middle cerebral artery damaged
GG	81	M	5 yrs	R	Hearing	Residential Deaf School	Deaf	Deaf	Sign	——	Right superior temporal and middle temporal gyri extending into the angular gyrus

Fig. 2. Summary of characteristics of deaf brain-damaged signers.

Karen L. and Paul D.) and their deaf control subjects showed that all three left hemisphere damaged patients had impaired signing relative to their deaf control subjects. Furthermore, their signing did not break down in a uniform manner; the profiles of the three patients were very different (Poizner et al., 1987b). Linguistic analysis of the signing of these patients revealed the nature of the differential linguistic impairments: one was agrammatic, the second had grammatically correct signing but with 'phonemic' errors; and the third had a breakdown at the grammatical level of structure in sign language, consisting of many paragrammatisms and errors in the use of spatialized syntax.

Gail D.: agrammatic sign aphasia

Of the three deaf patients with left hemisphere damage, one patient (Gail D.) was grossly impaired in her sign output after her stroke. Her signing was dysfluent, reduced to single sign utterances of largely referential signs, shorn of syntactic and morphological markings, even though American Sign Language, as already indicated, is a heavily inflected language, in which signs frequently involve many grammatical morphemes concurrent with the sign stem. Her language profile was, in fact, classically like that of hearing patients classified as Broca's aphasic; her signing was *agrammatic.* Gail D.'s limited output was generated through continuous prompting by the examiner. Her signs were produced in an extremely effortful manner much of the time, and she was clearly frustrated in her attempts to communicate further information. Her difficulties were intermittent; occasionally she produced single signs fluently and with little hesitation. She tended to have great difficulty in expression; her narratives were severely limited, effortfully produced, and – significantly – without any of the grammatical apparatus of ASL. Gail D. omitted all grammatical formatives, including most pronouns, inflectional and derivational processes, as well as all aspects of spatially organized syntax. Her case shows the

devastating effect that left hemisphere damage can have on a visual-gestural language.

Karen L.: grammatical signing with sublexical impairment

Karen L. appeared to be the least impaired of the three left hemisphere damaged signers. Karen L. was first studied by Chiarello et al. (1982), and then by Poizner et al. (1987). Unlike Gail D., she was not agrammatic, but instead had a fluent sign aphasia. She effortlessly produced long strings of signs which showed a wide range of correct grammatical forms. These included the rich derivational and inflectional morphology of ASL, and nearly all aspects of the spatially organized syntax. However, this left hemisphere damaged patient showed primary impairment at the *sublexical* level, making frequent errors which would be the equivalent of phonemic errors in a spoken language. Her errors in ongoing signing tended to be almost exclusively sublexical paraphasias; they involved substitutions within the parameters of the sublexical structure of signs – substitution of one handshape for another, substitution within place of articulation or within movement. These were not articulatory problems; rather they were substitutions within the sublexical parameters of signs, equivalent to, for example, phonemic substitutions in spoken languages.

In addition, Karen L.'s signing appared vague. Linguistic analysis revealed that she exhibited a specific problem with specifying who or what she was referring to with her freely used pronouns. She tended to use pronominal indices in ASL very freely and also indexed verbs to spatial loci frequently. In ASL, both pronouns and indexed verbs involve association with spatial loci. Karen L.'s deficit arose in failing to specify the nouns associated with the indices. It was her frequent use of pronouns and indexed verbs without specifying associated nouns that gave rise to the impression that her signing was 'vague' and somewhat empty of content. In summary, her signing errors were in two domains: in failure to specify nominal referents for pronouns and in substitution of handshapes, movements and locations within signs. These errors were in contrast to her well-preserved lexical semantics and her inclusion of derivational and inflectional morphology. Furthermore, Karen L. had a marked and lasting sign comprehension loss. Her sign aphasia contrasted with that of another left hemisphere damaged patient (Paul D., to be described in next section), in that she showed preserved grammar and impaired 'phonology' and he exhibited an opposite pattern.

Paul D.: paragrammatic sign aphasia

The third left hemisphere damaged patient is Paul D., reported first by Battison and Padden (1974) and then extensively studied by Poizner et al. (1987). Paul D. also had a fluent sign aphasia after his stroke, yet showed primary impairment at the *grammatical* level. His signing before his stroke was articulate, even eloquent. After his stroke, he produced many semantically and grammatically inappropriate signs in the context of fluent sign output. His signing (as his written English) displayed errors of selection at the semantic and grammatical levels.

Paragrammatisms. What was remarkable about Paul D.'s signing was the occurrence of morphological substitutions, often involving an appropriate root form, but an inappropriate inflection or derivation. He also on occasion substituted one inflectional form for another and even produced nonsense inflections. Fig. 3 shows examples of Paul D.'s morphological errors, and illustrates his tendency to select morphologically complex forms where simple ones would be linguistically appropriate. Furthermore, he produced an abundance of sign neologisms, even creating morphologically *illegal* combinations.

Spatial syntactic impairment. Paul D.'s grammatical impairment was evident not only in his frequent paragrammatisms but also at another level in terms of the spatially organized syntax and discourse. He tended to overuse nominals and appeared to avoid spatial indexing (the equivalent of

pronouns in ASL). Furthermore, he often failed to use verb indexing, even where it is required. When he used it, the verb agreement, as conveyed through spatial indexing, was often incorrect.

Paul D.'s specific problems at the inflectional and derivational level indicate that lexical and grammatical structure can break down independently in a sign language. The structure of Paul D.'s lexical signs was relatively preserved, in the face of his grammatical deficits. This is particularly interesting, given that ASL conveys the two levels of structure concurrently, rather than sequentially.

On the basis of these three left hemisphere damaged signers, the following conclusion is warranted: certain areas of the left hemisphere are crucial to language function in deaf signers whose primary language is a sign language. However, without examining the effects of right hemisphere damage, it cannot be concluded that the left hemisphere is dominant for sign language, and certainly not that the left hemisphere is specialized specifically for sign language functioning. In fact, the brains of deaf signers might yet be bilaterally organized, with lesions to the right hemisphere producing similar aphasias, or other aphasias, but aphasias nonetheless. Before discussing the language capacities of right-lesioned signers, we turn briefly to their nonlanguage visuospatial deficits.

Nonlanguage visuospatial capacities

Selected tests were administered which are sensitive distinguishers of visuospatial performance in left versus right hemisphere damaged hearing patients. The tests were administered both to the left hemisphere damaged signers and to the signers with right hemisphere damage. These tests involved drawing, block design, selective attention, line orientation, facial recognition and visual closure. The signers with right hemisphere damage, in contrast to those with left hemisphere damage, showed severe spatial disorganization across a range of tasks. One patient with right hemisphere damage

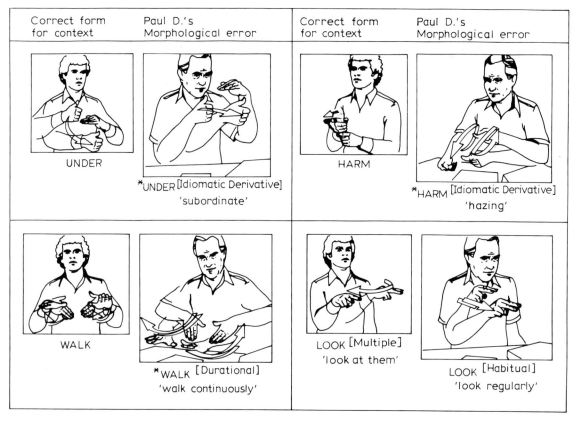

Fig. 3. Errors of paragrammatic left hemisphere lesioned signer. (Correct signs are shown in insets.) Note paragrammatisms of Paul D.

(Brenda I.) showed topographic disorientation. Another (Gilbert G.), who had specialized in building and repairing from blueprints before his stroke, was unable to do simple block designs afterwards. A third (Sarah M.), who had been an artist before her stroke, also showed severe visuo-spatial impairment, including highly distorted drawings, inability to indicate perspective and neglect of left hemispace. The spatial deficits in Sara M.'s drawings are in marked contrast to her good artistic abilities before her stroke, revealed in oil paintings.

To illustrate how nonlanguage spatial capacities of left-lesioned signers differ from those of right-lesioned signers, results are presented from drawing to copy from the BDAE (Fig. 4). The drawings of the right hemisphere damaged patients tended to show severe spatial disorganization, whereas those of the left hemisphere damaged patients did not. The right hemisphere damaged patients did not indicate perspective; several neglected the left side of space, and did not preserve the overall spatial configuration. The drawings of the left hemisphere damaged patients showed marked superiority. The overall outlines were preserved, as well as the spatial relations of the objects presented. Internal details, however, were sometimes omitted.

There were clear-cut differences between left- and right-lesioned signers across a range of nonlanguage spatial tasks. On a block design task of the WAIS-R, for example, the left hemisphere damaged signers produced absolutely correct constructions on simple designs, and even on the more complicated designs they maintained the overall spatial configurations. In contrast, the right-lesioned signers produced incorrect constructions, and tended to break the external configuration of the designs (Poizner et al., 1987). The general difficulty of the right-lesioned signers with the designs and their consistent tendency towards breaking external configurations is in opposition to the preserved performance of left-lesioned signers.

The right-lesioned patients, in summary, showed many of the classic visuospatial impairments seen in hearing individuals with right hemisphere damage (Kaplan and Goodglass, 1981; Goodglass and Kaplan, 1979). These impairments stand in contrast to the relatively preserved nonlanguage spatial functions of the left-lesioned signers.

Language in right-lesioned signers

The signers with right hemisphere damage present special issues in testing for language impairments; sign language makes linguistic use of space and these signers show nonlanguage spatial deficits. For example, they show left hemispatial neglect, which may introduce particular difficulties for users of a sign language; as addressee, the patient with left hemispatial neglect may well have to either receive signs in his neglected visual field or shift his gaze to the left, and thus away from the person addressing him. Given their obvious perceptual deficits and their impairment on nonlanguage visuospatial tasks, one might have expected a profound effect on sign language func-

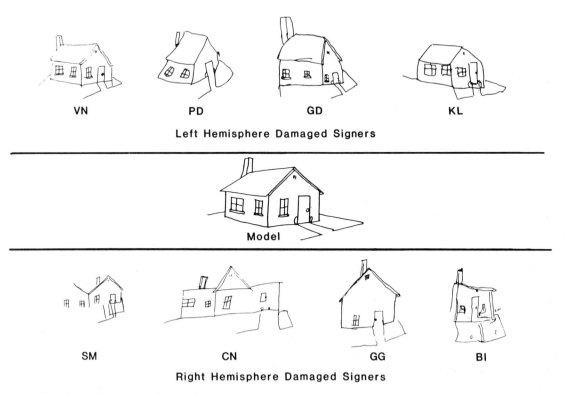

Fig. 4. Drawings of houses by left- and right-lesioned signers.

tions at all levels. But the three right hemisphere damaged patients were not aphasic at all for sign language. On the whole, they exhibited error-free signing with good range of grammatical forms, no agrammatism and no signing deficits.

When viewing signs, right-lesioned Sarah M. did indeed shift her gaze away from the signer. Remarkably, even with this unusual eye-gaze pattern, Sara M.'s comprehension of sign language was very good. Sara M. was an artist before her stroke, and showed severe spatial disorganization afterwards, including neglect of left hemispace, inability to indicate perspective, and so forth; and yet her sign language (including spatially expressed syntax) was completely unimpaired. Her sentences were grammatical and her signs were without error. In the light of her severe visuospatial deficit for nonlanguage tasks, Sarah M.'s correct use of the spatial mechanisms for sign syntax may point to the abstract nature of these mechanisms in American Sign Language.

Language profiles of left- and right-lesioned signers

Given their obvious perceptual deficits and their impairment on nonlanguage visuospatial tasks, one might have expected a profound effect on language functions at all levels, such as that found in patients with left hemisphere lesions. The rating scale profiles from the BDAE for the three left hemisphere lesioned signers showed that the scores were scattered, spanning virtually the entire range of values on most of the scales. The data point to the marked impairments of the left-lesioned patients. Furthermore, the individual profiles of the left-lesioned signers deviated from normal in separate ways and represent distinct patterns of sign aphasia. Recall that one left hemisphere damaged patient was agrammatic, another was grammatical in her signing but made sublexical errors and failed to specify her pronominal indexes, and a third was paragrammatic and had failure in spatially organized syntax.

In contrast to the left-lesioned signers, the three right hemisphere lesioned signers (Brenda I., Sarah M. and Gilbert G.) were not aphasic for sign language. Remarkably, they exhibited error-free signing with a large range of correct grammatical forms, good selection of signs, good sign phonology and no signing deficits. The signing of all three was fluent and varied, with conversational engagement and good understanding of everyday communication. The rating scale profiles of their sign characteristics reflected this grammatical (nonaphasic) signing; in fact, their scales were much like those of the control subjects. Furthermore, the left hemisphere damaged patients, but not those with right hemisphere damage, were impaired on tests of processing American Sign Language structures at different linguistic levels. Across a range of language tests given (tapping the phonology and the morphology of ASL), the right hemisphere damaged signers tested showed better performance than the left hemisphere damaged signers.

Spatial language and cognitive capacities contrasted

Thus, the deaf patients with right hemisphere damage showed severe spatial disorganization on nonlanguage tasks. Their signing, in contrast, was fluent, grammatical, of good phrase length and conveyed information well. This double dissociation of capacities — relatively preserved nonlanguage spatial capacities, but impaired signing in the left hemisphere damaged patients, and the reverse pattern in the right hemisphere damaged patients — clearly indicated the separation in hemispheric function that can occur for language and nonlanguage processing even when both are visuospatial. Since deaf signers do show hemispheric specialization, hearing and speech cannot be necessary for the development of hemispheric specialization. Rather, the differing functions of the two cerebral hemispheres emerge for space and for language, even for users of a visuospatial language.

Dissociation between spatial syntax and spatial mapping

As mentioned earlier, one of the distinguishing aspects of sign language, and one that may be among the most crucial for understanding brain organization for language, is the unique role of space, which figures structurally at all linguistic levels. For syntactic functions, arbitrary reference points in space are associated with nominals introduced into the discourse; pronoun signs are directed toward these points and verb signs obligatorily move between them in specifying grammatical relations (subject of, object of). As opposed to its syntactic use, space in ASL also functions in a *topographic* way: the space within which signs are articulated can be used to reflect more or less directly the layout of objects in space. In such spatial mapping, spatial relations among a selected set of sign forms that specify size and shape, for example, correspond in a topographic manner to actual spatial relations among objects described. What is the effect on the organization of the brain for language in its broadest sense when spatial relations have a topographic as opposed to grammatical function?

Patients were asked to describe the spatial layout of their living quarters from memory. In this task, signing space is used to indicate the positions of objects in actual space, and actual spatial relations are thus significant. Descriptions by some right hemisphere damaged patients were grossly distorted spatially; the major items of furniture were indicated, but in incorrect spatial relationships. In contrast, although the descriptions of two left hemisphere damaged patients showed omissions and had linguistic errors, there were no evident spatial distortions.

When space is used in the language to represent syntactic relations, however, the pattern was reversed, with left hemisphere damaged patients impaired, and right hemisphere damaged patients unimpaired. Thus, within signing, the use of space to represent *syntactic* relations and the use of space to represent *spatial* relations may be differentially affected, with the former disrupted by left hemisphere damage and the latter by right hemisphere damage (Poizner et al., 1987).

Apraxia and sign aphasia

In a long-standing controversy over the nature of aphasic disorders, certain investigators have proposed a common underlying basis for disorders of gesture and disorders of language (Kimura, 1982; Goldstein, 1948). Some attribute the specialization of the left hemisphere specifically for the control of changes in the position of both oral and manual articulators. In this view, disorders of language occur as a result of more primary disorders of movement control. A second position is that both apraxia and aphasia result from an underlying deficit in the capacity to express and comprehend symbols. Since gesture and linguistic symbol are transmitted in the same modality in sign language, the breakdown of the two can be directly compared. In addition to an array of language tests, a series of apraxia tests was administered to the deaf patients, including tests of production and of imitation of representational and nonrepresentational movements.

Sign aphasia without apraxia

The sign language adaptation of the Ideomotor Apraxia Tests of the BDAE consists of a three-fold classification of apraxia: buccofacial movements, intransitive limb movements (e.g., 'wave goodbye') and transitive limb movements (e.g., 'throw a ball'). If subjects are unable to carry out a movement to command ('Show me how you would . . .'), the examiner demonstrates the movement and asks the subject to copy it. Fig. 5 presents results from testing the six brain-damaged signers that were studied. The figure shows that no right-lesioned signer had ideomotor apraxia, and that one left-lesioned signer did (the agrammatic sign aphasic).

Studies such as these should allow one to determine the separability of sign aphasia and manual apraxia. The three right hemisphere damaged signers studied so far showed no evidence of either aphasia or apraxia. However, for the left hemisphere patients, all of whom were aphasic for sign language, some strong dissociations emerged between their capacities for sign language and their nonlanguage gesture and motor capacities (Poizner et al., 1984). The language deficits of these patients were on the whole related to specific *linguistic components of sign language* rather than to an underlying motor disorder, or to an underlying disorder in the capacity to express and comprehend symbols of any kind.

Competition between gesture and sign

Since gesture and linguistic symbol are transmitted in the same modality in sign language, the breakdown of the two can be directly compared. The results of the studies reported so far show a dissociation between apraxia and certain types of sign aphasia. A new case has recently emerged which also shows differential control over gesture and signs, in a very modality-specific way: a competition between language and gesture was found that could only be seen in a gestural language (Poizner et al., 1986b). The linguistic and gestural capacities of a 67-year-old prelingually deaf signer with a left hemisphere lesion were studied. Magnetic resonance imaging brain scan showed a subcortical lesion to the left basal ganglia (putamen and globus pallidus) and a number of very small lesions to the deep hemispheric white matter. The patient was not aphasic for sign language nor did he show ideomotor apraxia. (It is important to note that this man's lesion was not one that would be expected to lead to an aphasia for spoken or signed language.) However, in testing for ideomotor apraxia, an unusual pattern of behavior specific to sign language emerged.

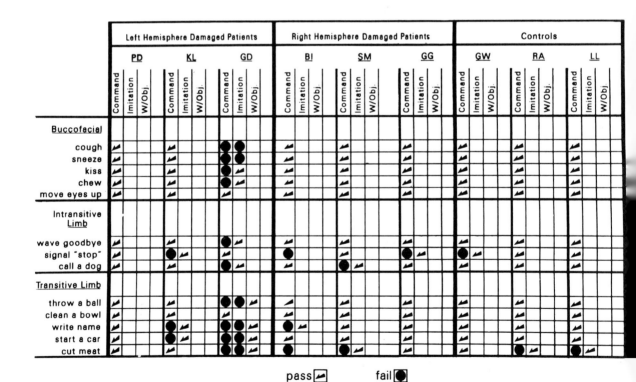

Fig. 5. Apraxia testing across right- and left-lesioned signers.

When asked to mime the use of objects with his left hand, his performance was nearly perfect. However, when then asked to mime the use of these same objects using his right hand, he showed a substantial number of intrusions from ASL (see Fig. 6). Fig. 6 also illustrates the contrast between one sign intrusion by the right hand and the gesture correctly performed by the left hand. When asked to mime the use of a razor, the patient correctly gestured with his left hand, as Fig. 6 shows. However, when asked to mime using his right hand, he intruded the ASL sign SHAVE, which differs from the gesture. The ASL sign uses a different configuration of the hand, is made in a different and more restricted location, and uses a different and more circumscribed movement than the gesture.

One interpretation of these unilateral sign intrusions is the following: A gesture can invoke two representations, one iconic (gestural), the other linguistic (ASL sign). The iconic, gestural representation can enter the right motor system and activate the left hand. In the left hemisphere, however, a competition could result between the linguistic and iconic representations. Both representations could be co-activated, with a resulting conflict, and the linguistic representation could dominate and activate the right hand in some

cases. These data indicate that mime and sign are different, and converge with the previously reported data to indicate that gesture and language are represented in the brain very differently, even for a gestural language. (We are grateful to Dr. Antonio Damasio for suggesting this interpretation.)

Three-dimensional computergraphic modeling

In recent investigations, new procedures for the three-dimensional computergraphic analysis of movement are being used (Poizner et al., 1986c; Jennings and Poizner, 1988) to examine the differential capacities of brain-lesioned signers to control movements that are equated in formational complexity at different levels. The linguistic and nonlinguistic movements are digitized and reconstructed in three dimensions, and then undergo numeric and graphic analyses. Fig. 7 presents three-dimensional reconstructions of the impaired movement of a hearing subject with ideomotor apraxia and a matched control subject (Poizner et al., in press). Such quantitative procedures clearly help specify more precisely the nature of language and movement disorders.

From these studies, it is becoming clear that the underlying basis of the left hemisphere specializa-

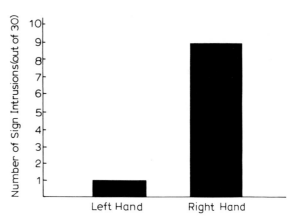

Gesture   ASL Sign   SIGN INTRUSIONS DURING APRAXIA TEST

Fig. 6. Competition between language and gesture in a brain-damaged signer. Note correct left-handed miming gesture for 'shave,' but right-handed intrusion from the ASL sign SHAVE.

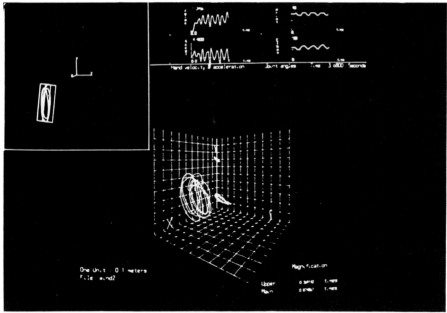

CONTROL

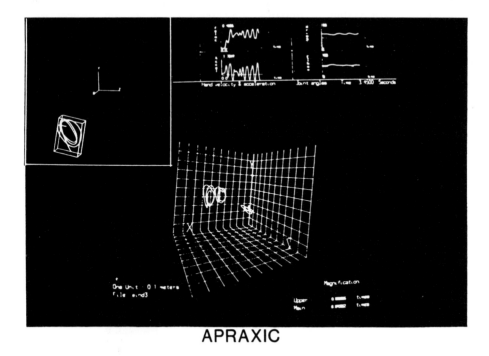

APRAXIC

Fig. 7. Three-dimensional computergraphic analysis of movement disorders.

tion for language does not rest fundamentally on capacities for movement sequencing, but rather on specific linguistic capacities. The investigation of the breakdown of movement control in relation to language marks a significant advance and broadens our understanding of how the brain controls movement at three different levels – *linguistic, symbolic* and *motoric*.

Summary

Patterns of language breakdown and preservation in the left- as opposed to right-lesioned signers examined so far suggest the following conclusions. Because the left-lesioned signers showed frank sign language aphasias and the right-lesioned signers showed preserved language function, it appears that it is, indeed, the left cerebral hemisphere that is specialized for sign language, or at least for the grammatical aspects of sign language investigated so far. This provides support for the proposition that the left cerebral hemisphere in humans may have an innate predisposition for language. Thus there appear to be anatomical structures within the left hemisphere that emerge as special-purpose linguistic processors in persons who have profound and lifelong auditory deprivation and who communicate with a linguistic system that uses radically different channels of reception and transmission from that of speech. In this respect brain organization for language in deaf signers parallels that in hearing, speaking individuals.

On the other hand, the data also suggest the possibility that those anatomical structures within the left hemisphere that subserve visual-gestural language may differ from those that subserve auditory-vocal language. In this regard, one of the left-lesioned signers studied, Karen L., had a marked and lasting sign comprehension loss that would not be expected, given her lesion, if she were hearing. Her lesion spares both the traditional Broca's area and Wernicke's area. It involves the left inferior parietal lobule, an area of the brain known to function for higher-order spatial analysis. Her case suggests that the inferior parietal lobule may play a stronger mediating role for signed than for spoken language.

Clearly, many more cases are needed before one can attempt to map the underlying neural substrate for sign language. But if one can uncover the neural circuitry for sign language, one will be further along in uncovering the ways in which the neural circuitry for language (whether spoken or signed) operates for linguistic processing independently of language modality and the ways in which the circuitry is modality-bound.

Acknowledgements

This paper was supported in part by the National Institutes of Health Grants NS 15175, NS 19096, NS 25149 and HD 13249 as well as National Science Foundation grant BNS86-09085 to the Salk Institute for Biological Studies.

References

Battison R: Linguistic Aspects of Aphasia in Deaf Signers. Manuscript, Northeastern University, 1979.

Battison R, Padden CA. Sign language Aphasia: A Case Study.' Paper presented at the 49th Annual Meeting of the Linguistics Society of America, New York, December, 1974.

Bellugi U: The structuring of language: clues from the similarities between signed and spoken language. In Bellugi U, Studdert-Kennedy M (Editors), *Signed and Spoken Language: Biological Constraints on Linguistic Form.* Dahlem Konferenzen. Weinheim/Deerfield Beach, FL: Verlag Chemie, pp. 115 – 140, 1980.

Chiarello C, Knight R, Mandel M: Aphasia in a prelingually deaf woman. *Brain: 105,* 29 – 51, 1982.

Critchley MD: Aphasia in a prelingually deaf woman. *Brain: 61,* 163 – 166, 1938.

Douglass E, Richardson JC: Aphasia in a congenital deaf mute. *Brain: 82,* 68 – 80, 1959.

Goldstein K: *Language and Language Disturbance.* New York: Grune and Stratton, 1948.

Goodglass H, Kaplan E: Assessment of cognitive deficit in the brain-injured patient. In Gazzaniga M. (Editor), *Handbook of Behavioral Neurobiology, Vol. 2.* New York: Plenum, 1979.

Goodglass H, Kaplan E: *The Assessment of Aphasia and Related Disorders.* Philadelphia: Lea and Febiger, 1972. Revised, 1983.

Jennings P, Poizner, H: Computergraphic modeling and analysis II: three dimensional reconstruction and interactive analysis. *J. Neurosci. Methods: 24,* 44 – 45, 1988.

Kaplan E, Goodglass H: Aphasia-related disorders. In *Ac-*

quired Aphasia. New York: Academic Press, 1981.

Kettrick C, Hatfield N: Bilingualism in a visuo-gestural mode. In Vaid J. (Editor), *Language Processing in Bilinguals.* Hillsdale, NJ: LEA Press, pp. 253 – 273, 1986.

Kimura D: Neuromotor mechanisms in the evolution of human communication. In Steklis H. D., Raleigh M.J. (Editors), *Studies in Neurolinguistics,* Vol. 2. New York: Academic Press Inc, pp. 197 – 219, 1979.

Kimura D: Neural mechanisms in manual signing. *Sign Lang. Stud.: 33,* 291 – 312, 1981.

Kimura D: Left hemisphere control of oral and brachial movements and their relation to communication. *Phil. Trans. R. Soc. Lond.: B298,* 135 – 149, 1982.

Kimura D, Davidson W, McCormick CW: No impairment in sign language after right hemisphere stroke. *Brain Cognition: 17,* 359 – 362, 1982.

Klima ES, Bellugi U: *The Signs of Language.* Cambridge, MA: Harvard University Press, 1979.

Lane H, Grosjean F: (Editors) *Recent Perspectives on American Sign Language.* Hillsdale, NJ: Lawrence Erlbaum Associates, 1980.

Leischner A: Die 'Aphasie' der Taubstummen. *Arch. Psychiatrie Nervenkr.: 115,* 469 – 548, 1943.

Liddell S: THINK and BELIEVE: sequentiality in ASL. *Language: 60,* 372 – 399, 1984.

Neville HJ, Bellugi U: Patterns of cerebral specialization in congenitally deaf adults. In Siple P. (Editor), *Understanding Language through Sign Language Research.* New York: Academic Press Inc, pp. 239 – 257, 1978.

Padden CA, Perlmutter DM: American Sign Language and the architecture of phonological theory. *Natural Lang. Ling. Theory: 5,* 335 – 375, 1987.

Poizner H, Battison R: Cerebral asymmetry for sign language: clinical and experimental evidence. In Lane H., Grosjean F. (Editors), *Recent Perspectives on American Sign Language.* Hillsdale, NJ: Lawrence Erlbaum Associates, pp. 79 – 101, 1980.

Poizner H, Bellugi U: Hemispheric specialization for a visual-gestural language. Paper presented at International Neuropsychology Society, Houston, TX, 1984.

Poizner H, Battison R, Lane H: Cerebral asymmetry of American Sign Language: effects of moving stimuli. *Brain lang.: 7,* 351 – 362, 1979.

Poizner H, Bellugi U, Lutes-Driscoll V: Perception of American Sign Language in dynamic point-light displays. *J. Exp. Psychol. Hum. Percept. Performance: 7,* 430 – 440, 1981.

Poizner H, Bellugi U, Iragui V: Apraxia and aphasia in a visual-gestural language. *Am. J. Physiol. Regulat. Integrative Comp. Physiol.: 246,* R868 – R883, 1984.

Poizner H, Klima ES, Bellugi U, Livingston R. Motion analysis of grammatical processes in a visual-gestural language. In Balzano G, McCabe V (Editors), *Event Cognition.* Hillsdale, NJ: Lawrence Erlbaum Associates, pp. 155 – 174, 1986a.

Poizner H, Bellugi U, Klima E, Kritchevsky M: *Competition Between Gesture and Language in a Brain-Damaged Signer.* Nashville, TN: Academy of Aphasia, 1986b.

Poizner H, Wooten E, Salot D: Computergraphic modeling and analysis: a portable system for tracking arm movements in three-dimensional space. *Beh. Res. Methods Instrum. Comput.; Special Issue Comput. Vision: 18,* 427 – 433, 1986c.

Poizner H, Klima ES, Bellugi U: *What the Hands Reveal about the Brain.* Cambridge, MA: MIT Press/Bradford Books, 1987.

Poizner H, Mack L, Verfaille M, Rothi L, Heilman K: Three-dimensional computergraphic analysis of apraxia: neural representations of learned movement. *Brain,* in press.

Ross P: Cerebral specialization in deaf individuals. In Segalowitz S. (Editor), *Language Functions and Brain Organization.* New York: Academic Press, pp. 287 – 313, 1983.

Sarno J, Swisher L, Sarno M: Aphasia in a congenitally deaf man. *Cortex: 5,* 398 – 414, 1969.

© 1989 Elsevier Science Publishers B.V. (Biomedical Division)
Handbook of Neuropsychology, Vol. 2
F. Boller and J. Grafman (Eds)

CHAPTER 9

Aphasia in left-handers and crossed aphasia

Yves Joanette

*Laboratoire Théophile-Alajouanine, C.H. Côte-des-Neiges, Montréal, and Faculté de Médecine, Université de Montréal,
Canada*

Introduction

Marc Dax, a physician of the Napoleonic army posted at Sommières in southern France, is credited with being the first to have stated, back in 1836, that aphasia is to be found only when the left hemisphere is lesioned. It was only some 50 years later that this conception of the brain-language relationship was made explicit and popularized by Paul Broca in Paris, in June of 1865. However, whereas Dax made no mention of the relationship between left-hemisphere language and handedness, Broca restricted the left-hemisphere dominance for language to right-handers, suggesting a right-hemisphere dominance for left-handers. If the first part of Broca's hypothesis has found support from clinical aphasiology and experimental neuropsychology, the second part was not so successful. As early as 1899, Byrom Bramwell introduced the term 'crossed aphasia' to denote the existence of exceptions to Broca's dogma; Bramwell attempted to account for the fact that aphasia could sometimes result from a lesion of the hemisphere ipsilateral to the preferred hand, that is from left-hemisphere damage in left-handers as well as from right-hemisphere damage in right-handers. However, with time, it became obvious that, whereas the incidence of so-called 'crossed' aphasia was

more or less the rule among left-handers, it was relatively exceptional among right-handers. Thus, the functional organization of the brain in left-handers, and particularly its lateralization component, was not simply the mirror image of that in right-handers, as Broca viewed it, but rather something different. At the same time, the literature was conveying an increasing and nontrivial number of case reports of right-handed aphasics presenting lesions of the right hemisphere, cases for which the use of the term 'crossed' aphasia is now usually restricted. Thus, the present chapter is concerned with two aspects of originally a single problem which has since evolved into two complementary but different domains: aphasia among left-handers, to which the first section of this chapter is devoted; and crossed aphasia in dextrals, which will be the topic of the second section of this chapter.

Aphasia in left-handers

This section on aphasia in left-handers will first consider the problem of handedness, which is more than a mere opposition between right- and left-handers. Then, the characteristics of aphasia in left-handers will be summarized with regard to both lesion lateralization and aphasia semiology.

Right-handers and left-handers

As alluded to earlier, the world is not simply divid-

Requests for reprints should be sent to: Yves Joanette, Ph.D.,
Laboratoire Théophile-Alajouanine, CHCN 4565 chemin de la
Reine-Marie, Montréal, Québec, Canada H3W 1W5.

ed into left-handers and right-handers. Following an initial dichotomous opposition, ambidextrals were also taken into account, thus establishing a trichotomy; others, like Subirana (1952), suggested a further distinction between absolute right- or left-handers and preferential ones, thus ending up with five sub-groups. In fact, it is now acknowledged that any division of the general population according to handedness is rather artificial and should only be considered as indicative and a useful way of clustering individuals. Human handedness appears to be distributed on a continuum, extending from those individuals who exclusively use their right hand to those few individuals who exclusively use their left hand, even though the exact nature of the distribution – unimodal, bimodal, J-shaped – has not yet been determined.

Distribution of right- and left-handers

According to Hécaen and Ajuriaguerra (1963), who reviewed nearly 50 studies on this topic, the incidence of left-handedness ranges from 1 to 30%, more than half of those studies reporting a range between 4 and 10%. These figures are illustrative of the diversity with which investigators evaluate the incidence of left-handedness. Annett (1985) suggests at least three causes for this discrepancy: first, the existence of genuine differences between different categories of individuals according to factors such as sex or level of education; second, differences in the way handedness is assessed (see below); and third, differences in the criteria used to establish that a given hand is preferred. Using the above-mentioned five-part distinction, Subirana (1952) submitted a general population to different manual tasks and observed the following distribution of the preferred hand: 25% of the subjects used the right hand exclusively, 40% used mostly the right hand, 25% used both hands and 10% used mostly the left hand. In this series, subjects using only their left hand were found to be exceptional. Comparable figures are suggested by Annett (1985): 66% of individuals show a more or less pronounced right-

hand preference, as opposed to 4% for left-hand preference, and 30% with mixed preference. However, it is pointed out by Annett (1985) that there can be a considerable amount of intra-subject variability with regard to hand preference; up to 30% of individuals may exhibit a mixed left-/right-hand preference.

Hand preference versus hand skill

Several studies have examined the relationship between hand preference and hand skill, the latter being observed in tasks requiring normal manipulations (e.g., dynamometer, tapping, peg moving). Whereas a number of studies did not find any significant relationship between preference and skill (Porac and Coren, 1981) Annett (1985) proposes that there is a stable relationship between these two different aspects of handedness. The latter appears to be distributed as a unimodal, quasi-normal distribution whose peak is shifted to the right, whereas the former appears to be distributed as a J-shape curve. Thus, the difference of distribution between hand skill and preference is an important factor in evaluating handedness.

Handedness evaluation

Handedness has been evaluated through self-report, reports of relatives, the use of questionnaires (Annett, 1970; Crovitz and Zener, 1962; Oldfield, 1971), direct observation of tool manipulation, and measurement of skill performances (Annett, 1970; Benton, 1962). Both self-reports and reports of relatives are, at best, only indicative of the feeling of belonging to one particular group in a left-/right-hander dichotomy, which can sometimes be pushed towards a trichotomy when it includes ambidextrality. However, these methods give only a gross indication of preferred hand and do not permit distinction of the degree of handedness. Most questionnaires have the advantage of providing a laterality quotient on the basis of an individual's preference for a given hand in activities such as writing, using scissors, striking matches or unscrewing lids. However, they can become difficult to answer and, moreover, they give equal weight to activities which may be very different with regard to their cognitive involvement or the degree of dexterity they require. Direct observation of an individual using asymmetrical tools, such as scissors or golf clubs, or threading a needle, can be useful, though not always easy to perform in a clinical context. Finally, assessment of manual skill through the use of tasks requiring manipulative dexterity, such as moving pegs, does provide a more accurate and discriminative evaluation of handedness. However, such measures relate to hand skill and, as previously seen, its relationship with hand preference is not acknowledged by all authors. Most studies which have compared self-reports with questionnaires, as well as the latter versus direct observation or the use of performance tasks, have found some degree of inconsistency (Annett, 1985). The evaluation of handedness is a problem that has not yet been resolved. Thus, given the lack of sophistication in handedness evaluation, subjects considered as 'left-handers', or more generally as 'non-right-handers', do not necessarily form a homogeneous group.

Significance of left-handedness

Another reason to consider non-right-handers as forming a heterogeneous group is the significance of left-handedness. According to Satz (1973), there are two types of left-hander: 'natural' and 'pathological'. The latter type of left-hander, less numerous than the former, is considered to exist because left-handers are over-represented in a certain number of pathological populations such as mental retardates, epileptics, stutterers, cerebral-palsied children, development dysphasics and dyslexics (Bradshaw and Nettleton, 1983). For this reason, sinistrality may sometimes be the expression of possible birth stressors (Satz, 1973). However, this hypothesis remains to be confirmed. Most left-handers can be considered of the 'natural' type. In the latter case, a number of potential explanations for the under-representation of left-handers in the general population have been put forward. These accounts range from the

most environmentally based to the most genetic. Even though none of these models can fully account for the distribution of handedness in the general population, including the particular case of twins, genetic models tend to offer the best approximation. In particular, models put forward by Annett (1972) and the two-gene, four allele one proposed by Levy and Nagylaki (1972) are the ones to which most reference is made.

Lateralization of lesions

Data on lateralization of aphasiogenic lesions in left-handers are not of equal quality. Zangwill (1967) and Annett (1975) identify, in the literature, five series of unselected patients for both handedness and lesion laterality. These series concern consecutive patients with unilateral lesion and aphasia; they are by Bingley (1958), Conrad (1949), Hécaen and Ajuriaguerra (1963) (as well as a more complete report by Hécaen and Sauguet (1971)) Newcombe and Ratcliff (1973) and Penfield and Roberts (1959). Most of these studies deal with war-wound patients; that by Penfield and Roberts (1959) deals with a special population: epileptics who had undergone surgery. According to Annett (1975), there is a considerable degree of variability between these studies. For example, the study by Hécaen and Ajuriaguerra (1963) found a more or less equal number of aphasics among left-brain-damaged (LBD) or right-brain-damaged (RBD) left-handers (22 out of 37 (59.5%) among LBD versus 11 out of 22 (50.0%) RBD right-handers), whereas the study by Penfield and Roberts (1959) reports a much larger proportion of aphasics among LBD (13/18 or 72.2%) than among RBD (1/15 or 6.7%) left-handers. However, the general tendency appears to be a much more distributed lateralization of lesions among left-handers than among right-handers. Newcombe and Ratcliff (1973) typify this finding: they observed a slightly larger proportion of aphasia among LBD (11/30 or 36.7%) than among RBD (8/33 or 24.8%) left-handers. The most widely-accepted idea among clinicians is that aphasia in left-handers is mainly associated with left-brain lesions, but that the occurrence of right-brain lesions is not at all infrequent.

One of the reasons why there is such a discrepancy between these studies, as far as lateralization of the aphasiogenic lesion in left-handers is concerned, lies in the definition of left-handedness and the method used to evaluate it. Thus, the studies might not be totally comparable. Another problem lies in the definition of 'aphasia'; for example, in some studies, all aphasic or dysphasic signs are considered, including transient dysphasic signs, whereas in other studies only non-transient aphasias are considered. Since there appears to be a larger proportion of transient dysphasia among left-handers, whatever the side of the lesion (Hécaen and Ajuriaguerra, 1963), this might be a confounding factor. As far as the total incidence of aphasia in left-handers is concerned, some authors suggest that there may be an overall greater incidence of aphasia among left-handers, whatever the side of the lesion (Hécaen and Ajuriaguerra, 1963; Hécaen and Sauguet, 1971; Gloning et al., 1969). However, this interpretation has not yet been fully acknowledged by most authors.

All in all, the data suggest that the lateralization of lesions among left-handers – and thus the lateralization of language function in these individuals – is much more heterogeneous than in right-handers. Among other things, it is suggested that there may be a proportion of left-handers with bilateral language representation. For example, Hécaen and Sauguet (1971) consider left-handers as being composed of at least three groups: those with a unilateral left language representation, those with a unilateral right representation, and those with a somewhat bilateral representation. Moreover, Hécaen and Sauguet (1971) and Hécaen et al. (1981) consider that those left-handers for whom language representation is most ambilateral are those showing the presence of familial sinistrality (FS +), defined as the presence of at least one left-hander among the members of the immediate family (parents, brothers or sisters, as well as children). However, this latter concept is questioned by Annett (1985), who considers studies on the effect of unilateral aphasiogenic lesion in left-handers, with or without left-handed relatives, to yield very few significant differences.

Satz (1980) conducted an extensive review of the literature on the laterality of aphasiogenic lesions among left-handers and applied these data to four models of brain lateralization for language. In these models, language representation is considered to be either (a) unilateral, (b) variable unilateral, i.e. unilateral but with some interindividual variations, (c) mostly variable unilateral as well as bilateral, or (d) mostly bilateral as well as variable unilateral. Satz postulates that the latter model best fits the observed aphasiological data. On the basis of these results, Satz (1980) suggests that a majority of left-handers might be either left-brain lateralized (40%) or unlateralized (40%), whereas only a minority (20%) would be right-brain lateralized. Of course, these figures are only to be taken as indicative, even more so since other authors consider ambilaterality among left-handers as being much more infrequent (Annett, 1985).

The classic data on the use of the Wada test among left-handers tend to support the presence of a certain percentage of left-handers with bilateral representation for language. Even though this approach has its own limitations, given the nature of the test and the subjects, the intra-carotid injection of sodium amytal in a left-handed population has shown that, among a group of 74 left-handers and ambidextrals without evidence of early brain lesion, 69% had left-hemisphere-based language versus only 18% with right-hemisphere-based language. The remaining 13% of the subjects exhibited a bilateral representation for language, since both the left and the right carotid injection indicated some degree of speech disturbance in these subjects. One interesting point to note here is that, in the latter case, left and right carotid injections did not always yield similar dysphasic disturbances.

In conclusion, laterality of aphasiogenic lesion among left-handers is much more heterogeneous than among right-handers. It may be said that, even though some left-handers do have right-hemisphere representation for language, and some others have a more bilateral representation, the majority of left-handers depend on their left hemisphere for language. Thus, aphasiogenic lesions among left-handers will, in most cases, involve the left hemisphere, even though right-hemisphere aphasiogenic lesions will not be as infrequent as in right-handers. As Annett (1985) pointed out, there is no generally agreed-upon theory as to the brainedness of left-handers.

Clinical aspects

Few studies have examined in detail the clinical aspects of aphasia in left-handers. However, it is generally acknowledged among clinicians that the manifestation of aphasia among left-handers is not identical to that in right-handers. Moreover, the recovery from aphasia is undoubtedly different in the left-handed individual, though not enough research has been devoted to this topic. Both these aspects will be reviewed here, despite the limited number of studies on this topic.

Semiology of aphasia in left-handers

One of the few systematic studies on the semiology of aphasia among left-handers is that of Hécaen and Ajuriaguerra (1963). They examined the clinical signs of 59 aphasic left-handers, 37 of whom had a left-hemisphere lesion and 22 a right-hemisphere one. A general comment by Hécaen and Ajuriaguerra (1963) is that, on the whole, aphasic signs in left-handers tend to be less severe than among right-handers.

Specifically, Hécaen and Ajuriaguerra (1963) examined their subjects according to a number of parameters, including the presence of expressive or comprehension disorders, the presence of an anomia, as well as the occurrence of agraphic or alexic signs. The main feature they found is the smaller incidence of comprehension deficits among left-handed aphasics, whatever the side of the lesion. Indeed, whereas nearly 40% of LBD right-

handers present some degree of comprehension disorder, only 13.5% of LBD and 9.1% of RBD show such a sign. Another characteristic of left-handers' aphasia is the proportionally larger incidence of expressive disorders. Again, whereas fewer than 35% of LBD right-handers show some degree of expressive disorder, 59.5% of LBD and 50% of RBD left-handers present such a deficit. However, unlike the difference for comprehension deficits, this difference tends to diminish with time, since a larger proportion of expressive disorders among left-handers are transient. Thus, after a certain time, the incidence of expressive disorders in left-handed aphasics resembles that in right-handed aphasics. The relatively higher incidence of expressive disorders in left-handers, combined with the lower incidence of comprehension deficits, as well as the greater variability in lateralization of aphasiogenic lesions, led Hécaen and Ajuriaguerra to suggest a parallel between left-handers' and children's functional organization for language. These authors suggest that both left-handers and children show a lesser degree of 'encephalization' of their brain's functional organization, at least as far as language is concerned. However, this hypothesis remains to be tested.

The only difference Hécaen and Ajuriaguerra (1963) noted, with regard to aphasic signs resulting from left- versus right-hemisphere lesion in left-handers, is in the incidence of alexia. Reading disorders are as frequent in left-handed LBD aphasics as in right-handed aphasics. However, these disorders seem to be much less frequent among RBD left-handed aphasics. It appears that reading difficulties are more often associated with lesions of the left hemisphere, whatever the patient's handedness. As far as writing disorders are concerned, they are also somewhat less frequent among RBD left-handed aphasics than both RBD left-handed and right-handed aphasics, even though they are nonetheless more frequent than reading disorders among RBD left-handed aphasics. However, it should be noted that Hécaen and Ajuriaguerra considered as a writing disorder the expression of spatial neglect. Thus, as they mention themselves, many of the writing disorders are in RBD left-handed aphasics of the spatial type (Hécaen and Albert, 1978).

The familial handedness factor was investigated by Hécaen and Sauguet (1971) in order to see if it was related to some difference in aphasic symptomatology. These authors found that LBD left-handed aphasics tend to be more impaired for writing than for oral language when they had no familial sinistrality. However, these results remain incomplete, and based on too small a number of observations to be conclusive. This factor remains to be thoroughly investigated.

Finally, one important aspect is the relationship between aphasic clinical signs and other neuropsychological signs in left-handers. One of the most striking features is that, still according to Hécaen and Ajuriaguerra (1963), neuropsychological deficits other than linguistic ones in left-handed aphasics tend to be much more like those observed in right-handers. Indeed, aphasic symptoms in LBD left-handed aphasics resemble those of right-handed aphasics, except for the lower incidence of comprehension disorders. On the other hand, the effect of a right-hemisphere lesion in left-handed aphasics is a neuropsychological semiology which is like that found in non-aphasic RBD right-handers, expressing itself for example through the presence of spatial neglect. In other words, the neuropsychological syndrome of a right-hemisphere lesion in left-handers is quite similar to that described in right-handers with the exception that language disorders are much less infrequent.

Recovery from aphasia
A certain controversy exists with regard to the rate of recovery from aphasia in left-handers. Some authors have claimed that left-handers might recover more rapidly from aphasia, thus supporting the theory that their functional organization for language might be more equally distributed over the two hemispheres. This view is supported by Subirana (1958) as well as by Luria (1947). According to Hécaen and Ajuriaguerra (1963), recovery from aphasia is more rapid among right-

handers with familial sinistrality. However, a number of studies were not able to support such a claim (Newcombe and Ratcliff, 1973; Russell and Espir, 1961). Thus, no strong claim can be made with reference to this problem. As Annett (1985) puts it: 'There are a number of indications that left-handers are more likely to recover from dysphasia than right-handers, but one test of a large sample found no evidence for such a difference' (p. 141). If such a tendency to recover more rapidly in left-handers does indeed exist, then according to Annett (1985), it might be more prevalent among left-handers with a right-hemisphere lesion than among those with a left-hemisphere lesion.

Crossed aphasia

As specified earlier, even though the term 'crossed' aphasia refers, strictly speaking, to any aphasia following a lesion ipsilateral to the preferred hand, it is now used *only* for those rare cases of aphasia in right-handers following a lesion of the right hemisphere. The prevalence of crossed aphasia in dextrals is currently estimated at between 0.4 and 3.5% of right-hemisphere lesions (Sweet et al., 1984). More than 75 case reports of crossed aphasia in dextrals have been published since the late XIXth century (see Joanette et al., 1982, for a detailed list). These observations challenge the current teaching with regard to the functional lateralization of the brain for language. In this context, they represent exceptional cases that are not only interesting, but also may throw some light on some still unknown factors that influence functional lateralization of the brain.

Cases of crossed aphasia in dextrals reported in the literature do not make a coherent ensemble, nor are they all convincing. For example, arguments in favor of an exclusively right-hemisphere lesion, and against the involvement of the left hemisphere, are not provided in every case. This is more evident in the earlier studies. This is not the principal confounding factor, however. As we have stated in a previous paper (Joanette et al.,

1982), many of the already known, or suspected, factors associated with a change in the functional lateralization of the brain for language can be found in most of these observations. If such factors are not taken into consideration, one could be placed in a position where cases of crossed aphasia of different origins would be compared. In other words, it seems much more preferable not to consider cases of crossed aphasia in dextrals in which some particular factor could account, partially or totally, for the presence of such a syndrome. Following a review of the 72 cases published up to that time, Joanette et al. (1982) and Habib et al. (1983) retained only 11 case reports that could satisfy the following criteria:

'(a) there is no doubt about right manual preference of the subject as well as his siblings and parents, (b) nature and localization of the lesion are such that the right hemisphere is the only one directly affected, (c) aphasic semiology is sufficiently documented, and (d) none of the environmental factors suspected to be related with a different brain functional organization (e.g., bilingualism, illiteracy, tone language) is present' (Habib et al., 1983, p. 413)

Moreover, as indicated by Sapir et al. (1986), subjects should not have sustained brain injury in childhood that could have caused changes in functional lateralization for language. The following description only pertains to cases of crossed aphasia in dextrals, respecting these criteria.

Clinical aspects

In the past, certain authors have suggested that there is a semiology common to nearly all crossed aphasics; for example, Brown and Wilson (1973) suggested that nearly all crossed aphasias in dextrals show agrammatism, or at least an aphasia of the 'anterior' type. This does not appear to be the case. In a review of the literature, Joanette et al. (1982) found that different aphasic syndromes can be found among the 11 cases of crossed aphasias in dextrals respecting the above-mentioned criteria (Angelergues et al., 1962; Assal et al., 1981; Brown and Wilson, 1973; Carr et al., 1981, case 3; Denes

and Caviezel, 1981; Fernandez-Martin et al., 1968; Habib et al., 1983; Pillon et al., 1979, 2 cases; Puel et al., 1982; Urbain et al., 1978). Given the large variation between authors with regard to the exact definition of a given type of aphasia, it was decided to describe crossed aphasia in these cases in semiological terms rather than by reference to some concept of aphasia taxonomy.

The first thing that should be mentioned is that language comprehension, whether oral or written, is only infrequently impaired among crossed aphasics. When there is a comprehension deficit, written language seems to be more affected than oral language. As far as expression is concerned, it is reduced in the majority of cases. However, the presence of a logorrheic jargon has been reported in some cases (e.g., Puel et al., 1982). One of the clinical signs that most frequently accompanies reduced expressive speech is some degree of agrammatism or, in some cases, of dyssyntaxia (paragrammatism). Phonemic paraphasias are also reported in the majority of cases, whereas arthric disorders and verbal paraphasias are less frequently mentioned.

Written expression is different from oral expression. Not only is the presence of a quantitative reduction much less frequent, but the presence of some logorrheic jargonagraphia is not infrequently reported (Habib et al., 1983; Pillon et al., 1979). In general, orthographic disorders are very common. In some cases, impairments include some degree of agrammatism or dyssyntaxia but usually less frequently than is the case for oral expression. In most cases, transpositions (reading aloud, repetition, copying and taking dictation) are affected. Among these, taking dictation is the most severely affected of all, reflecting the frequency of dysorthographia. This particular disturbance of written language has recently been further confirmed (Basso et al., 1985).

In terms of aphasia type, it can be said that most of the retained cases (6/11) can be considered as some form of Broca's aphasia. However, the remaining cases are difficult to classify, since certain clinical signs that are found in Wernicke's aphasia (oral and/or written jargon) exist in the absence of any comprehension deficit. Thus, even though crossed aphasia in dextrals tends to manifest itself as a Broca's aphasia, other types of aphasia are also to be found. However, it seems that aphasic syndromes are somewhat different from those of left-brain-damaged 'standard' right-handed aphasics, an aspect which has received further confirmation by Basso et al. (1985). Among other things, the relative frequency of impairments in written expression – including the presence of some jargonagraphia – and the relative infrequency of comprehension disorders are to be emphasized. Finally, the presence, in some cases, of a strong dissociation between reduced oral expression and the presence of a jargon in written expression is to be noted.

Recovery from aphasia seems rapid among crossed aphasics. Indeed, 6 out of the 11 cases reported here had a relatively rapid and complete recovery. However, in 4 cases, aphasic signs are reported as long-lasting, with only a small degree of recovery.

Neurological and neuropsychological semiology also reveals some interesting aspects. In all cases of crossed aphasia reported by Joanette et al. (1982), there is a left hemiplegia or hemiparesis accompanied by a sensory deficit in half of the cases. This neurological semiology is probably the reflection of some lesion characteristics (see below). Even though the presence of neuropsychological signs other than the aphasia is unequally documented, one is struck by the fact that visuo-constructive apraxia and dyscalculia are relatively frequent. In four cases, there is also some degree of left neglect. Finally, one interesting observation is the presence in two cases of some degree of temporal dysfunction, i.e., problems with the evaluation of time. This last neuropsychological sign is surprising, since it is only exceptionally reported in other brain-damaged populations. In summary, it can be concluded that 7 of the 11 cases here reported show some neuropsychological signs usually associated with a lesion of the right hemisphere in right-handers. Thus, it seems that the right hemisphere of crossed aphasics plays both an 'unusual' role in language as well as its 'usual' role as far as cognitive functions other than language are concerned (Basso et al., 1985).

According to Habib et al. (1983), the localization of aphasiogenic lesions in crossed aphasia appears to be somewhat different from localization in more standard left-hemisphere lesions among dextrals. Among other things, it appears to these authors that an involvement of sub-cortical structures (i.e., thalamus, basal ganglia and internal capsule) is much more frequent in crossed aphasia. Some recent case reports tend to corroborate this observation (Sapir et al., 1986) despite contradictory results in others (Basso et al., 1985). If such a characteristic of the lesion site is eventually confirmed, then it could indicate a privileged role of sub-cortical structures in language among those dextrals who will present crossed aphasia.

Theoretical implications

The existence of aphasia following a right-hemisphere lesion in dextrals respecting the above criteria is a challenge to contemporary conceptions about the functional lateralization of the brain for language. It should be mentioned, however, that the existence of crossed aphasia in dextrals does not necessarily mean that language in these subjects is sustained exclusively by the right hemisphere. Indeed, it could be that language is represented across both hemispheres. Studies of crossed aphasics with subsequent lesion of the left hemisphere would be the only source of incontestable data in this respect. However, the existence of cases of extended left-brain damage in some dextrals without the presence of aphasia (Boller, 1973) tends to confirm the possibility that language functions might be mostly, if not exclusively, represented within the right hemisphere in certain cases.

Many different accounts have been given in the literature with respect to crossed aphasia in dextrals, ranging from the most anatomical – and far-fetched – to the most functional ones.

Anatomical aberration. Among the first explanations for crossed aphasia is the one in which these individuals evidence some form of anatomical abnormality, or aberration, taking the form of an absence of decussation of cortico-spinal tracts (sic) (Souques, 1910; Ardin-Delteil et al., 1923). Thus, a left hemiplegia could coexist with the presence of a left-hemisphere aphasiogenic lesion. Of course, this explanation has since been ruled out!

Genetic factor. According to some authors, the existence of crossed aphasias in dextrals might mean either that the right-handedness/left-brainedness genetic factor is too weak to have influenced both handedness and brainedness, in this particular case having influenced only handedness (Ettlinger et al., 1955), or that handedness and brainedness are determined by two independent alleles which are usually associated but which can express themselves independently in exceptional cases (Levy and Nagylaki, 1972).

Incomplete lateralization. According to Jason Brown (Brown, 1976; Brown and Hécaen, 1976; Brown and Jaffe, 1975), the existence of crossed aphasia in dextrals could reflect the fact that, in some right-handers, the process of lateralization of cognitive function has been stopped at a given point for some unknown reason. This hypothesis relies on the fact that, in many crossed aphasics, the semiology somewhat resembles that of aphasia in children (e.g., few comprehension deficits and frequent agrammatism). However, the existence of crossed jargonaphasics is a challenge to such an explanation.

Early functional reorganization. According to many authors, crossed aphasia occurs in individuals having suffered discrete and undetected brain damage early in life. Thus, given the maximal functional plasticity of childhood, brain organization would have accordingly rearranged itself. However, no direct support for this explanation has yet been provided.

Basic functional aberration. Some authors, such as Carr et al. (1981), tend to present crossed aphasia in dextrals as the expression of some essential or basic functional aberration of brain organization. This concept presupposes more or less the possible existence of a functional situs inversus at the brain level in some individuals. However, not only does this explanation not provide the reasons for this basic aberration, but the presence of the usual right-hemisphere semiology in crossed aphasics would also mean that the functional situs inversus affects only language representation. This explanation has yet to be tested.

Cortical-subcortical dissociation for degree of lateralization. According to Habib et al. (1983), and given the higher frequency of lesions involving subcortical structures (thalamus, basal ganglia), the existence of crossed aphasias could mean that the left functional advantage for language could be more true for properly cortical structures than for subcortical structures, the latter now being recognized as part of the language areas. In other words, it could be that functional lateralization to the left may be less absolute for these phylogenetically older structures. If this were the case, reversed lateralization would be less exceptional at the subcortical than at the cortical level. However, this explanation is challenged by some contradictory results (Basso et al. 1985) and has yet to be confirmed.

In summary, there is no satisfactory account for the existence of exceptional cases of crossed aphasia among dextrals. It would be most surprising if a single explanation could account for all these cases. Most probably, multiple factors may intervene, some of which might be still unsuspected environmental or genetic factors that could, at least partially, determine the functional lateralization of the brain for language in a given individual.

Acknowledgements

Yves Joanette is Scientist of the Conseil de recherches médicales du Canada. This research was supported by Program Grant PG-28 of the Conseil de recherches médicales du Canada. The author wishes to thank John Boeglin and John Ryalls for their valuable comments on early versions of this paper.

References

Angelergues R, Hécaen H, Djindjian R, Jarrie-Hazan N: Un cas d'aphasie croisée. *Rev. Neurol. (Paris): 107,* 543 – 545, 1962.

Annett M: A classification of hand preference by association analysis. *Br. J. Psychol.: 61,* 303 – 321, 1970.

Annett M: The distribution of manual asymmetry. *Br. J. Psychol.: 63,* 343 – 358, 1972.

Annett M: Hand preference and the laterality of cerebral speech. *Cortex: 11,* 305 – 328, 1975.

Annett M: *Left, Right, Hand and Brain: The Right Shift Theory.* London (UK) and Hillsdale (New Jersey): Lawrence Erlbaum Associates, Publishers, 1985.

Ardin-Delteil, Lévi-Valensi, Derrieu: Deux cas d'aphasie. I. Aphasie de Broca par lésion de l'hémisphère droit chez une droitière. II. Aphasie avec hémiplégie droite chez une gauchère. *Rev. Neurol. (Paris): 30,* 14 – 24, 1923.

Assal G, Perentes E, Deruaz JP: Crossed aphasia in a right-handed patient. *Arch. Neurol. (Chicago): 38,* 455 – 458, 1981.

Basso A, Capitani E, Laiacona M, Zanobio ME: Crossed aphasia: one or more syndromes? *Cortex: 21,* 25 – 45, 1985.

Benton AL: Clinical symptomatology in right and left hemisphere lesions. In Mountcastle VB (Editor), *Interhemispheric Relations and Cerebral Dominance.* Baltimore: Johns Hopkins Press, 1962.

Bingley T: Mental symptoms in temporal lobe epilepsy and temporal lobe gliomas. *Acta Psychiatr. Neurol. Scand.: Suppl. 120,* 33, 1958.

Boller F: Destruction of Wernicke's area without language disturbance: a fresh look at crossed aphasia. *Neuropsychologia: 11,* 243 – 246, 1973.

Bradshaw JL, Nettleton NC: *Human Cerebral Asymmetry.* Englewood Cliffs (New Jersey): Prentice Hall, Inc., 1983.

Bramwell B: On 'crossed aphasia' and the factors which go to determine whether the 'leading' or 'driving' speech-centres shall be located in the left or in the right hemisphere of the brain, with notes of a case of 'crossed' aphasia (aphasia with right-side hemiplegia) in a left-handed man. *Lancet: i,* 1473 – 1479, 1899.

Broca P: Sur le siège de la Faculté du langage articulé. *Bull. Soc. Anthropol.: t.VI,* 337 – 393, 1865.

Brown JW: The neural organization of language: aphasia and lateralization. *Brain Lang.: 3,* 482 – 494, 1976.

Brown JW, Hécaen H: Lateralization and language representation. *Neurology: 26,* 183 – 189, 1976.

Brown JW, Jaffe J: Hypothesis on cerebral dominance. *Neuropsychologia: 13,* 107 – 110, 1975.

Brown JW, Wilson FR: Crossed aphasia in a dextral. *Neurology: 23,* 907 – 911, 1973.

Carr MS, Jacobson T, Boller F: Crossed aphasia: analysis of four cases. *Brain Lang.: 14,* 190 – 202, 1981.

Conrad K: Über aphasische Sprachstörungen bei Hirnverletzten Linkshänder. *Nervenarzt: 20,* 148 – 154, 1949.

Crovitz HF, Zener KA: A group test for assessing hand and eye dominance. *Am. J. Psychol.: 75,* 271 – 276, 1962.

Dax MG: Lésion de la moitié gauche de l'encéphale coïncidait avec l'oubli des signes de la pensée. Lu au congrès méridional tenu à Montpellier en 1836, par le docteur Marc Dax. *Gaz. Hebd. Méd. Chir.: t. XXXIII, 227(4),* 259 – 262, 1865.

Denes G, Caviezel F: Dichotic listening in crossed aphasia. 'Paradoxical' ipsilateral suppression. *Arch. Neurol. (Chicago): 38,* 182 – 185, 1981.

Ettlinger G, Jackson CV, Zangwill OL: Dysphasia following right temporal lobectomy in a right-handed man. *J. Neurol. Neurosurg. Psychiatry: 18,* 214 – 217, 1955.

Fernandez-Martin F, Martinez-Lage JM, Madoz P, Maravi E: La afasia cruzada. *J. Neurol. Sci.: 7,* 565 – 570, 1968.

Gloning I, Gloning K, Haub G, Quatember R: Comparison of verbal behavior in right-handed and non-right-handed patients with anatomically verified lesion of one hemisphere. *Cortex: 5,* 43 – 52, 1969.

Habib M, Joanette Y, Ali-Chérif A, Poncet M: Crossed aphasia in dextrals: a case report with special reference to site of lesion. *Neuropsychologia: 21,* 413 – 418, 1983.

Hécaen H, Ajuriaguerra, J de: *Les gauchers. Prévalence manuelle et dominance cérébrale.* Paris: Presses Universitaires de France, 1963.

Hécaen H, Albert ML: *Human neuropsychology.* New York: John Wiley & Sons, 1978.

Hécaen H, De Agostini M, Monzon-Montes A: Cerebral organization in left handers. *Brain Lang.: 12,* 261 – 284, 1981.

Hécaen H, Sauget J: Cerebral dominance in left-handed subjects. *Cortex: 7,* 19 – 48, 1971.

Joanette Y, Puel M, Nespoulous JL, Rascol A, Lecours AR: Aphasie croisée chez les droitiers. I. Revue de la littérature. *Rev. Neurol. (Paris): 138,* 575 – 586, 1982.

Levy J, Nagylaki T: A model for the genetics of handedness. *Genetics: 72,* 117 – 128, 1972.

Luria AR: *Traumatic Aphasia: Its Syndromes, Psychopathology and Treatment.* Moscow: Academy of Medical Sciences, 1947.

Newcombe F, Ratcliff GG: Handedness, speech lateralization and ability. *Neuropsychologia: 11,* 399 – 407, 1973.

Oldfield RC: The assessment and analysis of handedness: The Edinburgh Inventory. *Neuropsychologia: 9,* 97 – 114, 1971.

Penfield W, Roberts L: *Speech and Brain Mechanisms.* Princeton (New Jersey): Princeton University Press, 1959.

Pillon B, Desi M, Lhermitte F: Deux cas d'aphasie croisée avec jargonagraphie chez des droitiers. *Rev. Neurol. (Paris): 135,* 15 – 30, 1979.

Porac C, Coren S. *Lateral Preferences and Human Behavior.* New York: Springer Verlag, 1981.

Puel M, Joanette Y, Levrat M, Nespoulous JL, Viala MF, Lecours AR & Rascol A: Aphasie croisée chez les droitiers. II. Etude neurolinguistique et neuropsychologique d'un cas. Evolution sur deux ans. *Rev. Neurol. (Paris): 138,* 587 – 600, 1982.

Russell WR, Espir MLE: *Traumatic Aphasia.* Oxford: Oxford University Press, 1961.

Sapir S, Kokmen E, Rogers PJ: Subcortical crossed aphasia: a case report. *J. Speech Hear. Disord.: 51,* 172 – 176, 1986.

Satz P: Left-handedness and early brain insult: an explanation.

Neuropsychologia: 11, 115 – 117, 1973.

Satz P: Incidence of aphasia in left-handers: a test of some hypothetical models of cerebral speech organization. In Herron J (Editor), *Neuropsychology of Left-Handedness.* New York: Academic Press, Ch. 7, pp. 189 – 198, 1980.

Souques MA: Aphasie avec hémiplégie gauche chez un droitier. *Rev. Neurol. (Paris): 20,* 547 – 549, 1910.

Subirana A: La droiterie. *Schweiz. Arch. Neurol., Neurochir. Psychiatrie: 69,* 321, 1952.

Subirana A: The prognosis in aphasia in relation to the factor of cerebral dominance and handedness. *Brain: 8,* 415 – 425, 1958.

Sweet EWS, Panis W, Levine DN: Crossed Wernicke's aphasia. *Neurology: 34,* 475 – 479, 1984.

Urbain E, Seron X, Remits A, Linden M: Aphasie croisée chez une droitière. *Rev. Neurol. (Paris): 134,* 751 – 759, 1978.

Zangwill OL: Speech and the minor hemisphere. *Acta Neurol. Psychiatr. Belg.: 67,* 1013 – 1020, 1967.

© 1989 Elsevier Science Publishers B.V. (Biomedical Division)
Handbook of Neuropsychology, Vol. 2
F. Boller and J. Grafman (Eds)

CHAPTER 10

Non-verbal conceptual impairment in aphasia

Luigi Amedeo Vignolo

Clinica Neurologica dell'Universita, Spedali Civili, Brescia 25125, Italy

Purpose of chapter and some empirical definitions

This chapter discusses a number of empirical studies, some based on clinical observation alone, and some, more recently, on the systematic administration of non-verbal standardized tests, providing evidence of possible conceptual disorders associated with aphasia. In this clinical-experimental context, *concept* may be tentatively defined as a representation formed in the mind by generalizing from particulars, and *conceptual thinking* as the process of performing the operations required to form and handle concepts. *Abstraction* is used here in two ways, first, as the process by which a concept is obtained, and second, as a general idea, considered apart from the particulars perceived by the senses. *Abstract thinking* is opposed to concrete thinking, while *abstract attitude* underlines the *intentionality* of the conceptual operation. Categorical (or *'categoreal'*) thinking belongs to the wider sphere of conceptual thinking, stressing, however, the classificatory activity. Finally, *symbol* is used here in its broadest meaning, including both one thing representing another and, improperly, an arbitrary sign such as a word. Symbols thus defined constitute an essential instrument of *conceptual* thinking.

These widely overlapping definitions designate only some aspects of the broader notions of 'general intelligence' and 'cognition', and, in particular, they do not encompass the purely spatial organizational abilities. These terms are generally employed in order to explain the empirical findings of different clinical observations and experiments, and are often used loosely as synonymous, which admittedly is incorrect from a rigorously philosophical viewpoint.

Among the reviews on the broader topics of general intelligence and cognition in aphasia are the earlier works of Isserlin (1936), Weisenburg and McBride (1935), Ombrédane (1951) and Ajuriaguerra and Hécaen (1959) and the more recent studies by Hamsher (1981) and Gainotti (1988).

History

Clinical and unsystematic observations

As early as 1869 the pioneer Broca recognized some sort of intellectual defect in aphasia, and since the late nineteenth century a number of clinicians have studied it. The evidence used in these studies, based as it was mostly on either one or a few case-reports and heavily loaded with theoretical assumptions, was of questionable worth, and only a few examples need to be mentioned here. Trousseau (1864, 1865) stressed the fact that reading, writing and sometimes the imitation of gestures were as impaired as oral expression, and on this fragile basis he argued that aphasic patients suffer from a partial, but significant, loss of intelligence. Finkelnburg (1870) noticing an inability to recognize pantomimed actions and various conventional symbols (such as coins and military signs of rank) in aphasics, suggested subsuming these non-verbal disorders as well as those of oral and written language under the comprehensive concept of 'disorders of the symbolic function' or 'asymbolia', encompassing both the expression and the reception of symbols. On the basis of two post-mortem cases, he went so far as to indicate that the lesion was in the left insula and neighbouring temporal and parietal lobes. Jackson (1878) is credited with being the first in the English literature to suggest that aphasia involves an intellectual element. He observed that pantomime may be impaired and stated that aphasics are 'lame in thinking', in as much as 'speech is a part of thought' and that they often suffer from a 'loss or defect in symbolizing relations of things in any way'. These now oft-quoted statements were virtually ignored until Head revived Jackson's work in 1915 and developed it in his comprehensive book of 1926. He observed that patients were often unable to carry out a number of partially non-verbal tasks, such as pointing to their eye and ear both on command and on imitation, setting the hands of a clock, performing simple arithmetical calculations, assessing the comparative value of coins, and executing what would now be called 'constructional' tasks. He concluded that aphasia is a defect of 'symbolic formulation and expression', which to some extent transcends the linguistic sphere – a definition which enjoyed great success among Anglo-saxon researchers until the mid 1960s.

The Continental counterparts of the Jackson–Head line of thought were Marie's views in France and Goldstein's and Bay's in Germany. Marie (1906, 1926), based on his clinical observation of about one hundred cases, in 1906 undertook an epoch-making 'revision of the question of aphasia', and in this context he emphatically argued that 'true aphasia' is an intellectual impairment. By 'true' aphasia he meant Wernicke's aphasia (including, in a unified way, all forms that are nowadays subsumed under the heading of 'fluent' aphasia), while Broca's aphasia (corresponding to all 'non-fluent aphasia' forms, including global aphasia) also had an essential in-

tellectual element in it, being merely a combination of 'true aphasia' and an articulatory defect ('anarthria'). Marie maintained that the intellectual impairment of aphasics, unlike that of demented patients, is confined to 'didactically acquired procedures'. It is both general (affecting the association of ideas, memory, professional knowledge, and conventional and descriptive mimicry) and specific to language (affecting the comprehension of oral and written language, reading and writing). A well-known example of what Marie regarded as an intellectual deficit is the description of the striking errors made by an aphasic patient, a cook by profession, in the simple task of frying an egg – a grossly defective behavior which would now be diagnosed as a severe apraxia of use.

The idea that the aphasic's disorder of thinking may reflect a specific conceptual impairment did not arise until the work of Goldstein, whose often intricate arguments leading to this conclusion are found in a number of papers spanning several decades (e.g. Goldstein, 1919, 1927, 1942, 1948). This author's distinction between a concrete and an abstract (categorical, conceptual) attitude is central to our topic, and it is clearly stated in his book of 1942 (page 89):

'We can distinguish normally two different kinds of attitudes toward the world: a concrete and an abstract one. In the concrete attitude we are given over and bound to the immediate experience of a given thing or situation in its uniqueness. Our thinking and acting are directed by the immediate claims that one particular aspect of the object or situation in the environment makes. [. . .] We respond unreflectively to these claims. In the abstract attitude we transcend the immediately given, or sense impression; we *abstract* from particular properties. We are oriented in our actions by a conceptual point of view, be it the conception of a category, a class, or a general meaning under which the particular object before us falls. Our actions are determined not so much by the objects before us as by what we think about them. We detach ourselves from the immediate impression, and the individual thing becomes an accidental example or representative of a category. Therefore, we also call this attitude the categorical or conceptual attitude'.

Thus, according to Goldstein, the aphasic's basic disorder is the loss of the abstract attitude, which entails (a) language disruption, particularly, in amnesic aphasia (Goldstein, 1924), and (b) inability to perform non-verbal tasks requiring the patient to pick out (in gestalt terms) the essential in a field, to hold the figure clearly against the ground and, if necessary, to shift intentionally from a concept-directed classification to another (Goldstein and Scheerer, 1941). Two such tasks are, for example, Weigl's (1927) Color-Form Sorting Test, in which the patient classifies different cuts of wood according to color and form, and Gottschaldt's (1926, 1929) Hidden Figures Test, which evaluates the ability to disengage a geometrical figure from a distracting background which has been constructed using known field factors to produce maximal concealment.

Bay's theory (1962, 1963, 1964, 1974) incorporated both Marie's view of the 'true' aphasia and Goldstein's contention of the primary role played by categorical impairment in the disruption of language. He stressed that the intellectual defect in aphasia can be traced back to a specific disorder of 'concept formation' and actualization. As non-verbal evidence of such a disorder he described the remarkable errors made by some aphasics when requested to shape a plastic substance into three-dimensional models of common animals or objects. For example, when asked to reproduce a giraffe, a patient modelled an animal with a short neck but a very long tail, thereby showing that he was unable to form the exact concept of the giraffe, although he still had a vague idea that a salient feature of this animal was a long body part attached at one extremity of the trunk. Likewise, a tea-cup became, in the patient's reproduction, a much wider and flatter container, endowed, however, with a handle. Unfortunately, Bay provided no norms for such a task, nor did he rule out the possibility that his patient's errors were due to constructional apraxia – a disorder which cannot be considered a good marker of defective 'concept formation'. The same criticism applies to similar tasks, such as spontaneous drawing and drawing to command.

Most of the above authors not only believed that aphasia entails an intellectual defect, they further

maintained that the language disorder is merely one component of a more comprehensive and basic cognitive disorder of thinking. The opposite view was upheld by other workers, such as Wernicke (1874), Kleist (1934), Ajuriaguerra and Hécaen (1959) and Geschwind (1974) among others, all of whom minimized the importance of the cognitive impairment and maintained that disruption of the language mechanisms is an independent disorder. Wernicke, for example (1874), though well aware that aphasics did in fact sometimes show some intellectual deficits, explicitly warned that 'nothing could be worse for the study of aphasia than to consider the intellectual disturbance associated with aphasia as an essential part of the disease picture'. This lengthy controversy, sometimes referred to, in the French literature, as the 'noeticians vs. anti-noeticians' debate, was inconclusive and indeed, as Benton (1985) rightly observed, proved to be 'a rather fruitless exercise'. Nevertheless, it is both interesting and relevant for the present state of knowledge, because it contains some issues which are revived in more cautious terms in current hypotheses about the role of the conceptual impairment in aphasia.

First experimental studies 1930 – 1960

Methodologically, among the main drawbacks of the research reviewed so far were the lack of a clear differentiation between verbal and non-verbal performances, the undue generalization from single cases and the absence of normative values for the tests employed to assess cognitive impairment. A substantial advance in this respect was made by Weisenburg and McBride (1935), who were the first to administer a standard battery, including non-verbal as well as verbal tasks, to representative samples of aphasics ($n = 60$), non-aphasic brain-damaged patients ($n = 38$) and 'normal' controls ($n = 85$). The most relevant finding was that not only the verbal but also the non-verbal tests were performed more poorly by aphasics as a group than by the controls. However, the non-verbal battery included form-boards, mosaics, picture completion and drawing tests, thus involving first and foremost a visual constructional element, which is spatial rather than conceptual in nature. As Zangwill (1964) rightly pointed out, 'estimates of intelligence in aphasic patients should be based on performance tests only if constructional apraxia has been satisfactorily excluded' – which unfortunately does not apply to Weisenburg and McBride's results. Finally, these authors observed that, among aphasics, 'non-language performance . . . may suffer unequally. Variations are great and no general rule can be laid down for aphasia as a whole'. This inter-individual variation has been confirmed by subsequent investigation of non-verbal intelligence in aphasia, and it is now considered (Benton, 1985) a crucial problem whenever aphasics are studied as a homogeneous group.

Further experimental research was carried out by Teuber and Weinstein (1956), who, setting out to investigate perceptual selectivity in brain-damaged patients, did in fact contribute to our knowledge of the abstraction deficit in aphasics. They gave Gottschald's Hidden Figures Test to controls and brain-damaged patients who had suffered penetrating missile wounds about ten years before the testing. Brain-damaged patients were found to perform consistently worse than controls. Within the brain-damaged sample, aphasics as a group, irrespective of presence or absence of visual field defects and/or somatosensory symptoms, were significantly more defective than the other patients. This difference also persisted when the influence of 'general intelligence' (expressed by the Army General Classification Test score) on Gottschaldt's scores was ruled out by co-variance. These findings led Teuber and Weinstein to conclude that the disorder disclosed by Gottschaldt's test was intellectual rather than sensory-specific in nature. It appeared, however, that such a deficit could not be identified sic et simpliciter with general intellectual deterioration, but was a disorder of abstraction, conceived in its original meaning of mentally 'isolating from' *(abs-trahere).*

Dissenting evidence came from the work of Meyers (1948) and Bauer and Beck (1954), who found no significant inferiority in aphasics as compared to controls. Zangwill (1964), stressing the importance of these negative contributions, added quasi-anecdotal evidence of his own that pointed to the poor correspondence between severity of aphasia and number of errors in the Progressive Matrices Test (Raven, 1962) and concluded by taking a skeptical stand on the alleged co-occurrence of abstract thinking impairment and aphasia. It should be noted, however, that the Progressive Matrices were subsequently shown to be performed significantly worse by aphasics (although not selectively so) in carefully controlled experimental studies (see below). The intrinsic difficulty of the topic, the too often contrasting results and the admixture of empirical evidence with theoretical dogmas brought about a certain disaffection for the problem (cf. Zangwill, 1969, 1975).

Current research

Revival of research after the 1960s

Impairment on non-verbal association tasks
Indirect (and unexpected) evidence of a non-verbal conceptual disorder in aphasia came from a number of quantitative studies in the 1960s and early 1970s, most of which were originally aimed at investigating the possible concomitance of aphasia and the hemispheric side of the lesion with the classical agnosias, i.e. the non-verbal recognition defects. The mechanism of the agnosias, like that of the apraxias, is an obscure problem in clinical neurology, and it is not surprising, therefore, that this line of research was started off experimentally by the Milan group of neuropsychology, which at the time was entirely made up of neurologists.

Non-verbal recognition in various modalities (such as audition and vision of different types of stimulus) was assessed by means of ad hoc quantitative tests, administered to large unselected samples of right-handed patients, either without cerebral lesions ('controls') or with stabilized lesions confined to one hemisphere. The latter were further subdivided according to presence/absence of aphasia, as assessed by standard language batteries, and often also by the presence/absence of a visual field defect (VFD), which was considered evidence of postrolandic extension of the lesion. Auditory verbal comprehension scores were usually chosen as a measure of the severity of language disruption in the broader sense, since oral expression measures could be biased by concomitant articulatory difficulties. The control group scores were used to establish norms, i.e. to determine to what extent the imperfect performance of any given hemisphere-damaged patients could still be considered to fall within normal limits, or had to be defined as 'abnormal'. In spite of variations in recognition modality, test construction and scoring criteria, the common and crucial aspect of such non-verbal tasks is that they involved the *association* or matching of meaningful items (e.g. braying noise with donkey, red color with cherry etc.). Results were often compared with those of another type of task, entailing the perceptual *discrimination* of *meaningless* items (e.g., nondescript noises, different shades of the same color, etc.). Aphasics as a group selectively failed on the association tasks, but not on the perceptual discrimination tasks (when administered). These, by contrast, were selectively impaired in right-brain-damaged patients with posterior lesions. The consistent and specific concomitance of aphasia with failure on the association tasks, irrespective of the recognition modality (especially in the presence of good perceptual discrimination), led to the hypothesis that the aphasics' failure on these tests involved the high-level recognition of their meaning rather than the low-level, formal differentiation of their perceptual characteristics. This possibility fuelled new interest in the problem of conceptual impairment in aphasia. The main pertinent studies will be discussed in some detail.

Sound-to-picture association. In an investigation of auditory agnosia, Spinnler and Vignolo (1966) examined three samples of patients with unilateral hemispheric damage (aphasic, non-aphasic left-brain-damaged, right-brain-damaged and 'normal'

controls) by means of a sound-recognition test requiring the identification of meaningful sounds or noises.

The subject was asked to listen to the sound on a tape-recorder and to indicate which of four pictures shown to him represented the natural source of the sound he had just heard. To obtain information about the quality of the recognition disorder, the test was arranged in such a way that the picture corresponding to a given sound (e.g., the song of a canary) represented respectively (1) the correct natural source of the song (e.g., a canary singing); (2) the natural source of a sound *acoustically* very similar to the presented sound (e.g., a boy whistling); (3) a sound-producing event or object belonging to the same *semantic* category of the natural source of the presented sound, but producing a sound completely different from the presented one from an *acoustic* standpoint (e.g., a cock crowing); and (4) a sound-producing event or object unrelated to the presented sound either acoustically or semantically (e.g., a train in motion). Thus, three types of error were possible; *acoustic* errors, when the patient pointed to picture 2; *semantic* errors when he pointed to picture 3; *odd* errors, when he pointed to picture 4.

It was found that while non-aphasic left- and right-brain-damaged patients performed virtually the same as normal controls on the test, about one-fourth of aphasics (26%) fell below the normal cut-off score. Moreover, aphasics made significantly more semantic than acoustic errors, while the reverse trend occurred in the remaining groups. These results were confirmed by Faglioni et al. (1969), employing two different ad hoc tests. The first (the Meaningful Sounds Identification Test) was similar to that used in the preceding study and was intended to test the ability to identify the exact *meaning* of sounds. The second (the Meaningless Sound Discrimination Test) was intended to test the ability to accurately discriminate the *acoustic pattern* of sounds: the patients heard two successive nondescript noises and had to say whether they were 'the same' or 'different'. Aphasics, while specifically failing on the first test, were unimpaired on the second, which, by contrast, was particularly vulnerable to lesions of the right hemisphere. This double dissociation was recently confirmed by Vignolo (1982), who checked the hemispheric side of the lesion by means of a CT scan, while Varney and Damasio (1986) showed that the associative defect may be concomitant with several lesion sites in the left hemisphere. The aphasic's inability to match meaningful sounds and noises with their meaning is now well established (see also Doehring et al., 1967; Strohner et al., 1978; Varney, 1980, 1982a). The percentage of aphasics selectively impaired varies according to the testing techniques and experimental design from 26% (Spinnler and Vignolo, 1966) to 45% (Faglioni et al., 1969; Varney, 1980) and 43% (Varney, 1982a). On the whole, global and Wernicke's aphasia patients did worse than the other aphasics. In spite of the criticisms of Strohner et al. (1978), who found that semantic errors were no longer predominant when corrected for odd errors, all the above findings are rather consistent. They do show that impaired sound recognition, characteristic of aphasics, is due mainly to the inability to associate the perceived sound with its correct meaning, rather than to a defect of acoustic discrimination.

Color-to-picture association. In a study of color agnosia, De Renzi and Spinnler (1967) showed that aphasics, in contrast with other groups of brain-damaged patients and controls, were specifically impaired on a test requiring the subject to choose the typical color of a given object. The patient was given a set of colored pencils and a sheet of paper with a number of black-and-white line drawings of common objects having a typical color, such as a banana, a cherry, a cigar, and so on. The patient was asked to color each drawing with a few strokes, choosing the appropriate pencil. On the other hand, Scotti and Spinnler (1970) found that aphasics had no difficulty in carrying out tasks of subtle chromatic perception and discrimination, such as required by Farnsworth's (1943) 100 Hues Test, which was performed significantly more poorly by the right-brain-damaged patients with posterior lesions. These data were confirmed by De Renzi et al. (1972a), who concluded that the aphasics' poor performance in the color-to-picture task 'may be, at least in part, contingent upon a more general disorder of cognition, associated with, but not directly dependent on, the language derangement'.

This defect, which, whenever reported, was found in about one-third of the aphasic samples under study, has been confirmed by a number of investigations (Basso et al., 1976; Assal and Buttet, 1976; Cohen and Kelter, 1979; Varney, 1982b; Basso et al., 1985). However, the presence of color-to-picture impairment in the absence of a major aphasic syndrome (though associated with color anomia and alexia) has been described in single case reports by Stengel (1948), Kinsbourne and Warrington (1964) and Varney and Digre (1983).

Object-to-picture association. A study of visual form agnosia, carried out by De Renzi et al. (1969), showed that aphasics, in contrast to other samples of brain-damaged patients and controls, were selectively impaired in a task requiring the subject to match a picture with the corresponding object. Ten different objects were displayed on the table in front of the patient, who was then handed, in succession, ten realistic, colored pictures representing the same objects. He was asked to point to the correct object. The test was so designed that the picture was not an exact copy of the corresponding real object, but belonged to a different type of the same category. For example, the real key put on the table was a small, flat, white-metal car key, while the pictured one was a big, thick, black iron, old fashioned gate key. As a consequence, a correct matching could rely very little (or, most often, not at all) on the mere perceptual features of the two items, while it implied a categorization of the matched objects, leading to the awareness that both the real and the depicted object were subsumed under the same concept, e.g. the concept 'key'.

In contrast to their poor performance in this associative test, aphasics were not selectively impaired on the perceptual tasks of the Overlapping Figures Test (Poppelreuter, 1917) and a Face Recognition Test. These were specifically vulnerable in patients with right posterior hemispheric lesions.

The concomitance of aphasia with poor picture-to-object matching has been recently confirmed by Della Sala (1987), who found that the defect involved 37% of the aphasic sample and tended to be more frequent, though not significantly so, in Wernicke's and global aphasias.

Object-to-gesture and gesture-to-picture association. In a study of so-called 'agnosia of use' (Morlaas, 1928) or 'apraxia of use', which belongs to the wider category of ideational apraxia (De Renzi et al., 1968), the patient was given, successively, a number of objects frequently employed in everyday life, such as a hammer, and he was asked to take it into his hands and show how he would use it. This simple task was performed well by all experimental groups, except 34% of aphasics, and the deficit tended to be both more frequent and more conspicuous in global (80%) and severe Wernicke's aphasia (50% affected). Comparison with the scores obtained on a parallel test of imitation of gestures ruled out the possibility that poor performances were due to ideomotor apraxia, and indicated that the low scores resulted from *inability to choose the gesture normally associated with the appropriate use of the object.* In other words, here again the basic disturbance of aphasic patients was associative rather than psychomotor, and it could be tentatively described as the failure to synthesize different aspects of the same concept − a definition very reminiscent of Bay's (1964) view of impaired 'concept formation'.

Conversely, a series of studies investigating the patient's ability to recognize gestures and pantomimes performed by the examiner and point to the corresponding picture presented in a multiple-choice array (e.g. Gainotti and Lemmo, 1976; Duffy and Duffy, 1981; Varney, 1982a; Duffy and Watkins, 1984; Daniloff et al., 1982; see also reviews by Peterson and Kirshner, 1981, and by Christopoulou and Bonvillian, 1985) yielded results that, on the whole, are in line with the above-mentioned research. Thus, even when gestures were demonstrated for the patient, rather than requested of him, their association with the correct picture was significantly impaired in aphasics, from 41% (Varney, 1982a) to 62% (Gainotti and Lemmo, 1976) of the examined sample, but not in non-aphasic brain-damaged pa-

tients. When the type of mismatch was specifically investigated (Varney and Benton, 1982), semantic errors were found to be predominant, representing 80−100% of the total errors of aphasics. This strongly suggested that aphasics had a 'semantically vague' understanding of the pantomimes, rather than a complete lack of understanding. This finding was parallel to what was observed with the identification of meaningful sounds.

***

The above evidence clearly indicates a preferential concomitance of aphasia in general with failure on non-verbal association tasks. Such failure constitutes the so-called 'associative-semantic' level of agnosia (consisting of faulty identification of the *meaning* of percepts), as opposed to the purely 'perceptual-discriminative' level (consisting of impaired discrimination of the *form* of percepts) (Vignolo, 1972). This isolation of the semantic-conceptual level of the non-verbal recognition disorder can be traced back to earlier clinically based theories. For example, Kleist (1928) discussed agnosia for non-verbal sound and noises by contrasting the 'deafness-for-the-meaning-of-noises' ('Gerauschsinntaubheit') with the 'deafness-for-the-form-of-noises' ('Gerauschformtaubheit'). Lewandowski (1907) described a specific inability to connect the appropriate color with the corresponding line drawings. Lissauer (1890) isolated an 'associative' form of visual object agnosia, to be distinguished from an 'apperceptual' form. Finkelnburg's (1870) view that defective pantomime recognition reflected a higher, symbolic disorder has already been mentioned. The experimental findings reviewed so far added to the theoretical autonomy of these high-level non-verbal disorders *the important qualification that they were specifically associated with left-hemisphere lesions and aphasia.*

The reason the matching defects can be considered 'conceptual' in nature deserves comment. In spite of their seeming differences (association of sound to figure, color to figure, object to figure, object to gesture and vice versa) it may be argued that they require basically similar conceptual operations, since all essentially challenge the ability to grasp and handle the *meaning* of the presented stimuli. To correctly match stimuli which are perceptually very different, such as a miaowing sound and the picture of a cat, a blue pencil and a line drawing of waves, a realistic picture of a big, old-fashioned black iron key and a small, white-metal flat locker key, etc., one must realize that the members of each pair *signify* the same thing. In other words, one must recognize them, beyond the appearances, as representative of the same concept and thus associate them. Likewise, since the gesture of hammering is a constituent element of the concept of hammer (as are the object itself, its typical shape, the sound of the blows, etc.), it is difficult not to see in so-called 'apraxia of use' still another instance of the same conceptual disorder. This analogy also applies to the whole series of tasks requiring gesture-to-figure matching, investigated on the receptive rather than the expressive side. Therefore, it is not surprising that even pantomime recognition, like all association tasks, is specifically impaired in aphasic patients.

Impairment on a non-verbal task specifically requiring the handling of concepts

The conceptual disorder revealed by the failure of a sizeable proportion of aphasic patients on non-verbal association tasks can be examined more directly by means of a classic test of 'categoreal' thinking, such as the Color-Form Sorting Test, devised by Weigl in 1927 and included in Goldstein's battery (Goldstein, 1948).

The sorting behavior required by Weigl's test depends upon an ability to deal with concepts which, although at a higher degree of difficulty, is quite similar to that involved in the non-verbal association tasks. To sort and group together all round blocks, for example, it is necessary to temporarily disregard their individual differences in color, size, etc., and to focus on form alone, thereby realizing that they all belong to the same

concept, the concept of circle. Likewise, in matching a gesture to the corresponding figure, etc., it is necessary to disregard their differences in the formal and/or perceptual modality and to understand that they represent the same thing.

In the modified version, adopted by De Renzi et al. (1966), the patient was given 12 pieces of wood which, although all different from one another, could be sorted according to five discrete categories, i.e. color, form, suit (symbol), thickness and size. He was then asked to group them by 'putting together all the blocks which had something in common.' If he failed to find a correct solution within 3 minutes, the examiner sorted the items himself and asked the patient to indicate (by word, gesture and/or replication of the sorting) the category employed. A correct performance implied the ability to sort out, one at a time, each single feature of the blocks (e.g., color), leaving aside the other features.

Aphasics scored significantly worse than the right, left non-aphasic control groups, whose performance was not significantly different from one another. These results were at variance with those of a previous experiment by McFie and Piercy (1952), in that they indicated that impairment on Weigl's Test is specifically associated with aphasia, and not merely with lesions of the left hemisphere. In addition they failed to establish a poorer performance by amnesic aphasics (contrary to Goldstein, 1924), probably because the authors chose only patients with very pure, hence rather mild, amnesic aphasia.

Not all non-verbal tasks proposed by Goldstein (1948) as specific tests of 'abstract' thinking proved to be equally adequate to the intended purpose, probably because they also involve non-conceptual abilities. This is the case with Holmgren's (1877) Skein Test and Gottschaldt's (1926, 1929) Hidden Figures Test, among others. The former requires primarily the capacity to perform subtle perceptual discriminations, while the latter is heavily loaded with a visuo-spatial component.

In Holmgren's (1877) Skein Test, the patient is presented with a number of woollen skeins of different hues and is asked to pick out all the skeins belonging to the same color category (e.g. all the reds, the greens, etc.) De Renzi et al. (1972b) found that not only aphasics but also right-brain-damaged patients with visual-field defects performed poorly on this test. When the scores obtained by the same patients on a test of hue discrimination (Farnsworth) and on Weigl's Test were introduced as covariates in the analysis of Holmgren's Test means, it was found that the former significantly adjusted Holmgren's scores, while the latter did not. Finally, Holmgren's scores were not significantly correlated in aphasics with auditory verbal comprehension scores. The authors concluded that, while the right-brain-damaged impairment was due to a defect of hue discrimination, the reason for the aphasics' impairment was obscure, but it certainly could not be explained as a defect of the abstract attitude, as maintained by Goldstein (1924). At any rate, Holmgren's Test does not appear to be sufficiently related to other sorting tasks to be considered a reliable measure of conceptual thinking (De Renzi et al., 1972b).

Performance on Gottschaldt's Hidden Figures Test (Gottschaldt, 1926, 1929), which, as mentioned above, requires the ability to single out a visual figure from a complex background, was considered by Goldstein (1948) to involve the same basic function as Weigl's Test, which consists of singling out one visual feature and using it as a criterion for sorting different items. As described above, Teuber and Weinstein (1956), examining patients with penetrating missile wounds of the hemispheres, pointed to a specific association between poor performance on the Hidden Figures Test and aphasia. However, a subsequent study (Russo and Vignolo, 1967) of stroke patients which employed a more sophisticated statistical analysis clearly showed that right-brain-damaged patients, in addition to aphasics, performed poorly on the test. This was interpreted as a consequence of the marked visual-spatial component of the task.

A brief digression seems appropriate here to recall that the same performance pattern was recently found with Raven's Matrices (1962, 1965) – a widely used visual-spatial intelligence test. From a thorough review of the contrasting results obtained by different investigators using the original set of the Coloured Matrices in hemisphere-damaged patients, Gainotti et al. (1986b) concluded that some discrepancies found in the literature might be due to the negative influence of unilateral spatial neglect on performance, particularly on that of right-brain-damaged patients. They therefore undertook a carefully controlled study employing a new version of the test, devised to minimize the influence of unilateral spatial neglect without changing the essential features of the original task. In spite of this, they found that aphasics and right-brain-damaged patients were almost equally impaired and significantly more so than non-aphasic left-brain-damaged patients and non-brain-damaged controls. The poor performance of the

right-brain-damaged patients, while not emphasized in the discussion (which focused mainly on the relationship between the level of language disruption and the failure on the Coloured Matrices in the aphasic group; see below), is an important finding, which is probably due to the strong visual-spatial component of the test.

In summary, the isolation of the semantic-conceptual level of agnosia alerted the investigators to the possibility of a non-verbal conceptual impairment in aphasia, and this hypothesis was confirmed by the use of Weigl's Test. Whenever other intellectual tests, implying subtle perceptual discrimination or visuo-spatial analysis, were employed, right-brain-damaged patients also performed poorly.

A pause for reflection: tentative hypotheses

The evidence reviewed so far indicates that disorders of non-verbal conceptual thinking were more severe and more frequent in aphasics, as a group, than in left and right non-aphasic brain-damaged patients and controls. However, closer scrutiny of the experimental findings disclosed a number of important details which pointed to the need to qualify such general findings. In particular the problems of (A) the unity or multiplicity of the verbal conceptual impairment and (B) the relationship to the language disruption remained quite obscure.

(A) Disorders of conceptual thought have been assessed, in the reviewed studies, by a welter of diverse empirical tasks. The more economical view, that one was dealing with a single basic Grundstörung, would require that the performances on these tasks of aphasics as a group should correlate with one another to a highly significant degree. The actual findings were unsatisfactory from this viewpoint. For example, the correlations between the tests of sound-to-picture, color-to-picture and object-to-picture matching, computed in 99 patients who had been administered the three tests together, were indeed found to be significant only among the 57 left-brain-damaged patients (virtually all aphasics) (Vignolo, 1972). However, as shown in Table 1, the degree of such correlations was not sufficiently high to point to one single basic disorder underlying failure on the three tasks. This reminds one that contingency data failed to indicate a close relationship between pantomime recognition and sound recognition, which led Varney (1982a) to cast doubt on the asymbolic, unitary nature of the impairment demonstrated on these tests.

(B) The correlation between the degree of the non-verbal conceptual defect and that of the auditory language comprehension defect for words and sentences (which in most studies was adopted as a crude measure of aphasia) was not as high as one would expect of two disorders linked by a strong functional tie (e.g. De Renzi et al., 1968). When the Token Test (De Renzi and Vignolo, 1962a) was used as a measure of auditory language comprehension and hence, by extension, of aphasia, the correlations were usually higher (e.g. 0.65, Faglioni et al., 1969; 0.66, De Renzi et al., 1972a). However, since this test itself has been considered by some authors to be, at least in part, a conceptual test (see below), these figures should be taken with caution. Besides, only a percentage of the aphasic samples, ranging approximately from one-third to two-thirds, according to different samplings, tasks and experimental designs, showed a disorder of conceptual thinking. Some severe aphasics did not show this defect, which, in contrast, was occasionally present, though to a less severe degree, in a few left-brain-damaged patients without aphasia. This variability leads one to the suspicion that the non-verbal impairment could not be associated with aphasia in general, but *only with a specific aspect of the language disruption,*

possibily an aspect which embodied so-called 'inner language'. As will be seen, later studies attempted to explore precisely this possibility.

Taken together, the above-discussed findings do not provide a basis for a satisfactory explanation based on a direct functional relationship between conceptual impairment and aphasia *in the wider sense.* Rather, they compel us to discard as unlikely the simple-minded view that aphasia *as a whole* is either the *consequence* or the *cause* of a conceptual disorder.

The first interpretation seems to be improbable a priori because it is difficult to see how conceptual impairment as such might encompass the manifold aphasic symptoms, and in particular those which depend on the disruption of the phonological level of language, such as phonemic paraphasias and phonemic jargon. Indeed, in the published case series reviewed above, more than half the aphasics, including severe aphasics, did not show a significant failure of the associative semantic type and, as previously mentioned, the correlations between non-verbal conceptual impairment and different measures of comprehension (i.e. of aphasia), though always significant, are too low to establish a strict cause-effect relationship.

Conversely, the reviewed findings also fail to support the opposite interpretation, according to which failure on the non-verbal associative and conceptual tasks would merely depend upon the general disruption of language. The argument implies that the correct performance of such tasks relies entirely on implicit verbal mediation and, as a consequence, is affected by the diminished availability of words brought about by aphasia. The absence of significant non-verbal conceptual disorders in patients with severe aphasia and their presence in a certain number of left-brain-damaged patients without aphasia (including Lissauer's patient) are additional arguments against the simple-minded view of a cause and effect relationship − in either direction − between the non-verbal conceptual impairment and aphasia sensu lato.

These considerations led most investigators in

TABLE 1

	Color to picture	Picture to object
Sound to picture	0.48***	0.36**
Color to picture	−	0.61***

** = $p < 0.01$ *** = $p < 0.001$

the 1960s and early 1970s to leave aside, for the time being, the hypothesis of a functional relationship, and to lean toward the less constricting view of the anatomical contiguity and overlapping of the areas underlying non-verbal conceptual and language processing (De Renzi et al., 1966; Basso et al., 1973). They maintained that the left-hemisphere areas underlying conceptual impairment and the aphasias were contiguous and partly overlapping.

An alternative possibility was considered after a critical review of the main findings to that date (Vignolo, 1972). It was suggested that both the failure on the conceptual tasks and *certain limited aspects* of the aphasic syndrome might well be due to the same underlying mechanism: 'for example, the semantic paraphasias and the auditory comprehension errors 'in the semantic sphere' disclose an inability to operate the junction between *signifié* and *signifiant* (in De Saussure's sense, 1960) which is analogous to the non-verbal association defect discussed in the preceding section, and which might well depend on the same basic disorder'. In this vein, a common clinical observation is worth mentioning: the so-called transcortical sensory aphasias – in which the phonemic level is virtually intact, while the semantic-lexical level is selectively disrupted, as witnessed by the abundance of semantic paraphasias and of comprehension errors 'in the semantic sphere' – are the dissociated forms of aphasia which show the severest degree of non-verbal cognitive impairment. This functional approach was eventually developed by the Rome group of neuropsychology of the Catholic University (see below). Before such evidence appeared, the hypothesis of anatomical contiguity and broad overlapping seemed the most promising.

Recent lines of research

The inability to formulate an acceptable hypothesis suggesting a primarily functional link between non-verbal conceptual impairment and aphasia *as a whole* indicated to investigators that both disorders are multi-faceted in nature, and that a more analytical approach was needed for future research. The notion of non-verbal conceptual impairment, though more restricted than that of 'intellectual' or 'cognitive' disorders, is multiform, as witnessed by the welter of behavioral definitions (embodied in the different experimental tasks) and by the overlapping of its meaning with that of other terms, such as disorder of abstract attitude, of symbolic thought, etc. On the other hand, aphasia encompasses several different clinical forms (Broca's, Wernicke's, etc.), modalities (oral and written expression, comprehension, etc.) and levels of language disruption (phonemic, syntactic and semantic-lexical).

If was not until the 1970s and 1980s that investigators fully realized the intricacy of the problem, and such newly acquired awareness guided a whole series of more circumscribed, specific experimental studies. With some degree of arbitrariness, two partially overlapping lines of research may be detected. (1) Some studies tried to identify the type of non-verbal conceptual operation which is particularly or exclusively impaired in aphasia; (2) others aimed at isolating, within the multiformity of the aphasic disorder, one (or more) modality or mechanism, disruption of which is associated with the non-verbal conceptual disorder. Moreover, evidence from these two trends, in addition to that of a few specific studies, provided some hints as to (3) the difficult issue of the nature of the functional interaction between the non-verbal and the verbal conceptual defect. A brief review follows.

Type of conceptual operation on which aphasics specifically fail

This area was investigated in several studies, especially by the Konstanz group of neuropsychologists and linguists. Cohen et al. (1975, 1976) and Kelter et al. (1976) unexpectedly found that aphasics, as compared to non-aphasic brain-damaged, schizophrenic and normal subjects, performed poorly on a non-verbal task requiring them to select which of two pictures (referent and non-referent) was related to a third picture (clue), when the mediator, i.e. the common aspect linking clue to referent, was 'perceptual' in nature.

The following examples may be explanatory: (a) referent picture (to be selected): swan/non-referent picture: turkey; clue picture: snowman; *mediator:* color white; (b) screw/nail; winding stairs; *mediator:* spiral. By contrast, aphasics performed as well as the other groups when the mediator was 'situational' rather than 'perceptual' in nature (e.g. (a) guitar/violin; bullfight; *mediator:* Spain; (b) grave/picture postcard from mountains; obituary card; *mediator:* death). In these and subsequent experiments the so-called 'perceptual' mediators in fact encompassed a wide range of characteristics. In general mediators consisted of a significant detail, either *physical* but not necessarily detectable on the black-and-white, equal-size drawings (e.g. spikes, as in rose/tulip: porcupine; size, as in Saint Bernard dog/Pekinese dog: dwarf; color, as in the above-mentioned example of swan/turkey: snowman), *functional* (e.g. movement, as in snail/toad: kangaroo), *relational* (e.g. danger, as in shark/antelope: tiger) or even *psychological* (e.g. vanity, as in peacock/turkey: lady powdering in front of a mirror). The term 'perceptual', applied to the mediator in these tasks, may be misleading, and it must be clarified.

As the above examples show, the so-called 'perceptual' tasks of the Konstanz authors did not entail a problem of subtle perceptual discrimination, but, rather, they involved the *conceptual* operations to be performed with *semantically relevant* 'perceptual' features. This point is worth stressing, since subtle perceptual discrimination (in Lissauer's (1890) sense of 'apperception') was found to be specifically impaired in right, not left, brain-damaged patients (whatever the modality of the stimulus) both in the investigations in the 1960s, as discussed earlier in the chapter, and in the recent study by Cohen et al. (1983). In the latter (see Experiment III) the presentation in pairs of nearly identical visual figures, such as Chinese ideograms differing in one small detail, was performed significantly worse by right-brain-damaged patients with visual-field defects than by aphasics.

The dissociation 'perceptual' vs. 'situational' was confirmed by Woll et al. (1979) and Cohen et al. (1980a), who contrasted a test of 'characteristic parts' (e.g. crown/traffic handsignaller: scepter) which was difficult for aphasics with one of 'situa-tions' (e.g. royal coach/throne: chair), which was easy for aphasics. Taken together, all these findings led to an interesting hypothesis, i.e. that the crucial non-verbal conceptual impairment of aphasics consists of the inability to perform the 'analytical isolation, identification and conceptual comparison of highly specific individual aspects' of different items. By contrast, conceptual operations mainly based on common situational contexts are relatively spared. In other words, aphasic patients are specifically impaired in categorizing items on the basis of single, individual attributes common to all of them, such attributes being often, but not necessarily, perceptual sensu strictiore, while they are unimpaired in categorizing items having in common a whole complex of associations and few individual features. This interesting hypothesis was not consistently confirmed by subsequent studies, such as those by Cohen et al. (1982, 1983). The inability to replicate the previously noticed difference may be due, at least in part, to employing tasks that are too easy — as the authors themselves admit when referring to the work of Wilkins and Moskovitch (1978), whose testing conditions were more stressful. At any rate, the hypothesis remains worth pursuing. Moreover, the above-mentioned contradictions teach a lesson in methods, as they have the merit of alerting workers in the field to the possible influence of the structure and the difficulty of the several empirically constructed tests in the research findings — a point which is often ignored in experimental clinical neuropsychology.

The subsequent work of Cohen and coworkers focused mainly on better defining their hypothesis of 'analytical handling of individual features'. For example, Cohen and Woll (1981) investigated whether or not performance is affected by being able to actually *see* the relevant feature, by means of two-picture-ordering tasks, in one of which ('perceptual') the feature which allowed the drawing to be sorted and ordered systematically could be seen directly in the drawings themselves (e.g., length of hair of different female heads), while in the other ('inferable') they had to be inferred from everyday knowledge about the depicted objects (e.g., speed of different vehicles). Aphasics tended to do worse than the other groups on both tasks, but the difference was more pronounced in the latter than in the former test. It should be noted that the 'inferable' attributes task was easier than the 'perceptual' one, and that the aphasic's impairment was on the whole rather slight.

The massive contribution of the Konstanz group, in spite of some conflicting findings, does suggest a provisional hypothesis about the type of conceptual operation on which aphasics specifically fail. It would appear that at least two aspects are essential in making a non-verbal conceptual task particularly difficult for aphasics. Firstly, the task must require an intentional search and sustained *focusing of attention* on one discrete characteristic, common to the otherwise heterogeneous presented material – the characteristic may or may not be actually perceivable in the presented items. Secondly, the task must necessitate *abstracting* such a common characteristic and thereby recognizing that seemingly different things actually are subsumed by the same concept. The fact of voluntarily assuming a searching disposition or set strongly reminds one of the intentionality which is inherent in Goldstein's 'abstract attitude'. It also stresses the active, analytical aspect of the conceptual operation, as opposed to the more passive recognition of the commonness of items which occurs when these belong to several, broadly overlapping semantic fields. The latter type of recognition, while seemingly abstract and conceptual, is in fact much more concrete in nature, because it imposes itself, as it were, automatically upon the mind. This is probably the reason why it is easy even for aphasics. As to the need for a focusing of attention, this view agrees with the idea that the left (language-dominant) hemisphere processes items by concentrating on specific distinctions, rather than in a global way (see Bradshaw and Nettleton, 1981 and 1983, for discussion of the available evidence, pro and con).

To conclude, the thinking of the Konstanz group is definitely in line with Goldstein's (and Bay's) conceptions, particularly as regards its insistence on the conceptual handling of percepts and the intentional characteristic of the whole operation.

Aspects of the aphasic disorder that are specifically associated with the non-verbal conceptual impairment

Another line of research stemmed from awareness of the unsatisfactory degree of relationship between the above-described conceptual defects and aphasia *in general*. This prompted some investigators to look more closely into the aphasic syndrome in search of a more sensitive, albeit partial, linguistic correlate of the non-verbal impairment. A number of studies, carried out in the 1970s and 1980s, yielded additional findings concerning the correlation between the failure on the non-verbal associative and conceptual tasks and (a) various *clinical types* of aphasia, (b) impairment of different language *modalities* and (c) impairment of a *specific level* of linguistic disruption.

(a) Non-verbal conceptual defects and clinical types of aphasia
The early trend showing patients with global and severe Wernicke's aphasias to be more impaired on non-verbal conceptual tasks than the remaining clinical types was confirmed in a few of the more recent studies (e.g. De Renzi et al., 1972a; Gainotti and Lemmo, 1976). In some other studies the non-verbal defect was preferentially or selectively associated with fluent aphasia sensu lato (Varney, 1980), with global aphasia (Gainotti and Lemmo, 1976), or even – surprisingly – with Broca's aphasia (probably, however, including some globals: Cohen and Woll, 1981). In several studies in which these clinical partitions were explored, no significant difference was found either among the different forms or among groupings thereof. By contrast, a number of patients *without* non-verbal conceptual impairment were found even among the more severe aphasic syndromes (e.g. in about half of Wernicke's patients in De Renzi et al.,

1972a). Possible factors contributing to such contrasting results may include (1) different behavioral criteria adopted to subdivide aphasia and to define aphasic syndromes; for example, global aphasic patients were considered a discrete subclass in some studies, while they were included in the non-fluent subclass in others; (2) different concomitant variables introduced in the covariance analysis to evaluate the significance of intersyndrome comparisons: these variables ranged from some basic clinical parameters, such as age, years of schooling and length of illness, to the scores of several other behavioral tests given to the same patients. Thus, these results proved somewhat unreliable and inconclusive, and call for more homogeneous research strategies.

(b) Non-verbal conceptual defects and modalities of language impairment

While essentially confirming earlier findings indicating the concomitance of non-verbal conceptual impairment and aphasia as a whole, some studies stressed that failure on the (meaningful) sound-to-picture task was specifically associated with defects in the auditory comprehension of single words (Varney, 1980), to the extent that intact sound-to-picture performance in the acute stage post-stroke could predict rapid and complete recovery of auditory verbal comprehension (Varney, 1984a). By contrast, reading comprehension defects, rather than auditory ones, were found to be the selective aphasic correlates of poor color-to-picture (Varney, 1982b) and especially of poor gesture-to-picture matching (Varney, 1978, 1982a; Ferro et al., 1980). In addition, the last task was closely related to footprint 'reading', as evaluated by a picture-to-picture matching of line drawings of animals with their footprints – a task considered 'a type of "ideogram reading" requiring no special training' (Varney, 1984b). These differential associations suggest the existence of modality-specific determinants (e.g., visual, auditory) of both non-verbal and verbal matching tasks, and tend to undermine the hypothesis of one basic conceptual disorder subserving the impairment of both language and thought irrespective of modality. However, Varney, with Sivan (1985a, b), showed that both color-to-picture and gesture-to-picture matching tasks are performed at a normal adult level not only by normal children from age 6 onwards, but also by dyslexic children – which indirectly contradicts the modality-specificity hypothesis advanced to explain the poor non-verbal association tasks in aphasic adults.

(c) Non-verbal conceptual defects and impairment of a specific level of linguistic disruption

A series of studies by the group of neurologists and neuropsychologists at the Catholic University in Rome aimed at verifying the hypothesis that the specific aphasic correlate of non-verbal conceptual impairment could be identified with the semantic-lexical level of language impairment, as opposed to the phonemic (or phonological) and the syntactic levels. The semantic-lexical level, defined as the processing of the meaning of words as unitary and significant entities, can be selectively disrupted in aphasia (Alajouanine et al., 1964; Lhermitte et al., 1971) and such disruption manifests itself through the utterance of semantically related verbal paraphasias during the expression tasks (Schuell and Jenkins, 1961; Rinnert and Whitaker, 1973; Buckingham and Rekart, 1979) and through the (not necessarily parallel) inability to point to the correct picture or object in an array of semantically similar items during comprehension tasks (Pizzamiglio and Appicciafuoco, 1971; Daujat et al., 1974).

The impairment of the semantic-lexical level, in the tasks to be reviewed here, was assessed by the Verbal Sound and Meaning Discrimination Test, sometimes supplemented by an Auditory Language Comprehension and a Reading Comprehension Test.

In the first test (Gainotti et al., 1975), the patients were shown a card with six colored pictures on it and instructed to point to the one corresponding to the word uttered by the examiner. One of the pictures corresponded to the stimulus word, the name of the second picture was phonemically similar to the test word, and the object represented in a third picture had a strong semantic link with the correct word, while the three remaining pictures and their names were unrelated to the test word either phonemically or semantically. In the other two tests (Gainotti et al., 1981) the patients were requested to point to the picture corresponding to the stimulus word in an array of three semantically similar choices. In all three tests, errors showing confusion between the correct item and the semantically similar choice were considered indicative of semantic-lexical impairment.

The non-verbal conceptual disorders were studied by means of several tasks, administered to the usual four experimental groups. Some such tests yielded results that both agreed with the bulk of the earlier (1960s) evidence and supported the new hypothesis, i.e. aphasics did significantly worse than the other groups and, among aphasics, those with semantic-lexical impairment did significantly worse than those without it, independently of the severity of aphasia. These tests, which will be described in some detail, explored (a) the gesture-to-picture association, (b) the strength of the conceptual relationships and (c) the 'categoreal' or classificatory activity.

(a) In the gesture-to-picture association task (Test of Symbolic Gesture Interpretation: Gainotti and Lemmo, 1976), both conventional communicative movements (e.g. making the sign of the cross) and simple pantomimes (e.g. of plaing the guitar) representing common objects were performed by the examiner, who then asked the patient to point to the corresponding picture (e.g. a guitar) presented in a 3-choice array, which also included an item conceptually associated with the correct one (e.g. a trumpet) and an item unrelated to it (e.g. a bird). Impairment on this task in aphasics was considered to be cognitive in nature since it was not strictly related to errors on a test of ideomotor apraxia.

(b) The Conceptual Relationships test (Gainotti et al., 1979) is designed to determine the patient's ability to evaluate the strength of the conceptual tie linking the picture of an object (e.g. a hammer) with other pictures, representing objects having different degrees of association with the stimulus (e.g. a nail – high degree, a screw – mild degree, a glass – zero degree of association). The patient was required to place each picture, as it was handed to him, in three different boxes, corresponding to the three different degrees of association. It should be noted that this was a modified non-verbal version of the test devised by Lhermitte et al. (1971) to study semantic fields in aphasia.

(c) The Class Intersection test (Gainotti et al., 1986a) explored the ability to classify pictures of objects using two different criteria simultaneously. In every item, the patient was shown two sets of colored pictures, each representing a given class (e.g., birds and yellow objects) and placed in a line in the middle

of two separate strips of paper. At the ends of the strips a free space allowed the patient to add a new class member. The two strips were placed perpendicularly to one another, with the intersection corresponding to one of the free ends. The patient was then given six more pictures and asked to select the one belonging only to the first class (another bird), the one belonging only to the second class (another yellow object) and finally the one belonging to both classes at the same time (a yellow bird, i.e. a canary). The picture belonging only to the first class should be put in the free space at the end of the first strip, that belonging to the second class should be put at the end of the second strip and that belonging to both classes should be put at the intersection. Misclassifications were differentially rated, depending on whether they involved one or both classes.

Aphasics as a group did not perform significantly worse than the right-brain-damaged patients on other tests which were meant to explore the 'actualization of concepts' in Bay's sense (Drawing from Memory test: Gainotti et al., 1983) and the ability to grasp the exact criterion of definition of a class (Class Inclusion test: Gainotti et al., 1986a) as well as on Raven's Coloured Matrices (Gainotti et al., 1986b). It should be stressed, however, that even on these tests aphasics with a lexical-semantic disorder did perform significantly worse than those without it.

The view that conceptual disorders are preferentially associated with impairment of the semantic-lexical level of language is indirectly supported by the finding that non-verbal conceptual tasks are poorly correlated with tests of words and sentence repetition (Koemeda-Lutz et al., 1987; Cohen et al., 1988). Indeed, intentional repetition is a language modality which selectively taps the phonemic (and, to a degree, the syntactic) levels of language, but not the semantic-lexical level. These data fit with Lesser's (1978) sensible observation that 'that part of language, phonological or syntactic, which relates to form rather than content is less likely to be relevant to the ability to use rational thought than is the semantic aspect of language'.

The hypothesis that non-verbal conceptual disorders are specifically linked to semantic-lexical impairment is both attractive and rather convincing to clinicians who are familiar with aphasia. Unfortunately, the supporting evidence to date is still essentially limited to the significantly poorer performances of the aphasics with semantic-lexical disorders as compared to all other aphasics. The correlations between the degrees of non-verbal and semantic-lexical impairment are almost never reported in the reviewed studies and, when reported (e.g. rs = 0.542 between gesture-to-picture association and lexical-semantic impairment: Gainotti and Lemmo, 1976), are significant, but not higher than those found in earlier investigations of non-verbal conceptual defects and overall measures of aphasia. ˋMoreover, the percentage of aphasics with semantic-lexical defects who perform the conceptual tasks below cut-off is also either not specified or not particularly high, ranging from 52% on the Conceptual Relationships test (to be compared with 35% of the whole aphasic group) to 70% on the Symbolic Gesture comprehension test. These important parameters need to be further explored in future studies.

Functional relationships between non-verbal conceptual and verbal defects

A functional relationship may be inferred whenever both non-verbal and verbal performances of aphasics display a basic similarity in the *quality* of the deviant behavior. Since studies in which identical tasks were employed in parallel to investigate both domains in the same patients are unfortunately very rare to date, the evidence derived from such studies must be complemented by that from other studies confined to either non-verbal conceptual or verbal disorders. A basic qualitative similarity appears in the following: (1) the type of error in multiple-choice tasks; (2) the type of impairment on the Token Test; (3) the changes of semantic-conceptual field; and (4) the break-down of a specific stage of semantic integration.

(1) It has often been observed that semantic errors on verbal expression and comprehension tasks are typical of aphasic patients (Schuell and Jenkins, 1961; De Renzi and Vignolo, 1962b) and the same type of response has been found to be

predominant in these patients since the introduction of non-verbal, multiple-choice association tasks in the 1960s (see above). The selection of alternatives which are *semantically related* to the correct response has been noted in a recent review by Cohen et al. (1988). Duffy and Watkins (1984) should be credited with the first experimental demonstration of a similar performance by the same groups of aphasics in tasks requiring verbal and non-verbal comprehension, irrespective of the severity of the defects. These authors compared performances on two parallel tasks involving gesture-to-picture and word-to-picture association (in other words, pantomime and auditory verbal word comprehension tasks) and found a significant, though moderate, correlation of 0.51 between the two tests for the effect due to semantic relatedness. This finding is consistent with those of Seron et al. (1979), Daniloff et al. (1982) and Varney and Benton (1982), who found that the errors on gesture-to-picture (pantomime comprehension) tasks were more frequently related to the target response than unrelated to it. This trend is reminiscent of that observed in most non-verbal association tasks since the inception of this kind of study (see for example Spinnler and Vignolo, 1966).

(2) The discovery by the Konstanz group that aphasics are impaired to a comparable extent in non-verbal and verbal versions of the Token Test (originally developed as a sensitive test of auditory verbal comprehension: De Renzi and Vignolo, 1962a) constitutes another analogy which may suggest a functional link between the verbal and the non-verbal aspect of conceptual disorganisation. Cohen et al. (1977) found that aphasics did significantly worse than controls in a task where a real token was used in place of the verbal commands of the Token Test. This was shown to the patient while the usual array of tokens in front of him was temporarily hidden from view, and the patient was asked to point to the identical token as soon as the array was uncovered. Essentially the same results (aphasics worse than non-aphasic patients) were found in another study (Cohen et al.,

1980b) in which the token that the patient was asked to indicate was 'described' by a list of features (form, color, size) presented non-verbally by means of a series of drawings. Such pictorial command, as it were, was presented for a time-period that was identical with the time required to give the corresponding verbal command, and the array of tokens was shown only after the patient had inspected the stimulus drawings.

As the authors noted, the aphasic patients' impairment on all these tasks could be due to a short-term memory deficit and/or an excessively short exposure time. To rule out these factors, aphasics were given in succession a token and either a sentence or a series of drawings describing it. No time limit was set. Patients were asked to signify whether or not the token corresponded to the presented description. Again, aphasics did worse than other patients, presumably because they needed more time to understand and process the series of features of a given token, independently of whether the presentation was verbal or non-verbal (Gutbrod et al., 1985).

These findings, taken together, suggest, according to the Konstanz investigators, that the Token Test assesses abilities that are crucial for conceptual thinking, i.e. cognitive handling of individual features (such as size, etc.) and maintaining awareness of reliable representation of these features. From this angle, auditory verbal comprehension is not the critical behavioral aspect specifically tapped by the test, but merely adds to its power to discriminate aphasics from other brain-damaged patients and from controls. Considering the wide use of the Token Test, this challenging view is certainly worth further confirmation, with special reference to its practical implications.

(3) Another parallel was discovered by Koemeda-Lutz and coworkers (1985, 1987) by means of an elaborate class inclusion test. To perform the task correctly, patients had to grasp the common feature or category linking three pictures of objects (e.g. soap-bubble, feather and spider-web; *common feature:* lightness; ostrich, hen, penguin;

common category: birds) and they were subsequently asked to decide whether each of ten successively presented items belonged to the previously discovered class. In a parallel version of this task, the written name of the category (e.g. lightness, birds) was additionally given to the patients. Aphasics were found to be impaired on both versions of the test, and the quality of the impairment was the same, inasmuch as they failed mostly in deciding class inclusion or exclusion of those items at the boundary of a given class (e.g., they showed difficulties and hesitancies in determining whether 'silk-stocking' belonged to the class 'lightness', or 'bat' to 'birds'). This disorder is reminiscent of the changes of semantic field found in aphasics in the linguistic domain. For example, Lhermitte et al. (1971) found, among other things, that severe aphasics (particularly Wernicke's with semantic jargon) sometimes had a broadening and sometimes a narrowing of the semantic field. Grossman (1978, 1981) found that narrowing of semantic boundaries was characteristic of anterior aphasics, while the posterior patients displayed first a narrowing and then a broadening of the field during the testing session. Contrary to these findings, Grober et al. (1980), probably the only workers to employ non-verbal as well as verbal materials in studying this problem, concluded that posterior aphasics show a narrowing of the semantic field, while broadening of the verbal category fields was reported by Kudo (1987).

These discrepancies among psycho-linguistic studies, probably resulting from different theoretical assumptions, do not undermine the view that some sort of link exists between the non-verbal and the verbal abnormal variations of the semantic sphere in aphasics. The nature of the interrelationships between the two imparments is, however, obscure, and in all likelihood complex. This is borne out by the puzzling finding of Koemeda-Lutz et al. (1987) that aphasics' classification of pictures in the above-mentioned experiment is helped by previously providing verbal labels, in addition to the three drawings, to define the criterion for categorization. If, as Kudo (1987) maintains, aphasics may retain partially normal semantic knowledge, the interaction of linguistic and non-linguistic information may have a facilitating effect in establishing the stable definition of a category, as required by the Koemeda-Lutz experiment.

(4) An important experimental and theoretical effort to get to the core of the question was made by Caramazza et al. (1982), who refined and extended the method of an earlier study (Whitehouse et al., 1978). They employed two tests, one non-verbal ('Similarity Judgement') and one verbal ('Labeling') using cup-like drawings which varied in terms of the diameter-to-length ratio and presence/absence of a handle. They isolated a subgroup of mostly posterior aphasics who performed poorly on both tests. A sophisticated statistical analysis and theoretical discussion of this finding led them to advance the view that, in this type of patient, the sequence of events leading to naming is affected at one specific stage, i.e. the stage at which the patient must employ his semantic or conceptual categories to select and interpret the perceptual components of the object. According to their hypothesis, the breakdown of this crucial stage provides an explanation for the functional relationship between the non-verbal categorization deficit and the naming defects sensu lato (anomia and semantic paraphasias), which often co-occur in posterior aphasics.

Practical implications

The effect of conceptual impairments (as assessed by the tasks reviewed above) in the patient' everyday life is much less apparent than one might think. Aphasics who perform quite poorly on non-verbal tests of conceptual thinking often display virtually normal judgement and categorizing ability in dealing with real-life situations. Those who do not usually have diffuse, massive focal unilateral or bilateral damage. This sometimes astonishing discrepancy between performance in the laboratory and performance at home is observed in other neuropsychological impairments due to

circumscribed hemispheric lesions, e.g. ideational apraxia, and it may be explained, at least in part, by the fact that the test situation is highly artificial and thus requires much more intentional effort on the part of the patient than the more automatic situations of everyday life. If this 'Jacksonian' interpretation is correct, test performances may still be useful for inferring a patient's ability to carry out highly *intentional* tasks even outside the clinical setting, such as making a valid will (see Critchley (1961) and Gloning et al. (1970) for discussions of testamentary capacity in aphasia). Studies on the occupational resettlement of patients while still aphasic (Hatfield and Zangwill, 1975; Carriero et al., 1987), compared with the findings of the conceptual tests, should prove a fruitful approach to clarifying this point.

Conclusions

The studies reviewed above strongly suggest that some kind of functional relationship exists between aphasia and the concomitant non-verbal conceptual impairment. Such a relationship is likely (though not yet proven) to selectively involve the semantic-lexical level of language disruption. Stated in terms of the traditional classification of aphasia, the clinical forms which are likely to be specifically linked with the non-verbal conceptual defect are those included in the term 'associative aphasias' (von Monakow, 1914), i.e. severe amnesic aphasia and transcortical sensory aphasia. While the former has been investigated from this viewpoint since Goldstein's time (Goldstein, 1924) with, however, equivocal findings (De Renzi et al., 1966) probably due to the fact that the language disorder in most amnesic aphasics is comparatively slight, the latter has not attracted the attention it deserves, probably because the very existence of transcortical sensory aphasia as a separate clinical entity has been denied by several authorities (see not only Marie, 1906, but also Déjerine, 1914). This is unfortunate, since transcortical sensory aphasia, however rare, is a clinically separable syndrome, and one in which severe semantic-lexical defects are found in what could be regarded as their most dissociated form. Specific studies of non-verbal conceptual defects associated with this particular type of aphasia should prove fruitful. On the other hand, the functional relationship hypothesis requires further experimental support, since, as mentioned previously, our current knowledge on the degree of statistical correlation between the verbal and non-verbal defects is still unsatisfactory. Likewise, future investigations must determine whether the semantic-lexical disorder is the cause or the consequence of the non-verbal defect, or, as the work of Caramazza et al. (1982) suggests, both depend upon the disruption of the same underlying mechanism.

The hypothesis advanced since the mid-1960s and upheld by the Milan group (see De Renzi et al., 1966; Vignolo, 1972; Basso et al., 1973), that the concurrence of verbal and non-verbal conceptual deficits in aphasia, whatever the underlying physiological mechanisms, points to an anatomical contiguity and broad overlapping between the cerebral areas crucial for language and those that process non-verbal conceptual generalizations, should also be considered. This hypothesis is not at all incompatible with the preceding one; on the contrary, it represents its anatomical counterpart. Indeed, in the 'associative aphasias' a posterior (retro-rolandic) lesion is found, damaging to different degrees the so-called 'marginal' language areas in the left temporal and parietal lobes (Luria, 1970) as confirmed by clinical-CT scan correlations (Vignolo, 1988). The same localization has been demonstrated in fluent aphasics with predominantly semantic-lexical expressive defects (Cappa et al., 1981). The criticism commonly found in the literature, i.e. that non-aphasic left-brain-damaged patients with conceptual impairment are rare, does not seem to undermine the hypothesis, but merely emphasizes that the degree of overlapping between the two contiguous areas must be great. Such overlapping in the posterior marginal zones appears to be crucial for the processing of both verbalized and non-verbalized concepts; damage to this area is therefore likely to disrupt the semantic organization in both spheres simultaneously.

References

Alajouanine T, Lhermitte F, Ledoux, Renaud D, Vignolo LA: Les composantes phonémiques et sémantiques de la jargonaphasie. *Rev. Neurol.: 110,* 5 – 20, 1964.

Ajuriaguerra J de, Hécaen H: *Le Cortex Cerebral.* Paris: Masson, 1959.

Assal G, Buttet J: Couleurs, attributs d'objects. Leurs déficits lors des lésions du cortex cérébral. *Lyon Méd.: 236,* 685 – 689, 1976.

Basso A, De Renzi E, Faglioni P, Scotti G, Spinnler H: Neuropsychological evidence for the existence of cerebral areas critical to the performance of intelligence tasks. *Brain: 96,* 715 – 728, 1973.

Basso A, Faglioni P, Spinnler H: Non-verbal color impairment in aphasics. *Neuropsychologia: 14,* 183 – 192, 1976.

Basso A, Capitani E, Luzzati C, Spinnler H, Zanobio E: Different basic components in the performance of Broca's and Wernicke's aphasics on the colour-figure matching test. *Neuropsychologia: 1,* 51 – 59, 1985.

Bauer K, Beck D: Intellect after cerebro-vascular accident. *J. Nerv. Mental Dis.: 120,* 379 – 395, 1954.

Bay E: Aphasia and non-verbal disorders of language. *Brain: 85,* 411 – 426, 1962.

Bay E: Aphasia and conceptional thinking. In Halpern L (Editor), *Problems of Dynamic Neurology.* Jerusalem: Jerusalem Post Press, pp. 88 – 100, 1963.

Bay E: Principles of classification and their influence on our concepts of aphasia. In De Reuck AVS, O'Connor M (Editors), *Disorders of Language.* Proceedings of Ciba Foundation Symposium. London: Churchill, pp. 122 – 142, 1964.

Bay E: Intelligence and aphasia. In Lebrun Y, Hoops R (Editors), *Neurolinguistics: Intelligence in Aphasia.* Amsterdam: Swets and Zeitlinger, 1974.

Benton A: Symbolic thinking and brain disease. *Rech. Sémeiot.: 5,* 225 – 239, 1985.

Bradshaw JL, Nettleton HC: The nature of hemispheric specialization in man. *Behav. Brain Sci.: 4,* 51 – 91, 1981; and *6,* 517 – 533, 1983.

Broca P: Sur le siége de la faculté du langage articulé. *Trib. Méd.: 75,* 265 – 269, 1869.

Buckingham HV, Rekart DM: Semantic paraphasia. *J. Commun. Disord.: 12,* 197 – 209 1979.

Cappa S, Cavallotti G, Vignolo LA: Phonemic and lexical errors in fluent aphasia: correlation with lesion site. *Neuropsychologia: 19,* 171 – 177, 1981.

Caramazza A, Sloan Berndt R, Brownell HH: The semantic deficit hypothesis: percentual parsing and object classification by aphasic patients. *Brain Lang.: 15,* 161 – 189, 1982.

Carriero MR, Faglia L, Vignolo LA: Resumption of gainful employment in aphasics: preliminary findings. *Cortex: 1987,* in press.

Christopoulou, Bonvillian JD: Sign language, pantomime and

gestural processing in aphasic persons: a review. *J. Commun. Dis.: 18,* 1 – 20, 1985.

Cohen R, Kelter S: Cognitive impairment of aphasics in a colour-to-picture matching task. *Cortex: 15,* 235 – 245, 1979.

Cohen R, Woll G: Facets of analytical processing in aphasia: a picture ordering task. *Cortex: 17,* 557 – 570, 1981.

Cohen R, Engel D, Kelter S, List G, Strohner H: Thought disorders in aphasia. In *Proc. First Eur. Neurosci. Meet.,* Munich, 9 – 13, September, 1975.

Cohen R, Engel D, Kelter S, List G, Strohner H: Restricted associations in aphasics and schizophrenics. *Arch. Psychiatrie Nervenkr.: 222,* 325 – 338, 1976.

Cohen R, Kelter S, Schafer B: Zum Einfluss des Sprachverstandnisses auf die Leistungen im Token Test. *Z. Klin. Psychol.: 6,* 1 – 14, 1977.

Cohen R, Kelter S, Woll G: Analytical competence and language impairment in aphasia. *Brain Lang.: 10,* 331 – 347, 1980a.

Cohen R, Lutzweiler W, Woll G: Zur Konstruktvalidität des Token Test. *Nervenartz: 51,* 30 – 35, 1980b.

Cohen R, Glokner-Rist A, Lutz M, Maier T, Meier E: Cognitive impairments of aphasics in picture sorting and matching tasks. *Arch. Psychiatrie Nervenkr.: 232,* 223 – 234, 1982.

Cohen R, Glokner A, Lutz M, Maier T, Meier E: Cognitive impairments in aphasia: new results and new problems. In Bauerle R, Schwarze C, von Stechow A (Editors), *Meaning, Use and Interpretation of Language.* Berlin, New York: Walter de Gruyter, pp. 30 – 45, 1983.

Cohen R, Kelter S, Koemeda-Lutz M, Meier E: Sprache und Denken: Beitrage aus der Aphasieforschung. In von Stechow A, Schepping MT (Editors), *Fortschritte in der Semantik: Grammatikalische und sprachliche Prozesse.* Weinheim. Vch Acta Humaniora, pp. 79 – 112, 1988.

Critchley M: Testamentary capacity in aphasia. *Neurology: 11,* 749 – 754, 1961.

Daujat C, Gainotti G, Tissot R: Sur quelques aspects des troubles de la comprehension dans l'aphasie. *Cortex: 10,* 347 – 365, 1974.

Daniloff JK, Noll JD, Fristoe M, Lloyd LL: Gesture recognition in patients with aphasia. *J. Speech Hear. Disord.: 47,* 43 – 49, 1982.

Déjerine J: *Séméiologie des Affections du Système Nerveux.* Paris, 1914.

Della Sala S: Figure-object matching: another frequent nonverbal impairment of aphasics. *Ital. J. Neurol. Sci.: 1,* 43 – 49, 1987.

De Renzi E, Spinnler H: Impaired performance on color tasks in patients with hemispheric damage. *Cortex: 3,* 194 – 217, 1967.

De Renzi E, Vignolo LA: The Token Test: a sensitive test to detect receptive disturbances in aphasics. *Brain: 85,* 556 – 678, 1962a.

De Renzi E, Vignolo LA: Fattori verbali ed extra-verbali della comprensione negli afasici. In *Proc. Congr. Soc. Ital. Neurol.,* pp. 443 – 468, 1962b.

De Renzi E, Faglioni P, Savoiardo M, Vignolo LA: The influence of aphasia and of the hemispheric side of the cerebral lesion on abstract thinking. *Cortex: 2,* 339 – 420, 1966.

De Renzi E, Pieczuro A, Vignolo LA: Ideational apraxia: A quantitative study. *Neuropsychologia: 6,* 41 – 52, 1968.

De Renzi E, Scotti G, Spinnler H: Perceptual and associative disorders of visual recognition: relationship to the side of the cerebral lesion. *Neurology: 19,* 634 – 642, 1969.

De Renzi E, Faglioni P, Scotti G, Spinnler H: Impairment in associating colour to form, concomitant with aphasia. *Brain: 95,* 293 – 304, 1972a.

De Renzi E, Faglioni P, Scotti G, Spinnler H: Impairment of color sorting behavior after hemispheric damage: an experimental study with the Holmgren Skein Test. *Cortex: 8,* 147 – 163, 1972b.

De Saussure F: *Cours de Linguistique Générale,* 5e Edn. Paris: Payot, 1960.

Doehring GD, Dudley JG, Coderre L: Programmed instruction in picture sound association for the aphasic. *Folia Phoniatr.: 19,* 414 – 426, 1967.

Duffy JR, Watkins LB: The effect of response choice relatedness on pantomime and verbal recognition ability in aphasic patients. *Brain Lang.: 21,* 291 – 306, 1984.

Duffy RJ, Duffy JR: Three studies of deficits in pantomimic recognition in aphasia. *J. Speech Hear. Res.: 24,* 70 – 84, 1981.

Faglioni P, Spinnler H, Vignolo LA: Contrasting behavior of right and left hemisphere-damaged patients on a discriminative and semantic task of auditory recognition. *Cortex: 5,* 336 – 389, 1969.

Farnsworth D: The Farnsworth-Munsell 100-hue and dichotomous tests for color vision. *J. Opt. Soc. Am.: 33,* 568 – 578, 1943.

Ferro JM, Santos ME, Castro-Caldas A, Mariano MG: Gesture recognition in aphasia. *J. Clin. Neuropsychol.: 2,* 277 – 292, 1980.

Finkelnburg FC: Niederrheinische Gesellschaft: Sitzung von 21 Maerz 1870 in Bonn. *Berl. Klin. Wochenschr.: 7,* 449 – 450: 460 – 462, 1870.

Gainotti G: Non-verbal cognitive disorders in aphasia. In Whitaker HA (Editor), *Contemporary Reviews of Neuropsychology.* New York: Springer, pp. 127 – 158, 1988.

Gainotti G, Lemmo MA: Comprehension of symbolic gestures in aphasia. *Brain Lang.: 3,* 451 – 460, 1976.

Gainotti G, Caltagirone C, Ibba A: Semantic and phonemic aspects of auditory language comprehension in aphasia. *Linguistics: 154/155,* 15 – 29, 1975.

Gainotti G, Miceli G, Caltagirone C: The relationships between conceptual and semantic lexical disorders in aphasia. *Int. J. Neurosci.: 10,* 45 – 50, 1979.

Gainotti G, Miceli G, Caltagirone C, Silveri MC, Masullo C: The relationship between type of naming error and semantic-lexical discrimination in aphasic patients. *Cortex: 17,* 401 – 410, 1981.

Gainotti G, Silveri MC, Villa G, Caltagirone C: Drawing objects from memory in aphasia. *Brain: 106,* 613 – 622, 1983.

Gainotti G, Carlomagno S, Craca A, Silveri MC: Disorders of classificatory activity in aphasia. *Brain Lang.: 28,* 181 – 195, 1986a.

Gainotti G, D'Erme P, Villa G, Caltagirone C: Focal brain lesions and intelligence: a study with a new version of Raven's colored matrices. *J. Clin. Exp. Neuropsychol.: 8,* 37 – 50, 1986b.

Geschwind N: *Selected Papers on Language and the Brain.* Boston: D. Reidel, 1974.

Gloning K, Maly J, Quatember R: Problem of forensic testimony of aphasia patients. *Beitr. Gerichtl. Med.: 27*, 401 – 406, 1970.

Goldstein K: *Die Behandlung, Fuersorge und Begutachtung der Hirnverletzten.* Leipzig: Vogel, 1919.

Goldstein K: Das Wesen der amnestischen Aphasie. Vorläufige Mitteilung gemeinsamer Untersuchungen mit A. Gelb. *Schweiz. Arch. Neurol. Psychiatrie: 15,* 163 – 175, 1924.

Goldstein K: Die Lokalisation in der Grosshirnrinde. In Bethe A, Fischer E (Editors), *Handbuch der normalen und pathologischen Physiologie.* Berlin: Springer, 1927.

Goldstein K: *After-effects of Brain Injuries in War.* London: William Heinemann, 1942.

Goldstein K: *Language and Language Disturbances.* New York: Grune and Stratton, 1948.

Goldstein K, Scheerer M: Abstract and concrete behavior: an experimental study with special tests. *Psychol. Mon.n.: 239, 53:* 1 – 151, 1941.

Gottschaldt K: Uber den Einfluss der Erfahrung auf die Wahrnehmung von Figuren. *Psychol. Forsch.: 8,* 261 – 317, 1926; and *12,* 1 – 87, 1929.

Grober E, Perecman E, Kellar L, Brown J: Lexical knowledge in anterior and posterior aphasics. *Brain Lang.: 10,* 318 – 330, 1980.

Grossman M: The game of the name: an examination of linguistic reference after brain damage. *Brain Lang.: 6,* 112 – 119, 1978.

Grossman M: A bird is a bird is a bird: making reference within and without superordinate categories. *Brain Lang.: 12,* 313 – 331, 1981.

Gutbrod K, Mager B, Meier E, Cohen R: Cognitive processing of tokens and their description in aphasia. *Brain lang.: 25,* 37 – 51, 1985.

Hamsher K: Intelligence and aphasia. In Taylor Sarno M (Editor), *Acquired Aphasia,* ch. 11, New York: Academic Press, 1981.

Hatfield FM, Zangwill OL: Occupational resettlement in aphasia. *Scand. J. Rehabil. Med.: 7,* 57 – 60, 1975.

Head H: Hughlings Jackson on aphasia and kindred affections of speech. *Brain: 38,* 1 – 27, 1915.

Head H: *Aphasia and Kindred Disorders of Speech.* New York: MacMillan, 1926.

Holmgren F: *De la Cécité dans ses Rapports avec les Chemins de Fer et la Marine.* Stockholm, 1877.

Isserlin M: Aphasie. In Bumke O, Foerster O (Editors), *Handbuch der Neurologie, Vol. VI.* Berlin: Springer, 1936.

Jackson JH: On affections of speech from disease of the brain. *Brain: 1,* 304 – 330, 1878.

Kelter S, Cohen R, Engel D, List G, Strohner H: Aphasic disorders in matching tasks involving conceptual analysis and covert naming. *Cortex: 12,* 383 – 394, 1976.

Kinsbourne M, Warrington E: Observation on color agnosia. *J. Neurol. Neurosurg. Psychiatry: 27,* 296 – 299, 1964.

Kleist C: *Gehirnpathologie.* Leipzig: Barth, 1934.

Kleist C: Gehirnpathologische und lokalisatorische Ergebnisse ueber Hörstorungen, Gerauschtaubheiten und Amusien. *Monatschr. Psychiatrie Neurol.: 68,* 853 – 860, 1928.

Koemeda-Lutz M: *Struktur und Abruf vom semantischen Wissen bei Aphasikern.* Konstanz: Hartung-Gorre Verlag, 1985.

Koemeda-Lutz M, Cohen R, Meier E: Organization of and access to semantic memory in aphasia. *Brain Lang.: 30,* 321 – 337, 1987.

Kudo T: Aphasic's appreciation of hierarchical semantic categories. *Brain Lang.: 30,* 33 – 51, 1987.

Lesser R: *Linguistic Investigations of Aphasia.* London: Edward Arnold, 1978.

Lewandowsky M: Abspaltung des Farbensinnes durch Herderkrankung des Gehirns. *Berl. Klin. Wochenschr.: 44,* 1444 – 1446, 1907.

Lhermitte F, Derouesné J, Lecours AR: Contribution à l'étude des troubles sémantiques dans l'aphasie. *Rev. Neurol.: 125,* 81 – 101, 1971.

Lissauer H: Ein Fall von Seelenblindheit nebst einem Beitrag zur Theorie derselben. *Arch. Psychiatrie Nervenkr.: 21,* 222 – 270, 1890.

Luria AR: *Traumatic Aphasia. Its Syndromes, Psychology and Treatment.* The Hague, Paris: Mouton, 1970.

Marie P: Que faut-il penser des aphasies sous-corticales? *Sem. Méd.: 42,* 493 – 500, 1906.

Marie P: *Travaux et Mémoires, Vol. 1.* Paris: Masson et Cie, 1928.

McFie J, Piercy MF: The relation of laterality of lesion to performance on Weigl's Sorting Test. *J. Mental Sci.: 98,* 229 – 305, 1952.

Meyers R: Relation of 'thinking' and language; an experimental approach using dysphasic patients. *Arch. Neurol. Psychiatry: 60,* 119 – 139, 1948.

Morlaas J: *Contribution à l'Étude de l'Apraxie.* Paris: Legrand, 1928.

Ombrédane A: *L'Aphasie et l'Élaboration de la Pensée Explicite.* Paris: P.U.F., 1951.

Peterson LN, Kirshner HS: Gestural impairment and gestural ability in aphasia. *Brain Lang.: 14,* 333 – 348, 1981.

Pizzamiglio L, Appicciafuoco A: Semantic comprehension in aphasia. *J. Commun. Disord.: 3,* 280 – 288, 1971.

Poppelreuter W: *Die psychischen Schaedigungen durch Kopfschuss im Kriege 1914 – 1916.* Leipzig: Voss, 1917.

Raven J: *Coloured Progressive Matrices Sets A, Ab, B.* London: H.K. Lewis, 1962 (originally published in 1938, revised order in 1956).

Raven JC: *Guide to using the Coloured Progressive Matrices Sets A, Ab, B.* London: H.K. Lewis, 1965.

Rinnert C. Whitaker HA: Semantic confusions by aphasic patients. *Cortex: 9,* 56 – 81, 1973.

Russo M, Vignolo LA: Visual figure-ground discrimination in patients with unilateral cerebral disease. *Cortex: 3,* 113 – 127, 1967.

Schuell H, Jenkins J: Reduction of vocabulary in aphasia. *Brain: 84,* 243 – 261, 1961.

Scotti G, Spinnler H: Colour imperception in unilateral hemisphere-damaged patients. *J. Neurol., Neurosurg. Psychiatry: 33,* 22 – 28, 1970.

Seron X, Van Der Kaa MA, Remitz A, Van Der Linden M: Pantomime interpretation and aphasia. *Neuropsychologia: 17,* 661 – 668, 1979.

Spinnler H, Vignolo LA: Impaired recognition of meaningful sounds in aphasia. *Cortex: 2,* 337 – 348, 1966.

Stengel E: The syndrome of visual alexia with color anomia. *J. Mental Sci.: 94,* 46 – 58, 1948.

Strohner H, Cohen R, Kelter S, Woll G: Semantic and acoustic errors of aphasic and schizophrenic patients in a sound-picture matching task. *Cortex: 14,* 391 – 403, 1978.

Teuber HL, Weinstein S: Ability to discover hidden figures after cerebral lesions. *A.M.A. Arch. Neurol. Psychiatry: 76,* 369 – 379, 1956.

Trousseau A: De l'aphasie, maladie décrite récemment sous le nom impropre d'aphémie. *Gazette des Hôpitaux 37, 1864; Clinique Médicale, 1865.*

Varney NR: Linguistic correlates of pantomime recognition in aphasic patients. *J. Neurol. Neurosurg. Psychiatry: 41,* 564, 1978.

Varney NR: Sound recognition in relation to aural language comprehension in aphasic patients. *J. Neurol. Neurosurg. Psychiatry: 43,* 71 – 75, 1980.

Varney NR: Pantomime recognition defect in aphasia: implications for the concept of asymbolia. *Brain Lang.: 15,* 32 – 39, 1982a.

Varney NR: Colour association and 'colour amnesia' in aphasia. *J. Neurol. Neurosurg. Psychiatry: 45,* 248 – 252, 1982b.

Varney NR: The prognostic significance of sound recognition in receptive aphasia. *Arch. Neurol. (Chicago): 41,* 181 – 182, 1984a.

Varney NR: Alexia for ideograms: implications for Kanji alexia. *Cortex: 20,* 535 – 542, 1984b.

Varney NR, Benton AL: Qualitative aspects of pantomime recognition defect in aphasia. *Brain Lang.: 1,* 132 – 139, 1982.

Varney NR, Damasio H: CT scan correlates of sound recognition defect in aphasia. *Cortex: 22,* 483 – 486, 1986.

Varney NR, Digre K: Color amnesia without aphasia. *Cortex: 19,* 545 – 550, 1983.

Varney NR, Sivan AB: Color association performances of dyslexic and normal children. *J. Clin. Exp. Neuropsychol.: 7,* 314 – 316, 1985a.

Varney NR, Sivan AB: Pantomime recognition in normal and dyslexic children. *Dev. Neuropsychol.: 1,* 49 – 52, 1985b.

Vignolo LA: Les deux niveaux de l'agnosie. In Hécaen H (Edi-

tor), *Neuropsychologie de la Perception Visuelle.* Paris: Masson, pp. 222 – 240, 1972.

Vignolo LA: Auditory agnosia. In Broadbent DE, Weiskrantz L (Editors), *The Neuropsychology of Cognitive Function. Proc. R. Soc. Discuss. Meet., 18 – 19 Nov. 1981.* London: The Royal Society, pp. 49 – 57, 1982.

Vignolo LA: The anatomical and pathological basis of aphasia. In Clifford Rose F, Whurr R, Wylke MA (Editors), *Aphasia.* London: Whurr Publishers, pp. 227 – 249, 1988.

Von Monakow C: *Die Lokalisation im Grosshirn und der Abbau der Funktion durch corticale Herde.* Wiesbaden: Bergmann, 1914.

Weigl E: Zur Psychologie sogenannter Abstraktionsprozesse. *Z. Psychol.: 103,* 2 – 45, 1927.

Weisenburg T, McBride KE: *Aphasia: a Clinical and Psychological Study.* New York: London: The Commonwealth Fund. Oxford University Press, 1935.

Wernicke C: *Der aphasische Symptomencomplex.* Breslau: Max Cohn und Weigert, 1874.

Whitehouse P, Caramazza A, Zurif E: Naming in aphasia: interacting effects of form and function. *Brain Lang.: 6,* 63 – 74, 1978.

Wilkins A, Moscovitch M: Selective impairment of semantic memory after temporal lobectomy. *Neuropsychologia: 16,* 73 – 79, 1978.

Woll G, Cohen R, Kelter S: Eine Untersuchung zur Konzeptfindung aphatischer Patienten. *Z. Klin. Psychol.: 8,* 221 – 223, 1979.

Zangwill OL: Intelligence in aphasia. In De Reuck AVS, O'Connor M (Editors), *Disorders of Language.* London: Churchill, pp. 261 – 274, 1964.

Zangwill OL: Intellectual status in aphasia. In Vinken PJ, Bruyn GW (Editors), *Handbook of Clinical Neurology, Vol. 4.* Amsterdam: Elsevier, Ch. 6, pp. 105 – 111, 1969.

Zangwill OL: The relation of non-cognitive functions to aphasia. In Lennenberg EH, Lennenberg E (Editors), *Foundations of Language Development: a Multidisciplinary Approach.* New York: Academic Press, vol. 2, 1975.

© 1989 Elsevier Science Publishers B.V. (Biomedical Division)
Handbook of Neuropsychology, Vol. 2
F. Boller and J. Grafman (Eds)

CHAPTER 11

Disorders of body awareness and body knowledge

Gianfranco Denes

Department of Neurology, University of Padova, Via Giustiniani 5, 35128 Padova, Italy

Introduction

As the preceding chapters have abundantly shown, a fruitful and time-honoured approach to understanding the nature of cognitive functions in normal people derives from investigation of their breakdown in brain-damaged people. The study of aphasic, amnesic and agnosic patients, true experiments of nature, has led to the development and modification of theoretical models subserving language, memory and perception. The existence of these cognitive skills was already firmly established when these theoretical models were developed and neuropsychological data could only refine or add more data to the bulk of existing knowledge in this field.

A totally different approach was taken in trying to understand the behaviour of some patients who, as a result of diffuse or focal brain damage, were impaired in tasks requiring the conscious awareness of body parts. At variance with other cognitive disturbances whose effect was evident in the patients' everyday behaviour, this symptomatology mostly appeared in test situations and thus not affecting subjects' performance on their body. Unfortunately, rather than experimentally investigating whether this pathological behaviour was primarily due to the methodological error of selective observation or to the presence of a more pervasive cognitive disorder, the concept of a cognitive function specifically subserving conscious awareness of the body or parts of it with its own neural substrate rapidly developed. Once this

theory had been established a great variety of symptoms were labelled as disturbances of the body schema or body image, the common denominator being defective perception of the body or impairment of the cognitive understanding of the body or parts of it, to the point of including body experience disturbances under the term of body schema disturbance.

A further contribution to the consolidation of the body schema concept was thought to be the phantom limb phenomenon, that is, the persistence of the feeling of a limb, or more generally of part of the body, despite its having been amputated.

While, as De Renzi (1971) has emphasized, no objection can be raised to the hypothesis that a series of engrams linked to tactile, proprioceptive and visual afferences of somatic origin is stored inside the central nervous system, the concept of the existence of an anatomo-functional apparatus which specifically subtends the mental representation of the body and its parts is still not at all clear.

In the following pages we will try to evaluate critically the contribution of neuropsychology to the solving of the following problems:

(1) Are there specific cognitive mechanisms involved in the conscious awareness of one's body?

(2) Are these functions subserved by specific neural mechanisms?

(3) Is body awareness topologically or propositionally organized?

(4) What, if any, are the relationships between the cognitive and neural mechanisms involved in

the conscious awareness of the body and those subserving knowledge of extrapersonal space?

(5) What are the most appropriate methods of testing perception, awareness and knowledge of the body?

Development of the concept of the body schema

The concept of body schema developed in a somewhat vague way at the end of the XIXth century and beginning of the XXth century, in an attempt to provide a theoretical explanation for some phenomena, mainly of psychiatric interest, which were interpreted as resulting from the absence or non-utilization by the consciousness of the organic sensations normally associated with sensory perceptions. For example, Deny and Camus (1905) described a case of 'aberrant hypochondria' and interpreted it as a 'loss of body consciousness'.

Bonnier (1905) was the first to make a clear distinction between the sense of existence and the sense of space and subjective orientation of the body with respect to the external world. For Bonnier, awareness of the body was not only the result of processing of sensory information from receptors in the internal organs, joints and skin, but also involved a spatial component linked to topographic awareness of the body part being stimulated. By means of this process a body schema was created, whose loss gives rise to 'aschematia', understood as anesthesia limited to loss of a sense of the body's spatial characteristics. However, Bonnier never mentioned the neural substrate of the body schema, and his cases – patients with labyrinthine vertigo, who described experiencing their own body as larger (hyperschématie), smaller (hyposchématie), spatially distorted (paraschématie) or having lost its boundaries (aschématie) – are far from the type of neurological pathology that could be legitimately related to disturbances of a putative body schema.

The problem of the neural substrate of body orientation was faced for the first time by Munk (1890), who presented a neurophysiological model explaining how we are able to maintain correct body orientation in spite of continual variation in position and continual changes in sensory afferences. This process is made possible by comparison with former sensations stored in the sensory motor cortex and recalled in the form of images. The process of building these images develops in infancy and childhood from reflex and locomotor movements. For Munk the anatomical substrate of the process of spatial orientation resided in the parietal lobes, with further specialization in areas specific for the mental representation of single parts of the body. A parietal lesion may thus lead to loss of the body image in proportion to the extent of the injured area, and may involve total loss of body image *(psychic paralysis and psychic anesthesia)*. Munk's concept was later adopted by Wernicke (1900) to distinguish psychoses characterized by altered representation of the ego *(auto- and somatopsychosis)* from psychoses whose pathogenetic nucleus was presumed to be defective mental representation of the external world *(allopsychosis)*.

However, it was Head and Holmes (1911/12) who first presented the body schema model which subsequently influenced most authors. In their opinion, body orientation occurs by means of two mechanisms, one preconscious and the other conscious: 'Every recognizable change of body posture is measured, at a preconscious level, against the preceding posture or movement. It's the product of this operation that enters into our consciousness, just as on a taxi meter the distance is presented to us already transformed in shillings and pence. So the final product of the task for the appreciation of postures rises into consciousness as a measured postural change (postural schema)'.

On the other hand, the conscious process which allows the precise localization of the locus of stimulation on the surface of the body is called superficial schema. It is to the integrated functioning of these two physiological mechanisms (unfortunately defined, as stressed by Poeck and Orgass (1971), in psychological terms) that we owe the power of projecting our recognition of posture and movement even beyond the limits of our bodies: anything which participates in the conscious movement of our bodies is added to the model of ourselves and becomes part of the schemata, from the spoon that we hold for eating to the feather on our hat.

Head and Holmes claimed that postural and superficial schemata may be separately impaired by brain lesions, as shown by their patient (case 14) who, although unable to tell the position of his hand, was able to point to the stimulated spot correctly. This dissociation, which is in fact very common in autotopoagnosic patients, has recently been taken up again by Paillard (1982) in an attempt to present a neurophysiological model of body orientation disturbances. They examined the ability of a patient who had a cerebral lesion involving the left posterior hemisphere to identify and to localize stimuli applied to her 'deafferented' right upper limb. A functional dissociation between localization and identification in both performance and subjective report was found. This finding was interpreted as a tactual analogue of 'blind sight' (Weiskrantz et al., 1974).

Pick (1908, 1915, 1922), to whom we owe the term Autotopoagnosia (AT), held the view that different schemata exist, specific for sensory modalities and for different parts of the body. In Pick's opinion, the formation of the body image occurs partly by means of proprioceptive afferences but mainly through visual images. That is, body awareness represents a cognitive process linked to thought rather than a process carried out at a preconscious level.

For Schilder (1935), the construction of the body concept is an essential aspect of behavior, the formation of which involves all sources of sensation and spatial relationship of the body schema as a predominantly visual image. Schilder's major contribution, however, was to interpret body schema and its disorders within the framework of psychoanalytic symbolism, discussing the libidinal structure of the body image.

According to Schilder, body image may be distorted in a number of conditions, including hemiplegia and amputation. In his words: 'There arises the problem of organic disease in connection with the postural model of the body. Organic disease provokes abnormal sensations; it immediately changes the image of the body, partly the picture side of it and partly the libidinous investment. The sensations immediately become a part of the general attitude and experience of the individual'.

It is at once clear how this model is used not so much to explain the lack of awareness of the spatial characteristic of one's body, as the patient's experience when faced with a disfigurement of the body — a psychological reality for which a neurological explanation is not really convincing.

The contributions made by Gerstmann (1924, 1927, 1930, 1940, 1942, 1957) are twofold: first he described 'finger agnosia' (FA), a key symptom in the syndrome to which he gave his name and which, in the light of more recent works, has enjoyed undeserved popularity. On the other hand, he proposed a qualitatively different interpretation of somatoagnosic disturbances due to lesions of the right or left hemisphere.

For Gerstmann, the left parietal lobe represented the anatomo-functional substrate for conscious awareness, understood as a kind of inner diagram representing one's body as a whole as well as its single parts according to their location and spatial interrelation. Consequently, lesion of the left parietal lobe may lead to the incapacity to localize the various body parts, a bilateral disturbance which may be total (AT) or partial (FA). On the other hand, it may lead to specific impairment of orientation (lack of right-left orientation).

Conscious awareness of information coming from the left hemispace is only possible by means of an interhemispheric link between the right parietal lobe and the corresponding areas of the left hemisphere. Thus a lesion of the right parietal lobe or its inter-hemispheric connections may make it impossible to integrate the left hemisoma in the body schema (hemisomatoagnosia).

Although split-brain patients are unable to perform, without visual control, any cross-loalization task, e.g., touching the corresponding finger-tip of the hand contralateral to that stimulated by the examiner (Bogen, 1985), the behavior of the right parietal patients cannot simply be explained by defective awareness of the spatial characteristics of the left side of the body. Rather, these patients exhibit somatic neglect which may, in contrast to disturbances resulting from a left hemisphere lesion which become evident only in testing situations, so deeply influence patients' behavior that they implicitly or explicitly deny the existence of one half of their bodies.

With Schilder and Gerstmann, therefore, the concept of body schema, understood as awareness of one's own bodily spatial characteristics, was extended beyond the framework of a neurological model to include *body experience,* i.e., all the psychological, situational and emotional factors linked to the body, its organic alteration and its experienced events.

In this review, greater emphasis will be given to the description and interpretation of disturbances of awareness of personal space whose cognitive nature has recently been at least partly clarified. This chapter also very briefly reviews phenomena included only by some authors (Frederiks, 1969, 1985) among body schema disturbances, such as autoscopia, macro- and microsomatoagnosia and the phantom limb, which may be classified as organically based somatognosic hallucinations or illusions, and for which no satisfactory explanation has yet been provided, from either the anatomical or the cognitive viewpoints.

Bilateral disorders of body space localization

An impairment in tasks involving bilateral conscious localization of body space can be found in over 20% of patients with left retrorolandic lesions (Hécaen, 1972), especially if the patients are aphasic. Conversely, patients whose only or dominant neuropsychological symptom is bilateral impairment of personal space knowledge are exceptionally rare: this impairment may occur either as a localization disorder involving the whole body (autotopoagnosia, AT) or a small part of it (finger agnosia, FA), or as defective localization of space with the body as the point of reference (right-left disorientation: RLD).

Autotopoagnosia. Following Pick's reports (1908, 1922) of two patients with diffuse cerebral atrophy who showed normal comprehension but a selective inability to point on verbal command to their own body parts, the concept of AT rapidly became popular among neurologists, despite the fact that very few AT patients have ever been described. However, since their inability was not confined to their own bodies but also included those of the examiner and of a mannikin, the use of the term *somatotopoagnosia* was suggested by Gerstmann (1942).

The localization disorder is evident even in nonverbal tasks. Patients may be unable, for example, to indicate on their own bodies the part corresponding to that touched by the examiner on her/his own body (De Renzi and Scotti, 1970; Ogden, 1985), or to point on their own bodies to the part corresponding to an isolated drawing of the single part shown by the examiner (Semenza, 1988).

On the other hand, performance on naming of body parts singled out by the examiner, pointing to or naming isolated drawings of body parts, or discovering errors made by the examiner pretending to be autotopoagnosic, is markedly superior and sometimes flawless. Similarly, patients have no difficulty in pointing on verbal command to items belonging to other semantic categories, even if semantically related to the body, e.g., clothes (Ogden, 1985).

When faced with drawings of animals, patients only have difficulty when asked to point to parts of the body which animals have in common with humans (eyes, ears), while they have no difficulty in indicating the animal's typical somatic elements (e.g., snout, tail).

Errors are sometimes off-target, e.g., touching a contiguous body part, and sometimes semantic (touching a body part semantically related to the target: ankle in place of wrist). Sometimes the patient eventually reaches the target but reveals uncertainty in locating the precise spot. When asked, for example, to point to his/her wrist, she/he may grope along the arm, elbow or shoulder.

Faced with this gross impairment in testing situations, it must be stressed that patients do not show any impairment in tasks involving their bodies: dressing apraxia practically never occurs, nor do patients have difficulty in activities such as shaving or putting on their glasses.

Testing procedure. Before facing the problem of the search for possible autotopoagnosic symptoms, it is essential to recall, on the one hand, task demands which may require verbal mediation and, on the other, the confusing effects of possible associated symptoms such as aphasia, mental deterioration, attention deficit, and so on. A complete neuropsychological examination must therefore be carried out, partly with the aim of eliminating the effect of more general factors which could interfere in some stage of the somatognosic process.

The ability to draw a human figure or to assemble a human face or figure from separate components has been claimed by some authors (Engerth, 1933; Angyal and Lorand, 1938) to be a good indicator of body topological knowledge, with the advantage that it excludes verbal mediation. However, such tests imply visual, spatial and contructional abilities to such a degree that they are practically useless.

In the last 30 years, numerous test batteries have been compiled with the aim of exploring body part localization, excluding the effect of possible concomitant factors. The batteries typically include the following tests (modified from Semenza and Goodglass, 1985):

(A) Tests requiring verbal mediation:

(1) subject points to her/his own body part on verbal command

(2) subject points to body parts of a sketch on verbal command

(3) on verbal command, subject points to drawing of single body part in isolation, presented in a multiple-choice paradigm.

(B) Non-verbal tests:

(4) subject points to the examiner's body or to a drawing of a part which the examiner has touched on the subject's body.

(5) subject points on her/his own body to the part which the examiner has shown as a single part drawing.

Localizing value. Bilateral impairment in body part localization tasks has a different localizing value according to whether this symptom is associated with other neuropsychological symptoms, notably aphasia, or whether it represents the only or dominant sign of neuropsychological impairment. In the former case, no anatomo-clinical correlation is possible except generic damage to the left hemisphere, especially retrorolandic. In the latter case, more precise correlation may be made with a lesion of the left parietal lobe, almost always tumoral, primitive and metastatic in nature (De Renzi and Faglioni, 1963; De Renzi and Scotti, 1970; Poncet et al., 1971; Ogden, 1985; Semenza, 1988). This obviously contrasts with clinical practice, in which the vast majority of acquired cognitive disorders are vascular in origin. One explanation may be that in most cases vascular damage involves not only the parietal but also the temporal lobe, with the concurrent appearance of aphasia and other neuropsychological signs thus complicating the picture.

At least in their initial phases, tumors may be very small and thus give rise to a specific disturbance of autotopoagnosic type.

Finger agnosia, right – left disorientation and the Gerstmann syndrome

In 1924 the Austrian neurologist Joseph Gerstmann described the case of an ambidextrous patient with a right parietal tumor, not aphasic but mentally deteriorated, who showed a loss 'of the ability to recognize, identify, differentiate, name, select, indicate and orient the individual fingers of either hand, the patient's own as well as those of other persons' (1957).

This symptom complex, which Gerstmann called

finger agnosia (FA) was interpreted as a disorder of the body schema in its most differentiated aspect.

Three years later (1927) Gerstmann reported the frequent co-occurrence of FA with agraphia. This association was not seen as casual, but as the expression of a new syndrome which was completed, in 1930, by the addition of right – left disorientation and acalculia. Gerstmann's idea was that his tetrad was an internally coherent syndrome whose kernel was FA. His argument for this was the following: a close connection between fingers and calculation is reflected by the widespread (although not universal!) use of the decimal system, which is as widespread as children's use of their fingers for counting and calculation. R – L orientation is usually established by making use of the hands. Writing, finally, requires a mastering of finger praxis closely connected to a normally developed finger sense: a partial support of this latter hypothesis can be bound in the Jackson and Zangwill (1952) and Benton (1959) studies where a correlation between finger localization and finger praxis abilities was found in both adults and children. With regard to the neurological substrate, Gerstmann located it in the left angular gyrus in its transition to the second occipital gyrus. As a primary disturbance, the syndrome should occur independently of mental deterioration, aphasia, apraxia and sensory or motor disorders.

Since Gerstmann's time, assessment of his syndrome and in particular its main symptom, FA, has rapidly become routine in neurological examinations. Only in recent years, with refined methods and the extensive use of group studies, have we begun to criticize both the functional and localizing significance of FA and of Gerstmann's syndrome in general (Benton, 1959, 1977; Critchley, 1966; Poeck and Orgass, 1969, 1971; Gainotti et al., 1972).

Analysis of the elements of Gerstmann's syndrome and testing procedures
Finger agnosia. As already mentioned for AT, patients with FA show a clear dissociation between failure on tests aimed at revealing the symptom and the knowledge and use they make of their finger in daily life, although there is sometimes a certain amount of clumsiness in using them, especially in tasks requiring imitation of meaningless gestures.

As defined by Gerstmann, FA is a very broad and ill-defined symptom, to the extent that the most recent literature prefers the term 'finger localization deficit' and various ad hoc testing batteries have been proposed (Benton, 1959; Ettlinger, 1963; Poeck and Orgass, 1969; Gainotti et al., 1972). Some subtests require verbal mediation: pointing to a given finger (one's own, the examiner's, a sketch of the hand on verbal command). Non-verbal tasks consist of indicating or moving the finger corresponding to that touched by the examiner on the contralateral hand or on a sketch. Some conditions exclude visual mediation. The results of the application of these batteries are disappointing with regard to clarifying the concept of the specific nature of FA.

Ettlinger (1963) reported results for a battery of 12 finger recognition tests, given to a group of 12 patients with cortical lesions limited to the dominant parietal lobe. Correlation between tests was not high: failure on one was not a good predictor of failure on the others.

Similar conclusions were reached by Poeck and Orgass (1969) in an unselected group of unilateral brain-damaged patients tested with a battery of verbal and nonverbal tests of finger localization. Tasks requiring verbal mediation (visuo-verbal and tactile-verbal) formed a cluster, and failure on them was correlated with aphasic disorders and low scores on the WAIS Verbal Scale. In contrast, failure on nonverbal finger identification tasks was more closely related with low WAIS performance.

The problem of testing finger sense through tests not involving verbal mediation and aimed at assessing the ability to analyse fingers as individual elements was addressed by Kinsbourne and Warrington (1962). They tested 12 patients with presumed Gerstmann's syndrome and compared their performance with that of 20 brain-damaged patients without these signs.

They found that Gerstmann patients failed at

least three out of five tests while no patient in the second group failed. Unfortunately, as pointed out by De Renzi (1982), some of the Gerstmann patients did not show any difficulty in finger naming or pointing, while the opposite was noted in 5 of the 20 control patients.

When considering the consequences of right hemisphere damage on finger recognition, the study by Gainotti et al. (1972) deserves mention: these authors found that bilateral impairment in non-verbal finger recognition tasks was of the same magnitude following right or left hemisphere lesion. The poor performance of the right hemisphere brain-damaged patients was associated with mental deterioration, while most of the left-brain-damaged patients showed concomitant aphasia and sensory impairment, although the correlation was not statistically significant. These results are in agreement with those of Sauguet et al. (1971).

Developmental disorders of finger recognition
Normative studies of the developmental aspects of finger recognition were carefully carried out by Benton and his group.

Both in preschool (Lefford et al., 1974) and school children (Benton, 1959), performance levels in finger recognition tasks were clearly shown to depend on the stimulus characteristics and response requirements of the specific tests presented; moreover, within the 3 – 12-year age-range, each task showed a regular developmental course.

The great majority of 3-year-old children, for example, can easily point to fingers that the examiner touches under the child's visual control. When the task requires intersensory integration (identifying the touched finger blindfolded) or representational thinking (localization on a model of a schematic hand of the finger touched by the examiner), performance drops to such a degree that even at the age of 12 the tactile localization of simultaneously stimulated pairs of fingers has not reached the level of performance of normal adults.

Clearly, improvement in finger localization

tasks co-occurs with the development of other cognitive skills such as language, spatial skills, etc., so that it is extremely difficult to evaluate the effect of concomitant variables. For example, Matthews and coworkers (1966) found a closer association in a group of mentally retarded children between non-verbal tasks of finger identification and the Wechsler Bellevue Performance Scale I.Q. than on the Verbal I.Q.

However, some children have been described, most often left-handed and of normal intelligence, who show a specific developmental disability in finger recognition coupled with calculation disturbances (Benson and Geschwind, 1970; Kinsbourne, 1968; Kinsbourne and Warrington, 1963a,b; Spellacy and Peter, 1978). The term 'developmental Gerstmann syndrome' has been proposed for this pattern.

One of the most frequent accompanying symptoms is dyslexia, although some of these children can read at normal levels. Spelling difficulties, constructional disabilities and impairment on visuo-perceptive tasks have also been described.

Given the variety of the concomitant symptomatology, it seems very unlikely that a single unitary cause for this rare developmental symptom complex can be postulated.

Right – left disorientation
R – L disorientation may be defined as a specific disorder of spatial orientation restricted to the sagittal plane of the subject's body or that of the confronting examiner, a mirror image or a sketch of a person.

It is characterized by the selective incapacity to apply the R – L distinction to symmetrical parts of the body. The specificity of the disorder has been claimed on the basis of sparing of other spatial concepts (up – down and front – back), unimpaired extrapersonal spatial orientation, and absence of aphasia. On this basis R – L disorientation was considered a specific body schema disorder and its presence as indicative of an impairment of the neural substrate of the corresponding ability, which Bonhöffer (1923), Gerstmann

(1924, 1930) and Head (1920) attributed to the left retrorolandic area.

R – L orientation is tested by examining the subject's ability to point to the side indicated by the examiner on verbal command or on imitation. The test may vary in difficulty from the execution of one step simple commands ('Show me your right hand') to multi-step commands involving simultaneous orientation towards one's own body and that of the confronting person (e.g., placing either left or right hand on a specified part of the confronting examiner either on verbal command or in imitation).

Before evaluating the clinical significance of disturbed R – L orientation, however, the nature of the task must be examined.

Correctly applying the R – L distinction is not easy: its development lags behind that of other spatial abilities (Benton, 1959), and it is common to observe confusion in normal adults in verbal labelling of right – left or identifying pictures of body parts as right – left. These findings seem more frequent in women than in men (Harris and Gitterman, 1978; Wolf, 1973; Bakan and Putnam, 1974).

As women are generally less proficient in spatial skills than men (for a review see De Renzi, 1982), the spatial nature of R – L orientation may be suggested. However, mastery of spatial skills is not a sufficient condition: in his careful analysis of R – L orientation Benton (1979) stressed the following elements:

Verbal factors: in order to correctly apply the verbal label 'right' or 'left' to the corresponding part of the body the subject must understand the term and retain it in short-term memory (STM) for the time necessary to execute the command.

Sensory factors: R – L labels are applied to the corresponding body part which has to be discriminated sensorily from the opposite one. This is particularly important in the developmental period, when a difference in excitation between the two sides of the body, mainly due to the development of manual performance, may provide an R – L gradient of excitation by which a given side is felt as different from the other.

Conceptual factors: if the orientation task requires manipulation of personal orientation in tasks of discriminating the right or left side of the confronting person, a high degree of conceptualization is required.

Visuo-spatial factors: some R – L orientation tasks make heavy demands on visuo-spatial factors, e.g. pointing in a sketch to the side touched on the subject's body by the examiner.

It is therefore not surprising that impairment in R – L orientation tasks may be found following brain damage. In an unselected group of brain-damaged patients, Benton (1959) found that more than two-thirds failed in R – L orientation tasks.

Given the verbal nature of most R – L orientation tests it is not surprising that most sensory aphasics fail on them (Benton, 1959; Poeck and Orgass, 1967; Orgass and Poeck, 1968; Sauguet et al., 1971).

The relationship between language comprehension impairment and R – L orientation verbal tasks is so close that both Head (1926) and Goodglass and Kaplan (1972) included tests of R – L discrimination in their language assessment battery. However, it should be recalled that the relationship between failure on lateral orientation tests and language comprehension is not simple, since some sensory aphasics show no signs of disturbance on these tasks (Sauguet et al., 1971).

Although right-brain-damaged patients do not usually show significant impairment in R – L discrimination tasks involving verbal mediation, they do usually show deficit in imitating lateral hand movements performed by the confronting examiner. In these cases, the impairment is proportional to the necessary spatial components of the testing situation (Sauguet et al., 1971).

The relationship between corporeal and extracorporeal orientation disorders will be treated below.

Other elements of the Gerstmann syndrome
Acalculia. Impairment in number-processing and calculation is a frequent accompanying symptom

of focal and diffuse brain damage and takes on a variety of different forms. Aphasic visuo-spatial dyscalculia and anarithmetia (a specific impairment of retrieving learned arithmetic values and/or manipulating them) have been described (Hécaen and Albert, 1978).

According to Gerstmann (1940), the acalculia shown by his patients was of the purest type (anarithmetia), reflecting the 'intimate relationship between differentiation of fingers and calculation'. Unfortunately, this assumption has not been supported by other authors. According to Critchley (1953), Hécaen (1972) and Orgogozo (1976) the calculation disturbance found in Gerstmann syndrome patients is mostly spatial: numbers lose their positional value (units, tens, hundreds) and are inverted in reading and in calculation. Oral calculations are better than written ones.

In the Gerstmann patients described by Kinsbourne and Warrington (1962), both aphasic and spatial acalculia were present. We may therefore conclude that no distinct pattern of acalculia is characteristic of the Gerstmann syndrome.

Agraphia. Writing disturbance presumed to be characteristic of the Gerstmann symptom complex shows the following features: letters are generally badly formed, although absolute agraphia seldom occurs (Pederson, 1936); alignment disturbances are frequent; spelling errors, both written and oral, mostly involve letter order rather than the substitutions or omissions characteristic of writing disturbances of aphasic type (Kinsbourne and Warrington, 1962). The disturbance is obvious, both on dictation and in copying. In a cognitive approach (Ellis, 1982) this pattern of error is suggestive of impairment at the most peripheral level of the writing process. However, further studies are needed for correct qualification of the writing features of parietal lobe patients.

In his strenuous defence of his syndrome, Gerstmann was well aware that one or more of its components could be an accompanying symptom of other broader neuropsychological deficits, but he stressed that when the four symptoms occurred together in an isolated form, they made up a distinctive constellation resulting from a defective body schema for the hand, suggesting a dominant parietal lobe lesion.

In the last forty years, however, a series of studies have cast some doubt both on the localizing value and on the theoretical 'Grundstörung' of the syndrome. In an unselected group of brain-damaged patients Benton (1961) assessed the interrelation between the four components of the Gerstmann syndrome and other neuropsychological variables, such as constructional praxis, reading and non-verbal memory: statistical analysis showed that the four Gerstmann symptoms were as closely correlated with each other as with the three non-Gerstmann symptoms. An analysis restricted to patients affected by left parietal lobe lesions produced similar results: the mean correlation coefficient between finger recognition and the other three Gerstmann components was not significantly higher than the correlation between the four Gerstmann components and constructional praxis and reading.

Similar conclusions were reached by Poeck and Orgass (1966). In an unselected group of 50 unilateral brain-damaged patients they found that the four Gerstmann components showed no closer correlation to each other than to a number of various neuropsychological deficits. Given the high correlation between aphasia and the concurrent presence of the four Gerstmann components, they suggested that a language impairment was a common denominator of the four symptoms. However, this should not mean that aphasia, as opposed to FA, is the 'Grundstörung' of the Gerstmann syndrome, but rather that its effect is evident in a number of behavioral deficits whose separation is an 'artificial exercise' (Russell, 1963).

Turning to localizing value, only when at least three Gerstmann components are found together may involvement of the left angular gyrus be reasonably supposed. However, the lesion usually extends well beyond the angular gyrus, is progressive or recurrent in nature and is accompanied by aphasia (Heimburger et al., 1964). The above study concluded that 'Gerstmann syndrome cannot be regarded as an autonomous entity but merges with numerous other deficits, notably aphasia'.

The autonomy and localizing value of the Gerstmann syndrome were defended by Kinsbourne and Warrington (1962), who maintained that the four symptoms were independent of language disturbances and stated that 'the conjunction of symptoms is more than coincidental'. Similarly, on the basis of a single case report, Strub and Geschwind (1974) stated that the Gerstmann syndrome is independent of aphasia. They described a patient, probably affected by presenile dementia, who showed a severe writing disorder, both on dictation and in copying, calculation disturbances, some difficulty in R – L orientation tasks, and an impairment in pointing to the examiner's fingers, although finger naming was perfect. The patient was not aphasic but showed severe constructional apraxia and visuo-spatial deficits. Without attempting to provide a theoretical basis for the syndrome, the authors concluded that the Gerstmann tetrad may exist in the absence of a significant degree of aphasia.

Lastly, two recent studies may support the possibility of the Gerstmann tetrad's appearing in the absence of aphasia or general mental impairment, and its localizing value. Roeltgen and colleagues (1983) described a patient who, following a lesion of the superior angular gyrus extended into the supramarginal gyrus and to a lesser extent into the superior parietal lobe, showed severe writing and calculation disturbances and some difficulty in understanding two-stage commands involving L – R orientation and performing finger localization tasks. He was not aphasic and his attention was reported to be normal. No attempt at a theoretical explanation of the syndrome was made. A transient Gerstmann syndrome was experimentally produced by Morris et al. (1984) following electrical stimulation of the posterior perisilvian area in an epileptic patient, before surgical removal of an epileptogenic focus.

Summarizing the results of the above studies, the following conclusions emerge:

FA, as originally proposed by Gerstmann, has lost its status as a primary deficit. At present an impairment in finger localization skills is considered an epiphenomenon of a broader neuropsychological deficit such as aphasia or general mental impairment. Furthermore, even if hypothetical 'finger sense' does exist, the co-occurrence of the former deficits prevents an experimental verification of it. For these reasons, a psychological explanation that goes beyond the mere application of a verbal label has not yet been offered.

On this basis the three other components that Gerstmann thought were a necessary consequence of the loss of the 'finger sense' must be considered functionally independent of FA.

As regards the localizing value, only when at least three elements of the syndrome occur concurrently may a left parietal lobe lesion be reasonably suspected.

Lastly, we are far from solving the problem of whether this aggregate of symptoms indicates the concurrent dysfunction of different functional systems which have a contiguous neural representation, or whether it denotes damage to a single functional mechanism involved in the execution of apparently different cognitive functions. However, in the light of the present evidence, the latter hypothesis seems very unlikely.

Mechanisms underlying bilateral disturbances of body knowlegde: modern views

The spatial hypothesis

The hypothesis of the spatial nature of some if not all bilateral body awareness disorders can be traced back to Badal (1888), who ascribed the deficit of finger localization shown by his patient Valerie to a loss of 'sense de l'éspace'. This quite vague notion of spatial deficit was later elaborated by Conrad (1933) in the framework of the Gestalt tradition: localizing and pointing to a specific body part requires the evocation of a clear mental image of the body, including the representation of the spatial relationships between the various parts in order to single out the target; if this faculty is lost a dissociation between 'what tasks' (tasks involving understanding, naming and describing the functions of the body part singled out by the examiner) and 'where tasks' (pointing to a specific body part on verbal command or imitation or describing the precise location of a specific body part in relation to other body parts) should appear (Engerth, 1933).

This dissociation is the main feature of AT (De Renzi and Faglioni, 1963; De Renzi and Scotti, 1970; Poncet et al., 1971; Ogden, 1985; Semenza, 1988), and body parts devoid of definite boundaries, such as joints or cheeks, are the most difficult for autotopoagnosic patients to localize.

We are still left with the question of the specificity of the processes of building and maintaining a clear image of how single parts of the body are related to one another. This problem was experimentally investigated by De Renzi and co-workers (De Renzi and Faglioni, 1963; De Renzi and Scotti, 1970). They convincingly demonstrated that AT was not an autonomous phenomenon but rather that it represents a fragment of a more generalized deficit which can be seen whenever the patient is asked to divide a whole into its components on an ideational, representative or perceptual level. The above authors' patients failed in pointing to parts of a bicycle or describing the relative position of the various parts of a car. More interestingly, although they were neither aphasic nor amnesic, they showed a striking difficulty in recalling the details of a complex scene or a well-known story in a logical sequence. If, however, they were asked definite and circumscribed questions, their performance was flawless. In the praxic sphere the same behavior appeared: use of single objects was correct, while carrying out a complex sequence of gestures was defective. According to De Renzi and Scotti (1971), this pattern of behavior was suggestive of a supramodal deficit reminiscent of Head's (1920) semantic aphasia and characterized by 'a loss of power to appreciate or to formulate the logical conclusion of a train of thought . . . This impairment extends to a number of non-linguistic performances such as drawing, topographical memory, etc.' Unfortunately AT was not tested in Head's patients. The same line of thought can be seen in the defective performance in recalling an itinerary, finding a town in an outline map of France, and oral spelling in the autotopoagnosic patient described by Poncet et al. (1971).

Impairment of spatial orientation has been suggested as the basis of FA, seen as a disorder of spatial orientation with respect to the actual sequence of fingers of the hand. Lange (1930) postulated the existence of a 'category of direction of space' which was impaired in patients with finger agnosia. On theoretical grounds Stengel (1944) viewed impairment in finger localization as the inability to appreciate the position of individual fingers among their fellows. This position, similar to that of Conrad (1933), was experimentally tested by Kinsbourne and Warrington (1962). They examined 12 patients clinically affected by Gerstmann's syndrome with a series of ingenious non-verbal tasks and, in comparison with 20 other brain-damaged patients, found a specific difficulty in relating the fingers to each other in the correct spatial sequence. The patients appeared to perceive the fingers as an undifferentiated mass as if they were 'fused into a solid lump'. Unfortunately, not all patients with defective bodily orientation fit the part-whole impairment model: neither Stengel (1944) nor Kinsbourne and Warrington (1962) tested their patients in non-body-related tasks requiring the ability to analyse wholes into parts. Neither Ogden's (1985) nor Semenza's (1988) autotopoagnosic patients showed any impairment in tasks requiring a general ability to analyse wholes into parts, suggesting an impairment in evoking a discrete body image, whose nature is unspecified.

Misreaching
Optic ataxia consists of difficulty in reaching a target outside the body under visual control: this symptom has been demonstrated in a series of ex-

perimental studies (Haaxma and Kuypers, 1975) and clinical observations (for reviews, see Rondot et al., 1977; Damasio and Benton, 1979) to involve a disconnection of the motor area from the striate area, producing a defect in visual guidance of contralateral hand and finger movements. Since some of the errors made by autotopoagnosic patients in localizing tasks are of the off-target type, the hypothesis of a disconnection between visual and tactile areas and motor areas is not unreasonable. However, as stressed by De Renzi (1985), most of these patients have no difficulty in reaching objects or even parts of their own or the examiner's body, once they have been touched by somebody else. Conversely, patients affected by optic ataxia usually have no difficulty in pointing to their own bodies.

Only a few exceptions are reported: some patients affected by Balint's syndrome (e.g., case No. 3 of Hécaen and Ajuriaguerra, 1952) have comparable difficulties in pointing to objects and body parts.

The autotopoagnosic patients described by Pick (1922) showed important disturbances of optic ataxia type: when trying to reach an object, the patient's hand gropes in space, behind or at the side of the target to be centered. More recently we (Denes et al., 1982) described a patient who, following an acute episode of eclampsia coupled with a mild pattern of conduction aphasia, displayed agraphia, constructional disturbances and a gross inability to reach targets outside and on her body, both with and without visual control. This symptom complex was thought to be a consequence of a disconnection between posterior and motor areas.

We must therefore suggest that a systematic examination of the ability to point correctly to body parts must be carried out in all patients showing optic ataxia and autotopoagnosia, with and without visual control, in order to discover the association between the two types of task.

The conceptual linguistic hypothesis
The relation between cognitive and anatomical structures subserving body orientation and those subserving language is not clear. The mere fact that most if not all cases of AT are not obviously aphasics does not necessarily imply that conscious awareness of the body is not totally or partially dependent on linguistic structures.

The specificity of body part names as a linguistic category which may be selectively impaired following brain damage was first proposed by Hécaen and Ajuriaguerra (1952) and further demonstrated in a series of observations in the following years.

Selecki and Heron (1965) discussed body awareness disorders in the light of a linguistically based model. They described five patients with left parieto-temporo-occipital lesions who showed significant impairment in understanding and naming body parts in comparison with the same tasks using other semantic categories. They proposed that the origin of this deficit was selective impairment of verbal body image: this linguistic category is the result of symbolic integration with the existing gnostic image which is in turn predominantly based on proprioceptive-vestibular-tactile-sensory interaction.

Dennis (1976) reported the case of a right-handed epileptic girl who, following left anterior temporal lobectomy for relief of seizures 3 years before examination, showed a selective deficit in lexical tasks involving body parts and right – left discrimination. In naming subtests her errors were either circumlocutions or paraphasias of the semantic type within the word category of body parts. Comprehension of body part names was equally deficient, but varied with the degree of selectional constraint (phonemic and semantic cueing). A dissociation between naming and comprehension of body parts was reported by McKenna and Warrington (1978), with naming better spared than comprehension, the reverse of the pattern for other semantic categories.

In two group studies Goodglass et al. (1966) and Assal and Buttet (1973) observed that Wernicke's aphasics were more impaired in understanding body part names than other categories of words. In two more detailed studies Goodglass and colleagues (1986, 1988) showed that body part names together with letters and colors stand out as specific semantic categories as demonstrated by selective impairment of naming and comprehension. They also offered an ingenious explanation for body part specificity: body part names, like letters and colors, are limited in number, learned early in life, and their category membership is clearly defined. This set of properties distinguishes what they call the 'fixed set category'. In addition, body parts are particularly rich in associative and semantic values. For these reasons it is reasonable to postulate that they deserve independent processing in both functional and neurological terms.

However, a purely linguistically based explanation for every case of body part unawareness does not seem fully tenable. Most autotopoagnosic patients are perfect in naming body parts, while the performance of Dennis's patients in pointing to body parts on imitation was flawless.

The relationship between verbally and non-verbally tested disturbances of 'body schema' (right – left orientation, finger naming and recognition, AT) and aphasia was investigated by Sauguet et al. (1971). They found that a significant proportion of Wernicke's aphasics failed on verbal and, to a lesser degree, on non-verbal tests of body orientation. However, since a number of patients with sensory aphasia performed most of the tests adequately, they postulated that a combination of somatosensory impairment with aphasic disorder is a sufficient condition for the occurrence of some types of 'body schema' disturbance.

In a more recent study Semenza and Goodglass (1985) added further support to the role of linguistic structures in the process of body awareness: a group of 32 aphasics was tested with a body part identification task; some tests required linguistic mediation, such as pointing to the body on verbal command, while others did not, e.g., pointing to a part of the body corresponding to an isolated drawing of the single parts shown by the examiner. They found that a common factor underlies identification of body parts independently of testing conditions: the greater its lexical frequency, the higher the probability of its being correctly identified and standing out as a whole even in a non-verbal context. They therefore proposed that body parts are conceptually organized in a hierarchical way, determined by their frequency of use in language. In other words, the strength and precision of the representation of the body part as an isolated concept seems to be linguistically determined.

The concept of semantic organization of body parts as opposed to topographical representation was further reinforced by analysis of the errors made by the above authors' patients, regardless of testing modality (verbal vs. non-verbal). Functional similarity errors (joint for joint, toe – thumb interchanges) and location similarities accounted for the majority of incorrect responses. In their study, however, no single patient showed body part identification impairment as a prominent neuropsychological symptom, nor did the authors compare body part identification tasks with other object or part-of-object identification tasks. However, this fallacy was recently overcome by the observation of a patient (Semenza, 1988) who, following a left parietal lesion and in the absence of significant aphasia, showed an almost isolated deficit in pointing to body parts as opposed to parts of other complex objects. This deficit was independent of the testing modality (verbal versus non-verbal) and a substantial proportion of her errors were semantically related.

As far as disturbances limited to specific parts of the body are concerned, the same line of thought was followed by Benton (1959) in relation to FA. He hypothesized that correct finger localization involves a symbolic process consisting of the 'ability to handle the symbols that relate to the fingers', postulating an impairment of language functions as the basis of bilateral finger agnosia, even when tested in non-verbal tasks. This hypothesis was partially supported by the results of Stone and Robinson (1968) and Gainotti et al. (1972), who showed that left-hemisphere brain-damaged patients were impaired in finger localization tests, independent of the verbal/non-verbal modality of testing. In the latter study, however, the relationship between the presence of aphasia and bilateral impairment in finger localization failed to reach statistical significance, the other detrimental factors being mental deterioration and somatosensory deficit, a finding which is in line with the results of Sauguet et al. (1971) reported above.

The role of linguistic mediation in the broad and less defined concept of body awareness, i.e., right – left orientation, is of course essential: understanding commands which involve the system of right – left orientation (e.g. touching the examiner's left hand with his/her right hand) requires considerable mastery of language skills, given the lack of other clues to facilitate the comprehension of the command, and a strict relationship between right – left orientation verbal task impairments and aphasia must obviously exist.

A series of studies starting from the single case study reported by Bonhoeffer (1923) and extending to Head (1920), Gerstmann (1930), Benton (1959), Poeck and Orgass (1967), McFie and Zangwill (1960) and Sauguet et al. (1971) has also shown a strict relationship between receptive language disorders and right – left orientation tasks, both verbal and non-verbal, thus supporting Head's assumption that even the imitation of lateralized movements involves verbal mediation.

Three conclusions thus seem to emerge from the above studies:

(i) Body parts stand out as a specific conceptual category, a notion in line with the hypothesis of the existence of cognitive systems based on a distinct module (for a review, see Shallice, 1987).

(ii) The internal structure of this category is hierarchically organized according to a linguistic principle, that is, lexical frequency of the various body parts.

(iii) This category can be selectively impaired following focal brain damage, with further specification according to task demands (linguistic vs. non-linguistic).

Unilateral disorders of body awareness

Two important features characterize impairment of body awareness following right hemisphere lesion:

(1) The disturbance of personal space knowledge involves the contralateral side of the body *(hemisomatoagnosia)*.

(2) While somatoagnosic disturbances following left hemisphere damage are evident only in testing situations, the daily behavior of affected patients being completely unaffected, hemisomatoagnosia (which usually occurs only with right brain damage) may appear with spectacular disorders of behavior, to the point at which the hemisomatoagnosic patient behaves as though she/he had lost one limb.

According to Frederiks (1969, 1985a), hemisomatoagnosia may take on two forms, conscious and non-conscious.

In conscious hemisomatoagnosia, a rarely described phenomenon (Lhermitte et al., 1928; Menninger-Lerchenthal, 1935; Frederiks, 1963), the patient spontaneously reports the experience of having lost the perception of half her/his body. The phenomenon usually occurs in paroxysmal forms during an epileptic seizure or a migraine attack. It may follow right or left hemisphere lesion, although at least one case of conscious hemisomatoagnosia has been described following brainstem lesion (Frederiks, 1963). No anatomo-clinical correlation or theoretical interpretation of this symptom can be given, in view of the rarity of reported cases.

Non-conscious hemisomatoagnosia is a phenomenon frequently found in clinical practice and may be considered as indicating a right retrorolandic lesion. Hécaen (1972) reports that 29% of patients with right hemisphere lesions show unilateral somatoagnosic disturbances, as opposed to only 3% with left hemisphere lesions, who generally only show a slight and transitory form. In non-conscious hemisomatoagnosia, the patient pays no attention to the left half of her/his body, and this behavior appears in various ways according to the situation and the tasks requested.

In daily living, hemisomatoagnosia influences day-to-day behavior: the patient seems to have forgotten that she/he has another half-body, e.g., only shaves one side of his face, does not put the left earpiece of a pair of glasses behind the left ear, and, if asked to sit down, will leave the left buttock off the chair.

Another interesting sign is *motor aspontaneity* or *motor akinesia,* e.g., the patient fails to use the left arm, although she/he is not greatly paretic, as shown by the standard neurological examination. Similarly, when asked to lift both arms simultaneously, she/he only raises the arm homolateral to the lesion, as if the contralateral limb did not exist (Castaigne et al., 1970; Valenstein and Heilman, 1981).

A lack of responsivity to sensory stimuli presented to the affected side, in the absence of any sensory or motor deficit severe enough to account for imperception, has frequently been reported, with various degrees of severity.

Tactile extinction may be defined as a lack of attention to or perception of a stimulus when a contralateral stimulus is simultaneously presented, even though the unreported stimulus is perceived normally when presented alone (Nathan, 1946; Critchley, 1953; Bender, 1952). Although unanimity has not been reached about the nature, frequency and localizing value of this phenomenon, most authors (Critchley, 1953; Schwartz et al., 1979) agree that right parietal lobe damage results in more instances of tactile extinction than injury to the left lobe, even when the data are covaried for the presence of aphasia which could prevent the testing of the most severe aphasic patients.

Alloesthesia or *allochiria* is a symptom by which a sensory stimulus applied to one side of the body is perceived in the corresponding area on the other side. Although first described in patients with spinal cord injury and hysteria (Obersteiner, 1880, 1881), the majority of reported cases follow right hemisphere lesion (for a recent review, see Kawamura et al., 1987). The clinical characteristics of the patients reported in the literature are very similar (Hécaen and Ajuriaguerra, 1952):

 — painful stimuli (cold, pinprick) are usually perceived after a short delay at the corresponding area of the side contralateral to the stimuli;

 — stimuli are sometimes felt as different from the sensations normally produced by them;

 — in only a few instances does alloesthesia affect the face and distal parts of the limbs, the most frequently affected areas being the trunk and proximal parts of the limbs;

 — a close topographical correspondence exists between pointing and verbal report of the spot thought to be stimulated;

 — alloesthesia following cortical damage is usually a transient symptom appearing in the acute stage, frequently accompanied by slight cloudiness of consciousness and anosognosia (see later);

 — of the 29 patients reported in the literature with alloesthesia following unilateral cortical damage, 27 had right hemisphere lesions, the majority after a hemorrhage involving the putamen (Kawamura et al., 1987).

In a meeting of the Société de Neurologie of Paris, Babinski (1914) drew attention to a disturbance he had observed in cases of hemiparesis or hemiplegia, in which patients 'ignorent ou paraissent d'ignorer l'existence de la paralysie dont ils sont atteints'. Babinski coined the term *anosognosia* to describe this phenomenon, and his note concluded with the words: 'Je ferai remarquer qu'il s'agissait dans les cas observés d'hémiplégie gauche. L'anosoagnosie serait-elle particulière aux lésions occupant l'hémisphère droit?'. Since that time, and in spite of the fact that some authors (for a review, see Weinstein and Kahn, 1955; Frederiks, 1985) have described anosognosia following lesions of the dominant hemisphere, the relationship between the symptom and right hemisphere lesion is the rule.

Two forms of anosognosia may be clearly distinguished: the verbal conscious form, and an unconscious, implicit form. Explicit verbal negation ranges from complete denial of being ill, projection of the disorder outside one's own body (*somatoparaphrenia:* the patient attributes the sick limb to another person), to time-shifts (the patient states that she/he has been hemiplegic in the past, but is now well). This picture, admittedly very rare in clinical practice, is found almost exclusively in the acute phase of a right retrorolandic *ictus,* often with clouded consciousness. Once the acute stage is over, the picture of an implicit denial of illness, with indifference to it *(anosodiaphoria)* is very common.

As regards the relationship between anosognosia and hemisomatoagnosia, the latter does predict the appearance of anosognosic behavior, although no clarification has yet been made of the factor which, added to the somatoagnosic deficit, causes altered consciousness of illness.

Mechanisms underlying hemisomatoagnosia
Physiological hypothesis. In discussing Babinski's (1918) report, Pierre Marie (1918) hypothesized that the various forms of hemisomatoagnosia were exclusively due to loss of deep sensation following parietal lobe lesion. However, although Babinski (1918) and Meige (1918) believed that a sensory deficit was a necessary presupposition, they did not think it was sufficient: this is indeed demonstrated by the fact that many hemianesthetic patients are not hemisomatoagnosic.

A physiological approach very popular in the 1950s and 1960s was that of Denny-Brown et al. (Denny-Brown et al., 1952; Denny-Brown and Banker, 1954) based on the concept of *amorphosynthesis,* understood as a disturbance of sensitivity due to the raised threshold related to spatial summation. Following a parietal lesion, the process of synthesis of multiple sensory afferences no longer takes place, giving rise to unawareness of the contralateral half of the body and of space. This disturbance may follow either right or left hemisphere lesion, but the concurrent appearance of language disturbances in left hemisphere lesions leads to the impossibility of showing a somatoagnosic disturbance in left hemisphere le-

sions (Brain, 1941).

However, only rarely does a lesion limited to the left parietal lobe cause aphasia so severe as to prevent the examiner from discovering a somatoagnosic deficit. Moreover, as seen above, the phenomenology and nature of somatoagnosic disturbances following left parietal lesions are far from hemisomatoagnosia.

Attentional hypothesis. An unawareness of extrapersonal space is the most frequent symptom of hemisomatoagnosia (Frederiks, 1969). This correlation led Critchley (1953) and more recently Watson et al. (1973, 1974) to state that hemisomatoagnosia is subtended by an attentional deficit for half the space, including the hemisoma. The leading role of the right hemisphere in attentional processes (for recent reviews, see De Renzi, 1982; Heilman et al., 1985) may explain the prevalence of hemisomatoagnosia following right hemisphere lesion. However, not all patients with unilateral spatial neglect show signs of hemisomatoagnosia, the latter being far less frequent (Hécaen and Angélergues, 1963; Cutting, 1978). The relationship between frequency and severity of extrapersonal and intrapersonal hemi-inattention was recently studied by Bisiach et al. (1986) in a group of right-hemisphere brain-damaged patients (RHBD). Personal neglect was tested by asking patients to touch the left hand with the right hand; extrapersonal neglect was tested by means of a cancellation task. Medium and severe personal neglect were found to be far less frequent than extrapersonal neglect of corresponding severity. Only one out of 97 RHBD showed personal neglect without extrapersonal neglect, while only 6 out of 35 patients with extrapersonal neglect showed personal neglect. Personal neglect occurred in association with marked impairment of motor, somatosensory and visual field defects, while extrapersonal neglect was doubly dissociated from such defects. In both cases of neglect, the lesion was retrorolandic and involved the inferoposterior parietal region. It therefore seems that in man there is an overlap of cortical areas involving personal and extrapersonal awareness of space.

However, given the discrepancy between the frequency of the two types of neglect, the existence of a single general-purpose mechanism subserving attention for personal and extrapersonal space has not been proven, suggesting that, at least in cases of faulty body localization limited to one part of the body, a body-specific attentional system may be suspected.

Neuropathology of hemisomatoagnosia Hemisomatoagnosia has been described almost exclusively following large retrorolandic right hemisphere lesion involving the parietal lobe and the underlying white matter. The etiology is usually vascular and onset acute (Critchley, 1953; Heilman et al., 1983; Bisiach et al., 1986). Very few cases have been described of intrapersonal neglect following subcortical lesion involving the reticular and cortico-limbic activating circuit (for a review, see Heilman et al., 1985). Anosognosia and somatoparaphrenia have been described following right thalamic lesion (Carreras et al., 1968). However, the specific contribution of the thalamus in producing intra- and extrapersonal neglect has recently been called into question by Perani et al. (1987) by means of perfusion studies. Their right hemisphere brain-damaged patients with subcortical neglect showed a significantly greater reduction of cortical perfusion on single photon emission tomography (SPECT) compared with patients affected by similar lesions but without neurological signs. The above authors concluded that a large cortical lesion probably due to diaschisis is the crucial factor in the appearance of neglect after a subcortical stroke.

Somatoagnosic illusions and hallucinations

Phantom limb

Since the first published description by Ambroise Paré (1551) of patients who, despite having had a limb amputated, still feel it as present, sometimes painfully, the term *phantom limb* (Mitchell, 1871, 1872, quoted by Weinstein, 1969) has gained universal popularity in both medical and literary establishments (for recent reviews, see Frederiks,

1969, 1985b; Weinstein, 1969). However, the phenomenon does not only follow an acquired loss of limb:

– phantoms have been described following amputation of other external organs such as breasts, male genitalia and facial parts;

– they may follow body part deafferentation, e.g., after spinal cord transection or brachial plexus injury;

– they are reported in the congenital absence of limbs (Poeck, 1964);

– exceptionally, phantoms may follow cerebral lesion or a transient epileptic episode.

For these reasons the original concept of phantom limb has been enlarged and may be operationally defined as the 'subjective report of the awareness of a non-existent or deafferented bodily part in a mentally competent individual' (Weinstein, 1969).

The interest shown by neuropsychologists in the phantom limb phenomenon is due to the fact that it seems to represent a kind of experimental proof of the existence of a mental representation of a body part which persists in spite of the lack of specific afferent impulses.

Characteristics of phantom limb

Phantoms following limb amputation are almost universal. They may appear in two forms which often occur together: real phantom limb, consisting of perception of the missing limb, including its spatial relationship to the rest of the body, and phantom limb sensations such as paresthesia, pain, etc., perceived as originating from the missing limb.

The phenomenon usually appears almost immediately after amputation and may persist for a long time. Sometimes, over the years, the phantom becomes smaller and less well-defined, until its distal portion mingles with the stump (telescoping: Weiss and Fishman, 1963).

Patients may provide somesthetic information on their phantom's size, length, weight, position and movement, and sometimes report sensations of voluntary movements.

Phantoms following the amputation of other organs are less frequent: of 203 women who underwent unilateral mastectomy, 33.5% reported phantoms of the missing breast (Weinstein et al., 1970). The appearance of the phantom was significantly associated with the side on which the mastectomy had been carried out (more often following left-sided operations), duration of the tumor before mastectomy, and patients' age at the time of surgery.

Phantoms following generally traumatic transection of the spinal cord involve parts of the body innervated by the lumbar, sacral and caudal nerves, and are frequently associated with burning and tingling sensations (Weinstein, 1969). Sensations of micturition and defecation are sometimes reported.

Theories regarding the nature of phantoms

Peripheral theory: the phantom arises from nerve stump endings, triggered by neuromata and scars. Unfortunately, neurosurgical modification of scar tissue may lead to opposing results, from disappearance to intensification of the phenomenon. Moreover, phantoms are not always eliminated by cordotomy or section of posterior roots.

Central theory: the phantom is due to the effects of the deafferented projection areas specific to the amputated or deafferented body part. Experimental support for this theory has been invoked on the basis of abolition of the phantom following cerebral lesion (Head and Holmes, 1911 – 12) or surgical ablation (Hécaen et al., 1956) of the parietal cortex contralateral to the affected part. Poeck's (1964) study on the occurrence of phantoms in amyelic children seems to confirm the hypothesis of a built-in cortical representation of the body. This presence seems to be a prerequisite for the experience of a phantom.

Need theory: the phantom represents emotional compensation for a loss. If this were true, most phantoms would deal with those parts of the body of greatest emotional significance. However, a series of studies (for a review, see Weinstein, 1969) did not show any statistically significant correlation between the psychological value of the part in question and the probability of the appearance of a phantom.

Somatoagnosic hallucinations

Since Bonnier's pioneering observations (1905) regarding patients who felt their bodies or parts of them as abnormally large or small, several psychosensory hallucinatory somatoagnosic disturbances have been described.

These disorders are usually paroxysmal and occur particularly during attacks of migraine or epilepsy. In the latter case the somatoagnosic hallucination may represent the beginning of a focal seizure. EEGs generally show that the focus is in the parieto-temporo-occipital region, although neither side is prevalent.

Somatoagnosic hallucinations have also been described following widespread lesions, focal lesions of the CNS, confused states of various origin, and psychosis. However, it should be stressed that some authors have also described these phenomena in perfectly normal subjects, e.g., upon falling asleep or waking.

They are classically distinguished as follows:

Autoscopy: this is the vision a person has of her/his own image or part of it, as in a mirror. This is therefore a psychosensory hallucination in which the body image is projected into external space; it may be more or less vivid, is sometimes transparent, and may reflect the patient's emotional state. It usually appears in the centre of the visual field (although some cases in which it is lateralized have been described) and sometimes in the hemianopic field. The phenomenon is generally transitory, not lasting more than a few seconds, although Conrad (1953) described a case of permanent autoscopy.

Macro- and microsomatoagnosia: these psychosensory somatoagnosis disturbances take place as segmentary changes, sometimes somatotopic, in which one part of the body (usually a limb) is perceived as larger than normal (marcosomatoagnosia) or smaller (microsomatoagnosia). Given the great variety of etiologies, neither an anatomo-clinical correlation nor a reasonable hypothesis regarding the basis of these bizarre phenomena seems to be possible. However, as Frederiks (1985b) points out that most cases of somatoagnosic hallucination are of organic origin, a careful medical examination must be carried out in every case. Detailed reviews on this subject may be found in Hécaen and Ajuriaguerra (1952), Lukianowitz (1958) and Frederiks (1969, 1985b).

Concluding remarks

Twenty years ago Poeck (1969) made some important methodological statements on the concept of body schema disorders.

(a) When both investigation methods and experimenters' ingenuity are increasingly refined and new neuropsychological examination procedures are applied to groups of brain-damaged patients, at least some subjects will do badly on the tests. However, it seems methodologically incorrect to infer from this the existence of a specific cognitive function equipped with its own neural substrate. It is more probable that the deficit mainly depends on task requirements whose nature has not been sufficiently analyzed.

(b) Before considering a neuropsychological symptom as 'primary', the following possibilities must be excluded:

– the symptom must not simply represent a previously undescribed aspect of a more extensive impairment of neuropsychological function, such as language, spatial orientation, etc.;

– the observed symptom must not depend on the patient's incapacity – due to the concurrent presence of associated neuropsychological deficits – to understand or carry out the requested task, since its nature is not known;

– the concurrent presence of more general psychological variables such as cognitive or memory deficits must not lead to a general lowering of all cognitive capacities.

This review has shown that most disorders of body schema are not primary, but represent the epiphenomenon of isolated or concurrent break-down of more extensive cognitive abilities, mainly language and spatial attention. Therefore, a specific psychological function equipped with its own neurological substrate such as somatoagnosia does not at present appear to be a workable hypothesis, although it must be recognized that there are patients affected by disorders of knowledge, conscious awareness and mental representations of the body whose nature has not yet been experimentally clarified.

From a practical viewpoint, therefore, we cannot simply be content with attaching a label such as 'body schema disorder' to any altered knowledge of personal space. We must follow Luria's (1964) thinking and state that only qualitative analysis of the symptom is effective.

Ulrich, the hero of Musil's novel 'Der Mann ohne Eigenschaften', says: (Vol. I, Part II, Chapter 83): 'There are some mathematical problems which do not allow of a general solution, but there are also single solutions which, combined, approach the general solution'. A similar consideration is pertinent to the problems discussed in this review.

Acknowledgements

The preparation of this chapter was partly supported by a Grant from the Consiglio Nazionale delle Ricerche to G.D. The critical reading by Carlo Semenza M.D. of earlier drafts of this chapter is acknowledged.

References

Angyal LV, Lorand B: Beiträge zu den Zeigenstörungen autotopoagnostisch Aphatischerkranken. *Arch. Psychiatr.: 108,* 493 – 516, 1938.
Assal G, Buttet J: Troubles du schéma corporel lors des atteints hémisphériques gauches. *Schweiz. Rundsch. Med.: 62,* 172 – 179, 1973.
Babinski J: Contribution à l'étude des troubles mentaux dans l'hémiplégie cérébrale. *Rev. Neurol.: 27,* 845 – 847, 1914.
Babinski J: Anosognosie. *Rev. Neurol.: 31,* 365 – 367, 1918.
Badal J: Contribution à l'étude des cécités psychiques. Alexie, agraphie, hémianopsie inférieure, trouble du sens de l'espace. *Arch. Ophtalmol.: 140,* 97 – 117, 1888.
Bakan P, Putnam W: Right-left discrimination and brain

lateralization. Sex differences. *Arch. Neurol. (Chicago): 30,* 334 – 335, 1974.

Bender MB: *Disorder of Perception.* Springfield, IL, Charles C Thomas, 1952.

Benson DF, Geschwind N: Developmental Gerstmann syndrome. *Neurology: 20,* 293 – 298, 1970.

Benton AL: *Right-Left Discrimination and Finger Localization. Development and Pathology.* New York, Hoeber-Harper, 1959.

Benton AL: The fiction of the 'Gerstmann Syndrome'. *J. Neurol. Neurosurg. Psychiatry.: 24,* 176 – 181, 1961.

Benton AL: Reflections on the Gerstmann syndrome. *Brain Lang. 4,* 45 – 62, 1977.

Benton AL: Body schema disturbance; finger agnosia and right-left disorientation. In Heilman KM, Valenstein E (Editors), *Clinical Neuropsychology.* New York: Oxford University Press, 1979.

Bisiach E, Perani D, Vallar G, Berti A: Unilateral neglect: personal and extrapersonal. *Neuropsychologia: 24,* (6), 759 – 767, 1986.

Bogen JE: Split-brain syndromes. In Frederiks JAM (Editor), *Handbook of Clinical Neurology. Vol. 1 (45): Clinical Neuropsychology.* Amsterdam: Elsevier, 1985.

Bonhöffer K: Zur Klinik und Lokalization des Agrammatismus und der Rechts-Links-Desorientierung. *Monatsschr. Psychiat. Neurol.: 54,* 11 – 42, 1923.

Bonnier P: L'aschématie. *Rev. Neurol.: 13,* 604 – 609, 1905.

Brain R: Visual disorientation with special reference to the lesions of the right cerebral hemisphere. *Brain: 64,* 244 – 272, 1941.

Carreras M, De Risio C, Visintini F: Osservazione a proposito di un caso di somatoparafrenia. In *Problemi di Neurologia e Psichiatria.* Roma: Il Pensiero Scientifico, 1968.

Castaigne P, Laplane D, Degos JD: Trois cas de négligence motrice par lésion rétrorolandique. *Rev. Neurol.: 122,* 233 – 242, 1970.

Conrad K: Das Körperschema. Eine kritische Studie und der Versuch einer Revision. *Z. Gesamte Neurol. Psychiatry.: 147,* 346 – 369, 1933.

Conrad K: Un cas singulier de 'fantôme spéculaire'. *Encéphale: 42,* 338 – 352, 1953.

Critchley M: *The Parietal Lobes.* London: Arnold, 1953.

Critchley M: The enigma of Gerstmann's syndrome. *Brain: 89,* 183 – 188, 1966.

Cutting J: Study of anosognosia. *J. Neurol. Neurosurg. Psychiatry: 41,* 548 – 555, 1978.

Damasio AR, Benton AL: Impairment of hand movements under visual guidance. *Neurology: 29,* 170 – 174, 1979.

Denes G, Caviezel F, Semenza C: Difficulty in reaching objects and body parts: a sensorimotor disconnection syndrome. *Cortex: 18,* 165 – 173, 1982.

Dennis M: Dissociated naming and locating of body parts after left anterior temporal lobe resection: an experimental case study. *Brain Lang.: 3,* 147 – 163, 1976.

Denny-Brown D, Banker BQ: Amorphosynthesis from left parietal lesions. *Arch. Neurol. Psychiatry: 71,* 302 – 313, 1954.

Denny-Brown D, Meyer JS, Horenstein S: The significance of perceptual rivalry resulting from parietal lesions. *Brain: 75,* 433 – 471, 1952.

Deny G, Camus P: Sur une forme d'hypocondrie aberrante due à la perte de la conscience du corps. *Rev. Neurol.: 9,* 461 – 467, 1905.

De Renzi E: Sull'utilità del concetto di schema corporeo nella patologia corticale. *Lav. Neuropsichiatr.: 44 (2),* 1395 – 1406, 1971.

De Renzi E: *Disorders of Space Exploration and Cognition.* Chichester: John Wiley and Sons, 1982.

De Renzi E, Faglioni P: L'autotopoagnosia. *Arch. Psicol. Neurol. Psichiatr.: 24,* 1 – 34, 1963.

De Renzi E, Scotti G: Autotopoagnosia: fiction or reality? *Arch. Neurol. (Chicago): 23,* 221 – 227, 1970.

Ellis AW: Spelling and writing (and reading and speaking). In Ellis A.W. (Editor), *Normality and Pathology in Cognitive Functions.* London: Academic Press, 1982.

Engerth G: Zeichenstörungen bei patienten mit Autotopoagnosie. *Z. Gesamte Neurol. Psychiatry: 143,* 381 – 402, 1933.

Ettlinger G: Defective identification of fingers. *Neuropsychologia: 1,* 39 – 45, 1963.

Frederiks JAM: Anosognosie et hémisomatoagnosie. *Rev. Neurol.: 5,* 585 – 597, 1963.

Frederiks JAM: Disorders of the body schema. In Vinken PJ, Bruyn GW (Editors), *Handbook of Clinical Neurology, Vol. 4.* Amsterdam: Elsevier, pp. 207 – 240, 1969.

Frederiks JAM (Editor): Disorders of the body schema. In *Handbook of Clinical Neurology, Vol. 1* (45): *Clinical Neuropsychology.* Amsterdam: Elsevier, 1985a.

Frederiks JAM (Editor): Phantom limb and phantom limb pain. In *Handbook of Clinical Neurology. Vol. 1 (45): Clinical Neuropsychology.* Amsterdam: Elsevier, 1985b.

Gainotti G, Cianchetti G, Tiacci C: The influence of hemispheric side of lesion on nonverbal tests of finger localization. *Cortex: 8,* 364 – 381, 1972.

Gerstmann J: Fingeragnosie: eine umschriebene Störung der Orientierung am eigenen Körper. *Wien. Klin. Wochenschr.: 37,* 1010 – 1012, 1924.

Gerstmann J: Fingeragnosie und isolierte Agraphie: ein neues Syndrom. *Z. Gesamte Neurol. Psychiatr.: 108,* 152 – 177, 1927.

Gerstmann J: Zur Symptomatologie der Hirnläsionen in Übergangsgebiet der unteren Parietal und mittleren Occipitalwindung. *Nervenarzt: 3,* 691 – 695, 1930.

Gerstmann J: Syndrome of finger agnosia, disorientation for right and left, agraphia and acalculia. *Arch. Neurol. Psychiatry (Chicago): 44,* 398 – 406, 1940.

Gerstmann J: Problem of imperception of disease and of impaired body territories with organic lesions. Relation to body scheme and its disorders. *Arch. Neurol. Psychiatry.: 48,* 890 – 913, 1942.

Gerstmann J: Some notes on the Gerstmann syndrome. *Neurology: 7,* 866 – 869, 1957.

Goodglass H, Kaplan E: *The Assessment of Aphasia and Related Disorders.* Philadelphia: Lea and Febiger, 1972.

Goodglass H, Budin C: Category and modality specific dissociations in word comprehension and concurrent phonological dyslexia. *Neuropsychologia: 26,* 67 – 78, 1988.

Goodglass H, Klein B, Carey P, Jones KJ: Specific semantic word categories in aphasia. *Cortex: 2,* 74 – 89, 1966.

Goodglass H, Wingfield A, Hyde MR, Theurkauf JC: Category specific dissociations in naming and recognition by aphasic patient. *Cortex: 22,* 87 – 102, 1986.

Haaxma R, Kuypers HGJM: Intrahemispheric cortical connexions and visual guidance of hand and finger movements in the rhesus monkey. *Brain: 98,* 253 – 260, 1975.

Harris LJ, Gitterman SR: Sex and handedness differences in well-educated adults' self-description of left-right confusability. *Arch. Neurol. (Chicago): 35,* 773, 1978.

Head H: Aphasia and kindred disorders of speech. *Brain: 43,* 89 – 165, 1920.

Head H, Holmes G: Sensory disturbances from cerebral lesions. *Brain: 34,* 102 – 254, 1911/12.

Hécaen H: *Introduction à la Neuropsychologie.* Paris: Larousse, 1972.

Hécaen H, Ajuriaguerra J: *Méconaissance et Hallucinations Corporelles: Intégration et Désintégration de la Somatoagnosie.* Paris: Masson, 1952.

Hécaen H, Ajuriaguerra J: Balint's syndrome (psychic paralysis of visual fixation and its minor forms). *Brain: 77,* 373 – 400, 1954.

Hécaen H, Albert ML: *Human Neuropsychology.* New York: Wiley, 1978.

Hécaen H, Angélergues R: *La Cecité Psychique.* Paris: Masson, 1963.

Hécaen H, Penfield W, Bertrand C, Malmo R: The syndrome of apractognosia due to lesions of the minor cerebral hemisphere. *Arch. Neurol. Psychiatry: 75,* 400 – 434, 1956.

Heilman KM, Valenstein E, Watson RT: Localization of neglect. In Kertesz A (Editor), *Localization in Neuropsychology.* New York: Academic Press, 1983.

Heilman KM, Valenstein E, Watson RT: The neglect syndrome. In Frederiks JAM (Editor), *Handbook of Clinical Neuropsychology, Vol. 1 (45): Clinical Neuropsychology.* Amsterdam: Elsevier, 1985.

Heimburger RF, De Meyer W, Reitan RM: Implications of Gerstmann's syndrome. *J. Neurol. Neurosurg. Psychiatry: 27,* 52 – 57, 1964.

Jackson CV, Zangwill OL: Experimental finger dyspraxia. *Q. J. Exp. Psychol.: 4,* 1 – 10, 1952.

Kawamura M, Hirayama K, Shinohara Y, Watanabe Y, Sugishita M: Alloaesthesia. *Brain: 110,* 225 – 236, 1987.

Kinsbourne M: Developmental Gerstmann syndrome. *Pediatr. Clin. North Am.: 15,* 771 – 778, 1968.

Kinsbourne M, Warrington EK: A study of finger agnosia. *Brain: 85,* 47 – 66, 1962.

Kinsbourne M, Warrington EK: The development of finger differentiation. *Q. J. Exp. Psychol.: 15,* 132 – 137, 1963a.

Kinsbourne M, Warrington EK: The developmental Gerstmann syndrome. *Arch. Neurol. (Chicago): 8,* 490 – 501, 1963b.

Lange J: Fingeragnosie und Agraphie (eine psychopathologische Studie). *Monatsschr. Psychiatr. Neurol.: 76,* 129 – 188, 1930.

Lefford A, Birch HG, Green G: The perceptual and cognitive bases for finger localization and selective finger movement in preschool children. *Child Dev.: 45,* 335 – 343, 1974.

Lhermitte J, De Massary J, Kyriaco N: Le role de la pensée spatiale dans l'apraxie. *Rev. Neurol.: 11,* 895 – 903, 1928.

Lukianowicz N: Autoscopic phenomena. *Arch. Neurol. Psychiatry: 80,* 199 – 220, 1958.

Luria AR: Neuropsychology in the local diagnosis of brain damage. *Cortex: 1,* 3 – 18, 1964.

Marie P: Cited in Babinski, 1918.

Matthews CG, Folk EG, Zerfas PG: Lateralized finger localization deficits and differential Wechsler-Bellevue results in retardates. *Am. J. Ment. Defic.: 70,* 695 – 702, 1966.

Meige H: Cited in Babinski, 1918.

McKenna P, Warrington EK: Category specific naming preservation: a single case study. *J. Neurol. Neurosurg. Psychiatry: 41,* 571 – 574, 1978.

McFie J, Zangwill OL: Visual-constructive disabilities associated with lesions of the left hemisphere. *Brain: 83,* 243 – 260, 1960.

Menninger-Lerchenthal E: *Das Truggebilde der eigenen Gestalt (Heautoskopie, Doppelgänger).* Berlin: S. Karger, 1935.

Mitchell SW: Phantom limbs. *Lippincott's Mag.: 8,* 563 – 569, 1871.

Mitchell SW: *Injuries of Nerves and Their Consequences.* Philadelphia, Lippincott and Co., 1872.

Morris HH, Lüders H, Lesser RP, Dinner DS, Hahn J: Transient neuropsychological abnormalities (including Gerstmann's syndrome) during cortical stimulation. *Neurology: 34,* 877 – 883, 1984.

Munk H: *Über die Functionen der gross Hirnrinde, 2 Aufl.* Berlin: Aug. Hirschwald, 1890.

Nathan PW: On simultaneous bilateral stimulation of the body in a lesion of the parietal lobe. *Brain: 69,* 325 – 334, 1946.

Obersteiner H: Über einige Sensibilitätsstörungen bei Neurosen. *Wien. Med. Presse: 21,* 1635 – 1636, 1880.

Obersteiner H: On allochiria: a peculiar sensory disorder. *Brain: 4,* 153 – 163, 1881.

Ogden JA: Autotopoagnosia. Occurrence in a patient without nominal aphasia with an intact ability to point to parts of animals and objects. *Brain: 108,* 1009 – 1022, 1985.

Orgass B, Poeck K: Rechts-Links-Störung oder Aphasie? Eine experimentelle Untersuchung zur diagnostischen Gultigkeit der Rechts-Links-Prüfung. *Dtsch. Z. Nervenheilkde: 194,* 261 – 279, 1968.

Orgogozo JM: Le syndrome de Gerstmann (revue critique de la littérature). *Encephale: II,* 41 – 53, 1976.

Paillard J: Le corps et ses langages d'espace. Nouvelles contributions psychophysiologiques à l'étude du schéma corporel. In Jeddi E. (Editor) *Le Corps en Psychiatrie.* Paris: Masson, pp. 52 – 69, 1982.

Paré A: *The Apologie and Treatise of Ambroise Paré.* Chicago: University of Chicago Press, quoted by Weinstein, 1969.

Pedersen O: Zur Kenntnis der Symptomatologie der parietooccipitalen Übergangsregion. *Archiv. Psychiatr. 105,* 535 – 549, 1936.

Perani D, Vallar G, Cappa S, Messa C, Fazio F: Aphasia and neglect after subcortical stroke. *Brain: 110,* 1211 – 1229, 1987.

Pick A: Über Störungen der Orientierung am eigenen Körper. Arbeiten aus der deutschen psychiatrischen Universitätsklinik in Prag. 1 – 19. Berlin: Karger, 1908.

Pick A: Zur Pathologie des Bewusstseins vom eigenen Körper. *Neurol. Zentralbl.: 34,* 257 – 265, 1915.

Pick A: Störung der Orientierung am eigenen Körper. *Psychol. Forsch.: 1,* 303 – 318, 1922.

Poeck K: Phantoms following amputation in early childhood and in congenital absence of limbs. *Cortex: 1,* 269 – 275, 1964.

Poeck K: Modern trends in neuropsychology. In Benton AL (Editor), *Contributions to Clinical Neuropsychology*. Chicago: Aldine Publishing Company, 1969.

Poeck K, Orgass B: Über Störungen der Rechts-Links-Orientierung. *Nervenarzt: 38*, 285 – 291, 1967.

Poeck K, Orgass B: An experimental investigation of finger agnosia. *Neurology: 19*, 801 – 807, 1969.

Poeck K, Orgass B: The concept of the body schema: a critical review and some experimental results. *Cortex: 7*, 254 – 277, 1971.

Poeck K, Orgass B: Gerstmann's syndrome and aphasia. *Cortex: 2*, 421 – 439, 1966.

Poncet M, Pellister JF, Sebahoun M, Nasser CJ: A propos d'un cas d'autotopoagnosie secondaire à une lésion pariéto-occipitale de l'hémisphere majeur. *Encéphale: 60*, 1 – 14, 1971.

Roeltgen DP, Sevush S, Heilman KM: Pure Gerstmann's syndrome from a focal lesion. *Arch. Neurol. (Chicago): 40*, 46 – 47, 1983.

Rondot P, De Recondot J, Ribadeau Dumas JL: Visuomotor ataxia. *Brain: 100*, 355 – 376, 1977.

Russell WR: Some anatomical aspects of aphasia. *Lancet: 2*, 1173 – 1177, 1963.

Sauguet J, Benton AL, Hécaen H: Disturbances of the body schema in relation to language impairment and hemispheric locus of lesion. *J. Neurol. Neurosurg. Psychiatry: 34*, 496 – 501, 1971.

Schilder P: The image and appearance of the human body. *Psych Monographs No. 4*. London: Kegan, 1935.

Schwartz AS, Marchok PL, Krenik CS, Flynn RE: The asymmetric lateralization of tactile extinction in patients with unilateral cerebral dysfunction. *Brain: 102*, 669 – 684, 1979.

Selecki BR, Herron JT: Disturbances of the verbal body image: a particular syndrome of sensory aphasia. *J. Nerv. Ment. Dis.: 141*, 42 – 52, 1965.

Semenza C: Impairment in localization of body parts following brain damage. *Cortex: 24*, 443 – 449, 1988.

Semenza C, Goodglass H: Localization of body parts in brain-injured subjects. *Neuropsychologia: 23 (2)*, 161 – 175, 1985.

Shallice T: Impairments of semantic processing: multiple dissociations. In Coltheart M, Sartori G, Job R (Editors), *The Cognitive Neuropsychology of Language*. London: Lawrence Erlbaum, 1987.

Spellacy F, Peter B: Dyscalculia and elements of developmental Gerstmann syndrome in school children. *Cortex: 14*, 197 – 206, 1978.

Stengel E: Loss of spatial orientation, constructional apraxia and Gerstmann's syndrome. *J. Ment. Sci.: 90*, 753 – 760, 1944.

Stone FB, Robinson B: The effect of response mode on finger localization errors. *Cortex: 4*, 233 – 244, 1968.

Strub R, Geschwind N: Gerstmann syndrome without aphasia. *Cortex: 10*, 378 – 387, 1974.

Valenstein E, Heilman KM: Unilateral hypokinesia and motor extinction. *Neurology: 31*, 445 – 448, 1981.

Watson RT, Heilman KM, Cauthen JC, King FA: Neglect after cingulectomy. *Neurology: 23*, 1003 – 1007, 1973.

Watson RT, Heilman KM, Miller BD, King FA: Neglect after mesencephalic reticular formatin lesions. *Neurology: 24*, 294 – 298, 1974.

Weinstein EA, Kahn RL: *Denial of Illness*. Springfield: Charles C Thomas, 1955.

Weinstein J: Neuropsychological studies of the phantom. In Benton AL (Editor), *Contributions to Clinical Neuropsychology*. Chicago: Aldina Publishing, 1969.

Weinstein J, Vetter J, Sersen EA: Phantoms following breast amputation. *Neuropsychologia: 8*, 185 – 197, 1970.

Weiskrantz L, Warrington EK, Sanders MD, et al: Visual capacity in the hemianopic field following a restricted occipital ablation. *Brain: 97*, 719 – 728, 1974.

Weiss SA, Fishman S: Extended and telescoped phantom limbs in unilateral amputees. *J. Abnorm. Soc. Psychol.: 66*, 489 – 497, 1963.

Wernicke C: *Grundriss der Psychiatrie in klinischen Vorlesungen*. Leipzig: Thieme, 1900.

Wolf SM: Difficulties in right-left discrimination in the normal population. *Arch. Neurol. (Chicago): 29*, 128 – 129, 1973.

© 1989 Elsevier Science Publishers B.V. (Biomedical Division)
Handbook of Neuropsychology, Vol. 2
F. Boller and J. Grafman (Eds)

CHAPTER 12

Motor control

Emilio Bizzi and Ferdinando A. Mussa-Ivaldi

Department of Brain and Cognitive Sciences, Massachusetts Institute of Technology, Cambridge, MA 02139, U.S.A.

Introduction

In this chapter, we will discuss some of the problems involved in the planning and execution of arm movements by reviewing the psychophysical and physiological data supporting the notion that these processes are separate. It is of interest that a distinction between planning and execution has also been proposed in the context of apraxic disorders. In Chapter 35, ideational and ideomotor apraxia are presented as disturbances affecting, respectively, planning and execution of voluntary movements.

In our discussion of these processes, we will focus on neural information processing, and we will discuss the importance of mechanical and geometrical properties of the motor system. In particular, we will consider the following four points:
1. coordinate transformations and planning
2. the execution of movement
3. role of proprioceptive reflexes
4. multi-joint posture and movement

Coordinate transformations and planning

The necessary first step in any planning of an arm trajectory must be for the central nervous system (CNS) to represent the position of the target to be reached. This initial step involves transforming the retinal image of the target into head-centered and, ultimately, body-centered coordinates. An insight into this process has been provided by Andersen et al. (1985, 1987), who recorded the activity of single neurons from area 7a of the posterior parietal cor-

tex in monkeys. They found that the responsiveness of these cells' receptive field to retinotopic stimuli is influenced by the angle of gaze. Therefore, their experiment demonstrated that there was an interaction between the system that represented the eye's position and the system that represented the retinal position. This interaction tuned parietal neurons to represent the location of targets in head-centered coordinates.

It is important to emphasize that this coordinate transformation occurs in the posterior parietal cortex, an area that appears to be crucial in the planning of voluntary actions. Lesions of the parietal lobe in humans produce an array of symptoms, including the inability to localize visual targets, the loss of spatial memories and deficits in motor coordination.

In addition to the representation of the target in head-centered coordinates, the CNS must also represent the initial arm configuration in order to plan the arm trajectory. If the hand's initial position is detected visually by the CNS, then the process is identical to the one utilized for locating the target. On the other hand, if the arm's configuration is perceived through a combination of proprioceptors (joint, muscle or tendon receptors), then a complex and poorly understood set of transformations must occur. In other words, the position of the hand must be derived from the activity of receptors which code their output in terms of muscle and joint coordinates. We do not know how the CNS would accomplish this complex read-out.

Once the hand's initial position and final target are represented in the same coordinate frame, then the CNS must solve the problem of representing the hand's trajectory. In short, the CNS must plan the path and the velocity of the hand in space. There is some evidence that this representation may be formed in the posterior parietal cortex and medial regions of the frontal lobe.

Recent results obtained by Georgopoulos et al. (1980), based on recordings from single neurons from the parietal cortex of monkeys, indicated a correlation between neural activity and the direction of the arm's movement. These experiments consisted of recording activity from individual cortical cells as the monkey executed movements from a fixed location to a set of targets placed around the starting point. Their results show that the curves relating the frequency of discharge of a cell to the direction of the arm's movement were characterized by a single maximum. For each cell, this maximum occurred at a specific movement direction, which was defined as the cell's 'preferred direction'. During any movement of the hand, the average direction of a cell ensemble was defined as the weighted sum of all the preferred directions with the weights given by the cell activities. This average was found to be in good agreement with the direction of hand movements. One possible conclusion from these data is that the activity of neurons in the motor cortex encodes the planned direction of hand movements (Georgopoulos et al., 1980). However, the same data have also been shown to be consistent with the hypothesis that cortical neuron activity encodes muscle-related variables (Mussa-Ivaldi, 1988). Further experimental studies are necessary to establish whether these neurons are more related to the planning or to the execution of arm movements.

Also relevant here are recent experiments by Gnadt et al. (1986) and Gnadt and Andersen (1988), which have shown that there is a class of cells in the lateral intraparietal area that encode the intended amplitude and direction of eye movements. These cells remained active while the experimental animal delayed making an eye move-

ment to a remembered target location. The discharge of these cells seemed to represent a memory-related signal coded in motor coordinates.

To sum up, a number of CNS processes clearly transform inputs available in the coordinates of the sensory systems into motor representations coded in the coordinates of the motor system. It should be stressed that these two sets of coordinates are very different and that the transformation from one to the other is an important step in movement production.

While there is little question that the CNS must perform these transformations, there is some disagreement among researchers whether movements of the arm are planned in muscle, joint or hand coordinates. One way to identify the coordinates involved in this planning stage has been to look for invariances in movement that would discriminate between the three possibilities.

Let us consider the following experimental situation: a human subject is asked to move the hand towards a target. This task does not specify a trajectory for the arm but merely a location in space which, given a starting position, can be reached through a wide variety of paths. If the CNS plans the arm's movement as displacements of the skeletal segments, one would expect that the hand trajectory would be obtained from some simple and invariant pattern of joint motions. Going from an initial to a final set of joint angles, the simplest solution is a monotonic change in joint angles for the whole duration of the movement. This choice would result in a predictable and significant curvature of the hand path between starting and final positions. By contrast, if the CNS plans the movement in hand coordinates, the hand would follow a straight path, that is a monotonic change in hand coordinates, and a more complex pattern of joint motion would be observed.

When this experiment was actually carried out (Morasso, 1981), it was found that trajectories were remarkably invariant if they were described in hand coordinates with respect to a fixed frame in the environment. Morasso instructed human subjects to move their hand from one target to another with no instruction regarding speed or accuracy (Fig. 1).

Fig. 1 indicates two findings of interest. First, the path taken by the hand from one target to another was found to be straight or only gently

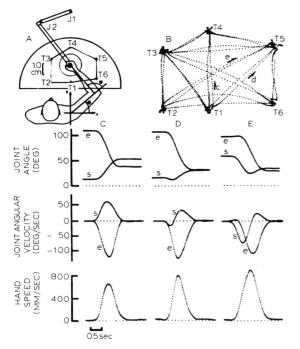

curved. This finding is of interest because hand movements must result from the combined effect of a rotation of both the shoulder and the elbow joints; convoluted hand trajectories would result if the two degrees of freedom were not perfectly co-ordinated. This tendency to produce straight hand paths suggests that path-planning may be occurring. Second is the finding reported by Morasso (1981) illustrated in Fig. 1C, D, and E, in which kinematic data are presented for three movements performed by the subjects in different parts of the work space. A plotting of the data showed that the traces for the two joints' positions and their velocities varied from movement to movement. In contrast, the speed of the hand was found to be always roughly bell-shaped, even when the joints' angular velo-cities were complex. The fact that the hand-speed profile was not dependent on the movement's loca-tion in the work space is consistent with the notion that the CNS plans a movement in terms of the hand kinematics.

It is worth noting that more than twenty years ago M. Bernstein wrote, 'The hypothesis that there exist in the higher levels of the CNS projections of space, and not projections of joints and muscles, seems to me to be at present more probable than any other' (Bernstein, 1967, p. 50).

In another experiment, human subjects were in-structed to approach targets by way of curved paths (Abend et al., 1982). No instruction was given regarding hand position or speed. The sub-jects first performed a series of movements in the absence of visual feedback about arm position and then repeated the experiment with feedback. There were two unexpected results, which are illustrated in Fig. 2. First, the trajectories of the hand ap-peared to be composed of a series of gently curved segments, which met at more highly curved regions. Arrowheads denoting local peaks in cur-vature appeared to divide movement 4 into four segments. Second, the hand-speed profiles were found to be irregular compared to those associated with straight trajectories. There were valleys or in-flections in the speed profile that were temporally associated with peaks in the path curvature; in

Fig. 1. A. Plan view of a seated subject grasping the handle of the two-joint hand-position transducer (designed by N. Hogan). The right arm was elevated to shoulder level and moved in a horizontal work space. Movement of the handle was measured with potentiometers located at the two mechanical joints of the apparatus (J1, J2). A horizontal semicircular plate located just above the handle carried the visual targets. Six visual target locations (T1 through T6) are illustrated as crosses. The digitiz-ed paths between targets and the curved path were obtained by moving the handle along a straight edge from one target to the next and then along a circular path; movement paths were reliably reproduced. B. A series of digitized handle paths (sampling rate, 100 Hz) performed by one subject in different parts of the movement space. The subject moved his hand to the illuminated target and then waited for the appearance of a new target. Targets presented in random order. Arrows show direc-tion of some of the hand movements. C, D, and E. Kinematic data for three of the movements, the paths of which are shown in (B). Letters show correspondence, for example, data under (C) are for path c in (B); e, elbow joint; s, shoulder, angles measured as indicated in (A). (From Bizzi and Abend: *Motor Control Mechanisms in Health and Disease*, edited by J.E. Desmedt, Raven Press, New York, pp. 31–45, 1983; modified from Morasso, 1982.)

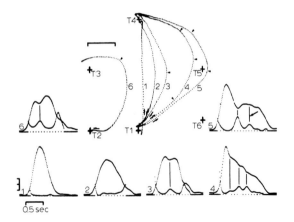

Fig. 2. Six movements performed by the same subject in the absence of visual feedback. Movement 1: Subject told only to move her hand to the target, T4. Movements 2, 3, 4, and 5: Subject told to move her hand between targets T1 and T4 by way of smoothly curved trajectories, ranging from shallow to highly curved ones. Movement 6: Subject told to make curved movement from T3 to T2. The 6 movement paths are superimposed on one set of target symbols. Arrows indicate the direction of hand movement along the path. Numbers indicate correspondence between the hand path of a movement and the superimposed hand speed and path curvature profiles. In each case, the curvature profile is the more shallow of the two curves. The data are plotted from the time of illumination of the target light. Because subjects often began and ended movements with paths so highly curved that the curvature values are off scale, the curvature is plotted only for those times during the movement when the hand speed is greater than 150 mm/s. Bar near hand paths = 10 cm. For the speed curvature profiles, full ordinate bar = speed of 200 mm/s; half bar = a curvature of 1/100 mm (inverse of radius of curvature). For paths 3, 4, 5 and 6 arrowheads = local curvature maxima along the trajectory; curvature maxima are also denoted by vertical lines over the curvature profiles. (From Bizzi and Abend: *Motor Control Mechanisms in Health and Disease*, edited by J.E. Desmedt, Raven Press, New York, pp. 31–45, 1983.)

other words, the hand tended to slow during the more highly curved parts of the trajectory. Curvature peaks with associated speed irregularities were typical of curved movements. In addition, Abend and colleagues showed that the movement's characteristics were independent of the part of the work space in which the movements took place (Fig. 2, movement 6).

Hogan (1984) and Flash and Hogan (1985) showed that a single optimization principle could account for both straight and curved trajectories. This principle posits that trajectories are maximal-

ly smooth, a hypothesis that implies that the chosen trajectory minimizes the mean-squared amplitude of the jerk (i.e., the rate of change of acceleration) associated with the motion of the hand (Flash, 1983; Flash and Hogan, 1985). Flash and Hogan showed that if the movement begins at rest in one position and ends at rest in another, the minimum-jerk movement turns out to have a bell-shaped velocity profile very similar to the experimental observation reported by Morasso (1981) (Fig. 1).

The minimum-jerk theory is also valid for curved movements like those recorded by Abend et al. (1982). The theory can generate curved motions by specifying a small number of 'via' points along the desired path of the hand. It is important to note that the theory succeeds only if the position of the limb is expressed in terms of the coordinates of the hand. In contrast, the minimum-jerk principle applied to joint coordinates would generate curved hand trajectories with asymmetrical velocity profiles. In Fig. 3 from Flash and Hogan (1985), typical measurements of a human subject's hand path are shown with the corresponding predicted minimum-jerk motions. Remarkably, the theoretical predictions agree with the experimental observations to within 4%.

In contrast to the views of those who have stressed that trajectory planning may be organized in the coordinates of the hand, other investigators have suggested that the planning of movement occurs in joint coordinates. For instance, Soechting and Laquaniti (1981) found a constancy in the ratio of elbow-to-shoulder joint velocities as the hand approached a set of targets located in the sagittal plane. These researchers concluded that the CNS plans movements of the arm by specifying joint-rate ratios.

Work of Hollerbach et al. (1986) supports the idea of motor planning in joint rather than hand coordinates on a different basis. They suggested that straight trajectories of the hand can be obtained if the CNS uses joint interpolation by introducing delays between the onset of movements in different joints ('staggered joint interpolation'). In

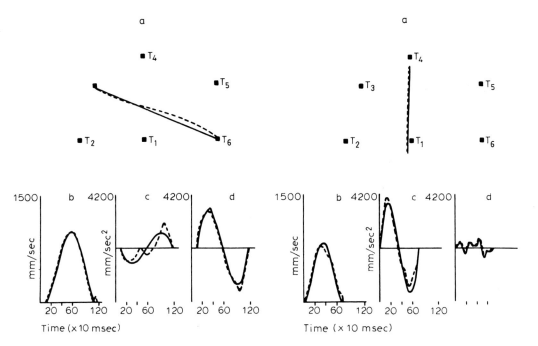

Fig. 3. Predicted minimum-jerk hand paths (a), time profiles of tangential speed (b), and acceleration components along two orthogonal directions (c and d) for two unconstrained point-to-point movements in the horizontal plane are shown by the solid lines. Typical measurements of a human subject's voluntary movements between the same points are shown by the dashed lines. Note the essentially straight paths and the characteristic bell-shaped profile. (From Flash and Hogan: *J. Neurosci.*: 5, 1688 – 1703, 1985.)

this hypothesis, the motion of each joint is still characterized as a monotonic change from the initial to the final angle. By controlling the delays between the joint motions, the CNS would be able to generate straight hand movements.

It should be stressed that in the hypothesis of staggered joint interpolation, problems arise because different delays are required by the motor system to obtain straight hand trajectories with different directions and in different regions of the workspace. Given an arbitrary hand movement, the computation by the CNS of the appropriate delays would seem to be a very complex task. For this reason, while the staggering mechanism is competent to obtain joint coordination, it does not seem to provide an appropriate representation for planning movements of the hand within the environment.

In addition, reversal of joint motions have been observed during the execution of planar arm tra-

jectories (Morasso, 1981). These reversals are necessary to maintain the hand on a straight path as movements occur in certain regions. For instance, to obtain straight hand movements in the horizontal plane, the shoulder must invert its motion as the forearm becomes orthogonal to the trajectory. In addition, the elbow must invert its motion as the hand passes through a point of minimum normal distance from the shoulder. It is evident that such joint reversals cannot be accounted for by the staggered joint interpolation theory, which assumes monotonic joint motions.

In summary, the issue of whether trajectory planning is done in hand or in joint coordinates is, at this point, still hotly debated among researchers in motor control. We favor the idea that movement planning is represented in the CNS in a way that is consistent with the metric of the environment rather than the metric of the musculoskeletal system. However, one should keep in mind that in some important cases, the configuration of the arm must be explicitly taken into account by the motor planner. This is the case, for example, when we move our arm in a cluttered environment and we want to avoid hitting obstacles not only with the hand, but also with other parts of the body such as the elbow. Then, the CNS can take advantage of the fact that the arm has more degrees of freedom than are necessary to specify the position of the hand.

The execution of movement

So far, we have considered the question of how the CNS plans arm trajectories. In order to generate movement, the brain must translate the plan into neural signals that activate muscles. In the past, physiologists have not specifically addressed this issue. The signals from motor areas were assumed to activate the segmental spinal cord apparatus to generate the desired movement. Very little attention was paid to the complex problem of how joint motions and joint torques are derived and how compensation for dynamic interactions is obtained. In this section, we will present a model that predicts the generation of torques by the CNS based on exploiting muscle mechanical and geometrical properties.

We believe that the mechanical properties of muscles deserve special study because it is likely that the features displayed by the neural controller have evolved as a result of its need not only to control but also to take advantage of the most salient features of the musculo-skeletal apparatus. A case for this approach was made by Feldman (1974a, b), who investigated the spring-like properties of the human arm. In addition, Rack and Westbury (1974) found that muscles do indeed behave like tunable springs in the sense that the force generated by the muscles is a function of their length and level of neural activation.

The force/length relationship in individual muscle fibers was studied by Gordon et al. (1966), who related the development of tension at different muscle lengths to the degree of overlap between ac-

tin and myosin filaments (Fig. 4). (In the structural organization of vertebrate striated muscles, sarcomeres are the units which are repeated longitudinally along the fibrils. These units consist primarily of comb-like arrays of overlapping actin and myosin filaments.) According to the sliding-filaments theory of muscle contraction (Huxley, 1963, 1969), the process of generating force within

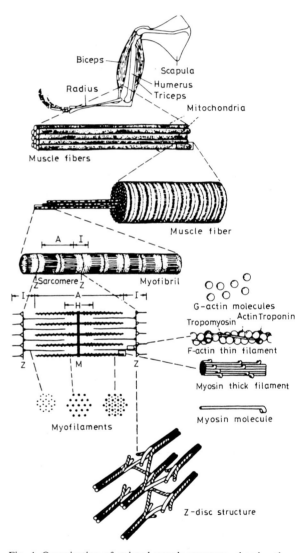

Fig. 4. Organization of striated muscle structure, showing the nomenclature applied to the bands and the proteins which make up the thick and thin filaments. (From T.A. McMahon: *Muscles, Reflexes, and Locomotion*, Princeton University Press, Princeton NJ, 1984.)

the muscles is caused by the physical interaction between myosin and actin filaments. This interaction leads to the formation of cross-bridges. The increase in muscle stiffness, observed as the motoneuronal drive to the muscle increases, is considered a direct consequence of the generation of new cross-bridges.

In addition, muscles are arranged about the joints in an agonist – antagonist configuration. If we attribute spring-like properties to muscles, then a limb's posture is maintained when the forces exerted by the agonist and antagonist muscle groups are equal and opposite. This fact implies that when an external force is applied, the limb is displaced by an amount that varies with both the external force and the stiffness of the muscles. When the external force is removed, the limb should return to the original position. Experimental studies of arm movements in monkeys have shown that a forearm posture is indeed an equilibrium point between opposing spring-like forces (Bizzi et al., 1976). The observation that posture is maintained by the equilibrium between the length – tension properties of opposing muscles led to the idea that movements result from a shift of the equilibrium point caused by a change in neural input. This hypothesis was first proposed by Feldman (1966). The studies by Bizzi et al. (1976), Kelso (1977) and Kelso and Holt (1980) provided the needed experimental evidence.

In particular, Bizzi et al. (1984) demonstrated that the transition from one forearm posture to another is achieved when the CNS adjusts the relative intensity of neural signals directed to each of the opposing muscles. This result suggests that a single-joint arm trajectory is controlled by neural signals which specify a series of equilibrium positions for the limb. Evidence supporting this important hypothesis has been provided by three sets of experiments, which will be briefly summarized here (Bizzi et al., 1984). The movements used in these experiments were single-joint elbow flexion and extension, which lasted approximately 700 ms for a 60° amplitude.

The first set of experiments was performed in both intact monkeys and in those deprived of sensory feedback. The monkey's arm was briefly held in its initial position after a target that indicated final position had been presented. Then, the arm was released. It was found that movements to the target were faster than control movements performed in the absence of a holding action. Fig. 5 shows a plot of the accelerative transients against the durations of the holding period in the same animal before and after interruption of the nerves conveying sensory information. The time course of the increasing amplitude of the accelerative transient was virtually identical in the two conditions. It was found that the initial acceleration after release of the forearm increased gradually with the duration of the holding period, reaching a steady-state value no sooner than 400 ms after muscles' activation. These results demonstrated that the CNS has programmed a slow, gradual shift of the equilibrium position instead of a sudden, discontinuous transition to the final position.

The same conclusions were supported by a second set of experiments in which the forearm was forced to a target position through an assisting tor-

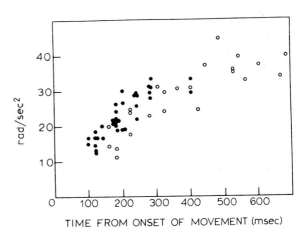

Fig. 5. The forearm of intact and deafferented animals was held in its initial position while the animal attempted to move toward a target light. Then, the forearm was released at various times. This figure is a plot of acceleration (immediately following release) versus holding time. The abscissa shows time in milliseconds; the ordinate shows radians per second squared. Solid circles: intact animal; open circles: deafferented animal. (From Bizzi et al.: *J. Neurosci.: 4*, 2738 – 2744, 1984.)

que pulse applied at the beginning of a visually triggered forearm movement. The goal of this experiment was to move the limb ahead of the equilibrium position with an externally imposed displacement in the direction of the target. It was found that the forearm, after being forced by the assisting pulse to the target position, returned to a point between the initial and the final position before moving to endpoint.

This return motion was caused by a restoring force generated by the elastic muscle properties. Note that if muscles merely generated force or if the elastic properties were negligible, we would not have seen the return motion of the limb. Since the same response to our torque pulse was also observed in monkeys deprived of sensory feedback, it was inferred that proprioceptive reflexes are not essential to the generation of restoring forces. Taken together, these results suggest that alpha motoneuronal activity specifies a series of equilibrium positions throughout the movement.

Finally, in a third set of experiments, the arm was not only driven to the target location, but also held there for a variable amount of time (1 – 3 s) after which, the target light at the new position was activated. A cover prevented the animal from seeing its arm (Fig. 6). After the monkey reacted to the presentation of the light, it activated the arm muscles (flexors in the case of Fig. 6) to reach the target position. At this point, the servo which held the arm was deactivated.

The results were as follows. The arm returned to a point intermediate between the initial and the target positions before moving back to the target position. Note that during the return movement, requiring extension, flexor activity was evident. The amplitude of the return movement was a function of the duration of the holding action. If enough time elapsed between activation of the target light and deactivation of the servo, the arm remained in the target position upon release.

These observations provided further support for the view that motoneuronal activity specifies a series of equilibrium positions throughout a movement. If the muscles merely generated force during

the transient phase of a movement, we would not have seen the pronounced return motion of the limb during flexor muscle activity.

The sequence of static equilibrium positions encoded during movement by the motoneuronal activity has been labelled a 'virtual trajectory' (Hogan, 1984), to be distinguished from the actual trajectory followed by the limb. The virtual trajectory is based on length – tension relationships under static conditions. By contrast, the actual tra-

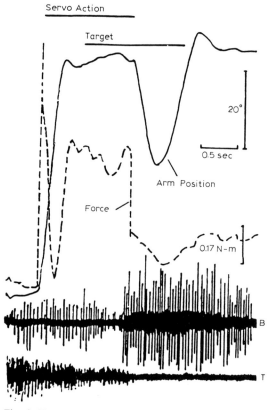

Fig. 6. Forearm movements of deafferented monkeys with a holding action in the final position. While the target light remained off, the servo moved the arm to the target position. Then the target light was activated and the servo was turned off. The arm returned to a position intermediate between the initial and target positions before moving back to the target position. Similar results were obtained in many trials in two monkeys. The upper bar indicates duration of servo action. The lower bar indicates onset of the target light. The broad trace shows arm position; the dashed trace shows torque. B: flexor (biceps); T: extensor (triceps). (From Bizzi et al.: *J. Neurosci.: 4*, 2738 – 2744, 1984.)

jectory is the observable result of the interaction between the elastic forces and other dynamic components such as limb inertia, muscle velocity – tension properties and joint viscosity.

An important consequence of this notion is that the virtual trajectory can be used to avoid the computation of inverse dynamics. The inertial and viscous components of the limb may be viewed as 'perturbing torques' which make the arm deviate from the virtual trajectory. At low speeds and accelerations, the difference between actual and virtual trajectory is small and can be neglected by the motor controller. However, as the speed and acceleration of the movement increase, limb inertia and viscosity are expected to cause larger deviations from the virtual trajectory. These deviations can be corrected if the CNS increases muscle stiffness or modifies the virtual trajectory itself.

The spring-like properties of the muscle also provide built-in stability to the movement (Hogan, 1985). In a computational approach based on the solution of equations of motion, problems arise when an external perturbation (such as the arm's hitting an obstacle) causes a deviation from the preprogrammed path. If this happens, the motor controller must recompute or provide some special servo-control mechanisms. In contrast, if movement is obtained by shifting the equilibrium position defined by elastic actuators, a deviation from the intended path simply results in larger restoring forces without the need of computation or of particular control schemes (McKeon et al., 1984).

Finally, we would like to stress another important feature of the moving equilibrium hypothesis. Traditionally, in motor control, behaviors like maintaining posture, generating movements and generating forces have been considered separate endeavors requiring different control schemes. In contrast, the experiments of Bizzi et al. (1984) show that these apparently diverse behaviors share a common information-processing scheme.

So far we have described the moving equilibrium point as a centrally specified set of motor commands to the motoneurons without any consideration for those neural signals that originate from the muscles, joints and tendons. It is well known that these signals directly, via monosynaptic excitation, and indirectly, via polysynaptic pathways, set up a complex pattern of activation of the motoneurons. In the next section, we will review how both centrally driven and reflex activities cooperate to control muscle mechanical properties.

Role of proprioceptive reflexes

There is little doubt that the sensory impulses originating from the muscle spindles, from the Golgi tendon organs and from the joint receptors collectively play an important role in modulating centrally generated motor patterns. The activity from these receptors is of great importance for stable posture and movement. With respect to limb stabilization, experimental evidence has shown that limb tremor and drifts in posture will result when proprioceptive feedback is interrupted in humans (Marsden et al., 1984; Rothwell et al., 1982; Sanes et al., 1985). Interestingly, the CNS, even without the assistance of reflex activity, generates signals that will produce the limb's movement to a target. However, without proprioceptive feedback, newly acquired posture can be maintained only for 2 – 3 s. After this time, a slow drift will gradually lead to a change in posture. The presence of feedback is thus critical for stabilization of centrally driven postural states.

Another important stabilizing property of the proprioceptive apparatus was described by Nichols and Houk (1976). They demonstrated that the force generated by the soleus muscle following a stretch depends upon the integrity of the reflex pathway. They also showed that muscle force fell during a muscle stretch in spinal cats whose dorsal roots were sectioned. However, such behavior was not displayed by the soleus when reflexes were intact.

Signals from actively contracting muscles and from stretched antagonists provide information to the spinal cord about the initial configuration of the joints (Hasan and Stuart, 1984; Matthews and Watson, 1981). An example of the importance of afferent information for multi-joint coordination has been reported by Polit and Bizzi (1979). In their experiments, they used two sets of monkeys, one set deprived of proprioceptive feedback, the other set intact. The deprived monkeys executed elbow flexion and extension movements following the presentation of a target light while the shoulder was kept stable. However, when the shoulder's position with respect to the target lights was changed by the experimenters, the animal made significant errors in performing the task. In contrast, intact animals adapted and performed without error after 2 – 3 trials even if there was a change in shoulder position. This set of experiments demonstrated the role played by proprioceptive afferents in providing the CNS with the appropriate signals for coordinating multi-joint motions.

The proprioceptive apparatus also plays an important role when unexpected perturbations impinge upon the body during posture. The resulting corrective actions may or may not conform to the traditional view of stretch reflexes. For instance, Nashner et al. (1979) showed that if, in normal human subjects, the support surface for the legs is suddenly raised, the gastrocnemius muscle becomes active even though no stretch of this muscle is produced. They also demonstrated that when one foot is raised and the other is simultaneously lowered, electromyographic (EMG) activity is observed in muscles underlying shortening. Taken together, these experiments have led Nashner and colleagues to postulate the existence of 'functional synergies' which are elicited by sudden perturbations. The EMG activity characteristic of these synergies cannot be explained on the basis of what we know about stretch reflexes.

In addition to playing a role in postural stabilization, proprioceptive signals play a role during movement, especially when unexpected perturbations are encountered.

The effectiveness of signals from the muscle spindles is greatly dependent upon a linkage between alpha and gamma motoneurons. The sensitivity of a spindle can, in fact, be modified by the activity of alpha motoneurons which affect the state of length and tension of the spindle itself. There is substantial evidence that there is a variable degree of alpha – gamma coactivation during centrally programmed movements. This coactivation has been observed by many investigators in a number of systems (Granit et al., 1955; Vallbo, 1970, 1973).

In particular, the experiments of Severin et al. (1967) have shown that during locomotion in cats, reflex activity from muscle-spindle receptors is greater from the shortening agonist muscles than it is from the lengthening antagonists. Results such as these indicate that gamma impulses are sent to the muscle spindles just prior to or during extrafusal contraction, thus producing intrafusal muscle contraction. As a result, there is an increase of reflex activity. It has been suggested that through this coactivation of alpha and gamma elements, a mobile part of the body is servo-assisted so as to adjust force output to compensate for changes in load (Matthews, 1972).

However, to properly evaluate the complexities underlying load compensation, it is important to consider some of the interacting processes that occur at spinal and supraspinal levels following the application of a load. With respect to these processes, it is relevant that alpha motoneurons receive not only facilitation from muscle spindle afferents but also an inhibitory input from Golgi tendon organs. In addition, afferent proprioceptive impulses reach subcortical and cortical areas (Brooks et al., 1976; Conrad et al., 1974; Evarts, 1973), generating impulses that play back on the spinal cord apparatus via corticospinal pathways. These long-loop reflexes may be influenced by pre-existing sets of instructions (Evarts and Tanji, 1976). These few examples suggest an exceedingly complex situation characterized by parallel processing along various spinal and supraspinal pathways.

Recent experimental evidence has provided some answers concerning the contributions made by the reflex and mechanical properties to the increased force produced by muscles when loads are unexpectedly applied during centrally programmed movements.

The question of evaluating the increment of the reflex and mechanical torque generated by an animal was approached by comparing head movements before and after surgical interruption of the sensory pathways in monkeys (Bizzi et al., 1978). The results indicated that the compensatory torque of reflex origin, stimulated by the unexpected application of an opposing force, was from 10 – 30% of the torque required for perfect compensation. However, the larger fraction of the observed compensation was due to the mechanical (inertial, viscous, and elastic) properties of the neck musculature.

These results, as well as those of Vallbo (1973) in normal human subjects, of Grillner (1972) in cats, and of Allum (1975) on postural resetting, show how muscle mechanical properties and reflex activity cooperate when a limb is confronted by an unexpected perturbation. A load disturbance is initially resisted by the elastic action of the activated musculature and then, after a brief delay (40 – 60 ms), by the reflexes.

Multi-joint posture and movement

One of the main results derived from the single-joint experiments described above is that movement is nothing more than a series of sequentially implemented postures. In the following section, we will extend this idea to the multi-joint case.

The study of multi-joint arm movement presents radically different problems than does the case of the single joint. For example, in single-joint studies, it was found that the CNS achieved a stable posture of the forearm by selecting appropriate length – tension curves of the elbow muscles so that at the desired elbow angle, the torque generated by the flexors was equal and opposite to the torque generated by the extensors. As a small external perturbation displaced the limb $\delta\theta$ degrees from its equilibrium location, the elastic muscle properties generated a restoring torque δT. The ratio of this torque to the imposed displacement was a single number expressing the stiffness

of the elbow.

By contrast, in a multi-joint situation, if a displacement is externally imposed on the hand, rather than on a single articulation, the amount of stretch experienced by the muscles depends not only upon the amplitude of the perturbation, but also upon its direction. Then, a single number is no longer sufficient to describe the force – displacement relation. This relation is now expressed by a matrix whose elements characterize the ratio of each component of the restoring force vector to each component of the applied displacement vector.

To deal with this more complex situation, a new experimental approach to the study of posture and movement was developed (Mussa-Ivaldi et al., 1985). This approach was based on measuring the net spring-like behavior of the multi-joint arm by displacing the hand in several directions in the horizontal plane (See Fig. 7). As the hand came to rest at the end of each displacement, the force, $F = (F_x, F_y)$, exerted by the subject on the handle was measured. Since the hand was stationary, this force had no viscous or inertial components and could therefore only be due to muscle length – tension properties (including reflex components).

With a small displacement of the hand, $\delta r = (\delta x, \delta y)$, it was legitimate to assume a linear relation of the form:

$$
\begin{aligned}
F_x &= K_{xx}\,\delta x + K_{xy}\,\delta y \\
F_y &= K_{yx}\,\delta x + K_{yy}\,\delta y.
\end{aligned}
\tag{1}
$$

Then, by measuring forces and displacements in different directions, it was possible to estimate the K coefficients from a linear regression applied independently to both the above expressions. These coefficients could be represented by a single entity: a table, or matrix, expressing the multi-dimensional stiffness of the hand:

$$
K = \begin{bmatrix} K_{xx} & K_{xy} \\ K_{yx} & K_{yy} \end{bmatrix}
$$

With this notation, Equation 1 assumes a more compact form, $F = K \, \delta r$.

The hand stiffness in the vicinity of equilibrium is given by a matrix which was estimated by analyzing the force and displacement vectors. The hand-stiffness matrix was represented as an ellipse characterized by three parameters: magnitude (the total area derived from the determinant of the stiffness matrix); orientation (the direction of maximum stiffness); and shape (the ratio between maximum and minimum stiffness). The ellipse captures the main geometrical features of the elastic-force field associated with a given hand posture and provides an understanding of how the arm interacts with the environment.

Fig. 8 shows the hand stiffness of four human subjects while they maintained the hand in a number of workspace locations. The stiffness ellipses measured at given hand postures are also shown along with a schematic display of the corresponding arm configurations. A remarkable feature of these data was the similarity between the different subjects with respect to stiffness shape and orientation. By contrast, the stiffness magnitude varied considerably. This graphical representation provides a 'gestalt' and affords a qualitative understanding of the way in which the hand may interact with external forces that could change its posture.

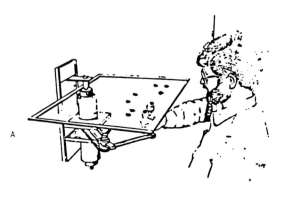

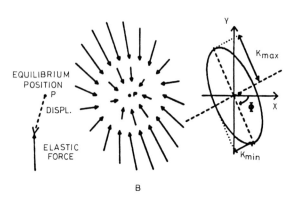

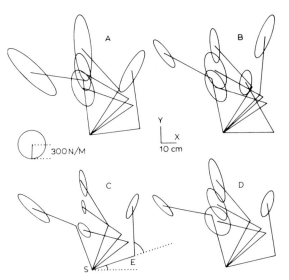

Fig. 7. A. Experimental setup: sketch of the apparatus in a typical experimental situation. B. Stiffness representation. Left: when the hand is displaced from its equilibrium position, an elastic restoring force is observed which in general, is not co-linear with the displacement vector. Center: several displacements of variable amplitude and direction are plotted together with the restoring forces computed from a measured hand stiffness. Right: the trajectory of the force vectors obtained by means of the previous procedure is an ellipse with the major and minor axes indicated, respectively, by K_{max} and K_{min}. The angle, Φ, between the major axis and the fixed x-axis is the stiffness orientation. The shape is given by the ratio, K_{max}/K_{min}, and the size, or magnitude, is the area enclosed by the ellipse. (Modified figure from Mussa-Ivaldi et al.: *J. Neurosci.: 5,* 2732–2743, 1985.)

Fig. 8. Stiffness ellipses obtained from four subjects during the postural task. Each ellipse has been derived by regression on about 60 force and displacement vectors. The upper arm and the forearm are indicated schematically by two line segments, and the ellipses are placed on the hand. The calibration for the stiffness is provided by the circle to the left which represents an isotropic hand stiffness of 300 N/m. (From Mussa-Ivaldi et al.: *J. Neurosci.: 5,* 2732–2743, 1985.)

It was found that one way to affect the stiffness shape and orientation was to change the configuration of the arm while the hand remained in a given position. This finding suggests that an effective strategy for modifying all parameters of the postural stiffness may be to combine variations of neural input to the muscles with variations of configuration of the 'extra' or redundant degrees of freedom of the limb.

Changes in configuration also have a relevant effect on other components of motor impedance. Indeed, changing arm configuration is the only way the CNS can change the endpoint inertia of the limb (Hogan, 1985). From this point of view, it can be seen that the configuration of the limb should be regarded as one of the 'commanding inputs' available to the CNS for controlling posture. Redundancy of the musculoskeletal system is usually regarded as a problem to be overcome by the CNS in coordinating limb movements (Bernstein, 1967); instead, the results reported here show that redundancy may also offer alternative ways to control postural dynamics.

To sum up, the experimental evidence indicates that the equilibrium position of the hand is established by the coordinated interaction of elastic forces generated by the arm muscles (Mussa-Ivaldi et al., 1985). According to the equilibrium trajectory hypothesis, which was tested first in the context of single-joint movements, multi-joint arm trajectories are achieved by gradually shifting the arm equilibrium between the initial and final positions. In this control scheme, the hand tracks its equilibrium point, and torque is not an explicitly computed variable.

Evidence supporting this hypothesis in the context of multi-joint hand movements has been obtained by combining observations of hand movements with computer simulation studies. A model developed by Flash (1987) has successfully captured the kinematic features of measured planar arm trajectories. As shown by Morasso (1981), planar hand movements between pairs of targets are characterized by approximately straight hand paths. However, if the same movements are

analyzed at a finer level of detail, the paths present a modest degree of inflexion and curvature, depending on the direction of movement and on the workspace location. In the simulation, Flash made the assumption that the hand equilibrium trajectories (but not necessarily the actual trajectories) are invariantly straight. In addition, she assumed that the equilibrium trajectories have unimodal velocity profile, regardless of the target locations in the workspace.

To test this hypothesis (Flash, 1987), the arm dynamics were simulated obtaining torques from the difference between actual and equilibrium positions multiplied by the stiffness. It must be stressed that the stiffness parameters used in the simulation of movements were derived from experimentally measured postural stiffness values. In particular, Mussa-Ivaldi et al. (1985, 1987) observed that the shape and the orientation of the hand stiffness were insensitive to changes in the net force output. This result provided the evidence for assuming that these parameters may not change when the hand moves through the locations at which the field was measured.

The results of the simulation showed that with straight equilibrium trajectories, the actual movements were slightly curved. Moveover, the direction of curvature, in different workspace locations and with different movement directions, was in good agreement with the experimentally observed movements (Fig. 9). This result suggests that during movement planning, the CNS ignores the inertial and viscous properties of the arm and directly translates the desired trajectory into a sequence of static postures. Then, when the movement is executed, the inertial and viscous forces act as perturbations, causing deviations of the actual path with respect to the planned path.

The success of the simulation in capturing the kinematic details of measured arm movements is important as a step towards providing us with a new intellectual framework for understanding trajectory formation in the multi-joint context. This work indicates a planning strategy whereby the motor controller may avoid complex computational problems such as the solution of dynamics.

A directly testable consequence of the equilibrium trajectory hypothesis would be a built-in stability in movement. For example, if during the execution of a hand trajectory, an unpredicted disturbance displaces the hand from the planned path, then according to the equilibrium-trajectory hypothesis, the muscle's elastic properties and the proprioceptive reflexes generate a force attracting the hand towards the original path.

This prediction was experimentally confirmed by McKeon et al. (1984). They asked human subjects to perform pointing movements between two targets while gripping the handle of a two-link manipulandum similar to that shown in Fig. 5. A clutch mounted on the inner joint of the manipulandum was used to brake the inner link under computer control. As the clutch was activated at the onset of a movement, the hand trajectory was restricted to a circular path with a radius equal to the length of the outer link of the manipulandum. While the clutch was engaged, the handle force was

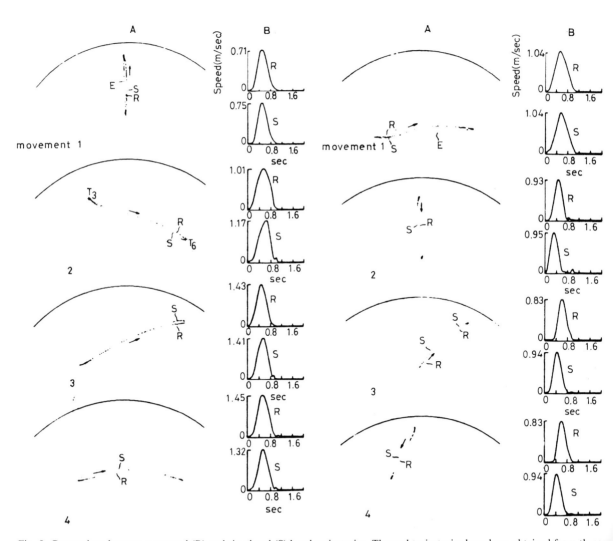

Fig. 9. Comparison between measured (R) and simulated (S) hand trajectories. The real trajectories have been obtained from three subjects. The simulated trajectories were derived with a straight virtual trajectory (E) from start to target position. A: trajectories; B: hand velocities versus time. (From Flash: *Biol. Cybern.: 57*, 257–274, 1987.)

found to be always strongly oriented so as to restore the hand to the unconstrained path and not to the end-point of the path.

According to the equilibrium-trajectory hypothesis, the muscle's spring-like properties are responsible for generating the necessary joint torques, thus implicitly providing an approximated solution to the dynamics problem. As the approximation becomes inadequate at higher speeds of acceleration, the stiffness can be increased and the equilibrium trajectory can be modified on the basis of the difference between the actual and the planned path. The task of the CNS is then to transform the planned trajectory into a different sequence of equilibrium positions and stiffnesses.

Conclusion

At the present time, the problems of how coordinate transformations are achieved and how torques are produced are the main concerns of investigators of motor functions in artificial and biological systems. In this paper, we have reviewed current ideas and put forward a new biological perspective on planning and execution of movements. Beyond what has been discussed here, there are many problems of fundamental importance which, because of their complexity, have not yet been tackled by motor control experimenters. Examples of such problems include the question of modular and hierarchical organization of the motor system, the specification of time, and the way in which we use memory both in controlling specialized, highly learned skills and in the solution of novel motor tasks.

Acknowledgements

This research was supported by National Institute of Neurological Disease and Stroke Research Grant NS09343, National Institute of Arthritis and Musculoskeletal and Skin Diseases Grant AR26710, and the National Eye Institute Grant EY02621.

References

Abend W, Bizzi E, Morasso P: Human arm trajectory formation. *Brain: 105*, 331 – 348, 1982.

Allum JHJ: Responses to load disturbances in human shoulder muscles: the hypothesis that one component is a pulse test information signal. *Exp. Brain Res.: 22*, 307 – 326, 1975.

Andersen RA, Essick GK, Siegel RM: Encoding spatial location by posterior parietal neurons. *Science: 230*, 456 – 458, 1985.

Andersen RA, Essick GK, Siegel RM: Neurons of area 7 activated by both visual stimuli and oculomotor behavior. *Exp. Brain Res.: 67*, 316 – 322, 1987.

Bernstein M: *The Co-ordination and Regulation of Movements.* Oxford: Pergamon Press, 1967.

Bizzi E, Accornero N, Chapple W, Hogan N: Posture control and trajectory formation during arm movement. *J. Neurosci.: 4*, 2738 – 2744, 1984.

Bizzi E, Dev P, Morasso P, Polit A: Effect of load disturbances during centrally initiated movements. *J. Neurophysiol.: 39*, 435 – 444, 1978.

Bizzi E, Polit A, Morasso P: Mechanisms underlying achievement of final head position. *J. Neurophysiol.: 39*, 435 – 444, 1976.

Brooks VB, Hore J, Meyer-Lohmann J, Vilis T: Cerebellar pathway for precentral responses following arm perturbations. *Neurosci. Abstr.: 2*, 516, 1976.

Conrad B, Matsunami C, Meyer-Lohmann J, Wiesendanger M, Brooks VB: Cortical load compensation during voluntary elbow movements. *Brain Res.: 81*, 507 – 514, 1974.

Evarts EV: Motor cortex reflexes associated with learned movement. *Science: 179*, 501 – 503, 1973.

Evarts EV, Tanji J: Reflex and intended responses in motor pyramidal tract neurons of monkey. *J. Neurophysiol.: 39*, 1069 – 1080, 1976.

Feldman AG: Functional tuning of the nervous system during control of movement or maintenance of a steady posture. III. Mechanographic analysis of the execution by man of the simplest motor tasks. *Biophysics: 11*, 766 – 775, 1966.

Feldman AG: Change of muscle length due to shift of the equilibrium point of the muscle-load system. *Biofizika: 19*, 534 – 538, 1974a.

Feldman AG: Control of muscle length. *Biofizika: 19*, 749 – 751, 1974b.

Flash T: Organizing principles underlying the formation of hand trajectories. Ph.D. Dissertation: Harvard/MIT Division of Health Sciences and Technology, MIT, Cambridge, MA, 1983.

Flash T: The control of hand equilibrium trajectories in multijoint arm movements. *Biol. Cybern.: 57*, 257 – 274, 1987.

Flash T, Hogan N: The coordination of arm movements: an experimentally confirmed mathematical model. *J. Neurosci.: 5*, 1688 – 1703, 1985.

Georgopoulos AP, Kalaska JF, Massey JT: Cortical mechanisms of two-dimensional aiming arm movements. I. Aiming at different target locations. *Soc. Neurosci. Abstr.: 6*, 156, 1980.

Gnadt JW, Andersen RA: Memory related motor planning activity in posterior parietal cortex of macaque. *Exp. Brain Res.: 70,* 216 – 220, 1988.

Gnadt JW, Andersen RA, Blatt GJ: Spatial, memory, and motor-planning properties of saccade-related activity in the lateral intraparietal area (LIP) of macaque. *Soc. Neurosci. Abstr.: 12,* 458, 1986.

Gordon AM, Huxley AF, Julian FJ: The variation in isometric tension with sarcomere length in vertebrate muscle fibers. *J. Physiol. (London): 184,* 170 – 192, 1966.

Granit R, Holmgren B, Merton PA: The two routes for excitation of muscle and their subservience to the cerebellum. *J. Physiol. (London): 130,* 213 – 224, 1955.

Grillner S: The role of muscle stiffness in meeting the changing postural and locomotor requirements for force development of the ankle extensors. *Acta Physiol. Scand.: 86,* 92 – 108, 1972.

Hasan Z, Stuart DG: Mammalian muscle receptors. In Davidoff RA (Editor), *Handbook of the Spinal Cord.* New York: Marcel Dekker, Ch. 3, pp. 559 – 607, 1984.

Hogan N: An organizing principle for a class of voluntary movements. *J. Neurosci.: 4,* 2745 – 2754, 1984.

Hogan N: The mechanics of multi-joint posture and movement control. *Biol. Cybern.: 52,* 315 – 331, 1985.

Hollerbach JM, Moore SP, Atkeson CG: Workspace effect in arm movement kinematics derived by joint interpolation. In Gantchev G, Dimitrov G, Gatev P (Editors), *Motor Control.* New York: Plenum Press, pp. 197 – 208, 1986.

Huxley HE: Electron microscope studies on the structure of natural and synthetic protein filaments from striated muscle. *J. Mol. Biol.: 7,* 281 – 308, 1963.

Huxley HE: The mechanism of muscular contraction. *Science: 164,* 1356 – 1366, 1969.

Kelso JAS: Motor control mechanisms underlying human movement reproduction. *J. Exp. Psychol.: 3,* 529 – 543, 1977.

Kelso JAS, Holt KG: Exploring a vibratory system analysis of human movement production. *J. Neurophysiol.: 43,* 1183 – 1196, 1980.

Marsden CD, Rothwell JC, Day BL: The use of peripheral feedback in the control of movement. *Trends Neurosci.: 7,* 253 – 257, 1984.

Matthews PBC: *Mammalian Muscle Receptors and Their Central Actions.* Baltimore: Williams and Wilkins, 1972.

Matthews PBC, Watson JDC: Effect of vibrating agonist or antagonist muscle on the reflex response to sinusoidal displacement of the human forearm. *J. Physiol. (London): 321,* 297 – 316, 1981.

McKeon B, Hogan N, Bizzi E: Effect of temporary path constraint during planar arm movements. *Neurosci. Abstr.: 10,* 337, 1984.

Morasso P: Spatial control of arm movements. *Exp. Brain Res.: 42,* 223 – 227, 1981.

Mussa-Ivaldi FA: Do neurons in the motor cortex encode movement direction? An alternative hypothesis. *Neurosci. Lett.: 91,* 106 – 111, 1988.

Mussa-Ivaldi FA, Hogan N, Bizzi E: Neural, mechanical and geometric factors subserving arm posture in humans. *J. Neurosci.: 5,* 2732 – 2743, 1985.

Mussa-Ivaldi FA, Hogan N, Bizzi E: The role of geometrical constraints in the control of multi-joint posture and movement. *Neurosci. Abstr.: 13,* 347, 1987.

Nashner LM, Woollacott M, Thuma G: Organization of rapid responses to postural and locomotor-like perturbations of standing man. *Exp. Brain Res.: 36,* 463 – 476, 1979.

Nichols TR, Houk JC: Improvement in linearity and regulation of stiffness that results from actions of stretch reflex. *J. Neurophysiol.: 39,* 119 – 142, 1976.

Polit A, Bizzi E: Characteristics of the motor programs underlying arm movements in monkeys. *J. Neurophysiol.: 42,* 183 – 194, 1979.

Rack PMH, Westbury DR: The short range stiffness of active mammalian muscle and its effect on mechanical properties. *J. Physiol. (London): 240,* 331 – 350, 1974.

Rothwell JCM, Traub MM, Day BL, Obeso JA, Thomas PK, Marsden CD: Manual motor performance in a deafferented man. *Brain: 105,* 515 – 542, 1982.

Sanes JN, Mauritz K-H, Dalakas MC, Evarts EV: Motor control in humans with large-fiber sensory neuropathy. *Hum. Neurobiol.: 4,* 101 – 114, 1985.

Severin FV, Orlovsky GN, Shik ML: Work of the muscle receptors during controlled locomotion. *Biophysics: 12,* 575 – 586, 1967.

Soechting JF, Laquaniti F: Invariant characteristics of a pointing movement in man. *J. Neurosci.: 1,* 710 – 720, 1981.

Vallbo AB: Slowly adapting muscle receptors in man. *Acta Physiol. Scand.: 78,* 315 – 333, 1970.

Vallbo AB: The significance of intramuscular receptors in load compensation during voluntary contractions in man. In Stein RB, Person KG, Smith RS, Redford JB (Editors), *Control of Posture and Locomotion.* New York: Plenum Press, pp. 211 – 226, 1973.

© 1989 Elsevier Science Publishers B.V. (Biomedical Division)
Handbook of Neuropsychology, Vol. 2
F. Boller and J. Grafman (Eds)

CHAPTER 13

Apraxia

Ennio De Renzi

Clinica Neurologica, Universita di Modena, Via del Pozzo 71, 4100 Modena, Italy

The term apraxia covers a spectrum of disorders affecting the purposeful execution of movements carried out deliberately and out of context, in the absence of elementary motor-sensory deficits, perceptual and comprehension impairment and severe mental deterioration. The crucial point is that the patient has all the sensory-motor potentialities for proper execution of the movement, and in fact succeeds in many circumstances, but fails when the act must be performed in response to the examiner's request. Thus, although in the most severe cases even daily routines are impaired, it is rather common to see a patient who fails to make the sign of the cross or to demonstrate the use of a toothbrush on command, and nevertheless crosses her/himself on entering a church and brushes her/his teeth in the bathroom. This dissociation between everyday behavior and test performance accounts for the underestimation of the disorder by the patient, her/his family and even physicians, many of whom would be surprised to know that apraxia occurs in approximately one-third of unselected left-brain-damaged patients, tested in the acute stage of a stroke (De Renzi et al., 1980). It follows that the interest apraxia has for the neurologist is more because of the light it sheds on the neural organization of movement planning than because of its practical consequences.

In neurological parlance the term apraxia has been used to cover disorders of motor activity which have little in common with the kind of deficits to which it was originally applied, e.g., constructional apraxia, dressing apraxia, gaze apraxia, gait apraxia, etc. The first two forms probably depend on a space-perceptual disorder, while the latter two concern automatic movements. They will not be treated here.

Ideomotor apraxia

When a subject is requested to execute a gesture, he/she must first remember its general configuration and then transform it in a well-coordinated pattern of innervations to be transmitted to the executive motor centers (Roy and Square, 1985). Either of these stages can break down, resulting in two distinct forms of apraxia: ideational apraxia (IA), where the very concept of the gesture is lacking (the patient does not know what to do); and ideomotor apraxia (IMA), where it is the implementation of the gesture in a precise motor program that is disrupted (the patient knows what to do but not how to do it). The two disorders frequently occur together, but must be kept separate, because they reflect the disruption of different mechanisms and are subserved by discrete structures. IMA is by far the best-researched and well-defined form of apraxia and it will, therefore, be treated first.

Testing procedure
The errors made by ideomotor apraxics do not concern the general configuration of the gesture, which can generally be recognized, unless it is spoiled by perseveration, but rather the unfolding

of the single elements constituting the action, the choice of the correct muscular innervations, the positioning of the limb in space, etc. For instance, when requested to salute, the patient may put the back of her/his hand on the forehead with the fingers outstretched and abducted; when requested to flip a coin, she/he alternately opens and closes her/his fingers. It must be recognized, however, that it is not always easy to decide whether the patient has the representation of the gesture clear in her/his mind, especially when the ideomotor deficit is severe, and this is one of the reasons why imitation tests are often preferable to verbal commands in testing IMA. Since the examiner provides the model of the action and the patient must simply copy it, errors can only be due to an executive deficit. Another advantage of imitation tasks is that verbal comprehension difficulties, which in some aphasics may hinder the understanding of commands (Goodglass and Kaplan, 1963), are bypassed and apraxia tests can be confidently administered to severe Wernicke's or global aphasics (De Renzi, 1985).

However, since apraxia is traditionally conceived of as a disorder of gestures, i.e. of movements that are expressive of ideas, intentions or emotions, many authors (Goodglass and Kaplan, 1972; Brown, 1972; Kertesz and Ferro, 1984; Gonzales Rothi and Heilman, 1984) request the execution on verbal command of conventional symbolic gestures (to salute, to wave goodbye, etc.) and pretended object manipulation (show me how you would use a hammer, a key, etc). If the patient fails, the gesture is requested on imitation, in order to rule out a comprehension deficit. Hécaen and Rondot (1985) proposed a rather sophisticated classification of gestures as a basis for a comprehensive examination, distinguishing between symbolic, iconic expressive and indexical (i.e. describing the utilization of objects) gestures, but the relevance of this categorization to clinical purposes remains to be demonstrated.

Yet there is no convincing reason for arguing that the symbolic, meaningful nature of the action is critical for bringing out the deficit of execution

that characterizes IMA. De Renzi et al. (1980) and Lehmkuhl et al. (1983) found no difference between the sensitivity of meaningful and meaningless movements to the consequence of left brain damage, and Pieczuro and Vignolo (1967) reported that the latter rather than the former were performed more poorly by left-hemisphere patients, in comparison with normal controls. Haaland and Flaherty (1984) claimed that only the imitation of pretended object use movements and not that of representative and non-representative/intransitive movements was significantly associated with left-brain damage. This finding is at variance with what was reported in the great majority of studies (Pieczuro and Vignolo, 1967; De Renzi et al., 1980; Kimura, 1982), and it is also difficult to explain, since the distinction among different types of movement is of dubious psychological meaning in imitation tasks. What is the difference between imitating the gesture of snapping fingers (a representative, intransitive gesture) and that of pretending to flip a coin (an object use gesture)?

We use a 24-item test (De Renzi et al., 1980), made up in equal proportion of finger movements and whole arm movements, half of which are meaningful and half meaningless. The presentation of each item may be repeated up to three times if the patient performance is not flawless, and a score of 3, 2, 1 or 0 is assigned, depending on whether the correct imitation is achieved on the first, second or third presentation, or never. This scoring system is simple and reliable and the administration of the test to control patients permits the identification of a cut-off point discriminating a normal from a pathological performance.

Imitation tasks can be supplemented by tests in which the information eliciting the movement is conveyed through a single sensory channel (verbal, visual, tactile). Thus the patient may be given the command to pretend to use a hammer, or can be shown a hammer and asked to pantomime its use, or can be handed a hammer, which is kept hidden from sight, and requested to use it. The purpose of this procedure is to compare the performance across the modalities and to evaluate whether failures are specific for one of them. De Renzi et al. (1982) have found that this may be the case for a few patients.

An activity that may be sensitive to the disruption of motor programs is writing. Apraxic agraphia is a disorder characterized by a profound impairment in grapheme formation by either hand, though the letter choice is correct, as shown by the absence of errors when the patient types or assembles words with anagram letters (Coslett et al., 1986). A subtype of this disorder is 'ideational apraxia', which has been recently reported (Baxter and Warrington, 1986) in a patient showing a striking dissociation between his preserved ability to copy letters and his failure to write them to dictation. Apraxic agraphia must be distinguished from aphasic agraphia, where spelling errors predominate, callosal agraphia, which is confined to the left hand, and spatial agraphia, marked by a distorted spatial orientation of lines and words and/or ignoring of the left side of the page. The interesting finding with apraxic agraphia is that it may be unaccompanied by hand apraxia and may, on the other hand, be absent in the presence of hand apraxia (Coslett et al., 1986), thus suggesting that the motor programme subserving letter formation is independent of those guiding other manual activities.

Left hemisphere dominance

A basic feature of apraxia is its close relationship to left hemisphere damage. This was first ascertained by Liepmann (1908), who compared 41 patients with right hemiplegia and 42 patients with left hemiplegia and found an impaired execution of gestures in 20 patients (i.e., approximately 50%) of the former group and in none of the latter. Since the performance was carried out with the non-paralysed limb (i.e. the left one in left-brain-damaged patients), Liepmann inferred that the left hemisphere controlled the organization of motor activity of either side of the brain. Subsequent studies have provided unequivocal evidence in support of this claim. Table 1 summarizes the data from investigations carried out with quantitative tests which based the diagnosis of apraxia on the determination of a cut-off score, usually corresponding to the poorest score found in a normal control group. The limb ipsilateral to the damaged hemisphere was always used. Approximately one-third of left-brain-damaged patients were found to be apraxic. The proportion of right brain-damaged patients falling below the cut-off score is remarkably lower in the five studies where they have been examined.

The prevalence of apraxia following left brain damage does not imply that the right hemisphere lacks any potential for planning movements. In some patients the two sides of the brain are apparently able to act independently, as suggested by two cases that have become famous in the history of apraxia: the first patient described by Liepmann (1900), the Regierungsrat, and the callosal patient of Geschwind and Kaplan (1962). Both were able to carry out gestures on imitation and the Regierungsrat also on command with the left hand, in spite of a callosal lesion blocking the

TABLE 1

Incidence of apraxia in hemisphere-damaged patients in different studies

Authors	Kind of test	Percentage of apraxics	
		LBD	RBD
Pieczuro and Vignolo (1967)	Imitation	46% (70)*	9% (35)
De Renzi et al. (1968)	Imitation	28% (35)	2% (45)
Basso et al. (1980)	Imitation	39% (123)	
De Renzi et al. (1980)	Imitation	32% (100)	6% (70)
De Renzi et al. (1982)	Imitation	32% (150)	2% (110)
	Object use pantomime	34% (150)	6% (110)
Kertesz and Ferro (1984)**	Command and imitation	55% (acute cases) 40% (chronic cases)	
Basso et al. (1985)	Imitation	45% (152)	

* Numbers in brackets refer to the total number of patients examined.
** Also includes cases of oral apraxia.

transmission of information from the left to the right side. Their behavior was, in this respect, markedly different from that of other patients with pathological damage of the callosum (see for instance Liepmann and Maas, 1907; Watson and Heilman, 1983; Graff-Radford et al., 1987) and more similar to that of epileptic callosotomized patients (Gazzaniga et al., 1967; Zaidel and Sperry, 1977). That these patients are not an exception is suggested by the finding (Kertesz et al., 1984) that there are right-handed patients with large left-sided infarcts involving the parietal-frontal region who are not apraxic in the acute stage.

Thus while the dominance of the left hemisphere in movement planning is likely to be the rule, the degree of its intensity is variable from subject to subject and there can be cases of equipotentiality.

Relationship of left hemisphere dominance for praxis to manual preference and language dominance

The nature of the left brain dominance for praxis in right-handers has been the subject of many speculations. Some authors (Liepmann, 1920; Geschwind, 1975b) emphasized its close relationship to right hand preference, and submitted that both depended on the fact that learned movement engrams are stored in the left brain. They would be immediately available to the motor cortex guiding the right limbs, but only through callosal transmission to that governing the left limbs. Hence the great adroitness of the right over the left hand. By the same token, the left hand would become apraxic, when left brain damage or a callosal interruption makes the engrams unavailable to the right motor cortex. The opposite pattern is to be expected in left-handers. This hypothesis is more convincing in explaining apraxia than hand preference, because it is not clear why the transfer of motor engrams from one side of the brain to the other should entail such a marked and persistent information degrading as to justify the left hand lag in acquiring new skills. Moreover, if the same mechanism accounts for handedness and movement organization, damage to the hemisphere ip-

silateral to the preferred hand, whether the right or the left, should never result in apraxia, or, in other words, apraxia should always follow left brain lesion in right-handers and right brain lesion in left-handers. There is evidence that this rule does not always hold in left-handers. Although there are 10 cases in the literature of apraxia in left-handers following right brain damage (in addition to those gleaned by Poeck and Kerschensteiner, 1971; see Heilman et al., 1973; Valenstein and Heilman, 1979; and Margolin, 1980) the number of apraxics following left brain damage is greater, and from a careful review of the literature Signoret and North (1979) were led to conclude that in left-handers 'gesture apraxia is usually observed following a left-sided lesion'. As to right-handers, some cases of crossed aphasia (i.e., of aphasia associated with right brain damage in right-handers) have been reported which showed limb apraxia (Assal et al., 1981; Henderson, 1983; Basso et al., 1985a). Moreover, a performance definitely below the cut-off point has been found in the left hand of a minority of right-handers following right brain damage (see Table 1). These findings, even if infrequent, cannot be reconciled with the assumption that the same basic mechanism underpins manual preference and gesture planning.

Apraxia is very frequently associated with aphasia and a correlation around 0.40 between the severity of the two disorders has been reported in two studies (De Renzi et al., 1968; Kertesz et al., 1984). Though significant, this correlation is too low to support the idea that there is a causal link between the two symptoms (Goodglass and Kaplan, 1963), as suggested by authors who view apraxia as a disorder in communication. This hypothesis might be entertained if symbolic gestures only were affected, but it can hardly explain the fruitless attempts the patient makes to imitate a meaningless action carried out by the examiner. The association between the two symptoms is therefore likely to be due to the encroachment of the lesion upon contiguous structures, differentially specialized for language and praxis. The independence of apraxia from aphasia is further supported by single case reports of right-handed patients who, following left brain damage, had severe apraxia but no or only minimal aphasia, because language representation was shifted to the right hemisphere (Goodglass and Kaplan, 1963; Heilman et al., 1974; Selnes et al., 1982; Junqué et al., 1986).

The nature of the apraxic deficit

There have been many attempts to define more precisely the nature of the apraxic deficit. Based on the greater sensitivity of multiple action than single hand position tests to left brain damage, Kimura and Archibald (1974) submitted that apraxia is basically a sequencing disorder, emerging when the rapid transition from one motor position to another must be monitored. The assumption that single hand postures are not impaired in left-brain-damaged patients is, however, at variance with clinical experience, as Kimura herself (1977) subsequently recognized, and left hemisphere patients were found by Jason (1983) not to be impaired in comparison with right hemisphere patients when they had to perform a sequence of hand positions under time pressure, i.e., in a condition that should favour the occurrence of sequential errors.

Other authors have argued that apraxia reflects a deficit in learning rather than in performance. Left-brain-damaged patients, whether affected by a cerebrovascular injury (Jason, 1983) or submitted to circumscribed temporal or frontal cortical excisions (Jason, 1985), were found to be poorer than comparable right-sided groups in learning a sequence of four or five hand positions, while they were not impaired in reproducing them after a delay of 28 – 45 min. Jason (1985) inferred that the left hemisphere is specialized in acquisition rather than storage or retrieval of manual sequences. Gonzales Rothi and Heilman (1984) in turn interpreted the poor performances shown by apraxic as compared to non-apraxic left-brain-damaged patients on learning a sequence of 12 gestures as evidence of a deficit in consolidating the motor engrams in memory. The learning deficit shown by apraxics was held consistent with the hypothesis

that the left parietal lobe, which was damaged in all of them, is the repository of visuokinesthetic motor engrams, needed to program skilled movements. The evidence that left-brain-damaged patients in general and apraxics in particular show a deficit in memorizing sequences cannot be disputed. Its relevance to the interpretation of apraxia is, however, questionable, since severe apraxics also fail to reproduce a single hand position, whether meaningful or meaningless, when the model is present. The many attempts they make to choose the appropriate finger movement and to reach the correct spatial position attest not to a memory deficit, but to a difficulty in selecting from the repertoire of motor innervations those suited to implement the proposed action. Once the programme has been built up, it can be easily repeated, as shown by the fact that apraxics did not differ from non-apraxic left-brain-damaged patients on skilful performances, such as finger tapping (Kimura, 1977; Haaland et al., 1980), screw rotation (Pieczuro and Vignolo, 1967; Kimura, 1979) and grooved pegboard (Haaland et al., 1980), where the same action must be repeated over and over again. However, if an action that has eventually been executed is presented afresh after a delay, the difficulty in making the correct choice is again present.

Anatomo-functional models of apraxia

Eighty years since its original formulation, Liepmann's (1908, 1920) interpretation of apraxia still retains much of its interest and provides the basic framework within which most of the findings of subsequent investigations can be accommodated. This is not to say that it does not require modifications or refinements, or that it convincingly explains every aspect of the symptomatology, but its main tenet – that IMA follows the isolation of the primary motor cortex innervating the limb from the left hemisphere areas where the movement is programmed – remains valid.

Liepmann posited that the sensory information eliciting the movement, whether collected from the right or the left brain, must be processed by the left hemisphere, where a motor programme (Bewe-gungsentwurf) is built up specifying the ordering and spatial arrangement of the single movements composing the action. He remained vague about where and how this programme is made, but assumed that it had to be transmitted to the left sensory-motor cortex (sensomotorium), where the tactile and kinesthetic memories of the innerva-tions suited to implement the movement are arous-ed and excite the motor cortex. Nowadays the con-cept of sensomotorium has been abandoned and substituted by that of association motor cortex, or area 6 (Geschwind, 1965). If the left limb must be used, the commands are transferred to the right area 6, travelling through the corpus callosum. Ideomotor apraxia ensues when a lesion interrupts at different points the transfer of the plan of action to the executive centers.

Taking into account the contributions of other authors, Liepmann (1908) considered three forms of apraxia: (1) ideational apraxia, where the pa-tient fails to attain the general project of the ac-tion; (2) ideomotor apraxia, where the lesion prevents the transfer of the motor plan to the areas storing the innervatory engrams (sensomotorium); (3) melokinethic apraxia, due to the loss of the in-nervatory engrams. This form, which was first proposed by Kleist (1907), has never been describ-ed with sufficient accuracy to be distinguishable from a mild form of paresis and to gain acceptance by neurologists.

Liepmann, however, mainly focussed on IMA, which would appear in three clinical contexts, depending on the locus of lesion:

Parietal apraxia, due to the interruption of the pathways connecting the associative sensory areas with the sensomotorium and affecting both limbs. Liepmann surmised that the impairment was more severe in the right than in the left limb, since the latter can to a certain extent benefit from right hemisphere guidance, but Kimura and Archibald (1974), Kimura (1977) and Lehmkuhl et al. (1983) could not confirm this claim.

Frontal apraxia, consequent to the damage of the left premotor cortex, where the innervatory

engrams are stored. The lesion almost always in-volves the adjacent motor area, causing a right limb paresis, so that only the left limb apraxia is apparent.

Callosal apraxia, due to interruption of the outflow from left area 6 to right area 6, causing apraxia of the left limb.

We will now assess the body of evidence support-ing this model and the modifications that have been suggested by subsequent studies.

Parietal and frontal apraxia   A first issue to ad-dress is whether the transmission of information to the premotor cortex, storing the innervatory engrams, must be preceded by its processing in a center where the movements needed to implement the action are chosen and organized in a sequence. If so, the parietal cortex is a likely candidate for harboring this center, for it is reciprocally con-nected with area 6 and receives inputs from all sen-sory associative cortices.

Liepmann (1908) and Geschwind (1965) took ex-ception to this hypothesis and maintained that parietal damage caused apraxia only by interrupt-ing the arcuate fasciculus, which runs in the white matter of the supramarginal gyrus. This fasciculus is formed by fibers from the temporal, parietal and occipital cortex which are directed to the frontal cortex. They constitute a compact bundle only deep to the parietal opercule, where a lesion can in-volve all of them (Dejerine, 1895). Fig. 1 shows its position. Kertesz and Ferro (1984) proposed that the lesion of the occipito-frontal bundle, which transmits visual information to the premotor cor-tex, also contributes to apraxia, but, as shown in Fig. 1, it runs much more medially, at the external angle of the lateral ventricle, above the head of caudate nucleus and is, therefore, rarely involved by most of the infarcts of the middle cerebral artery.

The reason adduced by Geschwind (1965) to re-ject the hypothesis of a parietal center is the occur-rence of left-hand apraxia in association with left pre-rolandic damage. A left parietal center, he argued, would be connected with the homologous region of the right hemisphere and would transfer the information it processes to it and thence forward to the right premotor area, thus bypassing the block represented by a left frontal injury. The cogency of the argument depends on the finding that frontal apraxia is at least as frequent and severe as parietal apraxia. The available clinical and experimental evidence questions this assumption. Faglioni and Basso (1985) have reviewed the case reports in the older literature and have found a surprisingly scanty number of patients whose apraxia could be unequivocally attributed to a left frontal lesion, in contrast with the abundant documentation of parietal apraxia. Quantitative studies carried out on consecutive series of patients corroborate this difference. On a single hand posture imitation test only left parietal patients and not left frontal patients were impaired com-

pared to corresponding right-sided groups (Kimura, 1982), and De Renzi et al. (1983) found that parietal apraxics were not only more numerous (75% vs. 25%), but also more severely impaired than frontal apraxics. Consistent with this finding, Basso et al. (1985b) reported apraxia in 62% of parietal patients as against 24% of frontal patients. When multiple manual position tests were given, again left parietal patients performed more poorly than left frontal patients. The difference was significant in Kolb and Milner's (1981) and De Renzi et al.'s (1983) study, but not in Kimura's (1982) study.

Particularly relevant to the issue of the role played by the left parietal cortex are the data of Kolb and Milner (1981), who investigated patients submitted to left parietal and frontal cortex removal for the relief of epilepsy. The finding that parietal patients were significantly more impaired than frontal patients cannot be reconciled with the hypothesis that parietal apraxia is contingent on white matter lesion, and points to a specific role of the parietal cortex in programming movements. It is true that, as Kolb and Wishaw (1985) point out, the deficit associated with left parietal cortex excision was remarkably less severe than that found in left hemisphere stroke patients and only emerged in the reproduction of a three-movement sequence and not when patients were asked to pantomime the use of objects and to make symbolic gestures to verbal command. However, it must be remembered that these patients underwent the removal of the parietal cortex just because it was thought to be the seat of a long-standing lesion. Compensatory mechanisms may well have developed, reducing the role played by the area in the normal individual.

On the whole, the bulk of evidence argues against assigning the same role to parietal and frontal lesions and challenges the view that the impulses arousing the innervatory engrams of the left hand must first be transmitted to the premotor area and then travel through the fibers connecting the left with the right premotor cortex. As suggested by Kleist (1934), fibers originating in the left

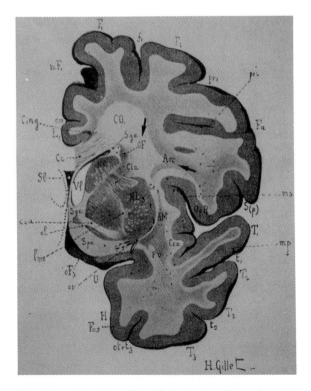

Fig. 1. Frontal section of the left hemisphere 60 mm from the frontal pole. Arrows point to the location of the arcuate fascicle (Arc) and the occipito-frontal fascicle (OF). (Fig. 244, page 447, of Dejerine J: *Anatomie des Centres Nerveux*. Paris: Rueff, 1985).

parietal lobe and crossing the callosum on their way to the right hemisphere may constitute an alternative pathway which partially compensates for left premotor area damage. This hypothesis implies that the parietal cortex and not simply the subjacent white matter is implicated in the transmission of information to the premotor areas.

Cerebral blood flow studies, carried out in normals, bear out the participation of both the parietal and premotor cortex in guiding motor activity. When the subject executes complex movements carried out in external space, such as tracing a spiral in the air or moving her/his forefinger along the cells of a maze following verbal instructions, the sensory-motor area contralateral to the moving hand and the parietal and premotor regions of both sides show a blood flow increase (Roland et al., 1980). The latter areas but not the former are also activated when the movement is not actually carried out, but simply imagined (Ingvar and Philipson, 1977). Cortical stimulation experiments, carried out in man during operation, also corroborate the view that the parietal cortex participates in movement organization. The execution of a sequence of three oral movements was disrupted following the stimulation of the parietal or the premotor area (Ojemann and Mateer, 1979).

In principle, animal studies should be highly informative in discriminating between cortical and white matter contribution to the execution of movements. However, most of them meet with the important limitation that the conditional motor performances required are repetitive and stereotyped, whereas apraxia typically affects movements which must be programmed anew and not the reiteration of the same movement (remember that screwing and unscrewing were found to be unimpaired by Pieczuro and Vignolo, 1967, and Kimura, 1979). Also, it is difficult to determine to what extent alterations of finger positions or limb trajectories exhibited by parietally lesioned monkeys reflect a deficit of motor organization or a spatial disorder, given the well-known parietal lobe specialization in space analysis (Ettlinger, 1977). By and large, the evidence provided by animal ablation studies is meager. A monkey with a cortical lesion of the inferior parietal lobe was reported by Haaxma and Kuypers (1975) to show a mild impairment in adapting the position of contralateral fingers to the grooves giving access to a food pellet. An incorrect posture of the contralateral hand with abnormally extended fingers was reported (Faugier-Grimaud et al., 1978) in monkeys submitted to subpial suction of area 7, which corresponds to the inferior parietal lobule of man, whereas a lesion of the same area did not affect the animal's capacity to open boxes of increasing complexity (Deuel, 1977).

The question may be raised as to whether the parietal and frontal cortex participate in the organization of motor acts at the same functional level, or whether they are hierarchically related, with the former providing the program for the choice and ordering of the single movements and the latter the innervatory patterns for the activation of the motor cortex. If so, qualitative differences between the praxic impairment associated with the two localizations might be expected, but no evidence supporting this prediction has so far been provided (Lehmkuhl et al., 1983).

Denny-Brown (1958) contrasted repellent apraxia with magnetic apraxia, positing that the former was associated with parietal damage and the latter with frontal damage, a distinction that has not been endorsed by subsequent investigators. Luria (1966) contrasted afferent apraxia, linked to parieto-occipital damage, where the spatial organization of action would be impaired, with efferent apraxia, due to frontal lesion, where the organization of an action over time would disintegrate, but empirical rules for making this distinction were not given. Heilman et al. (1982) recently pleaded for the recognition of two distinguishable forms of IMA, one related to parietal injury and the other to an injury disconnecting the parietal cortex from the premotor area, and based the difference on performance in pantomime recognition tests. They argued that if the parietal cortex stores the visuokinesthetic engrams of the movement, parietal apraxics should be expected to meet with difficulty in the discrimination of correct from incorrect videotaped gestures, while apraxics with more anterior damage would not. Their findings were apparently consistent with this prediction, but their cogency is undermined by the questionable criteria adopted to classify apraxics as parietal or non-parietal (when CT scan data were not available, the fluency – non-fluency dimension of oral speech was used). In a second paper (Gonzales Rothi et al., 1985) apraxic aphasics were reported to perform more poorly than non-apraxic aphasics on a pantomime comprehension test, in spite of equal impairment in overall severity of aphasia. Unfortunately, no data were available on the lesion localization, except that all patients had unilateral infarctions of the left hemisphere.

It has recently been suggested (Kimura, 1983) that the organization of praxis in the left hemisphere is related to the sex of the patient, with women becoming apraxic following an anterior lesion and men following both posterior and anterior lesion. Data collected in our laboratory are at variance with the claim that posterior lesion does not produce apraxia in women. In an unpublished series of 103 left-brain-damaged patients (56 M and 47 F) we found apraxia in 22 men (39%) and 19 women (40%). The disorder was associated with posterior (post-rolandic) damage in 12 (56%) of apraxic males and in 10 (53%) of apraxic females. Also Jason (1985) did not confirm sex differences in cerebral organization of manual praxis.

Callosal apraxia Liepmann and Maas's (1907) patient Ochs was the first documentation of callosal apraxia. It has been followed by a substantial number of case reports (reviewed by Faglioni and Basso, 1985), which have confirmed that tumoral, vascular and traumatic lesions interrupting the callosal pathways result in apraxia of the left limbs. Unfortunately, the rarity of this localization has so far prevented systematic studies of a consecutive series of callosal patients in order to evaluate the relative frequency of positive and negative cases (some of the latter were reported in the older literature; see Berlucchi, 1926). It would also be interesting to know with more precision which part of the callosum is critical for transferring information relevant to the motor act execution. The only study available in humans (De Lacoste et al., 1985) is based on callosal retrograde degeneration associated with the anatomical sites of focal cortical lesions. It indicates that fibers from the inferior and middle frontal gyri run in the genu and rostrum, while fibers from the temporo-parieto-occipital junction run in the posterior two-fifths of the corpus callosum. No apraxia of the left limb was observed in patients who underwent splenial section in the course of tumor removal (Trescher and Ford, 1937; Damasio et al., 1980) and even patients with section of the posterior half of the truncus or its leftward outflow (Sugishita et al., 1980; Gersh and Damasio, 1981) did not show left limb apraxia, but simply left hand agraphia. Unfortunately, no case has been reported with a lesion confined to the anterior half of the truncus of the corpus callosum.

It is fair to recognize, however, that the idea that the integrity of callosal pathways is needed to ensure normal left hand praxis is challenged by data from patients with callosal agenesis and patients submitted to callosal section for the relief of a drug-resistant epilepsy. In the former condition refined testing procedures have brought out a certain degree of motor impairment, consisting in a decreased accuracy of movements, especially those involving bi-manual coordination (Ferris and Dorsen, 1975; Gott and Saul, 1978) and the inter-hand transfer of manual learning (Gott and Saul, 1978), but no apraxia (Ettlinger et al., 1972, 1974). A slowing in the performance of motor coordination and manual dexterity tests and an impairment on tasks requiring alternating motion was also found in commissurotomized patients (Zaidel and Sperry, 1977), but again no clear evidence of left limb apraxia. The testing procedure is critical. When the information eliciting the movement was confined to a hemisphere and the motor response was made by the other hemisphere, the patient made errors in executing gesture, especially if they involved the distal musculature. Thus she/he met with difficulty in assuming finger positions with the left hand in response to a verbal command or on imitation of a model projected to the right visual field. The same was true if it was the right hand that had to reproduce a position flashed to the left visual field (Gazzaniga et al., 1967; Zaidel and Sperry, 1977). These deficits, however, have little to do with the left brain dominance in motor planning and simply attest to the fact that the sensory message could not reach the contralateral motor cortex and that the motor cortex did not have good control over the ipsilateral hand. The crucial experiment for testing the hypothesis that the right hemisphere is in trouble when it cannot avail itself of left brain guidance is the tachistoscopic presentation of finger postures to the left visual field and their reproduction by the left hand. No error was found in this condition (Gazzaniga et al., 1967; Zaidel and Sperry, 1977; Volpe et al., 1982). A possible interpretation of this puzzling negative finding is that the long-lasting lesion which underlies the epilepsy of these patients has favored a reorganization of cerebral dominance and has resulted in a right hemisphere autonomy in movement planning (Faglioni and Basso, 1985). What is not completely satisfactory in this ad hoc explanation is that it implies a functional rearrangement of motor dominance in every callosotomized patient, while very few of them showed independent right hemisphere competence for language. Alternatively, the discrepancy between the impairment observed in naturally occurring callosal diseases and the normal performance of surgical cases might be accounted for by assuming that in the former the involvement of paramedian frontal structures (especially the supplementary motor area) contributes to apraxia. In a review of the published cases of left hand callosal apraxia, Goldenberg et al. (1985) pointed out that damage always impinged upon the medial frontal lobe, especially the left one, and surmised that its involvement was influential in producing apraxia. This was not, however, the case in two recently published callosal patients (Watson and Heilman,

1983; Graff-Radford et al., 1987). Two cases of bilateral apraxia associated with left mesial hemisphere infarcts which included the supplementary motor area have been reported by Watson et al. (1986), but this finding must compete with the many negative cases in the literature and with the outcome of a study (Freund and Hummelshein, 1985) carried out on 13 patients with damage confined to the left medial frontal lobe, but sparing the precentral motor cortex (11 had anterior cerebral artery infarcts and two had tumors). Ideomotor apraxia was never observed.

The issue is further complicated by a recent study by Milner and Kolb (1985), who did find impairment in the reproduction of motor positions following callosotomy. They examined four patients, two with a complete section of the commissures and two with a section limited to the anterior commissure, the anterior 5 cm of the corpus callosum and probably the hippocampal commissure. All were requested to imitate a three-movement sequence test that the authors had previously used with patients submitted to circumscribed cortical removal (Kolb and Milner, 1981), and which had shown an impairment in frontal patients of either side and a more marked one in left parietal patients. Unexpectedly, callosal patients were as deficient as left parietal patients and significantly more so than frontal patients, independently of the hand used to carry out the task. This finding apparently argues against left hemisphere dominance in praxis. Yet, however interesting on its own, it may not be relevant to the issue of apraxia. Taken in conjunction with data from frontal excisions, the callosal patients' data do show that the cooperation of the two frontal areas is needed to ensure good performance of either the right or the left hand in a manual sequence task, but the specificity of the test for apraxic disorders is open to question. Do the callosal patients fail because of the praxic demands of the task, or, as the authors themselves surmise, because of its mnestic load, which may be too heavy for patients who are known to be impaired on verbal and visual memory tests (Zaidel and

Sperry, 1977)? Considering the bulk of evidence marshalled on apraxia and the negative findings of commissurotomized patients, the latter interpretation would appear more likely, but it must be recognized that data from surgical sections remain difficult to interpret in the context of current theorization on apraxia.

Participation of deep nuclei

As envisaged by the classical theory, the circuitry subserving the transmission of motor programs to area 4 would be confined to the cortical areas and their connecting pathways, and would not implicate the subcortical grey structures. Quite recently, however, a few cases of severe apraxia, with CT scan documentation of damage restricted to the left deep nuclei (basal ganglia and thalamus), have been reported (Agostoni et al., 1983; Basso and Della Sala, 1986; De Renzi et al., 1986). Other cases have occasionally been mentioned by the literature (see De Renzi et al., 1986, for review) but have not excited much attention. In most of these cases there is no evidence of an encroachement of the lesion upon the arcuate fasciculus. These patients raise the same kind of problem posed by aphasia or hemi-inattention following deep lesions. Do they imply a participation of the basal ganglia and thalamus in functions traditionally thought to be the province of the cortex? In the case of apraxia, this would mean that the loop connecting the parietal cortex with the neostriatum, the globus pallidus, the lateral thalamic nuclei and thence with area 4 and 6 is implicated in the transmission of motor programs, and represents a subsidiary route to the arcuate fasciculus. Perani et al. (1987) recently proposed the concept of diaschisis, i.e., transient functional depression occurring at a distance from the lesion, for explaining the presence of neuropsychological symptoms in subcortical aphasia and neglect. They found a greater reduction of cortical perfusion on I-123 HIPDM and SPECT in left-brain-damaged patients showing aphasia and right-brain-damaged patients showing neglect following a deep lesion than in patients having comparable lesion sites (but

smaller size) and free from neuropsychological symptoms. These remote cortical effects were tentatively attributed to cortical deafferentation, consequent on lack of input from afferents originating in the injured area (Powers and Raichle, 1985). Whatever the mechanism, the fact remains that a defective functional integration between cortical and subcortical centers can give rise to neuropsychological symptoms, apraxia included.

Evolution in IMA

Very few studies have assessed the evolution of IMA. One of them investigated Alzheimer patients and found, predictably, that IMA deteriorates in the course of the disease (Della Sala et al., 1987). The question of the recovery from apraxia following a stroke was addressed by Basso et al. (1987). Twenty-six patients with left brain damage, found to be apraxic in the first month post-stroke, were retested at a mean interval of eight months. Only 13 of them were still apraxic on the second examination and only five on a third examination, carried out at least six months later. There was a trend for patients with sparing of the temporoparietal or parietal-occipital region to improve more than those who had these areas damaged (as was the case for all of the patients who were still apraxic on the third examination). Other variables – sex, age, lesion size, aphasia type, comprehension deficit – were not related to the outcome of apraxia.

Ideational apraxia

Approximately at the same time as Liepmann was investigating IMA, Pick (1902, 1905) reported a few patients who showed impressive errors in demonstrating the use of objects that had been correctly recognized and named. The impairment was particularly manifest when the patient was requested to carry out actions involving the utilization of more than one object (e.g., lighting a candle, or putting a letter into an envelope), but also appeared with single objects. For instance, a patient (Pick, 1905) tried to comb her hair with a knife, put a match in her mouth when asked to use it, and turned key and scissors over in her hands without being able to show their use. The majority of these patients suffered from generalized brain impairment (daily epileptic seizures, dementia), but at least one case (Pick's, 1905, patient No. 3) was affected by an infarct, presumably located in the posterior region of the left hemisphere. Pick called this form motor apraxia (since he wanted to contrast it with sensory apraxia, i.e., apraxia secondary to deficits of recognition) but the name was soon abandoned in favour of that of ideational apraxia. He submitted that it was due to the faulty representation of the aim of the movement (Zielvorstellung) consequent on a disorder of attention. Liepmann (1908) first considered IA as an extreme manifestation of a severe form of IMA, but ultimately (1920) admitted its autonomy and attributed it to a left hemisphere lesion, located in the parieto-occipital junction, posteriorly to that responsible for IMA.

IA is mentioned in every discussion of apraxia, but has seldom been the subject of specific studies, and there are very few case reports (Zangwill, 1960; Brown, 1972; Poeck and Lehmkuhl, 1980) documenting its features and the clinical context in which it occurs. It is, therefore, no wonder that many uncertainties persist with regard to its very nature, the way it must be tested and the kind of errors it produces. There is general consensus on the definition of IA as a disorder of the ideational plan of action, manifesting itself through the faulty use of objects when a complex sequence of acts must be organized. Yet opinions diverge as to its real autonomy with respect to other disorders, the reason why the patient fails to attain a clear representation of the general shape of movements and the localizing value of the symptom.

The autonomy of IA has been challenged from two viewpoints. A few authors (Sittig, 1931; Zangwill, 1960) revived the earlier position of Liepmann that IA is but an extreme form of IMA, so severe as to hinder the facilitation that the handling of an object normally exerts on its manipulation. Sittig (1931) remarked that many

ideomotor errors are difficult to distinguish from the ideational ones and that even faulty actions that apparently point to an ideational failure (e.g., blowing out the match before having lit the candle) might be due to an executive derailment and not reflect what the patient had in mind.

It is true that IMA and IA frequently coexist in the same patient and that the former can so deeply affect the movement execution as to produce an ineffective use of tools and make the ideational project unrecognizable, but instances of dissociation between the two disorders have been repeatedly reported (Poeck and Lemkuhl, 1980) and the quality of errors is often revealing of the nature of the deficit. In a systematic, quantitative investigation (De Renzi et al., 1968), where movement imitation was compared with object use, 11 left-brain-damaged patients performed in the normal range on the former test and were impaired on the latter. A non-significant correlation of 0.31 was recently found (De Renzi and Lucchelli, 1988) between the errors made by 20 left-brain-damaged patients on a test requiring the coordinated use of objects and the scores on a movement imitation test, and striking examples of dissociation between the performance on the two tests were observed. As to the error quality, it would be hard to attribute to an executive impairment errors such as putting the stamp inside the envelope, when a letter must be prepared for mailing, or striking the candle instead of the match when the task is to light a candle. Thus the autonomy of IA with respect to IMA seems to be well established.

The independence of IA has also been questioned from a different standpoint. The frequency with which it was reported, especially in the older literature, in association with diffuse disease (e.g., senile dementia, or post-epileptic confusional states) and the conceptual nature of its errors led some authors (Dejerine, 1914; Goldstein, 1948; Denny-Brown, 1958) to deny IA the status of a discrete symptom, and to conceive of it as a manifestation of global mental deterioration. Pick (1905) spoke of disorders of attention that would hamper the regulatory effect exerted on the single components of the action by the representation of its aim. Dejerine (1914) attributed the disruption of the logical ordering of acts to deficits of attention, memory and mental associations, although he rather unexpectedly added that higher intellectual functions, such as abstraction and reasoning, may remain intact in these patients. The interpretation of a cognitive deficit in terms of mental deterioration has recurred many times in the history of neuropsychology, but to be forcibly argued it needs more than the mere observation that some, or several, patients showing the deficit present with a global decline of intelligence, or with lapses of attention. Ajuriaguerra et al. (1960b) found that only patients at an advanced stage of senile dementia showed IA, while the symptom has been repeatedly observed in patients with focal lesions who were not mentally deteriorated. The mental deterioration hypothesis has been put to the test and rejected by De Renzi et al. (1968), since left-brain-damaged patients with IA were not found to perform significantly more poorly than those without IA on the Raven PM Test. As to the role played by weakening of attention (Pick, 1905), this is by no means the impression that most of these patients give to the observer, since they often display a serious effort to overcome their difficulties and may even ultimately attain the goal, through trial and error.

Granted that IA is a discrete symptom, deserving separate treatment, its ultimate nature remains open to question. The majority of authors conceive of it as a deficit in ordering the units of the action, the single acts being performed correctly, but out of sequence. Consequently, only tasks involving the coordinated use of multiple objects would be adequate to bring IA out. However, when systematically investigated, left-brain-damaged patients have also been found to be impaired in demonstrating the use of single objects (De Renzi et al., 1968). Is it legitimate to call this deficit IA? To answer this question and to gain a better understanding of IA, De Renzi and Lucchelli (1988) gave 20 left-brain-damaged patients both a multiple object and a single object test. The

former was made up of five tasks: to light a candle, to open and close a padlock, to open a bottle of water with a bottle-opener and to pour water into a glass, to prepare a letter for mailing, to prepare an expresso pot. The errors made in the execution of these tasks were categorized as follows. (1) Clumsiness: the action is appropriate for the object, but carried out in an awkward and ineffectual way. These errors probably reflect the presence of IMA. (2) Perplexity: the patients looks hesitatingly at the objects, attempts to use one of them, puts it down, tries with another object, etc. The behavior attests that she/he does not know what to do. (3) Omission: an action needed to complete the sequence is omitted (i.e., the stamp is put on the envelope, without moistening it, or the match is taken to the wick, without striking it). (4) Mislocation: the patient handles the object in an appropriate way, but carries out the action in the wrong place (e.g., she/he strikes the match and then tries to light the candlestick instead of the candle). (5) Misuse: the object is used in a conceptually inappropriate way (e.g. the bottle-opener is stirred inside the glass). (6) Sequence errors: the patient inverts the order in which the acts composing the action must follow each other (e.g. she/he seals the envelope before having put the letter inside it). Omission, misuse and mislocation were by far the most frequent errors, while errors of sequence were rare. Thus a deficit in evoking the appropriate use of the single objects rather than a disorder in ordering the acts composing the action would appear to be the most common cause of failure. In fact, comparable errors were also observed with the single object test where errors of perplexity, misuse (e.g., the patient used a key to hammer, or an eraser to comb himself) and mislocation (she/he wrote holding the pen upside down) were repeatedly observed. As the patient often named the object or specified what it was for, an agnosic impairment could be ruled out. The performance on the single object test correlated highly (0.85) with that on the multiple object test.

Morlaas (1928) was the first to emphasize that IA patients also failed with single objects and from this he drew the inference that IA is basically an agnosia of use. The term is equivocal and should be replaced with that of amnesia of use, which more clearly identifies IA as a particular form of semantic amnesia. The patient fails because she/he is unable to gain access to that particular aspect of the semantic repository where the memory of the way an object must be used is stored. Selective forms of semantic amnesia − i.e. the failure to recover on essential feature of a visually presented stimulus, in spite of its identification − have been repeatedly reported in left-brain-damaged patients: e.g., they may be unable to associate the shape of an object with its sound (Faglioni et al., 1969), its color (De Renzi and Spinnler, 1967), the pantomime displaying its use (Gainotti and Lemmo, 1976), etc. The correlation between these disorders and amnesia of use remains to be investigated.

Considered in this perspective, IA is a radically different symptom from IMA, since it belongs more to the realm of conceptual deficits than to that of movement disorders. Yet it is not an unspecific impairment due to a generalized dysfunction of the cortex, but points to a focalized left hemisphere disruption. IA has never been found to follow right brain damage (Ajuriaguerra et al., 1960a; De Renzi et al., 1968) and its occurrence in patients with senile dementia may well be an expression of left hemisphere disease, not different from what happens with aphasia. There is a consensus in the literature (Foix, 1916; Liepmann, 1920; Morlaas, 1928; Hécaen, 1972) that damage to the left temporo-parietal region plays a crucial role in determining IA, but the lack of studies carried out on unselected samples of patients, with lesions documented by autopsy, surgical or CT scan findings, prevents the drawing of firm conclusions on this point.

Oral apraxia

The inability to carry out purposeful non-verbal movements with the musculature of the mouth, lips, tongue and throat, not due to paresis or other elementary motor disorders, was the first example of apraxia reported in the literature. As early as 1878 Jackson commented upon the failure of some aphasics to protrude their tongue on command, although they were perfectly able to move it when chewing or licking their lips. A poignant description of these patients' behavior was given by Moutier (1908): 'Let us ask an anarthric patient to stick out his tongue; the patient opens his mouth, makes some desperate efforts, shows with his gesture that he has perfectly understood our command. Yet his tongue lies still in his mouth, or it barely moves'.

Other gestures suitable to demonstrate oral apraxia (OA) are whistling, kissing, puffing or blowing, clearing ones's throat, teeth chattering, etc. The deficit is not contingent on the verbal presentation of the command and can equally be shown by requiring the imitation of the examiner's performance, thus by-passing a possible deficit in language comprehension. Kerschensteiner and Poeck (1974) analysed the errors made by patients and classified them as substitution, augmentation and addition, deficient responses, trial and error groping and perseverations. Semantically unrelated substituted movements were the predominant error type, but no specific relationship of error patterns to discrete aphasic syndromes could be identified. No qualitative difference was observed between errors on verbal command and imitation, except in anomic aphasics who were more impaired on the former modality.

The same close relationship to left brain damage found for limb apraxia also holds for OA (De Renzi et al., 1966), but there are differences in the intrahemispheric organization of the two types of movement. While limb apraxia is more marked and frequent following parietal lesion, Tognola and Vignolo (1980) have shown, based on clinical − CT scan correlations, that OA most commonly results from damage to the frontal and central opercula and the anterior part of the insula and is associated with inferior parietal damage in no more than one-third of cases. Kimura's (1982) data concur with those of Tognola and Vignolo as far as the execution of single oral movements is concerned. A less consistent picture emerges when a sequence of three oral movements is given to imitate. Kimura (1982) found left frontal and left parietal patients equally impaired, while Kolb and Milner (1981), who investigated epileptic patients with removal of discrete cortical areas, reported a disruption after frontal lobe ablations of either side, but not after parietal lobe ablations. As already mentioned for limb apraxia, it is open to question whether sequence tests, with their non-negligible load on memory, are particularly relevant to apraxia. The doubt is enhanced by the finding (Milner and Kolb, 1985) that patients who had undergone commissurotomy for the relief of epilepsy scored even more poorly than frontal patients, which is at variance with the absence of oral apraxia following callosal damage, even when it was of a size sufficient to cause limb apraxia (Sweet, 1941; Geschwind and Kaplan, 1962; Watson and Heilman, 1983; Graff-Radford et al., 1987). It was just this finding that led Geschwind (1965) to hypothesize that, in contrast with what holds for limb movements, the left premotor area can control the oral-movement-producing brain stem nuclei of both sides without the intermediation of the right motor cortex. I believe that only single movements are appropriate to test OA and that the bulk of evidence points to the anterior cortex as the place where their planning occurs. Posterior damage may still interfere with the oral activity execution either by impairing the transition from one position to the other (Mateer and Kimura, 1977) or by interrupting the transfer of the command eliciting the movement, but will not disrupt its organization. If so, one would expect that oral and limb apraxia, though both subserved by the left hemisphere, can be dissociated. The data of De Renzi et al.'s (1966) study, where the two forms were assessed systematically, confirm this prediction. Out of 58 left-brain damaged patients who showed signs of OA, 30 (51%) were not limb apraxic, while 8 (22%) of the 36 patients with limb apraxia did not have OA. Thus, while the commonalities between the two forms of apraxia

are indisputable (Roy and Square, 1985), they must be kept distinct.

As concerns limb apraxia, OA does not usually impair the patient's daily routine, since the deficit becomes apparent only when the movement must be executed in an artificial situation, in response to the examiner's request, and not in spontaneous or context-dependent performances. Yet it has been maintained that the symptom may deserve special attention, because of its possible relationship to speech disorders of Broca's aphasics. A few authors (Liepmann, 1900; Ballet, 1908; Nathan, 1947; Bay, 1957) have assumed that both symptoms are dependent on the same mechanism. Of course the linguistic component of the patients' speech cannot be due to an apraxic mechanism; rather, their difficulty in producing appropriate verbal sounds may be secondary to the faulty positioning of the oral muscles. The term apraxia of speech (Johns and Darley, 1970) has become popular as a substitute for the more classical labels of aphemia, Broca's aphasia, anarthria, cortical dysarthria, efferent motor aphasia, etc., which had been proposed in the past to emphasize the lack of motor control in the production of phonological sounds and the discrepancy between the laborious, effortful articulation in purposeful speech and islands of fluency in automatic sequences. Many studies have attempted to outline the phonological, articulatory and acoustic features of apraxia of speech (for a review, see Miller, 1986). Both electromyographic (Shankweiler and Taylor, 1968; Fromm et al., 1982) and fiberscopic and X-ray investigations (Itoh and Sasanuma, 1984) have provided evidence of a disordered pattern of motor activity, 'at the level of the motor programming of articulators' (Itoh and Sasanuma, 1984), distinct from that observed in purely dysarthric patients.

The question is whether apraxia of speech is but the articulatory counterpart of the impairment in controlling bucco-facial non-verbal movements found in OA. Nathan (1947) said: 'as facial apraxia is a common accompaniment of aphasia, it should be considered as a possible cause of dysarthria, whenever the aphasia is of the type known as

Broca's aphasia (aphasia and dysarthria)'. It is indisputable that the two phenomena are highly correlated: De Renzi et al. (1966) found OA in 90% of Broca's aphasics as against only 6% of Wernicke's aphasics, and Mateer and Kimura (1977) and Mateer (1978) reported that only non-fluent aphasics were impaired in the imitation of single oral movements. However, this may be due to the contiguity of the motor association areas involved by apraxia of speech and OA and does not imply that the same mechanism underlies the control of non-verbal movements and the production of linguistic sounds. Both La Pointe and Wertz (1974) and Bowman et al. (1980) found no close relationship between the severity of apraxia of speech and OA. Also the finding that a few patients show OA without disorders of the phonological-articulatory production argues against the view that the two phenomena denote the disruption of the same structures, although the mechanism may be similar.

Trunk apraxia

Geschwind (1975a, b) emphasized the frequent preservation of axial movements, i.e., those carried out with the musculature of the neck and trunk, in patients with severe limb apraxia. When the instructions are given verbally the patient would correctly execute the command to bow, kneel, walk backwards and even dance and take the position of a boxer, in sharp contrast with her/his failure to make a fist, punch, salute, etc. Nothing was said of the patients' performance on imitation. This discrepancy was accounted for by assuming the existence of alternative routes, directly linking the language area of the temporal lobe with the subcortical motor system and eventually the spinal nuclei, which would permit the by-passing of the lesion block. The alternative route cannot be used for carrying out distal limb movements, because they require the mediation of the pyramidal pathway and thus the intact connection of Wernicke's area with areas 4 and 6. Geschwind's claim was based on anecdotal evidence. Poeck et

al. (1982) put it to the test by comparing the performance of four groups of aphasics (global, Wernicke's, Broca's and amnesic) on limb and axial movement tasks, although the latter mainly involved eye and neck muscles, while Geschwind was primarily concerned with trunk and proximal limb muscles. All groups scored lower on limb than axial movements when the command was given in the verbal modality, but the difference was significant only in global aphasics. When imitation was requested, the rate of correct responses was approximately the same for both types of movement. On the whole, the data lend weak support to the thesis of a different anatomical organization of hand as compared to axial praxis, although there is some suggestion that axial movement commands may be more easily comprehended by severe aphasics, possibly because, as Geschwind (1975a) intimated, they are bilaterally decoded.

References

Agostoni E, Coletti A, Orlando G, Tredici G: Apraxia in deep cerebral lesions. *J. Neurol. Neurosurg. Psychiatry: 46,* 804 – 808, 1983.

Ajuriaguerra J, Hécaen H, Angelergues R: Les apraxies: varietés cliniques et latéralization lésionelle. *Rev. Neurol.: 102,* 566 – 594, 1960a.

Ajuriaguerra J, Muller M, Tissot R: A propos de quelques problèmes posés par l'apraxie dans les démences. *Encephale: 49,* 375 – 401, 1960b.

Assal G, Perentes E, Dervaz JP: Crossed aphasia in a right-handed patient: post-mortem findings. *Arch. Neurol. (Chicago): 38,* 455 – 458, 1981.

Ballet G: Apraxie faciale (impossibilité de souffler) associée à de l'aphasie complexe (aphasie motrice et aphasie sensorielle). Apraxie et aphemie. *Rev. Neurol.: 2,* 445 – 447, 1908.

Basso A, Della Sala S: Ideomotor apraxia arising from a purely deep lesion. *J. Neurol. Neurosurg. Psychiatry: 49,* 458 – 465, 1986.

Basso A, Luzzatti C, Spinnler H: Is ideomotor apraxia the outcome of damage to well-defined regions of the left hemisphere? Neuropsychological study of CAT correlations. *J. Neurol. Neurosurg. Psychiatry: 43,* 118 – 126, 1980.

Basso A, Capitani E, Laiacona M, Zanobio ME: Crossed aphasia: one or more syndromes? *Cortex: 21,* 25 – 45, 1985a.

Basso A, Faglioni P, Luzzatto C: Methods in neuroanatomical research and an experimental study of limb apraxia. In Roy EA (Editor), *Neuropsychological Studies of Apraxia and Related Disorders.* Amsterdam: North Holland, Ch. 8, pp. 179 – 202, 1985b.

Basso A, Capitani E, Della Sala S, Laiacona M, Spinnler H: Recovery from ideomotor apraxia: a study on acute stroke patients. *Brain: 110,* 747 – 760, 1987.

Baxter MD, Warringon EK: Ideational agraphia: a single case study. *J. Neurol. Neurosurg. Psychiatry: 49,* 369 – 374, 1986.

Bay E: Die corticale Dysarthrie und ihre Beziehungen zur sogenannten motorische Aphasie. *Dtsch. Z. Nervenheilk.: 176,* 553 – 594, 1957.

Berlucchi C: Corpo calloso e disturbi disprassici. *Cervello: 5,* 1 – 8, 1926.

Bowman C, Hodson B, Simpson R: Oral apraxia and aphasic misarticulations. In Brookshire R (Editor), *Clinical Aphasiology, Conference Proceedings.* Minneapolis: BRK, 1980.

Brown JW: *Aphasia, Apraxia, Agnosia.* Springfield: Thomas, 1972.

Coslett HB, Gonzales Rothi LJ, Valenstein E, Heilman KM: Dissociations of writing and praxis: two cases in point. *Brain Lang.: 28,* 357 – 369, 1986.

Damasio AR, Chui HC, Corbett J, Kassel N: Posterior callosal section in a non- epileptic patient. *J. Neurol. Neurosurg. Psychiatry: 43,* 351 – 356, 1980.

Dejerine J: *Anatomie des Centres Nerveux.* Paris: Rueff, 1895.

Dejerine J: *Semiologie des Affections du Système Nerveux.* Paris: Masson, 1914.

De Lacoste MC, Kirkpatrick JB, Ross E: Topography of the human corpus callosum. *J. Neuropathol. Exp. Neurol.: 44,* 578 – 591, 1985.

Della Sala S, Lucchelli F, Spinnler H: Ideomotor apraxia in patients with dementia of Alzheimer type. *J. Neurol.: 234,* 91 – 93, 1987.

Denny-Brown D: The nature of apraxia. *J. Nerv. Mental Dis.: 126,* 9 – 32, 1958.

De Renzi E. Methods of limb apraxia examination and their bearing on the interpretation of the disorder. In Roy EA, (Editor), *Neuropsychological Studies of Apraxia and Related Disorders.* Amsterdam: North Holland, Ch. 2, pp. 45 – 64, 1985.

De Renzi E, Lucchelli F: Ideational apraxia. *Brain: 111,* 1173 – 1185, 1988.

De Renzi E, Spinnler H: Impaired performance on color tasks in patients with hemispheric damage. *Cortex: 3,* 194 – 216, 1967.

De Renzi E, Pieczuro A, Vignolo LA: Oral apraxia and aphasia. *Cortex: 2,* 50 – 73, 1966.

De Renzi E, Pieczuro A, Vignolo LA: Ideational apraxia: a quantitative study. *Neuropsychologia: 6,* 41 – 52, 1968.

De Renzi E, Motti F, Nichelli P: Imitating gestures: a quantitative approach to ideomotor apraxia. *Arch. Neurol. (Chicago): 37,* 6 – 18, 1980.

De Renzi E, Faglioni P, Sorgato P: Modality-specific and supramodal mechanisms of apraxia. *Brain: 105,* 301 – 312, 1982.

De Renzi E, Faglioni P, Lodesani M, Vecchi A: Impairment of left brain-damaged patients on imitation of single movements and motor sequences. Frontal- and parietal-injured patients compared. *Cortex: 19,* 333 – 343, 1983.

De Renzi E, Faglioni P, Scarpa M, Crisi G: Limb apraxia in patients with damage confined to the left basal ganglia and thalamus. *J. Neurol. Neurosurg. Psychiatry: 49,* 1030 – 1038, 1986.

Deuel RK: Loss of motor habits after cortical lesions. *Neuropsychologia: 15,* 205 – 215, 1977.

Ettlinger G: Parietal cortex in visual orientation. In Rose FC (Editor), *Physiological Aspects of Clinical Neurology.* Oxford: Blackwell, 1977.

Ettlinger G, Blakemore CB, Milner AD, Wilson J: Agenesis of the corpus callosum: A behavioral investigation. *Brain: 95,* 327 – 346, 1972.

Ettlinger G, Blakemore CB, Milner AD, Wilson J: Agenesis of the corpus callosum: A further behavioural investigation. *Brain: 97,* 225 – 234, 1974.

Faglioni P, Basso A: Historical perspectives on neuroanatomical correlates of limb apraxia. In Roy EA (Editor). *Neuropsychological Studies of Apraxia and Related Disorders.* Amsterdam: North Holland, Ch. 1, pp. 3 – 44, 1985.

Faglioni P, Spinnler H, Vignolo LA: Contrasting behavior of right and left brain-damaged patients on a discriminative and a semantic test of auditory recognition. *Cortex: 5,* 366 – 389, 1969.

Faugier-Grimaud S, Frenois C, Stein DG: Effects of posterior parietal lesions on visually guided behavior in monkeys. *Neuropsychologia: 16,* 151 – 168, 1978.

Ferris GS, Dorsen MM: Agenesis of the corpus callosum. 1. Neuropsychological studies. *Cortex: 11,* 95 – 122, 1975.

Foix MCh: Contribution a l'étude de l'apraxie idéomotrice, de son anatomie pathologique et des ses rapports avec les syndromes qui ordinairement l'accompagnent. *Rev. Neurol.: 1,* 283 – 298, 1916.

Freund HJ, Hummelshein H: Lesions of premotor cortex in man. *Brain: 108,* 697 – 733, 1985.

Fromm D, Abbs J, McNeil M, Rosenbek J: Simultaneous perceptual-physiological method for studying apraxia of speech. In Brookshire (Editor), *Clinical Aphasiology, Conference Proceedings.* Minneapolis: BRK, 1982.

Gainotti G, Lemmo MA: Comprehension of symbolic gestures in aphasia. *Brain Lang.: 2,* 451 – 460, 1976.

Gazzaniga MS, Bogen JE, Sperry RW: Dyspraxia following division of the cerebral commissures. *Arch. Neurol. (Chicago): 16,* 606 – 612, 1967.

Gazzaniga MS, Le Doux JE, Wilson DH: Language, praxis and the right hemisphere. Clues to mechanisms of consciousness. *Neurology: 27,* 1144 – 1147, 1977.

Gersh F, Damasio AR: Praxis and writing of the left hand may be served by different callosal pathways. *Arch. Neurol. (Chicago): 38,* 634 – 636, 1981.

Geschwind N: Disconnexion syndromes in animal and man. *Brain: 88,* 237 – 294, 1965.

Geschwind N: Preservation of axial movements to verbal command in cases of apraxia or comprehension deficit. In: Michel F, Schott B (Editors): *Les Syndromes de Disconnexion Calleuse chez l'Homme.* Actes du Colloque International de Lyon. Hopital neurologique, Lyon, pp. 301 – 307, 1975a.

Geschwind N: The apraxias: neural mechanisms of disorders of learned movement. *Am. Sci.: 63,* 188 – 195, 1975b.

Geschwind N, Kaplan E: A human cerebral deconnection syndrome. *Neurology: 12,* 675 – 685, 1962.

Goldenberg G, Wimmer A, Holzner F, Wessely P: Apraxia of the left limbs in a case of callosal disconnection: the contribution of medial frontal lobe damage. *Cortex: 21,*

135 – 148, 1985.

Goldstein K: *Language and Language Disturbances*. New York: Grune and Stratton, 1948.

Gonzales Rothi LJ, Heilman KM: Acquisition and retention of gestures by apraxic patients. *Brain Cognition: 3,* 426 – 437, 1984.

Gonzales Rothi LJ, Heilman KM, Watson RT: Pantomime comprehension and ideomotor apraxia. *J. Neurol. Neurosurg. Psychiatry: 48,* 207 – 210, 1985.

Goodglass H, Kaplan E: Disturbances of gesture and pantomime in aphasia. *Brain: 86* 703 – 720, 1963.

Goodglass H, Kaplan E: *The Assessment of Aphasia and Related Disorders*. Philadelphia: Lea and Fabiger, 1972.

Gott PS, Saul RE: Agenesis of the corpus callosum: limits of functional compensation. *Neurology: 28,* 1272 – 1279, 1978.

Graff-Radford NR, Welsch K, Godersky J: Callosal apraxia. *Neurology: 37,* 100 – 105, 1987.

Haaland KY, Flaherty D: The different types of limb apraxia errors made by patients with left vs. right hemisphere damage. *Brain Cognition: 3,* 370 – 384, 1984.

Haaland KY, Porch B, Delaney HD: Limb apraxia and motor performance. *Brain Lang.: 9,* 315 – 323, 1980.

Haaxma R, Kuypers HGJM: Intrahemispheric cortical connections and visual guidance of hand and finger movements in the rhesus monkey. *Brain: 98,* 239 – 260, 1975.

Hécaen H: *Introduction à la Neuropsychologie*. Paris: Larousse, 1972.

Hécaen H, Rondot P: Apraxia as a disorder of a system of signs. In Roy EA (Editor), *Neuropsychological Studies of Apraxia and Related Disorders*. Amsterdam: North-Holland, Ch. 4, pp. 75 – 97, 1985.

Heilman KM, Coyle IM, Gonyea EF, Geschwind N: Apraxia and agraphia in a left-hander. *Brain: 96,* 21 – 28, 1973.

Heilman KM, Gonyea EF, Geschwind N: Apraxia and agraphia in a right-hander. *Cortex: 10,* 284 – 288, 1974.

Heilman KM, Rothi LJ, Valenstein E: Two forms of ideomotor apraxia. *Neurology: 32,* 342 – 346, 1982.

Henderson VW: Speech fluency in crossed aphasia. *Brain: 106,* 837 – 857, 1983.

Ingvar DH, Philipson L: Distribution of cerebral blood flow in the dominant hemisphere during motor ideation and motor performance. *Ann. Neurol.: 2,* 230 – 237, 1977.

Itoh M, Sasanuma S: Articulatory movements in apraxia of speech. In Rosenbek J, McNeil M, Aronson A (Editors), *Apraxia of Speech*. San Diego: College Hill, 1984.

Jackson JH: Remark on non-protrusion of the tongue in some cases of aphasia, 1878. In: *Selected Writings,* London: Hodder and Stoughton, Vol. 2, pp. 153 – 154, 1932.

Jason GW: Hemispheric asymmetries in motor functions: II. Ordering does not contribute to left hemisphere specialization. *Neuropsychologia: 21,* 47 – 58, 1983.

Jason GW: Manual sequence learning after focal cortical lesions. *Neuropsychologia: 23,* 483 – 496, 1985.

Johns DF, Darley FL: Phonemic variability and apraxia of speech. *J. Speech Hear. Res.: 13,* 556 – 583, 1970.

Junqué C, Litvan I, Vendrell P: Does reversed laterality really exist in dextral? A case study. *Neuropsychologia: 24,* 241 – 254, 1986.

Kerschensteiner M, Poeck K: Bewegungsanalyse bei buccofacialer Apraxie. *Nervenartz: 45,* 9 – 15, 1974.

Kertesz A, Ferro JM: Lesion size and localization in ideomotor apraxia. *Brain: 107,* 921 – 933, 1984.

Kertesz A, Ferro JM, Shewan CM: Apraxia and aphasia. The functional anatomical basis for their dissociation. *Neurology: 30,* 40 – 47, 1984.

Kimura D: Acquisition of a motor skill after left-hemisphere damage. *Brain: 100,* 527 – 542, 1977.

Kimura D: Neuromotor mechanisms in the evolution of human communication. In Steklis HD, Raleigh MI (Editors), *Neurobiology of Social Communication in Primates*. New York: Academic Press, Ch. 7, pp. 197 – 219, 1979.

Kimura D: Left hemisphere control of oral and brachial movements and their relation to communication. In Broadbent DE, Weiskrantz L (Editors), *The Neuropsychology of Cognitive Function*. London: The Royal Society, Ch. 10, pp. 135 – 149, 1982.

Kimura D: Sex differences in cerebral organization for speech and praxis functions. *Can J. Psychol.: 37,* 19 – 35, 1983.

Kimura D, Archibald Y: Motor functions of the left hemisphere. *Brain: 97,* 337 – 350, 1974.

Kleist K: Korticale (innervatorische) Apraxie. *Jahrb. Psychiatrie Neurol.: 28,* 46 – 112, 1907.

Kleist K: *Gehirnpathologie vornehmlich auf Grund der Kriegersfahrungen*. Leipzig: Barth, 1934.

Kolb B, Milner B: Performance of complex arm and facial movements after focal brain lesions. *Neuropsychologia: 19,* 491 – 503, 1981.

Kolb B, Wishaw IQ: Can the study of praxis in animals aid in the study of apraxia of humans? In Roy EA (Editor), *Neuropsychological Studies of Apraxia and Related Disorders*. Amsterdam: North-Holland, Ch. 9, pp. 203 – 223, 1985.

La Pointe L, Wertz R: Oral movement abilities and articulatory characteristics of brain injured adults. *Percept. Motor Skills: 39,* 39 – 46, 1974.

Lehmkuhl G, Poeck K, Willmes K: Ideomotor apraxia and aphasia: an examination of types and manifestations of apraxic symptoms. *Neuropsychologia: 21,* 199 – 212, 1983.

Liepmann H: Das Krankheitsbild der Apraxie (motorische Asymbolie) auf Grund eines Falles von einseitiger Apraxie. *Monatschr. Psychiatrie Neurol.: 8,* 15 – 44, 102 – 132, 182 – 197, 1900.

Liepmann H: *Drei Aufsatze aus dem Apraxiegebiet*. Berlin: Karger, 1908.

Liepmann H: Apraxie. *Ergeb. gesamt. Med.: 1,* 516 – 543, 1920.

Liepmann H, Mass O: Ein Fall von linseitiger Agraphie und Apraxie bei rechtseitiger Lähmung. *Monatschr. Psychiatrie Neurol.: 10,* 214 – 227, 1907.

Luria AR: *Higher Cortical Functions in Man*. New York: Basic Books, 1966.

Margolin DI: Right hemisphere dominance for praxis and left hemisphere dominance for speech in a left-hander. *Neuropsychologia: 18,* 715 – 719, 1980.

Mateer C: Impairments of nonverbal oral movements after left hemisphere damage: A follow-up analysis of errors. *Brain Lang.: 6,* 334 – 341, 1978.

Mateer C, Kimura D: Impairment of nonverbal oral movements in aphasia. *Brain Lang.: 4,* 262 – 276, 1977.

Miller N: *Dyspraxia and its Management*. London: Croom

Helm, 1986.

Milner B, Kolb B: Performance of complex arm and facial movements after cerebral commissurotomy. *Neuropsychologia: 23,* 791–799, 1985.

Morlaas J: *Contribution a l'Etude de l'Apraxie.* Paris: Legrand, 1928.

Moutier F: *L'Aphasie de Broca.* Paris: Stenheil, 1908.

Nathan PW: Facial apraxia and apraxic dysarthria. *Brain: 70,* 449–478, 1947.

Ojemann G, Mateer C: Human language cortex: localization of memory, syntax and sequential motor-phoneme identification system. *Science: 206,* 1401–1403, 1979.

Perani D, Vallar G, Cappa S, Messa C, Fazio F: Aphasia and neglect after subcortical stroke. A clinical-cerebral perfusion correlation study. *Brain: 110,* 1211–1229, 1987.

Pick A: Zur Psychologie der motorischen Apraxie. *Neurol. Zentralbl.: 21,* 994–1000, 1902.

Pick A: *Studien über motorische Apraxie und ihre nahesthende Erscheinungen: ihre Bedeutung in der Symptonatologie psychopathologischer Symptomenkomplexe.* Leipzig: Deuticke, 1905.

Pieczuro A, Vignolo LA: Studio sperimentale sull'aprassia ideomotoria. *Sist. Nerv.: 19,* 131–143, 1967.

Poeck K, Kerschensteiner M: Ideomotor apraxia following right-sided cerebral lesion in a left-handed subject. *Neuropsychologia: 9,* 359–361, 1971.

Poeck K, Lehmkuhl G: Das Syndrom der ideatorischen Apraxie und seine Localization. *Nervenartz: 51,* 217–225, 1980.

Poeck K, Lehmkuhl G, Willms K: Axial movements in ideomotor apraxia. *J. Neurol. Neurosurg. Psychiatry: 45,* 1125–1129, 1982.

Powers WJ, Raichle ME: Positron emission tomography and its application to the study of cerebrovascular disease in man. *Stroke: 16,* 361–376, 1985.

Roland PE, Skinhoj E, Lassen NA, Larsen B: Different cortical areas in man in organization of voluntary movements in extrapersonal space. *J. Neurophysiol.: 43,* 137–150, 1980.

Roy EA, Square PA: Common considerations in the study of limb, verbal and oral apraxia. In Roy EA (Editor), *Neuropsychological Studies of Apraxia and Related Disorders.* Amsterdam: North-Holland, Ch. 6, pp. 111–161, 1985.

Selnes OA, Rubens AL, Risse GL, Levy RS: Transient aphasia with persistent apraxia. *Arch. Neurol. (Chicago): 39,* 122–126, 1982.

Shankweiler D, Taylor M: Electromyographic studies of articulation in aphasia. *Arch. Phys. Med. Rehabil.: 49,* 1–8, 1968.

Signoret JL, North P: *Les Apraxies Gestuelles.* Paris: Masson, 1979.

Sitting O: *Ueber Apraxie.* Berlin: Karger, 1931.

Sugishita M, Toyokura Y, Yoshioka M, Yamada R: Unilateral agraphia after section of the posterior half of the truncus of the corpus callosum. *Brain Lang.: 9,* 215–225, 1980.

Sweet WH: Seeping intracranial aneurysm simulating neoplasm. *Arch. Neurol. Psychiatry: 45,* 86–104, 1941.

Tognola G, Vignolo LA: Brain lesions associated with oral apraxia in stroke patients: a clinico-neuroradiological investigation with the CT scan. *Neuropsychologia: 18,* 257–281, 1980.

Trescher JH, Ford FR: Colloid cyst of the third ventricle. Report of a case; operative removal with section of corpus callosum. *Arch. Neurol. Psychiatry: 37,* 959–973, 1937.

Valenstein E, Heilman KM: Apractic agraphia with neglect-induced paragraphia. *Arch. Neurol. (Chicago): 36,* 506–508, 1979.

Volpe BT, Sidtis JJ, Holtzman JD, Wilson DH, Gazzaniga MS: Cortical mechanisms involved in praxis: observations following partial and complete section of the corpus callosum in man. *Neurology: 32,* 645–650, 1982.

Watson RT, Heilman KM: Callosal apraxia. *Brain: 100,* 391–403, 1983.

Watson RT, Fleet WS, Gonzales Rothi L, Heilman KM: Apraxia and the supplementary motor area. *Arch. Neurol. (Chicago): 46,* 787–792, 1986.

Zaidel D, Sperry RW: Some long-term motor effects of cerebral commissurotomy in man. *Neuropsychologia: 15,* 193–204, 1977.

Zangwill OL: Le probléme de l'apraxie ideatoire. *Rev. Neurol.: 102,* 595–603, 1960.

Section 4

Disorders of Visual Behavior

editor

A.R. Damasio

CHAPTER 14

Neural mechanisms of visual processing in monkeys

Robert Desimone and Leslie G. Ungerleider

Laboratory of Neuropsychology, National Institute of Mental Health, Bethesda, MD 20892, U.S.A.

Object vision and spatial vision: two cortical systems

Anatomical and physiological studies have revealed at least twenty cortical areas with visual functions in monkeys, and there could possibly be an even greater number of visual areas in man (for reviews, see Weller and Kaas (1981) and Van Essen (1985)). In reviewing the contributions of these multiple areas to vision, we will rely on two recently discovered principles of organization, which help not only in understanding the functions of these areas but also, fortunately, in writing about them. The first principle is that the multiple cortical areas are organized within processing *systems*. According to a model originally proposed by Ungerleider and Mishkin (1982) there are two major processing systems, or 'pathways', both of which originate in the striate cortex. One of the pathways is directed ventrally into the temporal lobe and is crucial for object recognition. The other is directed dorsally into the parietal lobe and is crucial for spatial perception and visuomotor performance.

The original evidence for separate processing systems for pattern vision and spatial vision was the contrasting effects of posterior parietal and inferior temporal cortical lesions in monkeys (see Ungerleider and Mishkin (1982) and Mishkin et al. (1983), for references). Lesions of inferior temporal cortex cause severe deficits in performance of a wide variety of visual discrimination learning tasks but not visuospatial tasks. By contrast, posterior parietal lesions do not affect visual discrimination performance but instead cause severe deficits in visuospatial performance, such as visually guided reaching and judging which of two identical objects is located closer to a visual landmark (Fig. 1). Recent evidence indicates that this pathway also plays a role in oculomotor control and motion perception. Although pattern vision and spatial vision are commonly associated with the geniculostriate and tectofugal systems, respectively, it has been shown in primates that both pattern recognition and visuospatial functions are dependent on striate cortex. Lesions of striate cortex (but not the superior colliculus) severely impair both pattern and spatial vision (Mishkin and Ungerleider, 1982) and nearly eliminate visually driven activity in both the inferior temporal and the posterior parietal cortex

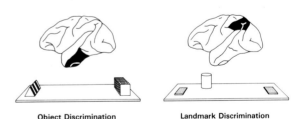

Object Discrimination   **Landmark Discrimination**

Fig. 1. Two behavioral tasks that distinguish between the functions of the inferior temporal and posterior parietal cortex. Inferior temporal lesions (left, in black) cause a severe impairment in learning to discriminate two objects based on their features but do not affect spatial tasks. Posterior parietal lesions (right, in black) cause an impairment in spatial tasks, such as judging which of two identical plaques is located closer to a visual landmark (cylinder), but do not affect object discrimination learning. From Mishkin et al. (1983).

(Rocha-Miranda et al., 1975; M. Goldberg, personal communication). Thus, it appears that the inferior temporal cortex is part of a system that originates in striate cortex and is necessary for recognizing objects, while the posterior parietal cortex is part of a system that also originates in striate cortex but is necessary for appreciating the spatial relationships among objects.

The second simplifying principle of organization is that within each of the two major cortical pathways, visual areas form processing *hierarchies*. Anatomical studies have shown that virtually all connections between successive pairs of areas in the occipitotemporal processing pathway are reciprocal, i.e. projections from one area to the next are reciprocated by projections from the se-

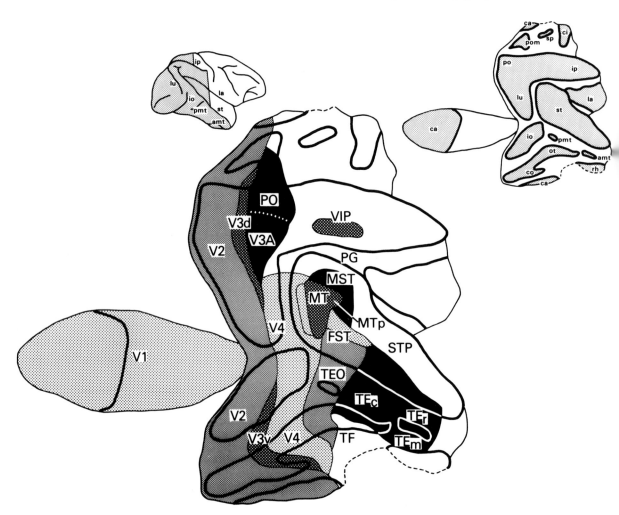

Fig. 2. Cortical visual areas in the macaque, shown on a flattened representation of the cortex. The portion of the cortex flattened is shown in grey on the small lateral view of the hemisphere (upper left). The major sulci are shown in grey on the small flattened map (upper right). It was necessary to 'cut' the map at the border of V1 in order to flatten it (Van Essen and Maunsell, 1980). The large map shows the locations of many of the known visual areas. Areas PG, TF and STP are shown in white without borders, since the boundaries and/or subdivisions of their visual portions are not yet clear. Abbreviations: amt, anterior middle temporal sulcus; ca, calcarine fissure; ci, cingulate sulcus; co, collateral sulcus; io, inferior occipital sulcus; ip, intraparietal sulcus; la, lateral sulcus; lu, lunate sulcus; ot, occipitotemporal sulcus; po, parieto-occipital sulcus; pmt, posterior middle temporal sulcus; pom, medial parieto-occipital sulcus; rh, rhinal fissure; sp, subparietal sulcus; st, superior temporal sulcus. Figure adapted from Ungerleider and Desimone (1986).

cond area back onto the first. Yet, in spite of this reciprocity of anatomical connections, physiological and behavioral studies indicate that much of the processing in this system is actually sequential, or hierarchical (for reviews, see Van Essen and Maunsell, 1983; Ungerleider, 1985; Desimone et al., 1985; Maunsell and Newsome, 1987). The earliest neuronal response latencies found in

physiological recordings increase steadily as one proceeds from the retina towards the inferior temporal cortex. Likewise, the average receptive field size also increases as one moves along the pathway towards the temporal lobe, consistent with the notion that the receptive fields of cells in later areas are built up from those in earlier areas. Finally, in studies in which neurons in area V2 or the inferior

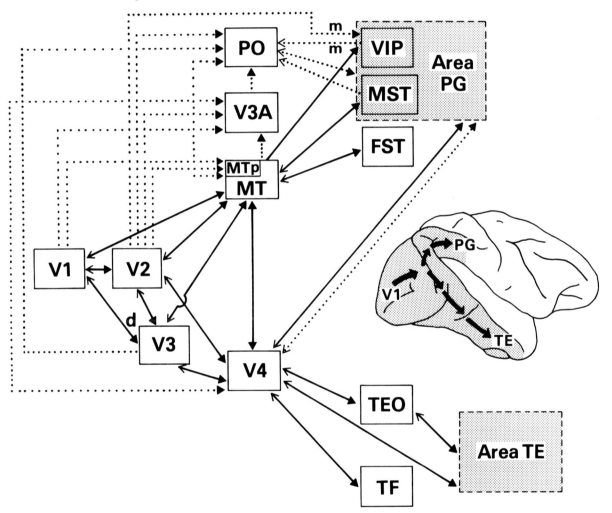

Fig. 3. Schematic diagram of the cortical visual areas in the macaque and their interconnections. Solid lines indicate projections involving all portions of the visual field representation in an area, whereas dotted lines indicate projections limited to the representation of the peripheral visual field. The connections between area V4 and PG are shown in both solid and dotted lines to indicate that the projection is heavier from the peripheral visual field. Heavy arrowheads indicate 'forward' projections, which terminate predominantly in layer 4, light arrowheads indicate 'backward' projections, which tend to avoid granular layer 4 and terminate instead in the supragranular and infragranular layers, and lines with two reciprocal arrowheads indicate intermediate projections (Tigges et al., 1973, 1974; Rockland and Pandya, 1979; Van Essen and Maunsell 1983; Ungerleider, 1985; Ungerleider and Desimone, 1986). 'd' indicates that the projection from V1 and V3 is limited to the dorsal portion of V3. 'm' indicates that the connections of VIP with both V2 and PO are limited to VIP's medial portion. Adapted from Ungerleider and Desimone (1986).

temporal cortex have been studied following removal of striate cortex, the neurons were found to be completely unresponsive (Rocha-Miranda et al., 1975; Schiller and Malpeli, 1977). Conversely, neurons in striate cortex appear to be largely unaffected by removal of area V2 (Sandell and Schiller, 1982) or, indeed, most of the non-visual association cortex (Nakamura et al., 1986). Like the occipitotemporal pathway, the early parts of the occipitoparietal pathway also have a hierarchical organization, although the hierarchy probably gives way to parallel processing among numerous small cortical areas at the later stations of this pathway (Figs. 2 and 3). Interestingly, while the cortical areas of the somatosensory system were originally thought to be organized in parallel, there is recent evidence for hierarchical processing within this system as well (Pons et al., 1987), suggesting that hierarchical processing is a general principle of sensory systems. As we shall see later in this review, some aspects of visual processing are, indeed, massively parallel, but much of this parallel processing takes place within each cortical area rather than across areas.

Thus, it is possible to view much of the neural mechanism for vision, especially object vision, as a 'bottom-up' process, in which the low-level inputs provided by the retina are transformed into a more useful representation through successive stages of processing. In the first part of this chapter we will follow the transformation of visual information that occurs at each successive level of the two cortical pathways, after briefly reviewing processing in the retina and lateral geniculate nucleus. Our focus will be on object recognition, as spatial vision is the topic of the following chapter, by Goldberg and Colby (Ch. 15). Since the early portions of the two pathways have many structures in common, we will consider them together through area V3, after which the pathways, and their treatments in this review, diverge. At the end of the chapter we will consider some 'top-down' aspects of visual processing that may rely on projections from higher-order processing stations back to the lower-order ones and on possible interactions between the two major pathways.

Population codes for objects

If the object recognition system is organized hierarchically, then it is important to understand its ultimate goal. An early idea was that each cell in the highest, or last, visual area would code a particular complex object. A popular example was that even one's grandmother might be represented by a single, highly specialized, cell and this notion came to be known as the 'grandmother cell' theory of recognition. As will become clear in the following sections of this chapter, this theory is no longer tenable. Rather, at all levels of the visual system, complex objects appear to be coded by the activity of populations, or networks, of cells, and the representation of a particular object may be widely distributed throughout one or more visual areas. That said, the goal of the anatomical pathway for object recognition becomes less obvious. The photoreceptors are a population of cells, for example, and they are necessarily capable of coding, by their population response, any conceivable stimulus. Why are subsequent populations needed?

There are a variety of answers to this question, but the most important is probably best illustrated by example. Consider how the visual system might recognize a coffee cup. At the level of the photoreceptors, where a cell codes only the presence of light over a specific spot, a coffee cup will cause a complex pattern of receptor activation which will be highly dependent on the exact position, orientation, size, shape and illumination of the cup. Since a small change in any feature could cause a completely different pattern of photoreceptors to become active, a great deal of neural computation would be required to recognize the cup from the receptor activity. Now consider a population of cells at a higher level of the visual system, in which instead of simply coding the presence of light at specific locations, cells code features more directly related to the overall properties of objects, such as object length, width, color, three-dimensional curvature, texture and volume, independent of the exact position or illumination. Furthermore, imagine that variations in the shape of an object cause the pattern of activation within the high-level population to vary in predictable and straightforward ways. Even though many different objects will activate a given cell in this high-level population (i.e. the cells are not grandmother cells), and even though the number of cells in the high-level population required to code a particular object might even be comparable to the number of activated receptors (i.e. the population size will still be large), the computation required to recognize a cup based on the activity of the high-level population would be far less than would be required from the receptors.

If one accepts this notion of distributed representations, or population coding, then the ultimate goal of the recognition system would seem to be to construct a representation of objects in which cells code features related to invariant and/or global object properties rather than to local patterns of light and dark on the retina. One might say that the visual system transforms information that is *implicit* in the activity of low-level populations into information that is *explicit* in the activity of higher-level populations. Some of the actual transformations performed at the different levels will be described in this review.

Population codes for features

One can attempt to push the notion of distributed representations even further and ask whether the representation not only of objects but even of individual object features is distributed across populations of cells. In the early days of visual neurophysiology, it was common to speak of feature 'detectors', such as bar and edge detectors, which were presumably specialized to detect a single feature, sometimes termed the 'trigger feature'. Later, it was recognized that cells at all levels of the visual system do not respond in an all-or-none fashion to one specific stimulus, but rather give graded, or tuned, responses as a stimulus is varied in any of a number of ways.

Visual cells therefore seem more like multidimensional 'filters' rather than feature 'detectors'. For the visual system to extract a specific piece of information about a feature such as length or orientation would require a comparison of the outputs of many cells.

A simple example of a population code based on tuned filters is provided by the cones. Each of the three cone classes is, in a sense, a broadly tuned spectral filter, whose output is a function of stimulus intensity and wavelength. A specific response from just a single cone class specifies virtually no information about wavelength, since the response could have resulted from a virtually unlimited number of combinations of different wavelengths and intensities. Yet, because the three classes of cones have different spectral sensitivities which are only partially overlapping, a given spectral stimulus will cause a unique trio of responses from the cone population, and the visual system can thereby extract many thousands of different shades of color and brightness.

Whereas the cones are influenced by only two stimulus variables, wavelength and intensity, the number of variables that influences cells at higher levels of the visual system may be much larger. Some cells in the striate cortex, for example, are reported to be sensitive to stimulus orientation, color, contrast, disparity, spatial frequency and size. Thus, just as a comparison of the activity of opposing cones is necessary to extract stimulus wavelength independent of intensity, a comparison of the responses of cells sensitive to different orientations and wavelengths might be required to extract stimulus wavelength independent of its orientation. This is a controversial issue, however, and many believe that stimulus qualities such as color and form are eventually coded by separate populations of cells. In the course of this review, we will consider the possible separation of stimulus qualities at the different levels of the visual system.

Retina and lateral geniculate nucleus

Since it is only through the retinal ganglion cells

that the retina sends information to the rest of the brain, we shall start our review with these cells. The description of the retinal ganglion cells will also apply to cells in the lateral geniculate nucleus (LGN), as the response properties of cells there appear to be very similar to those of the ganglion cells. These two groups of cells represent an early stage in the transformation from the raw intensity values coded by the photoreceptors into a representation based on object features. When stimulated with achromatic stimuli, most retinal ganglion and LGN cells respond much better to regions of illumination *change*, i.e. contrast, than to regions of uniform illumination (for reviews, see Zrenner (1983) and De Monasterio (1981)). Thus, neuronal activity is enhanced at the locations of object features such as surface shadings, textures, borders, scratches, etc.

The enhancement of neuronal responses at regions of local contrast results from the structure of retinal ganglion and LGN receptive fields, which are concentrically organized. The receptive fields of the majority of cells have either excitatory inputs to the center and inhibitory inputs to the surround or vice versa, such that light increments or decrements are excitatory in the field center or surround but not in both.

The above description of retinal and LGN activity applies only to stimulation by achromatic contrast. When stimulated with chromatic contrast, some cells, as we shall see, provide information relevant to color as well as form.

Color opponency

There are two main classes of retinal ganglion cells which appear to have very different roles in color vision. One class, which comprises the majority of cells, has small cell bodies and projects to the parvocellular layers of the LGN. Although these cells have been given a variety of different names in the literature, for simplicity we will term both the small ganglion cells and the parvocellular LGN cells 'P' cells (Shapley and Perry, 1986; Schein and De Monasterio, 1987). A second class of retinal ganglion cells has large cell bodies and projects to

the magnocellular layers of the LGN. For simplicity, we will term these cells 'M' cells.

When P cells are stimulated by chromatic stimuli that cover both the center and surround of the receptive field, they exhibit very different spectral behavior from that of individual cones (for reviews, see Zrenner (1983) and De Monasterio (1981, 1984)). This difference is due to the fact that the cone inputs to the center and surround of the P-cell receptive field are from different cone classes and are of opposite synaptic sign. A red/green, or R + G − , cell, for example, receives excitatory inputs from red cones to the center and inhibitory inputs from green cones to the surround (Fig. 4). Other common types include R − G + , G − R + , G + R − and B + (RG) − . When both the center and surround of a P-cell receptive field are stimulated by the same colored stimulus,

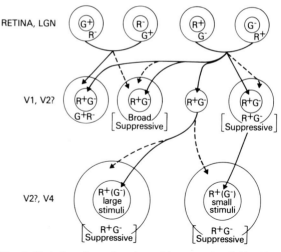

Fig. 4. Varieties of wavelength-sensitive receptive fields. Sizes are not drawn to scale. Arrows suggest how receptive fields at higher levels of the visual system might be built up from those at lower levels. Solid lines indicate excitatory connections, and dashed lines indicate suppressive connections. Cells with receptive fields shown in the middle and bottom rows would receive inputs from many cells with overlapping receptive fields in the prior row. The receptive fields shown in the middle row for V1 and V2 are only suggestive, as there is not yet common agreement on receptive field structure in these areas. The receptive fields shown in the bottom row for V2 and V4 indicate a possible receptive field structure for cells that respond best to colored stimuli that fill the field center (left) and for cells that respond best to small stimuli anywhere within a large excitatory center (right).

the response of the cell will reflect the *difference* between the spectral sensitivities of two or more cone types. Thus, the spectral sensitivity of the P cells is much narrower than that of any individual cone and their peak sensitivities are displaced from those of the cones.

In contrast to the P cell inputs, the inputs to the M cells arise from the *sum* of at least two cone types (the red and green cones, and possibly the blue cones), and the cone inputs are the same for both the center and the surround of the receptive field. Thus, the M cells have a spectral sensitivity even broader than that of the cones and are therefore nearly incapable of providing information about wavelength. In compensation, the M cells have stronger responses to low stimulus contrast (less than 10%) than do P cells (Shapley et al., 1981; Hicks et al., 1983; Derrington and Lennie, 1984; Kaplan and Shapley, 1986) and have a higher conduction velocity (Gouras, 1969; Schiller and Malpeli, 1977).

Although it is tempting to equate the P cells and M cells with the chromatic and achromatic mechanisms underlying the opponent color theory of color perception, these cells probably represent too early a stage of visual processing to serve that purpose. Opponent color theory, first put forth by Hering (1878), proposes that the three spectral signals arising from the cones yield six basic sensations occurring in two chromatic and one achromatic opponent pairs: red/green, blue/yellow and black/white. Whereas there is a superficial similarity between the R/G and B/Y P cells, on the one hand, and the red/green and blue/yellow mechanisms, on the other, the strong response of P cells to achromatic stimuli indicates that the P cells perform 'double duty' and contribute to the black/white as well as the color mechanism. In particular, the P cells' small receptive fields, high spatial frequency selectivity and large numbers suggest that they are responsible for the fine acuity of achromatic vision. M cells also contribute to the achromatic mechanism, especially at low contrast. As we shall see in the next section, M cells may also play a unique role in motion perception.

Striate cortex

While the neural representation of form and color in the LGN is apparently little different from that in the retina, a major transformation takes place in striate cortex, or V1. The magnitude of V1's contribution can be guessed at from the number of V1 cells: there are upwards of 250 million cells in striate cortex of one hemisphere compared to only 1 – 1.5 million cells in the LGN (Connolly and Van Essen, 1984). Given the large number of different cell types and their complex horizontal and vertical arrangement, it will be possible in this short review to present only a synopsis, rather than a comprehensive analysis, of color and form processing.

The analysis of form

Although properties of cells in layer 4C of striate cortex are reported to be very similar to those of cells in the LGN, from which they receive direct inputs, the properties of many of the cells both above and below layer 4C differ from those of the LGN in a number of striking ways, including the presence of binocular inputs, sensitivity to binocular disparity, and orientation specificity.

In their classic paper on the properties of cells in striate cortex of the cat, Hubel and Wiesel (1962) classified orientation selective cells into two groups, which they termed 'simple' and 'complex'. The receptive fields of the simple cells had elongated, mutually antagonistic excitatory and inhibitory subregions, the shapes of which could be used to predict the response to any arbitrary moving or stationary stimulus. The receptive fields of complex cells were often somewhat larger and did not appear to have subregions. Rather, antagonistic interactions among light and dark stimuli could normally occur within an apparently uniform excitatory region, and, thus, the responses to an arbitrary stimulus could not be predicted from a map of the receptive field.

What is the functional significance of simple and complex cells? According to the original Hubel and Wiesel model, simple cells functioned as detectors for lines and edges of particular orientation and location, and complex cells generalized the detection of lines and edges over a slightly larger retinal area. It was proposed that complex cells transmitted this information to a subsequent stage of visual processing for the eventual construction of a line and edge representation of objects. Later, it was demonstrated that simple and complex cells responded not only to lines and edges but also to stimuli such as sinusoidal gratings, which have a very different sort of luminance profile. The finding that V1 cells respond to gratings within their receptive fields, coupled with the realization that simple cells approximate a linear system, led to the hypothesis that the visual system computes the Fourier transform of objects rather than representing them by lines and edges (for reviews, see DeValois and DeValois (1980), Pollen and Ronner (1983), Shapley and Lennie (1985), and Kulikowski and Kranda (1986)). This hypothesis required that simple cells ultimately supply cells at a later stage of visual processing which extract the sinusoidal components of the entire retinal image. However, since cells with all the properties required of the global Fourier transform were never found in any visual area, the Fourier hypothesis in its original form was eventually abandoned.

Most recently it has become generally accepted that V1 neurons function as general-purpose spatial filters that transform the visual image in a number of useful ways. Whether the filtering properties are best described in spatial terms, such as responses to light or dark within excitatory and inhibitory regions of the receptive field, or in frequency terms is often a matter of the experimenter's choice. In either case, the goal is to understand how cells make explicit the information that is coded implicitly by the cells that supply their inputs. Stimulus orientation, for example, is much more directly coded by V1 neurons than LGN cells, and recent evidence suggests that simple cells may provide useful information about surface shading, three-dimensional surface curvature and broad contours, whereas complex cells may provide the most useful information about fine surface textures (Hammond and Mackay, 1977;

Zucker, 1985; Dobbins et al., 1987; Lehky and Sejnowski, 1988). This distinction between simple and complex cells may also be carried forward into other visual areas, since cells with somewhat similar properties have been described in areas V2 and V4 of extrastriate cortex (Foster et al., 1985; Desimone and Schein, 1987). Other sorts of information provided by specialized cell types in striate cortex will become clearer as we understand more about the later stages of the object recognition system.

The analysis of color

The parvocellular layers of the LGN send projections primarily into layer $4C\beta$ of striate cortex, and cells in this layer project, in turn, to cells in the supragranular and infragranular layers (Wiesel and Hubel, 1966; Hubel and Wiesel, 1972; Lund and Boothe, 1975). In terms of basic spectral sensitivity, the spectral properties of most color-sensitive V1 cells are very similar to those of P cells. Like P cells, the action spectra of color-sensitive cells in striate cortex appear to fall largely within four classes which correspond, at least qualitatively, to the four primary colors of opponent color theory, namely, red, green, blue and yellow (De Monasterio and Schein, 1982; Vautin and Dow, 1985). Thus, as in the retina and LGN, a specific color is not coded in V1 by the response of a specific cell devoted to detect that color, but rather by the graded responses of many cells among the different color classes.

While their basic spectral sensitivity is similar to that of P cells, the receptive field properties of most V1 cells are more varied and complex than those of P cells (Dow, 1974; Poggio et al., 1975; Michael, 1978a – c, 1979; Livingstone and Hubel, 1984; Thorell et al., 1984). One difference is that whereas color opponency in the LGN arises only as a result of the opposed cone inputs to the center and surrounds of the receptive fields, color opponency in V1 often occurs within homogeneous receptive fields. For example, an R + G − color-opponent V1 cell will commonly show excitation to red stimuli and inhibition to green stimuli at the same locations throughout the receptive field. This homogeneity may arise as a result of the V1 cell simply summing the outputs of many R + G − (and possibly G − R +) P cells with partially overlapping receptive fields (Fig. 4). One consequence of a uniform field is that the spectral sensitivity of many V1 cells is invariant with regard to stimulus position, unlike the case for P cells, whose spectral sensitivity depends on whether the stimulus is located in the field center, in the surround, or in both. In addition, the overlapping inputs derived ultimately from opposing cones may explain why some striate color cells are reported to give weaker responses to white stimuli than do P cells. These particular V1 cells may provide a basis for the pure chromatic mechanisms of opponent color theory.

A second major difference between the LGN and V1 is that whereas P cells respond well and are best tuned to broad or full-field color stimuli, the same is not true of a class of cells in V1 termed 'double color opponent', or DCO (Poggio et al., 1975; Michael, 1978a,b, 1979; Livingstone and Hubel, 1984). DCO cells respond well to a stimulus of a particular color confined to the center of the receptive field but, unlike P cells, respond poorly if the stimulus extends into the surround. The receptive field organization that accounts for this behavior is still unknown (see Fig. 4). In the goldfish retina, where DCO cells were first described, the surrounds of these cells receive opponent inputs that are *opposite* to those of the excitatory field (Daw, 1973). A typical goldfish DCO cell, for example, might have a homogeneous R + G − field center and a homogeneous R − G + surround. In V1, it is not yet clear whether the surrounds of DCO cells give explicit opponent responses like those in the goldfish (Michael, 1978a,b, 1979; Livingstone and Hubel, 1984), whether the surrounds simply provide antagonism when the field centers are also stimulated, but are otherwise silent (Tso et al., 1986; Hubel and Livingstone, 1987), or whether both types of organization are present. Furthermore, it is possible that the surrounds are not even color-specific, but have broad-band inhibitory properties (Tso et al., 1986). Regardless of

the final answer, the fact that DCO cells respond better to the edges of colored stimuli than to their interior may account for the fact that the perceived color of a surface seems to be determined largely by the color at its boundary. In the absence of surface information to the contrary, the visual system appears to use the surface boundary color to 'fill-in' the interior perceptually, much the way that patterns extending across a scotoma are perceptually filled in.

The M-cell pathway and the analysis of motion
Whereas the projections of the parvocellular layers of the LGN terminate in layer 4Cβ of striate cortex, the projections of the magnocellular layers terminate in layer 4Cα (Hubel and Wiesel, 1972; Lund and Boothe, 1975). Layer 4Cα cells, in turn, send major projections to cells in the layer just above them, layer 4B (Lund, 1973; Lund and Boothe, 1975; Fitzpatrick et al., 1985), and cells in 4B project to layers 2, 3 and 6 (Blasdel et al., 1985). As would be expected from the source of their inputs in the magnocellular LGN, cells in both 4Cα and 4B show broad-band spectral properties and sensitivity to low contrast (Dow, 1974; Livingstone and Hubel, 1984; Hawkin and Parker, 1984). In striking contrast to cells in the LGN, however, cells in layer 4B respond selectively according to the direction of stimulus motion (Dow, 1974; Livingstone and Hubel, 1984). Because cells in layer 4B are also known to project to areas MT and dorsal V3 in extrastriate cortex, each of which contains many directionally selective cells (Zeki, 1974; Felleman and Van Essen, 1987), a major function of this M-cell pathway may be to supply information to a cortical system concerned with motion analysis.

A functional architecture for color analysis?
According to the original model proposed by Hubel and Wiesel (1974), stimulus orientation was processed by cells located outside layer 4C and was systematically represented in a series of orientation columns which overlapped with a separate system of ocular dominance columns. Not surprisingly,

this first model was somewhat too simplistic and has been continually revised by both Hubel and Wiesel and others. One architectural feature that has recently been discovered is an array of cortical zones rich in the metabolic enzyme cytochrome oxidase (Wong-Riley, 1979; Hendrickson et al., 1981; Horton and Hubel, 1981; Hendrickson, 1985). These ellipsoid zones, commonly termed 'blobs', are regularly spaced along the centers of the ocular dominance columns within the infragranular and supragranular layers but are not present in layer 4C. The inputs to the blobs are not yet known, but most likely they arise from cells in layer $4C\beta$ and from the interlaminar cells of the LGN (Fitzpatrick et al., 1983). It is also likely that the blobs receive additional information indirectly from the magnocellular layers of the LGN via layer 4B (see Livingstone and Hubel, 1987b). Hubel and Livingstone (1987) have reported that cells in the blobs are unoriented and that most are double color opponent, whereas most supra- and infragranular layer cells outside the blobs (in the interblob regions) are oriented and not selective for color. This apparent segregation of properties has led these investigators to suggest that the blobs constitute a system for the analysis of color whereas the interblob regions constitute a system for the analysis of form and/or orientation. One problem with this notion of strict segregation of systems for orientation and color is that other investigators have found numerous oriented, color-selective cells outside the blobs (Michael, 1978b,c, 1979; Thorell et al., 1984; Dow and Vautin, 1987; Tso et al., 1986). Furthermore, as Allman (personal communication) has noted, the owl monkey has a well-developed blob system but little or no color vision.

Area V2

Cells in V2 have been far less extensively studied than cells in V1; nevertheless, the evidence so far indicates that cells in V2 have many properties similar to those of cells in V1, including sensitivity to bar length, orientation, color, direction of mo-

tion, and the spatial frequency of sinusoidal gratings, and that V2 even contains cells with simple and complex receptive field properties (Baizer et al., 1977; Kruger and Gouras, 1980; Foster et al., 1985; DeYoe and Van Essen, 1985; Shipp and Zeki, 1985; Hubel and Livingstone, 1987). Like cells in V1, with their multidimensional filtering properties, cells in V2 do not seem to 'detect' specific stimuli, but rather respond in a tuned fashion along several different stimulus dimensions. Nonetheless, two newly discovered properties of cells in V2 suggest ways in which object features are coded more explicitly in this area than in V1. The first is the ability of V2 but not V1 cells to respond to illusory contours (von der Heydt et al., 1984). Illusory here refers to contours that are physically broken or discontinuous, but which are 'filled-in' and thus perceived to be continuous (although not perceptually identical to physically continuous contours). Cells in V2 of awake monkeys have been shown to respond to illusory contours even when the physical pattern that generates the illusory contour does not include the receptive field. This is the best evidence yet that V2 cells actually 'extract' contours and provide an explicit or abstract representation of them. By contrast, individual cells in V1 do not seem to treat contours per se differently from other types of luminance change (although the presence of a contour must ultimately be coded by the relative activity of many different types of striate cells). The second newly discovered neuronal property of V2 is evidenced by a type of cell termed a 'spot' cell by Baizer et al. (1977) and an 'unoriented complex' cell by Hubel and Livingstone (1987). These cells are commonly tuned to the color and size of small spots within a relatively large receptive field. Thus, the cells combine color selectivity with a type of primitive shape selectivity, and, unlike individual cells in V1, maintain this selectivity over relatively large shifts in stimulus position. As we shall see in a later section, this type of neuronal property seems to be further elaborated in area V4 and the inferior temporal cortex.

Functional architecture in V2

It has recently been found that, when viewed in tangential section through the supragranular or infragranular layers, cytochrome oxidase-rich cortex in V2 appears as an alternating series of thin and thick 'stripes' separated by interstripe, or palestripe, regions of low cytochrome oxidase concentration (Livingstone and Hubel, 1982, 1984; Tootell et al., 1983). These three anatomical zones differ strikingly in their inputs and/or outputs. The thin stripes receive inputs from cells in the blobs of V1 and project to area V4, the interstripes receive inputs from the interblob regions of V1 and also project to area V4, and the thick stripes receive inputs from cells in layer 4B of V1 and project to area MT (Livingstone and Hubel, 1984, 1987a; DeYoe and Van Essen, 1985; Shipp and Zeki, 1985).

The three anatomical subregions of V2 also differ in their neuronal properties, although the extent of this difference is not yet clear. Hubel and Livingstone (1987) have reported a nearly complete segregation of neuronal properties within the three zones: unoriented cells selective for color are located in the thin stripes; cells selective for orientation, disparity and (to a lesser extent) direction of motion are located in the thick stripes; and cells selective for length and orientation are located in the interstripes. By contrast, although DeYoe and Van Essen (1985) report a tendency towards the sort of segregation reported by Hubel and Livingstone (1987), the former investigators found a substantial number of cells sensitive to each of the different stimulus qualities in each of the anatomical subdivisions. The most pronounced specialization they found was for direction of motion, which was largely a property of cells in the thick stripes and of cells projecting to MT. The difference between the results of the two studies is probably explained by differing styles of experimentation. Hubel and Livingstone attempted to place cells in a few categories such as 'color cell' or 'disparity cell' based on a cluster of neuronal properties judged qualitatively, whereas DeYoe and Van Essen measured the sensitivity of cells to different

stimulus dimensions independently of one another, and then asked how the quantitative measures related to the underlying anatomy. From the two studies taken together, it appears that a typical cell in one anatomical zone differs qualitatively from a typical cell in another, but that individual stimulus properties may not be represented exclusively in any one zone.

Relationship of P and M systems to the occipitotemporal and occipitoparietal pathways

Although there may well be incomplete segregation of the stimulus properties processed within the separate anatomical subregions of V2, the relative differences in neuronal properties among the subregions as well as their differing connections with the occipitotemporal and occipitoparietal pathways suggest corresponding differences in the types of information processed within these two systems. As delineated above, an anatomical system for motion analysis appears to form a major (but not the sole) component of the occipitoparietal pathway. This motion system derives largely from the M cells of the LGN and further involves layer 4B of V1, the thick stripes of V2, areas V3 and MT, and a series of additional visual areas within the superior temporal sulcus. Conversely, an anatomical system specialized for form and color is a major component of the occipitotemporal pathway. This latter system derives primarily from the P cells of the LGN and further involves the blob and interblob regions of V1, the thin and interstripe regions of V2, and area V4 and the inferior temporal cortex (area TE). These associations of the occipitoparietal pathway with the M-cell system, on the one hand, and the occipitotemporal pathway with the P-cell system, on the other hand (Livingstone and Hubel, 1987b), are probably not exclusive, however, as illustrated in Fig. 5. For example, the occipitotemporal system has access to information derived from M cells over a number of routes, including connections between cells in layer 4B and cells in layers 2 and 3 of V1, and projections from both V3 and MT to V4. Likewise, the occipitoparietal pathway probably has access to information derived from P cells via projections from area V4 both to MT and to regions within the posterior parietal cortex (area PG). What is the function of these interconnections between the two pathways? One possibility is that the P-cell input into the occipitoparietal pathway contributes to spatial functions other than motion perception, and that the M-cell input into the occipitotemporal pathway contributes to form perception at low contrast. In addition, the interconnections may allow for form and color to influence the processing of motion and for motion to influence the processing of form and color perception. For example, forms can be perceived in dynamic random dot displays in which the surface boundaries are defined only on the basis of differences in motion. This coding of shape from motion may very well rely on a two-stage process, in which the moving surface boundaries are first extracted by neurons within the occipitoparietal pathway, and the shape is then coded by neurons within the occipitotemporal pathway.

Recently, Livingstone and Hubel (1987b) have

proposed an alternative model of anatomical specialization, in which the M-cell system plays a more critical role in vision than in the scheme outlined above. Based on both physiological and psychophysical evidence, Livingstone and Hubel have proposed that the M-cell system alone can support virtually all aspects of vision except for color, and that it provides the exclusive basis not only for motion perception, but also for stereopsis, perception of the three-dimensionality of objects based on perspective and shading, and most of the Gestalt phenomena of 'linking operations'. According to this model, the only contributions of the P-cell system to perception are color and a two-fold increase in the resolution of simple achromatic patterns. If this notion is correct, then either the occipitoparietal pathway plays a far more important role in object vision than previously thought, or the M-cell system makes a larger contribution to the occipitotemporal pathway than the anatomy so far suggests.

The major physiological evidence that the M-cell system provides an exclusive basis for a specific perceptual capacity other than motion perception is the report of Hubel and Livingstone (1987) that disparity-sensitive cells in V2 are confined to the thick stripes. However, as described in the previous section, this finding is in disagreement with the results of DeYoe and Van Essen (1985) in V2, and it also conflicts with the results of Poggio and his colleagues (Poggio and Fisher, 1977; Poggio et al., 1985), who find that the large majority of cells in V1 and V2 are disparity-sensitive. The reason for this apparent discrepancy is not yet clear. Much of the psychophysical evidence for the Livingstone and Hubel model derives from studies utilizing isoluminant color images, i.e., images in which borders are formed solely on the basis of color rather than luminance differences. Such images are reported by some investigators to stimulate P cells in the LGN but not M cells (Kruger, 1979; Hicks et al., 1983; but see Schiller and Colby, 1983). It has been known for some time that many common perceptual phenomena, such as motion perception, are altered or absent

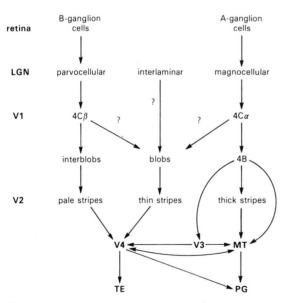

Fig. 5. The P-cell (left) and M-cell (right) streams. Modified from Livingstone and Hubel (1987b).

altogether when a subject views an isoluminant display. For example, if a red and green drifting grating is made isoluminant, the perceived speed of the grating is far less than the actual speed, and the grating may seem to stop moving entirely (Cavanagh et al., 1984; Livingstone and Hubel, 1987b). This effect of isoluminance on motion perception is consistent with a large body of psychophysical and physiological evidence that the M-cell system is the main contributor to the neural mechanism for motion analysis. More surprising effects of isoluminance on perception are the loss of depth perception in isoluminant random dot stereograms, the loss of the perception of three-dimensionality in isoluminant shaded surfaces, the loss of illusory contours and certain figure/ground phenomena in isoluminant displays, and the loss of many perceptual illusions, such as the Muller-Lyer illusion, that depend on perspective cues (see Livingstone and Hubel (1987b), for references). Most of these perceptual losses make sense from an evolutionary point of view, in that pure spectral contrast is much rarer in the environment than luminance contrast. Consequently, the visual system may not have evolved equivalent mechanisms for utilizing spectral and luminance contrast. Shadows, for example, arise solely from luminance contrast, almost by definition, and it is therefore not too surprising that the perception of surface shading is lost in isoluminant displays. The question, however, is whether such perceptual losses at isoluminance reflect only the loss of M-cell responses, or whether they also reflect the loss of cortical achromatic mechanisms deriving from P cells. Additional physiological studies of cortical neurons are necessary to answer this important question.

Area V3

V3 occupies a narrow strip of cortex adjacent to V2 (Zeki, 1969). Because the portion of V3 lying on the ventral aspect of the hemisphere (representing the upper visual field) has inputs and neuronal properties somewhat different from those of the portion lying on the dorsal aspect (representing the lower visual field), some consider the upper field representation to be a separate visual area, termed VP (Burkhalter et al., 1986). We prefer to consider the two representations to be part of the same area, and we use the terms V3d and V3v to distinguish between the dorsal and ventral parts of V3, respectively.

V3d receives inputs from both layer 4B of V1 (Felleman and Van Essen, 1984; Ungerleider, unpublished data) and from V2, preferentially from its thick stripe portion (Felleman et al., 1988), suggesting that it belongs largely to the M-cell system. V3v also receives inputs from V2, but it is not yet known from which portions. Since V3 projects to V4 as well as MT, V3 may provide a route for information derived from M cells to enter the occipitotemporal pathway. Less is known about neuronal properties in V3, compared to those of either V1 or V2, but it seems clear that V3 contains at least come cells selective for direction of motion, orientation, color, and/or disparity (Zeki, 1978; Baizer, 1982; Burkhalter and Van Essen, 1986; Felleman and Van Essen, 1987).

The pathway for object vision

Area V4

One of the major projection fields of V2 is area V4 (Zeki, 1971; Ungerleider et al., 1983; Felleman and Van Essen, 1983; Fenstemacher et al., 1984). V4 was first described by Zeki (1971), who defined it as a visual area on the dorsal aspect of the cerebral hemisphere, occupying the prelunate gyrus and portions of the adjacent banks of the lunate and superior temporal sulci (also see Van Essen and Zeki, 1978). Later work indicated that V4 had a coarse visuotopic organization, and that the portion on the prelunate convexity constituted only the representation of the lower visual field (Ungerleider et al., 1983; Ungerleider, 1985; Gattass et al., 1988). The upper field representation of V4 lies on the ventral aspect of the hemisphere, across from the upper field representations of V2 and V3. Some aspects of visual topography in V4 suggest that V4 contains one or more subdivisions, including a region termed V4t by Ungerleider and Desimone (1986), and regions termed AL and PM by Maguire and Baizer (1984). There is also recent anatomical evidence that V4 contains numerous small subunits which are not distinguishable on the basis of cytochrome oxidase staining but which have differential connections with the stripe and interstripe regions of V2 (DeYoe et al., 1988).

V4 has probably been the subject of more neurophysiological studies, and more controversy, than any area in extrastriate cortex. Zeki originally proposed that V4 was specialized almost exclusively for the analysis of color (1973, 1978, 1980, 1983a – c). This apparent specialization for color in V4, in conjunction with Zeki's finding of motion specialization in area MT (1974), was the primary support for a 'division of labor' theory of extrastriate cortex, according to which each visual area analysed a separate stimulus attribute in parallel with one another. More recently, however, both the specific notion of color specialization in V4 and the general notion of a division of labor among cortical areas based on simple features have been challenged by studies that have found that V4 contains many cells sensitive to stimulus form, many cells sensitive to wavelength, and many cells sensitive to both (Desimone et al., 1985; Tanaka, M., et al., 1986; Desimone and Schein, 1987). Like V1 and V2, V4 seems to be as much a 'form' area as a 'color' area. Thus, notwithstanding the gross segregation of function between the occipitotemporal and occipitoparietal pathways, much of the segregation of elemental features *within* the occipitotemporal pathway probably occurs at the level of columns, stripes and laminae within each area rather than at the level of entire areas.

The analysis of stimulus form   So far, all the stimulus qualities related to form that are coded by cells in V1 and V2 appear to be coded by cells in V4, including orientation, length, width, spatial frequency and (for a few cells) direction of motion (Desimone et al., 1985; Tanaka, M., et al., 1986; Desimone and Schein, 1987). As in V2, there are

even cells in V4 with properties analogous to those of simple and complex cells. Furthermore, although V4 cells have not been specifically tested for responses to illusory contours, some V4 cells respond only to stimuli with sharp edges, such as bars and square-wave gratings, suggesting that contours are explicitly represented in V4, as they are in V2.

Although receptive fields in V4 are often 20 – 100 times larger in area than fields in V1, the ability of cells in V4 to distinguish very fine features may also be comparable to that of cells in V1 and V2. For example, some cells in V4 give a peak response to bars only 0.05° in width, or to gratings with a spatial period of only 0.125° (the narrowest period that has been tested), which is about the receptive field width of many cells in the foveal representation of V1 (Desimone and Schein, 1987).

As with cells in V1 and V2, individual cells in V4 respond in a multidimensional fashion to stimuli, but continue the trend observed in V2 of coding invariant object features more explicitly than is the case in V1. First, many cells in V4 are tuned to both the length and the width of stimuli within a large receptive field (Fig. 6), and the tuning of some cells for shape is maintained over shifts in stimulus position. Many of these cells are also selective for the color of the stimulus, and thus seem to combine some degree of shape and color selectivity (Fig. 4). These shape-selective V4 cells resemble the 'spot cells' and 'unoriented complex' cells reported in V2, in that they prefer stimuli much smaller than their excitatory receptive fields, but the selectivity of the V4 cells for shape is not confined to spots. This generalization of response over retinal position found in V4, which is continued even more dramatically in the inferior temporal cortex (see below), may contribute to the perceptual equivalence of objects over retinal translation. By contrast, the specificity of individual V1 cells for width is poor, and no V1 cells have been reported to show invariance of length and width tuning over shifts in stimulus position (Schiller et al., 1976a,b; Albrecht et al., 1980).

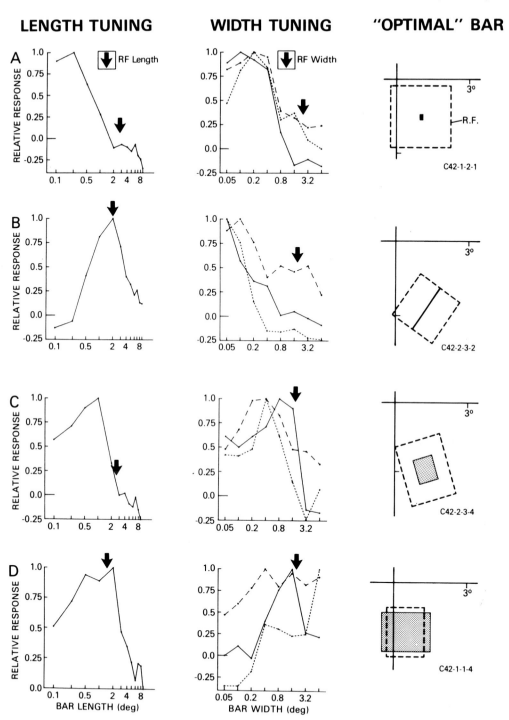

LENGTH TUNING   **WIDTH TUNING**   **"OPTIMAL" BAR**

Fig. 6. Examples of selectivity for stimulus length and width in area V4. Length and width selectivity appeared to vary independently, with different cells preferring bars of different 'shapes'. The length tuning curves were derived from the average firing rate to moving bars. The width tuning curves shown with dotted lines or dashed lines are derived from the average or peak response, respectively, to moving bars, and the curves shown with solid lines are derived from the average response to flashed bars. The heavy arrows on the length and width tuning curves indicate the length and width, respectively, of the receptive field. The cell shown in A responded selectively to black bars, the cells in B and C to green bars, and the cell in D to white bars. From Desimone and Schein (1987).

A second way individual cells in V4 may code form more explicitly than individual cells in V1 is also related to receptive field size. Because of their larger receptive fields, cells in V4 can not only generalize their response over a larger retinal area, but can code larger stimulus features than individual cells in V1. Although V1 cells will respond to the edges of large stimuli, an individual V1 cell stimulated by the edge of a bar probably cannot distinguish between an edge that belongs to a bar, say, 2 – 3° in width and an edge that belongs to a bar that is much wider, whereas this ability is common among V4 cells. In this respect, cells in V4 of the macaque resemble cells in area DL of the owl monkey (Petersen et al., 1980), a likely homology of V4.

A third, and possibly most important, receptive field difference between cells in V4 and V1 is the existence of large silent suppressive zones surrounding the excitatory receptive fields of cells in V4 (Desimone et al., 1985; Desimone and Schein, 1987). These zones are termed 'silent' because stimulation of the zones does not normally cause any change from the cell's baseline activity but can have a powerful effect on the response to a receptive field stimulus. Results from preliminary studies (Desimone et al., 1985) in which the receptive field and surround stimuli have been varied independently indicate that the stimulus-selective properties of the excitatory receptive field and the suppressive surround are often matched, e.g. the orientation or spatial frequency of the surround stimulus that elicits maximal suppression is the same that elicits maximal excitation inside the receptive field (Fig. 7). As a consequence, many V4 cells respond maximally to a stimulus only if it stands out from its background on the basis of a difference in form. This sensitivity to receptive field/surround differences may be useful for figure/ground separation, or 'breaking camouflage', an essential element of form vision.

The analysis of color   The proportion of color-selective cells reported in V4 has varied widely across studies (e.g. Zeki, 1978; Van Essen and

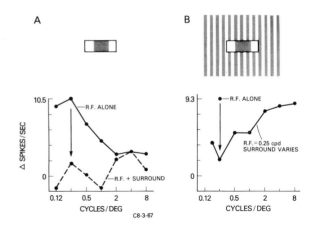

Fig. 7. Example of spatial frequency specific interaction between the excitatory receptive field and surround of a V4 neuron. (A) Responses to gratings restricted to the receptive field compared to responses to gratings that covered both the excitatory receptive field (1° in width) and the surround (10° in width). (B) Responses to an optimal grating (0.25 cycles/deg) within the excitatory receptive field presented simultaneously with a grating (0.12 – 8 cycles/deg) in the surround. For comparison the response to an optimal grating restricted to the receptive field is shown at the top left of the graph. When the frequency of the grating in the surround matched that of the grating in the receptive field, the response to the receptive field grating was maximally suppressed, whereas the suppression gradually diminished as the frequency of the surround grating was increased or decreased from that of the receptive field grating. From Desimone et al. (1985).

Zeki, 1978; Kruger and Gouras, 1980; Schein et al., 1982; De Monasterio and Schein, 1982; Schein et al., 1983; Desimone et al., 1985), due in part to differing definitions of color selectivity. When the responses of V4 cells to chromatic and achromatic stimuli are measured quantitatively, values for the bandwidths of the spectral tuning curves and the relative responses to chromatic and achromatic stimuli are continuously distributed across cells, with no obvious division between color and non-color selective cells (Schein et al., 1983; Desimone et al., 1985; Schein and Desimone, in preparation). Depending on where along these distributions one makes the division between color and non-color, one can arrive at very different percentages of cells in the two categories, which may explain some of the apparent discrepancies among the reported percentages of color cells. Regardless of how one classifies them, however, it is clear that most V4 cells show both significant tuning to wavelength and moderate responsiveness to achromatic stimuli, not unlike P cells in the LGN.

Since the basic wavelength sensitivity of V4 cells does not appear to differ much from that of prior areas, what do V4 cells contribute to color vision? The most striking claim of a unique contribution of V4 to color perception has come from Zeki (1980, 1983b,c), who has found that many V4 cells exhibit color constancy. Color constancy refers to the fact that perceived object color is largely invariant over changes in the wavelength of the ambient illumination, even though such changes may cause large differences in the actual wavelength composition of the light from an object entering the eye. To take an everyday example, objects appear to have the same color indoors as outdoors, even though indoor illumination (and thus the wavelength of light reflecting off the object) is far more 'yellow' than outdoor. Thus, the visual system is capable of taking into account the wavelength composition of the overall scene in computing the 'intrinsic' color (as defined by the spectral reflectance function) of an object in the scene. The powerful effects of context on perceived object color have been dramatically illustrated by Land (1977), who has manipulated independently the wavelength composition of a light illuminating a test surface and a light illuminating the surrounding scene. Using complex 'Mondrian' stimuli with many different colored patches for the test patch and scene, he has shown that the perceived color of the test patch remains constant when the wavelength of the light illuminating the entire Mondrian is varied but, conversely, that the perceived color of the test patch changes dramatically when only the wavelength of the light illuminating the surround is varied.

Zeki has conducted experiments with Mondrians analogous to those of Land, but with V4 neurons as test subjects. When a colored patch on the Mondrian is used as a stimulus, the response of some

V4 neurons to the patch appears to be invariant over large changes in the wavelength composition of the light illuminating the Mondrian. Thus, V4 cells, like observers, take into account or 'subtract out' the color of the overall illumination of a scene in the process of identifying the true color of an object within it.

A possible mechanism for color constancy in V4 is suggested by the finding that the suppressive surrounds of V4 receptive fields are often specific not only for form but for wavelength as well (Schein et al., 1983; Desimone et al., 1985). The maximally suppressive wavelength in the surround is normally the same as the maximally exciting wavelength within the excitatory receptive field. For example, the response of a red-sensitive V4 cell to an optimal red stimulus inside the excitatory receptive field is in some cases completely suppressed by a simultaneously presented large red stimulus in the surround. Since the surrounds of V4 cells are very large (sometimes 30° in diameter; see below), they may provide a mechanism for 'subtracting' the color of the background illumination from the color of a foreground object. Although this proposed mechanism for color constancy in V4 has not yet been tested experimentally, Hurlbert and Poggio (1988) have recently reported a computational model of color constancy that is based on receptive fields with similar properties to those of V4 cells. Another possible function for the receptive field and surround interactions in V4 is figure/ground separation based on color differences, but a role in this function and a role in color constancy are not mutually exclusive.

The role of the corpus callosum in V4 Although callosal terminations in V1 and V2 are limited to the representation of the vertical meridian (Kennedy et al., 1986), those in the rest of extrastriate cortex are far more extensive (Van Essen and Zeki, 1978; Van Essen et al., 1982). In V4, excitatory receptive fields are largely restricted to the contralateral visual field, rarely extending across the midline more than $1-2°$. Yet callosal connections are widespread in V4, even in regions where receptive fields do not include the vertical midline. If these connections do not provide a representation of the ipsilateral visual field in V4, then what is their purpose? A possible explanation has been offered by Moran et al. (1983), who found that the suppressive surrounds of V4 receptive fields sometimes extend up to 15° into the ipsilateral visual field. The ipsilateral components of the suppressive surrounds must be dependent on the corpus callosum, since they are eliminated by callosum transection. Thus, the influence of the callosum in V4 appears to be largely suppressive, and may serve to integrate across the midline the mechanisms for either color constancy or figure/ground separation, or both. The recent discovery that the receptive fields of cells in area MT have large suppressive surrounds sensitive to motion (Allman et al., 1985; Tanaka, K., et al., 1986) suggests that the callosum may serve suppressive functions in extrastriate areas other than V4.

Effects of lesions Two recent studies have examined the contribution of area V4 to color and form vision. In one, the prelunate portion of V4 representing the lower visual field was removed, and two animals were tested for their ability to perform tasks involving color constancy, hue discrimination and form discrimination (Wild et al., 1985). It was reported that the lesion impaired only color constancy, although eventually one of the two animals appeared to regain even this ability. The absence of an impairment in form and hue discrimination may have been due to the fact that the lesion involved only a part of the visual field representation in V4. Indeed, color constancy, which depends on integrating spectral information over much of the visual field, would be expected to be more sensitive to partial lesions than would form or hue discrimination. This possibility is supported by the results of a study with more extensive V4 lesions, which included not only the lower field representation but also part of the upper field representation (Heywood and Cowey, 1987). This latter study found impairments in both form and

hue discrimination, which is consistent with the notion that V4 processes both form and color and relays this information into the inferior temporal cortex.

Impairments of both color and form vision after V4 lesions may seem at odds with reports of achromatopsia following certain extrastriate lesions in humans (Meadows, 1974; Damasio et al., 1980). However, the lesion that most commonly results in achromatopsia in humans is in the ventral occipitotemporal region, far from where one would surmise the homolog of V4 to be located (especially the lower field representation of V4, which lies on the dorsal aspect of the hemisphere in monkeys). Curiously, the site of the lesion that causes achromatopsia is near the critical site of the lesion that causes prosopagnosia, a clinical syndrome whose most striking characteristic is the inability to recognize faces. Achromatopsia and prosopagnosia frequently arise together from the same lesion. Indeed, achromatopsia and prosopagnosia share a common characteristic in that both can be interpreted as an inability to distinguish among items belonging to the same perceptual category. Since there is now evidence that many prosopagnosic patients have difficulty distinguishing among items within categories other than that of faces (Damasio et al., 1982), within-category distinctions may be a general function of the ventral occipitotemporal cortex in humans, not unlike one of the functions proposed for the inferior temporal cortex in monkeys (see below).

Inferior temporal cortex
The inferior temporal cortex (IT) receives a major projection from area V4, and appears to be the last exclusively visual region in the cortical system for object recognition (Desimone et al., 1980, 1985). Regional variations in anatomical connections, neuronal properties and behavioral effects of lesions all suggest that IT contains several functionally distinct subareas, although the exact number and location of areas remain unclear. Most investigators would agree, however, that the more posterior portions of IT (including a subarea

termed 'TEO') have smaller receptive fields and less complex neuronal properties than the anterior portions (Desimone and Gross, 1979; Tanaka et al., 1987), and that posterior lesions have a greater effect on perceptual abilities such as visual discrimination, whereas anterior lesions (especially the anterior portions of cytoarchitectonic area TE) have a greater effect on mnemonic abilities, such as visual recognition (see Iwai and Mishkin, 1969; Cowey and Gross, 1970; Mishkin, 1972; Gross, 1973; Dean, 1982; Horel and Pytko, 1982; Iwai, 1985). Some of the proposed subdivisions of IT are illustrated in Fig. 2.

The analysis of form The trend of increasing neuronal receptive field size observed in moving from V1 to V4 continues into IT, where the median size of receptive fields is 26 × 26° (Gross et al., 1972; Desimone and Gross, 1979). These large receptive fields commonly include the center of gaze within or on their borders, and most cross the vertical meridian into the ipsilateral field. Although V4 neurons are also influenced by stimuli within the ipsilateral visual field, this influence, as indicated above, is usually to suppress the response of the V4 neuron to receptive field stimuli in the contralateral visual field. By contrast, neurons in IT give stimulus-specific, excitatory responses to stimuli within the ipsilateral field (Gross et al., 1972), suggesting that information from the ipsilateral visual field plays a far different role in IT than in V4. This conclusion is supported by metabolic mapping studies, which have found significant trans-callosal visual activation of IT but not prestriate areas (Macko and Mishkin, 1985).

Gross and Mishkin (1977) have proposed that one of the functions of the large, bilateral receptive fields in IT is to mediate the perceptual equivalence of objects over translation in retinal position. In fact, the loss of this perceptual equivalence may be one factor underlying impaired discrimination learning by monkeys with IT lesions. Since an object is normally seen at a somewhat different retinal locus from one trial to the next, animals with IT lesions, unlike normal monkeys, may have to learn the same discrimination separately for each of these different loci. Some support for this idea comes from a study by Seacord et al. (1979), who found that monkeys with both IT lesions and section of the optic chiasm showed no evidence of transfer of information from one visual hemifield to the other. Whether this would hold for information transfer between any two loci in the visual field remains to be determined.

What sort of information about objects is coded within the large receptive fields of IT neurons has been a matter of controversy. In the first study of neuronal properties in IT, Gross et al. (1972) reported that although many IT neurons responded to simple stimuli such as bars of light, a few neurons responded exclusively to the outline of a hand (a monkey's hand was best) and a few responded exclusively to faces. As described above under 'Population codes for objects', these findings led some theorists to propose that specific objects were coded by individual cells, an idea that came to be known as the 'grandmother cell' theory of recognition.

The grandmother cell theory lost favor over the years as subsequent studies by Gross and others found that most IT neurons appeared to respond selectively on the basis of object *features*, such as color, shape and texture, rather than to specific objects (Schwartz et al., 1983; Desimone et al., 1984; Saito et al., 1987). A typical cell is illustrated in Fig. 8. The cell responded well to objects with jagged edges throughout a large receptive field and poorly or not at all to objects with smooth edges, suggesting that the neuron was selective for some general feature of shape. By contrast, the only evidence for 'grandmother cells' in IT was persistent reports of a small proportion of cells selective for faces and, more rarely, for hands. Thus, except for such cells, which will be discussed below, the evidence indicates that the neural code for objects in IT must be a population code based on object features, as it is in other visual areas.

Even though IT neurons are clearly sensitive to object features such as shape and color, there is little understanding so far of how they actually code these features. In one attempt to probe the shape-sensitivity of IT neurons, Schwartz et al. (1983) tested cells with a set of stimuli based on shape descriptors known as the Fourier Descriptors (FDs). These descriptors can, in principle, be used to construct any arbitrary two-dimensional shape. Although the responses of many IT neurons varied systematically with the boundary curvature of the shapes, a subsequent study found that the responses to the FDs were in fact not useful in predicting the responses to other complex shapes

constructed from the FDs (Albright et al., 1985). Presumably, then, the code for shape is more complex than the FDs, and may even be based on three-dimensional features rather than two-dimensional (see Pentland, 1986). Alternatively, if shape is coded by a network of cells, the properties of any individual cell in the network may not resemble those of any particular shape primitive. In such a case, an individual cell's shape selectivity might only be understandable in the context of the network in which it is embedded.

Face-selective cells   Several laboratories have now reported the existence of face-selective cells in the temporal cortex (Gross et al., 1972; Bruce et al., 1981; Desimone et al., 1984; Baylis et al., 1985; Rolls et al., 1985; Perrett et al., 1982, 1985, 1987). A few such cells have been found throughout IT, but most authors agree that they are concentrated within the superior temporal sulcus. Baylis et al. (1985) have reported that there are two such zones of face-selective cells, in the upper and lower banks of the sulcus, respectively, sparing the floor in between. The zone in the upper bank is located within the superior temporal polysensory area (Desimone and Gross, 1979; Bruce et al., 1981), an area which receives multimodal inputs. The zone in the lower bank is located within cortex traditionally considered part of IT, which is exclusively visual.

The responses of a typical face-selective cell are illustrated in Fig. 9 (Desimone et al., 1984). The cell responded well to profiles of faces, but not at all to an isolated component or feature of the face. Some cells responded to all faces regardless of orientation, but others responded selectively to full-frontal views of faces, suggesting that the orientation of the head in the three-dimensional plane may be a critical feature for some of these cells. Cells that responded to an isolated component of a face, such as an eye or hair, were excluded by definition from the category of 'face-selective' by Desimone et al. (1984), but Rolls and Perrett and their colleagues have observed such 'face-component' cells intermingled with cells selective for intact faces (Baylis et al., 1985; Rolls

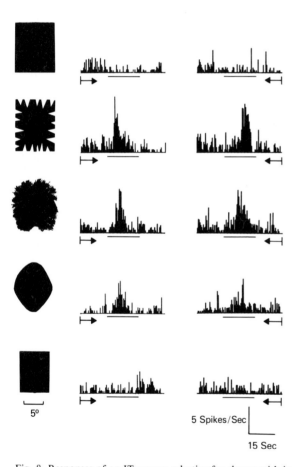

Fig. 8. Responses of an IT neuron selective for shapes with irregular edges. Stimuli were projected on a tangent screen, moving at 1.2°/s over a receptive field approximately 24° in width, indicated by the dark lines under the histograms. Stimuli with irregular edges elicited the best response, while stimuli with straight edges were ineffective. From Desimone et al. (1984).

et al., 1985; Perrett et al., 1982, 1987).

Why should IT treat faces differently from other objects? First, it should be noted that even the face-selective cells are not, strictly speaking, 'grandmother' cells, in that each cell does not respond exclusively to one face. Rather, since individual face-selective cells vary in their response to different expressions and orientations, they seem to form a distributed network for the coding of faces (Perrett et al., 1987), just as other cells in IT seem to form a distributed network for the coding of general object features.

A second answer to why the coding of faces may be specialized is that faces are extremely important to primates, not only for the recognition of specific

individuals in the troop or social group but also for social communication by facial expression. Given this importance, there may have been selective pressure to evolve neural mechanisms for the analysis of faces and facial expression. Desimone et al. (1984) have noted that there are at least two examples of specialized neural mechanisms that have evolved to facilitate social communication in other species. One is the specialized structures that mediate the perception and generation of song in birds (Leppelsack and Vogt, 1966; McCasland and Konishi, 1981), and another is the cortex specialized for language in humans. In each case, specialized perceptual mechanisms have evolved that are separate from those of audition in general. In man,

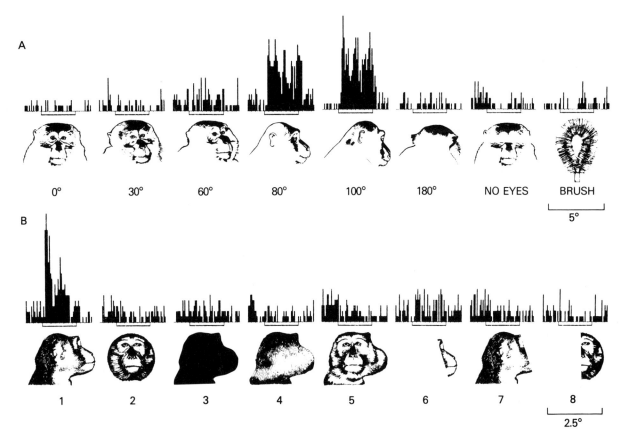

Fig. 9. Responses of an IT neuron that responded better to profiles of faces than to any other stimulus tested. Stimuli were colored slides projected with a slight oscillatory motion onto a tangent screen, centered over the receptive field. (A) Responses to a monkey face in different degrees of rotation. (B) Responses to profile of face and to profile with components removed or altered. The responses of this neuron appeared to depend on the overall configuration of several facial features. From Desimone et al. (1984).

the supramodal language cortex of the temporal lobe is located within the second temporal convolution, adjacent to the auditory association cortex (Rasmussen and Milner, 1975). Interestingly, the cortex that occupies this location in monkeys is the superior temporal sulcus, which contains both face-selective and polysensory cells. Thus, this portion of the primate brain may be a fertile zone for the development of supramodal mechanisms for communication.

Effects of lesions It is well established that the visual discrimination learning impairment resulting from IT lesions is not due to an impairment of basic sensory capacities such as visual acuity or color vision. Rather, the behavioral impairment seems to result from the loss of a 'high-level' mechanism, although the precise nature of this mechanism is controversial. One model initially proposed by Dean (1976, 1982) and recently expanded upon by Gaffan et al. (1986) is that monkeys with IT lesions have fewer perceptual 'categories' than normal. For example, a brush and a wooden block of the same general shape and color would probably fall within different perceptual categories for a normal monkey but might fall within the same category for an animal with an IT lesion. In a visual discrimination task, learning to associate the brush with reward and the block with nonreward might be as difficult for an animal with an IT lesion as a normal monkey would find learning to discriminate between two slightly different brushes. This concept fits with current models of prosopagnosia in humans, in which it is thought that the underlying impairment may be in discriminating among objects within the same perceptual category, rather than in discriminating faces per se (Damasio et al., 1982).

In contrast, Mishkin has argued that a reduction in the number of perceptual categories cannot fully explain the impairments that follow IT lesions. He has proposed that IT lesions also cause a loss of certain perceptual constancies (see section on 'The analysis of form'), a reduction in the visual inputs to a 'habit' learning system involving the basal ganglia, and a profound loss of visual memories (Mishkin, 1982; Mishkin et al., 1984; Mishkin and Appenzeller, 1987; Phillips et al., 1988). The memory loss is suggested by studies that have shown that animals with IT lesions cannot recognize an object seen as recently as 30–60 seconds previously. Mishkin has proposed that IT contains the 'central representations' for visual objects, and that the loss of IT leads to an inability to form new memories as well as to the loss of old memories. In this view, the role of the amygdala and hippocampus in visual memory is to facilitate the consolidation of new memories within IT. Thus, bilateral lesions of IT should cause a more devastating impairment in visual memory for an animal (or human) than lesions of temporal limbic structures, since limbic lesions impair the acquisition of new memories but spare memories consolidated before the lesion (e.g. see Squire, 1987). Although there are some suggestive neurophysiological data that IT could be the site of memory storage (Fuster and Jervey, 1981; Brown et al., 1987), definitive data on this issue are sorely lacking.

The occipitoparietal pathway for spatial vision

For many years, the route by which the parietal lobe received its visual information remained a mystery. Indeed, early anatomical investigations of parietal cortex demonstrated that the major connections of the inferior parietal lobule, or architectonic area PG, were with polysensory regions located in the prefrontal and cingulate cortex and within the depths of the superior temporal sulcus (Jones and Powell, 1970; Mesulam et al., 1977). No direct input from modality-specific visual cortex was reported. It is now known that a major route from the occipital lobe into the parietal lobe is via prestriate area MT (Maunsell and Van Essen, 1983c; Ungerleider and Desimone, 1986). In the sections below, we will briefly describe area MT, the areas to which MT projects, and some additional features of the occipitoparietal pathway (also see Chapter 15 of this volume).

Area MT

MT is a visuotopically organized area, which in macaques is located on the posterior bank and floor of the caudal portion of the superior temporal sulcus (Zeki, 1974; Gattass and Gross, 1981; Van Essen et al., 1981). The area is commonly called MT because in owl monkeys, in which it was first described (Allman and Kaas, 1971), the homologous area is located in the middle part of the temporal lobe. In all species of monkeys, both Old World and New World, MT can be identified by a pattern of heavy myelination occupying the lower cortical layers (Allman and Kaas, 1971; Spatz and Tigges, 1972; Ungerleider and Mishkin, 1979). As described previously in this chapter, the major inputs to MT appear to be dominated by the M-cell pathway, via layer 4B of V1, the thick stripes of area V2, and area V3 (Zeki, 1976; Van Essen et al., 1981; Weller and Kaas, 1983; DeYoe and Van Essen, 1985; Shipp and Zeki, 1985; Ungerleider and Desimone, 1986).

Physiological studies have shown that neurons in MT are insensitive to the color of a visual stimulus but are highly selective for binocular disparity and the speed and direction of stimulus motion (Zeki, 1976; Maunsell and Van Essen, 1983a,b; Albright, 1984). Furthermore, MT contains a columnar organization for the axis of stimulus motion that is similar in many respects to the columnar system for stimulus orientation found in V1 (Baker et al., 1981; Albright et al., 1984; Albright and Desimone, 1987).

Within MT, at least three transformations of the information provided by striate cells take place. First, MT cells have receptive fields about 8 – 10 times larger in linear dimension, or 60 – 100 times larger in area, than receptive fields of cells in V1 at comparable eccentricities (Gattass and Gross, 1981; Desimone and Ungerleider, 1986; Albright et al., 1984; Albright and Desimone, 1987). Second, whereas cells in V1 are sensitive to the direction of motion of the component gratings in a complex pattern, many MT cells are sensitive to the global motion of the pattern, that is, the vector sum of the component motions (Movshon et al., 1985).

Third, as described above, MT neurons have large, silent suppressive zones surrounding their classically defined receptive fields. These suppressive zones are selective for the direction of stimulus motion, so that the optimal motion for a typical MT cell is a stimulus moving against its background (Allman et al., 1985; Tanaka, K., et al., 1986).

Lesions in MT have virtually no effect on contrast sensitivity or the ability to saccade to a target but they impair the ability to detect the correlated motion of dots in a moving random dot display (Newsome and Pare, 1988), to detect shearing motion and structure-from-motion (Siegel and Andersen, 1986), and to match the velocity of pursuit eye movements to the velocity of the target (Newsome et al., 1985). These impairments in motion perception are consistent with the high proportion of directionally selective cells found in MT; however, most of the impairments largely disappear with time, suggesting that at least some motion information is independently available in other areas of the occipitoparietal pathway or perhaps even of the occipitotemporal pathway.

Further extensions of the cortical system for motion analysis

Beyond MT, the next transformation of motion information occurs in areas MST and FST, to which MT projects (Ungerleider and Desimone, 1986). These areas are located adjacent to MT on the medial bank and floor, respectively, of the superior temporal sulcus. Like neurons in MT, a majority of those in MST and about a third in FST are directionally selective (Desimone and Ungerleider, 1986). (MT also projects to area VIP, located in the ventral portion of the intraparietal sulcus, but it is not known whether VIP represents an extension of the motion system, since the properties of neurons in this area have not yet been studied.) Cells in MST and FST have even larger receptive fields than cells in MT, and some MST cells are not only selective for the direction of stimulus motion in the tangent plane, like cells in MT, but are also selective for the expanding or contracting image of an object moving in two dimensions (Desimone and Ungerleider, 1986; Saito et al., 1986).

Like MT lesions, lesions in MST acutely impair smooth pursuit eye movements, but, unlike the defect after MT lesions, the defect may be more a motor than a sensory one, since unilateral lesions involving MST impair contraversive tracking eye movements in both visual hemifields (Dursteler et al., 1987). Furthermore, cells in MST respond during tracking eye movements when no visual stimulus is present, suggesting there is some motor component to the neuronal discharge (Komatsu and Wurtz, 1988; Newsome et al., 1988).

Both MST and FST provide inputs to widespread regions within cytoarchitectonic area PG, including the lateral bank of the intraparietal sulcus and the inferior parietal lobule (Boussaoud et al., 1987). Either of these parietal regions, or both, may contain the next stage of motion-processing (Sakata et al., 1983; Motter and Mountcastle, 1981). For visually responsive cells in PG cortex, receptive fields are even larger than those in MST or FST; some receptive fields in PG include the entire contralateral visual field or even the entire bilateral visual field (Robinson et al., 1978; Motter and Mountcastle, 1981). Although some of the properties of cells in PG cortex resemble those of cells in MST, such as sensitivity to tracking eye movements and movement in depth, other properties appear to emerge for the first time. Some cells in PG cortex, for example, respond selectively to motion directed toward or away from the fovea (Motter and Mountcastle, 1981), that is, motion that would be produced by optical flow. In addition, some PG cells receive polysensory inputs (Hyvärinen and Shelepin, 1979; Leinonen et al., 1979). Thus, neurons along the sequence of areas from V1 through MT to MST and FST and then to PG cortex integrate motion information over an increasingly large portion of the retina, respond to inputs from additional sensory modalities, and may become more directly involved in oculomotor control. This motion-analysis system could also form the basis, at least in part, for visually guided behaviors other than oculomotor.

The motion-analysis system may turn out to be far more extensive than previously thought. Recent anatomical studies have shown that MST and FST project not only to areas in parietal cortex, but also to areas in the superior temporal sulcus (Boussaoud et al., 1987), including but not limited to the superior temporal polysensory area, or STP (Desimone and Gross, 1979). Cells in STP resemble those in parietal cortex, in that some respond selectively to movement in depth, rotational movement, and movement directed toward or away from the fovea (Bruce et al., 1981). Moreover, the receptive fields of most STP neurons include virtually the entire visual field, including both monocular crescents. The role of this temporal lobe component of the motion-analysis system in visuospatial function remains to be explored.

Peripheral field inputs to parietal cortex

The occipitoparietal pathway for spatial vision consists of more than just the motion-analysis system. Although area MT provides a major route from V1 into the parietal lobe, it is not the sole route. Area V4, for example, projects to PG cortex within the intraparietal sulcus (Ungerleider et al., 1986). In addition, Ungerleider and Desimone (1986) have noted that there appears to be a preferential projection into the parietal lobe from the peripheral field representations of several of the lower-order visual areas. The peripheral field representations of V1, V2, and V3 project to either V3A or PO, or both (Ungerleider, 1985; Colby et al., 1988). PO, in turn, is connected with several areas in the parietal lobe, including MST, VIP and additional unexplored regions in the intraparietal sulcus (Colby et al., 1988). Therefore, projections to PO, or to PO via V3A, have a route into parietal cortex separate from the one through MT. The convergence of inputs to the parietal cortex from the peripheral visual field is not surprising given the importance of the peripheral field in spatial vision (Mishkin and Ungerleider, 1982).

Top-down mechanisms: the influence of selective attention

In a typical visual scene there are a myriad of shapes, colors and textures stimulating our retinas simultaneously. Just as we cannot make an eye or limb movement to all objects at once, so also we cannot be fully aware of, or store in memory, more than one or two objects in a given moment. Thus, much of the unwanted information on the retina must be filtered out centrally. In part, some of the reduction of visual 'clutter' from a scene occurs preattentively as a result of both early neuronal mechanisms, such as edge enhancement (see above, under 'Retina and lateral geniculate nucleus'), and late mechanisms, such as figure/ground separation, which extract objects from their background (see above, 'Area V4'). Yet, even after figure/ground separation, there often remain too many extracted figures in a scene to be fully processed all at once (Julesz, 1981; Treisman, 1986). The selection of specific items for further processing or as the target for an eye or limb movement is commonly attributed to 'attention'.

Until recently, most neurophysiological work on visual attention was focused on either oculomotor structures or the posterior parietal cortex (see Mountcastle, 1978; Lynch, 1980; and Goldberg and Colby, Ch. 15 of this volume). Evidence from both neurophysiological and ablation studies suggests that the posterior parietal cortex is one of the structures involved in the control of spatial attention, especially the process of switching attention from one location to another (see Posner and Presti (1987) and Posner et al. (1987) for references). Posner et al. (1984, 1987) have reported that humans with unilateral lesions in the posterior parietal cortex show normal reaction times for the detection of stimuli within the visual fields both ipsilateral and contralateral to the lesion, indicating that it is possible for the subjects to 'attend' per se. However, if the subject's attention is first directed into the ipsilateral field, subjects with parietal lesions are very slow to detect a stimulus subsequent-ly presented within the contralateral field. Similar results have now been found in monkeys (D.L. Robinson, personal communication). These results suggest that, in addition to its role in spatial vision, the posterior parietal cortex plays an important role in disengaging attention from one locus so that it can be redirected to another, an interpretation that is consistent with a number of other behavioral impairments, such as contralateral neglect and extinction reported after posterior parietal lesions in monkeys and humans (for review, see Mesulam, 1981). In fact, impairments in spatial attention may underlie some of the deficits that have been commonly attributed to impairments in spatial perception following posterior parietal lesions (Lawler and Cowey, 1987).

Although some of the neural mechanisms underlying the control of spatial attention may lie in the posterior parietal cortex, we would expect that since this region does not itself contain the neural mechanisms for object recognition, its influence on the selection of objects for visual processing would result from interactions with the occipitotemporal pathway. How attention might serve to reduce unwanted information within the occipitotemporal pathway has been unclear. Receptive field size increases steadily along this pathway, so that by the inferior temporal cortex the receptive field of an individual neuron may encompass an entire scene. Thus, paradoxically, individual neurons would seem to be confronted with more and more information, rather than less and less, as one progresses to higher levels of the system. A possible solution to this puzzle was proposed by Moran and Desimone (1985), based on recordings in areas V4 and IT. They trained monkeys to attend to one or another of two stimuli within the receptive field of a V4 or IT neuron and found that the neuron's response was gated by the locus of the animal's attention within the receptive field. If a neuron responded selectively to red but not green stimuli, for example, both a red and a green stimulus would be placed simultaneously inside the neuron's receptive field. When the animal was instructed (as a result of task demands) to attend to the locus of the red stimulus, the neuron would give a good response, but if the animal was instructed to attend to the locus of the green stimulus, the neuron would give a poor response (Fig. 10). In each case, the neuron responded as if the receptive field had contracted around the attended stimulus, suggesting that attention serves not only to filter out unwanted information, but also to increase the spatial resolution of neurons with large receptive fields (Fig. 11). Results from

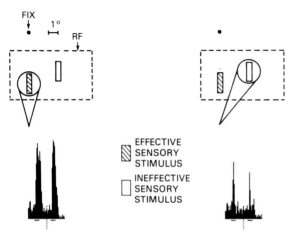

Fig. 10. Effect of selective attention on the responses of a neuron in extrastriate area V4. The neuronal responses shown are from when the monkey attended to one location inside the receptive field (RF) and ignored another. At the attended location (circled), two stimuli (sample and test) were presented sequentially, and the monkey responded differently depending on whether they were the same or different. Irrelevant stimuli were presented simultaneously with the sample and test but at a separate location in the receptive field. In the initial mapping of the field, the cell responded well to red bars but not at all to green bars. A horizontal or a vertical red bar (effective sensory stimuli) was then placed at one location in the field and a horizontal or a vertical green bar (ineffective sensory stimuli) at another. When the animal attended to the location of the effective sensory stimulus at the time of presentation of either the sample or the test, the cell gave a good response (left), but when the animal attended to the location of the ineffective stimulus, the cell gave only a small response (right) even though the sensory conditions were identical to the previous condition. Thus, the responses of the cell were determined predominantly by the attended stimulus. The horizontal bars under the histograms indicate the 200 ms period when the sample and test stimuli were on. Because of the random delay between the sample and test presentations, the histograms were synchronized separately at the onsets of the sample and test stimuli (indicated by the vertical dashed lines). Adapted from Moran and Desimone (1985).

IT neurons consistent with these results in V4 have now been found by Spitzer and Richmond (in preparation). No such effects were found by Moran and Desimone in either V1 or V2, indicating that V4 is probably the first area in the occipitotemporal pathway where responses are gated by spatial attention.

Surprisingly, the attentional effects observed by Moran and Desimone (1985) in V4 depended on both the attended and the ignored stimuli being located within the recorded neuron's receptive field. If one stimulus was located within the receptive field and one outside, the locus of the animal's attention had no effect on the neuron's response. Thus, attention appears to work only locally in V4, possibly at the level of a cortical module. By contrast, the receptive fields in IT were so large, and the attentional effects covered such a large spatial range, that it was not possible to test the effects of the animal attending outside the receptive field. These results suggest that the filtering of unwanted information is at least a two-stage process, with the first stage working over a small spatial range in V4, and a second stage working over a much larger spatial range in IT.

In addition to filtering unwanted information based on spatial location, a number of other effects of attention on sensory processing have been reported in extrastriate cortex. In both V4 and IT, the response of neurons to a stimulus composed of two features, such as a textured pattern or a colored grid, varies depending on which feature is relevant for the task the animal is performing (Braitman, 1984; Fuster and Jervey, 1981; Spitzer and Richmond, 1985; Hochstein and Maunsell, 1985). In V4, neuronal responses are stronger and more tightly tuned to orientation and color when the animal is performing a difficult discrimination than when performing an easier one (Spitzer et al., 1988). Furthermore, if the animal is performing a matching task, responses to a stimulus are stronger if it is a match to a previously presented sample than if it is a nonmatch (Haenny and Schiller, 1988; Haenny et al., 1988). In IT, neuronal responses are stronger when the animal is perform-

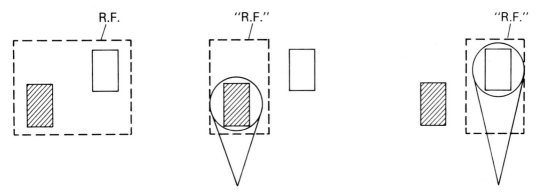

Fig. 11. Schematic representation of the effects of attention on cells in V4. When two stimuli are located within the receptive field (R.F.), and the animal attends to just one, a cell responds as if its receptive field had contracted around this attended stimulus. In the absence of attention, or if attention is directed outside the receptive field, the response of a cell will reflect the properties of all the stimuli within its field. In such a case, information about an individual stimulus, including its specific location, may be lost. From Desimone et al. (1989).

ing a discrimination task than when it is performing a detection task (Richmond and Sato, 1987). Finally, in areas V1 to IT, neuronal responses to an extrafoveally presented stimulus are reported to be stronger when the target used by the animal to maintain fixation is extinguished than when the target is present (Richmond et al., 1983; Richmond and Sato, 1987; Fischer and Boch, 1981; Boch, 1986). In each of these examples, behavioral context appears to modulate sensory processing, often to a very high degree. As we advance the exploration of perceptual mechanisms into higher-order cortical areas, it will be increasingly important to take such non-sensory factors into account.

Acknowledgements

We thank Mortimer Mishkin for his support and encouragement, and for comments on an earlier version of the manuscript. Joan Baizer also provided valuable comments on the manuscript, and Linda Thomas assisted in its preparation.

References

Albrecht DG, De Valois RL, Thorell LG: Visual cortical neurons: are bars or gratings the optimal stimuli? *Science: 207,* 77 – 90, 1980.

Albright TD: Direction and orientation selectivity of neurons in visual area MT of the macaque. *J. Neurophysiol.: 52,* 1106 – 1130, 1984.

Albright TD, Desimone R: Local precision of visuotopic organization in the middle temporal area (MT) of the macaque. *Exp. Brain Res.: 65,* 582 – 592, 1987.

Albright TD, Desimone R, Gross CG: Columnar organization of directionally selective cells in visual area MT of the macaque. *J. Neurophysiol.: 51,* 16 – 31, 1984.

Albright TD, Charles RA, Gross CG: Inferior temporal neurons do not seem to code shape by the method of the fourier descriptors. *Soc. Neurosci. Abstr.: 11,* 1013, 1985.

Allman JM, Kaas JH: A representation of the visual field in the caudal third of the middle temporal gyrus of the owl monkey (*Aotus trivirgatus*). *Brain Res.: 31,* 85 – 105, 1971.

Allman J, Miezin F, McGuinness E: Direction- and velocity-specific responses from beyond the classical receptive field in the middle temporal area (MT). *Perception: 14,* 105 – 126, 1985.

Baizer JS: Receptive field properties of V3 neurons in monkey. *Invest. Ophthalmol. Visual Sci.: 23,* 87 – 95, 1982.

Baizer JS, Robinson DL, Dow BM: Visual responses of area 18 neurons in awake, behaving monkey. *J. Neurophysiol.: 40,* 1024 – 1037, 1977.

Baker JF, Petersen SE, Newsome WT, Allman JM: Visual response properties of neurons in four extrastriate visual areas of the owl monkey (*Aotus trivirgatus*): a quantitative comparison of medial, dorsomedial, dorsolateral, and middle temporal areas. *J. Neurophysiol.: 45,* 397 – 416, 1981.

Baylis GC, Rolls ET, Leonard CM: Selectivity between faces in the responses of a population of neurons in the cortex in the superior temporal sulcus of the monkey. *Brain Res.: 342,* 91 – 102, 1985.

Blasdel GG, Lund JS, Fitzpatrick D: Intrinsic connections of macaque striate cortex: axonal projections of cells outside lamina 4C. *J. Neurosci.: 5,* 3350 – 3369, 1985.

Boch R: Behavioral activation of visual neurons in monkey striate cortex. *Soc. Neurosci. Abstr.: 12,* 1367, 1986.

Boussaoud D, Ungerleider LG, Desimone R: Cortical pathways for motion analysis: connections of visual areas MST and FST in macaques. *Soc. Neurosci. Abstr.: 13,* 1625, 1987.

Braitman DJ: Activity of neurons in monkey posterior temporal cortex during multidimensional visual discrimination tasks. *Brain Res.: 307,* 17–28, 1984.

Brown MW, Wilson FAW, Riches IP: Neuronal evidence that inferomedial temporal cortex is more important than hippocampus in certain processes underlying recognition memory. *Brain Res.: 409,* 158–162, 1987.

Bruce CJ, Desimone R, Gross CG: Visual properties of neurons in a polysensory area in superior temporal sulcus of the macaque. *J. Neurophysiol.: 46,* 369–384, 1981.

Burkhalter A, Van Essen DC: Processing of color, form and disparity in visual areas V2 and VP of ventral extrastriate cortex in the macaque. *J. Neurosci.: 6,* 2327–2351, 1986.

Burkhalter A, Felleman DJ, Newsome WT, Van Essen DC: Anatomical and physiological asymmetries related to visual areas V3 and VP in macaque extrastriate cortex. *Vision Res.: 26,* 63–80, 1986.

Cavanagh P, Tyler CW, Favreau OE: Perceived velocity of moving chromatic gratings. *J. Opt. Soc. Am. (American Optical Image Science Series): 1,* 893–899, 1984.

Colby CL, Gattass R, Olson CR, Gross CG: Topographical organization of cortical afferents to extrastriate visual area PO in the macaque: a dual tracer study. *J. Comp. Neurol.: 269,* 392–413, 1988.

Connolly M, Van Essen D: The representation of the visual field in parvicellular and magnocellular layers of the lateral geniculate nucleus in the macaque monkey. *J. Comp. Neurol.: 226,* 544–564, 1984.

Cowey A, Gross CG; Effects of foveal prestriate and inferotemporal lesions on visual discrimination by rhesus monkeys. *Exp. Brain Res.: 11,* 128–144, 1970.

Damasio AR, Yamada T, Damasio H, Corbett J, McKee J: Central achromatopsia: behavioral, anatomic, and physiologic aspects. *Neurology: 30,* 1064–1071, 1980.

Damasio, AR, Damasio H, Van Hoesen GW: Prosopagnosia: anatomic basis and behavioral mechanisms. *Neurology: 32,* 331–341, 1982.

Daw NW: Neurophysiology of color vision. *Physiol. Rev.: 53,* 571–611, 1973.

Dean P: Effects of inferotemporal lesions on the behavior of monkeys. *Psychol. Bull.: 83,* 41–71, 1976.

Dean P: Visual behavior in monkeys with inferotemporal lesions. In Ingle DJ, Goodale MA, Mansfield RJW (Editors), *Analysis of Visual Behavior.* Cambridge, MA: MIT press, pp. 587–628, 1982.

De Monasterio FM: Functional properties and presumed roles of retinal ganglion cells of the monkey. In Szentagothai J, Hamori J, Palkovits M (Editors), *Advances in Physiological Science. Vol. 2. Regulatory Functions of the CNS Subsystems.* 28th International Congress of Physiological Sciences, Budapest 1980. Budapest: Akademiai Kiado, pp. 261–270, 1981.

De Monasterio FM: Electrophysiology of color vision. I. Cellular level. In Verriest G (Editor), *Colour Vision Deficiencies VII.* The Hague: Dr. W. Junk Publishers, pp. 9–28,

1984.

De Monasterio FM, Schein SJ: Spectral bandwidths of color-opponent cells of geniculocortical pathway of macaque monkeys. *J. Neurophysiol.: 47,* 214–224, 1982.

Derrington AM, Lennie P: Spatial and temporal contrast sensitivities of neurones in lateral geniculate nucleus of macaque. *J. Physiol. (London): 357,* 219–240, 1984.

Desimone R, Gross CG: Visual areas in the temporal cortex of the macaque. *Brain Res.: 178,* 363–380, 1979.

Desimone R, Schein SJ: Visual properties of neurons in area V4 of the macaque: sensitivity to stimulus form. *J. Neurophysiol.: 57,* 835–868, 1987.

Desimone R, Ungerleider LG: Multiple visual areas in the caudal superior temporal sulcus of the macaque. *J. Comp. Neurol.: 248,* 164–189, 1986.

Desimone R, Fleming J, Gross CG: Prestriate afferents to inferior temporal cortex: an HRP study. *Brain Res.: 184,* 41–55, 1980.

Desimone R, Albright TD, Gross CG, Bruce C: Stimulus selective properties of inferior temporal neurons in the macaque. *J. Neurosci.: 4,* 2051–2062, 1984.

Desimone R, Schein SJ, Moran J, Ungerleider LG: Contour, color and shape analysis beyond the striate cortex. *Vision Res.: 25,* 441–452, 1985.

Desimone R, Moran J, Spitzer H: Neural mechanisms of attention in extrastriate cortex of monkeys. In Arbib MA, Amari S (Editors), *Dynamic Interactions in Neural Networks: Models and Data.* New York: Springer Verlag, pp. 169–182, 1989.

De Valois RL, De Valois KK: Spatial vision. *Annu. Rev. Psychol.: 31,* 309–341, 1980.

DeYoe EA, Van Essen DC: Segregation of efferent connections and receptive field properties in visual area V2 of the macaque. *Nature (London): 317,* 58–61, 1985.

DeYoe EA, Felleman DJ, Knierim JJ, Olavarria J, Van Essen DC: Heterogeneous subregions of macaque visual area V4 receive selective projections from V2 thin-stripe and interstripe subregions. *Invest. Ophthalmol. Visual Sci. (Suppl.): 29,* 115, 1988.

Dobbins A, Zucker SW, Cynader MS: Endstopped neurons in the visual cortex as a substrate for calculating curvature. *Nature (London): 329,* 438–441, 1987.

Dow BM: Functional classes of cells and their laminar distribution in monkey visual cortex. *J. Neurophysiol.: 37,* 927–946, 1974.

Dow BM, Vautin RG: Horizontal segregation of color information in the middle layers of foveal striate cortex. *J. Neurophysiol.: 57,* 712–739, 1987.

Dursteler MR, Wurtz RH, Newsome WT: Directional pursuit deficits following lesions of the foveal representation within the superior temporal sulcus of the macaque monkey. *J. Neurophysiol.: 57,* 1262–1287, 1987.

Felleman DJ, Van Essen DC: The connections of area V4 of macaque monkey extrastriate cortex. *Soc. Neurosci. Abstr.: 9,* 153, 1983.

Felleman DJ, Van Essen DC: Cortical connections of area V3 in macaque extrastriate cortex. *Soc. Neurosci. Abstr.: 10,* 933, 1984.

Felleman DJ, Van Essen DC: Receptive field properties of neurons in area V3 of macaque monkey extrastriate cortex.

J. Neurophysiol.: 57, 889 – 920, 1987.

Felleman DJ, DeYoe EA, Knierim JJ, Olavarria J, Van Essen DC: Compartmental organization of projections from V2 to extrastriate areas V3, V3A, and V4t in macaque monkeys. *Invest. Ophthalmol. Visual Sci. (Suppl.): 29*, 115, 1988.

Fenstemacher SB, Olson CR, Gross CG: Afferent connections of macaque visual areas V4 and TEO. *Invest. Ophthalmol. Visual Sci. (Suppl.): 25*, 213, 1984.

Fischer B, Boch R: Enhanced activation of neurons in prelunate cortex before visually guided saccades of trained rhesus monkeys. *Exp. Brain Res.: 44*, 129 – 137, 1981.

Fitzpatrick D, Itoh K, Diamond IT: The laminar organization of the lateral geniculate body and the striate cortex in the squirrel monkey (*Saimiri sciureus*). *J. Neurosci.: 3*, 673 – 702, 1983.

Fitzpatrick D, Lund JS, Blasdel GG: Intrinsic connections of macaque striate cortex: afferent and efferent connections of lamina 4C. *J. Neurosci.: 5*, 3324 – 3349, 1985.

Foster KH, Gaska JP, Nagler M, Pollen DA: Spatial and temporal frequency selectivity of neurones in visual cortical areas V1 and V2 of the macaque monkey. *J. Physiol. (London): 365*, 331 – 363, 1985.

Fuster JM, Jervey JP: Inferotemporal neurons distinguish and retain behaviorally relevant features of visual stimuli. *Science: 212*, 952 – 954, 1981.

Gaffan D, Harrison S, Gaffan EA: Visual identification following inferotemporal ablation in the monkey. *Q. J. Exp. Psychol.: 38B*, 5 – 30, 1986.

Gattass R, Gross CG: Visual topography of striate projection zone (MT) in posterior superior temporal sulcus of the macaque. *J. Neurophysiol.: 46*, 621 – 638, 1981.

Gattass R, Sousa APB, Gross CG: Visuotopic organization and extent of V3 and V4 of the macaque. *J. Neurosci.: 8*, 1831 – 1845, 1988.

Gouras P: Antidromic responses of orthodromically identified ganglion cells in monkey retina. *J. Physiol. (London): 204*, 407 – 419, 1969.

Gross CG: Visual functions of inferotemporal cortex. In Jung R (Editor), *Handbook of Sensory Physiology, Vol. VII/3B*, Berlin: Springer-Verlag, pp. 451 – 482, 1973.

Gross CG, Mishkin M: The neural basis of stimulus equivalence across retinal translation. In Harned S, Doty R, Jaynes J, Goldberg L, Krauthamer G (Editors), *Lateralization in the Nervous System*. New York: Academic Press, pp. 109 – 122, 1977.

Gross CG, Rocha-Miranda CE, Bender DB: Visual properties of neurons in inferotemporal cortex of the macaque. *J. Neurophysiol.: 35*, 96 – 111, 1972.

Haenny PE, Schiller PH: State dependent activity in monkey visual cortex. I. Single cell activity in V1 and V4 on visual tasks. *Exp. Brain Res.: 69*, 225 – 244, 1988.

Haenny PE, Maunsell JHR, Schiller PH: State dependent activity in monkey visual cortex. II. Retinal and extraretinal factors in V4. *Exp. Brain Res.: 69*, 245 – 259, 1988.

Hammond P, Mackay DM: Differential responsiveness of simple and complex cells in cat striate cortex to visual texture. *Exp. Brain Res.: 30*, 275 – 296, 1977.

Hawkin MJ, Parker AJ: Contrast sensitivity and orientation selectivity in lamina IV of the striate cortex of old world monkeys. *Exp. Brain Res.: 54*, 367 – 372, 1984.

Hendrickson AE: Dots, stripes and columns in monkey visual cortex. *Trends Neurosci.: 8*, 406 – 410, 1985.

Hendrickson AE, Hunt SP, Wu JY: Immunocytochemical localization of glutamic acid decarboxylase in monkey striate cortex. *Nature (London): 292*, 605 – 607, 1981.

Hering E: Zur Lehre vom Lichtsinne. Wien: Carl Gerold's Sohn, 1878.

Heywood CA, Cowey A: On the role of cortical area V4 in the discrimination of hue and pattern in macaque monkeys. *J. Neurosci.: 7*, 2601 – 2617, 1987.

Hicks TP, Lee BB, Vidyasagar TR: The responses of cells in macaque lateral geniculate nucleus to sinusoidal gratings. *J. Physiol. (London): 337*, 183 – 200, 1983.

Hochstein S, Maunsell JHR: Dimensional attention effects in the responses of V4 neurons of the macaque monkey. *Soc. Neurosci. Abstr.: 11*, 1244, 1985.

Horel JA, Pytko DE: Behavioral effect of local cooling in temporal lobe of monkeys. *J. Neurophysiol.: 47*, 11 – 22, 1982.

Horton JC, Hubel DH: A regular patchy distribution of cytochrome-oxidase staining in primary visual cortex of macaque monkey. *Nature (London): 292*, 762 – 764, 1981.

Hubel DH, Livingstone MS: Segregation of form, color and stereopsis in primate area 18. *J. Neurosci.: 7*, 3378 – 3415, 1987.

Hubel DH, Wiesel TN: Receptive fields, binocular interaction and functional architecture in the cat's visual cortex. *J. Physiol. (London): 160*, 106 – 154, 1962.

Hubel DH, Wiesel TN: Laminar and columnar distribution of geniculo-cortical fibers in the macaque monkey. *J. Comp. Neurol.: 146*, 421 – 450, 1972.

Hubel DH, Wiesel TN: Sequence regularity and geometry of orientation columns in the monkey striate cortex. *J. Comp. Neurol.: 158*, 267 – 294, 1974.

Hurlbert AC, Poggio TA: Synthesizing a color algorithm from examples. *Science: 239*, 482 – 485, 1988.

Hyvärinen J, Shelepin Y: Distribution of visual and somatic functions in the parietal associative area 7 of the monkey. *Brain Res.: 169*, 561 – 564, 1979.

Iwai E: Neurophysiological basis of pattern vision in macaque monkeys. *Vision Res.: 25*, 425 – 439, 1985.

Iwai E, Mishkin M: Further evidence on the locus of the visual area in the temporal lobe of the monkey. *Exp. Neurol.: 25*, 585 – 594, 1969.

Jones EG, Powell TPS: An anatomical study of converging sensory pathways within the cerebral cortex of the monkey. *Brain: 93*, 793 – 820, 1970.

Julesz B: Textons, the elements of texture perception, and their interactions. *Nature (London): 290*, 91 – 97, 1981.

Kaplan E, Shapley RM: The primate retina contains two types of ganglion cells, with high and low contrast sensitivity. *Proc. Nat. Acad. Sci. USA: 83*, 2755 – 2757, 1986.

Kennedy H, Dehay C, Bullier J: Organization of the callosal connections of visual areas V1 and V2 in the macaque monkey. *J. Comp. Neurol.: 247*, 398 – 415, 1986.

Komatsu H, Wurtz RH: Relation of cortical areas MT and MST to pursuit eye movements. I. Localization and visual properties of neurons. *J. Neurophysiol.: 60*, 580 – 603, 1988.

Kruger J: Responses to wavelength contrast in the afferent visual systems of the cat and the rhesus monkey. *Vision Res.: 19*, 1351 – 1358, 1979.

Kruger J, Gouras P: Spectral selectivity of cells and its dependence on slit length in monkey visual cortex. *J. Neurophysiol.: 43,* 1055 – 1069, 1980.

Kulikowski JJ, Kranda K: Image analysis performed by the visual system: feature versus Fourier analysis and adaptable filtering. In Pettigrew JD, Sanderson KJ, Levick WR (Editors), *Visual Neuroscience.* New York: Cambridge University Press, Ch. 26, pp. 381 – 404, 1986.

Land EH: The retinex theory of color vision. *Sci. Am.: 237,* 108 – 128, 1977.

Lawler KA, Cowey A: On the role of posterior parietal and prefrontal cortex in visuo-spatial perception and attention. *Exp. Brain Res.: 65,* 695 – 698, 1987.

Lehky SR, Sejnowski TJ: Neural network model for the cortical representation of surface curvature from images of shaded surfaces. In Lund JS (Editor), *Sensory Processing.* Oxford: Oxford University Press, 1988.

Leinonen L, Hyvärinen J, Nyman G, Linnankoski I: I. Functional properties of neurons in lateral part of associative area 7 in awake monkeys. *Exp. Brain Res.: 34,* 299 – 320, 1979.

Leppelsack HJ, Vogt M: Responses of auditory neurons in the forebrain of the songbird to stimulation with species-specific sounds. *J. Comp. Physiol.: 107,* 263 – 274, 1966.

Livingstone MS, Hubel DH: Thalamic inputs to cytochrome oxidase-rich regions in monkey visual cortex. *Proc. Natl. Acad. Sci. USA: 79,* 6098 – 6101, 1982.

Livingstone MS, Hubel DH: Anatomy and physiology of a color system in the primate visual cortex. *J. Neurosci.: 4,* 309 – 356, 1984.

Livingstone MS, Hubel DH: Connections between layer 4B of area 17 and the thick cytochrome oxidase stripes of area 18 in the squirrel monkey. *J. Neurosci.: 7,* 3371 – 3377, 1987a.

Livingstone MS, Hubel DH: Psychophysical evidence for separate channels for the perception of form, color, movement, and depth. *J. Neurosci.: 7,* 3416 – 3468, 1987b.

Lund JS: Organization of neurons in the visual cortex, area 17, of the monkey (*Macaca mulatta*). *J. Comp. Neurol.: 147,* 455 – 496, 1973.

Lund JS, Boothe RG: Interlaminar connections and pyramidal neuron organization in the visual cortex, area 17, of the macaque monkey. *J. Comp. Neurol.: 159,* 305 – 334, 1975.

Lynch, JC: The functional organization of posterior parietal association cortex. *Behav. Brain Sci.: 3,* 485 – 534, 1980.

Macko KA, Mishkin M: Metabolic mapping of higher-order visual areas in the monkey. In Sokoloff L (Editor), *Brain Imaging and Brain Function.* New York: Raven Press, pp. 73 – 86, 1985.

Maguire WM, Baizer JS: Visuotopic organization of the prelunate gyrus in rhesus monkey. *J. Neurosci.: 4,* 1690 – 1704, 1984.

Maunsell JHR, Newsome WT: Visual processing in monkey extrastriate cortex. *Annu. Rev. Neurosci.: 10,* 363 – 401, 1987.

Maunsell JHR, Van Essen DC: Functional properties of neurons in middle temporal visual area of the macaque monkey. I. Selectivity for stimulus direction, speed, and orientation. *J. Neurophysiol.: 49,* 1127 – 1147, 1983a.

Maunsell JHR, Van Essen DC: Functional properties of neurons in middle temporal visual area of the macaque monkey. II. Binocular interactions and sensitivity to binocular disparity. *J. Neurophysiol.: 49,* 1148 – 1167, 1983b.

Maunsell JHR, Van Essen DC: The connections of the middle temporal visual area (MT) and their relationship to a cortical hierarchy in the macaque monkey. *J. Neurosci.: 3,* 2563 – 2586, 1983c.

McCasland J, Konishi M: Interactions between auditory and motor activities in an avian song control nucleus. *Proc. Natl. Acad. Sci. USA: 178,* 7815 – 7819, 1981.

Meadows JC: The anatomical basis of prosopagnosia. *J. Neurol. Neurosurg. Psychiatr.: 37,* 489 – 501, 1974.

Mesulam M-M: A cortical network for directed attention and unilateral neglect. *Ann. Neurol.: 10,* 309 – 325, 1981.

Mesulam M-M, Van Hoesen GW, Pandya DN, Geschwind N: Limbic and sensory connections of the inferior parietal lobule (area PG) in the rhesus monkey: a study with a new method for horseradish peroxidase histochemistry. *Brain Res.: 136,* 393 – 414, 1977.

Michael CR: Color vision mechanisms in monkey striate cortex: dual-opponent cells with concentric receptive fields. *J. Neurophysiol.: 41,* 572 – 588, 1978a.

Michael CR: Color vision mechanisms in monkey striate cortex: simple cells with dual opponent-color receptive fields. *J. Neurophysiol.: 41,* 1233 – 1249, 1978b.

Michael CR: Color-sensitive complex cells in monkey striate cortex. *J. Neurophysiol.: 41,* 1250 – 1266, 1978c.

Michael CR: Color-sensitive hypercomplex cells in monkey striate cortex. *J. Neurophysiol.: 42,* 726 – 744, 1979.

Mishkin M: Cortical visual areas and their interactions. In Karczmar AG, Eccles JC (Editors), *Brain and Human Behavior.* Berlin: Springer-Verlag, pp. 187 – 208, 1972.

Mishkin M: A memory system in the monkey. *Philos. Trans. R. Soc. London: B298,* 85 – 95, 1982.

Mishkin M, Appenzeller T: The anatomy of memory. *Sci. Am.: 256,* 80 – 89, 1987.

Mishkin M, Ungerleider LG: Contribution of striate inputs to the visuospatial functions of parieto-preoccipital cortex in monkeys. *Behav. Brain Res.: 6,* 57 – 77, 1982.

Mishkin M, Ungerleider LG, Macko KA: Object vision and spatial vision: two cortical pathways. *Trends Neurosci.: 6,* 414 – 417, 1983.

Mishkin M, Malamut B, Bachevalier J: Memories and habits: two neural systems. In Lynch G, McGaugh JL, Weinberger NM (Editors), *Neurobiology of Learning and Memory.* New York: The Guilford Press, pp. 65 – 77, 1984.

Moran J, Desimone R: Selective attention gates visual processing in the extrastriate cortex. *Science: 229,* 782 – 784, 1985.

Moran J, Desimone R, Schein SJ, Mishkin M: Suppression from ipsilateral visual field in area V4 of the macaque. *Soc. Neurosci. Abstr.: 9,* 957, 1983.

Motter BC, Mountcastle VB: The functional properties of the light-sensitive neurons of the posterior parietal cortex studied in waking monkeys: foveal sparing and opponent vector organization. *J. Neurosci.: 1,* 3 – 26, 1981.

Mountcastle VB: Brain mechanisms for directed attention. *J. R. Soc. Med.: 71,* 14 – 28, 1978.

Movshon JA, Adelson EH, Gizzi MS, Newsome WT: The analysis of moving visual patterns. In Chagas C, Gattass R, Gross C (Editors), *Pattern Recognition Mechanisms.* Vatican City: Pontifical Academy of Sciences, pp. 117 – 151, 1985.

Nakamura RK, Schein SJ, Desimone R: Visual responses from

cells in striate cortex of monkeys rendered chronically 'blind' by lesions of nonvisual cortex. *Exp. Brain Res.: 63,* 185 – 190, 1986.

Newsome WT, Pare EB: A selective impairment of motion perception following lesions of the middle temporal visual area (MT). *J. Neurosci.: 8,* 2201 – 2211, 1988.

Newsome WT, Wurtz RH, Dursteler MR, Mikami A: Deficits in visual motion processing following ibotenic acid lesions of the middle temporal visual area of the macaque monkey. *J. Neurosci.: 5,* 825 – 840, 1985.

Newsome WT, Wurtz RH, Komatsu H: Relation of cortical areas MT and MST to pursuit eye movements. II. Differentiation of retinal from extraretinal inputs. *J. Neurophysiol.: 60,* 604 – 620, 1988.

Pentland A: Perceptual organization and the representation of natural form. *Artif. Intell.: 25,* 1 – 38, 1986.

Perrett DI, Rolls ET, Caan W: Visual neurons responsive to faces in the monkey temporal cortex. *Exp. Brain Res.: 47,* 329 – 342, 1982.

Perrett DI, Smith PAJ, Potter DD, Mistlin AJ, Head AS, Milner AD, Jeeves MA: Visual cells in the temporal cortex sensitive to face view and gaze direction. *Proc. R. Soc. London: B223,* 293 – 317, 1985.

Perrett DI, Mistlin AJ, Chitty AJ: Visual neurones responsive to faces. *Trends Neurosci.: 10,* 358 – 364, 1987.

Petersen SE, Baker JF, Allman JM: Dimensional selectivity of neurons in the dorsolateral visual area of the owl monkey. *Brain Res.: 197,* 507 – 511, 1980.

Phillips RR, Malamut BL, Bachevalier J, Mishkin M: Dissociation of the effects of inferior temporal and limbic lesions on object discrimination learning with 24-h intertrial intervals. *Behav. Brain Res.: 27,* 99 – 107, 1988.

Poggio GF, Fischer B: Binocular interaction and depth sensitivity in striate and prestriate cortex of behaving rhesus monkey. *J. Neurophysiol.: 40,* 1392 – 1405, 1977.

Poggio GF, Baker FH, Mansfield RJW, Sillito A, Grigg P: Spatial and chromatic properties of neurons subserving foveal and parafoveal vision in rhesus monkey. *Brain Res.: 100,* 25 – 59, 1975.

Poggio GF, Motter BC, Squatrito S, Trotter Y: Responses of neurons in visual cortex (V1 and V2) of the alert macaque to dynamic random-dot stereograms. *Vision Res.: 25,* 397 – 406, 1985.

Pollen DA, Ronner SF: Visual cortical neurons as localized spatial frequency filters. *IEEE Trans. Syst. Man Cybern.: SMC-13(5),* 907 – 916, 1983.

Pons TP, Garraghty PE, Friedman DP, Mishkin M: Physiological evidence for serial processing in somatosensory cortex. *Science: 237,* 417 – 420, 1987.

Posner MI, Presti DE: Selective attention and cognitive control. *Trends Neurosci.: 10,* 13 – 17, 1987.

Posner MI, Walker JA, Friedrich FJ, Rafal RD: Effects of parietal lobe injury on covert orienting of visual attention. *J. Neurosci.: 4,* 1863 – 1874, 1984.

Posner MI, Walker JA, Friedrich FJ, Rafal RD: How do the parietal lobes direct covert attention? *Neuropsychologia: 25,* 135 – 145, 1987.

Rasmussen T, Milner B: Clinical and surgical studies of the cerebral speech areas in man. In Zulch KJ, Creutzfeldt O, Galbraith GC (Editors), *Cerebral Localization.* Berlin:

Springer-Verlag, pp. 238 – 257, 1975.

Richmond BJ, Sato T: Enhancement of inferior temporal neurons during visual discrimination. *J. Neurophysiol.: 56,* 1292 – 1306, 1987.

Richmond BJ, Wurtz RH, Sato T: Visual responses of inferior temporal neurons in awake rhesus monkey. *J. Neurophysiol.: 50,* 1415 – 1432, 1983.

Robinson DL, Goldberg ME, Stanton GB: Parietal association cortex in the primate: sensory mechanisms and behavioral modulations. *J. Neurophysiol.: 41,* 910 – 932, 1978.

Rocha-Miranda CE, Bender DB, Gross CG, Mishkin M: Visual activation of neurons in inferotemporal cortex depends on striate cortex and forebrain commissures. *J. Neurophysiol.: 38,* 475 – 491, 1975.

Rockland KS, Pandya DN: Laminar origins and terminations of cortical connections of the occipital lobe in the rhesus monkey. *Brain Res.: 179,* 3 – 20, 1979.

Rolls ET, Baylis GC, Leonard CM: Role of low and high spatial frequencies in the face-selective responses of neurons in the cortex in the superior temporal sulcus in the monkey. *Vision Res.: 25,* 1021 – 1035, 1985.

Saito H, Yukie M, Tanaka K, Hikosaka K, Fukada Y, Iwai E: Integration of direction signals of image motion in the superior temporal sulcus of the macaque monkey. *J. Neurosci.: 6,* 145 – 157, 1986.

Saito H, Tanaka K, Fukumoto M, Fukada Y: The inferior temporal cortex of the macaque monkey. II. The level of complexity in the integration of pattern information. *Soc. Neurosci. Abstr.: 13,* 628, 1987.

Sakata H, Shibutani H, Kawano K: Functional properties of visual tracking neurons in posterior parietal association cortex of the monkey. *J. Neurophysiol.: 49,* 1364 – 1380, 1983.

Sandell JH, Schiller PH: Effects of cooling area 18 on striate cortex cells in the squirrel monkey. *J. Neurophysiol.: 48,* 38 – 48, 1982.

Schein SJ, De Monasterio FM: Mapping of retinal and geniculate neurons onto striate cortex of macaque. *J. Neurosci.: 7,* 996 – 1009, 1987.

Schein SJ, Marrocco RT, De Monasterio FM: Is there a high concentration of color-selective cells in area V4 of monkey visual cortex? *J. Neurophysiol.: 47,* 193 – 213, 1982.

Schein SJ, Desimone R, De Monasterio FM: Spectral properties of V4 cells in macaque monkey. *Invest. Ophthalmol. Visual Sci. (Suppl.): 24,* 107, 1983.

Schiller PH, Colby CL: The responses of single cells in the lateral geniculate nucleus of the rhesus monkey to color and luminance contrast. *Vision Res.: 23,* 1631 – 1641, 1983.

Schiller PH, Malpeli JG: Properties and tectal projections of monkey retinal ganglion cells. *J. Neurophysiol.: 40,* 428 – 445, 1977.

Schiller PH, Finlay BL, Volman SF: Quantitative studies of single-cell properties in monkey striate cortex. I. Spatiotemporal organization of receptive fields. *J. Neurophysiol.: 39,* 1288 – 1319, 1976a.

Schiller PH, Finlay BL, Volman SF: Quantitative studies of single-cell properties in monkey striate cortex. III. Spatial frequency. *J. Neurophysiol.: 39,* 1334 – 1351, 1976b.

Schwartz EL, Desimone R, Albright TD, Gross CG: Shape recognition and inferior temporal neurons. *Proc. Natl. Acad. Sci. USA: 80,* 5776 – 5778, 1983.

Seacord L, Gross CG, Mishkin M: Role of inferior temporal cortex in interhemispheric transfer. *Brain Res.: 167,* 259 – 272, 1979.

Shapley R, Lennie P: Spatial frequency analysis in the visual system. *Annu. Rev. Neurosci.: 8,* 547 – 583, 1985.

Shapley R, Perry VH: Cat and monkey retinal ganglion cells and their visual functional roles. *Trends Neurosci.: 9,* 229 – 235, 1986.

Shapley R, Kaplan E, Soodak R: Spatial summation and contrast sensitivity of X and Y cells in the lateral geniculate nucleus of the macaque. *Nature (London): 292,* 543 – 545, 1981.

Shipp S, Zeki S: Segregation of pathways leading from area V2 to areas V4 and V5 of macaque monkey visual cortex. *Nature (London): 315,* 322 – 325, 1985.

Siegel RM, Andersen RA: Motion perceptual deficits following ibotenic acid lesions of the middle temporal area (MT) in the behaving rhesus monkey. *Soc. Neurosci. Abstr.: 12,* 1183, 1986.

Spatz WB, Tigges J: Experimental-anatomical studies on the 'middle temporal visual area (MT)' in primates. I. Efferent cortico-cortical connections in the marmoset *Callithrix jacchus. J. Comp. Neurol.: 146,* 451 – 464, 1972.

Spitzer H, Richmond BJ: Visual selective attention modifies single unit activity in inferior temporal cortex. *Soc. Neurosci. Abstr.: 11,* 1245, 1985.

Spitzer H, Desimone R, Moran J: Increased attention enhances both behavioral and neuronal performance. *Science: 240,* 338 – 340, 1988.

Squire LR: *Memory and Brain.* New York: Oxford University Press, 1987.

Tanaka K, Hikosaka K, Saito H, Yukie M, Fukada Y, Iwai E: Analysis of local and wide-field movements in the superior temporal visual areas of the macaque monkey. *J. Neurosci.: 6,* 134 – 144, 1986.

Tanaka K, Fukada Y, Fukumoto M, Saito H: The inferior temporal cortex of the macaque monkey. I. Regional difference in response properties of cells. *Soc. Neurosci. Abstr.: 13,* 627, 1987.

Tanaka M, Weber H, Creutzfeldt OD: Visual properties and spatial distribution of neurones in the visual association area on the prelunate gyrus of the awake monkey. *Exp. Brain Res.: 65,* 11 – 37, 1986.

Thorell LG, De Valois RL, Albrecht DG: Spatial mapping of monkey V1 cells with pure color and luminance stimuli. *Vision Res., 24,* 751 – 769, 1984.

Tigges J, Spatz WB, Tigges M: Reciprocal point-to-point connections between parastriate and striate cortex in the squirrel monkey. *J. Comp. Neurol.: 148,* 481 – 490, 1973.

Tigges J, Spatz WB, Tigges M: Efferent cortico-cortical fiber connections of area 18 in the squirrel monkey (*Saimiri). J. Comp. Neurol.: 158,* 219 – 236, 1974.

Tootell RBH, Silverman MS, De Valois RL, Jacobs GH: Functional organization of the second cortical visual area in primates. *Science: 220,* 737 – 739, 1983.

Treisman A: Features and objects in visual processing. *Sci. Am.: 255,* 114B – 125, 1986.

Tso DY, Gilbert CD, Wiesel TN: Relationships between color-specific cells in cytochrome oxidase-rich patches of monkey striate cortex. *Soc. Neurosci. Abstr.: 12,* 1497, 1986.

Ungerleider LG: The corticocortical pathways for object recognition and spatial perception. In Chagas C, Gattass R, Gross C (Editors), *Pattern Recognition Mechanisms.* Vatican City: Pontifical Academy of Sciences, pp. 21 – 37, 1985.

Ungerleider LG, Desimone R: Cortical projections of visual area MT in the macaque. *J. Comp. Neurol.: 248,* 190 – 222, 1986.

Ungerleider LG, Mishkin M: The striate projection zone in the superior temporal sulcus of *Macaca mulatta*: location and topographic organization. *J. Comp. Neurol.: 188,* 347 – 366, 1979.

Ungerleider LG, Mishkin M: Two cortical visual systems. In Ingle DJ, Goodale MA, Mansfield RJW (Editors), *Analysis of Visual Behavior.* Cambridge: MIT Press, pp. 549 – 586, 1982.

Ungerleider LG, Gattass R, Sousa APB, Mishkin M: Projections of area V2 in the macaque. *Soc. Neurosci. Abstr.: 9,* 152, 1983.

Ungerleider LG, Desimone R, Moran J: Asymmetry of central and peripheral field inputs from area V4 into the temporal and parietal lobes of the macaque. *Soc. Neurosci. Abstr.: 12,* 1182, 1986.

Van Essen DC: Functional organization of primate visual cortex. In Jones EG, Peters AA (Editors), *Cerebral Cortex, Vol. 3.* New York: Plenum Press, pp. 259 – 329, 1985.

Van Essen DC, Maunsell JHR: Two-dimensional maps of the cerebral cortex. *J. Comp. Neurol.: 191,* 255 – 281, 1980.

Van Essen DC, Maunsell JHR: Hierarchical organization and functional streams in the visual cortex. *Trends Neurosci.: 6,* 370 – 375, 1983.

Van Essen DC, Zeki SM: The topographic organization of rhesus monkey prestriate cortex. *J. Physiol. (London): 277,* 193 – 226, 1978.

Van Essen DC, Maunsell JHR, Bixby JL: The middle temporal visual area in the macaque: myeloarchitecture, connections, functional properties and topographic organization. *J. Comp. Neurol.: 199,* 293 – 326, 1981.

Van Essen DC, Newsome WT, Bixby JL: The pattern of interhemispheric connections and its relationship to extrastriate visual areas in the macaque monkey. *J. Neurosci.: 2,* 265 – 283, 1982.

Vautin RG, Dow BM: Color cell groups in foveal striate cortex of the behaving macaque. *J. Neurophysiol.: 54,* 273 – 292, 1985.

von der Heydt R, Peterhans E, Baumgartner G: Illusory contours and cortical neuron responses. *Science: 224,* 1260 – 1262, 1984.

Weller RE, Kaas JH: Cortical and subcortical connections of visual cortex in primates. In Woolsey CN (Editor), *Cortical Sensory Organization, Vol. 2, Multiple Visual Areas.* Clifton, NJ: Humana Press, pp. 121 – 155, 1981.

Weller RE, Kaas JH: Retinotopic patterns of connections of area 17 with visual areas V-II and MT in macaque monkeys. *J. Comp. Neurol.: 220,* 253 – 279, 1983.

Wiesel TN, Hubel DH: Spatial and chromatic interactions in the lateral geniculate body of the rhesus monkey. *J. Neurophysiol.: 29,* 1115 – 1156, 1966.

Wild HM, Butler SR, Carden D, Kulikowski JJ: Primate cortical area V4 important for colour constancy but not wavelength discrimination. *Nature (London): 313,* 133 – 135,

1985.

Wong-Riley M: Changes in the visual system of monocularly sutured or enucleated cats demonstrable with cytochrome oxidase histochemistry. *Brain Res.: 171,* 11 – 28, 1979.

Zeki SM: Representation of central visual fields in prestriate cortex of monkey. *Brain Res.: 14,* 271 – 291, 1969.

Zeki SM: Cortical projections from two striate areas in the monkey. *Brain Res.: 34,* 19 – 35, 1971.

Zeki SM: Colour coding in rhesus monkey prestriate cortex. *Brain Res.: 53,* 422 – 427, 1973.

Zeki SM: Functional organization of a visual area in the posterior bank of the superior temporal sulcus of the rhesus monkey. *J. Physiol. (London): 236,* 549 – 573, 1974.

Zeki SM: The projections to the superior temporal sulcus from areas 17 and 18 in the rhesus monkey. *Proc. R. Soc. London: B193,* 199 – 207, 1976.

Zeki SM: Uniformity and diversity of structure and function in rhesus monkey prestriate visual cortex. *J. Physiol. (London): 277,* 273 – 290, 1978.

Zeki SM: The representation of colours in the cerebral cortex. *Nature (London): 284,* 412 – 418, 1980.

Zeki SM: The distribution of wavelength and orientation selective cells in different areas of monkey visual cortex. *Proc. R. Soc. London: B217,* 449 – 470, 1983a.

Zeki SM: Colour coding in the cerebral cortex: the reaction of cells in monkey visual cortex to wavelengths and colours. *Neuroscience: 9,* 741 – 765, 1983b.

Zeki SM: Colour coding in the cerebral cortex: the responses of wavelength-selective and colour-coded cells in monkey visual cortex to changes in wavelength composition. *Neuroscience: 9,* 767 – 781, 1983c.

Zrenner E: *Studies of Brain Function. 9: Neurophysiological Aspects of Color Vision in Primates.* Berlin: Springer-Verlag, 1983.

Zucker SW: Early orientation selection: tangent fields and the dimensionality of their support. Department of Electrical Engineering Technical Report 85 – 13 – R. Montreal, Canada: McGill University Press, pp. 1 – 33, 1985.

CHAPTER 15

The neurophysiology of spatial vision

Michael E. Goldberg and Carol L. Colby

Laboratory of Sensorimotor Research, National Eye Institute, Bethesda, MD 20892, U.S.A.

Introduction

Visual information enters the brain by exciting cells in the retinae, a pair of two-dimensional receptor mosaics which transform light into electrical signals. From the information encoded by these devices the brain constructs a representation of visual space so that the organism can successfully interact with those objects in the environment not directly in contact with its body: catch them, flee them, pursue them, or even throw a baseball at them. Space is not an exclusively visual construct. Even Shakespeare knew this: in *King Lear* Goneril tells the newly blinded Gloucester to 'smell his way to Dover'. One useful way to view space is as a motor construct: we can gauge the accuracy of our spatial analysis by judging the accuracy of movements we make toward objects in space (Jeannerod and Biguer, 1987). Much of our understanding about spatial vision comes from analysing the mechanisms whereby visual information is transformed into spatially accurate targeting information. It is plausible that the mechanisms that we shall discuss are in fact those that the brain uses to construct our and Goneril's idea of space. The reader must bear in mind, however, the great, so far unbridged, gap between plausibility and truth in our understanding of spatial vision.

Spatial vision requires both specifying where on the receptor surface an object is and making an estimate of the object's distance in depth. The visual system uses two sets of cues in particular to determine distance in depth: motion parallax cues, which can contribute to the estimation of depth by a single retina, and binocular disparity, which contributes to depth perception by calculating the difference in retinal position of an object in each eye. Spatial vision then requires that a limited set of objects be selected from the retina for further analysis, the process of visuospatial attention. Finally, spatial vision requires relating the retina's position to an extraretinal coordinate system so a correlation can be drawn between the position of a target on a movable retina and that target's position in an inertial space through which the organism must move. In this review we will concentrate on how certain cortical regions in the monkey's brain solve aspects of the problem of spatial vision. The first three sections deal with the anatomy and physiology underlying the detection of target position. The last two sections discuss target selection and the transformation from retinal to spatial coordinates.

The anatomical substrate of spatial vision

The visual cortex of primates contains multiple representations of visual space. Each of these representations, or areas, contains a map of all or part of the receptor surface. Single neurons in each area differ in their sensitivity to stimulus properties such as orientation, direction, speed and binocular disparity. Analysis of the connections of extrastriate visual cortex has yielded two major insights into its organization. First, extrastriate areas can be arranged in a hierarchy on the basis of the laminar pattern of connections among areas (Rockland and Pandya, 1979; Maunsell and Van Essen, 1983c) (Fig. 1). Second, this hierarchy can be subdivided into two 'streams', a dorsal stream, leading into parietal cortex, and a ventral stream, leading into temporal cortex (see Chapter 14 of this volume). These streams are physiologically distinct and participate in different visual functions (Van Essen and Maunsell, 1983; Desimone et al., 1985). The dorsal stream, comprising most of the areas shown in the top half of the figure, is particularly concerned with spatial vision and visuomotor functions.

Motion processing in visual cortex

Calculating depth from motion parallax cues requires a sophisticated visual motion analysis system. In primates this is thought to be a cortical function. A substantial proportion of cells in both striate cortex and V2 are selective for speed and direction of stimulus motion (Hubel and Wiesel, 1968; Schiller et al., 1976; Burkhalter and Van Essen, 1986). These motion-selective cells are concentrated in layer IVb of striate cortex (Dow, 1974) and in the cytochrome-dense zones of V2 (DeYoe and Van Essen, 1985) which provide the major inputs to area MT, a motion area in the superior temporal sulcus (Lund et al., 1976). Neurons in MT have a broad range of speed selectivities (Maunsell and Van Essen, 1983a) and a very high percentage of directionally selective neurons (Dubner and Zeki, 1971). Interactions between stimuli within the classically defined receptive field and stimuli well outside it suggest that cells in MT are capable of coding relative motion (Allman et al., 1985; Tanaka et al., 1986).

Area MT projects primarily to two other extrastriate areas, MST in the medial superior tem-

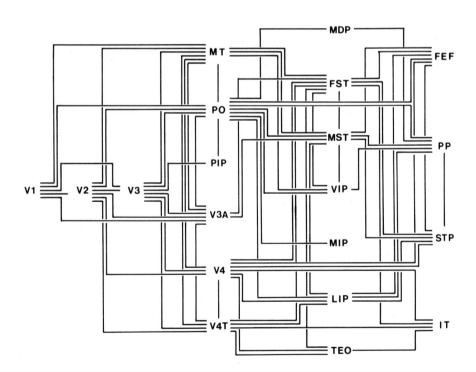

Fig. 1. Visual areas in cortex of macaque monkey. Areas are arranged in left-to-right order by hierarchical level, determined by laminar patterns of interconnecting pathways. Dorsal stream areas (MT, MST, VIP, PO, PP) are strongly interconnected and have relatively few projections to ventral stream areas (V4, TEO, IT).

poral sulcus and VIP in the intraparietal sulcus (Maunsell and Van Essen, 1983; Ungerleider and Desimone, 1986). Cells in MST are also strongly direction-selective (Desimone and Ungerleider, 1986) but differ from those in MT in that their responsiveness can depend on the task being performed by the animal. Some cells in MST give non-equivalent responses to identical visual stimulation when the monkey tracks a visual stimulus as compared to maintaining stationary fixation of a target (Newsome et al., 1988). Further, some MST cells are selective for expansion or contraction of a stimulus and some respond selectively to rotation, either in the frontoparallel plane or in depth (Saito et al., 1986). Areas MT and MST have multiple direct and indirect inputs to parietal cortex (Fig. 1) and presumably provide the motion information upon which its spatial functions are based.

Depth perception and binocular disparity

One of the most important cues for depth perception is binocular disparity, that is, the slight differences in the positions of the images formed in the two eyes. How cells in the brain encode and use this disparity to determine depth has been the subject of numerous investigations.

Striate cortex
In the geniculostriate pathway, the first appreciable convergence of signals from the two eyes onto single cells occurs in primary visual cortex. Neurons in striate cortex receive input from corresponding points on the two retinae. These binocular receptive fields have similar stimulus requirements for each eye so that orientation and direction selectivity are consistent for each of the two monocular fields when mapped separately. The interaction between the two fields, however, takes a number of different forms. Early investigations in anesthetized, paralysed cats showed that many cortical cells respond maximally when stimuli are placed in exactly corresponding positions within the two monocular receptive fields, while others prefer small offsets between the

stimuli (Barlow et al., 1967; Nikara et al., 1968; Pettigrew et al., 1968). These cells are said to be tuned to particular disparities: the disparities which produce responses may be exact superposition (zero disparity), slightly convergent or slightly divergent. Joshua and Bishop (1970) proposed that these cells subserve binocular single vision and depth discrimination.

In addition to the various types of tuned cell, Poggio and Fischer (1977), studying alert monkeys, found a second class of disparity-sensitive cells with a reciprocal receptive field organization. 'Far' neurons have an excitatory response over a range of uncrossed disparities, those beyond the fixation plane, and give an inhibitory response to stimuli with crossed disparity. 'Near' neurons have the opposite organization and give excitatory responses to stimuli with crossed disparities, those nearer than the fixation plane. These two cell types differ from the tuned neurons both in the shape of the tuning curve and in the range of disparities which will activate the cell, as shown in Fig. 2.

In striate cortex of alert monkey, $60-70\%$ of neurons are disparity-sensitive. Of these, about half are tuned excitatory cells; the peak response occurs for stimuli close to superposition. Tuned inhibitory cells are suppressed over a comparable range. The responses of reciprocal neurons typically change suddenly from maximal inhibition to maximal excitation, with the crossover point at or near zero disparity. In both cat (Ferster, 1981) and monkey (Poggio and Poggio, 1984) there is no correspondence between the simple/complex cell classification (see Chapter 14) and tuned or reciprocal responses to bar stimuli.

The cell types described thus far are thought to be involved in the detection of local stereopsis, that is, the position in depth of isolated line segments based on their binocular disparity. Humans and monkeys are also able to detect form and movement in stereoscopic depth in random-dot stereograms (Julesz, 1971; Bough, 1970). In this technique, different random-dot patterns are presented to each eye. The patterns are identical except for one region in which there is a consistent horizontal disparity between the two. The region of disparity is perceived as a shape standing out in front of or behind the rest of the pattern. When either pattern is viewed alone with one or both eyes no such pattern is seen. The visual system must match each point in the two stimuli correctly in order to differentiate figure from ground. This process has been called cyclopean vision or 'global' stereopsis to distinguish it from the process involved in detecting the disparity of isolated contours. While it was known from Julesz's psychophysical work that this process must occur relatively early in visual processing it was nonetheless surprising when Poggio et al. (1985) discovered that cells even in striate cortex can discriminate shapes that

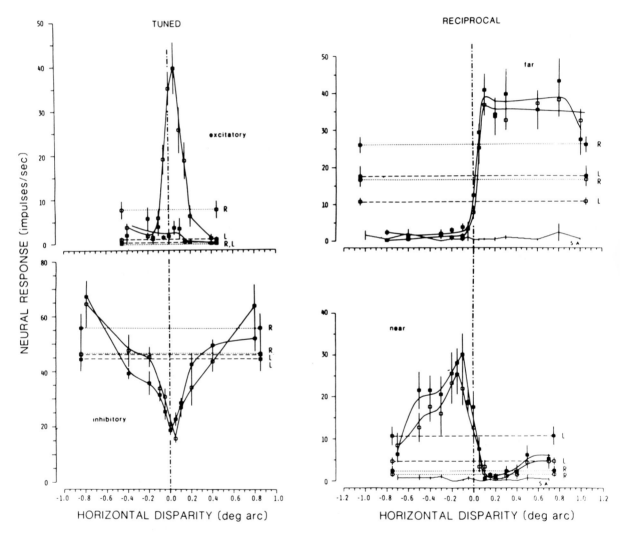

Fig. 2. Tuning curves for disparity selectivity in foveal cortical neurons of the macaque. Each panel shows the response magnitude for a single neuron tested at several different horizontal disparities. The stimuli were lines moving perpendicular to the preferred orientation of each cell. The filled and open symbols indicate opposite directions of stimulus motion. The dashed and dotted lines show response magnitude for monocular stimulation in each direction. Error bars indicate 1 SE of the mean. Tuned neurons respond over a very narrow range of stimulus disparities close to superposition. Reciprocal neurons have a broader response range with a sudden change from maximal to minimal responsiveness near zero disparity. Reproduced with permission from Annual Review of Neuroscience (Poggio and Poggio, 1984).

emerge only in the binocular viewing of random-dot stereograms. Optimal stimuli for such cells are typically many times larger than the conventionally defined receptive field and need not match the orientation selectivity of the cell as studied with solid stimuli. About 30% of the striate cells tested are sensitive to disparity in random-dot stimuli as well as to disparity in conventional bar stimuli and may be involved in processing cues for both global and local stereopsis. While their tuning characteristics do not differ from other disparity-sensitive cells when tested with isolated line segments, all such cyclopean cells are of the complex type and do not exhibit direction selectivity. Monkeys lacking binocular neurons in the striate cortex are unable to detect depth in dynamic random-dot stereograms (Crawford et al., 1984).

Extrastriate cortex

Several higher-order visual areas beyond striate cortex contain disparity-sensitive cells (Hubel and Wiesel, 1970; Zeki, 1974). While many of these neurons exhibit responses similar to those described for V1, a number of new features have also been noted.

In area V2 there is a greater proportion of disparity-selective neurons than in V1 (Poggio and Fischer, 1977; Poggio and Talbot, 1981). These neurons are concentrated in clusters within those portions of V2 that send efferents to area MT, the next stage in a chain of areas thought to subserve the analysis of visual motion (DeYoe and Van Essen, 1985).

Area MT has the highest percentage of disparity-selective cells among those areas of extrastriate cortex where the question has been examined (Felleman and Van Essen, 1987). Cells in MT are very sensitive to motion and nearly all are binocular, receiving approximately equal inputs from the two eyes (Zeki, 1974; Van Essen et al., 1981; Maunsell and Van Essen, 1983b). They are also selective for orientation, direction, speed and disparity (Maunsell and Van Essen, 1983a; Albright, 1984). MT neurons are thus particularly well suited for the analysis of motion in space. The types of disparity-selective neuron found in MT closely parallel those found at previous stages, namely near cells, far cells, tuned excitatory and tuned inhibitory. An important point concerning these cells is that they are tuned for fixed and not for chang-

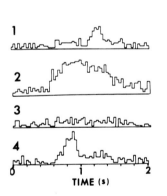

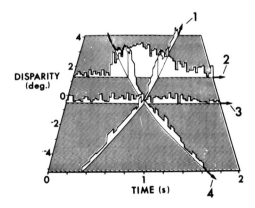

Fig. 3. The 3-D receptive field of a single neuron in MT. In the left panel, response histograms are shown for movement in the frontoparallel plane (trajectories 2 and 3) and for motions in depth (1 and 4). The unit responded well over a broad range (0.5 to 3,5 deg) of crossed (near) disparities when tested with frontoparallel motion (not shown). Responses to motions in depth whose center-points occur at a nonpreferred disparity have peaks at different points in time. For trajectory 1, the stimulus begins far from the animal and moves nearer, producing a response late in the movement. For trajectory 4, the stimulus appears near the animal and moves away, producing a response early in the movement. In the right panel, the same four histograms are plotted on a plane to show the spatial relationships of their peaks. The frontoparallel motions (2 and 3) are plotted running straight across from left to right at their respective disparities. The motions in depth (1 and 4) cut across disparities as they move. The peaks for these histograms occur at times when the stimuli have a disparity close to the preferred disparity. The maximal response occurs for frontoparallel motion. Reproduced with permission from Journal of Neurophysiology (Maunsell and Van Essen, 1983b).

ing disparities. An object moving obliquely in depth presents a stimulus of constantly changing disparity. Maunsell and Van Essen (1983b) carefully tested MT neurons to see whether they were selective for fixed or changing disparity and concluded that in every case the most effective stimulus was one moving parallel to the fixation plane, indicating that MT neurons code fixed disparities and are not selective for object motion toward or away from the eye. An apparent motion in depth response occurs only when cells are tested along trajectories whose center point is at a non-preferred disparity. MT neurons can be thought of as having three dimensional receptive fields, as illustrated in Fig. 3. For this cell, there is a significant response to any stimulus moving in a particular direction (left to right) regardless of whether it is also moving in depth. Note also that the cell responds to both an approaching stimulus (histogram 4) and a receding stimulus (histogram 1) within a restricted zone, that is, whenever the stimulus has a disparity close to the preferred fixed disparity. Maunsell and Van Essen conclude that there is as yet no convincing evidence for true motion in depth cells in extrastriate cortex. Information about object motion in depth may nonetheless be derived from the activity of the population of disparity-sensitive cells, since these cells represent a range of preferred depths.

Object perception in random-dot stereograms may arise from either motion or form disparity cues. Disparity-selective neurons should therefore exist in extrastriate areas in both the form and motion pathways. A substantial number of cells in V3d, V3v, V3A and V4 are disparity-selective (Burkhalter and Van Essen, 1986; Felleman and Van Essen, 1987; Poggio et al., 1988). The majority of disparity-tuned cells in V3 respond to patterns embedded in dynamic random-dot stereograms. This sensitivity to global stereopsis cues appears to increase as one ascends the hierarchy of visual areas (Poggio et al., 1988).

Enhancement of visual responses and visuospatial attention

A critical step in spatial analysis is the selection of targets from the environment for further analysis – the process of visuospatial attention (Heilman et al., 1987). For many years clinicians have postulated that these functions are located in the posterior parietal and, to a lesser extent, frontal cortices because patients with lesions in these areas frequently neglect the area of space contralateral to the lesion. A neural phenomenon which could subserve this process is that of behavioral enhancement of visual responsiveness. Neurons in many areas of the visual system share this property, first

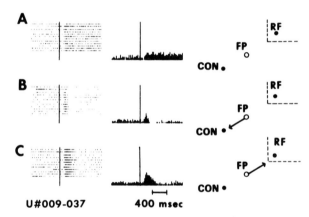

Fig. 4. Enhancement of a visual response in the monkey frontal eye field. Each section shows cell activity on the left and a cartoon of the behavior on the right. Cell activity is depicted as a raster (left) and as a histogram (center). In the raster each dot represents a neural discharge. Each row represents a 2 – s epoch of activity. Successive lines are synchronized on the appearance of the visual stimulus, depicted by the vertical trigger line. Histograms sum the activity of the rasters, with a bin width of 12 ms. **A**: Response of cell to appearance of two stimuli, one in the receptive field (RF), the other a control stimulus (CON) outside the receptive field, while the monkey looks at the fixation point (FP). **B**: Response of the neuron when the monkey makes a saccade from FP to CON. **C**: Response of the neuron when the monkey makes a saccade from FP to RF. The visual response is enhanced when the monkey uses the stimulus as the target for a saccade. Reproduced with permission from Journal of Neurophysiology (Goldberg and Bushnell, 1981).

described in the superior colliculus by Goldberg and Wurtz (1972). This phenomenon has also been observed in posterior parietal cortex (Yin and Mountcastle, 1977; Robinson et al., 1978), prelunate gyrus (Fischer and Boch, 1981), striate cortex (Wurtz and Mohler, 1976), V4 (Moran and Desimone, 1985), frontal eye field (Goldberg and Bushnell, 1981) and periprincipal cortex (Boch and Goldberg, 1987). The general outlines of the phenomenon are the same in each region: the visual response of a neuron is more intense when the monkey is about to use the stimulus as the object for some behavior. Fig. 4 shows an example of enhancement before saccadic eye movements in the monkey frontal eye field but the illustration could just as easily have been selected from periprincipal cortex or posterior parietal cortex. Fig. 4A shows the response of a neuron to the appearance of two stimuli, one in its receptive field and the other, a control stimulus, outside the receptive field. In this first task the monkey is required to look at the fixation point and not look at either of the other two stimuli when they appear. The cell gives a brisk discharge on the appearance of the stimulus and continues to discharge as long as the stimulus stays in the receptive field. When the monkey makes a saccade to the stimulus in the receptive field (Fig. 4C) the neuron discharges at a higher rate, although the activity is truncated by the beginning of the saccade. This enhancement of the visual response could result from various non-specific changes related to saccadic eye movements, such as pupillary dilatation or changes in the general level of arousal in the monkey. It does not occur when the monkey makes a saccade to the control stimulus (Fig. 4B). The enhancement is thus specific to the monkey's making a saccade to a stimulus in the receptive field. This spatially selective enhancement is found in prefrontal cortex, frontal eye field and posterior parietal cortex.

When Goldberg and Wurtz first described presaccadic enhancement in the superior colliculus, they postulated that the phenomenon was a substrate for general visuospatial attention because saccades are intimately connected with attention (Yarbus, 1967). However, Wurtz and Mohler (1976) suggested that because attention is not necessarily related to saccades it was important to study neurons under a condition in which attention and eye movements were dissociated. They trained monkeys to respond to a luminance change in either a peripheral target or a central fixation point without making a saccade to the peripheral target. Since the monkey responded to the peripheral stimulus in this difficult task they inferred that the monkey had attends to it. Surprisingly, neurons in the superior colliculus did not yield an enhanced response to a stimulus in the receptive field when the monkey attended to the stimulus without making a saccade to it. Thus, although presaccadic enhancement might have been a substrate for visuospatial attention, it is not so in the superior colliculus. Conversely, Bushnell et al. (1981) found that neurons in posterior parietal cortex yield enhanced responses to a stimulus whenever the monkey attends to it, whether or

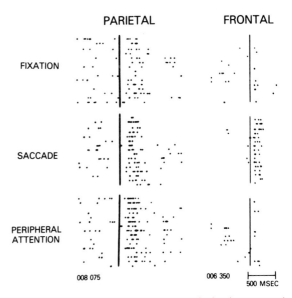

Fig. 5. Comparison of enhancement of visual response in parietal and frontal cortex for fixation, saccade and peripheral attention tasks. A parietal neuron is illustrated on left, and a frontal eye field neuron on right. Note that the response of the parietal neuron is enhanced in both tasks but the frontal response is enhanced only in the saccade task. Each raster is synchronized on the appearance of the visual stimulus.

not the monkey actually makes a saccade to the stimulus. They studied not only the peripheral attention task but also a hand-reach task in which the monkey had to reach out and touch a stimulus without looking at it. For cells in the parietal cortex there was an excellent correlation between enhancement in the saccade and non-saccade tasks: when the cells yielded enhanced responses in the saccade task, they also yielded enhanced responses in both no-saccade tasks. In the frontal eye field, just as in the superior colliculus, enhancement occurs only in association with eye movements. Fig. 5 compares parietal and frontal neurons in fixation, peripheral attention and saccade tasks. Note that the parietal neuron has an enhanced response in each of the tasks (peripheral attention and saccade) in which the monkey had to attend to the stimuli but that the frontal neuron shows enhancement only in the saccade task.

Not all modulation of neuronal activity is related to the spatial aspects of attention. In V4, where neurons are thought to process form vision (see Chapter 14), Moran and Desimone (1985) showed that neuronal activity was attenuated when the monkey had to attend to an ineffective stimulus within the neuron's receptive field. No such modulation was seen when the monkey had to attend to an ineffective stimulus outside the receptive field. Thus for V4 the critical variable is not the spatial location of the stimulus but its form. Attention serves to blunt the response to an irrelevant stimulus once its spatial location has been chosen rather than to select the location as enhancement does in posterior parietal cortex. A similar independence from spatial selection has been demonstrated in inferior temporal cortex by Richmond and Sato (1987). In this region there is an attenuation of response to a stimulus in the peripheral attention task, which could be considered a luminance-change-detection task. There is an enhancement when the same stimulus is used in a pattern discrimination task. Thus the enhancement does not signify the relevance of the spatial location of the stimulus but rather its relevance in a pattern discrimination.

The maintenance of spatial accuracy by a system tied to a roving retina

The retina is mapped onto the brain in a relatively hard-wired fashion, so that the retinal field is remapped over and over again in various parts of the brain (Van Essen and Maunsell, 1983). A given region of striate cortex, for example, corresponds to a given region of each retina. As the eyes move through the orbit, an object which occupies a constant region in space stimulates a series of different regions in striate cortex. How can the brain equate continuously shifting retinal activity with a constant object in space?

An intuitively appealing way to solve the problem is for the brain to create a map of the visual environment in some egocentric or inertial coor-

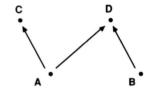

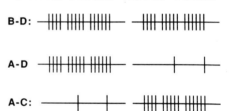

Fig. 6. Spatial and vector coding. A, B, C and D are four visual stimuli arranged at the corners of a parallelogram. Six idealized neuronal spike trains are illustrated. Each spike train begins at the appearance of the visual stimulus. The column on the left shows what would be expected in each situation for spatial coding, and the column on the right shows what would be expected for vector coding. When the monkey looks at B and the stimulus appears at D (B-D) the neuron discharges in response to the appearance of D. In spatial coding, the neuron discharges when the monkey looks at A and the stimulus appears at D (A-D) but not when the monkey looks at A and the stimulus appears at C (A-C). In vector coding, the neuron discharges when the monkey looks at A and the stimulus appears at C but not when the monkey looks at A and the stimulus appears at D.

dinate system, so that a stimulus located at a single place in visual space would excite the same neurons regardless of where the eyes were positioned in the orbit. This solution is called spatial coding, and it is contrasted in Fig. 6 with vector coding, the coding of stimuli by their distance and direction from the center of gaze rather than by their position in some supraretinal space. Consider a neuron that discharges when the subject looks at B and a stimulus appears at D. When the animal looks at A, a spatially coded neuron would discharge when the stimulus appears at D, because the stimulus at D is at the same spatial position, although at a different retinal position. A vector-coded neuron would discharge instead when the stimulus appears at C, because the two vectors A→C and B→D are identical, even though the spatial positions of the two stimuli differ. Robinson has postulated such a neuron in his model of the saccadic system (Robinson, 1981). Unfortunately, such a 'target position in space' neuron has never been found. Instead, neurons throughout the visual and oculomotor system are coded in vector coordinates relative to the fovea. Although the intensity of visual activity of some neurons in the posterior parietal cortex (Sakata et al., 1980; Andersen et al., 1985) and posterior thalamus (Schlag and Schlag-Rey, 1984) can be influenced by the position of the eye in the orbit, the retinal locations of the receptive fields do not seem to be affected by the orbital position. Thus the effect of a stimulus on a cell is a complicated function of its spatial position and the position of the eye in the orbit. In order to extract actual spatial position from such a neuron one would have to combine its activity with a neuron that signals position of the eye in the orbit. Such neurons have been found in parietal cortex by Sakata et al. (1980) and in central thalamus by Schlag-Rey and Schlag (1984).

Studies in the oculomotor system have provided some insight into another solution for the problem of spatial constancy. Motor neurons in the saccadic system, from the frontal eye field to the pons, are vector-coded (Fuchs et al., 1985). Visual neurons in the saccadic system, from the frontal eye field (Bruce and Goldberg, 1985) to the superior colliculus (Goldberg and Wurtz, 1972) are also vector-coded. Yet Hallett and Lightstone (1976) showed that humans can make accurate saccades to the spatial location of flashed targets even when there is a dissonance between the retinal location of the target and the eye movement necessary to fixate the target. Monkeys have a similar capability (Mays and Sparks, 1980), and movement neurons in the superior colliculus give spatially accurate vector movement signals, which must mean that by the time the oculomotor signal reaches the superior colliculus it has already been adjusted for the previous saccade (Sparks and Porter, 1983). Monkeys can also make accurate saccades to a flashed target if their eye position has been changed by electrical stimulation of the superior colliculus (Sparks and Mays, 1983). Since ablation of the oculomotor proprioceptive neurons in the trigeminal ganglion has no effect on a monkey's compensation for electrical stimulation, Sparks and Porter (1983) postulated that the brain used a corollary discharge from the oculomotor system to calculate the desired saccade.

Studies in the frontal eye field of the monkey suggest that the corollary discharge may act on visual neurons in the frontal eye field (Goldberg and Bruce, 1981). These neurons seem to maintain spatial accuracy when there is a dissonance be-

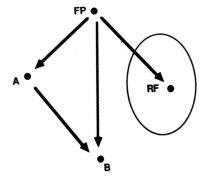

Fig. 7. Hypothetical retinal receptive field and eye movement vectors present when multiple saccades are made to briefly appearing stimuli. FP, A, B and RF are visual stimuli, and the oval surrounding RF is the receptive field as determined during a simple fixation task. Black arrows are possible saccades.

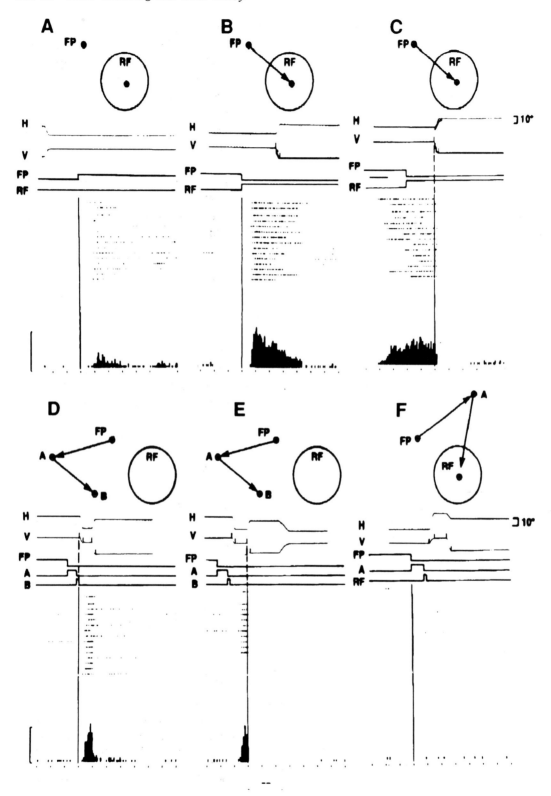

tween retinal vector of a stimulus and the movement vector of the saccade necessary to acquire that stimulus. We define the retinal vector as the vector drawn from the fovea to the location of the stimulus on the retina, and the movement vector as the direction and amplitude of the saccade. Usually these two vectors are identical but on occasion, because of an intervening saccade, there can be a dissonance between the two. Fig. 7 illustrates the problem faced by a cell dealing with this dissonance. Consider a cell with the receptive field depicted by the oval in the lower right quadrant. When the monkey makes a saccade from the fixation point (FP) to a stimulus in the receptive field (RF), the cell discharges in response to the stimulus and the retinal vector and movement vector are identical. When the monkey makes saccades from FP to the stimuli at A and B, the cell does not discharge. However, if stimuli are flashed briefly at A and B, and the monkey makes saccades in total darkness from FP to A and then A to B, the second saccade (from A to B) has the same vector as the original saccade (from FP to RF) but their retinal vectors (FP to B and FP to RF) are different.

In the frontal eye field, a number of visually active neurons have retinal receptive fields that change their topographic location when the retinal location of the stimulus evoking a certain eye movement is different from the direction of the eye movement. For these neurons the critical parameter is the vector of the saccade rather than the retinal location of the stimulus. Any stimulus could theoretically evoke a visual response from the neuron as long as, by virtue of the intervening saccade, the saccade necessary to acquire the place where the stimulus had been is the proper saccade for the cell. Nonetheless this is visual activity because the cells do not discharge before saccades made in total darkness. This phenomenon is illustrated in Fig. 8, which shows a frontal eye field neuron that discharges in response to the appearance of a stimulus in its receptive field (Fig. 8A), and in response to the stimulus for a visually guided saccade (Fig. 8B and C). The cell also discharges in double-jump tasks in which both stimuli appear sequentially and then disappear before the monkey moves its eyes. When the monkey performed the double-jump task, from FP to A to B, the cell began to discharge after the monkey had made a saccade to A, and before the saccade to B, even though neither spot ever appeared in the cell's retinal receptive field (Fig. 8D). This discharge terminated at the beginning of the saccade from A to B (Fig. 8E). When the monkey made a saccade from FP to A to RF (Fig. 8F), there was no discharge even though the stimulus appeared in the retinal receptive field. This cell had no postsaccadic activity, so the activity of the neuron could not be ascribed merely to a response to the first saccade. It also did not discharge in response to the presentation of the A and B stimuli alone. Instead, the activity in the double saccade task must be considered as a change in the retinal

Fig. 8. Activity of visuomovement neuron during double-step and control tasks. Each panel shows horizontal (H) and vertical (V) eye position traces and stimulus (FP, RF, A, B) status lines for a sample trial. Above each raster and histogram is a cartoon describing the experiment. RF, receptive field diagramed as an oval. FP is the fixation point, and A and B are other target positions. If in a given panel a light actually appeared then the light is marked by a dot. If the monkey made a saccade in that experiment, then the saccade is marked by an arrow. **A**: Activity in no-saccade task, with rasters synchronized on the appearance of stimulus in the receptive field. The stimulus was flashed for 50 ms. Raster and histogram synchronized on appearance of the stimulus. **B**: Brisk response in visually guided saccade task. Monkey began by fixating FP, which disappears when target at RF appears, and then made the saccade symbolized by the arrow. Raster and histogram are synchronized on target onset. **C**: Same task and trials as in **B**, with raster and histogram synchronized on saccade from FP to RF. **D – F** show the neuron's activity during double-jump tasks. **D**: Brisk activity when lights were flashed at A and then B, and the monkey made saccades from FP to A and then from A to B. Note that the A→B saccade had the same movement vector as the FP→RF saccade in panels **B** and **C**, but no target appeared in the initial receptive field of the cell. The raster and histogram are synchronized on the FP→A saccade. **E**: Same trials as in **D**, but synchronized on beginning of A→B saccade. **F**: Absence of response when stimuli appeared at A and RF, and the monkey made saccades from FP to A and A to RF. There was no response either to the visual stimuli or to the movement even though a stimulus appeared in the retinal receptive field as determined in **A**.

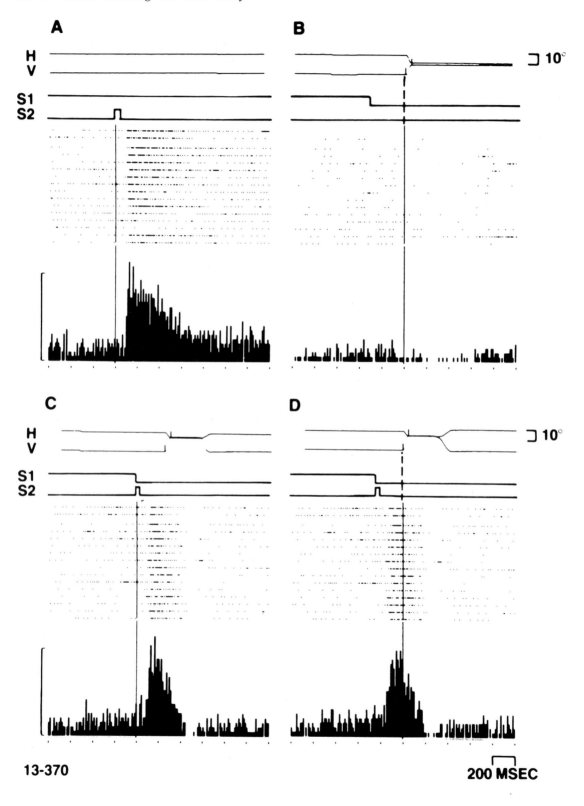

A

H
V

S1
S2

B

⊐ 10°

C

H
V

S1
S2

D

⊐ 10°

13-370

200 MSEC

receptive field of the neuron. The visual activity describes the presence of a visual target not in retinal coordinates but in motor coordinates. The cell signals that there is a visual stimulus which can evoke a saccade of certain dimensions, rather than that there is a stimulus in a certain part of a retinal receptive field.

The mechanism by which a receptive field can be changed is unclear. The process can be simply described by the formalism of vector subtraction. The vector $A \rightarrow B = FP \rightarrow A - FP \rightarrow B$, so it is possible to calculate the desired eye movement from the retinal location of the target and the dimensions of the previous eye movement. Both the components for such a calculation are present in the frontal eye field: cells that carry the retinal location of the target (Mohler et al., 1973) and cells that carry the dimensions of the previous saccade (Bizzi, 1968). That these two signals can interact is illustrated in Fig. 9. This frontal eye field cell discharges tonically in response to a briefly flashed stimulus: the firing continues for over a second (Fig. 9A). The cell has no activity at all before a learned saccade in total darkness (Fig. 9B). Even though the neuron discharges tonically in response to a briefly flashed stimulus, the tonic activity is truncated by the occurrence of a saccade (Fig. 9C, D). Presumably the same signal both turns off this neuron and turns on another neuron which begins to fire when a visual stimulus can be acquired by its output saccade. The effect of this processing is to transform visual activity from a retinal coordinate system to a motor coordinate system. The message of such a neuron is that there is a visual stimulus which can be acquired by a saccade of certain dimensions. This process ensures that the frontal eye field is able to maintain spatial ac-

curacy of saccades in the face of a dissonance between the retinal location of the target and the saccade needed to acquire it. It is important to emphasize that although the cell carries a spatially accurate signal, it is not a spatial signal per se because such a signal would discharge whenever a stimulus is in a certain spatial location, regardless of orbital position. This is not true for spatially accurate frontal eye field neurons.

These results demonstrate that the oculomotor system can maintain spatial accuracy by having the dynamics of previous saccades operate on the retinal map. This coordinate transformation model achieves spatial accuracy for saccades despite a moving retina by using neural components that have all been described, rather than requiring a component, target position in space, that has eluded discovery. One can hypothesize that the mechanism described for the maintenance of spatial accuracy in the saccadic system is generalizable to the problem of spatial perception: the coding of space would be not in absolute or inertial terms but in relative terms. Our perception of the spatial location of a target might be derived not from an inertial map, but by a backward analysis of targeting information for potential movement.

References

Albright TD: Direction and orientation selectivity of neurons in visual area MT of the macaque. *J. Neurophysiol.:* 52, 1106–1130, 1984.

Allman, JM, Miezin F, McGuinness E: Direction and velocity-specific responses from beyond the classical receptive field in the middle temporal visual area (MT). *Perception:* 14, 105–126, 1985.

Andersen, RA, Essick GK, Siegel RM: Encoding of spatial location by posterior parietal neurons. *Science:* 230, 456–458, 1985.

Fig. 9. Interaction of eye movement and visual stimulus in frontal eye field neuron. Each panel shows horizontal (H) and vertical (V) eye position, and the condition of the fixation point (S1) and peripheral stimulus (S2) positioned above a raster and histogram. **A**: Maintained discharge of a frontal eye field neuron to briefly (50 ms) flashed stimulus in the fixation task. Raster and histogram aligned on appearance of visual stimulus. **B**: Discharge of the neuron in association with a saccade to a remembered target. Note that there is no activity in this condition, although there may be a suppression of the background activity. Raster and histogram aligned on the beginning of the saccade. **C**: Discharge of the neuron when the monkey makes a saccade in total darkness to the flashed stimulus. Raster and histogram synchronized on target appearance. **D**: Same trials synchronized on beginning of saccade. Reproduced with permission from Journal of Neurophysiology (Bruce and Goldberg, 1985).

Barlow H, Blakemore C, Pettigrew JD: The neural mechanism of binocular depth discrimination. *J. Physiol.: 193,* 327 – 342, 1967.

Bizzi E: Discharge of frontal eye field neurons during saccadic and following eye movements in unanesthetized monkeys. *Exp. Brain Res.: 6,* 69 – 80, 1968.

Boch R, Goldberg ME: Saccade-related modulation of visual activity in monkey prefrontal cortex. *Invest. Ophthalmol.: 28* (Suppl), 124, 1987.

Bough EW: Stereoscopic vision in the macaque monkey: A behavioral demonstration. *Nature: 225,* 42 – 44, 1970.

Bruce CJ, Goldberg ME: Primate frontal eye fields: I. Single neurons discharging before saccades. *J. Neurophysiol.: 53,* 603 – 635, 1985.

Burkhalter A, Van Essen DC: Processing of color, form and disparity information in visual areas VP and V2 of ventral extrastriate cortex in the macaque monkey. *J. Neurosci.: 6,* 2327 – 2351, 1986.

Bushnell MC, Goldberg ME, Robinson DL: Behavioral enhancement of visual responses in monkey cerebral cortex: I. Modulation in posterior parietal cortex related to selective visual attention. *J. Neurophysiol.: 46,* 755 – 772, 1981.

Colby CL, Gattass R, Olson CR, Gross CG: Topographic organization of cortical afferents to extrastriate visual area PO in the macaque: a dual tracer study. *J. Comp. Neurol.: 238,* 1257 – 1299, 1988.

Crawford MLJ, Smith EL, Harwerth RS, von Noorden GK: Stereoblind monkeys have few binocular neurons. *Invest. Ophthalmol. Vis. Sci.: 25,* 779 – 781, 1984.

DeYoe EA, Van Essen DC: Segregation of efferent connections and receptive field properties in visual area V2 of the macaque. *Nature: 317,* 58 – 61, 1985.

Desimone R, Ungerleider LG: Multiple visual areas in the caudal superior temporal sulcus of the macaque. *J. Comp. Neurol.: 248,* 164 – 189, 1986.

Desimone R, Schein SJ, Moran J, Ungerleider LG: Contour, color and shape analysis beyond the striate cortex. *Vision Res.: 25,* 441 – 452, 1985.

Dow BM: Functional classes of cells and their laminar distribution in monkey visual cortex. *J. Neurophysiol.: 37,* 927 – 946, 1974.

Dubner R, Zeki SM: Response properties and receptive fields of cells in an anatomically defined region of the superior temporal sulcus in the monkey. *Brain Res.: 35,* 528 – 532, 1971.

Felleman DJ, Van Essen DC: Receptive field properties of neurons in area V3 of macaque monkey extrastriate cortex. *J. Neurophysiol.: 57,* 889 – 920, 1987.

Ferster D: A comparison of binocular depth mechanisms in areas 17 and 18 of the cat visual cortex. *J. Physiol.: 311,* 623 – 655, 1981.

Fischer B, Boch R: Enhanced activation of neurons in prelunate cortex before visually guided saccades of trained rhesus monkeys. *Exp. Brain Res.: 44,* 129 – 137, 1981.

Fuchs AF, Kaneko CRS, Scudder CA: Brainstem control of saccadic eye movements. *Annu. Rev. Neurosci.: 8,* 307 – 337, 1985.

Goldberg ME, Bruce CJ: Frontal eye fields in the monkey: eye movements remap the effective coordinates of visual stimuli. *Soc. Neurosci. Abstr.: 7,* 131, 1981.

Goldberg ME, Bushnell MC: Behavioral enhancement of visual responses in monkey cerebral cortex. II. Modulation in frontal eye fields specifically related to saccades. *J. Neurophysiol.: 46,* 773 – 787, 1981.

Goldberg ME, Wurtz RH: Activity of superior colliculus in behaving monkey: I. Visual receptive fields of single neurons. *J. Neurophysiol.: 35,* 542 – 559, 1972.

Goldberg ME, Wurtz RH: Activity of superior colliculus in behaving monkey: II. The effect of attention on neuronal responses. *J. Neurophysiol.: 35,* 560 – 574, 1972.

Guthrie BL, Porter JD, Sparks DL: Corollary discharge provides accurate eye position information to the oculomotor system. *Science: 221,* 1193 – 1195, 1983.

Hallett PE, Lightstone AD: Saccadic eye movements to flashed targets. *Vision Res.: 16,* 107 – 114, 1976.

Heilman KM, Watson RT, Valenstein E, Goldberg ME: Attention: behavior and neural mechanisms. In *Handbook of Physiology, Section I: The Nervous System. Vol. V: Plum F (Editor), Higher Functions of the Brain, Part. 1.* Bethesda, MD: American Physiological Society, pp. 461 – 481, 1987.

Hubel DH, Wiesel TN: Receptive fields and functional architecture of monkey striate cortex. *J. Physiol. (London): 195,* 215 – 243, 1968.

Hubel DH, Wiesel TN: Cells sensitive to binocular depth in area 18 of the macaque monkey cortex. *Nature: 255,* 41 – 42, 1970.

Jeannerod M, Biguer B: The directional coding of reaching movements. A visuomotor conception of spatial neglect. In Jeannerod M (Editor), *Neurophysiological and Neuropsychological Aspects of Spatial Neglect.* Amsterdam: Elsevier, pp. 87 – 114, 1987.

Joshua DE, Bishop PO: Binocular single vision and depth discrimination. Receptive field disparities for central and peripheral vision and binocular interaction on peripheral units in cat striate cortex. *Exp. Brain Res.: 10,* 389 – 416, 1970.

Julesz B: *Foundation of Cyclopean Perception.* London: University of Chicago Press, 1971.

Lund JS, Lund RD, Hendrickson AE, Bunt AH, Fuchs AF: The origin of efferent pathways from the primary visual cortex, area 17, of the macaque monkey as shown by retrograde transport of horseradish peroxidase. *J. Comp. Neurol.: 164,* 287 – 304, 1976.

Maunsell JHR, Van Essen DC: Functional properties of neurons in middle temporal visual area of the macaque monkey. I. Selectivity for stimulus direction, speed, and orientation. *J. Neurophysiol.: 49,* 1127 – 1147, 1983a.

Maunsell JHR, Van Essen DC: Functional properties of neurons in middle temporal visual area of the macaque monkey. II. Binocular interactions and sensitivity to binocular disparity. *J. Neurophysiol.: 49,* 1148 – 1167, 1983b.

Maunsell JHR, Van Essen DC: The connections of the middle temporal visual area (MT) and their relationship to a cortical hierarchy in the macaque monkey. *J. Neurosci.: 3,* 2563 – 2586, 1983c.

Mays LE, Sparks DL: Dissociation of visual and saccade-related responses in superior colliculus neurons. *J. Neurophysiol.: 43,* 207 – 232, 1980.

Mohler CW, Goldberg ME, Wurtz RH: Visual receptive fields of frontal eye field neurons. *Brain Res.: 61,* 385 – 389, 1973.

Moran J, Desimone R: Selective attention gates visual processing in extrastriate cortex. *Science:* 229, 782 – 784, 1985.

Newsome WT, Wurtz RH, Komatsu H: Relation of cortical areas MT and MST to pursuit eye movements. II. Differentiation of retinal from extraretinal inputs. *J. Neurophysiol.:* 639, 1234 – 5678, 1988.

Nikara T, Bishop PO, Pettigrew JD: Analysis of retinal correspondence by studing receptive fields of binocular signal units in cat striate cortex. *Exp. Brain Res.:* 6, 353 – 372, 1968.

Pettigrew JD, Nikara T, Bishop PO: Binocular interaction on single units in cat striate cortex: simultaneous stimulation by single moving slits with receptive fields in correspondence. *Exp. Brain Res.:* 6, 391 – 410, 1968.

Poggio GF, Fischer B: Binocular interaction and depth sensitivity in striate and prestriate cortex of behaving rhesus monkey. *J. Neurophysiol.:* 40, 1392 – 1405, 1977.

Poggio GF, Poggio T: The analysis of stereopsis. *Annu. Rev. Neurosci.:* 7, 379 – 412, 1984.

Poggio GF, Talbot WH: Mechanisms of static and dynamic stereopsis in foveal cortex of the rhesus monkey. *J. Physiol.:* 315, 469 – 492, 1981.

Poggio GF, Motter BC, Squatrito S, Trotter Y: Responses of neurons in visual cortex (V1 and V2) of the alert macaque to dynamic random-dot stereograms. *Vision Res.:* 25, 397 – 406, 1985.

Poggio GF, Gonzalez F, Krause F: Stereoscopic mechanisms in monkey visual cortex: binocular correlation and disparity selectivity. *J. Neurosci.:* 8, 4531 – 4550, 1988.

Richmond BJ, Sato T: Enhancement of inferior temporal neurons during visual discrimination. *J. Neurophysiol.:* in press, 1987.

Robinson DA: Control of eye movements. In *Handbook of Physiology, Section 1: The Nervous System, Vol. II, Part 2:* Brooks BV (Editor). Bethesda, MD: American Physiological Society, pp. 1275 – 1320, 1981.

Robinson DL, Goldberg ME, Stanton GB: Parietal association cortex in the primate: sensory mechanisms and behavioral modulations. *J. Neurophysiol.:* 41, 910 – 932, 1978.

Rockland KS, Pandya DN: Laminar origins and termination of cortical connections of the occipital lobe in the rhesus monkey. *Brain Res.:* 179, 3 – 20.

Saito HA, Yukie M, Tanaka K, Hikosaka K, Fukada Y, Iwai E: Integration of direction signals of image motion in the superior temporal sulcus of the macaque monkey. *J. Neurosci.:* 6, 145 – 157, 1986.

Sakata H, Shibutani H, Kawano K: Spatial properties of visual fixation neurons in posterior parietal association cortex of the monkey. *J. Neurophysiol.:* 43, 1654 – 1672, 1980.

Schiller PH, Finlay BL, Volman SF: Quantitative studies of single-cell properties in monkey striate cortex. I. Spatiotemporal organization of receptive fields. *J. Neurophysiol.:* 39, 1288 – 1319, 1976.

Schlag J, Schlag-Rey M: Visuomotor functions of central thalamus in the monkey. II. Unit activity related to visual events, targeting and fixation. *J. Neurophysiol.:* 51, 1175 – 1195, 1984.

Sparks DL, Mays LE: Spatial localization of saccade targets. I. Compensation for stimulation-induced perturbations in eye position. *J. Neurophysiol.:* 49, 45 – 63, 1983.

Sparks DL, Porter JD: Spatial localization of saccade targets. II. Activity of superior colliculus neurons preceding compensatory saccades. *J. Neurophysiol.:* 49, 64 – 74, 1983.

Tanaka K, Hikosaka K, Saito H-A, Yukie M, Fukada Y, Iwai E: Analysis of local and wide-field movements in the superior temporal visual areas of the macaque monkey. *J. Neurosci.:* 6, 134 – 144, 1986.

Ungerleider LG, Desimone R: Cortical connections of visual area MT in the macaque. *J. Comp. Neurol.:* 248, 190 – 222, 1986.

Van Essen DC, Maunsell JHR: Hierarchical organization and functional streams in the visual cortex. *Trends. Neurosci.:* 6, 370 – 375, 1983.

Van Essen DC, Maunsell JHR, Bixby JL: The middle temporal visual area in the macaque: myeloarchitecture, connections, functional properties and topographic organization. *J. Comp. Neurol.:* 199, 293 – 326, 1981.

Wurtz RH, Mohler CW: Organization of monkey superior colliculus: enhanced visual response of superficial layer cells. *J. Neurophysiol.:* 39, 745 – 765, 1976.

Wurtz RH, Mohler CW: Enhancement of visual response in monkey striate cortex and frontal eye fields. *J. Neurophysiol.:* 39, 766 – 772, 1976.

Yarbus AL: *Eye Movements and Vision.* New York: Plenum, pp. 1 – 222, 1967.

Yin TCT, Mountcastle VB: Visual input to the visuomotor mechanisms of the monkey's parietal lobe. *Science:* 197, 1381 – 1383, 1977.

Zeki SM: Cells responding to changing image size and disparity in the cortex of the rhesus monkey. *J. Physiol. (London):* 242, 827 – 841, 1974.

CHAPTER 16

Disorders of visual recognition

Antonio R. Damasio, Daniel Tranel and Hanna Damasio

Department of Neurology, Division of Behavioral Neurology and Cognitive Neuroscience, University of Iowa College of Medicine, Iowa City, IA, U.S.A.

Scope and limitations of the concept of agnosia

The shorthand for the notion of disorders of recognition is the Greek-derived term *agnosia*, which signifies 'absence of knowledge.' It was introduced by Freud in the course of his landmark discussion on aphasia (Freud, 1891), to designate the impaired recognition of a stimulus, as distinct from the impaired naming that characterized aphasia.

The concept of agnosia evolved largely through the study of its visual variety. At first, two types of visual agnosia were identified by Lissauer (1890). One, termed *apperceptive agnosia*, was thought to be due to the disturbed integration of otherwise normally perceived components of a stimulus. The other occurred in relation to normally integrated percepts, was deemed to be a more 'pure' recognition defect, and was termed *associative agnosia*. In a sense, both concepts appear to be valid and to fit the modern concept of agnosia as articulated by Teuber in 1968: 'A normal percept that has somehow been stripped of its meaning.'

Some qualification is necessary regarding the normalcy of perception in agnosia. Affirming the intactness of perception, though useful from a clinical perspective and helpful in the overall conceptualization of the defect, assumes that perceptual processes stop at some given point, beyond which recognition would presumably take over. This assumption is no longer tenable, if it ever was, except perhaps as a heuristic caricature. We simply

have no way of distinguishing what might be conceived of as the higher echelons of perception from the lower echelons of recognition. In other words, there is no definable point of demarcation between perception and recognition, and it might be reasonably argued that pure associative agnosics do in fact suffer from subtle deficiencies of the perceptual apprehension of reality, relative to certain features or dimensions critical for the recognition of certain stimuli. To say that perception is normal in visual agnosia simply means that the patient does see the stimulus clearly, i.e., without blurring or distortion, and does see enough of its form to describe it in a way that matches the observer's own description. As noted below, assessment of visual acuity, spatial contrast sensitivity, perception of texture, and even drawing of the stimulus from copy, all help substantiate the judgment that perception is indeed 'sufficient' for recognition to take place.

Provided the above qualification is considered, our current operational definition of agnosia sees it as a modality-specific impairment of the ability to recognize previously learned stimuli (or to recognize stimuli that would normally have been learned after adequate exposure), which occurs in the absence of disturbances of perception, intellect or language, and which is the result of acquired cerebral damage. In essence, then, agnosia is a malfunction of memory confined to certain stimuli presented through one specific sensory channel but not through others. Thus, visual agnosia is: *a*

317

disorder of recognition confined to the visual realm, in which an alert individual with normal attention, intellect, language and visual perception fails to arrive at the meaning of previously known non-verbal visual stimuli. In most instances the defect covers anterograde learning as well, so that stimuli which would normally have been learned will also go unrecognized.

Confirming the diagnosis of visual agnosia

The proper assessment of a presumed visual agnosic patient requires the establishment that (1) the impairment cannot be explained by an elementary disturbance of perception or intellect and that (2) the defect goes beyond an inability to name or describe verbally a stimulus with which the patient is otherwise familiar. Let us elaborate the latter. Visual agnosics must have normal language and be able to give verbal reports of experiences prompted by perception through non-affected channels, while being unable to *either recognize or name* stimuli that are presented via the affected modality. They are unable to generate a description of many of the pertinent features of the stimulus under scrutiny, such as its function, operation, etc. By contrast, patients with anomia, though unable to retrieve the specific verbal tag pertaining to the stimulus, can produce a description of characteristics, operation or use, which unequivocally establishes their knowledge of the stimulus.

An interesting problem, which is the object of current research efforts and does not pose a significant diagnostic problem, is the anomic patient who does have true visual agnosia for some stimuli, although visual recognition is normal in most instances. The existence of such subjects underscores the fact that if the boundaries between perception and recognition are fuzzy, so are the boundaries between recognition and naming.

Major perceptual impairments are not compatible with normal recognition, and the observer must make sure that the patient perceives enough of a stimulus to permit recognition.

The patient's neuro-ophthalmological status should be assessed in detail. Patients with agnosia for faces generally have a field defect for form vision, often a superior quadrantanopia or a hemianopia. However, at least one half but more often three-quarters of central vision is intact. Visual acuity and contrast sensitivity should be tested in all patients and proven to be within form vision ranges. The examiner should obtain a verbal account of what the patient sees in the intact portion of the visual field. A wide variety of stimuli should be used – objects, faces, colors, meaningful and meaningless geometric forms, and signs, linguistic and not. As will be noted below, the agnosic defect can be so selective for certain categories of stimuli and even for certain stimuli within categories that too narrow a sampling of stimuli may fail to reveal otherwise blatant defects. Real objects as well as graphic representations should be used. In some instances, a pictorial representation is not recognized whereas the real object may well be. Static as well as moving stimuli should be shown, the reason being that the revelation of shape through motion, as occurs in the turning of an object, may 'deblock' the recognition of a stimulus unidentified in its static presentation (the term 'static object agnosia' has been used for such situations). Accurate description of general shape, number and position of stimuli establishes that visual form perception is normal. Drawing stimuli from copy, or matching a stimulus with the appropriate drawing or photograph of a similar stimulus, suggests sufficient vision of the stimulus.

The presence of normal or near normal perception can be judged with demanding tasks such as Benton and Van Allen's test of facial discrimination (Benton et al., 1983), which requires the subject to match pictures of unfamiliar faces which vary in dimensions such as angle and lighting. Other standardized probes of visual perception include the Judgment of Line Orientation test and the 3-Dimensional Block Construction test (Benton et al., 1983). The Complex Figure Test (Lezak, 1983) can be used to assess drawing to copy, as it is standardized and comes in alternative forms (the Rey-Osterrieth and the Taylor). Additional useful neuropsychological probes include the Mooney Faces test and the Hooper Visual Organization Test. Patients affected by true visual agnosia will perform normally or near-normally in all of these procedures. A statement by the patient to the effect that vision is 'blurred' or 'foggy' rules out the diagnosis of visual agnosia.

The subject's intention to cooperate with the observer, as well as intellectual ability, must be intact for the patient to qualify as agnosic. The notion that agnosia would result from a combination of perceptual and intellectual defects, which once held sway, is no longer acceptable. Intellectual integrity should be assessed with a standardized instrument, such as the widely used Wechsler Adult Intelligence Scale-Revised (WAIS-R; Wechsler, 1981). Severe intellectual compromise will prohibit the patients' ability to report reliably on the contents of their own consciousness, thus precluding the diagnosis of agnosia. Severe attentional defects also preclude the label of agnosia; i.e., a patient who is distractible, or who cannot maintain a normal level of sustained alertness, or who cannot focus appropriately on salient and relevant stimulus characteristics, should not be diagnosed as agnosic. To document these clinically detectable impairments, tests of auditory and visual attention should be administered, including Digit Span (forwards and backwards) and Digit Symbol Substitution from the WAIS-R, and the Line Cancellation test (Lezak, 1983). Tests such as the Wisconsin Card Sorting Test (Heaton, 1981) and the Stroop Color and Word Test (Golden, 1978) are good measures to judge distractibility and ability to maintain a normal response set.

Agnosia must be distinguished from so-called 'global amnesia.' In global amnesia, the recognition and learning of stimuli presented through all sensory modalities is impaired. Although it is reasonable to conceptualize global amnesia as a 'multimodal agnosia,' it is important from the clinical standpoint to retain the term agnosia for those instances in which the recognition and learning defect is modality confined, and reserve the term amnesia for conditions in which recognition and learning are disturbed across different sensory systems. The latter term, of course, is entirely compatible with multimodal manifestations of the phenomenon of agnosia.

Profiles of visual agnosia and their anatomical correlates

As alluded to above, the phenomenon of visual agnosia can occur in relatively pure form, i.e., without learning and recognition defects in modalities other than visual, or in the setting of learning and recognition defects for stimuli presented through other modalities, in which case the term amnesia applies.

The critical loci of cerebral damage associated with visual agnosic responses are: (a) the posterior and inferior occipital visual association cortices; (b) the posterior temporal association cortices; (c) the superior occipital and parietal visual association cortices; and (d) the anterotemporal higher-order cortices and limbic system structures. The description of the principal types of visual agnosia presented below is keyed to those critical locations (see Fig. 1).

Visual agnosia following inferior occipital and posterior temporal association cortices

Agnosia for faces
Bilateral damage within some sectors of the occipitotemporal association cortices impairs the recognition of facial identity for any previously known face, including the face of the self as seen in a mirror or photograph. The subject is acutely aware of the complete inability to relate a face to any previously known person. By contrast, the subject promptly recognizes the identity of the possessor of the face upon hearing the voice, an indication that use of another sensory channel permits access to pertinent memoranda on the basis of which identification can take place (Damasio et al., 1982). Another contrast is the ability to recognize the identity of the possessor of the face from visual but non-face information such as

characteristics of gait or posture, e.g., stride, a stoop, and so on. Such a contrast indicates that the separation of perceptual processes as well as the

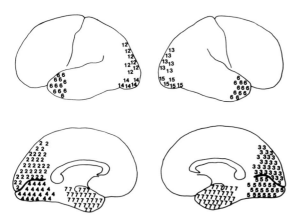

Fig. 1. Anatomical location of lesions associated with visual recognition defects. Bilateral lesions in subcalcarine visual association cortices (regions marked by 4 and 5) cause classical face agnosia with relative preservation of the recognition of most object categories. Recognition based on motion cues or on nonvisual modalities is normal. Bilateral damage in anterotemporal structures, both mesially (region marked by 7) and laterally (region marked by 6), cause impairments of visual recognition in the setting of amnesia, i.e., recognition of stimuli presented through other sensory modalities is also impaired. Bilateral damage in supracalcarine association cortices (regions marked by 2, 3, 12 and 13) can impair the recognition of identity based on motion cues. Such lesions also cause visual disorientation. Lesions confined to the left subcalcarine visual association cortices (region 4), and thus not involving the homologous area in the right hemisphere, generally do not cause visual recognition defects for objects or faces but preclude the recognition of visual-verbal symbols and thus impair reading (provided damage is placed deeply enough to involve the subjacent periventricular area, which surrounds the occipital horn of the left ventricle). Shallow lesions in this area cause loss of color perception in the contralateral hemifield (right hemiachromatopsia). Lesions confined to the right subcalcarine visual association cortices (region marked by 5) also cause hemifield defects in color perception (left hemiachromatopsia). In addition, facial recognition is defective, at the level of precise facial identity, i.e., recognition is slow and often inaccurate but not as pervasively impaired as in cases of face agnosia with bilateral lesions, i.e., lesions in regions marked by 4 *and* 5. Lesions confined to the left hemisphere in the territories marked by 4, 2, 12 and 14 can cause visual object agnosia in the absence of face agnosia. Lesions in the equivalent territory of the right hemisphere (encompassing regions marked by 5, 3, 13 and 15) impair the recognition of locations and routes, a disturbance covered by the term topographic disorientation. Such patients may be able to recognize the identity of faces.

separation of representations applies not only to different sensory modalities but also to different features and dimensions within the same modality.

Face agnosics also retain the ability to guess identity on the basis of salient features within the face or body of the target, e.g., a birthmark or a characteristic hairdo. As in the case of recovery of identity from characteristic motion, the success of the subject's guessing is largely dependent on context. If the context is appropriate the subject may be successful, but when context is impoverished or removed the subject guesses incorrectly or not at all. This can be proven experimentally by placing the telltale features in a stimulus which has been removed from its context, or in a stimulus which is dislocated to an inappropriate context. The hit rate for correct identification is then no better than chance. It should be clear that in all of these instances the subjects are not performing recognition of identity from faces but rather from parallel visual cues that do co-relate with the face and with the identity.

Most face agnosics retain the ability to read although some do so more slowly than before the onset of the condition. No face agnosic in our experience had difficulty recognizing faces as faces or telling human faces from nonhuman faces, and all but one had no trouble recognizing the meaning of facial expressions, assigning gender to faces, and making reasonable estimates of the ages of faces (Tranel et al., 1988). The exceptional patient, unable to recognize facial expressions normally, had significant direct damage to the inferior and early visual association cortices rather than a mere undercut of the connectivity of that region.

It is noteworthy that the problem with expressions occurred only with static expressions, as shown in a photograph, but not when the expressions were enacted in the real setting and thus accompanied by movement. The patient was able to recognize an expression of surprise or a smile when he literally watched it unfold as movement over time. This patient as well as all other face agnosics in our experience could produce a full repertoire of facial expressions with his own face.

Neuropsychological profile of face agnosics Some face agnosics have impaired appreciation of texture (Newcombe, 1979), and most have defective color perception (Meadows, 1974; Damasio et al., 1980), although neither texture nor color perception is a critical factor in the recognition of the specific identity of faces. The visual acuity of face agnosics is normal but they may have partial field cuts for form vision, especially in upper quadrants (Damasio, 1985a). Spatial contrast sensitivity is either normal or impaired in levels that cannot account for the recognition defect (Rizzo et al., 1986). Stereopsis is normal (Damasio et al., 1980; Rizzo and Damasio, 1985) and so are the scanpaths with which agnosics inspect faces (Rizzo et al., 1987).

Face agnosics perform normally in tasks in which they are required to match unfamiliar and differently lit photographs of faces but not requested to recognize their identity (Tzavaras et al., 1970; Benton and Van Allen, 1972; Benton, 1980). They can distinguish figure from ground, and can sketch the contours of figures shown in photographs or diagrams. As noted above, the perception of movement is remarkably intact. Face agnosics can localize stimuli in space, by pointing or by describing relative spatial position. Face agnosics can attend to stimuli anywhere in their visual panorama. Their visual experience has the same perspective as that of the observer (Benton, 1980; Damasio, 1985b). In virtually every aspect, then, face agnosics differ from patients with Balint syndrome, whose visual experience and gaze are disjointed, erratic, and controllable by neither the examiner's command nor the subject's will (Damasio, 1985a). They also differ from patients with right parietal damage, whose visuoperceptive abilities are severely impaired (Benton, 1980; Damasio, 1985a). Curiously, most of those perceptually disturbed patients can recognize previously known faces provided enough time is allowed for face features to be analysed (Meier and French, 1965; Damasio, 1985a).

Impaired recognition of non-face visual stimuli by face agnosics

1. The problem with unique non-face stimuli. Patients with face agnosia often appear to have intact visual recognition of non-face stimuli. As we have pointed out elsewhere, however, that impression is an artifact caused by the overwhelming importance of faces, on the one hand, and by the mode of testing for recognition of non-face stimuli, on the other. In fact, face agnosics fail to recognize any other previously known visual stimulus provided that they are required to recognize a unique exemplar, at subordinate level, rather than membership in progressively more generic categories of stimuli, e.g., 'Laura's Mercedes,' versus 'Mercedes cars,' versus 'German sedans,' versus 'passenger cars,' versus 'vehicles.' Face agnosics cannot recognize their cars, houses or a variety of familiar landmarks (buildings and their architectural or interior decoration details).

2. The problem with non-unique, non-face stimuli. Face agnosics are also impaired in the recognition of some objects even when they are not asked to recognize them as unique exemplars but rather as mere members of a category. The range of examples is wide and includes animals, some food ingredients, makes of cars, articles of clothing, and musical instruments to name but a few (Faust, 1955; Pallis, 1955; Bornstein, 1963; Lhermitte et al., 1972; Damasio et al., 1982, 1987). In other words, within a number of conceptual categories of stimuli, some exemplars fail to be properly identified either at the 'basic object' level, or at some intermediate subordinate level less specific than the 'unique subordinate' level. Superordinate identification is never impaired. In short, subjects with face agnosia have difficulties that go well beyond the identification of unique exemplars. Their defect is most marked for a variety of natural kinds, such as animals or fruits, and certain manmade kinds such as musical instruments. This relative dissociation has also been observed by Warrington (Warrington and Shallice, 1984), and referred to as 'category-specific'. Our view is that although the defects prevail within certain categories they are 'category-related' rather than 'category-specific' (Damasio, 1989a). The subjects fail to recognize some exemplars within certain categories, but have no difficulty with the recognition of other exemplars from the same categories. Within animal categories, subjects have trouble recognizing members of the cat family (distinguishing a tiger, a lion and a domestic cat) but invariably recognize an elephant. For man-made kinds, the recognition impairments fail to follow any category drawn on the basis of a concept or verbal label. For example, while most musical instruments are just as man-made and manipulable as carpentry or garden tools, the recognition of musical instruments is always defective but tools are visually recognized without difficulty.

Recognition of fragments of stimuli by face agnosics   We have found that face agnosic subjects who fail to recognize a stimulus as a whole may recognize a part of that stimulus as an independently meaningful fragment, even when the identification proposed for the fragment is in conflict with the correct identity for the whole (Damasio et al., 1987). An example is the recognition of a 'knot,' or 'snake's tail,' or 'rope,' when the patient is asked to view the line drawing of a pretzel. Several fragments of the drawing, if taken in isolation, do look like a knot in a rope, or some part of a snake. The responses are unquestionably reasonable at the fragment scale. The astonishing fact is that the patient can disregard the whole and concentrate only on a part. These responses are not found in normal controls, even elderly controls. Based on our preliminary evidence, face agnosics are at the mercy of fragment recognition and at their poorest level of performance when the potential meaning of local fragments of a whole stimulus is in conflict with the meaning of the global frame. This was apparent in an experiment which consisted of assessing recognition in relation to two sets of line drawings: one set contained drawings which could be decomposed into fragments with independent meanings that were semantically not concordant with the meaning of the global frame; the other set contained drawings whose fragments were always concordant with the global frame.

Recognition performance for the 'concordant' set was superior. Elsewhere, we have concluded that the agnosic's difficulty is not one of building the internal description of parts of stimuli, but it may be that of binding into a coherent whole whatever part or parts they happen to describe well.

Non-conscious recognition of faces   Recognition can occur at a nonconscious level. A patient may be unable to experience familiarity with a stimulus and be unable to evoke any related record consciously, and yet be capable of generating responses which indicate that the stimulus has indeed established contact with previously learned and pertinent records. In short, the patient as a sentient being does not recognize but the brain does. The prime example of this phenomenon is the discrimination of familiar faces by face agnosics as indexed by autonomic skin conductance responses to face stimuli (Tranel and Damasio, 1985, 1988), or to face – name matches (Bauer, 1984). Comparable results were obtained by De Haan et al. (1987) and Bruyer et al. (1983), using other paradigms. The responses clearly separate familiar from unfamiliar faces, a separation which the patients are consciously unable to make. Experimental forced-choice paradigms, involving the choice of one face from a set of two in relation to a specific cue, have also provided evidence for non-conscious recognition of stimuli (Tranel et al., 1987).

Anatomical correlates of face agnosia   The lesions that cause face agnosia disconnect or destroy visual association cortices in Brodmann's fields 18 and 19, and largely spare the primary visual cortices (area 17) (Damasio, 1985a). The sector of areas 18 and 19 compromised by these lesions includes several functional subfields related to the processing of form, color, and texture (see Van Essen and Maunsell, 1983; Allman et al., 1985; Damasio, 1985a; Livingstone and Hubel, 1987). This is the sector of the central visual system that is preferentially related to the functional 'stream' of visual information flow dedicated to the analysis of the physical characteristics of stimuli (shape, color, texture), rather than to the detection of the position of stimuli in space (Damasio and Damasio, 1982; Damasio et al., 1982; Ungerleider and Mishkin, 1982).

Twelve post-mortem studies have now been conducted in patients with face agnosia, and all have had bilateral lesions (Damasio et al., 1982; Nardelli et al., 1982). This points to the likely bilaterality of the neural processes underlying facial recognition. The evidence currently available from the modern neuroimaging era is comparable. All our cases of face agnosia without manifest visuoperceptive disturbances have bilateral lesions, while a review of our cases of unilateral left and right occipital lesions has not turned up a single case of pervasive and stable prosopagnosia. Evidence from cases of surgical callosal section also speaks in favor of the bilaterality of the facial recognition system. Split-brain subjects continue to recognize familiar faces with each isolated hemisphere (Sperry et al., 1979), and each isolated hemisphere can process unfamiliar faces albeit with different mechanisms and efficiency (Levy et al., 1972; Gazzaniga and Smylie, 1983).

Although most available studies from other investigations reveal the same results there are some reports of unilateral lesions associated with face recognition defects (Whitely and Warrington, 1977; De Renzi, 1986; Landis et al., 1986; Sergent and Poncet, 1988). We believe that all such cases have face recognition defects in the setting of visuoperceptive (and visuoconstructive) disturbances and we have hesitated to lump them together with more perceptually 'pure' face agnosics. Furthermore, our findings indicate that the unilateral right cases have lesions that encompass *both* the inferior and the superior occipital regions and even extend into the right parietal region. Clearly this matter requires further analysis. For instance, although visuoperceptive disturbances are present it is not clear whether they play a role in the recognition defect.

In general, unilateral lesions are associated with partial face recognition defects even when the pic-

ture of pervasive face agnosia is missing. Patients with right-sided lesions in the subcalcarine region have a slow and laborious process of recognition that may lead to the successful identification of faces with which they are thoroughly familiar, but lead to recognition errors for less well known faces. By contrast, patients with left occipital lesions produce quicker but semantically off-target responses. The right hemisphere examples approach faces on the basis of local fragments and use the fragments to guide a deliberate search for identity. The patients have no difficulty with the recognition of objects at categorical level. The left hemisphere examples appear to seize the general identity of the target rapidly and correctly, to the point of detecting their geographic and professional placement, but the final assignation of specific identity goes off-target. The patients use different strategies to perceive faces, as has been suggested by studies of facial recognition in split-brain patients and in normals. The right occipitotemporal region appears the best endowed for rapid grasping of the global, configurational aspects of the stimulus, while the left operates in a slower, fragment-related, feature approach.

The concept of visual object agnosia

The designation 'visual object agnosia' has been used for patients who fail to recognize many common objects even at the categorical, non-unique level, and who generally do not recognize any objects at unique level either. The reader may well ask how such patients differ from the face agnosics described above. The answer is two-fold. First, in most such cases of visual object agnosia, the magnitude and extension of the defect are greater. Secondly, curiously enough, in some of those cases face agnosia is actually absent while object agnosia is more pervasive. Since more often than not the patients are of the former variety, the label visual object agnosia does not capture the scope of the defect any more than face agnosia does. The designation visual object agnosia should be reserved for patients who can recognize faces and are impaired only in non-face domains.

Visual object agnosia is infrequent. Further-more, the condition may be transient. Large bilateral infarctions or tumors involving the visual association cortices are the usual neuropatho-logical correlates. In some of the few patients in whom the defect is stable and confined to objects, as the designation implies, a unilateral lesion in the left visual association cortices has been found (Hé-caen and Ajuriaguerra, 1956; Feinberg et al., 1985). Some of those patients may be able to recognize a stimulus when the actual object is presented in motion, rather than statically or in a pictorial representation (e.g., line drawing), an in-dication that the physiological substrate is dif-ferent from that in face agnosia.

Visual agnosia following superior occipital and parietal lesions

Subjects with bilateral superior occipital lesions or with bilateral superior occipital and parietal lesions are unable to recognize identity from movements, pantomime or visuomotor signs such as American Sign Language. It is remarkable that such subjects, provided the stimuli are presented in the normally functioning part of their visual fields, can recognize the identity of objects and faces, although they may be unable to place those stimuli in their proper location in space and may be unable to follow their trajectory. Their agnosia, in the traditional sense, as applied to non-verbal stimuli, is of little consequence to their lives, since recogni-tion of objects from movement or pantomime is hardly a major requirement for normal social in-teraction. The agnosia for visuomotor signs is also of little consequence unless those signs have linguistic value, as in ASL. A disturbance of visuomotor linguistic sign recognition is the pro-vince of aphasia. In short, the visual agnosia of pa-tients with superior lesions is likely to go undetected unless specifically tested for. What such patients do have is *visual disorientation*, the main symptom of the Balint syndrome (Damasio, 1985a). This consists of a loss of normal acuity in all but a small sector of the visual field, most of which is kept in a form of haze. In addition, the sector of clear vision is unstable and its position may shift erratically about the visual field. The subjects are unable to construct a spatially coherent visual panorama (see Chapter 17 of this volume).

Visual agnosia following damage to higher-order anterotemporal cortices and limbic system structures in the anterior temporal region

Visual recognition defects in humans can also be caused by lesions in higher-order association cor-tices in the anterior temporal region, and by lesions in limbic system structures of the mesial temporal region (entorhinal cortex, hippocampus and amygdala). Patient HM, who sustained bilateral surgical ablations to entorhinal cortex and hip-pocampus, has not been able to learn the identity behind the many faces he has come into contact with since he sustained his lesions (Corkin, 1984). It appears that HM can otherwise recognize previously acquired object categories normally, provided recognition is not required at unique ex-emplar level.

Patients with damage to both bilateral mesial limbic system structures and bilateral higher-order neocortices have provided further evidence (Damasio, 1985a). Patient Boswell is unable to recognize the identities of faces learned before his condition, and is equally unable to learn the identi-ty of any new face he has come into contact with during the 13 years following the onset of his le-sions. The main difference between the visual recognition defects of Boswell and the defects in the 'pure' visual agnosics is that in the latter the defect is confined to the visual modality whereas in the former it covers all modalities. The persons whose identity Boswell fails to recognize visually, he also cannot recognize from the sound of the voice or any other sensory clues.

Boswell's lesions spare the primary and early visual association cortices in areas 17, 18 and 19. His lesions destroy the entorhinal cortex, the hip-pocampus, the amygdala, and the cortices of areas

20, 21, 37, 35, 36 and 38. These cortices receive projections from the early association cortices in occipital and posterior temporal regions, and project back to those same cortices. They also project to paralimbic cortices (such as the entorhinal cortex in area 28), while the latter projects to the hippocampus proper (Van Hoesen and Pandya, 1975a,b). The lesions found in Boswell compromise the same bidirectional lines affected in the 'pure' agnosics described above but the damage is located more anteriorly. The processing is thus disrupted downstream. These findings indicate that the identity of unique faces cannot be learned or recognized as a result of the operation of early visual cortices alone. The evocation of pertinent records on the basis of which recognition of unique identity is established requires neural units in anterior temporal neocortices and in limbic structures. This mechanism of recognition failure is discussed in more detail below.

The physiology of recognition

From records of physical structure to records of other pertinently linked characteristics and relations: the multiple representations of entities and events

The normal recognition of a stimulus presented through a single sensory modality, whichever it may be, calls not only for the appropriate perceptual description of the stimulus (which we term perceptual activation) but also for the co-activation, at conscious level, of numerous memory records pertinent to the stimulus. Those memory records may be evoked from stores within the same and other sensory modalities, and may be both non-verbal and verbal. For instance, the recognition of a guitar presented visually may evoke memoranda regarding its usual placement in the universe, its usual interaction with a perceiver or user, its operation, and the outcome of that operation, specifically, its sound. While placement and interaction with a passive perceiver constitute information probably recorded in visual association cortices, the key interaction with a user undoubtedly depends on somatosensory recordings away from visual cortices. Likewise, while the operation of a guitar can be represented and recorded in visual and somatosensory manner, the outcome of the operation must be recorded in auditory association cortices. Note that no verbal tag whatsoever is necessary for the recognition of a guitar as such. All that is minimally required is that the presentation of the stimulus generate an activation of pertinently associated records, of sufficient type and number. Inevitably, the activation of many nonverbal cross-references will bring with it the activation of related name tags. However, while verbal tags probably assist with the speed and precision of recognition, they are not necessary for recognition to take place. It is not necessary at all to evoke the word 'guitar' in order to recognize a guitar. This point bears on the distinction between 'anomia' and 'agnosia.' The lack of evocation of a specific name tag can occur even when recognition has taken place and only in this situation is the term *anomia* appropriate. Naturally, lack of recognition or *agnosia*, subsumes failure to activate the name tag.

Recognition of a stimulus presented through one sensory channel, as tested at the bedside or in a controlled experimental situation, thus appears to proceed from a percept description achieved within a single modality cortex (albeit in several segregated functional regions), towards a multiple record evocation that generally occurs, though not necessarily, in multiple modality systems, each of which possesses several functional regions. In our model, the sense or feeling of familiarity experienced by the perceiving subject is thus the result of the activation of multiple evocations pertinently related to the stimulus, at conscious level, occurring in multiple regions of the cerebral cortices but attended to by the perceiver during the same time-locked window.

The physical structure of the guitar in our example will be recorded in separate and fragmentary representations that correspond, at diverse scales, to its shape, texture, typical operation and outcome of operation, to mention but a few of those generated by single or repeated interactions with such an object. But not only are representations built through different modalities (sensory and motor), they are also of different 'levels' or 'hierarchies,' some being secondary to others. For instance, shape is derived from more elementary computations of form, color, texture and even movement, all of which can contribute to its representation. Likewise, the representations built around a particular person are multiple across features, dimensions and modalities. Human faces draw on representations of physical structure, e.g., form, shape, texture, color, and typical motion of facial moving parts. But as an object, a familiar person offers to the perceiver other representable components, for instance, typical posture or characteristic gait. While all of these representations are visually based, they rely on different aspects of the visual system for their construction and storage. Furthermore, these different types of representation are not equivalent in terms of their power to offer recognition of identity without the assistance of contextual cues, i.e., while it is possible to recognize identity on the basis of the physical structure of a face alone, it is only possible to recognize identity on the basis of gait when the context changes the base rates, i.e., makes it probable that one among a relatively finite number of persons is the possessor of that gait.

The point to be made here is that any stimulus is likely to be represented in the brain in multiple forms, across different sensory modalities and different sensory maps within modalities. Almost invariably it is also represented in terms of the motor interaction engaged in by the perceiver's previous encounters with the stimulus. Finally, representations of the somatic states that accompanied the encounters are also laid down, i.e., the emotional and affective states of the perceiver as characterized by parameters of internal milieu, visceral states, state of smooth and striated musculature, and so forth. The magnitude of each of such varied representations differs for different stimuli, and is influenced by the history of each perceiver, and by context during acquisition. The characteristics of certain stimuli, in terms of their physical structure, operation and intrinsic value in the universe, are different, and so are the values of different stimuli for the perceiving organism. The latter will determine the kind of somatic state that accompanies interactions with the stimulus, and in so doing, determine the importance of somatic state representation in what one might term the overall mapping of a particular object. In this view, the mapping of a unique face of a friend is, by this reason alone, different from the mapping of a shovel. In short, the overall mapping of any entity and, by extension, any event is the potential sum total of sub-representations available in sensory and motor cortices. It follows from this view that the recognition of an object is determined by which feature, dimension and context is offered perceptually or in internally generated recall, to the available overall representation. In most natural situations, stimuli offer more than one characteristic to the perceiver and thus initiate parallel processes whereby different features or dimensions, intrinsic or contextual, can trigger the activation of past records, and rapidly generate the reconstitution of an internal set of activations that define, when properly attended, the identity of the stimulus.

The wealth of possibilities in such a system allows recognition to operate on the basis of partial or imperfect fits. When a stimulus provides the brain with part of a previously represented characteristic, that part alone may be sufficient to trigger recognition. This means that the processes of recognition are made easier, one might say possible, by the multiplicity and richness of representations, as well as by the relatively low level of sufficiency needed for single features to initiate an effective process of co-activation.

Domains and taxonomic levels

While the early literature on agnosia emphasized distinctions by sensory modality, e.g., visual, auditory, tactile, etc., current research at our laboratory and others indicates that the subject matter of stimuli to be recognized or learned and their level of uniqueness are the keys to the processes of learning and recognition, and to the profile of their breakdown following brain damage. The evidence indicates that the entities and events whose physical structures impress the brain through its sensory systems become naturally grouped (categorized) by different features and dimensions, and constitute relatively individualized domains of reality (Damasio et al., 1989a).

Taking the visual world as the example, primary domains include human faces, other natural kinds such as animals and botanical specimens, man-made objects of different varieties, words, numbers, and so on. Differently placed brain lesions can cause the prevalent breakdown of recognition of some of these domains or categories, while leaving others largely untouched. Lesions thus produce striking dissociations such as the preservation of recognition of words and numbers in a patient unable to recognize faces and other natural kinds (Damasio et al., 1989a; Damasio and Damasio, 1983; Warrington and Shallice, 1984; Warrington and McCarthy, 1987; Goodglass et al., 1986). It should be clear that we do not see domains as having rigid boundaries and certainly not as groups of stimuli sharing precisely all defining characteristics. Also, domains are not concepts nor are they to be misunderstood for verbal labels attributable to them under certain contexts. Domains are naturally occurring superimpositions of characteristics shared by a number of entities and events. All bona fide members share a core but the amount of non-core characteristics varies greatly. As expected, when we say that there are dissociations in the recognition (or lack thereof) of domains, we never mean that one domain is necessarily *all* unrecognized or *all* preserved (Damasio et al., 1987). It is merely mostly so and exceptions are almost always present.

The taxonomic level at which the entities or events are considered in recognition encounters or experimental tasks is no less important. As an example, most familiar faces are usefully recognized only at the level of unique identity, the finest and most subordinate taxonomic level. Recognition of faces as faces, or of facial expressions, calls for less unique and more generic levels of processing. For instance, the broader categories of happy or sad facial expressions can be found in any human face, and are entirely independent of the unique identity of any face. The recognition of most non-face natural kinds, and most man-made objects, occurs at non-unique taxonomic levels, for instance, the recognition of a tool, utensil, vehicle, animal, and so on. Exceptions include the recognition of a personal pet, or car, or house. The evidence for selective breakdowns in relation to taxonomic level indicates that almost invariably, focal cerebral damage impairs the recognition of unique identity and allows for recognition of broader categories.

Taxonomic level and domain are interacting constraints. For instance, patients who cannot recognize the unique identity of faces generally cannot recognize the unique identity of animals, houses or vehicles. The size and constitution of the domain to which stimuli belong are of great relevance. Stimuli that belong to domains made up of *many different* but *physically similar* members are especially difficult to recognize and are mostly not recognized by agnosics. An example is certain groups of animals, e.g., cats, or similar car makes. Agnosic patients recognize normally at superordinate and basic object level, i.e., they can appropriately recognize an exemplar as an animal or vehicle, but fail to distinguish among exemplars at subordinate level. The subordinate position of some of those items which do not require unique recognition is different from and higher than the subordinate position of unique items, i.e., they are closer to the 'basic object' level than to the 'unique subordinate' level and yet their recognition is disturbed. Familiar faces are at an even greater distance from the basic object level (deeper and more subordinate) and at that level the recognition operation of visual agnosics collapses entirely. Some exemplars within certain domains share some of the recognition burdens of familiar faces in that they constitute visually 'ambiguous' groupings. The ambiguity, however, is not evenly distributed across the domain. For instance, many animal species show remarkable similarity among exemplars, and yet there are numerous exemplars whose distinctiveness ensures optimal recognition by even the most severe agnosic.

In addition to the characteristics of physical structure of a stimulus, and to physical structure ambiguity (the size of the class constituted by members with the same physical structure), several other factors play an important role in the processes of recognition and in the type of recognition failures that follow certain areas of brain damage. One is the operation and outcome of operation of the entity referring to the usual action of an object, what it is capable of performing, what effect it produces on the user and on the environment, etc. Knowledge about operation and outcome is likely to be mapped in locations different from those used for representations of physical structure. Another is the frequency, and the significance of a stimulus in the environment is an additional important factor, and it may well influence recognition success and failure. Taking extreme ends of the continuum, for example, human faces or buildings are so frequently encountered in the environment and have such a prominent significance in the environment that their extensive representations, all other things being equal, must be less vulnerable to recognition failure, at the generic level. A closely related factor is the significance of the object to the perceiver, a factor composed of multiple ingredients, such as survival value, attractiveness, etc. It would be expected, and our evidence supports this, that highly significant stimuli enjoy more extensive mapping, and may fare better when normal recognition is disrupted. Finally, the extent to which a stimulus is mapped in several different sensory modalities as opposed to a single modality, influences the degree of vulnerability to recognition failure.

The substrates of knowledge: a model for the neural basis of recognition

Based on some of the evidence discussed above and on other evidence from neuropsychology, neuro-

anatomy and neurophysiology, we have proposed a model of the cognitive/neural architecture necessary for learning, memory and recognition, applicable to visual processing and its disorders (see Damasio, 1989b). The essentials of the framework, development, base structures and operation of such a model are outlined below.

Framework

The model described here is governed by two sets of constraints. The first, termed *neurobiological constraints*, corresponds to the anatomical design of the nervous system and to neuroanatomically embodied values of the organism. The other, termed *reality constraints*, corresponds to the characteristics of physical structure, operation, frequency of occurrence of entities and events external to the perceiver's entire organism (environmental) and of entities and events external to the perceiver's brain but internal to the body, i.e., somatic. During perceptual interactions between the perceiver's brain and reality, the two sets of constraints lead to:

(1) *domain formation*, which is a process of feature, entity, and event grouping based on *physical structure similarity, spatial placement, temporal sequence,* and *temporal coincidence*;

(2) the creation of records of *contextual complexity*, which register the temporal coincidence of entities and their interrelationships within an event;

(3) *functional regionalization* (a process of assignment of the groupings described above to different regions of brain structure).

Cognitive structures and neural substrates

The fundamental cognitive structures of the model are:

(1) records of fragments of component features within perceptual and motor events;

(2) records of the combinatorial arrangement binding the occurrence of the above representations in temporal and spatial terms.

The neuroanatomical substrates for the fundamental cognitive structures are:

(1) primary and early association cortices, both sensory and motor, which constitute the substrate for feature records;

(2) association cortices of different orders, both sensory and motor, some limbic structures (entorhinal cortex, hippocampus, amygdala, cingulate cortices, the neostriatum and the cerebellum, which constitute the substrate for the binding code records (convergence zones);

(3) feedforward and feedback connectivity interrelating (1) and (2);

(4) servosystem structures in the thalamus, basal forebrain, hypothalamus and brain stem nuclei.

Operations

The cognitive/neural architecture outlined above can perform (1) perceptuomotor interactions with the perceiver's surround and (2) learning of above. It can also (3) attempt the reconstitution of perceptuomotor interactions in internal recall and motor performance, (4) solve problems and make decisions, and (5) plan and create.

The critical operation for the understanding of recognition and its disorders is the attempted perceptuomotor reconstitution. This process is based on a multiregional co-activation of sensory and motor records laid down in primary/early association cortices and brought about by feedback retroactivation from convergence zones. At a specified threshold of neuronal activities, the multiregionally distributed retroactivations become attended to and emerge as evocations in consciousness.

According to this model, and unlike traditional neurological models, there is *no localizable single store* for the meaning of a given stimulus within a cortical region. Rather, meaning is arrived at by widespread multiregional activation of records pertinent to a stimulus, wherever such records may be distributively stored within a large array of sensory and motor structures, cortical and not. The process is dynamic and virtually starts from scratch for every new instance of recognition. In

other words, a display of the meaning of a stimulus does not exist in permanent fashion, but is recreated for each and every instantiation. The same stimulus does not need to produce the same precise evocations every time it is presented, although there is a good likelihood that many of the same or similar sets of records will be evoked in relation to the same or comparable stimuli. The records that pertain to a given entity are thus distributed in the telencephalon both in the sense that they are mapped over sizeable neuron populations and also in the sense that they are to be found in multiple loci in the cerebral cortices and some subcortical nuclei. The diversity of records is engendered by the diversity of reality, as appreciated by the senses, and by the intrinsic values of the organism, which bias perceptuo-motor interactions. As elaborated above, the physical structure and operation of an entity, the interaction between the entity and the perceiver, and the value of the entity for the perceiver (in the perspective of its innate and acquired goals) are key determinants of the recording of knowledge.

Reinterpreting visual agnosia

On the basis of the above model, it is possible to delineate some key mechanisms underlying visual agnosia. The first would correspond to insufficient mapping of physical structure of entities, at the level of the early visual association cortices. In this situation, visual perception is intact to the point of allowing clear vision, permitting the patient to give a report of the visual world that generally corresponds to the examiner's view. Nonetheless, the mapping of the visual world is imprecise and incomplete, and this limits the co-activation of pertinent records in nearby local convergence zones, i.e., records that are stored in fairly caudal visual association cortices. In this situation, there is considerable disruption of visual recognition at generic level, in addition to impairment of recognition at the unique exemplar level. The recognition defect encompasses several taxonomic levels, and compromises both recognition of unique identity and recognition of categories. In the case of faces, both facial identity recognition and recognition of facial expressions are disrupted. Operating in other domains of stimuli, this form of defect will be more or less manifest, depending upon the constraints and principles elaborated above. Recognition of objects, for example, will be impaired for exemplars belonging to classes formed by many members sharing a high degree of visual similarity. The defect will be especially marked when the exemplars require precise distinctions among members in such classes.

Another mechanism of dysfunction would come from interruption of the chain of processing further downstream in the system. The anatomical referent in this case would be the cortices within the occipitotemporal junction. Damage here would not interfere with normal and comprehensive mapping of physical structure in primary and early visual association cortices, allowing for normal visual recognition, provided there is no requirement for recognition of unique exemplars from within a visually similar set. Even recognition of faces at categorical levels, e.g., facial expressions and gender, would be normal. Further downstream, however, the system would fail in at least two ways. One is to render records and convergence zones in visual association cortices inaccessible. Although sufficiently co-activated, these records would not establish contact with other records further forward in the system. Another mode of failure is insufficient co-activation of such records and convergence zones. Defective convergence zones at this level, for example, might prevent the retroactivation, via feedback connectivity, of records of physical structure in the more caudal sectors of the system, which would prevent disambiguation of a particular visual stimulus, so that, for example, it would not be possible to reach the point at which unique identity could be assigned.

The discriminatory electrodermal responses of face agnosics described above can also be interpreted in this framework. In our view, these responses are evidence that re-encounter with a previously learned face can activate pertinent records, i.e., upon re-presentation of all or some part of the face (under conditions which are generally at variance with the original learning conditions in terms of lighting, viewing angle, context, etc.), the brain activates a set of records which correspond to that face and that face alone. This operation depends on local feedforward activation of convergence zones and on backprojection and co-activation of neuronal ensembles which hold distributed storage of maps of physical structure of the face being perceived. The rich experience of the visual world that agnosic subjects are able to conjure up requires that such a wealth of co-activations does indeed occur. In turn, co-activation can trigger autonomic responses, one aspect of which is the skin conductance response. The discriminatory electrodermal responses in face agnosics are not the result of some primitive form of perceptual process, but rather an index of the rich retro-co-activation generated when re-presentations of faces activate previously acquired, non-damaged and accessible face records.

There is another possible mechanism of dysfunction to be found in patients with anterior temporal (mesial and/or lateral) damage, such as patient Boswell or patient HM. In these patients, there is either destruction of the machinery responsible for construction of the binding codes that allow the reconstitution and retrieval of unique memories, or loss of the binding codes themselves. This sort of damage virtually precludes the system from operating at subordinate taxonomic levels. Thus, the success of recall and recognition will be entirely at the mercy of other constraints and largely dependent upon the domain. For example, whenever a unique exemplar is called for, there will be complete failure of recall and recognition. For recognition at basic object level or for certain types of categorical face recognition (e.g., facial expressions, gender, age estimation), the system operates normally, since there is no need for input from the more anterior binding code regions, and the recognition problem can be successfully solved at local and more caudal zones. In essence, then, the success of the system in these patients depends entirely on the combined influence of taxonomic level and domain.

It is interesting, in this respect, to consider the differences between patient Boswell and our other face agnosic patients, on the skin conductance paradigms. The other patients, those with damage in the occipitotemporal junction and nearby fields, show preserved non-conscious face recognition *even in the anterograde compartment* (Tranel and Damasio, 1988). Obviously, they still have enough local feedforward and feedback operation to allow formation of records rich enough to permit discriminatory skin conductance responses. The effect in the anterograde compartment, as we have noted previously, is smaller than that in the retrograde bin, which makes good sense considering that in the latter compartment there will be a much richer set of co-activation triggered by the initial perception of a familiar face. But the effect is there, nonetheless, and it was demonstrated clearly and significantly by all three patients tested.

By contrast, patient Boswell never showed electrodermal discrimination of any visual stimulus, from the anterograde compartment, including faces. He simply gives absolutely no indication, at any level, conscious or non-conscious, overt or covert, of learning any new visual entity. This finding supports the critical role of the binding machinery in the anterior temporal lobe, in the formation of codes that allow new learning at the level of unique episodes. There is, of course, evidence that patient Boswell can acquire certain types of anterograde knowledge covertly (affective and motor configurations) (Damasio et al., 1989b). This learning, however, is not possible for stimuli that require an internal visual output for proper recall or recognition.

Acknowledgement

This study was supported by NINCDS Grant PO1 NS19632.

References

Allman J, Miezin F, McGuinnes E: Stimulus specific responses from beyond the classical receptive field: neurophysiological mechanisms for local-global comparisons in visual neurons. *Ann. Rev. Neurosci.: 8*, 407 – 430, 1985.

Bauer RM: Autonomic recognition of names and faces in prosopagnosia: a neurophysiological application of the Guilty Knowledge Test. *Neuropsychologia 22*, 457 – 469, 1984.

Benton AL: The neuropsychology of face recognition. *Am. Psychol. 35;* 176 – 186, 1980.

Benton AL, Van Allen MW: Prosopagnosia and facial discrimination. *J. Neurol.: Sci.: 15*, 167 – 172, 1972.

Benton AL, Hamsher K, Varney N, Spreen O: *Contributions to Neuropsychological Assessment.* New York: Oxford University Press, 1983.

Bornstein B: Prosopagnosia. In Halpern L (Editor), *Problems of Dynamic Neurology.* Jerusalem: Hadassah Medical Organization, 283 – 318, 1963.

Bruyer R, Laterre C, Seron X, Feyereisen P, Strypstein E, Pierrard E, Rectem D: A case of prosopagnosia with some preserved covert remembrance of familiar faces. *Brain Cognition 2*, 257 – 284, 1983.

Corkin S: Lasting consequences of bilateral medial temporal lobectomy: clinical course and experimental findings in HM. *Semin. Neurol. 4*, 249 – 259, 1984.

Damasio A: Disorders of complex visual processing. In MM Mesulam (Editor), *Principles of Behavioral Neurology, (Contemporary Neurology Series 26).* Philadelphia: Davis, pp. 259 – 288, 1985a.

Damasio A: Prosopagnosia. *Trends Neurosci.: 8*, 132 – 135, 1985b.

Damasio A: Category-related recognition defects and the organization of meaning systems. *Trends Neurosci.:* 1989a (in press).

Damasio A: Multiregional retroactivation: A systems level model for some neural substrates of cognition. *Cognition:* 1989b (in press).

Damasio A, Damasio H: Cerebral localization of complex visual manifestations: clinical and physiologic significance. *Neurology: 32*, 96, 1982.

Damasio A, Damasio H: Anatomical basis of pure alexia. *Neurology: 33*, 1573 – 1583, 1983.

Damasio A, Yamada T, Damasio H, Corbett J, McKee J: Central achromatopsia: behavioral, anatomical and physiologic aspects. *Neurology: 30*, 1064 – 1071, 1980.

Damasio AR, Damasio H, Van Hoesen GW: Prosopagnosia: anatomic basis and behavioral mechanisms. *Neurology: 32*, 331 – 341, 1982.

Damasio AR, Welsh K, Damasio H: The neural substrate of visual recognition impairments. *Neurology: 37;* 129, 1987.

Damasio AR, Damasio H, Tranel D: Impairments of visual recognition as clues to the processes of memory. In Edelman G, Gall E, Cowan M (Editors), *Signal and Sense: Local and Global Order in Perceptual Maps.* Neuroscience Institute Monograph, Wiley & Sons, 1989a.

Damasio AR, Damasio H, Tranel D: New evidence in amnesic

patient Boswell: implications for the understanding of memory. *J. Clin. Exp. Neuropsychol.: 11*, 61, 1989b.

De Haan EHF, Young A and Newcombe F: Face recognition without awareness. *Cognitive Neuropsychology: 4*, 385–415, 1987.

De Renzi E: Prosopagnosia in two patients with CT scan evidence of damage confined to the right hemisphere. *Neuropsychologia: 24*, 385–389, 1986.

Faust C: *Die zerebralen Herdstorungen bei Hinterhauptsverletzungen und ihr Beurteilung.* Stuttgart: Thieme, 1955.

Feinberg T, Heilman KM, Rothi LG: Multimodal agnosia. *Neurology: 35*, 119, 1985.

Freud S: *On Aphasia.* New York: International University Press, 1891/1953.

Gazzaniga MS, Smylie CS: Facial recognition and brain asymmetries: clues to underlying mechanisms. *Ann. Neurol.: 13*, 536–540, 1983.

Golden CJ: *Stroop Color and Word Test Manual.* Chicago: Stoelting Co., 1978.

Goodglass H, Wingfield A, Hyde M, Theurkauf J: Category specific dissociations in naming and recognition by aphasic patients. *Cortex 22*, 87–102, 1986.

Heaton RK: *Wisconsin Card Sorting Test Manual.* Odessa, FL: Psychological Assessment Resources, Inc. 1981.

Hécaen H, de Ajuriaguerra J: Agnosie visuelle pour les objects inanimes par lésion unilatérale gauche. *Rev. Neurol.: 94*, 222–233, 1956.

Landis T, Cummings JL, Christen L, Bogen JE, Imhof H-G: Are unilateral right posterior cerebral lesions sufficient to cause prosopagnosia? Clinical and radiological findings in six additional patients. *Cortex: 22*, 243–252, 1986.

Levy J, Trevarthen C, Sperry RW: Perception of bilateral chimeric figures following hemispheric disconnection. *Brain 95*, 61–78, 1972.

Lezak M: *Neuropsychological Assessment.* Vol. 2, New York: Oxford University Press, 1983.

Lhermitte J, Chain F, Escourolle R, Ducarne B, Pillon B: Etude anatomoclinique d'un cas de prosopagnosie. *Rev. Neurol.: 126*, 329–346, 1972.

Lissauer H: Ein fall von Seelenblindheit nebst einem Beitrag zur Theorie derselben. *Arch. Psychiatr. Nervenkrankh.: 21*, 22–70, 1890.

Livingstone MS, Hubel DH: Psychophysical evidence for separate channels for the perception of form, color, movement, and depth. *J. Neurosci.: 7*, 3416–3468, 1987.

Meadows JC: The anatomical basis of prosopagnosia. *J. Neurol. Neurosurg. Psychiatry: 37*, 489–501, 1974.

Meier MJ, French LA: Lateralized deficits in complex visual discrimination and bilateral transfer or reminiscence following unilateral temporary lobectomy. *Neuropsychologia: 3*, 261–272, 1965.

Nardelli E, Buonanno F, Coccia G, Fiaschi A, Terzian H, Rissuto N: Prosopagnosia: report of four cases. *Eur. Neurol.: 21*, 289–297, 1982.

Newcombe F: The processing of visual information in prosopagnosia and acquired dyslexia: functional versus physiological interpretation. In Osborne DJ, Gruneberg MM, Eiser JR (Editors), *Research in Psychology and Medicine.* London: Academic Press, Vol. 1, pp. 315–322, 1979.

Pallis CA: Impaired identification of faces and places with agnosia for colours. *J. Neurol. Neurosurg. Psychiatry: 18*, 218–224, 1955.

Rizzo M, Damasio H: Impairment of stereopsis with focal brain lesions, *Ann. Neurol.: 18*, 147, 1985.

Rizzo M, Corbett JJ, Thompson HS, Damasio AR: Spatial contrast sensitivity in facial recognition. *Neurology: 36*, 1254–1256, 1986.

Rizzo M, Hurtig R, Damasio A: The role of scanpaths in facial recognition and learning. *Ann. Neurol.: 22*, 41–45, 1987.

Sergent J, Poncet M: Patterns of perceptual deficits in two prosopagnosia patients. *J. Clin. Exp. Neuropsychol.: 10*, 50, 1988.

Sperry R, Zaidel E, Zaidel D: Self recognition and social awareness in the deconnected minor hemisphere. *Neuropsychologia: 17*, 153–166, 1979.

Teuber HL. Alterations of perception and memory in man: reflections on methods. In Weiskrantz L (Editor), *Analysis of Behavioral Change.* New York: Harper & Row, 1968.

Tranel D, Damasio AR: Knowledge without awareness: an autonomic index of facial recognition by prosopagnosics. *Science: 228*, 1453–1454, 1985.

Tranel D, Damasio AR: Nonconscious face recognition in patients with face agnosia. *Behav. Brain Res.: 30*, 235–249, 1988.

Tranel D, Damasio AR, Damasio H: Covert discrimination of familiar stimuli other than faces in patients with visual recognition impairments caused by occipitotemporal damage. *Soc. Neurosci.: 13*, 1453, 1987.

Tranel D, Damasio AR, Damasio H: Intact recognition of facial expression, gender, and age, in patients with impaired recognition of face identity. *Neurology: 38*, 690–696, 1988.

Tzavaras A, Hécaen H, Le Bras H: Le problème de la spécificité du déficit de la réconnaissance du visage humain lors des lesions hémisphériques unilaterales. *Neuropsychologia: 8*, 403–416, 1970.

Ungerleider LG, Mishkin M: Two cortical visual systems. In Ingle DJ, Mansfield RJW, Goodale MA (Editors), *The Analysis of Visual Behavior.* Cambridge: MIT Press, 1982.

Van Essen DC, Maunsell JHR: Hierarchical organization and functional streams in the visual cortex. *Trends Neurosci.: 6*, 370–375, 1983.

Van Hoesen GW, Pandya DN: Some connections of the entorhinal (area 28) and perirhinal (area 35) cortices in the rhesus monkey. I. Temporal lobe afferents. *Brain Res.: 95*, 1–24, 1975a.

Van Hoesen GW, Pandya DN: Some connections of the entorhinal (area 28) and perirhinal (area 35) cortices in the rhesus monkey. III. Entorhinal cortex efferents. *Brain Res.: 95*, 39–59, 1975b.

Warrington EK, McCarthy RA: Categories of knowledge: further fractionations and an attempted integration. *Brain: 110*, 1273–1296, 1987.

Warrington EK, Shallice T: Category specific semantic impairments. *Brain: 107*, 829–854, 1984.

Wechsler DA: *The Wechsler Adult Intelligence Scale-Revised.* New York: The Psychological Corporation, 1981.

Whiteley AM, Warrington EK: Prosopagnosia: a clinical, psychological, and anatomical study of three patients. *J. Neurol. Neurosur. Psychiatry: 40*, 395–403, 1977.

CHAPTER 17

Disorders of visuospatial analysis

Freda Newcombe[1] and Graham Ratcliff[2]

[1] *Neuropsychology Unit, University Department of Clinical Neurology, The Radcliffe Infirmary, Oxford OX2 6HE, England,
and* [2] *Harmarville Rehabilitation Center, P.O. Box 11460, Guys Run Road, Pittsburgh, PA 15238, U.S.A.*

Introduction

Attempts to select and organize findings from neuropsychological studies of visuospatial disorders into a coherent and comprehensive schema are fraught with the problems facing any reviewer in any field, only perhaps to a greater degree. The nature of the data, the absence of a clearly defined conceptual framework, and a history of confusing and inconsistent terminology all result in bias and lack of clarity. We have to deal with reports of complex behaviours which are almost certainly multifactorial and which were originally recognized as entities (e.g. Gerstmann's syndrome; Balint's syndrome) more because of their clinical presentation and presumed medical relevance than because of a clearly identifiable cognitive deficit which can be specified in terms of cognitive mechanism or anatomical substrate. Further, the traditional terminology of clinical neurology (apraxia, agnosia and aphasia) does not always accurately accommodate these disorders (c.f. constructional apraxia and visual spatial agnosia) and may carry unwarranted implications about their basis. The result is that it is often difficult to distinguish between description and interpretation in accounts of visuospatial disorder, and the legacy of previous interpretive descriptions has probably influenced the observations which subsequent investigators make when examining new cases.

The literature on Balint's syndrome (Balint, 1909), which will be discussed in more detail below, provides a good example of these problems. The syndrome is generally considered to involve three components, usually described as an inadequacy of visual attention, an abnormality in the redirection of gaze, and some form of inaccuracy in visually guided reaching. Yet the syndrome appears quite different in different accounts. Thus Damasio (1985, p. 275) describes Balint's syndrome as an '*acquired* disturbance of the *ability to perceive the visual field as a whole,* resulting in the *unpredictable perception and recognition of only parts of it*'. He equates the deficit with simultanagnosia and although he points out that, in the case of Balint's syndrome, this disorder is accompanied by impairments in pointing and the inability to shift gaze to new visual stimuli (sometimes called ocular apraxia), there is no doubt that he regards the attentional component as primary. Yet Cogan (1965, p. 288) described cases of oculomotor apraxia 'which is also called Balint's syndrome' and Joynt et al. (1985, p. 55) conceived the syndrome as 'a defect in refixation in the presence of intact gnosis', suggesting that these authors regarded the gaze disturbance as primary, although they do mention the other components of the syndrome. Finally, one of us gave prominence to the disorder of reaching in previous references (Ratcliff, 1982) to the syndrome in order to emphasize that inadequate perception of the position of visual stimuli in relation to the observer appeared to be the crux of the syndrome.

The situation is further complicated by differing

uses of the confusing terminology associated with the syndrome. Thus Luria et al. (1963) use the term 'optic ataxia' in comparing the oculomotor deficit in their simultanagnosic patient with that seen in Balint's syndrome, whereas most authors have used this term with reference to the reaching disorder. Holmes (1918, p. 449) introduced the term 'disturbance of visual orientation' to mean 'an affection of the power of localizing the position in space and the distance of objects by sight alone' in connection with the inaccurate reaching and faulty refixation of his patients who resembled Balint's case in several respects. Holmes did recognize the presence of a concomitant attentional disorder in his cases but he considered it to be independent of the visual disorientation. However, the term 'visual disorientation' has subsequently been used to label the whole symptom complex he described (Ratcliff and Davies-Jones, 1972), the misreaching component (e.g. Riddoch, 1935) and the simultanagnosic component (Damasio, 1985). In contrast, Godwin-Austen's (1965) report of a 'case of visual disorientation' stressed the importance of distinguishing this disorder from simultanagnosia.

The point is not that any one of the authors is more correct than the others but that the raw data and the clinical picture of the behaviours which they describe are liable to become blurred and distorted by the overlay of interpretation and inconsistent terminology which is at best vague and at worst misleading. We began our review with a discussion of these issues because we felt that readers might gain a clearer understanding of visuospatial disorders if they were alerted to the problem involved in doing so. But we do not set out to reform terminology; previous attempts to do so have not gained general acceptance and can yield unwieldy taxonomies (Nielsen, 1936). However, we do propose to make explicit our criteria for including material in this review and our rationale for imposing a particular organization on it in the hope that this will help the reader to determine our biases and distinguish interpretation from data.

We focus on disorders which seem to indicate a 'faulty appreciation of the spatial aspects of visual experience' (Benton, 1985a, p. 169) in that they affect the perception of spatial relationships between an observer and an object, between objects in extra-corporal space or the orientation of external stimuli. We also discuss difficulty in remembering this kind of information, difficulty in using it to guide behaviour and difficulty performing mental spatial operations, while acknowledging that it is sometimes not clear which of these is at the root of a particular behavioural deficit. We include discussion of disorders affecting the ability to locate and name body parts, although we believe these belong to a separate category which is clearly dissociable from the other spatial disorders. Conversely, we do not discuss constructional apraxia or visuospatial neglect (which are treated elsewhere in this volume), although both could be regarded as 'spatial' in the sense outlined above.

We distinguish these spatial disorders from those affecting the perception of form and the recognition of objects, while conceding that virtually all visual stimuli are spatial in that they have position and extension in space and that the very notion of form implies a network of spatial relationships within its individual space (*l'espace des formes*, Paillard, 1971). The functional dissociation between spatial disorders and other visuoperceptual deficits was originally suggested on the basis of clinical evidence (Newcombe and Russell, 1969) and has now been confirmed by neurophysiological and anatomical studies (Ungerleider and Mishkin, 1982; Pandya and Yeterian, 1984; Desimone et al., 1984, 1985; Ungerleider, 1985) as well as by further clinical work (Eslinger and Benton, 1983; Brouwers et al., 1984; Martin, 1987; Newcombe et al., 1987). We now seem to be on reasonably secure ground in linking spatial disorders with damage to the dorsal, occipito-parietal projections of the visual system, while pattern recognition seems to rely more on the occipito-temporal pathway (Damasio, 1985). Further discussion of the two cortical visual systems and of the complexities of form and pattern recognition can be found elsewhere in this volume.

Within the spatial domain, we are confining our attention mainly to spatial disorders within the visual modality. The use of tactual analogues in neuropsychological examination has been informative in two respects: it has demonstrated the supramodal nature of some (mainly right hemisphere) spatial deficits and it has ruled out hemianopic visual field defects as a primary and sufficient cause of the visuospatial disorders observed in patients with posterior right hemisphere lesions (De Renzi, 1982). It may, however, be misleading to draw too close an analogy between performance in the visual and tactual modalities: Hermelin and O'Connor (1982, p. 50) concluded on the basis of their developmental research that 'visual processing led to a stable and invariant organization of points in space, whereas when touch was applied without vision, the spatial framework was structured in subjective and relative terms'. Their comment implicitly touches the issue of egocentric and allocentric space, which provides an important variable in visuospatial processing.

We think it important to consider visuospatial disorders in the light of what we know about human information-processing, although the attempt to do so is complicated by the lack of a universal and coherent theory of spatial cognition. In its absence we have suggested a rough distinction between disorders which appear to result from dysfunction at early, relatively simple stages of processing and those which suggest a disturbance of later, more complex processes. We also refer to different spatial coordinate systems presumed to be involved at different stages and in different tasks (Hein and Jeannerod, 1983) and to the internal representation of spatial information. These concepts are well-established in the literature of cognitive psychology and artificial intelligence. Moscovitch (1979) argued that functional hemispheric asymmetries emerge at later stages of processing, while earlier, sensory stages of processing are performed in a similar manner by both hemispheres. Ratcliff and Cowey (1979) applied this distinction to visual perceptual disorders, using the term 'disorders of sensory analysis' to refer to

those presumed to occur at early stages. More recently, theoretical models of visual information-processing have begun to appear which propose increasingly complex levels of representation to deal with more complex spatial relationships.

Hinton's (1981) model, for example, proposes three frames of reference – the retinal frame, the object frame and the scene frame – to deal with the position of elements relative to the retina and the position of objects relative to the rest of the scene. While the details of the models proposed by other authors may differ (Feldman (1985), for example, favours a four-frame model) the principle of a hierarchy of frameworks or representations handling progressively more complex relationships is gaining wide acceptance. In general, the earlier stages of processing or levels of representation would seem to be most amenable to coding in terms of an egocentric coordinate system. In contrast, an allocentric coordinate system, which bears more resemblance to what we usually think of as a map, may be more useful at later stages of processing where the spatial relationships obtaining between external stimuli (rather than their individual position with respect to the observer) need to be encoded.

The related notion of an internal representation has been used to explain the phenomenon of neglect of one half of the 'representational' space which Bisiach and Luzzatti's (1978) patients were asked to imagine; and Farah's analysis (see Chapter 21 of this volume) of the neurological basis of mental imagery illustrates the utility of taking an information-processing approach to clinical data. Accordingly, we refer to cognitive constructs whenever we consider that they have potential relevance, although we admit that the concepts and models of cognitive psychology and the clinical data cannot invariably be mapped onto each other satisfactorily.

Balint-Holmes syndrome

Although the patients described by Holmes (1918; Holmes and Horrax, 1919) differed in some respects from the earlier case reported by Balint (1909), we follow De Renzi (1985) in reviewing the group of symptoms identified by these authors under the joint heading of Balint-Holmes syndrome because the similarities between their patients seem to outweigh the differences. The true syndrome consists of a triad of disorders − oculomotor apraxia or psychic paralysis of gaze, spatial restriction of attention and optic ataxia − but subsequent authors have reported partial forms in which any of these symptoms may occur in isolation or in modified form. We include them here because they seem to us to help to clarify the causes of the deficits.

The full syndrome affects the subject bilaterally and is caused by a bilateral, though not necessarily symmetrical, lesion involving the parietal or parieto-occipital region. Most of the early cases were the result of gunshot wounds but in civilian practice it is most frequently encountered as a result of infarction in the posterior border-zone territory associated with severe hypotension (Damasio, 1985). The disorder, particularly in its partial forms, is probably considerably more common than the relatively infrequent reports would suggest.

Gaze apraxia

The oculomotor symptomatology in cases of Balint's syndrome has been reviewed by Girotti et al. (1982). The disorder can be generally characterized as an inability to shift the gaze so as to bring peripherally exposed stimuli into fixation. The gaze is typically described as wandering, apparently aimlessly, until the target is located as though by chance; and there may be difficulty maintaining fixation once it is acquired. When they have been studied, convergence and pursuit eye-movements have typically been found to be abnormal, though Balint did not report any such deficits in his patient. It is quite clear that these difficulties are not the result of an actual gaze paresis, as most authors have reported that patients' eyes will move spontaneously and in many cases they are able to move their eyes to verbal command,

although some authors who have examined eye movements particularly carefully have found them to be hypometric, to have increased latency, and to be easily fatiguable or inconsistent even when no visual target is involved (Garein et al., 1967; Vighetto and Perenin, 1981; Rousseaux et al., 1986). Some patients are able to fixate and follow their own finger as it is brought near to their face or bring their eyes promptly to a stimulus, such as a part of their body or the source of a sound, which they can presumably locate by non-visual means. In contrast, they may be unable to converge or fixate on the examiner's finger (Holmes, 1918; Holmes and Horrax, 1919; Godwin-Austen, 1965) but this is not always the case (Holmes, 1918).

A dissociation similar to that between redirection of gaze to visual and non-visual targets is seen with respect to reaching: patients can sometimes reach accurately for points on their own body but not for external stimuli. This has been taken to imply that the disorder reflects inadequate specification of the position of the stimulus by the visual system (Holmes, 1918; Ratcliff, 1982) and this is probably at least a contributory cause in some patients. However, this is unlikely to be the explanation for those cases where localization of non-visual targets is impaired and in whom a more truly praxic component seems to be implicated. Nor could it explain the puzzling cases who can reach accurately for visually presented targets but not direct their gaze to them (Waltz, 1961; Monaco et al., 1980). But it should be noted that the lesions in these two patients included substantial frontal damage and the aetiology of the gaze disturbance may have been different from that seen in the more typical Balint's syndrome associated with posterior cerebral dysfunction. Nevertheless, these cases do show that disordered eye movements and presumably a resulting disruption of the orderly scanning of the environment do not necessarily lead to inaccurate reaching.

Restriction of attention

A further problem affecting visual search in some

patients is a difficulty in initiating a refixation saccade, which appears to be attributable to an inability to unlock the gaze from the target on which
it is currently fixed. This aspect of the oculomotor
disorder was named 'spasm of fixation' by Holmes
(1930), who attributed it to a disinhibition of the
occipital fixation reflex and commented that
'spasm of fixation is not effective when . . . attention is not arrested by an object of special interest'.
This observation raises the possibility that the difficulty in moving the eyes is associated with a difficulty in shifting attention, and a number of lines
of evidence implicate the parietal lobes – damaged in the Balint-Holmes syndrome – in the
maintenance and distribution of attention to visual
stimuli. In the monkey, neurones in Brodman's
area 7 exhibit an enhanced response to a peripheral
stimulus when that stimulus can be assumed to be
the subject of the monkey's attention, even if the
experimental situation prevents the monkey from
looking or reaching towards it (Robinson et al.,
1978), although it is possible that these attention-
related changes are the result of the control of this
area by another brain region such as the pulvinar
(Andersen, 1987). Posner and his colleagues (1984)
have shown that parietal lobe damage can result in
an impairment of the ability to disengage attention
from its current focus, and impairment of this
disengaging operation is seen in patients with clinical neglect (Morrow and Ratcliff, 1987). It is
reasonable to assume that shifts of gaze are preceded (or, at least, accompanied) by shift of visual attention, particularly when the goal of the eye
movement is to bring a peripherally exposed target
into fixation. This is just the situation in which patients with Balint-Holmes syndrome are most likely to have difficulty initiating the saccade and it
seems likely that, in some cases, the spasm of fixation is secondary to restriction of visual attention.
This does not exclude the possibility that, in other
cases, there may be a primary inability to initiate
voluntary eye movements either to command or to
visual targets, and several authors have suggested
that, when this is the case, the frontal lobes are involved (Monaco et al., 1980; Hauser et al., 1980;

Hécaen and Ajuriaguerra, 1954). Just as one might
think of the spatial restriction of attention in the
Balint-Holmes syndrome as a bilateral form of the
much more common unilateral visuospatial neglect,
one could compare the inability to initiate eye
movements to a bilateral conjugate gaze palsy.

More direct evidence for the restriction of visual
attention in some of these patients comes from the
observation that they may appear to be able to see
only one object or part of an object at a given time.
Thus one of Hécaen and Ajuriaguerra's (1954) patients had difficulty lighting a cigarette because he
could not see the cigarette and match simultaneously (although this could also have resulted from
the associated optic ataxia). The patient of Girotti
et al. (1982) is said to have been able to read an
advertisement while watching motor racing on tele-
vision but not to have noticed the cars speeding
past the placard. Although the patients may have
visual field cuts, predominantly in the lower
quadrants, their failure to notice visual stimuli is
not the result of absolute visual field loss. Rather
it seems that a new peripheral stimulus is less
salient than would normally be the case although
it can be detected if attention is appropriately
directed. This state of affairs may explain the apparently variable visual fields noted in some cases.
In Balint's original case attention was consistently
directed $30° - 40°$ into the right half-field, while
stimuli on the left were only noticed if his attention
was specifically summoned to them. This asymmetry of attention has been noted in other patients
and makes the disorder all the more reminiscent of
unilateral neglect. As in the classical cases of
simultanagnosia (Wolpert, 1924; Kinsbourne and
Warrington, 1963) the inability to read and make
sense of complex scenes may be affected but it is
not certain that the mechanism is the same for the
two disorders. An elevated tachistoscopic recognition threshold for double stimuli (e.g. pairs of letters or shapes), in the presence of relatively normal
thresholds for recognition of single stimuli, has
been considered the hallmark of simultanagnosia
(Kinsbourne and Warrington, 1963; Levine and
Calvanio, 1978), but Godwin-Austen's (1965) case

of visual disorientation recognized double stimuli at quite short exposure durations.

Optic ataxia

Sometimes described as visuomotor ataxia or defective visual localization, the third component of the Balint-Holmes syndrome is an impairment of the ability to reach accurately for visually presented stimuli although non-visual stimuli may be located accurately. On finger – nose testing, the patient will touch his nose accurately but miss the examiner's finger. In its full form in patients with bilateral lesions, the disorder affects stimuli in all parts of the visual field and impairs reaching with both arms, but defective reaching has been described limited to the half-field contralateral to unilateral parietal lesions (Ratcliff and Davies-Jones, 1972) or the contralateral half of space even if gaze was directed to a stimulus on that side (Vighetto and Perenin, 1981), with only one arm as in Balint's original case (Balint, 1909) or with some specific combination of arm and half-field (Rondot, Recondo and Ribadeau Dumas, 1977).

The disorder has been attributed to a disconnection of visual input from the motor mechanisms involved in programming a reaching movement (Rondot et al., 1977; Boller et al., 1975) and this is almost certainly the explanation for those cases in which the disorder is limited to a specific combination of arm and half-field. However, as with the re-direction of gaze, it is plausible to suggest that, in some cases, defective reaching is a result of inadequate specification of the position of a visual stimulus caused by damage to a mechanism which provides target information to the motor system rather than by the cutting of a simple connection. The neurones of Areas 5 and 7 would seem to be well suited to such a rôle and, although the earlier literature suggested that the lesion responsible for defective localization was in the supra-marginal and angular gyri, more recent evidence implicates areas higher in the parietal lobe (Ratcliff and Davies-Jones, 1972; Käse et al., 1977; Damasio and Benton, 1979).

In addition to their probable involvement in the redirection of visual attention, it has been suggested that these neurones play a rôle in the programming of reaching movements (Mountcastle et al., 1975), update the spatial relationships between external stimuli and the moving animal (Leinonen et al., 1979), and act as an interface between sensory and motor systems that accomplish motor movement under sensory guidance (Andersen, 1987). A number of authors working with human patients (e.g. De Renzi, 1982; Ratcliff, 1982) and animals (e.g. Soper, 1979; Mountcastle et al., 1975; Andersen, 1987) have seen the parallel between the consequences of parietal damage in man and the neurophysiology of parietal cortex as revealed by single unit and ablation studies in primates. Further elucidation of this relationship is one of the more intriguing possibilities for clinico-physiological correlation in the near future.

In summary, the position to date is that parietal or parieto-occipital lesions can cause attentional disturbances and a difficulty in specifying the position of visual stimuli with respect to the individual, which are at once consistent with what we know of the physiology of this part of the brain and sufficient to account for many of the manifestations of the Balint-Holmes syndrome. Further, it seems that the locating difficulty and attentional disturbance can occur independently and that one or the other underlies optic ataxia − at least as they occur in the Balint-Holmes syndrome.

In cognitive terms, it would be sufficient to suppose that a relatively simple mechanism coding space in an egocentric reference frame was disturbed in these cases, though adequate coding at this level might be a prerequisite of later more sophisticated spatial information-processing.

Disorders of sensory analysis and elementary perception

These disorders are presumed to occur at a relatively early stage of visuospatial processing but the relationship between early (subtle) sensory loss and higher-order visuoperceptual and visuospatial ability is still a subject of controversy. The balance of evidence suggests that sensory loss is not a sufficient condition for the emergence of 'higher-order' perceptual and visuospatial defects (Ettlinger, 1956; Levine et al., 1980; Ratcliff and Ross, 1981; Warrington, 1985).

Localization

Gross disorders of localization have already been discussed in relation to Balint's syndrome. A less severe impairment localizing objects in pericorporal space is a fairly frequent concomitant of posterior cerebral lesions. Those studies that have required patients to test localization in *central* vision, by asking patients to make same/different judgements regarding the position of a dot on two sample cards (Warrington and Rabin, 1970), or to identify the location of single and paired dots (Hannay et al., 1976), have indicated more frequent and severe impairment in patients with right hemisphere lesions, not invariably associated with neglect (Hannay et al., 1976). This hemispheric difference did not emerge when Ratcliff and Davies-Jones (1972) examined localization in the *peripheral* visual field. These authors found a highly significant impairment of localization in men with stable focal posterior brain lesions, regardless of laterality. Conflicting anatomical conclusions drawn from localization studies have been attributed to differences in task demand, notably their execution in either relative or absolute space (De Renzi, 1982; Benton, 1985a), i.e. the role of body-centred versus extrapersonal referents (see also Ventre et al., 1984). Undoubtedly, other factors need to be considered, including the distinction between central and peripheral visual channels (Paillard, 1982a), and the fact that the subjects of Ratcliff and Davies-Jones used a pointing response. The latter authors (Ratcliff and Davies-Jones, 1972, pp. 58 – 59) stress the unusual finding of 'gross localization defects throughout the peripheral visual field in the absence of defective localization in central vision'.

Depth perception

Depth perception has been assessed in a variety of ways: by asking subjects to estimate distance in the natural environment or to judge the relative distance of real, three-dimensional objects under more controlled conditions, by measuring the acuity of stereoscopic vision per se, and by investigating the ability to achieve 'global' stereopsis by seeing form and depth in random-element stereograms. These different forms of depth perception represent different processes and are not necessarily affected together by cerebral lesions.

The estimation of distance may be grossly impaired as part of the spatial disturbance associated with the complete forms of the Balint-Holmes syndrome in patients with bilateral cerebral lesions, and quantitative testing may reveal less severe impairments of the ability to judge relative distance in patients with lesions in a variety of locations on either hemisphere, although they are usually in the posterior part of the brain (Danta et al., 1978). Similar results are obtained when 'local' stereopsis or stereoacuity is assessed by measuring the smallest degree of retinal disparity between the images of well-defined, stereoscopically exposed pairs of forms which can give an impression of depth; patients with lesions in either hemisphere may be impaired (Lawler, 1981; Lehman and Wälchi, 1975; Rothstein and Sacks, 1972).

The situation is less clear in the case of global stereopsis, which is assessed using random-element stereograms of the kind devised by Julesz (1971). These differ from the stereo images used in conventional tests of stereoacuity in that they typically employ much larger disparities and consequently do not tax stereoacuity per se. However, they also differ in that no shape is perceptible in monocular vision − the stimuli appear randomly speckled − and the perception of surface depth requires that the visual system select the solution which would be consistent with the 'global' impression of a shape standing out in depth from the large number of possible local disparity matches between individual specks. Global stereopsis is typically made more difficult by reducing the correspondence between the two images so that there is no solution that is entirely consistent and the visual system has to settle for the best fit.

This is clearly a complex task in which depth and form perception are interdependent. Most studies have suggested a right hemisphere dominance for stereopsis (Benton and Hécaen, 1970; Carmon and Bechtoldt, 1969; Hamsher, 1978) but this has not been invariably confirmed (Lawler, 1981; see also the reservations of Ross, 1983). Lawler compared the performance of particularly well-matched unilateral patient groups of two different aetiologies: men who had undergone unilateral temporal lobectomy and ex-servicemen who had sustained penetrating missile injuries of the brain some 30 years prior to examination. Both missile injury groups showed an impairment of stereoacuity on a more sensitive measure than that used in some previous studies but neither of them showed any impairment of global stereopsis. The temporal lobectomy groups were not significantly impaired on either task, although the right temporal lobe group began to show a mild impairment on stereograms with reduced binocular correlation. This finding is particularly interesting in view of the heavy form perception component in global stereopsis, which raises the possibility that the inferior, temporal cortical visual pathway may be involved and the suggestion that global stereopsis in monkeys requires the integrity of infero-temporal cortex (Cowey and Porter, 1979).

The above evidence would be consistent with the view that prestriate areas in both hemispheres are involved in stereoacuity (Ratcliff and Cowey, 1979; Lawler, 1981) but allow the possibility that right hemisphere lesions, perhaps especially in the temporal lobe, may make an additional contribution to global stereopsis. The complexity of the situation is underscored by one of Lawler's patients who reports a persistent and marked defect in depth perception but showed no impairment on any of her three quantitative measures of stereopsis.

Line orientation

An early study by Lenz (1944, p. 63, cited by McFie et al., 1950) of the ability to reproduce vertical and horizontal lines (by drawing or with stick

models) in six of 56 cases of penetrating missile injury, suggested to him that the right occipito-parietal region had 'great relevance . . . for all directional operations in the visual and sensory motor space'. Partial support for his conclusion came from a study by Bender and Jung (1948, p. 204) of 100 brain-injured patients. These authors concluded that 'right sided cerebral injuries give rise to more marked deviations of the subjective vertical and horizontal than do comparable injuries of the left side', and noted that the direction and extent of error varied with laterality of lesion: errors in patients with right hemisphere lesions occurred in an anti-clockwise direction whereas clockwise errors were found in patients with left hemisphere lesions. Their data were reanalysed by McFie et al. (1950), who indicated a site-by-lesion effect: the right hemisphere deficit was pronounced only with frontal and parietal lesions; with temporal and occipital lesions, it was the group with left hemisphere injury that differed significantly from the normal controls. In the same publication, McFie and co-workers reported orientation defects in four of the subset of five patients, in their own study of visual spatial agnosia in eight selected cases with posterior lesions.

In large-scale studies, however, setting a rod to the vertical (when the examiner moves the indicator) proves to be a relatively easy task. Interesting interactions were nevertheless found (Birch et al., 1961) when patients had to judge the true vertical position of a luminous rod in a darkened room, either without structure or when the rod appeared within a luminous square frame tilted 22° in an anti-clockwise direction. Twenty patients (all suffering from vascular disease) were selected according to the following criteria: a hemiplegia present for at least seven months; no gross expressive or receptive language disturbance; and no hemianopia which appeared to influence visual perception significantly. The orthopaedic control subjects were matched for age and sex. The five patients who had hemianopic visual field defects were unimpaired at depth perception, form perception and reading; and none reported visual difficulties in daily life. Against the completely dark background (egocentric reference), patients with brain lesions did not meet the same consistent standard of performance as control subjects. Conversely, they were relatively better able to judge verticality against a structured (frame) background, whereas the control subjects were relatively less efficient in this condition with a conflictual item of information, than when responding within a strictly egocentric frame of reference.

Regarding perception of directional orientation, Benton (1985a, p. 170) has postulated that 'the perception of directional orientation is mediated primarily by the right hemisphere in right-handed subjects.' His work and that of colleagues has suggested an overwhelming right hemisphere contribution (particularly marked in patients with posterior lesions) in visually guided judgements of line direction (Benton et al., 1975, 1978), such that almost half the patients with right hemisphere lesions were worse than the most impaired subject with a left hemisphere lesion. Similarly, De Renzi and colleagues (1971) observed a strong association between right hemisphere injury and inaccuracy in setting a rod at an oblique angle to match a standard. A similar predominance of right hemisphere deficit was found on simpler tasks requiring same/different judgements of slope, without an overt motor component (Warrington and Rabin, 1970), although not invariably achieving statistical significance (Bisiach et al., 1976). There is, however, some recent evidence of a left hemisphere contribution to judgements of line orientation when the standard matching-to-sample format is used (Kim et al., 1984; Mehta et al., 1987).

Disorders of spatial cognition

Mental rotation

The ability to imagine 'movements, transformations, or other changes in visual objects' was presumed by Guildford and Zimmerman (1948, p. 28) to be the process underlying a mathematically derived factor. This putative mental process was initially investigated with form-boards (De Renzi

and Faglioni, 1967; Dee, 1970; Meier, 1970) when no clear hemispheric differences emerged. Likewise, Butters et al. (1970), in studies of 'reversable operations', found that both 'severe' parietal groups were impaired. Only on Piaget's village scene test (with its presumably heavier perceptual and attentional demands) were the 'severe' right parietals significantly worse than those with left parietal lesions. A more pronounced right posterior deficit was reported by Ratcliff (1979) using an adaptation of Benson and Gedye's (1963) mannikin task. These patients had difficulty in judging which hand of the schematic figure held a flag only when the figure was inverted upside-down. Thus, the difficulty was not in ascribing the label 'right' or 'left' as such. Ratcliff concluded that patients with right posterior lesions had difficulty in mentally reorienting the inverted stimuli.

More recently, Mehta et al. (1988) have investigated performance on mental rotation tasks in men with chronic, unilateral focal brain lesions, using Thurstone's flags (Thurstone and Jeffrey, 1983) and Vandenberg's (1983) three-dimensional 'spatial visualization' test based on the Shepard and Metzler (1971) paradigm. Again, in keeping with most of the earlier studies, no hemispheric differences were found. In fact, marginally greater left than right hemisphere deficits emerged when Mehta (1988) examined rotation judgements using a simpler experimental task involving same/different judgements.

In a theoretical discussion of the rotation paradigm, Corballis (1982, p. 194) links it closely with imagery and concludes that it entails both propositional (Pylyshyn, 1979a,b, 1981) and analogue (Kosslyn and Pomerantz, 1977; Kosslyn and Schwartz, 1977) elements (see also Shepard and Cooper, 1982). He perceives an analogue quality in the mapping of left and right and its disorder in the phenomenon of visuospatial neglect. He suggests that 'images are *stored* in propositional fashion but "displayed" in analogue format'. Hence, 'operations on the image, such as mental rotation, may occur at the level of the analogue display rather than at the level of the propositions used to generate the display' (Corballis, 1982, p. 195). Distributive processing of this kind may go some way towards explaining the participation of both cerebral hemispheres in mental rotation. Ratcliff (1979) imputed the right hemisphere deficit in mental rotation to a failure to operate on a spatial representation. A left hemisphere deficit might involve a failure to generate appropriate mental images (Farah, 1984).

Memory for location
There is some justification for distinguishing between 'visual' and 'spatial' memory from the dissociations occurring with temporal and parietal lobe disease respectively. We reported a case, with post-mortem data, displaying a marked impairment of 'spatial' learning on a visually guided stylus maze but good delayed visual recall in the drawing from memory of a complex geometrical figure (Newcombe et al. 1987). Moreover, the distinction has some support from experimental psychological studies, suggesting a spatially based working memory system, relatively independent of visual processing (Baddeley and Lieberman, 1980). But the evidence is, as yet, inconsistent on this issue (compare Pezdek and Evans, 1979, and Salthouse, 1974, with Brooks, 1970, and Beech, 1984).

The short-term aspect of spatial memory is measured by tasks such as the Corsi block span and experimental tasks requiring the subject to recall location, e.g. the position of a circle on a line (Corsi, cited by Milner, 1971). On the latter task, Corsi found that the magnitude of error was related to extent of right hippocampal excision; patients who had undergone a left temporal-lobe resection were unimpaired. We would expect some patients with parietal-lobe disease to show deficits on this task that could well be more severe than those displayed after right temporal-lobe resection.

Long-term spatial memory has been investigated by Smith and Milner (1981), in an adapted version of Kim's game. Sixteen toy-objects were displayed in a fixed position on a board. Subjects were asked to name the toy and estimate the average price of the real object. They then moved to a different

position in the room, out of sight of the display, where they had to recall as many objects as possible and thereafter to place a set of the same 16 toy-objects on a blank board, in exactly the same position in which they were initially displayed for price estimation. Delayed recall for object-names and positions was again tested 24 hours later.

It is incidental recall of location which concerns us here. Patients who had undergone a right temporal lobectomy were impaired at location (for which both absolute and relative measures were used) and again the magnitude of error was related to extent of right hippocampal removal. However the authors, in reporting this association between encoding of location and mesial structures of the temporal lobe, indicate the rich connectivity of these structures with both frontal and parietal cortex. Data from our current studies of the long-term effects of focal missile injury suggest that posterior lesions, regardless of laterality, are associated with impaired performance on this task.

Maze learning
It is important, first of all, to distinguish the different processing requirements of the heterogeneous cluster of maze tasks. Thus, Ratcliff and Newcombe (1973) reported a clear dissociation in performance on locomotor and stylus maze tasks: deficits on the former were associated with bilateral and those on the latter with right posterior brain lesions. Likewise, there is no a priori reason for assuming identical processing demands and strategies in the solution of a stylus maze task, compared with a lattice maze (Elithorn, 1955), in which the solution is constrained by the number of nodes through which the subject must pass, or the Porteus maze, in which errors are clearly marked cul-de-sacs (Porteus and Peters, 1947). Studies using the lattice maze have consistently reported a right hemisphere deficit without implicating any particular region of the brain (Benton et al., 1963; Colonna and Faglioni, 1966; Archibald, 1978). In contrast, the Porteus test, with its forward-planning requirements, may be more sensitive to anterior lesions (Crown, 1951): although a

unilateral right-sided deficit has clearly emerged only in Parkinson's patients after subthalamotomy (Meier and Story, 1967).

We shall focus on the stylus maze with its relatively heavy demand on working and long-term spatial memory. Early studies by Milner (1965) emphasize the deficits shown by patients with large right hippocampal lesions in temporal lobectomy patients, deficits also reflected in a tactual analogue of the task (Corkin, 1965). Both authors also noted deficits in right frontal patients associated with rule-breaking behaviour. A more substantial body of data now suggests that posterior, parietal lesions are frequently associated with disproportionately severe maze-learning deficits (Newcombe and Russell, 1969; Ratcliff and Newcombe, 1973; De Renzi et al., 1977). Newcombe and Russell (1969) associated the more severe maze-learning deficits with high right parietal lesions, in the region of area 7 and adjacent cortices, for which supportive evidence has been found in a post-mortem study (Newcombe, Ratcliff and Damasio, 1987).

Spatial memory: short-term vs. long-term
De Renzi (1982, p. 226) clearly indicated the putative dissociation between short-term and long-term spatial memory. Two patients with right posterior lesions were markedly impaired on Corsi's non-verbal block span task (described by Milner, 1971) but unimpaired on tasks of perception, spatial exploration and maze learning. Newcombe et al. (1987) reported the reverse pattern. As De Renzi pointed out, these dissociations are similar to those envisaged for verbal memory (Warrington and Weiskrantz, 1973) and have corresponding implications for memory models. However, impairment of short-term spatial memory span (as measured by Corsi's test) is not consistently associated with right hemisphere lesions. Significant reduction of non-verbal span has been reported, regardless of laterality (De Renzi and Nichelli, 1975; De Renzi et al., 1977; Mehta et al., 1988), although when the memory load is increased, by testing the retention of a three-block sequence after 9 and 16 second delays and adding interpolated activity (counting), in a modification of the Bauer-Petersen procedure, the posterior right hemisphere deficit is thrown into sharper relief (De Renzi et al., 1977). Similarly, difficulty in learning a spatial sequence in excess of span was strongly associated with right posterior lesions (De Renzi et al., 1977).

Topographical orientation

Disorders of topographical orientation and memory are relatively infrequent (Hécaen and Angelergues, 1963) but nevertheless varied in expression. They embrace the loss of memory for familiar surroundings, the inability to locate countries and cities on a map, and the inability to find one's way either within one's own home or in the external environment. Such disorders are not infrequently associated with other visuospatial deficits (Landis et al., 1986), including unilateral spatial neglect (Brain, 1941; Hécaen, 1962), prosopagnosia and achromatopsia (Pallis, 1955), disorders of visual perception and exploration (Paterson and Zangwill, 1945), visual and spatial memory impairments (Whitty and Newcombe, 1973) and post-traumatic amnesia and confusion (Paterson and Zangwill, 1944a). Nevertheless, there is reasonably convincing clinical evidence that topographical disorders can be disproportionately severe if not the only striking symptom of cognitive dysfunction. Thus, a patient has been described with intact perceptual and spatial skills but a selective topographical disorder (Whiteley and Warrington, 1978) and, conversely, an amnesic patient without topographical disorientation (De Renzi et al., 1977, case RA). Likewise, contrasting patterns of recovery point to the relative independence of topographical functions: patients showing a persistent topographical disorder despite a rapid improvement in face recognition (Landis et al., 1986) or a marked improvement in memory and orientation (Paterson and Zangwill, 1944a).

Individual case studies reflect different forms of topographical disorder and provide a first assay of the mechanisms involved. A preliminary distinction can be made between the loss of topographical memory and a more perceptually based failure to recognize localities and their landmarks, with 'their unique orientating value' (Landis et al., 1986, p. 135). The loss of memory for localities and routes that were well-known prior to disease has to be distinguished clearly from the loss of geographical knowledge; topographically impaired patients may continue to locate their home or cities on a map (Landis et al., 1986, case 1).

One can also draw an operational distinction between the loss of premorbid topographical memories and the inability to construct and remember new spatial schemata, which De Renzi et al. (1977) have compared with retrograde and anterograde amnesia respectively. This dissociation is evident in studies of recovery. Cases 1 and 2 of the four patients with topographical problems described by Habib and Sirigu (1987) apparently recovered topographical memory (in the sense described above) but continued to report orientation problems in unfamiliar surroundings. We have also observed difficulty in topographical orientation in unfamiliar surroundings, without frank topographical memory loss, in men with chronic focal missile lesions in the posterior area of the right hemisphere; they complain that it invariably takes them longer to learn their way around than other family members when on holiday, although they are not aware of difficulty on familiar routes in their daily life.

Topographical memory loss is usually, if not invariably, associated with a loss of the capacity to visualize familiar places. A patient with a topographical disturbance of 30 years duration could not visualize or describe the lay-out of his own home or of the home town in which he had lived most of his life (Whitty and Newcombe, 1973).

However, the reverse is not necessarily true. In marked contrast to patients who present with a loss of topographical memory are those whose perception of their topographical environment has changed. Thus, a well-studied case by Pallis (1955, p. 219) complained: 'In my mind's eye I know exactly

where places are, what they look like. I can visualize T . . . square without difficulty, and the streets that come into it . . . I know the order of the shops . . . I can draw you a plan of the roads from Cardiff to the Rhondda Valley . . . it's when I'm out that the trouble starts. My reason tells me I must be in a certain place and yet I don't recognize it'. The perceptual and mnestic aspects of topographical disorder were also well distinguished in a case study by Wilbrand (1887, cited by Critchley, 1969, p. 313). This intelligent and articulate 63-year-old lady was unable to visualize the streets of her native city, Hamburg, or her own home after a stroke. Subsequently, her topographical memory had somewhat improved whereas perception was still markedly impaired: 'I could quite well walk through Hamburg with my eyes closed, but when I actually stand in the street I don't know which way to turn; with my eyes shut, I see the old Hamburg in front of me again'. Her comment points to the interesting distinction between data-driven and conceptually driven responses, discussed by Martin (1987), who also drew our attention to Goldstein's illustration of the phenomenon (Goldstein, 1940, pp. 39 – 43).

The perceptual component of some topographic disorders is not necessarily at the relatively elementary level of depth perception, stereoscopic vision, judgement of location, etc. Thus De Renzi and Faglioni (1962) and Whiteley and Warrington (1978) report cases whose topographical difficulties appeared to be compounded by difficulty in recognizing landmarks. Moreover, Pallis (1955, p. 223) concluded that his patient, a 51-year-old mining engineer and colliery manager (whose symptoms resulted from a cerebral embolism), had retained his sense of orientation in abstract space, noting his 'excellent performance in drawing maps of places familiar to him before his illness'. He could outline an appropriate route on a map but had difficulty when following it in practice: 'The places are all strange, yet commonsense tells me they are not new to me'. Pallis concluded that he was unable to appreciate the topographical significance of landmarks in the environment. Interestingly, he still played chess.

Many of the patients with topographical disorders use compensatory strategies: verbal directions and distinctive features in the landscape or scene frame. So case 2, described by Landis et al. (1986), located her room door as first on the left after the fire escape; and the ex-serviceman with a right posterior missile injury, studied by Paterson and Zangwill (1945, p. 11), identified the interview room in which he was consistently examined only by a small notice, 'AC plugs'.

Further insights into the mechanisms supporting topographical orientation and memory can presumably be expected from developmental studies and cognitive modelling. In a discussion of the requisites of normal spatial orientation, Byrne (1982, p. 241 and pp. 246–249) specifies the need for a compass (for the detection of orientation in relation to a 'fixed, external frame of reference'), a place-keeper (for recording and updating position on a map, by monitoring movements and recognizing landmarks) and a map ('any representation which subserves navigation'). He distinguishes between a 'network-map', essentially consisting of strings and nodes (branch points, landmarks etc.), and thus similar to a schematic map of a subway or underground train system, and a vector-map, which is 'isomorphic to the real world when viewed from above', as represented by an ordnance survey map. Most subjects appear to rely on a network map (Linde and Labov, 1975), either when describing their own department or when giving instructions to strangers. There are considerable individual differences in the ability to construct and use a vector-map, and ecological demands and priorities are probably important: Australian aborigines are expert (with a mean error of less than 5 degrees) at pointing to invisible but highly significant landmarks, the sacred places (Byrne, 1982). Byrne suggests that some patients with topographical disorders reflect the functional distinction between these maps: the patient reported by Paterson and Zangwill (1945) could not recognize landmarks or use network-map representations but retained a vector-map of his home town. Patho-

physiology may provide further dissociations, e.g. in place-keeping, in that some patients would appear to have a problem in recognizing the topographical significance of landmarks whereas others may have difficulty in monitoring their movements in space, whether navigating in real life or following a laboratory map (Semmes et al., 1955, 1963; Ratcliff and Newcombe, 1973). An interesting patient studied by Cole and Perez-Cruet (1964, p. 241) was able to locate cities on a map of the United States and to draw a plan of the ward and the hospital wing but could not find his way to the examiners' laboratory, close to the ward 'after many attempts and instructions and was unable to describe various routes around the hospital': apparently a selective disorder of topographical orientation.

Neuropsychological studies of topographical disorder tend to be limited to tests of previous factual (geographic and topographic) knowledge and/or performance on stylus maze and locomotor map-reading tasks. From empirical studies of laboratory performance and clinical symptomatology, De Renzi et al. (1977) have concluded that maze tasks are the best available laboratory tools for the examination of topographical memory. Such maze tasks require the subject, who is stationary, to appreciate and learn the turns at a sequence of choice-points. In contrast, the locomotor maze requires the moving subject to navigate in a 3 × 3 matrix with a map (held in a fixed orientation to his body) to which his own changing orientation has continually to be related and on which he has continually to update his position. The emphasis is on spatial computation and transformation rather than on spatial memory *tout court*. Not surprisingly, performance on these two differing tasks has been dissociated experimentally and related to unilateral right posterior and bilateral lesions respectively (Ratcliff and Newcombe, 1973; and see Orbach, 1959, for a functional and anatomical dissociation in performance in monkey on two different maze tasks).

The cognitive demands in the locomotor task are relatively complex; a variety of strategies, potentially sustained by either hemisphere, could be used to solve it. Hence, unilateral posterior lesions produced a mild defect, whereas bilateral lesions (not in this case associated with significantly poorer performance on many other cognitive tasks) provoked a highly significant impairment, with little overlap between bilateral and unilateral groups: a contrast reminiscent of the qualitatively different nature of memory impairment associated with unilateral and bilateral temporal-lobe lesions.

De Renzi et al. (1977, p. 504) have concluded that: 'for an isolated, severe topographical amnesia to occur, injury to the right posterior neocortex is a necessary prerequisite'. The possibility of specialization within the hemispheres (especially the right hemisphere) for different components of topographical orientation follows ineluctably. It seems no accident that the more perceptual form of the disorder involving failure to recognize landmarks may occur with prosopagnosia and central achromatopsia and is associated with a more inferiorly placed lesion (Damasio et al., 1982). When more widespread visual memory deficits are found then the hippocampus and the parahippocampal gyrus (Habib and Sirigu, 1987) may be involved. When spatial memory or learning is significantly impaired or the task demands substantial spatial computation, then it would appear that the parietal cortex is implicated (De Renzi, 1982; Newcombe et al., 1987). Recent papers (Landis et al., 1986; Habib and Sirigu, 1987) point to the frequency of cerebrovascular disease — specifically, infarction of the right posterior cerebral artery — in the genesis of these disorders.

Spatial disorientation has been reported as a developmental disorder and specifically in conjunction with the Dyke-Davidoff-Masson syndrome (Fine et al., 1980). Fine et al. describe a 60-year-old male patient who had repeatedly been admitted to hospital between 1948 and 1977 because of focal seizures. He showed the typical features of the syndrome, with limb atrophy, dysmorphia, and elevation of sphenoid ridge and frontal sinus. As a child, he was frequently lost in the neighbourhood and was poor at geography at school although able to cope with English and mathematics. During military service, he was relegated to a non-combat unit because he misdirected the squadron while on field exercises. As a truck driver, he was frequently lost when making deliveries and was obliged to use a written check-list of familiar landmarks (streets, traffic lights, turnings), prepared by kindly colleagues. When examined in later life he had a left facial paresis and a left hyperreflexia. Sensation was intact except for graphaesthesia, baragnosis, position sense, and two-point discrimination in the left hand. He had a normal verbal IQ; language and face recognition skills were intact. However, he had a constellation of deficits, including failures of categorization and visual search and impairment of visual integration and constructional apraxia, ascribed by these authors to frontal and parietal dysfunction respectively. His severe and lifelong inability to use a map was discussed by the authors in the light of observations by Kohn and Dennis (1974) that right hemisphere lesions before the age of ten cause more disability than those occurring in adolescence on tasks requiring the reading of road maps and the maintenance of extrapersonal orientation.

Disorders of body image and personal orientation

Disorders of body-centred space-coordinate systems can give rise to a variety of symptoms, ranging from gross misconception of one's body image to finger agnosia. The notion of body schema has been subjected to considerable criticism and it may therefore be helpful to distinguish conceptually the main components of egocentric spatial reference (Head and Holmes, 1911–1912; Paillard, 1982b). First, there is *postural reference* as a component of geocentric calibration; second, *the body schema*, which presupposes a spatially organized concept of one's own body that allows the spatial indexing of sensory input and is involved in the triggering and guidance of movement; third, the *body image* itself, which is a conscious representation, coded by its sensory characteristics of quality, form and intensity. Within that framework, we can consider some of the disorders of body image and personal orientation associated with disease of the central nervous system. The origin of these disorders can be diverse and multifactorial. Hence it is far from clear whether they are independent syndromes and to what extent they can be related to a disturbance of body image per se.

Anosognosia

Gross disorders in the perception of one's own body can occur in the acute period after a cerebrovascular accident. The symptoms may include neglect or denial of paralysis, a defective appreciation of the extent of the defect, the experience of a phantom limb, and a failure to distinguish between one's own body and that of the examiner. Explicit denial of paralysis has been ascribed to 'kinesthetic hallucinations' resulting from partial sensory deprivation (Frederiks, 1985). Behavioural neglect of limbs may occur despite their normal use in coordinated motor activities such as walking and dressing (Critchley, 1969).

The interpretation of anosognosic disorders is varied. They may be ascribed to aphasia, more diffuse disorientation, and intellectual deterioration (Poeck and Orgass, 1971). Alternatively, they may be regarded as selective disorders (Alajouanine and Lhermitte, 1957) and accorded a more focal neurophysiological basis: for example, a failure to integrate somatosensory afference from the contralateral half of the body (Denny-Brown, 1962; Denny-Brown and Banker, 1954). There is, however, a consensus of opinion that these disorders are frequently associated with damage to the posterior area of the right hemisphere. Thus, Critchley (1969, p. 411) reports that 'the peculiar role of the parietal lobe − or lobes − in the building-up of the postural schema of the body leads to an important association with corporeal awareness, imagery and memory'.

Autotopagnosia

The label 'autotopagnosia' − signifying the in-

ability to identify or point to body parts on verbal instruction − covers a cluster of symptoms that are not always systematically studied and of which the mechanisms are ill-understood. We will discuss separately three aspects of autotopagnosia − disorders of personal orientation, finger agnosia and right − left disorientation − which may occur, albeit rarely, as relatively isolated symptoms in the absence of dysphasia, dyspraxia or disorders of pointing.

Disorders of personal orientation and body-part identification

Personal orientation is measured by the ability to locate body parts in response to verbal command, demonstration or markings on a schematic figure. It is distinguished from *extrapersonal* orientation as measured by the subject's ability at locomotor map-reading (Semmes et al. 1955, 1963). This conceptual distinction was supported by behavioural evidence of dissociable deficits in groups of ex-servicemen with chronic, focal missile injuries of the brain. Thus, men with parietal lesions (right or left) were impaired at locomotor map-reading, whereas those with anterior (especially left) lesions and those with left parieto-occipital lesions were impaired on the personal orientation task. As Semmes and co-workers (1963, p. 769) conceded, the dissociation was not clear-cut: performance on the two tasks was significantly related, suggesting 'both common and independent elements in these two forms of orientation'. A clearer dissociation emerged in the comparison of left anterior and right posterior lesions: anterior lesions tended to impair personal but not extrapersonal orientation, whereas the converse was the case for right posterior lesions. The authors repudiated the notion that difficulties in personal orientation can be reduced to lower-order visual sensory loss and doubted that they were of a spatial nature; they suggested, on the basis of correlations between performance on personal orientation and sorting tasks, that the difficulty in 'shifting from one perceptual organization to another' (p. 267), associated with anterior lesions, could represent the common underlying mechanism.

In addition to the work of Semmes et al. (1963) and Teuber and Mishkin (1954), there is a study by Butters et al. (1972) which supports the dissociation between personal and extrapersonal orientation. On what is described as a 'personal' spatial task (Money's road-map test of directional sense: Money et al., 1965) patients with left frontal lesions were more impaired, whereas right parietal patients were relatively inferior on the 'extrapersonal' spatial test (copying stick patterns in a matched and reversal condition). Physiological research has also supported a distinction between predominantly egocentric and predominantly allocentric orientation (Pohl, 1973; Ungerleider and Brody, 1977; Paillard, 1987).

Moreover, the various tests of personal orientation tap different skills which are plausibly dissociable and differentially affected by pathophysiology. Localization of body parts may require the ability to assign a correct verbal label, to distinguish between left and right on the body of oneself and others, and to transform or rotate mentally locations on the examiner's body or on diagrams presented in different (back/front, upright/inverted) views. Thus aphasia, right−left disorientation and disorders of spatial cognition could variously affect performance on one or several versions of these personal orientation tasks.

A careful study of body-part identification by Semenza and Goodglass (1985) failed to demonstrate selective failures of body-part identification associated with sensory modality of stimulus or response mode. Thirty-two aphasic patients were studied on a wide range of body-part identification tasks. In initial trials, none of the subjects with 'pure right hemisphere lesions' made errors on the nine experimental conditions, which included pointing in verbal and non-verbal conditions, imitating the examiner or touching a part previously located by a tactile stimulus. The authors concluded that performance on all these tasks depended on 'strength and precision of the conceptual representation of the individual body parts, whether indicated by name, by visual pointing or by touch'

(Semenza and Goodglass, 1985, p. 173). They could not support the notion of a general disorder of awareness of body topology and were not able to attribute particular importance to axial versus peripheral components of the task or detect a substantial contribution from problems of pointing and reaching. The pattern of errors did not support an earlier view (De Renzi and Scotti, 1970) that body localization errors were a special example of failure to isolate parts within a whole, although they concede that this interpretation might hold for some cases. They indicated that errors in body localization were generally not random but displayed functional similarities (e.g. TOE − thumb; KNEE − elbow) or were in the vicinity of the target. An interesting problem arises as to whether some patients may show a selective difficulty in naming body parts to verbal command (Goodglass et al., 1976). Some recent reports of category-specific naming difficulties (Yamadori and Albert, 1973; Warrington and Shallice, 1984; Temple, 1986) suggest that the notion is not entirely implausible.

The study by Semenza and Goodglass (1985), however, focussed on a selected population of aphasic patients. From other clinical studies, it would appear that disorders of personal orientation merit some claim for quasi-independent status, dissociated alike from aphasia (Poncet et al., 1971) and nominal defects (De Renzi and Scotti, 1970) as well as from disorders of extra-personal orientation.

Finger agnosia

Finger agnosia, together with right/left disorientation, dysgraphia and dyscalculia, is regarded as a key attribute of Gerstmann's syndrome (Gerstmann, 1940). It does not imply a motor apraxia. Gerstmann's (1924) first patient could thread a needle and sew, and one of Lange's (1936) patients continued to play the piano well. Lange suggested that highly automatized activities are preserved but that patients can no longer differentiate the individual fingers or apply them individually as tools.

In a scholarly critique of this syndrome, Critchley (1969, p. 210) draws attention to the inconsistencies of early case studies yet recognizes the occurrence of this symptom-complex and its frequent association with left parietal-lobe disease. He also raises the interesting question as to why the fingers have assumed this unusual significance in body-schema disorders. He points to the 'peculiar role (of the hand) in human ecology' as 'the most efficient organ or tool' and 'the principal instrument of touch'. We could add that it is an important marker of fine spatial coordinates in touching and reaching. Moreover, increasing physiological evidence of the extensive cortical representation of the hand, with its several anatomically (and presumably functionally) distinct maps, emphasizes the key role of the hand as an executive tool of visuomotor coordination and motor command (Paillard, 1988).

Contemporary neuropsychology tends to question the 'purity' of the Gerstmann syndrome (compare Benton, 1961, and Strub and Geschwind, 1983), because of its frequent association with other symptoms of cognitive disorder. When tested in a verbal mode, finger agnosia shows a definite, but not invariable, association with language comprehension problems (Poeck and Orgass, 1969; Sauguet et al., 1971), although the deficit has been found in non-aphasic patients with left hemisphere lesions as well as those with right hemisphere lesions (Sauguet et al., 1971; Gainotti et al., 1972). The failure to find clear-cut hemispheric differences when patients with receptive aphasia are excluded was originally attributed by Benton (1959) to a disturbance of body schema combined with an impairment in symbolic comprehension, a view endorsed by Sauguet et al. (1971). But other factors have been adduced to account for the syndrome, including apraxia (Herrmann and Pötzl, 1926) and a failure to appreciate spatial relationships (Stengel and Vienna, 1944).

Furthermore, Benton's (1959) developmental work has shown that the identification of fingers on an outline drawing appears to make fairly complex cognitive demands such that normal children of nine may fail the task. Likewise, some related skills, for example, the tactile localization of simultaneously presented stimulus pairs, do not reach maturity until after the age of twelve.

Right/left disorientation

The inability to distinguish right from left (on oneself, on the examiner, or on a schematic figure) is another feature of the Gerstmann syndrome but it occurs in other clinical groups as a component of impaired personal orientation. Right/left judgements on the self usually require body-part identification and naming skills, both of a relatively simple order. Identification at this basic level is seldom impaired except in severe receptive dysphasia or diffuse intellectual impairment. When such confusion does occur, outside the setting of intellectual deterioration and severe comprehension loss, it can be a rare but striking symptom of parietal-lobe dysfunction; and it has also been reported as a developmental disorder. Critchley (1969) points to unfortunate servicemen who must originally have been considered eligible for the armed forces but then proved unable to move in the required direction on the parade-ground or to distinguish port from starboard.

Increasing the spatial complexity of the task obviously requires additional cognitive skills, including that of mental rotation or spatial transformation. This emerges clearly when the patient has to identify right and left body parts on the examiner sitting opposite or on schematic figures which may be presented, as on Ratcliff's (1979) task, in different spatial orientations, including the most difficult version (a mannikin presented upside down and back to front). In Ratcliff's study, the inverted condition evoked a posterior *right* hemisphere deficit, specifically ascribed to the demand for mental rotation.

As Benton's (1959) developmental studies demonstrated, right/left orientation is relatively late to develop reliably. Moreover, a small proportion of the normal population consistently make errors, including a slightly higher percentage of women than men (Wolf, 1973; Harris and Gitterman,

1978). There is also some interesting developmental evidence for a clear dissociation between right – left judgements on one's own body and performance on the more complex road-map test of directional sense (Money et al., 1965). The latter task presents a schematic map of city blocks on which a route has been traced. Subjects have to imagine walking along the route and then to state whether they make a right-hand or a left-hand turn at each choice-point. The map cannot be turned. The path sometimes turns towards the subject's body, changing the perspective from which the right/left judgement must be made. Children with Turner's syndrome were more severely impaired on this task though they had little difficulty with simple right/left judgements (N. Newcombe, cited by Corballis, 1982).

Concluding remarks

The disorders discussed here are important for both clinical and theoretical reasons. Clinically, evidence for the presence of spatial disorder may be extracted from the patient's history by the alert examiner even though it may not be the presenting complaint. The early signs of spatial disorder may include a history of losing one's way, 'forgetting' where one has parked one's car or failure to locate common items in a familiar supermarket, difficulty getting arms or legs into the appropriate parts of clothes, misplacing objects so that they fall past the edge of the surface on which they were to be placed, repeatedly bumping the kerb (when driving on the left) or crossing the median when driving, difficulty telling the time on an analogue clock, loss of skill in drawing, and reading difficulty or poor arrangement of lines on the page when writing. By appropriate questions and, if necessary, by formal testing, the informed examiner will generally be able to determine whether these symptoms suggest topographical disorientation, dressing apraxia, optic ataxia, unilateral neglect, impaired perception of line orientation or constructional apraxia and distinguish them from the disorders of memory, praxis and language (or normal human

error) which may cause similar phenomena.

In terms of the actual examination of the patient, most of the spatial disorders described in this chapter are probably less salient than the other manifestations of spatial impairment discussed in chapters on neglect and constructional apraxia, as the latter deficits are amongst the easiest signs of spatial disorders to elicit. However, the symptoms of the Balint-Holmes syndrome stand apart in being quite dramatic, in their full form, and probably sufficiently common in minor forms that at least a screening test for them should be part of a comprehensive examination of the central nervous system. It is also important to appreciate the distinction between disorders of personal and extra-personal orientation and the sheer variety of (frequently) dissociable spatial disorders. It is simply inappropriate to lump them together in an undifferentiated category of 'perceptual disorder' or to assume that the possibility of visuospatial disorder has been excluded when one or two perceptual tests have been performed normally.

From the academic point of view, the neuropsychology of visuospatial disorder is in an unusual, perhaps even unique, position to serve as an interface between neurophysiology and cognitive science. The visuospatial systems have been a rich source of data for neurophysiologists, at least since the pioneering work of Mountcastle and his colleagues (1975) and of Hubel and Wiesel (1977). But now that techniques are available for studying the awake behaving animal and visual processing has been traced from striate and pre-striate cortex well out into the temporal and parietal lobes, brain structure and function can be related to increasingly complex forms of behaviour. If the spatial disorders seen in patients with cerebral lesions are consistent with the known neurophysiology and neuroanatomy (and vice-versa), then the assumption that the infra-human primate data can be applied to man is strongly supported and the data gain in significance. This seems to be the case with the disorders of attention and reaching associated with parietal lobe damage (see Andersen, 1987, for a review). This correspondence not only suggests ways of thinking about the clinical symptoms but also confirms the behavioural significance of the physiological and anatomical findings. This two-way approach to the brain not only provides a pathway to the study of perception via the view from within (Mountcastle, 1975); it is also a route to the study of brain function from the perspective of the behavioural scene outside (Ratcliff, 1987).

The interface with cognitive science is, as yet, less well developed but there have already been several instances in which conceptual frameworks or theories from cognitive psychology (e.g. Marr, 1982) or artificial intelligence have been applied to the analysis of clinical data (Farah, 1984; Ratcliff and Newcombe, 1982) to good effect and some recent models of spatial perception and orientation show considerable promise in this respect (Hinton, 1981; Lieblich and Arbib, 1982; Feldman, 1985). Again, the benefits go in both directions. For example, the clinical and neurophysiological data now strongly suggest a greater separation between form and spatial vision – the 'what' and 'where' systems – than is reflected in some of the above models. This may need to be taken into account in future theories if the goal is to model the particular solutions to the problem of seeing adopted by the human brain rather than achieving the most economical explanation that accounts for some aspects of visual capacity.

It is premature to speculate in detail on what such a model would look like but it seems to us that, in general terms, it is likely to involve a series of representations of space which become increasingly more abstract, relational and remote. The earlier representations probably employ some form of egocentric coding and are applicable primarily to space which is within reach of the hand or eye (or within sight of the organism). Visual sensory data are initially retinotopic but probably need to be transformed into a body-centred framework by taking account of eye position, head position, body orientation and, possibly, the gravitational vertical before they are used to guide behaviour. We presume that this is accomplished by the visuo-motor mechanisms of the parietal and frontal lobes working in concert with subcortical visual centres and liken it to the sensorimotor encoding of Paillard (1987) or the absolute localization of Benton (1969).

It seems to us that the more remote space involved in route-finding and topographical knowledge would be better represented in an allocentric framework and the same is probably true of the more complex spatial relationships obtaining between elements of a visual scene (e.g. the relationship between positions of chess pieces, landmarks on a cartographic map or parts of the Rey figure) when it is their interrelationship rather than individual positions with respect to the observer that is crucial. How many levels of this form of representation are required is uncertain and their neural basis is less clear, but again it certainly involves posterior cerebral cortex and, in man, probably the right parietal lobe (but see Paterson and Zangwill, 1944b, and Newcombe et al., 1987, for some reservations). Conceivably, the neural mechanisms which accomplish sensory-motor encoding could also be applied to allocentric coding, subserving a similar mapping function but operating on different data and in a different reference frame. The fact that patients with severe forms of the Balint-Holmes syndrome are typically disoriented in large-scale space suggests either that the same or neighbouring mechanisms are involved or that earlier sensorimotor encoding is a precursor of later allocentric encoding. The role of the hippocampus, which has been reported to serve as a cognitive map in animals (O'Keefe and Nadel, 1978), is less clear in man but, in our view, it is more likely to be involved in the evocation (see Chapter 16) of spatial information than in decoding or encoding representations of that information.

Acknowledgements

We are very much indebted to our colleagues – Ziyah Mehta and Jacques Paillard – for valuable criticism of the text and to Joan Smith for most skilful secretarial assistance. Part of this work was carried out under Medical Research Council Grant (PG 7301443).

References

Alajouanine T, Lhermitte F: Des anosognosies électives. *Encéphale: 46*, 505 – 519, 1957.

Andersen RA: Inferior parietal lobe function in spatial perception and visuomotor integration. In Mountcastle VB, Plum F, Geiger SR (Editors), *Handbook of Physiology*. Bethesda: American Physiological Soceity, Chap. 12, pp. 483 – 518, 1987.

Archibald YM: Time as a variable in the performance of hemisphere-damaged patients on the Elithorn Perceptual Maze Test. *Cortex: 14*, 22 – 31, 1978.

Baddeley AD, Lieberman K: Spatial working memory. In Nickerson RS (Editor), *Attention and Performance VIII*. Hillsdale, NJ: Erlbaum, Ch. 26, pp. 521 – 539, 1980.

Balint R: Seelenlähmung des 'Schauens', optische Ataxie, raümliche Störung der Aufmerksamkeit. *Monatsschr. Psychiatr. Neurol.: 25*, 51 – 81, 1909.

Beech JR: The effects of visual and spatial interference on spatial working memory. *J. Gen. Psychol.: 110*, 141 – 149, 1984.

Bender N, Jung R: Abweichungen der subjectiven optischen Verticalen und Horizontalen bei Gesunden und Hirnverletzen. *Arch. Psychiatry: 181*, 193 – 212, 1948.

Benson AJ, Gedye JL: Logical processes in the resolution of orientation conflict. *R.A.F. Institute of Aviation Med. Rep. 259*. Ministry of Defence (Air) London, 1963.

Benton AL: *Right-Left Discrimination and Finger Localization: Development and Pathology*. New York: Hoeber-Harper, 1959.

Benton AL: The fiction of the 'Gerstmann syndrome'. *J. Neurol. Neurosurg. Psychiatry: 24*, 176 – 181, 1961.

Benton AL: Disorders of spatial orientation in man. In Vinken PJ, Bruyn GW (Editors), *Handbook of Clinical Neurology*. Amsterdam: Elsevier, Vol. 3, pp. 212 – 228, 1969.

Benton AL: Visuoperceptive, visuospatial, and visuoconstructive disorders. In Heilman KM, Valenstein E (Editors), *Clinical Neuropsychology*. New York: Oxford University Press, Ch. 8, pp. 151 – 185, 1985a.

Benton AL: Body schema disturbances: finger agnosia and right-left disorientation. In Heilman KM, Valenstein E (Editors), *Clinical Neuropsychology*. New York: Oxford University Press, Ch. 6, pp. 115 – 129, 1985b.

Benton AL, Hécaen H: Stereoscopic vision in patients with unilateral brain disease. *Neurology: 20*, 1084 – 1088, 1970.

Benton AL, Elithorn A, Fogel ML, Kerr M: A perceptual maze test sensitive to brain damage. *J. Neurol. Neurosurg. Psychiatry: 26*, 540 – 544, 1963.

Benton AL, Hannay J, Varney NR: Visual perception of line direction in patients with unilateral brain disease. *Neurology: 25*, 907 – 910, 1975.

Benton AL, Varney NR, Hamsher K deS: Visuospatial judgment: a clinical test. *Arch. Neurol. (Chicago): 35*, 364 – 367, 1978.

Birch HG, Belmont I, Reilly T, Belmont L: Visual verticality in hemiplegia. *Arch. Neurol. (Chicago): 5*, 444 – 453, 1961.

Bisiach E, Luzzatti C: Unilateral neglect of representational space. *Cortex: 14*, 129 – 133, 1978.

Bisiach E, Nichelli P, Spinnler H: Hemispheric functional asymmetry in visual discrimination between univariate stimuli: an analysis of sensitivity and response criterion. *Neuropsychologia: 14*, 335 – 342, 1976.

Boller F, Cole M, Kim Y, Mack JL, Patawaran C: Optic ataxia: clinical-radiological correlations with the EMI scan. *J. Neurol. Neurosurg. Psychiatry: 38*, 954 – 958, 1975.

Brain WR: Visual disorientation with special reference to lesions of the right cerebral hemisphere. *Brain: 64*, 244 – 272, 1941.

Brooks LR: An extension of the conflict between visualization and reading. *Q. J. Exp. Psychol.: 22*, 91 – 96, 1970.

Brouwers P, Cox C, Martin A, Chase T, Fedio P: Differential perceptual spatial impairment in Huntington's and Alzheimer's dementias. *Arch. Neurol. (Chicago): 41*, 1073 – 1076, 1984.

Butters N, Barton M, Brody BA: Role of the right parietal lobe in the mediation of cross-modal associations and reversible operations in space. *Cortex: 6*, 174 – 190, 1970.

Butters N, Soeldner C, Fedio P: Comparison of parietal and frontal lobe spatial deficits in man: extrapersonal vs personal (egocentric) space. *Percept. Motor Skills: 34*, 27 – 34, 1972.

Byrne RW: Geographical knowledge and orientation. In Ellis AW (Editor) *Normality and Pathology in Cognitive Functions*. London: Academic Press, Ch. 8, pp. 239 – 264, 1982.

Carmon A, Bechtoldt HP: Dominance of the right cerebral hemisphere for stereopsis. *Neuropsychologia: 7*, 29 – 39, 1969.

Cogan DG: Ophthalmic manifestations of bilateral non-occipital cerebral lesions. *Br. J. Ophthalmol.: 49*, 281 – 297, 1965.

Cole M, Perez-Cruet J: Prosopagnosia. *Neuropsychologia: 2*, 237 – 246, 1964.

Cole M, Schutta HS, Warrington EK: Visual disorientation in homonymous half-fields. *Neurology: 12*, 257 – 263, 1962.

Colonna A, Faglioni P: The performance of hemisphere-damaged patients on spatial intelligence tests. *Cortex: 2*, 293 – 307, 1966.

Corballis MC: Mental rotation: anatomy of a paradigm. In Potegal M (Editor) *Spatial Abilities: Development and Physiological Foundations*. New York: Academic Press, Ch. 8, pp. 173 – 198, 1982.

Corkin S: Tactually-guided maze learning in man: effects of unilateral cortical excisions and bilateral hippocampal lesions. *Neuropsychologia: 3*, 339 – 351, 1965.

Cowey A, Porter J: Brain damage and global stereopsis. *Proc. R. Soc. Lond. B: 204*, 339 – 407, 1979.

Critchley M: The parietal lobes. New York: Hafner, 1969.

Crown S: Psychological changes following prefrontal leucotomy. A review. *J. Mental Sci.:* Jan. 1951.

Damasio A: Disorders of complex visual processing: agnosias, achromatopsia, Balint's syndrome, and related difficulties of orientation and construction. In Mesulam MM (Editor), *Principles of Behavioral Neurology. Contemporary Neurology Series*. Philadelphia: F.A. Davis, Ch. 7, pp. 259 – 288, 1985.

Damasio AR, Benton AL: Impairment of hand movements

under visual guidance. *Neurology: 29,* 170 – 174, 1979.

Damasio AR, Damasio V, Van Hoesen GW: Prosopagnosia: anatomical basis and behavioral mechanisms. *Neurology: 32,* 331 – 341, 1982.

Danta G, Hilton RC, O'Boyle DJ: Hemisphere function and binocular depth perception. *Brain: 101,* 569 – 589, 1978.

Dee HL: Visuoconstructive and visuoperceptive deficit in patients with unilateral cerebral lesions. *Neuropsychologia: 8,* 305 – 314, 1970.

De Renzi E: *Disorders of Space Exploration and Cognition.* Chichester: John Wiley, 1982.

De Renzi E: Disorders of spatial orientation. In Vinken PJ, Bruyn GW, Klawans HL (Editors), *Handbook of Clinical Neurology.* Amsterdam: Elsevier, Ch. 27, pp. 405 – 422, 1985.

De Renzi E, Faglioni P: Il Disorientamento spaziale da lesione cerebrale. *Sist. Nerv.: 14,* 409 – 436, 1962.

De Renzi E, Faglioni P: The relationship between visuo-spatial impairment and constructional apraxia. *Cortex: 3,* 327 – 342, 1967.

De Renzi E, Faglioni P, Previdi P: Spatial memory and hemispheric locus of lesion. *Cortex: 13,* 424 – 433, 1977.

De Renzi E, Faglioni P, Scotti G: Judgement of spatial orientation in patients with focal brain damage. *J. Neurol. Neurosurg. Psychiatry: 34,* 489 – 495, 1971.

De Renzi E, Faglioni P, Villa P: Topographical amnesia. *J. Neurol. Neurosurg. Psychiatry: 40,* 498 – 505, 1977.

De Renzi E, Nichelli P: Verbal and non-verbal short-term memory impairment following hemispheric damage. *Cortex: 11,* 341 – 354, 1975.

De Renzi E, Scotti G: Autotopagnosia: fiction or reality? Report of a case. *Arch. Neurol. (Chicago): 23,* 221 – 227, 1970.

Denny-Brown D: In Mountcastle VB (Editor), *Interhemispheric Relations and Cerebral Dominance* (Discussion). Baltimore: Johns Hopkins Press, 244 – 252, 1962.

Denny-Brown D, Banker BQ: Amorphosynthesis from left parietal lesions. *Arch. Neurol. Psychiatry: 71,* 302 – 313, 1954.

Desimone R, Albright TD, Gross CG, Bruce C: Stimulus-selective properties of inferior temporal neurons in the macaque. *J. Neurosci.: 4,* 2051 – 2062, 1984.

Desimone R, Schein SJ, Moran J, Ungerleider LG: Contour, color and shape analysis beyond the striate cortex. *Vision Res.: 25,* 441 – 452, 1985.

Elithorn A: A preliminary report on a perceptual maze test sensitive to brain damage. *J. Neurol. Neurosurg. Psychiatry: 18,* 287 – 292, 1955.

Eslinger PJ, Benton AL: Visuoperceptual performances in aging and dementia: clinical and theoretical implications. *J. Clin. Neuropsychol.: 5,* 213 – 220, 1983.

Ettlinger G: Sensory deficits in visual agnosia. *J. Neurol. Neurosurg. Psychiatry: 19,* 297 – 307, 1956.

Farah MJ: The neurological basis of mental imagery: a componential analysis. *Cognition: 18,* 245 – 272, 1984.

Feldman JA: Four frames suffice: a provisional model of vision and space. *Behav. Brain Sci.: 8,* 265 – 289, 1985.

Fine EJ, Mellstrom M, Mani SS, Timmins J: Spatial disorientation and the Dyke-Davidoff-Masson syndrome. *Cortex: 16,* 493 – 499, 1980.

Frederiks JAM (Editor): Disorders of the body schema. In *Handbook of Clinical Neurology, Vol. 1 (45): Clinical Neuropsychology.* Amsterdam: Elsevier, Ch. 25, pp. 373 – 393, 1985.

Gainotti G, Cianchetti C, Tiacci C: The influence of the hemispheric side of lesion on non-verbal tasks of finger localization. *Cortex: 8,* 364 – 381, 1972.

Garein R, Rondot P, de Recondo J: Ataxie optique localisée aux deux hémichamps homonymus gauches. *Rev. Neurol.: 116,* 707 – 714, 1967.

Gerstmann J: Fingeragnosie: Eine umschriebene Störung der Orientierung am eigenen Körper. *Wien. Klin. Wochenschr.: 37,* 1010 – 1012, 1924.

Gerstmann J: Syndrome of finger agnosia; disorientation for right and left, agraphia and acalculia. *Arch. Neurol. Psychiatry: 44,* 398 – 408, 1940.

Girotti F, Milanese C, Casazza M, Allegranza A, Corridori F, Avanzini G: Oculomotor disturbances in Balint's syndrome: anatomoclinical findings and electrooculographic analysis in a case. *Cortex: 8,* 603 – 614, 1982.

Godwin-Austen RB: A case of visual disorientation. *J. Neurol. Neurosurg. Psychiatry: 28,* 453 – 458, 1965.

Goldstein K: *Human Nature in the Light of Psychopathology.* Cambridge, Mass: Harvard University Press, 1940.

Goodglass H, Klein B, Carey P, Jones K: Specific semantic word categories in aphasia. *Cortex: 2,* 74 – 89, 1976.

Guildford JP, Zimmerman WS: The Guildford-Zimmerman Aptitude. *J. Appl. Psychol.: 32,* 24 – 34, 1948.

Habib M, Sirigu A: Pure topographical disorientation: a definition and anatomical basis. *Cortex: 23,* 73 – 85, 1987.

Hamsher K DeS: Stereopsis and unilateral brain disease. *Invest. Ophthalmol.: 17,* 336 – 343, 1978.

Hannay HJ, Varney NR, Benton AL: Visual localization in patients with unilateral brain disease. *J. Neurol. Neurosurg. Psychiatry: 39,* 307 – 313, 1976.

Harris LJ, Gitterman SR: University professors' self-descriptions of left-right confusability: sex and handedness differences. *Percept. Motor Skills: 47,* 819 – 823, 1978.

Head H, Holmes G: Sensory disturbances from cerebral lesions. *Brain: 34,* 102 – 254, 1911 – 1912.

Hécaen H: Clinical symptomatology in right and left hemispheric lesions. In Mountcastle VB (Editor), *Interhemispheric Relations and Cerebral Dominance.* Baltimore: The Johns Hopkins Press, Ch. 10, pp. 215 – 243, 1962.

Hécaen H, Ajuriaguerra J: Balint syndrome (psychic paralysis of visual fixation) and its minor forms. *Brain: 77,* 373 – 400, 1954.

Hein A, Jeannerod M (Editors): *Spatially Oriented Behavior.* New York: Springer, 1983.

Hermelin B, O'Connor N: Spatial modality coding in children with and without impairments. In Potegal M (Editor), *Spatial Abilities: Development and Physiological Foundations.* New York: Academic Press, Ch. 2, pp. 35 – 54, 1982.

Herrmann G, Pötzl O: *Ueber die Agraphie und ihre lokaldiagnostischen Beziehungen.* Berlin: Karger, 1926.

Hinton GE: A parallel computation that assigns canonical object-based frames of references. In *Proceedings of the Seventh International Joint Conference on Artificial Intelligence, Vol. 2.* University of British Columbia, Vancouver, pp. 683–685, 1981.

Holmes G: Disturbances of visual orientation. *Br. J. Ophthalmol.: 2,* 449–468, 506–516, 1918.

Holmes G: Spasm of fixation. *Trans. Ophthalmol. Soc.: 50,* 253–262, 1930.

Holmes G, Horrax G: Disturbances of spatial orientation and visual attention with loss of stereoscopic vision. *Arch. Neurol. Psychiatry: 1,* 385–407, 1919.

Hubel DH, Wiesel TN: Functional architecture of macaque monkey visual cortex. *Proc. R. Soc. Lond. B: 198,* 1–59, 1977.

Joynt RJ, Honch GW, Rubin AJ, Trudell RG: Occipital lobe syndromes. In Frederiks JAM (Editor), *Handbook of Clinical Neurology, Vol. 1 (45) Clinical Neuropsychology.* Amsterdam: Elsevier, Ch. 5, pp. 49–62, 1985.

Julesz B: *Foundations of Cyclopean Perception.* Chicago: Chicago University Press, 1971.

Käse CS, Troncoso JF, Court JE, Tapia JF, Mohr JP: Global spatial disorientation. *J. Neurol. Sci.: 34,* 267–278, 1977.

Kim Y, Morrow L, Passafiume D, Boller F: Visuoperceptual and visuomotor abilities and locus of lesion. *Neuropsychologia: 22,* 177–185, 1984.

Kinsbourne M, Warrington EK: The localizing significance of limited simultaneous form perception. *Brain: 86,* 697–702, 1963.

Kohn B, Dennis M: Selective impairments of visuo-spatial abilities in infantile hemiplegics after right cerebral hemidecortication. *Neuropsychologia: 12,* 505–512, 1974.

Kosslyn SM, Pomerantz JR: Imagery, propositions, and the form of internal representations. *Cognitive Psychol.: 9,* 52–76, 1977.

Kosslyn SM, Shwartz SP: A data-driven simulation of mental imagery. *Cognitive Sci.: 1,* 265–296, 1977.

Landis T, Cummings JL, Benson DF, Palmer EP: Loss of topographic familiarity: an enviromental agnosia. *Arch. Neurol. (Chicago): 43,* 132–136, 1986.

Lange J: Agnosien und Apraxien. In Bumke O, Foerster O (Editors), *Handbuch der Neurologie, Vol. VI.* Berlin: Springer, pp. 807–960, 1936.

Lawler KA: Aspects of spatial vision following brain damage. Unpublished D. Phil. thesis: Oxford University, 1981.

Lehmann D, Wälchli P: Depth perception and location of brain lesions. *J. Neurol.: 209,* 157–164, 1975.

Leinonen L, Hyvarinen J, Nyman G, Linnanonski J: Functional properties of neurons in lateral part of associative area 7 in awake monkeys. *Exp. Brain Res.: 34,* 299–320, 1979.

Lenz H: Raumsinnstörungen bei Hirnverletzungen. *Dtsch. Z. Nervenheilk.: 157,* 22–64, 1944.

Levine DN, Calvanio R: A study of the visual defect in verbal alexia-simultanagnosia. *Brain: 101,* 65–81, 1978.

Levine DN, Calvanio R, Wolf E: Disorders of visual behavior following bilateral posterior cerebral lesions. *Psychol. Res.: 41,* 217–234, 1980.

Lieblich I, Arbib MA: Multiple representations of space underlying behavior. *Behav. Brain Sci.: 5,* 627–659, 1982.

Linde C, Labov W: Spatial networks as a site for the study of language and thought. *Language: 51,* 924–939, 1975.

Luria AR, Pravdina-Vinarskaya EN, Yarbuss AL: Disorders of ocular movement in a case of simultanagnosia. *Brain: 86,* 219–228, 1963.

Marr D: *Vision: A Computational Investigation into the Human Representation and Processing of Visual Information.* San Francisco, WH Freeman, 1982.

Martin A: Representation of semantic and spatial knowledge in Alzheimer's patients: Implications for models of preserved learning in amnesia. *J. Clin. Exp. Neuropsychol.: 9,* 191–224, 1987.

McFie J, Piercy MF, Zangwill OL: Visual-spatial agnosia associated with lesions of the right cerebral hemisphere. *Brain: 73,* 167–190, 1950.

Mehta Z: Perceptual and spatial disorders: clinical dissociations and theoretical implications. Unpublished D.Phil. thesis: Oxford University, 1988.

Mehta Z, Newcombe F, Damasio H: A left hemisphere contribution to visuospatial processing. *Cortex: 23,* 447–461, 1987.

Mehta Z, Newcombe F, Ratcliff G: Patterns of hemispheric asymmetry set against clinical evidence. In Crawford J, Parker D (Editors), *Developments in Clinical and Experimental Neuropsychology.* New York; Plenum Press (in press), 1988.

Meier MJ: Effects of focal cerebral lesions on contralateral visuomotor adaptation to reversal and inversion of visual feedback. *Neuropsychologia: 8,* 269–279, 1970.

Meier MJ, Story, JL: Selective impairment of Porteus maze test performance after right subthalamotomy. *Neuropsychologia: 5,* 181–189, 1967.

Milner B: Visually-guided maze learning in man: effects of bilateral hippocampal, bilateral frontal, and unilateral cerebral lesions. *Neuropsychologia: 3,* 317–338, 1965.

Milner B: Interhemispheric differences in the localization of psychological processes in man. *Br. Med. Bull.: 27,* 272–277, 1971.

Monaco F, Pirisi A, Secchi GP, Cossu G: Acquired ocular-motor apraxia and right-sided cortical angioma. *Cortex: 16,* 159–167, 1980.

Money J, Alexander D, Walker HT Jr: *A Standardized Road-Map Test of Direction Sense.* Baltimore: The Johns Hopkins Press, 1965.

Morrow L, Ratcliff G: Attentional mechanisms in clinical neglect. *J. Clin. Exp. Neuropsychol.: 9,* 74–75, 1987.

Moscovitch M: Information processing and the cerebral hemispheres. In Gazzaniga MS (Editor), *Handbook of Behavioral Neurobiology, Vol. 2, Neuropsychology.* New York: Plenum, 379–446, 1979.

Mountcastle VB, Lynch JC, Georgopoulos A, Sakata H, Acuna C: Posterior parietal association cortex of the monkey: command functions for operations within extrapersonal space. *J. Neurophysiol.: 38,* 871–908, 1975.

Newcombe F, Russell WR: Dissociated visual perceptual and spatial deficits in focal lesions of the right hemisphere. *J. Neurol. Neurosurg. Psychiatry: 32,* 73–81, 1969.

Newcombe F, Ratcliff G, Damasio H: Dissociable visual and spatial impairments following right posterior cerebral lesions: clinical, neuropsychological and anatomical evidence. *Neuropsychologia: 25,* 149–161, 1987.

Nielsen JM: *Agnosia, Apraxia, Aphasia: Their Value in Cerebral Localization.* New York: Hafner, 1936, reprinted, 1962.

O'Keefe J, Nadel L: *The Hippocampus as a Cognitive Map.*

Oxford: Oxford University Press, 1978.

Orbach J: Disturbances of the maze habit following occipital cortex removals in blind monkeys. *Arch. Neurol. Psychiatry: 81,* 49 – 54, 1959.

Paillard J: Les determinants moteurs de l'organisation de l'espace. *Cah. Psychol.: 14,* 261 – 316, 1971.

Paillard J: The contribution of peripheral and central vision to visually-guided reaching. In Ingle DJ, Mansfield RJW, Goodale MS (Editors), *The Analysis of Visual Behavior.* Cambridge, Mass: MIT Press, 1982a.

Paillard J: Le corps et ses langages d'espace: Nouvelles contributions psychophysiologiques à l'étude du schéma corporel. In Jeddi E (Editor), *Le Corps en Psychiatrie.* Paris: Masson, pp. 53 – 69, 1982b.

Paillard J: Cognitive versus sensorimotor encoding of spatial information. In Ellen P, Thinus-Blanc C (Editors), *Cognitive Processes and Spatial Orientation in Animal and Man.* Dordrecht: Martinus Nijhoff, pp. 43 – 77, 1987.

Paillard J: Basic neurophysiological structures of eye-hand coordination. In Bard C, Fleury M, Hay L (Editors), *Development of Eye-Hand Coordination Across the Life Span.* Columbia: University of South Caroline Press. (in press).

Pallis CA: Impaired identification of faces and places with agnosia for colours: Report of a case due to cerebral embolism. *J. Neurol. Neurosurg. Pyschiatry: 18,* 218 – 224, 1955.

Pandya DN, Yeterian EH: Proposed neural circuitry for spatial memory in the primate brain. *Neuropsychologia: 22,* 109 – 122, 1984.

Paterson A, Zangwill OL: Recovery of spatial orientation in the post-traumatic confusional state. *Brain: 67,* 54 – 68, 1944a.

Paterson A, Zangwill OL: Disorders of visual space perception associated with lesions of the right cerebral hemisphere. *Brain: 67,* 331 – 358, 1944b.

Paterson A, Zangwill OL: A case of topographical disorientation associated with a unilateral cerebral lesion. *Brain: 68,* 188 – 212, 1945.

Pezdek K, Evans GW: Visual and verbal memory for objects and their spatial locations. *J. Exp. Psychol. Hum. Learn. Memory: 5,* 360 – 373, 1979.

Poeck K, Orgass B: An experimental investigation of finger agnosia. *Neurology: 19,* 801 – 807, 1969.

Poeck K, Orgass B: The concept of body schema: a critical review and some experimental results. *Cortex: 7,* 254 – 277, 1971.

Pohl W: Dissociation of spatial discrimination deficits following frontal and parietal lesions in monkeys. *J. Comp. Physiol. Psychol.: 82,* 227 – 239, 1973.

Poncet M, Pelissier JF, Sebahoun M, Nasser CJ: A propos d'un cas d'autotopoagnosie secondaire à un lésion pariéto-occipitale de l'hémisphère majeur. *Encéphale: 60,* 1 – 14, 1971.

Porteus SD, Peters H: Maze test validation and psychosurgery. *Genet. Psychol. Monogr.: 36,* 3 – 86, 1947.

Posner MI, Walker JA, Friedrich FJ, Rafal RD: Effects of parietal injury on covert orienting of attention. *J. Neurosci.: 4,* 1863 – 1874, 1984.

Pylyshyn ZW: The rate of 'mental rotation' of images: A test of a holistic analogue hypothesis. *Memory Cognition: 7,* 19 – 28, 1979a.

Pylyshyn ZW: Validating computational models: A critique of Anderson's indeterminacy of representation claim. *Psychol. Rev.: 86,* 383 – 394, 1979b.

Pylyshyn ZW: The imagery debate: analogue media versus tacit knowledge. *Psychol. Rev.: 88,* 16 – 45, 1981.

Ratcliff G: Spatial thought, mental rotation and the right cerebral hemisphere. *Neuropsychologia: 17,* 49 – 54, 1979.

Ratcliff G: Disturbances of spatial orientation associated with cerebral lesions. In Potegal M, (Editor), *Spatial Abilities: Development and Physiological Foundations.* New York: Academic Press, Ch. 13, pp. 301 – 331, 1982.

Ratcliff G: Spatial cognition in man: the evidence from cerebral lesions. In Ellen P, Tinus-Blanc, C (Editors), *Cognitive Processes and Spatial Orientation in Animal and Man, Vol. 2, Neurophysiology and Developmental Aspects.* NATO ASI Series. Dordrecht; Martinus Nijhoff, pp. 78 – 90, 1987.

Ratcliff G, Cowey A: Disturbances of visual perception following cerebral lesions. In Oborne DJ, Gruneberg MM, Eiser JR (Editors), *Research in Psychology and Medicine, Vol. 1.* London: Academic Press, pp. 307 – 314, 1979.

Ratcliff G, Davies-Jones GAB: Defective visual localization in focal brain wounds. *Brain: 95,* 49 – 60, 1972.

Ratcliff G, Newcombe F: Spatial orientation in man: effects of left, right, and bilateral posterior cerebral lesions. *J. Neurol. Neurosurg. Psychiatry: 36,* 448 – 454, 1973.

Ratcliff G, Newcombe F: Object recognition: some deductions from the clinical evidence. In Ellis AW (Editor), *Normality and Pathology in Cognitive Functions.* London: Academic Press, Ch. 5, pp. 147 – 171, 1982.

Ratcliff G, Ross J: Visual perception and perceptual disorder. *Br. Med. Bull.: 37,* 181 – 186, 1981.

Riddoch G: Visual disorientation in homonymous half-fields. *Brain: 58,* 376 – 382, 1935.

Robinson DL, Goldberg ME, Stanton GB: Parietal association cortex in primates: sensory mechanisms and behavioral modification. *J. Neurophysiol.: 41,* 910 – 932, 1978.

Rondot P, Recondo J de, Ribadeau Dumas JL: Visuomotor ataxia. *Brain: 100,* 355 – 376, 1977.

Ross JE: Disturbance of stereoscopic vision in patients with unilateral stroke. *Behav. Brain Res.: 7,* 99 – 112, 1983.

Rothstein TB, Sacks JG: Defective stereopsis in lesions of the parietal lobe. *Am. J. Ophthalmol.: 73,* 271 – 284, 1972.

Rousseaux M, Delafosse A, Devos P, Quint S, Lesoin F: Syndrome de Balint par infarctus biparietal: analyse neuropsychologique. *Cortex: 22,* 267 – 277, 1986.

Salthouse TA: Using selective attention to investigate spatial memory representations. *Memory Cognition: 2,* 749 – 757, 1974.

Sauguet J, Benton AL, Hécaen H: Disturbances of the body schema in relation to language impairment and hemispheric locus of lesion. *J. Neurol. Neurosurg. Psychiatry: 34,* 496 – 501, 1971.

Semenza C, Goodglass H: Localization of body parts in brain injured subjects. *Neuropsychologia: 23,* 161 – 175, 1985.

Semmes J, Weinstein S, Ghent L and Teuber H-L. Spatial orientation in man after cerebral injury: I. Analyses by locus of lesion. *J. Psychol.: 39,* 227 – 244, 1955.

Semmes J, Weinstein S, Ghent L, Teuber H-L: Correlates of impaired orientation in personal and extrapersonal space.

Brain: 86, 747 – 772, 1963.

Shepard RN, Cooper LA: *Mental Images and their Transformations.* London: MIT Press, 1982.

Shepard RN, Metzler J: Mental rotation of three-dimensional objects. *Science: 171,* 701 – 703, 1971.

Smith ML, Milner B: The role of the right hippocampus in the recall of spatial location. *Neuropsychologia: 19,* 781 – 793, 1981.

Soper HV: Principal sulcus and posterior parieto-occipital cortex lesions in the monkey. *Cortex: 15,* 83 – 96, 1979.

Stengel E, Vienna MD: Loss of spatial orientation, constructional apraxia and Gerstmann's syndrome. *J. Mental Sci.: 90,* 753 – 760, 1944.

Strub R, Geschwind N: Localization in Gerstmann syndrome. In Kertesz A (Editor), *Localization in Neuropsychology.* New York: Academic Press, CH 12, 295 – 321, 1983.

Temple CM: Anomia for animals in a child. Brain: 109, 1225 – 1242, 1986.

Teuber H-L, Mishkin M: Judgment of visual and postural vertical after brain injury. *J. Psychol.: 38,* 161 – 175, 1954.

Thurstone LL, Jeffrey TE: Flags: A test of spatial thinking. In Eliot J, Macfarlane Smith I (Editors), *An International Directory of Spatial Tests.* Windsor, Berks: NFER-Nelson, pp. 197 – 198, 1983.

Ungerleider LG: The corticocortical pathways for object recognition and spatial perception. In Chagas C, Gattass R, Gross G (Editors), *Pattern Recognition Mechanisms.* Pontifical Academy of Sciences, Vatican City, pp. 21 – 33, 1985.

Ungerleider LG, Brody BA: Extrapersonal spatial orientation: the role of posterior parietal, anterior frontal, and inferotemporal cortex. *Exp. Neurol.: 56,* 265 – 280, 1977.

Ungerleider LG, Mishkin M: Two cortical visual systems. In Ingle DJ, Mansfield RJW, Goodale MS (Editors), *The Analysis of Visual Behavior.* Cambridge, Mass: MIT Press, Ch. 18, pp. 549 – 586, 1982.

Vandenberg SG: Vandenberg's test of three-dimensional spatial visualization. In Eliot J, Macfarlane Smith I (Editors), *An International Directory of Spatial Tests.* Windsor, Berks: NFER-Nelson, pp. 322 – 323, 1983.

Ventre J, Flandrin JM, Jeannerod M: In search for the egocentric reference: a neurophysiological hypothesis. *Neuropsychologia: 22,* 797 – 806, 1984.

Vighetto A, Perenin MT: Ataxie optique: analyse des réponses oculaires et manuelles dans une tache de pointage vers une cible visuelle. *Rev. Neurol.: 137,* 357 – 372, 1981.

Waltz AG: Dyspraxias of gaze. *Arch. Neurol. (Chicago): 5,* 638 – 647, 1961.

Warrington EK: Agnosia: the impairment of object recognition. In Frederiks JAM (Editor), *Handbook of Clinical Neurology, Vol. 1 (45), Clinical Neuropsychology.* Amsterdam: Elsevier, Ch. 23, 333 – 349, 1985.

Warrington EK, Rabin P: Perceptual matching in patients with cerebral lesions. *Neuropsychologia: 8,* 475 – 487, 1970.

Warrington EK, Shallice T: Category specific semantic impairments. *Brain: 107,* 829 – 854, 1984.

Warrington EK, Weiskrantz L: An analysis of short-term and long-term memory defects in man. In Deutch JA (Editor), *The Physiological Basis of Memory.* London: Academic Press, pp. 365 – 395, 1973.

Whiteley AM, Warrington EK: Selective impairment of topographical memory: a single case study. *J. Neurol. Neurosurg. Psychiatry: 41,* 575 – 578, 1978.

Whitty CWM, Newcombe F: R.C. Oldfield's study of visual and topographic disturbances in a right occipito-parietal lesion of 30 years duration. *Neuropsychologia: 11,* 471 – 475, 1973.

Wolf SM: Difficulties in right-left discrimination in a normal population. *Arch. Neurol.: 29,* 128 – 129, 1973.

Wolpert I: Die Simultanagnosie-Störung der Gesamtauffassung. *Z. Gesamte Neurol. Psychiatr.: 93,* 397 – 415, 1924.

Yamadori A, Albert ML: Word category aphasia. *Cortex: 9,* 112 – 125, 1973.

© 1989 Elsevier Science Publishers B.V. (Biomedical Division)
Handbook of Neuropsychology, Vol. 2
F. Boller and J. Grafman (Eds)

CHAPTER 18

Neglect: hemispheric specialization, behavioral components and anatomical correlates

Sandra Weintraub and M.-Marsel Mesulam

Department of Neurology, Harvard Medical School, and Division of Neuroscience and Behavioral Neurology, Dana Research Institute, Beth Israel Hospital, Boston, MA, U.S.A.

Introduction

Adaptive behavior depends on the ability to scan the environment so as to detect and focus on events that are biologically relevant. This capacity can be disrupted by cerebral lesions that give rise to a syndrome known as hemispatial neglect. Neglect of the contralateral hemispace is a common outcome of unilateral brain injury. Although multimodal in its expression, neglect is most observable and often most disruptive to the patient's behavior when it occurs in the visual modality. This chapter will be concerned with visual neglect in humans, its cerebral localization, underlying mechanisms and relevance to theories of hemispheric specialization and localization.

Definitions

Hemispatial neglect is associated with several phenomena which have been referred to by such terms as 'inattention', 'hemispatial agnosia', 'hemispatial hypokinesia' and 'extinction'. These terms, however, have also been used as shorthand labels to refer to the various theoretical positions on the mechanisms underlying the neglect syndrome. In this chapter, neglect will be considered as a unitary disorder affecting the distribution of attention throughout the extrapersonal space, so

that the terms 'neglect' and 'spatial inattention' will be used interchangeably.

Clinical features

Hemispatial inattention, or neglect, is manifested in a variety of ways that range from the subtle to the dramatic. Following a unilateral cerebral lesion, some patients may deny ownership of the limbs on the contralateral side. Some patients are unaware of their unilateral sensory and motor deficits or, if aware, may minimize their significance. These puzzling and often bizarre symptoms related to denial of illness (anosognosia) and lack of concern about deficits (anosodiaphoria) have been described elsewhere (Weinstein and Friedland, 1977; Weinstein and Kahn, 1955).

Patients with neglect may tend to dress only one side of the body or groom one side of the face. Failure to eat food placed in the neglected visual field and bumping into walls and furniture in that field are also common. When addressed or approached from the affected sector of space, the patient may not respond at all or may behave as if the stimulus had instead come from the opposite, non-neglected side (allesthesia).

In other patients neglect may be subtle, requiring special clinical techniques in order to be elicited. Testing for extinction with the method of bilateral simultaneous stimulation in the auditory, visual and tactile modalities is one such technique that could reveal evidence of neglect in a patient who on observation appears otherwise unimpaired.

Localization of lesions causing neglect

Right vs. left hemisphere

The frequency of occurrence of neglect and its severity following right or left unilateral cerebral lesions has been a topic of considerable controversy. In 1941, Brain described three cases of left hemispatial inattention in patients with posterior right cerebral lesions. This report was followed by two other detailed accounts of the visuospatial disorders associated with right-sided lesions, which included contralateral hemispatial neglect (McFie et al., 1950; Paterson and Zangwill, 1944). It was subsequently argued, however, that this asymmetry in the pathology of neglect was due to the fact that patients with equally large left cerebral lesions were aphasic and therefore not testable, resulting in a spurious disproportion of patients with right cerebral lesions and neglect (Battersby et al., 1956; Denny-Brown et al., 1952; Zarit and Kahn, 1974).

Despite these objections, however, there has been mounting evidence that hemispatial inattention is, in fact, more frequent and severe following right hemispheric lesions than following left cerebral damage (Albert, 1973; Allen, 1948; Arrigoni and De Renzi, 1964; Chain et al., 1979; Costa et al., 1969; De Renzi et al., 1970; Faglioni et al., 1971; Gainotti, 1968; Gainotti and Tiacci, 1971; Hécaen, 1962; Hécaen et al., 1956; Oxbury et al., 1974; Weintraub and Mesulam, 1987, and in press). Hécaen (1962), reviewing a large series of patients with retrorolandic lesions, reported that of 59 patients with neglect, 51 had right-sided lesions, 4 had left-sided lesions and 4 had bilateral hemispheric damage. Furthermore, reports of persistent right-sided neglect of the body surface from a left unilateral cerebral lesion are rare. In the case

reported by Denny-Brown and Banker (1954) symptoms resolved within a few days.

The frequent association between neglect and right cerebral lesions has led to theories of right hemispheric dominance in the distribution of attention to extrapersonal space (Heilman and Valenstein, 1979; Heilman and Van Den Abell, 1979, 1980; Mesulam, 1981, 1985; Weintraub and Mesulam, 1987). These will be discussed in a later section.

Intrahemispheric localization

All three cases described by Brain (1941) had lesions affecting the parietal lobe or the parieto-temporo-occipital junction on the right. The association between parietal lesions and neglect and the relative rarity of neglect with lesions elsewhere in the brain has been emphasized by others as well (Battersby et al., 1956; Critchley, 1953; Denny-Brown and Banker, 1954; Denny-Brown and Chambers, 1958; De Renzi et al., 1970; Hécaen et al., 1962; McFie et al., 1950; Paterson and Zangwill, 1944).

In subsequent reports, however, neglect has been noted following frontal lesions (Castaigne et al., 1972; Chain et al., 1972; Damasio et al., 1980; Heilman and Valenstein, 1972; Van der Linden et al., 1980), thalamic infarcts (Watson and Heilman, 1979; Watson et al., 1981) and ventrolateral thalamotomy (Vilkki, 1984), caudate and putamenal hemorrhages (Hier et al., 1977) and lesions in other basal ganglia structures and subcortical white matter (Damasio et al., 1980; Ferro and Kertesz, 1984; Healton et al., 1982; Kertesz et al., 1986; Stein and Volpe, 1983). In a study of 110 patients with right cerebral lesions, however, Vallar and Perani (1986) reported that neglect was more common in patients with posterior parietal involvement. In those with subcortical lesions, neglect was more likely to occur if the lesion involved grey matter than if it was only in the white matter. Observing that neglect from frontal lesions tended to be less severe and to resolve more rapidly than that from parietal lesions, Damasio et al. (1980) have suggested that a hierarchy may exist in the anatomical control of spatially directed attention, with the parietal region exerting the dominant influence.

Psychological mechanisms underlying neglect

Several theories have been proposed to account for neglect behavior. Each reflects the influence of one of the many manifestations of this syndrome. The earliest formulation of the mechanism of neglect focused on its sensory manifestations. The observation that under conditions of double simultaneous stimulation there is a tendency to ignore or 'extinguish' the stimulus contralateral to the lesion led to the notion that degradation of sensory input into the damaged hemisphere through a process of stimulus rivalry lay at the root of neglect (Bender and Furlow, 1945). The importance of the parietal lobe for the integration of sensory information and the seemingly strong association between parietal lobe lesions and symptoms of neglect led to the theory that a defect of spatial sensory integration, or 'amorphosynthesis', was responsible for neglect of the contralateral hemispace (Denny-Brown and Banker, 1954; Denny-Brown and Chambers, 1958; Denny-Brown et al., 1952).

The validity of theories based on sensory processing was challenged when it was pointed out that extinction and other manifestations of neglect could be demonstrated in patients with no evidence of primary sensory defect (Critchley, 1949, 1953). Critchley suggested that the phenomenon of extinction represented an impairment not at the level of sensation but rather at the level of attention. During bilateral simultaneous stimulation which produces a state of stimulus rivalry, he argued that one stimulus ultimately distracts attention from the other. Lesions in the parietal lobe could also result in inattention to particular sectors of the body and extrapersonal space by disrupting sensory integration and the storage of a body schema (Critchley, 1949).

The finding that neglect could be demonstrated during the course of blindfolded tactile exploration (Chedru, 1976; De Renzi et al., 1970; Faglioni et

al., 1971) led to the hypothesis that the underlying defect in neglect was not in the perception of space but rather in its internal representation. De Renzi et al. (1970) recorded the amount of time required to find a marble on the right and left sides of a tactile finger maze. Tactile exploration of the maze, it was argued, relied on the construction of an internal representation of the area being explored from successive sensory inputs as the finger traced through the maze. Patients with lesions in either hemisphere took longer to locate the marble when it was placed on the side of the maze contralateral to the lesion. However, complete failure to find the marble in the maximum time allotted for each trial occurred only in patients with right-sided lesions.

In a series of experiments it was demonstrated that neglect could be elicited for the mental representation of scenes and geometric shapes. In two studies (Bisiach and Luzzatti, 1978; Bisiach et al., 1981) patients with right parietal lesions were asked to imagine and describe a well-known city square from one perspective. They recalled more details from the right side of the square than from the left. However, when they were then asked to assume a perspective directly opposite to the one they had just taken, they easily recalled features which were formerly in the left field but now in the right side of the imagined scene. In another study Bisiach et al. (1979) compared patients with left neglect to control subjects on a task in which they were required to detect differences on the right or left side of an irregularly shaped figure. The figure was not exposed in its entirety, however, but was slowly passed under a slit which permitted only part of the figure to be exposed at any one point in time. The patients made more errors than control subjects when the figures differed on the left side but performed as well as controls when the differences were on the right. Since performance required the generation of an internal image of the complete figure, these findings were cited as evidence that a breakdown in the mental representation of the left side of the object caused the neglect.

The findings from these studies have led to the

suggestion that lesions cause neglect by introducing a spatial bias into the internal representation of the extrapersonal space. A recent replication of the Bisiach and Luzzatti (1978) study, however, demonstrated that neglect of imagined space could be altered by changing the position of the patient's head and eyes (Meador et al., 1987). Turning the head to the left improved recall of details in that field. These results were taken to imply that the representation of space itself was intact but underactivated and that moving the head and eyes into the left field increased right hemispheric activation and hence access to the left part of the internal representation. Bisiach et al. (1985) had, in fact, demonstrated earlier that neglect on a tactile maze task could be diminished by changing the position of both the head and the trunk while the eyes were blindfolded. Thus, the internal representation of space would appear to employ a multiple coordinate system anchored alternatively to the head, body and perhaps to the eyes as well.

Yet another group of theories emphasizes the role of arousal in neglect. Kinsbourne (1970a,b) proposed that neglect was the result of an imbalance in the contralateral orienting tendencies of each cerebral hemisphere. According to this model, lateral shifts in attention occur when one hemisphere gains control of the brainstem orienting mechanism. Which hemisphere gains control is determined by stimulus factors and the nature of the task at any point in time, the left reacting more quickly to verbal information and the right to nonverbal, spatial material (Rizzolatti et al., 1971). Thus, verbal material should cause attention to be shifted to the right hemispace and nonverbal stimuli would shift attention to the left. Kinsbourne (1972), in fact, reported that normal right-handed subjects turned their head and eyes to the right while solving verbal problems and to the left while solving numerical and spatial problems. He attributed the apparent preponderance of neglect in patients with right cerebral lesions to an artifact of the clinical setting, where patients are constantly stimulated verbally, leading to excessive left hemispheric activation and, in turn, frequent

rightward orientation (Kinsbourne, 1970a).

According to an alternative and more anatomically based model proposed by Heilman and his colleagues (Heilman and Valenstein, 1979; Heilman and Watson, 1977), neglect is a result of the disruption of a cortico-limbic-reticular loop which mediates the orienting response to extrapersonal space. The resultant hypoarousal of the damaged hemisphere causes diminished intention to act (hypokinesia) in the hemifield contralateral to the lesion (Heilman et al., 1985; Heilman and Valenstein, 1979; Valenstein and Heilman, 1981).

Relationship between neglect and sensory-motor deficits

The frequency of visual field deficits and somatosensory and motor defects has been reported to be higher in patients with neglect than in those who do not neglect the contralateral hemispace (Battersby et al., 1956; Gainotti, 1968; Oxbury et al., 1974; Vallar and Perani, 1986; Zarit and Kahn, 1974). Albert (1973) and Chedru et al. (1973) reported that, in patients with right cerebral lesions, neglect was seen more often in association with visual field defects than with none. However, numerous observations indicate that neglect can occur in the absence of elementary disturbances of sensation or movement, indicating that these disturbances are neither necessary nor sufficient for neglect to occur (Albert, 1973; Allen, 1948; Chain et al., 1979; Leicester et al., 1969; Weintraub and Mesulam, 1987, and in press).

Oculomotor scanning and neglect

Contralateral gaze paresis has been reported to be more frequent, severe and long-lasting in patients with right cerebral damage than in those with left-sided lesions, suggesting that the control of eye movements is asymmetrically organized in the two cerebral hemispheres (De Renzi et al., 1982). This could contribute to the greater frequency of neglect observed following right-sided lesions.

Individual components of saccadic eye

movements (e.g., number, intersaccadic interval) may be disturbed in the neglected field (Girotti et al., 1983). In response to the appearance of targets in the contralateral hemifield, eye movement reaction times were longer in patients with right hemispheric damage than in those with left hemispheric lesions. Occasionally, patients with right-sided lesions failed to show any response to the visual stimulus. The slowing of reaction was felt to reflect decreased arousal, while the altered saccadic movements were seen as evidence of a separate oculomotor component in the observed neglect. Since it is also evident that neglect can occur in patients without oculomotor defects (Gainotti, 1968), it is hard to know whether the oculomotor defect is a cause or a result of the observed neglect.

Studies have shown that when the spatial area to be explored is large, patients with either right or left hemispheric lesions show some contralateral neglect; however, when the task necessitates that attention be focused on small portions of space, i.e., emphasizing foveation and minimizing eye movemevents, then neglect is more obvious in patients with right-sided lesions (Colombo et al., 1971; Gainotti et al., 1986). These findings have led to the suggestion that left hemispatial neglect is a function not so much of defective exploration as of an inability to extract information from the left side of stimuli during eye fixation (Gainotti et al., 1986).

Chedru et al. (1973) calculated the amount of time spent in each hemispace by measuring eye movements of patients with unilateral lesions while they searched a screen of randomly arrayed symbols for a target symbol. Lesions in either hemisphere resulted in longer search times in the contralateral hemispace but this was significantly different from the performance of control subjects only for patients with right cerebral lesions. Not only were saccadic components of movements disrupted but the entire exploratory approach was poorly organized.

Chain et al. (1979) demonstrated that in patients with left cerebral lesions the degree of neglect measured by eye movements varied with the symbolic content of the stimuli presented. As the symbolic content of stimulus pictures increased, the neglect increased in patients with left cerebral lesions. Patients with left-sided lesions also showed neglect when reading written text. In contrast, the severity of neglect in patients with right cerebral lesions was similar regardless of the symbolic content of pictures. However, in these patients, neglect was not observable while scanning printed text. This finding was attributed to the small premium placed on visuospatial processing capacity (and hence right hemispheric engagement) required by the linguistic material, leading to reduced neglect. Patients with left cerebral lesions had a tendency to 'hypercompensate' for visual field defects, forcing the search into the affected field, while patients with right hemispheric lesions did not show this tendency (also see Chedru et al., 1973).

Johnston and Diller (1986) reported a correlation between neglect as measured by standard bedside tasks (cancellation, drawing) and neglect as measured by oculographic recordings of the amount of time spent searching each hemispace while looking at an array of letters. This finding supports the notion that alterations in oculomotor scanning constitute one of the several behavioral manifestations associated with hemispatial inattention.

A recent study of patients' search strategies on visual target cancellation tasks provides further evidence that a disruption of exploratory programs may play a significant role in the unilateral neglect of patients with right-sided lesions (Weintraub and Mesulam, in press). Patients were given target cancellation tasks in which stimuli were arrayed either in rows and columns or were distributed randomly on a page. Control subjects and patients with left-sided lesions typically started the search on the left side of the page and scanned for targets systematically in rows or columns regardless of the stimulus array. In contrast, patients with right-sided lesions spontaneously adopted an unsystematic approach, beginning on the right side of the page and proceeding in a haphazard manner, particularly when the stimulus array was random. We do not yet know whether the tendency of control subjects to start scanning on the left will also hold in illiterate individuals or in those who use languages written from right to left.

Stimulus parameters affecting neglect

The degree of visual neglect manifested by a patient can vary greatly depending on the particular method used to detect it. Neglect that is very apparent in clock drawing may be virtually absent on a cancellation task and vice versa (Figs. 1 and 2). Changing stimulus attributes within the same paradigm can also affect the severity of neglect observed.

Neglect on visual search tasks seems to differ depending on whether the stimuli are verbal or nonverbal, but there is disagreement regarding the direction of this effect. On the one hand, Kinsbourne's (1970a,b, 1972) model would predict that in patients with right cerebral lesions neglect would increase with verbal stimuli and diminish

with nonverbal stimuli. This expectation was confirmed in a study by Heilman and Watson (1978). They gave patients with right cerebral lesions two cancellation tasks: in one, the goal was to detect from among an array of slanted lines those that were tilted at a certain angle; in the second, the patients were asked to find target words from an array of different words. Other studies, however, have not replicated this finding. In two studies, it was found that patients with right cerebral lesions had more hemispatial neglect for nonverbal stimuli, while patients with left-sided damage had more neglect for verbal material (Chain et al., 1979; Leicester et al., 1969). Another investigation found no difference in the severity of neglect observed on verbal and nonverbal cancellation tasks (Caplan, 1985). In our own studies of visual target cancellation (Weintraub and Mesulam, in press), target detection was influenced by a complex interaction between the type of material (letters and shapes) and the manner in which stimuli were positioned on the page (random or structured). In general, patients with right-sided lesions had more difficulty with shapes than with letters. These findings are in agreement with some

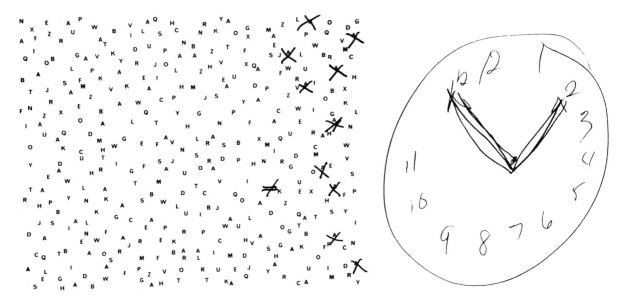

Fig. 1. (left) Sample of letter cancellation task taken from a 56-year-old woman with a right fronto-parieto-temporal lesion. The task was to circle all the 'A's. Neglect of the left side of the page is dramatic. (right) A clock drawn by the same patient. Evidence of neglect is subtle and far less prominent than on the cancellation task.

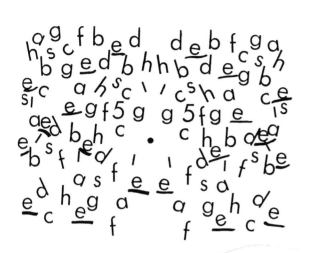

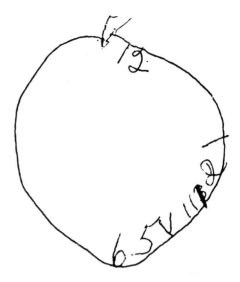

Fig. 2. (left) Sample of an early version of the letter cancellation task taken from a 74-year-old woman with a right parietal lobe lesion. The task was to underline the letter 'e', and none was missed by the patient. (right) Clock drawing by the same patient. Neglect of the left side is dramatic. These samples are in sharp contrast with those of Fig. 1.

previous reports Chain et al., 1979; Leicester et al., 1969) but opposed to others (Heilman and Watson, 1978).

It is difficult to reconcile these contradictory findings from target cancellation studies since the tasks differ from one study to another. However, one factor which could account for the differences and which has not been systematically studied is stimulus complexity. A comparison between performance on the Albert (1973) line-crossing test and our cancellation test revealed that, regardless of lesion site, patients omitted more targets on the cancellation task (Weintraub and Mesulam, 1987) (Fig. 3). This suggested that the lines were easier for patients to detect. It would be interesting to compare performance on a series of cancellation tasks in which stimulus complexity as well as type (verbal vs. nonverbal) was systematically varied. Leicester et al. (1969) found that the level of difficulty in a visual match-to-sample task influenced the severity of neglect manifested. The severity of neglect could be increased by making the discrimination between choices difficult (e.g., presenting for the target 'jkt' choices such as 'tjk', 'kjt', etc.) and diminished by presenting dissimilar

choices for the same target item (e.g., 'mnp', 'ltq').

Another factor which affects neglect is whether the task occurs in peripersonal or more distant extrapersonal space. A recent retrospective study reported that these two forms of neglect could be dissociated from one another (Bisiach et al., 1986). Personal neglect, measured by the ability of patients to touch the left hand with the right, was found only in association with severe motor, somatosensory and visual deficits, while extrapersonal neglect could occur in the absence of these defects. In the monkey, lesions in the postarcuate cortex or in the rostral sector of the inferior parietal lobule cause neglect of events in peripersonal space, while lesions in the frontral eye fields produce neglect of stimuli presented in far space (Rizzolatti et al., 1985). These observations imply that more than one spatial coordinate system may influence attentional behavior.

A cortical network for spatially directed attention and hemispatial neglect

Anatomical and behavioral evidence reviewed in

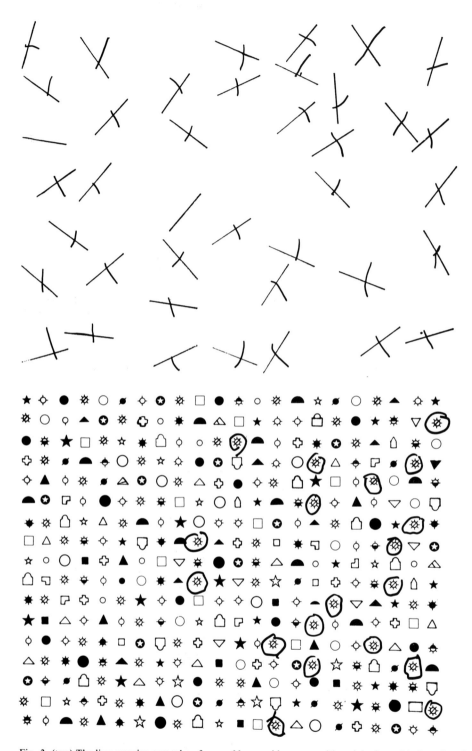

Fig. 3. (top) The line-crossing test taken from a 66-year-old woman with a right frontal lesion. One line on the extreme left and one slightly to the left of center are left uncrossed. (bottom) Sample of the shape cancellation task taken from the same patient shows many target omissions in the left hemispace and some failure to detect targets on the right as well.

detail elsewhere (Mesulam, 1981, 1985), argues for the existence of a widespread cerebral network mediating the distribution of attention throughout extrapersonal space. There are four main components in this network: a sensory-perceptual-representational component in the parietal cortex and pulvinar nucleus of the thalamus, an exploratory-motor component subserved by frontal cortex, superior colliculus and striatum, a limbic component mediated by the cingulate and retrosplenial areas and an arousal component provided by the intralaminar thalamic nuclei and brainstem reticular formation. These components are monosynaptically interconnected. When any of the anatomical regions in this network or their interconnections are damaged, neglect of the contralateral hemispace can occur. There is no one-to-one correspondence between behavioral manifestations and anatomical lesion site.

With respect to behavioral components, deficits in the *sensory component of directed attention* are apparent in such clinical manifestations as extinction and allesthesia. In the case of extinction, the brain appears to receive the sensory stimulus but ignores it (Volpe et al., 1979), while in allesthesia the stimulus is received but mislocated.

Experiments on the covert (without eye movements) orientation of attention have demonstrated that patients with right parietal lesions have difficulty with leftward attentional shifts when the task necessitates disengaging attention from another stimulus (Posner et al., 1984). Thus, impaired disengagement before leftward attentional shifts could provide another sensory component contributing to the diminished reactivity to the contralateral field.

Scanning or searching movements and reaching or ambulating into sectors of extrapersonal space are aspects of the *motor-exploratory component of directed attention*. Target cancellation tasks can reveal the efficiency of scanning strategies for visual exploration. Chedru et al. (1973) demonstrated that normal individuals typically scan a visual array by starting in the upper left quadrant and proceeding systematically in a clockwise circular direction. Patients with unilateral lesions, in contrast, begin the search in the ipsilateral field and searching eye movements are erratic. In that study, subjects were only asked to visually search for the targets. When the subject is permitted to make a motor response to the target with the limb (i.e., circle it with a pencil) then, as previously noted, we have found that patients with left-sided lesions proceed in systematic successive left-to-right horizontal or vertical sweeps of the page, while those with right cerebral lesions initiate the search on the right side of the page and proceed in an erratic fashion (Mesulam, 1985; Weintraub and Mesulam, 1985, and in press).

A recent study of manual spatial exploration without the benefit of visual guidance provides further evidence that the exploratory-motor component of attention is disturbed only in patients with right cerebral lesions (Weintraub and Mesulam, 1987). Blindfolded and asked to search by palpation for a small plastic pin fixed to a cork-covered board, patients with right-sided lesions took longer to locate the target in the contralateral field than in the ipsilateral field (17.85 vs. 5.99 seconds, respectively). Patients with left cerebral lesions, in contrast, performed similarly to control subjects in the ipsilateral and contralateral hemispaces. Alterations of reaction time could not account for this effect. Patients with right-sided lesions manually explored the left side of the board less well whether they were using the left hand (when not hemiparetic) or the right. Thus, the deficit is one of exploring the left hemispace regardless of which side of the body is being used for the task.

The *motivational (limbic) component of directed attention* plays an important role in determining what extrapersonal event will capture the focus of interest. Single cell studies in animals have shown that motivational relevance is a powerful trigger for activating posterior parietal and prefrontal neurons involved in directing spatial attention (Bushnell et al., 1981; Goldberg et al., 1981; Mountcastle et al., 1975; Robinson et al., 1978). Conceivably, contralateral neglect may also arise because sensory events lack behavioral relevance.

Not all behavioral components are equally salient in patients with neglect. In fact, there are reports of dissociation between neglect as tested by extinction and neglect manifested on drawing or cancellation tasks (Ogden, 1985; Vallar and Perani, 1986; Weintraub and Mesulam, 1987; Zarit and Kahn, 1974).

Hemispheric asymmetry in the spatial distribution of attention

From the available evidence it would appear appropriate to conclude that the right cerebral hemisphere in right-handed individuals plays a dominant role in the distribution of attention throughout the extrapersonal space (Heilman and Valenstein, 1979; Heilman and Van Den Abell, 1979, 1980; Mesulam, 1981, 1985; Weintraub and Mesulam, 1987). As already mentioned, studies of patients with unilateral brain damage have generally shown that neglect is more common and severe following right cerebral injury (Albert, 1973; Gainotti, 1968; De Renzi et al., 1970; Chain et al., 1979; Oxbury et al., 1974; Posner et al., 1984; Weintraub and Mesulam, 1987, and in press).

In addition, a number of studies with normal subjects support a dominant role for the right hemisphere in directed attention. In one study, Heilman and Van Den Abell (1980) observed EEG desynchronization (i.e., activation) in the left hemisphere only after stimulation of the contralateral right visual field whereas right hemispheric desynchronization occurred after stimulation of either visual field. In another study, a warning signal delivered to the left visual hemispace significantly reduced reaction times to visual stimuli in both the right and left hands (Heilman and Van Den Abell, 1979). A warning signal in the right hemispace reduced reaction time in the right hand but not to the same degree as it had been altered by stimulation of the left hemispace. With the method of positron emission tomography, it has been demonstrated that regional cerebral glucose metabolism increases significantly in the right inferior parietal lobule during visual and auditory vigilance tasks regardless of the hemispace stimulated (Reivich et al., 1983; Reivich, Alavi and Gur, 1984).

These observations would suggest that the right cerebral hemisphere contains the neural units for modulating attention within both the left and the right sides of space, while the left hemisphere contains units that pertain only to the contralateral right side (Fig. 4). A lesion in the left hemisphere would disrupt attention to the right side but the resultant neglect would be expected to be mild and transient, since the right hemisphere could assume

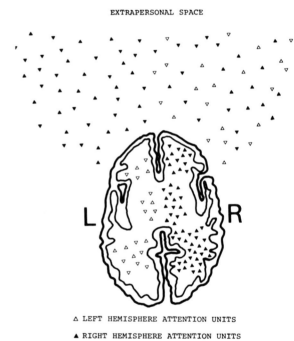

EXTRAPERSONAL SPACE

△ LEFT HEMISPHERE ATTENTION UNITS

▲ RIGHT HEMISPHERE ATTENTION UNITS

Fig. 4. A schematic model for right hemispheric dominance in the distribution of attention within extrapersonal space (from Weintraub and Mesulam, 1987). The left hemisphere contains the neural units for directing attention to the contralateral right hemispace (open triangles). The right hemisphere contains the neural units for directing attention to the contralateral left hemispace (dark triangles) and, to a lesser extent, the ipsilateral right hemispace. This model predicts three outcomes following brain damage: in the case of unilateral right-sided lesions, there would be left hemispatial neglect; with a lesion in the corpus callosum, no neglect would be expected; bilateral lesions would put the right hemispace in double jeopardy, leading to right neglect.

the function of surveying the right visual field. A lesion in the right hemisphere, in contrast, would disrupt attention in both visual fields, with a greater degree of severity in the contralateral field.

The occurrence of ipsilateral neglect is crucial to this theory of hemispheric dominance for the distribution of attention. On a visual target cancellation task, we observed that only patients with right-sided lesions also omitted a significant number of targets in the ipsilateral hemispace. While this finding was highly significant, the presence of ipsilateral neglect in the visual modality was difficult to interpret. The reason for this is that as the eyes move from left to right, more of the right hemispace enters the neglected left visual hemifield. Thus, ipsilateral neglect could simply have been an artifact of the interaction between neglect for retinocentric and somatocentric hemispaces. This argument was countered, however, by our demonstration that blindfolded manual exploration was significantly impaired not only in the contralateral hemispace but also in the ipsilateral hemispace in patients with right-sided lesions (but not in those with left hemisphere lesions). We also demonstrated that these bilateral exploration deficits could not be caused by an overall slowing of motor response speed.

In some individuals, the left hemisphere contribution to directed attention may be exceptionally minor so that unilateral right hemispheric injury could lead to severe attentional disturbances throughout the extrapersonal space. This may explain why some patients with unilateral right cerebral lesions develop what appears to be an acute confusional state rather than hemispatial neglect (Mesulam et al., 1976; Seltzer and Mesulam, 1988).

The anatomical basis for right hemisphere dominance in directed spatial attention is unknown. Conceivably, some components in the cortical network for the distribution of attention could be larger on the right side of the brain or the relevant interconnections could be organized differently. Some parietal regions and their corresponding thalamic nuclei do appear to be larger

in the right side of the brain (Eidelberg and Galaburda, 1984) and this could provide an anatomical substrate for this behavioral specialization.

Neglect of the right hemispace

Rarely, right hemineglect may occur in conjunction with strictly unilateral left-sided lesions. The frequency of this may approximate that of true crossed aphasia. However, in our experience severe right neglect most commonly occurs as a consequence of *bilateral* lesions. We have collected five consecutive cases of severe and persistent right-sided neglect and in each case CT scans have revealed bilateral hemispheric lesions (Fig. 5). A review of some of the cases reported in the early literature would also suggest that right-sided neglect seems to occur in the context of bilateral lesions. The case reported by Bender and Furlow (1945), who developed right visual field extinction following a left parieto-occipital head wound, in fact had sustained a previous injury on the right side. Furthermore, much of the early case material in which neglect was reported was obtained from patients with space-occupying lesions or penetrating missile wounds so that, in fact, the damage may not have been strictly confined to one cerebral hemisphere.

Testing for neglect

Neglect should be investigated in the context of a full neurological examination to document neighborhood signs such as primary sensory and motor deficits. There are a variety of ways to examine for neglect at the bedside. It is important to include tests of all the major components of neglect. Sensory neglect can be assessed by the technique of bilateral simultaneous stimulation. In the visual modality, the examiner can move his own fingers in the right and left visual fields; auditory extinction can be tested by snapping fingers to the right and left sides of the patient's head while standing behind him; light touches to the patient's face and extremities can be used to detect somatosensory extinction. Several trials in each modality with equal numbers of unilateral and bilateral stimulations allow a comparison of the severity of neglect in the three modalities.

Patients with left neglect can detect unilateral left-sided stimulation but may show sensory extinction if another stimulus is simultaneously delivered in the right hemispace. This technique is obviously only useful in patients without visual field, auditory or somatosensory defects. Sometimes, an incomplete or resolving hemianopia may be impossible to distinguish from extinction. Extinction may be so strong in some patients that even the ambient environment will be sufficient

stimulus to provoke it. In that case, it might be beneficial to test extinction in a darkened room using two points of light as stimuli.

The exploratory-motor components of visual neglect can be assessed at bedside with the use of cancellation tests. The line-crossing test (Albert, 1973) is convenient, particularly since it can be quickly improvised at bedside when neglect turns up unexpectedly in a patient. We have designed four cancellation tests which differ with respect to stimulus content (shapes vs. letters) and distribution of stimuli on the page (structured vs. random) (Weintraub and Mesulam, 1985, and in press). In each condition, there are 60 target stimuli surrounded by approximately 300 nontarget stimuli.

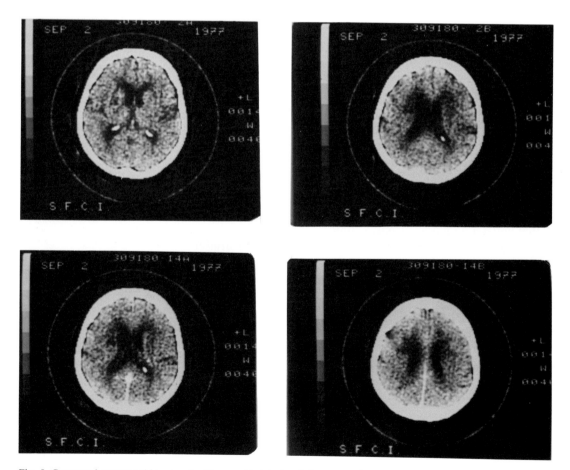

Fig. 5. Computed tomographic scan of a 75-year-old right-handed woman with severe gaze deviation to the left and neglect of the right hemispace. Bilateral lesions of the caudate nucleus are evident.

The targets are symmetrically distributed with respect to the right – left and top – bottom axes of the page. The page is aligned with the patient's body midline and the target is centrally displayed on an index card so as not to influence the patient's spontaneous search strategy. In order to record the search strategy, patients are handed pencils of different colors at regular intervals (based on targets detected or time elapsed) and told to circle all the targets. The examiner can tally the number of target omissions in each hemispace, record the time to complete the task and note the search strategy. Control subjects up to the age of 65 omit no more than 2 targets per hemispace, regardless of stimulus content or array, and can complete each task within 2 minutes. In patients who have clinically recovered from right hemispheric injury, a disorganized search or its initiation on the right side of the page may be the only residual symptom of neglect.

Exploratory neglect can also be tested by blindfolding the patient and asking him to search by palpation for a small object placed on the right or left side of a tray table. The amount of time required to locate the object can be calculated in each hemispace to obtain a quantitative measure

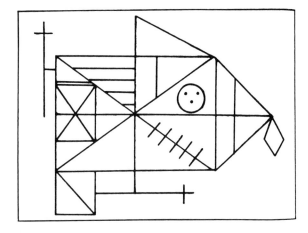

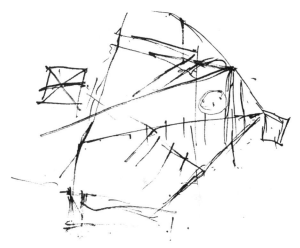

Fig. 7. (top) The Rey-Osterrieth complex figure (Osterrieth, 1944). (bottom) Copy of the Rey-Osterrieth figure done by a 70-year-old right-handed woman with a large right parietal lobe lesion. Neglect of the left side of the figure is dramatic.

Fig. 6. Attempt to copy a clock (on the left) by a 76-year-old woman with a right frontal lobe lesion.

which can then be used to chart the course of recovery. Patients should be tested with the ipsilateral (non-hemiparetic) limb and, when feasible, also with the other limb.

Another standard test of visual neglect is drawing. Asked to draw or even copy familiar objects such as a clock (Fig. 6), cube, flower or house, patients with neglect typically omit details from the side of the drawing contralateral to the lesion. Fig. 7 illustrates severe left hemispatial neglect in the copy of the Rey-Osterrieth complex figure (Osterrieth, 1944) done by a patient whose large right parietal lesion is illustrated in Fig. 8.

Neglect can be quantified on a task that requires the patient to bisect a single horizontal line but care has to be taken to note where the line is with respect to the patient's body orientation since this can affect the extent to which the midpoint of the line is displaced (Bradshaw et. al., 1985; Heilman and Valenstein, 1979; Schenkenberg et al., 1980).

Most of the tests for eliciting neglect are not pure tests of its individual behavioral components. Thus, visual cancellation tasks emphasize the exploratory-motor components of neglect but also rely on the sensory representation of the stimulus array. Drawing tasks require constructional ability

in addition to spatial planning. Right cerebral lesions can impair complex perceptual judgements apart from causing neglect (Benton et al., 1983) and this could confound the interpretation of neglect in tasks that stress this component. Reliable strategies for assessing the motivational aspects of neglect are not yet available.

A number of methodologies have been devised to measure neglect in the laboratory. One method is to measure eye movements while the subject is examining a visual array. The amount of time spent looking at each field can be used as a measure of neglect. Such precise measurements also permit evaluation of the degree of organization of the movements during searching. Motor

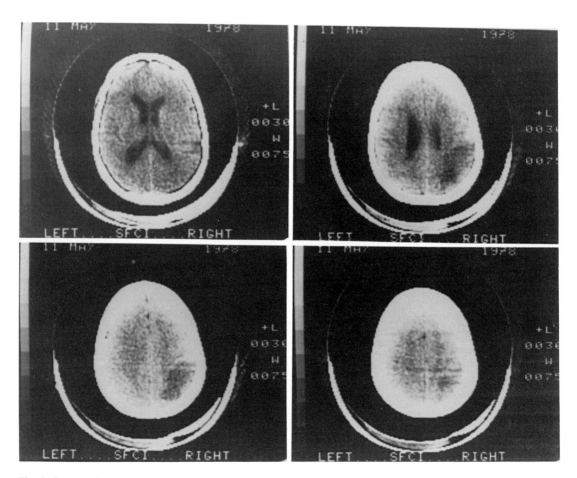

Fig. 8. Computed tomographic scan of the patient whose drawing is illustrated in Fig. 7. The lesion involves both the inferior and the superior parietal lobules.

neglect, or hypokinesia, can be measured with an apparatus that records the time to execute ballistic movements in one or the other hemispace (Heilman et al., 1985).

There has been a tendency to consider the various manifestations of neglect in an additive manner. For example, Ogden (1985), in a study of unselected patients with unilateral lesions, measured neglect with a series of five tasks and obtained a composite score for the severity of neglect. Neglect may be very severe by one measure and virtually undetectable by another, as illustrated in Figs. 1, 2 and 3. The presence of such dissociations suggests that an additive scale may not be legitimate.

Other symptoms commonly associated with neglect

In patients with right cerebral lesions, neglect is often accompanied by a number of other symptoms peculiar to right cerebral damage. These include: denial of illness (Weinstein and Friedland, 1977; Weinstein and Kahn, 1955), diminished concern, jocularity, dressing apraxia, constructional deficits (McFie and Piercy, 1950; Paterson and Zangwill, 1944), motor impersistence (Joynt and Goldstein, 1977) and disturbances of prosody (Ross, 1985).

Recovery of neglect and treatment issues

Prognosis for overall rehabilitation and recovery is adversely affected by the presence of neglect (Denes et al., 1982). Approaches to treating neglect in the rehabilitation setting have focused on enhancing awareness of deficits and improving visual search and scanning strategies (Diller and Weinberg, 1977; Weinberg et al., 1977). The possible use of dopaminergic substances in treating neglect arises from animal studies showing that an interruption of the nigrostriatal pathway leads to contralateral neglect (Feeney and Weir, 1979; Marshall, 1979).

Rubens (1985) reported that visual neglect diminished on several tasks in patients with right cerebral lesions during caloric stimulation. This was particularly apparent in those patients who had a brisk vestibulo-ocular response. It was suggested that caloric stimulation might lead to sustained facilitation of head- and eye-turning toward the neglected left side. While teaching a patient to attend to the left side appears a simple task, practice shows that left-sided neglect is remarkably recalcitrant to behavioral intervention. New and imaginative treatments are very much needed for this group of patients.

Conclusions

This chapter has reviewed a large body of information on the syndrome of hemispatial neglect. Even though there is a fair amount of disagreement regarding the localization and underlying mechanisms of neglect, some general trends emerge. The most convincing conclusions and those that are of greatest importance to behavioral neurology and neuropsychology have to do with right hemispheric dominance for neglect. The most parsimonious explanation is that the right hemisphere modulates the distribution of attention to both extrapersonal hemispaces, whereas the left hemisphere directs attention only to the contralateral right hemispace. Another conclusion concerns the behavioral heterogeneity of neglect behavior. Thus, neglect behavior has exploratory-motor, sensory-representational, motivational and arousal components. This behavioral heterogeneity is associated with a complex cerebral network which provides the anatomical substrate of directed attention. Important directions for future research will undoubtedly focus on the anatomical basis for the hemispheric asymmetry, on the clinical subtypes of neglect syndromes and on strategies for testing and treating neglect.

Acknowledgements

The preparation of this chapter was supported in part by an Alzheimer's Disease Research Center grant 1P50 AG05134 to the Harvard Medical School and a Jacob Javits Neuroscience Investigator Award and NINCDS grants NS 09211 and NS 20285 to Dr. Mesulam.

References

Albert ML: A simple test of visual neglect. *Neurology: 23,* 658 – 664, 1973.

Allen MI: Unilateral visual inattention. *N. Z. Med. J.: 47,* 605 – 617, 1948.

Arrigoni G, De Renzi E: Constructional apraxia and hemispheric locus of lesion. *Cortex: 1,* 170 – 197, 1964.

Battersby WS, Bender MB, Pollack M, Kahn RL: Unilateral 'spatial agnosia' ('inattention') in patients with cerebral lesions. *Brain: 79,* 68 – 93, 1956.

Bender MB, Furlow LT: Phenomenon of visual extinction in homonymous fields and psychologic principles involved. *Arch. Neurol. Psychiatry: 53,* 29 – 33, 1945.

Benton AL, Hamsher K, Varney NR, Spreen O: *Contributions to Neuropsychological Assessment.* New York: Oxford University Press, 1983.

Bisiach E, Luzzatti C: Unilateral neglect of representational space. *Cortex: 14,* 129 – 133, 1978.

Bisiach E, Luzzatti C, Perani D: Unilateral neglect, representational schema and consciousness. *Brain: 102,* 609 – 618, 1979.

Bisiach E, Capitani E, Luzzatti C, Perani D: Brain and conscious representation of outside reality. *Neuropsychologia: 19,* 543 – 551, 1981.

Bisiach E, Capitani E, Porta E: Two basic properties of space representation in the brain: evidence from unilateral neglect. *J. Neurol. Neurosurg. Psychiatry: 48,* 141 – 144, 1985.

Bisiach E, Perani D, Vallar G, Berti A: Unilateral neglect: personal and extrapersonal. *Neuropsychologia: 24,* 759 – 768, 1986.

Bradshaw JL, Nettleton NC, Nathan G, Wilson L: Bisecting rods and lines: effects of horizontal and vertical posture on left-side underestimation by normal subjects. *Neuropsychologia: 23,* 421 – 425, 1985.

Brain WR: Visual disorientation with special reference to lesions of the right cerebral hemisphere. *Brain: 64,* 244 – 272, 1941.

Bushnell MC, Goldberg ME, Robinson DL: Behavioral enhancement of visual responses in monkey cerebral cortex: 1. Modulation in posterior parietal cortex related to selective visual attention. *J. Neurophysiol.: 46,* 755 – 771, 1981.

Caplan B: Stimulus effects in unilateral neglect? *Cortex: 21,* 69 – 80, 1985.

Castaigne P, Laplane D, Degos JD: Trois cas de negligence motrice par lesion frontale pre-rolandique. *Rev. Neurol. (Paris): 126,* 5 – 15, 1972.

Chain F, Chedru F, Leblanc M, Lhermitte F: Renseignements fournis par l'enregistrement du regard dans les pseudo-hemianopsies d'orgine frontale chez l'homme. *Rev. Encephalographie Neurophysiol. Clin.: 2,* 223 – 231, 1972.

Chain F, Leblanc M, Chedru F, Lhermitte F: Negligence

visuelle dans les lesions posterieures de l'hemisphere gauche. *Rev. Neurol. (Paris): 135,* 105 – 126, 1979.

Chedru F: Space representation in unilateral spatial neglect. *J. Neurol. Neurosurg. Psychiatry: 39,* 1057 – 1061, 1976.

Chedru F, Leblanc M, Lhermitte F: Visual searching in normal and brain-damaged subjects. *Cortex: 9,* 94 – 111, 1973.

Colombo A, De Renzi E, Faglioni P: The occurrence of visual neglect in patients with unilateral cerebral disease. *Cortex: 12,* 221 – 231, 1976.

Costa LD, Vaughn HG, Horowitz M, Ritter W: Patterns of behavioral deficit associated with visual spatial neglect. *Cortex: 5,* 242 – 263, 1969.

Critchley M: The phenomenon of tactile inattention with special reference to parietal lesions. *Brain: 72,* 538 – 561, 1949.

Critchley M: *The Parietal Lobes.* London: Edward Arnold, 1953.

Damasio AR, Damasio H, Chang Chui H: Neglect following damage to frontal lobe or basal ganglia. *Neuropsychologia: 18,* 123 – 132, 1980.

Denes G, Semenza C, Stoppa E, Lis A: Unilateral spatial neglect and recovery from hemiplegia. *Brain: 105,* 543 – 552, 1982.

Denny-Brown D, Banker BQ: Amorphosynthesis from left parietal lesion. *Arch. Neurol. Psychiatry: 71,* 302 – 313, 1954.

Denny-Brown D, Chambers RA: The parietal lobe and behavior. *Proceedings of the Association for Research in Nervous and Mental Disease, Vol. 36.* Baltimore: Williams and Wilkins, Ch. 3, pp. 35 – 117, 1958.

Denny-Brown D, Meyer JS, Hornstein S: The significance of perceptual rivalry resulting from parietal lesion. *Brain: 75,* 434 – 471, 1952.

De Renzi E, Faglioni P, Scotti G: Hemispheric contribution to exploration of space through the visual and tactile modality. *Cortex: 6,* 191 – 203, 1970.

De Renzi E, Colombo A, Faglioni P, Gibertoni M: Conjugate gaze paresis in stroke patients with unilateral damage. *Arch. Neurol. (Chicago): 39,* 482 – 486, 1982.

Diller L, Weinberg J: Hemi-inattention in rehabilitation: the evaluation of a rational remediation program. In Weinstein EA, Friedland RP (Editors), *Advances in Neurology, Vol. 18.* New York: Raven Press, pp. 63 – 82, 1977.

Eidelberg D, Galaburda AM: Inferior parietal lobule: divergent architectonic asymmetries in the human brain. *Arch. Neurol. (Chicago): 41,* 843 – 852, 1984.

Faglioni P, Scotti G, Spinnler H: The performance of brain-damaged patients in spatial localization of visual and tactile stimuli. *Brain: 94,* 443 – 454, 1971.

Feeney DM, Weir CS: Sensory neglect after lesions of substantia nigra or lateral hypothalamus: differential severity and recovery of function. *Brain Res.: 178,* 329 – 346, 1979.

Ferro JM, Kertesz A: Posterior internal capsule infarction associated with neglect. *Arch. Neurol. (Chicago): 41,* 422 – 424, 1984.

Gainotti G: Les manifestations de negligence et d'inattention pour l'hemispace. *Cortex: 4,* 64 – 91, 1968.

Gainotti G, Tiacci C: The relationships between disorders of visual perception and unilateral spatial neglect. *Neuropsychologia: 9,* 451 – 458, 1971.

Gainotti G, D'Erme P, Monteleone D, Silveri MS: Mechanisms of unilateral spatial neglect in relation to laterality of cerebral lesions. *Brain: 109,* 599 – 612, 1986.

Girotti F, Casazza M, Musicco M, Avanzini G: Oculo-motor disorders in cortical lesions in man: the role of unilateral neglect. *Neuropsychologia: 21,* 543 – 553, 1983.

Goldberg ME, Bushnell MC: Behavioral enhancement of visual responses in monkey cerebral cortex: II. Modulation in frontal eye fields specifically related to saccades. *J. Neurophysiol.: 46,* 773 – 787, 1981.

Healton EB, Navarro C, Bressman S, Brust JCM: Subcortical neglect. *Neurology: 32,* 776 – 778, 1982.

Hécaen H: Clinical symptomatology in right and left hemispheric lesions. In Mountcastle VB (Editor), *Interhemispheric Relations and Cerebral Dominance.* Baltimore: The Johns Hopkins Press, Ch. X, pp. 215 – 243, 1962.

Hécaen H, Penfield W, Bertrand C, Malmo R: The syndrome of apractagnosia due to lesions of the minor hemisphere. *Arch. Neurol. Psychiatry: 75,* 400 – 434, 1956.

Heilman KM, Valenstein E: Frontal lobe neglect in man. *Neurology: 22,* 660 – 664, 1972.

Heilman KM, Valenstein E: Mechanisms underlying hemispatial neglect. *Ann. Neurol.: 5,* 166 – 170, 1979.

Heilman KM, Van Den Abell T: Right hemispheric dominance for mediating cerebral activation. *Neuropsychologia: 17,* 315 – 321, 1979.

Heilman KM, Van Den Abell T: Right hemispheric dominance for attention: the mechanism underlying hemispheric asymmetries of inattention. *Neurology: 30,* 327 – 330, 1980.

Heilman KM, Watson RT: Mechanisms underlying the unilateral neglect syndrome. In Weinstein EA, Friedland RP (Editors), *Advances in Neurology, Vol. 18.* New York: Raven Press, pp. 93 – 106, 1977.

Heilman KM, Watson RT: Changes in the symptoms of neglect induced by changing task strategy. *Arch. Neurol. (Chicago): 35,* 47 – 49, 1978.

Heilman KM, Bowers D, Coslett HB, Whelan H, Watson RT: Directional hypokinesia: prolonged reaction times for leftward movements in patients with right hemisphere lesions and neglect. *Neurology: 35,* 855 – 859, 1985.

Hier DB, Davis KR, Richardson EP, Mohr JP: Hypertensive putaminal hemorrhage. *Ann. Neurol.: 1,* 152 – 159, 1977.

Johnston CW, Diller L: Exploratory eye movements and visual hemineglect. *J. Clin. Exp. Neuropsychol.: 8,* 93 – 101, 1986.

Joynt RJ, Goldstein MN: Minor cerebral hemisphere. In Friedlander WJ (Editor), *Advances in Neurology, Vol. 7: Current Reviews of Higher Nervous System Dysfunction.* New York: Raven Press, pp. 147 – 183, 1977.

Kertesz A, Ferro JM, Black SE: Subcortical neglect: anatomic, behavioral and recovery aspects. *Neurology: 36* (Suppl.), 132, 1986.

Kinsbourne M: A model for the mechanism of unilateral neglect of space. *Trans. Am. Neurol. Assoc.: 95,* 143 – 146, 1970a.

Kinsbourne M: The cerebral basis of lateral asymmetries in attention. *Acta Psychol.: 33,* 193 – 201, 1970b.

Kinsbourne M: Head and eye turning indicates cerebral lateralization. *Science: 176,* 539 – 541, 1972.

Leicester J, Sidman M, Stoddard LT, Mohr JP: Some determinants of visual neglect. *J. Neurol. Neurosurg. Psychiatry:*

32, 580 – 587, 1969.

Lynch JC: The functional organization of posterior parietal association cortex. *Behav. Brain Sci.: 3,* 485 – 499, 1980.

Marshall JF: Somatosensory inattention after dopamine-depleting intracerebral 6-OHDA injections: spontaneous recovery and pharmacological control. *Brain Res.: 177,* 311 – 324, 1979.

McFie J, Piercy MF, Zangwill OL: Visual spatial agnosia associated with lesions of the right hemisphere. *Brain: 73,* 167 – 190, 1950.

Meador KJ, Loring DW, Bowers D, Heilman KM: Remote memory and neglect syndrome. *Neurology: 37,* 522 – 526, 1987.

Mesulam M-M: A cortical network for directed attention and unilateral neglect. *Ann. Neurol.: 10,* 309 – 325, 1981.

Mesulam M-M: Attention, confusional states and neglect. In Mesulam M-M (Editor), *Principles of Behavioral Neurology.* Philadelphia: FA Davis, Ch. 3, pp. 125 – 168, 1985.

Mesulam M-M, Waxman SG, Geschwind N, Sabin TD: Acute confusional states with right middle cerebral artery infarctions. *J. Neurol. Neurosurg. Psychiatry: 39,* 84 – 89, 1976.

Mountcastle VB, Lynch JC, Georgopoulos A, Sakata H, Acuna A: Posterior parietal association cortex of the monkey: command functions for operations within extrapersonal space. *J. Neurophysiol.: 38,* 871 – 908, 1975.

Ogden JA: Anterior-posterior interhemispheric differences in the loci of lesions producing visual hemineglect. *Brain Cognition: 4,* 59 – 75, 1985.

Osterrieth PA: Le test de copie d'une figure complexe. *Arch. Psychol.: 30,* 206 – 356, 1944.

Oxbury JM, Campbell DC, Oxbury SM: Unilateral spatial neglect and impairments of spatial analysis and visual perception. *Brain: 97,* 551 – 564, 1974.

Paterson A, Zangwill OL: Disorders of visual space perception associated with lesions of the right cerebral hemisphere. *Brain: 67,* 331 – 358, 1944.

Posner MI, Walker JA, Friedrich FJ, Rafal RD: Effects of parietal injury on covert orienting of attention. *J. Neurosci.: 4,* 1863 – 1874, 1984.

Reivich M, Gur R, Alavi A: Positron emission tomographic studies of sensory stimuli, cognitive processes and anxiety. *Hum. Neurobiol.: 2,* 25 – 33, 1983.

Reivich M, Alavi A, Gur RC: Positron emission tomographic studies of perceptual tasks. *Ann. Neurol.: 15* (Suppl.), S61 – S65, 1984.

Rizzolatti G, Umilta C, Berlucchi G: Opposite superiorities of the right and left cerebral hemispheres in discriminative reaction time to physiognomical and alphabetical material. *Brain: 94,* 431 – 442, 1971.

Rizzolatti G, Gentilucci M, Matelli M: Selective spatial attention: one center, one circuit or many circuits? In Posner MI, Marin OSM (Editors), *Attention and Performance XI.* Hillsdale, NJ: Lawrence Erlbaum, Ch. 13, pp. 251 – 265, 1985.

Robinson DL, Goldberg ME, Stanton GB: Parietal association cortex in the primate: Sensory mechanisms and behavioral modulations. *J. Neurophysiol.: 41,* 910 – 932, 1978.

Ross ED: Modulation of affect and nonverbal communication by the right hemisphere. In Mesulam M-M (Editor), *Principles of Behavioral Neurology.* Philadelphia: FA Davis, Ch.

6, pp. 239 – 258, 1985.

Rubens AB: Caloric stimulation and unilateral visual neglect. *Neurology: 35,* 1019 – 1024, 1985.

Schenkenberg T, Bradford D, Ajax E: Line bisection and unilateral visual neglect in patients with neurologic impairment. *Neurology: 30,* 509 – 517, 1980.

Seltzer B, Mesulam M-M: Confusional states and delirium as disorders of attention. In Boller F, Grafman J (Editors), *Handbook of Neuropsychology.* Amsterdam: Elsevier, Ch. 9, pp. 165 – 174, 1988.

Stein S, Volpe BT: Classical 'parietal' neglect syndrome after subcortical right frontal lobe infarction. *Neurology: 33,* 797 – 799, 1983.

Valenstein E, Heilman KM: Unilateral hypokinesia and motor extinction. *Neurology: 31,* 445 – 448, 1981.

Vallar G, Perani D: The anatomy of unilateral neglect after right-hemisphere stroke lesions. A clinical/CT-scan correlation study in man. *Neuropsychologia: 24,* 609 – 622, 1986.

Van der Linden M, Seron X, Gillet J, Bredart S: Heminegligence par lesion frontale droite. A propos de trois observations. *Acta Neurol. Belg.: 80,* 298 – 310, 1980.

Vilkki J: Hemi-inattention after ventrolateral thalamotomy. *Neuropsychologia: 22,* 399 – 408, 1984.

Volpe BT, Ledoux JE, Gazzaniga MS: Information processing of visual stimuli in an 'extinguished' field. *Nature: 282,* 722 – 724, 1979.

Watson RT, Heilman KM: Thalamic neglect. *Neurology: 29,* 690 – 694, 1979.

Watson RT, Valenstein E, Heilman KM: Thalamic neglect: possible role of the medial thalamus and nucleus reticularis in behavior. *Arch. Neurol. (Chicago): 38,* 501 – 506, 1981.

Weinberg J, Diller L, Gordon WA, Gerstman LJ, Lieberman A, Lakin P, Hodges G, Ezrachi O: Visual scanning training effect on reading-related task in acquired right brain damage. *Arch. Phys. Med. Rehabil.: 58,* 479 – 486, 1977.

Weinstein EA, Friedland RP (Editors); Behavioral disorders associated with hemi-inattention. In *Advances in Neurology, Vol. 18: Hemi-inattention and Hemisphere Specialization.* New York: Raven Press, pp. 51 – 62, 1977.

Weinstein EA, Kahn RL: *Denial of Illness.* Springfield, IL: Charles C. Thomas, 1955.

Weintraub S, Mesulam M-M: Mental state assessment of young and elderly adults in behavioral neurology. In Mesulam M-M (Editor), *Principles of Behavioral Neurology.* Philadelphia: FA Davis, Ch. 2, pp. 71 – 123, 1985.

Weintraub S, Mesulam M-M: Right cerebral dominance for directed attention: further evidence based on ipsilateral neglect. *Arch. Neurol. (Chicago): 44,* 421 – 425, 1987.

Weintraub S, Mesulam M-M: Visual hemispatial inattention: stimulus parameters and exploratory strategies. *J. Neurosurg. Neurol. Psychiatry:* in press.

Zarit SH, Kahn RL: Impairment and adaptation in chronic disabilities. Spatial inattention. *J. Nerv. Mental Dis.: 159,* 63 – 72, 1974.

© 1989 Elsevier Science Publishers B.V. (Biomedical Division)
Handbook of Neuropsychology, Vol. 2
F. Boller and J. Grafman (Eds)

CHAPTER 19

Blindsight

L. Weiskrantz

Department of Experimental Psychology, University of Oxford, South Parks Road, Oxford OX1 3UD, England

Introduction

In non-human primates, there are at least six visual pathways originating in the retina in addition to the major route to dorsal lateral geniculate nucleus and thence to striate cortex. These extra-striate pathways allow retinal information to reach the superior colliculus, the pretectal nucleus, the accessory optic tract nucleus, the suprachiasmatic region of the hypothalamus, the pulvinar, the pregeniculate nucleus, and of course their subsequent projections in turn. There is also a pathway from the dorsal lateral geniculate to *pre*striate cortex (although it is not clear whether this receives a direct retinal input). All of these extra-striate pathways remain open when the geniculostriate pathway is blocked or completely damaged (cf. Weiskrantz, 1972).

It is not surprising, therefore, that with complete removal of the striate cortex bilaterally and with consequent degeneration of the dorsal lateral geniculate nuclei, monkeys can still make visual discriminations, albeit not as skillfully as normal animals. They can detect and reach with reasonable accuracy for brief and small targets whose positions are randomly shifted from trial to trial (Weiskrantz et al., 1977), they can discriminate lines differing in orientation in the frontal plane by as little as 8 degrees from each other (Pasik and Pasik, 1980). Their visual acuity is reduced by about 2 octaves (Miller et al., 1980), but the resulting capacity – approximately 11 cycles/degree – is still better than that of the normal

cat. They may be capable of wavelength discriminations, although the evidence is unsettled on this point (cf. Humphrey, 1970; Schilder et al., 1972). With subtotal lesions of striate cortex, subtotal field defects arise with the shape and approximate size to be expected from the cortical projection map of the retina, but these scotomata still allow good detection and localization of stimuli within them. Indeed, with appropriate training, the field defects show some recovery of function and shrinkage (Cowey, 1963; Mohler and Wurtz, 1977; cf. also Cowey and Weiskrantz, 1963; Weiskrantz and Cowey, 1970). On the other hand, animals appear to be agnosic as regards the meaning of the stimuli that they can readily detect (Luciani, 1884; Cowey, 1963; Humphrey, 1974) except in the sense that detection per se can serve as a cue for reward and for trained discriminations.

Given the close similarity in anatomical organization of the human visual system to that of the infra-human primate, parsimoniously it would be expected that a comparable pattern of residual capacities would be found in man after damage to the striate cortex. But the typical clinical outcome of damage to the occipital lobes in man is a densely blind scotoma of a size and shape to be expected from the classical retinocortical maps (Holmes, 1918). And so the question that arises is whether these disparate patterns of results can be reconciled, or are man and monkey qualitatively different despite the similarity of their visual anatomy?

As simple as the question appears, there are some serious difficulties that stand in the way of an answer. The first is geometrical and straight-forward: the striate cortex of man is mainly buried in the medial surface in the calcarine fissure, whereas in the monkey the macular projection is on the lateral surface and readily accessible. It is rare, in man, for any lesion of the striate cortex to occur without damage to overlying tissue, including visual association cortex, whereas it is relatively easy for lesions restricted to striate cortex to be studied in experimental animals. The difference is important for two reasons. First, it has been reported that the effects of enlarging a striate cortex lesion in the monkey so as to include posterior association cortex leads to a significant reduction in residual visual capacity (Pasik and Pasik, 1971). Secondly, it is becoming clear that the outputs from striate cortex to more anterior cortical regions are functionally segregated and that their cortical targets – closely packed within a small distance of each other – therefore have specialized capacities of a modular type, e.g., colour, movement, spatial features, form, etc. (cf. Cowey, 1985). As at least some of these regions are likely to be damaged in man whenever striate cortex is also damaged, the pattern of deficits can differ considerably from patient to patient with relatively slight differences in the disposition of the lesions. Therefore, the comparisons with experimental striate lesions in monkey and clinically occurring lesions in man are not typically comparisons of like with like, and moreover there are inherent, but structurally sound, sources of variance in the clinical material. There is a further difference that often occurs – lesions to striate cortex in man may have a long or irregular history, or may even be present prenatally. The classical animal studies were based largely on mature animals with lesions that had an abrupt onset rather than a developmental history.

A second difficulty in answering the question of human/animal comparability is methodological. Residual vision in the animal is perforce studied behaviorally, typically by making reward contingent upon a particular choice between alternative responses which are arbitrarily linked to one

of two stimuli chosen by the experimenter for comparison. For systematic studies of particular dimensions or discrimination, or even of detection per se, a long history of training and large series of trials are entailed. Human visual assessment is rarely carried out in such a fashion clinically – it would be too tedious and time-consuming. Instead, patients are asked to respond verbally whether they 'see' a presented stimulus, and perhaps to describe it.

But when patients with field defects caused by occipital lesions are studied psychophysically with 'animal' forced-choice methodology, it emerges that visual capacities which are uncovered do not necessarily correlate with their reported experiences, and often are radically and surprisingly different. In some well-studied cases, good capacity can be demonstrated even when the patient acknowledges no visual experience whatever of the stimuli to which he or she responds and discriminates. That extreme situation gave rise to the term 'blindsight' – visual discrimination in the absence of acknowledged awareness (Sanders et al., 1974; Weiskrantz et al., 1974; Weiskrantz, 1986) – but generically it is subsumed under the larger topic of the residual capacity that might be possessed by the extra-striate pathways in man following damage to the striate cortex, when subjects are tested by forced-choice or non-verbal methodology rather than by verbal report or commentary. That is the subject of this review. The subject and the related background issues surrounding it are discussed more fully elsewhere (Weiskrantz, 1972, 1980, 1986).

Residual visual capacities within scotomata

Because of the lengthy testing required, and because selected cases may be especially relevant, much of the literature concerns single case or small group studies. As in other areas of neuropsychology, single cases are especially illuminating when they reveal what dissociations may be *possible*. The case that perhaps has been most extensively studied, D.B., who had what is thought to be a relatively restricted lesion of the right calcarine fissure (resulting from surgical removal of a benign angioma), is the subject of a detailed monograph, which also summarizes other cases in the literature and the implications (Weiskrantz, 1986).

Localizing Several subjects investigated by a large number of investigators have demonstrated a capacity to localize stimuli within their 'blind' fields. Sometimes the response has been a saccade to the supposed locus of the stimulus, typically a briefly flashed spot, after it has been terminated. Indeed, it was this response that first produced evidence for Pöppel et al. (1973) of residual visual function in the field defects, in war veterans with gunshot wounds of the occipital lobes. Sometimes, the response has been of pointing or touching the locus of a target on a perimeter screen. In one study, the subject was trained to give a numerical score on a ruled scale to successfully describe the locus. In all studies the accuracy is typically not as high as in the intact visual field, but nevertheless can be very impressive. Of course, success in this task necessarily entails successful detection of the stimulus per se, but detection has also been studied independently of localizing (Barbur et al., 1980; Stoerig, 1987; Stoerig et al., 1985; Stoerig and Pöppel, 1986; Weiskrantz, 1986).

Acuity Relatively few systematic studies have been carried out, but D.B.'s acuity has been measured both with Moiré fringe interference gratings (approximating to sine-wave gratings) and with photographic sine-wave gratings. Interestingly, his acuity is poorer very close (within $5 - 10$ degrees) to the vertical meridian than a bit more eccentrically, but beyond that point his acuity declines with increasing eccentricity, as expected, and his acuity in the scotoma is always poorer than in a corresponding point of the intact half-field. The reduction in acuity for the region $16 - 20$ degrees eccentric is about 2 octaves as compared to the mirror-symmetric region of the intact field (2.5 cycles/degree compared with 10 cycles/degree).

Orientation D.B. is unusual in repeatedly demonstrating a good discriminative capacity for orientation in the frontal plane. Although impaired relative to his good field, he could nevertheless discriminate a difference in orientation of 10 degrees between two successively presented gratings even at an eccentricity of 45 degrees in the impaired field. Most other subjects who have been tested have shown much less residual capacity for orientation (e.g., Barbur et al., 1980; Perenin, 1978).

Colour Evidence for wavelength discrimination has at best been marginal and slim (as in the destriated monkey). Typically investigators have taken the usual pains to ensure that differences in sensitivity per se could not account for the discrimination, i.e., to determine whether wavelength discrimination is possible even with brightnesses matched or randomly varied so as to be irrelevant. However, a recent study by Stoerig (1987) took a different tack and demonstrated good discrimination of 'colour' in scotomata (the inverted commas are because the subjects actually acknowledged seeing nothing at all, i.e., had blindsight.) Her stimuli were deliberately arranged to combine wavelength and intensity differences, and she reports a significant discriminative capacity in the scotomas of 6 out of 10 subjects. The control condition was one in which only achromatic intensity differences of the same order of magnitude were present between stimuli, and then the subjects' discriminations fell to chance.

Movement and transient stimuli A number of reports have been made of detection of moving stimuli by subjects in their impaired fields (Brindley et al., 1969; Barbur et al., 1980; Bridgeman and Staggs, 1982), and of course classically Riddoch (1917) and Poppelreuter (1917) described gunshot-wound cases who reported seeing moving but not stationary stimuli. But it is to be expected typically that moving stimuli would be more salient than static stimuli for all subjects, normal visual fields or no. And so the question that is central here is whether moving or otherwise transient stimuli (i.e., flickering or with rapid onset or offset) have a special and disproportionately strong value for cases with occipital damage. The evidence suggests that the scotomatous field is not especially or disproportionately tuned to transient stimuli. With D.B., at least, his movement thresholds by forced-choice 'guessing' were approximately normal, and he could detect very well the presence or absence of a stationary stimulus even when its onset gain was very slow (10 s to reach steady state; cf. Weiskrantz, 1986). (Interestingly, the best evidence for movement as a uniquely dissociable capacity comes from a case in which it was selectively *impaired*, without any loss in detection of static stimuli or for any other visual dimension; Zihl et al., 1983.)

'Form'   Most reports of evidence for form discrimination have been negative, or weak. An exception was the evidence, replicated several times, for D.B.'s ability to discriminate X from O (Weiskrantz et al., 1974; Weiskrantz, 1986). Weiskrantz and Warrington re-examined the issue by asking whether the subject's 'form' vision was actually derived from orientation differences between the major components of the discriminative stimuli, given that D.B. has good orientation discrimination. They concluded that this was the case, and that forms which are equated in orientational components are only poorly discriminated by him (cf. Weiskrantz, 1986). Another interesting exceptional report is that of Ptito et al. (1987) of hemispherectomy cases who could make successful 'same-different' discriminations of 3-D forms presented simultaneously to their hemianopic and their contralateral intact visual fields. 2-D versions of the same forms were less successful. Whether orientation turns out to be a relevant aspect of this result remains to be seen. Weiskrantz and Warrington also succeeded in demonstrating 'same-different' matches for simultaneous pairs of 2-D stimulus (X and O) between the impaired and contralateral intact fields of D.B., but interestingly

when the pairs of stimuli were confined to *within* the field defect such matches appeared to be much more difficult (Weiskrantz, 1986).

Issues

Stray light, intraocular diffusion, and other similar possible artifacts   Most investigators have, by now, tested strenuously for such factors, given (or despite) the dismissal of evidence of residual vision on such grounds by Campion et al. (1983). Controls include the use of comparison cases with scotomas caused by retinal pathology (who show no residual capacity), the use of bright masking fields to make the possible diffusion of light into the intact field indiscriminable (which does not abolish the discrimination within the scotoma), and the use of stimuli which would be severely degraded by diffusion, such as high spatial frequency gratings for measuring acuity in the impaired field. Continuous eye movement recordings have ruled out inadvertent fixation shifts, and stimuli too brief to outlast a saccade have often been used. The most stringent control comes from the use of the optic disc within the impaired field as a comparison target. If a light is not detectable on the disc, discriminable diffusion can be concluded to be less than half the diameter of the disc. Weiskrantz and Warrington (cf. Weiskrantz, 1986) and Stoerig et al. (1985; Stoerig, 1987) have used this control effectively. When the target falls on the disc, performance is at chance. When it falls off the disc, detection rises significantly above chance. D.B. did not 'see' any of the stimuli, but he dectected the stimulus when it fell in the neighbourhood of the disc but failed to detect it when it fell on the disc. The whole issue is discussed in more detail in Weiskrantz, 1986.

Is residual capacity just degraded normal capacity?   Those investigators who have specifically addressed this question have concluded, in line with a 'two visual system' hypothesis, that residual vision has particular biases towards detection and localization, with poor capacity for stimulus identification. This position has also been bolstered by the reports of a reasonable correspondence between psychophysical data on visual sensitivity with target velocity in the scotoma and the properties of superior colliculus single neurons, unusually low c.f.f. (Barbur et al., 1980), as well as attentional phenomena and inter-hemifield disinhibitory effects thought reasonably to mirror inter-collicular interactions (Singer et al., 1977). Weiskrantz and Warrington also directly pursued the question by seeking double dissociations between the intact and impaired fields of D.B. The fact that the conditions can be arranged so that the impaired field is poorer than the intact field for form discrimination, but can actually be made superior for a detection task (when retinal location is chosen appropriately for the test), strongly suggests a qualitative dissociation between form and detection between the intact and impaired fields (cf. Weiskrantz, 1986).

The quality, consistency and substance of verbal reports A number of different issues intrude here. First, there are several reports of excellent discriminative capacity even when the subject firmly and consistently denies having any experience – is 'just guessing.' These are not merely restricted to the shadowy boundary seen in normal subjects around threshold. For example, D.B. approached perfect performance in a number of tasks (such as orientation, acuity, movement) without any acknowledged visual experience, and with resolute and consistent unwillingness to admit having any such experience. Secondly, however, as some stimuli become more salient, e.g., with vigorous movement and/or high contrast, subjects *may* report a 'feeling' or even a visual sensation. But even then the visual experience tends to be non-veridical. For example, D.B. reports 'bending waves' in response to vigorous movement. Barbur et al.'s subject 'G' reports a change in 'darkness level' with high-contrast light stimuli on a darker ground. Thirdly, there may well be changes over time, especially as subjects themselves tend to become personally quite interested in the limits and

contents of their impaired fields. Fourthly, there may well be differences not only in subjects' accounts of their own experiences, but also in different experimenters' interest in, or even tolerance for, this aspect of the phenomenon. There is no doubt that subjects and experimenters alike find it easier to restrict the stimulus situations and their response categories to an actual report of 'seeing something' rather than just experience-less 'guessing'. But, finally, visual experience, even when acknowledged, just because it is a comfortable and accustomed mode of reporting for subjects, can actually impede the investigation of unexperienced 'implicit' processing of residual capacities. A number of examples of this were seen in D.B. by Weiskrantz and Warrington and it only gradually became apparent to us that it was actually better to use less salient stimuli to improve performance by switching the subject into an 'implicit' rather than an 'explicit' mode, in which he depended upon his real but non-veridical experiences (cf. Weiskrantz, 1986).

Response criteria There is an understandable but too easily seductive temptation to assume that the assignment of signal detection parameters, because they are quantitative, will somehow resolve the disjunction between a subject's professed lack of visual experience and the demonstrable visual capacity. But neither β nor d', as applied to the forced-choice performance itself, offers an adequate resolution. Thus, Stoerig et al. (1985) deliberately set out to vary the value of the response criterion, β, over a range from strict to lax in the conventional signal/detection manner by adjusting the proportion of stimuli to blanks in a detection task for a blindsight patient. The subject's performance in demonstrating positive discrimination remained impervious to such variations, and 'over and over again he claimed that he had no sensation whatsoever, that he was only guessing, and could hardly believe that his performance was above chance.' Stoerig and Pöppel (1986) and Stoerig (1987) adopted the same strategy in demonstrating the robustness of 'colour' discrimination, again with no acknowledged visual experience by the subjects.

As regards discriminative sensitivity, d', one can adjust D.B.'s suprathreshold performance in his blind field so that it matches (or even exceeds) that in the mirror-symmetric good field, using a forced-choice method with both. He will still insist that there is a simple but crucial difference − one stimulus he can 'see', the other he cannot. His performance in the impaired field can be pushed to a ceiling, and still he professes not to see. It would be impossible to make the stimuli more discriminable, and hence more 'seeable', because he is already at ceiling. Instead of changes in d' or β providing adequate accounts, what remains is the possibility that his sensitivity for 'seeing' per se has been markedly lowered in his blind field independently of any change in his discriminative capacity or response criterion as such. But that simply brings the issue around a full circle. The decreased sensitivity for acknowledged 'seeing', in the face of a demonstrable capacity of discrimination, is precisely what requires explanation. To redescribe the problem in signal detection terminology does not provide the explanation − it merely highlights the problem to be explained.

To the extent that blindsight is related to other modes of 'implicit' processing, as in priming effects in amnesic memory (Warrington and Weiskrantz, 1982) and normal memory (Tulving et al., 1982) or implicit face identification in the absence of explicit recognition in prosopagnosia (Bauer, 1984; Tranel and Damasio, 1985; DeHaan et al., 1987) or in residual capacity in the absence of acknowledged detection in central visual masking (Marcel, 1983a,b) or in any other examples of 'automatic' processing (cf. Schacter et al., 1988), the conceptual issue is a general and widespread one. The dissociation between 'implicit' and 'explicit' is deeper than can be solved by the mere assignment of parameters in signal detection terms.

Critical lesions and pathways   As there have been no post mortem examinations in any of the well-studied cases, one must depend on less secure sources of evidence or on inferential material. But the positive evidence of residual capacity reported for several cases of hemispherectomy (Perenin and Jeannerod, 1978; Perenin, 1978; Ptito et al., 1987) makes it extremely unlikely that there can be a sufficient explanation based on remaining intact striate cortex, as Campion et al. (1983) suggest. Given that residual capacity has been found in the monkey after total bilateral removal of striate cortex, there must be in that case a viable capacity conveyed over extra-striate pathways alone. But, assuming that the same organization exists in man, none of the well-studied cases was of bilateral and total striate cortical lesions. It is possible, therefore, that some aspects of residual capacity in these cases may depend upon information being processed not only within the damaged hemisphere but also, especially with hemispherectomy, reaching and being processed by the intact contralateral hemisphere, as Ptito et al. suggest is the situation with between-field matching of 3-D forms in their hemispherectomy cases. The route in such a case might well be via subcortical commissures, which have also been suggested to account for recent evidence of inter-hemispheric integration in split-brain patients (Sergent, 1987).

It seems likely, however, that no single alternative pathway will provide a complete answer, nor is there any reason why there should be such a dependence. Some aspects of residual capacity (e.g., large summation areas, sensitivity to high velocities of movement) are parsimoniously accounted for in terms of the midbrain projection pathway originating in the retina, with its distinctive class of P-gamma and P-epsilon retinal ganglion cells (Perry and Cowey, 1984). On the other hand, such cells show no differential response to wavelength, and a capacity for colour discrimination might therefore depend on a retinal projection of P-beta type cells to pulvinar or to cortex via the geniculate-prestriate projection, as suggested by Stoerig (1987). Still other aspects, e.g., orientation, may be 'emergent' properties from the selective convergence of connections onto intact specialized association cortex. Thus, even though orientation is not a trigger feature for superior colliculus neurons (just as it is not for lateral geniculate neurons), it may emerge through a convergence at a later stage beyond the colliculus via a posterior thalamic projection (just as it emerges in the projection from the geniculate to the striate cortex).

Another aspect that is orthogonal to the particulars of specific parallel pathways concerns long-term recovery *and* training. In the monkey it is clear that recovery can be made to take place with training, and apparently only with training, even with total unilateral removal of striate cortex (Cowey, 1963; Cowey and Weiskrantz, 1963; Weiskrantz and Cowey, 1970). The midbrain pathway has been definitely implicated in such a recovery (Mohler and Wurtz, 1977) but it seems likely that cortical shifts may also be involved in subtotal striate removals (cf. Weiskrantz, 1972).

Turning to human studies, there is suggestive evidence from cases of residual visual capacity following hemispherectomy that there is greater recovery when the original brain damage occurred earlier in life. Damasio et al. (1975) also report a striking case of a 34-year-old woman who had brain damage at the age of five, and a left hemispherectomy at age 20. Some years later the right eye showed 'almost normal vision. Testing of the fields showed no hemianopia.' Marquis (1935) also discusses a striking case of a boy with a porencephalic cyst (presumably of prenatal origin) in the posterior left hemisphere that was removed surgically at the age of 11. The surgeon, Jelsma, and Marquis himself were 'certain as to the absence of the occipital lobe' following surgery: 'the entire occipital lobe, with the complete calcarine fissure, was lacking.' But there was only slight constriction of the visual field on the right, and there were normal retinal zones of colour sensitivity. The issue of residual visual capacity in children clearly merits detailed and systematic study, although there are serious methodological difficulties to be overcome. Finally, as with the monkey, specific training has been reported to be effective in bringing about recovery of visual capacity in patients with some categories of occipital lesions (Zihl, 1980; Zihl and von Cramon, 1985).

Explicit methodology for implicit visual processes

There is no doubt that a requirement for forced-choice 'guessing' when the patient acknowledges no visual experience whatever, or, at best, reports unusual and non-veridical experience, is an uncomfortable one for many subjects. Indeed, some refuse to test altogether, commenting that they are unwilling to 'lie' or to 'bet' about events they cannot see. No doubt experimenters also vary in their skill or tolerance for putting subjects at their ease and convincing them to respond to visual stimuli without their actually 'seeing'.

As in the field of implicit memory testing and priming, where methods are used to reveal intact retention without direct reference to remembered events (cf. Warrington and Weiskrantz, 1968, 1982), 'blindsight' techniques have evolved which avoid any requirement for a reference to the visual impairment itself. All of the methods involve asking the subject to respond to events in the intact visual field, and evidence for implicit processing is inferred from the interactions of stimuli in the intact field with stimulus presented (typically, simultaneously) in the impaired field.

A good example is the recent study by Marzi et al. (1986), who exploited the fact that simple reaction times are typically quicker to two simultaneous visual stimuli than to one. With some subjects it was found that this was so when one of the two stimuli fell within the field defect. (And when a single stimulus was presented to the field defect itself, there was no response). There is no requirement that the subject attend or 'guess' about unseen events in the blind field. So far this technique has been successful in demonstrating residual vision in only a minority of tested subjects with field defects caused by occipital damage, but only a limited range of relatively small and low-contrast stimuli have been used to date.

Another example of interaction is found in the method used by Pizzamiglio et al. (1984), with a technique described for normal subjects by Dichgans et al. (1972). If a large disc, covered by random dots, is rotated in front of a subject, it produces a sensation of body rotation in the opposite direction (and cyclotorsion of the eyes in the same direction as the rotation). Pizzamiglio et al. (1984) showed that there is a larger effect in normal control subjects with full-field rotation than with half-field rotation. They argued that if the same summated effect applies in patients even when half of the rotation stimulus pattern lies within the field defect, it can be inferred that the 'blind' field is contributing to the perceptual effect. They reported positive effects in all of the seven subjects tested.

'Induced' effects in the good field by stimuli projected to the impaired field can be found in a number of different approaches. Torjussen (1976, 1978) used a type of veridical completion phenomenon. When a full circle was presented as a brief stimulus to hemianopic patients (with fixation in the center of the circle), it was reported that they 'saw' the completed circle. If only a half-circle was presented to the scotoma, nothing was reported. Equally, if a half-circle was presented only to the intact half-field, only a half-circle was reported. Torjussen found that mirror symmetry of the two halves of the stimulus was important. Marcel (personal communication) states that he has confirmed the essential features of Torjussen's findings in two cases. Another related positive confirmation has been reported by Perenin et al. (1986).

Another induced effect has been used by Ruddock et al. (personal communication; cf. Weiskrantz, 1986, for further details), employing 'imaginary' contours produced by Kaniza triangles (Gregory, 1972). If part of the inducing stimulus is placed in the blind field, and the other two corners in the intact field, an induced effect is found. In the critical comparison condition, an inappropriate stimulus is placed in the blind field. It was found that, in the latter case, the strength of

the induced effect was weaker than with the appropriate stimulus in the blind field. I have seen the same phenomenon in one subject, using the same stimulus material (unpublished), and Marcel (personal communication) also reports confirmation in two subjects.

Finally, an interesting adaptation and desensitization attentional phenomenon has been exploited by Singer et al. (1977). With repeated determinations of a detection threshold for peripherally located targets, sensitivity gradually declines. But sensitivity can be 'reset' to its original level if a mirror-symmetric region of the other half-field is adapted in turn. These effects are seen in normal subjects. The interesting finding is that the resetting in the good half-field occurred even when the stimuli were directed to the blind half-field of a hemianopic patient. The authors link their results conceptually to reciprocal electrophysiological interaction between mirror-symmetric regions of the superior colliculus.

While all of these are examples of implicit processes that make their mark upon explicitly acknowledged perception, one should not overlook conventional methods of measuring autonomic effects evoked by 'unseen' stimuli. Thus, Zihl et al. (1980) found that there were a significantly greater number of electrodermal responses to light stimuli in the 'blind' field of hemianopic patients than there were to 'blanks'. The responses to lights were also larger in amplitude. It is of interest that electrodermal responses have been put to effective application at a 'higher' level of visual processing by Tranel and Damasio (1985). They showed that two prosopagnosic patients who, in the usual way with such patients, completely failed to recognize familiar faces explicitly, nevertheless showed a stronger skin conductance response to photographs of familiar faces than they did to control unfamiliar faces.

Concluding comments

Enough evidence has been mustered to support a

conclusion that extra-striate pathways in man are capable of subserving visual function. The argument that there is a functional discontinuity in the visual systems of man relative to other primates, always a difficult argument evolutionarily and logically (cf. Weiskrantz, 1961), can be taken as a position of last resort rather than taken for granted prima facie. Nevertheless, only the early chapters of the story have been written. It is still not clear what the final catalogue will be of types of residual function that are possible following striate cortex blockade, interruption or removal in man. Given that there are a multiplicity of pathways emanating from the retina reaching a variety of extra-striate targets, and given that it would appear that many of the targets are organized as functional modules, a variety of unique dissociations might be expected to emerge (cf. Weiskrantz, 1980). Equally, however, given the arbitrariness of the limits of naturally occurring disease processes and accidents, and given the close packing of the several visual pathways and targets, uniformity in clinical populations is not to be expected. Finer analysis will depend upon animal experiments, but it is gratifying that these have made their contribution to the uncovering of hitherto unsuspected residual capacity in clinical patients.

It is too soon, even, to know how common the instances of residual visual function will turn out to be in clinical populations of patients with occipital damage. The recent advances in developing explicit methodologies to study implicit processes should make it easier to pursue the question. At this stage of the research, a multiplicity of new techniques is to be welcomed rather than deplored. But it is also clear, even with these techniques, as in many other areas of neuropsychology, that there can be a disproportionate gain from the intensive study of a few well-selected cases compared to a superficial study of larger heterogeneous groups.

The most intriguing and surprising aspect of the investigation of residual vision has been finding a disconnection, or at least a mismatch, between the subject's objectively determined capacity and his reported experience as communicated in verbal commentaries, including the complete absence of any such experience in a number of cases. Again, how common this will turn out to be is a question for future research. But by now there should not be any surprise or mystery in the possibility of such a disconnection. It is seen in much contemporary research, e.g., commissurotomies, amnesia, prosopaganosia (cf. Schacter et al., 1988, for a review). Much, perhaps even most, neural processing normally proceeds without any awareness or availability for verbal commentary whatsoever. Indeed, it might be said that awareness is a special privilege and luxury reserved for a very limited class of processes. If research on residual visual capacity helps to define that class more precisely, and to point to the critical neural pathways and systems involved, it will be a welcome major bonus which was not anticipated.

References

Barbur JL, Ruddock KH, Waterfield VA: Human visual responses in the absence of the geniculo-striate projection. *Brain: 102,* 905 – 928, 1980.

Bauer RM: Autonomic recognition of names and faces in prosopagnosia: a neuropsychological application of the guilty knowledge test. *Neuropsychologia: 22,* 457 – 469, 1984.

Bridgeman B, Staggs D: Plasticity in human blindsight. *Vision Res.: 22,* 1199 – 1203, 1982.

Brindley GS, Gautier-Smith PC, Lewin W: Cortical blindness and the functions of the non-geniculate fibres of the optic tracts. *J. Neurol. Neurosurg. Psychiatry: 32,* 259 – 264, 1969.

Campion J, Latto R, Smith YM: Is blindsight an effect of scattered light, spared cortex, and near-threshold vision? *Behav. Brain Sci. 6;* 423 – 448, 1983.

Cowey A: The basis of a method of perimetry with monkeys. *Q. J. Exp. Psychol.: 15,* 81 – 90, 1963.

Cowey A: Aspects of cortical organization related to selective impairments of visual perception. In Posner MI, Marin OSM (Editors), *Attention and Performance, 11.* Hillsdale, NJ: Lawrence Erlbaum, pp. 41 – 62, 1985.

Cowey A, Weiskrantz L: A perimetric study of visual field defects in monkeys. *Q. J. Exp. Psychol.: 15,* 91 – 115, 1963.

Damasio A, Lima A, Damasio H: Nervous function after right hemispherectomy. *Neurology: 25,* 89 – 93, 1975.

DeHaan EHF, Young A, Newcombe F: Face recognition without awareness. *Cognitive Psychol.: 4,* 385 – 415, 1987.

Dichgans J, Held R, Young L: Moving visual scenes influence the apparent direction of gravity. *Science: 178,* 1217 – 1219, 1972.

Gregory RL: Cognitive contours. Nature; 238, 51 – 52, 1972.

Holmes G: Disturbances of vision by cerebral lesions. *Br. J.*

Ophthalmol.: 2, 353 – 384, 1918.

Humphrey NK: What the frog's eye tells the monkey's brain. *Brain Behav. Evol.: 3,* 324 – 337, 1970.

Humphrey NK: Vision in a monkey without striate cortex: a case study. *Perception: 3,* 241 – 255, 1974.

Luciani L: On the sensorial localisations in the cortex cerebri. *Brain: 7,* 145 – 160, 1884.

Marcel AJ: Conscious and unconscious perception; experiments on visual masking and word recognition. *Cognitive Psychol.: 15,* 197 – 237, 1983a.

Marcel AJ: Conscious and unconscious perception: an approach to the relations between phenomenal experience and perceptual processes. *Cognitive Psychol.: 15,* 238 – 300, 1983b.

Marquis DG; Phylogenetic interpretation of the functions of visual cortex. *Arch. Neurol. Psychiatry: 33,* 807 – 815, 1935.

Marzi CA, Tassinari, G, Lutzemberger L, Aglioti A: Spatial summation across the vertical meridian in hemianopics. *Neuropsychologia: 24,* 749 – 758, 1986.

Miller M, Pasik P, Pasik T: Extrageniculate vision in the monkey. VII. Contrast sensitivity functions. *J. Neurophysiol.: 43,* 1510 – 1526, 1980.

Mohler CW, Wurtz RH: Role of striate cortex and superior colliculus in visual guidance of saccadic eye movements in monkeys. *J. Neurophysiol.: 40,* 74 – 94, 1977.

Pasik T, Pasik P: The visual world of monkeys deprived of striate cortex: effective stimulus parameters and the importance of the accessory optic system. In Shipley T, Dowling JE (Editors), *Visual Processes in Vertebrates, Vision Research Supplement No. 3.* Oxford: Pergamon Press, pp. 419 – 435, 1971.

Pasik T, Pasik P: Extrageniculate vision in primates. In Lessell S, van Dalen JTW (Editors), *Neuro-ophthalmology Vol. 1.* Amsterdam: Elsevier, pp. 95 – 119, 1980.

Perenin MT: Visual function within the hemianopic field following early cerebral hemidecortication in man. II. Pattern discrimination. *Neuropsychologia: 16,* 696 – 708, 1978.

Perenin MT, Jeannerod M: Visual function within the hemianopic field following early cerebral hemidecortication in man. I. Spatial localization. *Neuropsychologia: 16,* 1 – 13, 1978.

Perenin MT, Girard-Madoux P, Jeannerod M: From completion to residual vision in hemianopic patients. *Eur. Brain Behav. Soc. Abstr. Behav. Brain Res.: 20,* 130 – 131 (Abstr.), 1986.

Perry VH, Cowey A: Retinal ganglion cells that project to the superior colliculus and pretectum in the macaque monkey. *Neuroscience: 12,* 1125 – 1137, 1984.

Pizzamiglio L, Antonucci G, Francia A: Response of the cortically blind hemifields to a moving visual scene. *Cortex: 20,* 89 – 99, 1984.

Pöppel E, Held R, Frost D: Residual visual function after brain wounds involving the central visual pathways in man. *Nature: 243,* 295 – 296, 1973.

Poppelreuter W: *Die psychischen Schadigungen durch Kopfschuss in Kriege 1914 – 16; die Storungen der niederen und hoheren Sehleistungen durch Verletzungen des Okzipitalhirns, Vol. I.* Leipzig: Voss, 1917.

Ptito A, Lassonde M, Leporé F, Ptito M: Visual discrimination in hemispherectomized patients. *Neuropsychologia: 25,* 869 – 879, 1987.

Riddoch G: Dissociation of visual perceptions due to occipital injuries, with especial reference to appreciation of movement. *Brain; 40,* 15 – 57, 1917.

Sanders MD, Warrington EK, Marshall J, Weiskrantz L: 'Blindsight': vision in a field defect. *Lancet: April 20,* 707 – 708, 1974.

Schacter DL, McAndrews MP, Moscovitch M: Access to consciousness: dissociations between implicit and explicit knowledge in neuropsychological syndromes. In Weiskrantz L (Editor), *Thought Without Language.* Oxford, Oxford Univ. Press, pp. 242 – 278, 1988.

Schilder P, Pasik P, Pasik T: Extrageniculate vision in the monkey. III. Circle vs triangle and 'red vs green' discrimination. *Exp. Brain Res.: 14,* 436 – 448, 1972.

Sergent J: A new look at the human split brain. *Brain: 110,* 1375 – 1392, 1987.

Singer W, Zihl J, Pöppel E: Subcortical control of visual thresholds in humans: evidence for modality specific and retinotopically organized mechanisms of selective attention. *Exp. Brain Res.: 29,* 173 – 190, 1977.

Stoerig P: Chromaticity and achromaticity: evidence of a functional differentiation in visual field defects. *Brain: 110,* 869 – 886, 1987.

Stoerig P, Hübner M, Pöppel E: Signal detection analysis of residual vision in a field defect due to a post-geniculate lesion. *Neuropsychologia: 23,* 589 – 599, 1985.

Stoerig P, Pöppel E: Eccentricity-dependent residual target detection in visual defects. *Exp. Brain Res.: 64,* 469 – 475, 1986.

Torjussen T: Residual function in cortically blind hemifields. *Scand. J. Psychol.: 17,* 320 – 322, 1976.

Torjussen T: Visual processing in cortically blind hemifields. *Neuropsychologia: 16,* 15 – 21, 1978.

Tranel D, Damasio AR: Knowledge without awareness: an autonomic index of facial recognition by prosopagnosics. *Science: 228,* 1453 – 1455, 1985.

Tulving E, Schacter DL, Stark HA: Priming effects in word fragment completion are independent of recognition memory. *J. Exp. Psychol. Learn. Memory Cognition: 8,* 352 – 373, 1982.

Warrington EK, Weiskrantz L: New method of testing long-term retention with special reference to amnesic patients. *Nature: 217,* 972 – 974, 1968.

Warrington EK, Weiskrantz L: Amnesia: a disconnection syndrome? *Neuropsychologia: 20,* 233 – 248, 1982.

Weiskrantz L: Encephalisation and the scotoma. In Thorpe WH, Zangwill OL (Editors), *Current Problems in Animal Behaviour.* Cambridge; Cambridge Univ. Press, pp. 30 – 85, 1961.

Weiskrantz L: Behavioural analysis of the monkey's visual nervous system (Review Lecture). *Proc. R. Soc. B: 182,* 427 – 455, 1972.

Weiskrantz L: Varieties of residual experience. *Q. J. Exp. Psychol.: 32,* 365 – 386, 1980.

Weiskrantz L: *Blindsight. A Case Study and Implications.* Oxford: Oxford Univ. Press, 1986.

Weiskrantz L, Cowey A: Filling in the scotoma: a study of residual vision after striate cortex lesions in monkeys. In Stellar E, Sprague JM (Editors), *Progress in Physiological psychology, Vol. 3.* New York: Academic press, pp. 237 – 260, 1970.

Weiskrantz L, Warrington EK, Sanders MD, Marshall J: Visual capacity in the hemianopic field following a restricted occipital ablation. *Brain: 97,* 709 – 728. 1974.

Weiskrantz L, Cowey A, Passingham C: Spatial responses to brief stimuli by monkeys with striate cortex ablations. *Brain: 100,* 655 – 670, 1977.

Zihl J: 'Blindsight': improvement of visually guided eye movements by systematic practice in patients with cerebral blindness. *Neuropsychologia: 18,* 71 – 77, 1980.

Zihl J, Tretter F, Singer W: Phasic electrodermal responses after visual stimulation in the cortically blind hemifield. *Behav. Brain Res.: 1,* 197 – 203, 1980.

Zihl J, von Cramon D: Visual field recovery from scotoma in patients with postgeniculate damage: a review of 55 cases. *Brain: 106,* 313 – 340, 1983.

CHAPTER 20

Constructional apraxia

Arthur Benton

Department of Neurology, University of Iowa, College of Medicine, Iowa City, IA 52242, U.S.A.

Introduction

Visuoconstructional disabilities, as reflected in failure in drawing or assembling tasks, were of some interest to neurologists and psychologists as early as the 1880s, at which time they were usually interpreted as evidence of either 'loss of the spatial sense' or impairment of the capacity for 'combinatory activity'. When the German neurologist, Karl Kleist (Fig. 1), introduced the term and concept of 'constructional apraxia' in the 1920s to designate a specific defect in spatial-organizational or constructional activity, these disabilities became a topic of major concern in clinical neuropsychology.

Kleist's (1923, 1934) definition of constructional apraxia was fairly precise and restrictive. He conceived of the disorder as being what is now called a disconnection symptom (Geschwind, 1965), in which there is failure to integrate the visual and kinesthetic information required for successful constructional activity. On the one hand, constructional apraxia was to be distinguished from other constructional deficits that were clearly the results of impaired visuoperceptive capacity; on the other hand, although akin to the classical apraxias of Liepmann (1900, 1908), it was sufficiently distinctive to warrant a separate designation. The pure case of constructional apraxia shows adequate visual form perception, preserved capacity to localize objects in visual space and no signs of ideomotor apraxia. Thus the disorder is one of 'execution' or 'praxis' and not merely a behavioral expression of either perceptual impairment or motor disability.

Up to that time constructional apraxis generally had been viewed as a sign of bilateral occipitoparietal disease. In contrast, Kleist maintained that the visuomotor integrative process underly-

Fig. 1. Karl Kleist (1879 – 1960). (Reprinted from *Archiv für Psychiatrie und Nervenkrankheiten, Vol. 202,* 1961, by permission of Springer-Verlag.)

ing constructional performances took place in the left hemisphere and was conducted by way of the corpus callosum to the right hemisphere in order to mediate bilateral constructional activity. Following the reasoning of Liepmann with respect to unilateral ideomotor apraxia, he further maintained that a strategically placed callosal lesion which interrupted the pathways from the dominant to the subordinate hemisphere would produce a unilateral constructional apraxia confined to the left hand.

The disability which Kleist and his student, Hans Strauss (1924), described was readily accepted as a distinctive type of behavioral deficit associated with cerebral disease, and by the late 1920s the term 'constructional apraxia' had become part of the lexicon of clinical neurology. However, Kleist's precise definition of constructional apraxia as an executive type of disorder rather than as the motoric expression of visuoperceptual impairment was largely ignored, the term being applied to visuoconstructional failure whether or not it was associated with visuoperceptual impairment.

Types of defective performance

Kleist defined constructional apraxia as a disturbance 'in formative activities such as assembling, building and drawing, in which the spatial form of the product proves to be unsuccessful, without there being an apraxia of single movements'. This broad definition permitted the employment of diverse tasks to probe for the presence of the disability. The most frequently utilized procedures are listed below.

A. Stick construction. The patient is requested to make a pattern with sticks which is identical with a presented model. Fig. 2 reproduces an early illustration of a patient's performance on this task.

B. Block-arranging in the horizontal plane. An actual model is presented to the patient for reproduction (Fig. 3).

C. Block-building in the vertical plane: for example, building a cross or a pyramid from a presented model (Fig. 4).

D. Block designs. Instead of the actual model, a reduced, two-dimensional schematic representation of a block arrangement is presented for reproduction. This task, which was originally designed as an intelligence test and is a component of several intelligence test batteries, makes demands on the capacity to deliberate, analyse and

Fig. 2. An early illustration of defective stick-arranging. (Rieger, C: Ueber Apparate in den Hirn. *Arb. Psychiatr. Klin. Wuerzb. 5,* 72 – 77, 1909.)

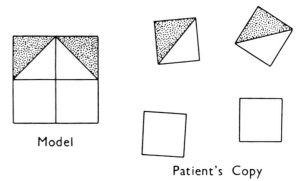

Model   Patient's Copy

Fig. 3. Defective block-arranging; correct blocks are selected but an 'open' square is constructed. (Reprinted from Critchley, M: *The Parietal Lobes.* London, Edward Arnold, 1953: courtesy of Dr. Macdonald Critchley.)

Fig. 4. An early illustration of defective vertical block-building. (Poppelreuter, W: *Die psychischen Schädigungen durch Kopf-schuss im Kriege 1914 – 1916*. Leipzig: Voss, 1917.)

As some of the illustrations indicate, these tasks may elicit striking evidence of lateral visual neglect, particularly in patients with right hemisphere lesions. Moreover, an association between neglect as manifested in drawings and neglect as clinically observed has been noted (Hier et al., 1983a).

Performance levels of brain-diseased patients on the different tasks have been found to be positively intercorrelated but the correlation coefficients (generally ranging from 0.60 to 0.80) are not so high as to warrant the assumption that a single test performance is a fully adequate measure of visuoconstructional capacity. There is suggestive evidence that assembling task performances cor-

plan. Hence it has to be regarded as a less specific measure of elementary visuoconstructional competence.

E. Three-dimensional block construction. Three-dimensional models are presented for reproduction (Fig. 5). Critchley (1953) was perhaps the first to point out that performance on this task may bring to light constructional difficulties which are not disclosed by two-dimensional tasks. A variant of this procedure involves the presentation of photographs of the three-dimensional models (Benton et al., 1983).

F. Drawing from a model. Line drawings (usually of abstract designs) are presented to be copied (Fig. 6). If scoring criteria are sufficiently liberal, with emphasis on essential spatial relationships rather than on graphomotor skill, the task can be given to patients who have to draw with the non-writing hand (Dee and Fontenot, 1969).

G. Drawing on verbal request. The patient is asked to draw a specific object such as a house, bicycle or clock.

Fig. 5. Defective three-dimensional block construction. Top: failure to construct left half of model. Bottom: 'closing-in' performance in which patient included part of model in his own construction. (Department of Neurology, University of Iowa Hospitals and Clinics).

Fig. 6. Defective design copying. Left: neglect of size differences. Right: failure to copy right peripheral figure. (Department of Neurology, University of Iowa Hospitals and Clinics).

relate more closely with each other than they do with drawing tasks (Benton, 1967). However, Hier et al. (1983a) have reported a relatively high correlation ($r = 0.79$) between a block-assembling task and the complex figure of Rey (Osterrieth, 1944; Lezak, 1983).

Lesional localization

Although Kleist specified that constructional apraxia was the product of a left hemisphere lesion resulting in a disconnection between perceptual and motor processes, early observers (e.g., Lange, 1936; Dide, 1938) reported that the defect was more frequently encountered in patients with right hemisphere disease. The finding was confirmed by subsequent studies and in fact was utilized to support the conception that the right hemisphere possessed distinctive functional properties (Paterson and Zangwill, 1944; Hécaen et al., 1951, 1956).

That constructional apraxia is more frequently shown by patients with right hemisphere disease that those with left hemisphere lesions, at least in non-aphasic patients, is now firmly established. The available data suggest a 3 to 1 'right – left ratio' as well as a greater severity of deficit in right-lesioned patients (Critchley, 1953; Benton, 1967, 1973; Mack and Levine, 1981; De Renzi, 1982). Of course, constructional apraxia is also found in patients with bilateral disease and is particularly

severe in those with occipitoparietal involvement (Critchley, 1953; Benton and Fogel, 1962).

However, there is a subgroup of patients with lesions of the left hemisphere, specifically aphasics with impairment in oral language comprehension, who also show an impressively high frequency of constructional disability (Benton, 1973). It is clear from the qualitative features of their performances and from the fact that they may succeed in other tasks requiring even greater verbal understanding that the poor performances of these patients cannot be ascribed to a failure to grasp the meaning of the test instructions. However, the possibility that their defective performances are due to an incapacity to maintain their orientation to the task cannot be excluded. In any case, the failure of many investigators to consider aphasic and non-aphasic patients (and, among aphasic patients, those with and without serious impairment of verbal understanding) separately in tabulating the performances of patients with left hemisphere disease is undoubtedly one reason for the inconsistent determinations of the 'right – left ratio' that are found in the literature.

In accordance with Kleist's original formulation, it has been generally assumed that the crucial lesion for constructional apraxia is to be found in the occipitoparietal territory, even though his specific placement in the left hemisphere has been discarded in favor of a predominant placement in the right hemisphere. However, it is not clear that this posterior lesional localization is fully justified. While many studies (e.g., Black and Strub, 1976; Mack and Levine, 1981; Hier et al., 1983a; Villa et al., 1986) have indeed found that patients with right posterior parietal lesions show particularly frequent and severe disabilities, other studies (e.g., Benson and Barton, 1970; Kertesz and Dobrowolski, 1981) report an essentially equal distribution of defective performances along the anterior – posterior dimension of locus of lesion. It is certainly not rare to encounter 'frontal' constructional apraxia in clinical practice, and at least one study found a relatively high frequency of defective three-dimensional block construction in patients with right frontal lobe lesions (Benton, 1968).

Reasons for these conflicting reports with respect to the question of intra-hemispheric locus of lesion have not been identified. Differences in the characteristics of the samples of subjects studied (e.g., patients seen a few days after stroke or surgery vs. those seen at a later stage of recovery; tumor patients vs. stroke patients; younger vs. older patients) may be one determinant. The type of task utilized to assess constructional praxis may shape the pattern of findings. Relatively complex tasks such as the Wechsler block designs or the complex figure of Rey, which make demands on the capacity for sustained attention and deliberation, may elicit defective performances independently of the locus of brain damage, while simpler tasks may have a sharper focus. Different scoring criteria may be influential. Right – left differences in constructional performance are enhanced when only extremely poor performances are classified as defective (Benton, 1967) and the same effect may apply to the problem of intra-hemispheric lesional localization. Rather unexpectedly, investigators have reported that they do not find a significant relationship between constructional impairment and overall size of lesion, as estimated by CT scan (Kertesz and Dobrowolski, 1981; Hier et al., 1983a). Nor has it been found that size of lesion is related to rate of recovery from constructional disability (Hier et al., 1983b).

Clinical and behavioral correlates

General mental impairment

As is true of practically all specific abilities, constructional performance is related to general intellectual level, and constructional disability is associated with general mental impairment or dementia (Benton et al., 1983; Villa et al., 1986). However, an early study of three-dimensional constructional praxis found that 40% of a sample of patients with general mental impairment (defined as a significant discrepancy between obtained and expected IQs) performed on a normal level, as compared to 75% of patients without evidence of general mental impairment (Benton and Fogel, 1962). A case report by Denes and Semenza (1982) describes strikingly intact constructional performance in a grossly demented patient. Thus it is clear that, within this context of a positive association, visuoconstructional capacity may be impaired in the absence of objective evidence of dementia and, conversely, may remain intact in patients with pervasive cognitive impairment. One implication of these findings is that assessment of constructional ability may play a useful role in the detection and evaluation of dementing illnesses.

Sensorimotor deficits

In patients with right hemisphere lesions the presence of visual field defects is only weakly associated with impaired constructional performances (De Renzi and Faglioni, 1967; Hier et al., 1983a). The association does not hold for left hemisphere lesioned patients. Even in right hemisphere cases there are so many exceptions to the rule (i.e., patients with field defects who perform adequately and those without field defects who are impaired) to make it evident that visual field defect per se is not a significant determinant of performance. Nor are visual field defects a determinant of lateral neglect in drawing performances. Similarly, the relationship between hemiparesis and constructional performance is quite tenuous. On the other hand, the presence of motor impersistence is associated with constructional impairment (Hier et al., 1983a). But general mental impairment and extent of lesion are almost certainly factors mediating this association.

Constructional apraxia and visuoperceptual impairment

This is a central issue, since it bears on the cogency of Kleist's restrictive definition of constructional apraxia. All studies agree in finding a close relationship between visuoconstructional and visuoperceptual performances in patients with right hemisphere disease (Piercy and Smyth, 1962; Dee,

1970; Arena and Gainotti, 1978; Mack and Levine, 1981; De Renzi, 1982; Kim et al., 1984; Griffiths and Cook, 1986). For example, Dee (1970), investigating the visuoperceptual performances of 22 constructional apraxics, identified only one patient who made normal scores on the perceptual tasks, and Mack and Levine (1981) found correlation coefficients of 0.56 and 0.84 between a constructional performance and scores on two visuoperceptual tasks. On the other hand, the findings for this constructional-perceptual relationship in patients with left hemisphere disease is less consistent. Piercy and Smyth (1962) found an equally close association between visuoconstructional and visuoperceptual performance in patients with right and left hemisphere lesions. In Dee's study, three of 22 constructional apraxics performed adequately on visuoperceptual tasks; thus although in general a substantial relationship between the constructional and perceptual performances was still evident, there were at least a few patients who conformed to Kleist's formulation. A more striking between-hemispheres difference was reported by Mack and Levine, who found no significant correlations between constructional and perceptual performances in their patients with left hemisphere disease, in contrast to the close associations observed in patients with right hemisphere disease. Griffiths and Cook (1986) found a closer relationship between copying and perceptual performances in right-lesioned than in left-lesioned patients. Thus there is a suggestion in some studies that the determinants of impaired constructional performance may be different according to side of lesion.

Neurobehavioral mechanisms

The salient finding that, in non-aphasic samples, visuoconstructional defect is more frequent and more severe in patients with right hemisphere disease but nevertheless is shown by a far from negligible proportion of patients with left hemisphere lesions has posed a problem of interpretation. There is obviously no 'dominance' of the right hemisphere for constructional praxis in the sense that the left hemisphere is 'dominant' for language functions in right-handed persons.

One proffered explanation for the moderate hemispheric asymmetry which is repeatedly observed is that failure on visuoconstructional tasks may reflect derangement of any one of a number of underlying neurocognitive mechanisms. It is proposed that, in accordance with Kleist's formulation, there is a perceptuomotor integrative mechanism in the occipitoparietal region of the left hemisphere that mediates the executive aspects of constructional activity. A lesion in this territory may disrupt the motoric-integrative component of performance, even in the absence of visuoperceptual defect. A patient with such a disruptive lesion would be Kleist's 'true' constructional apraxic, performing adequately on visuoperceptual tasks but failing when manipulative activity is required. A second mechanism, associated with right-hemispheric or bilateral occipitoparietal disease, underlies the perception of spatial relationships; its destruction produces visuoperceptual impairment which necessarily entails failure on visuoconstructional tasks.

Although this hypothesis of distinctive hemispherically associated mechanisms, originally proposed by Duensing (1953), has gained wide acceptance, it lacks substantial empirical support. The hypothesis predicts that visuoperceptual and visuoconstructional performances would be closely correlated in patients with right hemisphere lesions and uncorrelated (or at least much less closely correlated) in those with left hemisphere lesions. However, as has been seen, the evidence for such a difference is not strong. Only the study by Mack and Levine (1981) reports an impressive between-hemispheres difference in this respect. Thus it appears that Kleist's 'pure' constructional apraxia must be a fairly uncommon disorder.

Another approach to the problem of a between-hemispheric difference has been to postulate that derangement of distinctive mediating mechanisms will lead to qualitatively distinctive types of failing performance. For example, it has been predicted that right-lesioned patients with perceptual disability will make spatially disorganized, disintegrated reproductions, while the performances of left-lesioned patients with executive handicaps will be characterized by spatially intact but simplified constructions. This is a reasonable hypothesis that deserves continued exploration. However, as De Renzi's (1982) review of the question indicates, the outcome to date has been a mélange of conflicting findings.

The role of aphasic disorder as a correlate of constructional disability in patients with left hemisphere disease has not been fully elucidated. Some studies (e.g., Villa et al., 1986) do not differentiate between aphasic and nonaphasic patients in forming left hemisphere samples of cases. Other studies (e.g., Mack and Levine, 1981) do separate and compare the performances of aphasic and nonaphasic patients but give no information about the status of these patients' specific linguisitic capacities. One study (Benton, 1973) found an impressive frequency of constructional disability in aphasic patients with significant impairment in oral language comprehension (as assessed by the Token Test), while aphasics with only mild (or no) comprehension difficulties performed adequately on the constructional task. This is the only study that has gone beyond the global diagnosis of aphasia to examine a relationship between a specific linguistic disability and constructional performance. If its findings are confirmed, they would suggest another neurocognitive mechanism underlying constructional activity in which verbal mediation plays an essential role as well as another principle of classification, namely, whether or not an observed constructional disability appears to be language-dependent.

Some conclusions

Constructional apraxia (perhaps better designated 'visuoconstructional disability' in order to avoid unintended implications) is a sufficiently specific form of behavioral impairment to warrant special study as well as the inclusion of tests to probe for its presence in clinical evaluation. Performances on the diverse tasks that have been utilized as measures of constructional praxis have been found to be positively interrelated. However, the correlations are not so high as to exclude the possibility that neuropsychologically meaningful types of constructional ability can be identified. This is a question that deserves further examination. At the present time it would seem wise to employ at least two different types of task for the evaluation of 'constructional praxis' in clinical assessment and research studies.

The association between constructional apraxia and disease of the right hemisphere in nonaphasic patients is firmly established. Patients with lesions in the anterior, as well as posterior, areas of the right hemisphere may show impaired performance; hence its characterization as a 'posterior parietal' disability is not accurate. Constructional apraxia is also encountered in patients with disease of the left hemisphere. The role of aphasic disorder as a determinant of constructional performance in patients with left hemisphere disease remains unclear. The question warrants close scrutiny.

The (in part contradictory) findings of the many studies of constructional apraxia with their indications of diverse 'localizations' of the disability, of the importance of general mental impairment as a correlate and of the possible role of linguistic impairment as a determinant of performance level suggest that its neurological basis is not a single lesional locus but rather a number of loci in a widespread neural network.

References

Arena R, Gainotti G: Constructional apraxia and perceptual disabilities in relation to laterality of cerebral lesions. *Cortex: 14*, 463 – 476, 1978.

Benson DF, Barton MI: Disturbances in constructional ability. *Cortex: 6*, 19 – 46, 1970.

Benton AL: Constructional apraxia and the minor hemisphere. *Confin. Neurol.: 29*, 1 – 16, 1967.

Benton AL: Differential behavioral effects in frontal lobe disease. *Neuropsychologia: 6*, 53 – 60, 1968.

Benton AL: Visuoconstructive disability in patients with cerebral disease: its relationship to side of lesion and aphasia. *Doc. Ophthalmol.: 34*, 67 – 76, 1973.

Benton AL, Fogel ML: Three-dimensional constructional praxis: a clinical test. *Arch. Neurol. (Chicago): 7,* 347 – 354, 1962.

Benton AL, Hamsher K, Varney NR, Spreen O: *Contributions to Neuropsychological Assessment: A Clinical Manual.* New York: Oxford University Press, 1983.

Black FW, Strub RL: Constructional apraxia in patients with discrete missile wounds of the brain. *Cortex: 12,* 212 – 220, 1976.

Critchley M: *The Parietal Lobes.* London: Edward Arnold, 1953.

Dee HL: Visuoconstructive and visuoperceptive defects in patients with unilateral cerebral lesions. *Neuropsychologia: 8,* 305 – 314, 1970.

Dee HL, Fontenot DJ: Use of the non-preferred hand in graphomotor performance. *Confin. Neurol.: 31,* 273 – 289, 1969.

Denes, G, Semenza C: Sparing of constructional abilities in severe dementia. *Eur. Neurol.: 21,* 161 – 164, 1982.

De Renzi E: *Disorders of Space Exploration and Cognition.* New York: John Wiley & Sons, 1982.

De Renzi E, Faglioni E: The relationship between visuospatial impairment and constructional apraxia. *Cortex: 3,* 327 – 342, 1967.

Dide M: Les désorientations temporo-spatiales et la prépondérance de l'hémisphère droit dan les agnoso-akinésies proprioceptives. *Encéphale: 33,* 276 – 294, 1938.

Duensing F: Raumagnostische und ideatorisch-apraktische Störung des gestaltenden Handelns. *Dtsch. Z. Nervenheilk.: 170,* 72 – 94, 1953.

Geschwind N: Disconnexion syndromes in animals and man. *Brain: 88,* 237 – 294; 585 – 644, 1965.

Griffiths K, Cook M: Attribute processing in patients with graphical copying disability. *Neuropsychologia: 24,* 371 – 383, 1986.

Hécaen H, Ajuriaguerra J de, Massonet J: Les troubles visuoconstructives par lésion pariéto-occipitale droite. *Encéphale: 40,* 122 – 179, 1951.

Hécaen H, Penfield W, Bertrand C, Malmo R: The syndrome of apractognosia due to lesions of the minor cerebral hemisphere. *Arch. Neurol. Psychiatry: 75,* 400 – 434, 1956.

Hier DB, Mondlock BA, Caplan LR: Behavioral abnormalities after right hemisphere stroke. *Neurology: 33,* 337 – 344, 1983a.

Hier, DB, Mondlock BA, Caplan LR: Recovery of behavioral abnormalities after right hemisphere stroke. *Neurology: 33,* 345 – 350, 1983b.

Kertesz A, Dobrowolski S: Right-hemisphere deficits, lesion size and location. *J. Clin. Neuropsychol.: 3,* 283 – 299, 1981.

Kim Y, Morrow L, Passafiume D, Boller F: Visuoperceptual and visuomotor abilities and locus of lesion. *Neuropsychologia: 22,* 117 – 203, 1984.

Kleist K: Kriegsverletzungen des Gehirns in ihrer Bedeutung fuer die Hirnlokalisation und Hirnpathologie. In Von Schjerning O (Editor), *Handbuch der Aerztlichen Erfahrung im Weltkriege 1914/1918, BD IV, Geistes- und Nervenkrankheiten.* Leipzig: Barth, 1923.

Kleist K: *Gehirnpathologie.* Leipzig: Barth, 1934.

Lange J: Agnosien und Apraxien. In Bumke O. Foerster O (Editors), *Handbuch der Neurologie, Vol. 6.* Berlin: Springer, 1936.

Liepman H: Das Krankheitsbild der Apraxie (motorischen Asymbolie). *Monatschr. Psychiatr. Neurol.: 8,* 15 – 44; 102 – 132; 182 – 197; 1900.

Liepman H: *Drei Aufsätze aus dem Apraxiegebiet.* Berlin: Karger, 1908.

Lezak MD: *Neuropsychological assessment,* 2nd Edition. New York: Oxford University Press, 1983.

Mack JL, Levine RN: The basis of visual constructional disability in patients with unilateral cerebral lesions. *Cortex: 17,* 515 – 532, 1981.

Osterrieth PA: Le test de copie d'une figure complexe. *Arch. Psychol.: 30,* 206 – 356, 1944.

Paterson A, Zangwill OL: Disorders of visual space perception associated with lesions of the right cerebral hemisphere. *Brain: 67,* 331 – 358, 1944.

Piercy M, Smyth VOG: Right hemisphere dominance for certain nonverbal intellectual skills. *Brain: 85,* 775 – 790, 1962.

Poppelreuter W: *Die psychische Schaedigungen durch Kopfschuss im Kriege 1914 – 16: Die Stoerungen der niederen und hoeheren Sehleistungen durch Verletzungen des Okzipitalhirns.* Leipzig: Voss, 1917.

Rieger C: *Ueber Apparate in dem Hirn. Arbeiten aus der Psychiatrischen Klinik zu Wuerzburg, Heft 5.* Jena: Gustav Fischer, 1909.

Straus H: Ueber konstruktive Apraxie. *Monatsschr. Psychiatr. Neurol.: 63,* 739 – 748, 1924.

Villa G, Gainotti G, De Bonis C: Constructive disabilities in focal brain-damaged patients: influence of hemispheric side, locus of lesion and coexistent mental deterioration. *Neuropsychologia: 24,* 497 – 510, 1986.

Handbook of Neuropsychology, Vol. 2
F. Boller and J. Grafman (Eds)

CHAPTER 21

The neuropsychology of mental imagery

Martha J. Farah

Carnegie-Mellon University, Pittsburgh, PA 15213, U.S.A.

Introduction

Of the countless thoughts that pass through our minds each day, many take the form of mental images. Our ability to conjure up images and manipulate them is central to much of our nonverbal thinking and problem-solving. Imagery precedes verbal, analytic thought in the course of cognitive development (Piaget and Inhelder, 1971), and remains essential, even in adulthood, for such activities as mental arithmetic (Hayes, 1973), map reading (Shepard and Hurwitz, 1984) and mechanical reasoning (McKim, 1980). The history of science documents many instances of the crucial role of imagery in scientific creativity (Shepard, 1978).

The aim of this chapter is to outline what is known about the neuropsychology of imagery, within a theoretical framework derived from cognitive psychology. Particular attention will be paid to the ways in which the neuropsychological data relate to the following issues:

(1) *Relation of mental imagery to perception.* One of the oldest hypotheses about mental imagery is that it is the 'top-down,' or efferent, activation of perceptual representations by higher cognitive processes (Finke, 1980; Hebb, 1968; Hume, 1739/1969; Shepard, 1978, 1984). That is, to form an image of an object from memory is to activate by internal means some of the same representations in the visual system that would normally be activated upon viewing the object. This is an issue about mental imagery which has been much

debated within cognitive psychology, with some researchers questioning the empirical basis for the claim that imagery shares representations of objects with the visual system (e.g. Intons-Peterson, 1983; Pylyshyn, 1973). As we will see, neuropsychological data can be extremely informative on this issue.

(2) *The modularity of mental imagery.* Is mental imagery a distinct 'module' of the mind? In other words, are the processes that underlie the formation and manipulation of mental images separate from the cognitive processes underlying nonimagistic (e.g. verbal) thought? Introspection would suggest that imagery and verbal thought are distinct, and there is certainly some objective evidence for this as well (e.g. Pavio, 1971). However, the evidence has not been interpreted the same way by all psychologists, and some find it more parsimonious to assume that recalling an image from memory is no different from recalling nonimagistic memories in terms of the underlying information-processing primitives involved (Anderson, 1976; Pylyshyn, 1984). This is another example of an issue originally formulated in cognitive psychology for which neuropsychological data can be very informative.

(3) *Internal structure of the mental imagery system.* Just as language has identifiable subcomponents of processing, such as the retrieval of words and the grammatical parsing of sentences, and these subcomponents of language processing are associated with different neural substrates (see Zurif, 1984), it seems likely that mental imagery

also has an internal componential structure. Studies of mental imagery in cognitive psychology suggest ways in which the imagery system might be internally structured, which can guide neuro-psychological research on imagery. Reciprocally, neuropsychological data can inform us about the internal componential structure of imagery through patterns of association and dissociation among imagery abilities after brain damage.

(4) *Cerebral localization of mental imagery*. What parts of the brain are normally involved in mental imagery? Is imagery ability a function of modality-specific visual areas of the brain? Is it lateralized to one hemisphere? Do different components of mental imagery have different neural substrates?

For purposes of organizing this review, a somewhat arbitrary distinction will be drawn be-tween the mental representations underlying im-agery and the processes used to create and manipulate mental images. The first section will review what is known about imagery representa-tion. The second section will review recent research on the process of generating images from memory. The third section will review research on the pro-cesses of manipulating mental images, as ex-emplified by mental image rotation.

Representations underlying mental imagery

Introspectively, imagining an object is much like seeing it. This suggests that some of the same representations are involved in the two activities. In terms of a neuropsychological model of im-agery, this proposal amounts to the claim that im-agery is efferent activity in the brain's visual areas. Neuropsychological data from a variety of sources provide support for this view of imagery, and also suggest more specifically which visual areas might be shared with imagery.

There are many findings in neuropsychology that are relevant to the relationship between im-agery and perception. A detailed review may be found in Farah (1988). Representative findings will be summarized briefly here. These findings can be roughly grouped into two categories: those that localize imagery to specific visual processing areas of the brain and those that implicate shared func-tional mechanisms for visual imagery and visual perception through findings of parallel deficits in imagery and perception after brain damage.

Common neural substrates for imagery and perception

Regional cerebral blood flow during im-agery Roland and Friberg (1985) measured regional cerebral blood flow under four different conditions: resting, mental arithmetic (subtracting 3 repetitively starting at 50), memory scanning of an auditory stimulus (mentally jumping every se-cond word in a well-known musical jingle), and visual imagery (visualizing a walk through one's neighborhood making alternating right and left turns starting at one's front door). In each of the subjects tested, the pattern of blood flow in the visual imagery task showed massive activation of the posterior regions of the brain compared to the resting state, including the same areas that normal-ly show increased blood flow during visual-perceptual tasks (Mazziotta et al., 1983; Roland, 1982; Roland and Skinhoj, 1981). Furthermore, these areas did not show increases in blood flow compared to the resting state in the other two cognitive tasks.

Goldenberg et al. (1987) have investigated the blood flow changes that accompany imagery using an extremely simple and elegant design, including a control condition differing from the imagery condition only in the absence of imagery. Different groups of normal subjects were given the same auditorily presented lists of concrete words to learn under different instructional conditions: one group was told to just listen to the words and try to remember them, while the other group was told to visualize the referents of the words as a mnemonic strategy. Some subjects in the no-imagery group reported spontaneously imaging the words when questioned after the experiment, and they were re-classified as image condition subjects. Recall was higher overall for the imagery group, as would be expected if these subjects did indeed differ from the no-imagery group in their use of imagery. The patterns of blood flow recorded during the two conditions also differed, by two distinct measures. First, there was relatively more blood flow to the occipital lobes in the imagery condition than in the nonimagery condition in which the identical stimulus words were being memorized. Second, the pattern of covariation of blood flow among brain areas, which provides another index of regional brain activity, was also greater in the occipital and posterior temporal areas of the brain in the imagery condition compared to the nonimagery condition.

Goldenberg et al. (1988) have also studied the blood flow correlates of spontaneously evoked imagery, rather than imagery use evoked by instructions to image. They compared the patterns of regional blood flow while subjects tried to answer two types of question: questions requiring visual imagery to answer (e.g. 'Is the green of pine trees darker than the green of grass?') and questions which do not require imagery to answer (e.g. 'Is the categorical imperative an ancient grammatical form?'). Despite the superficial similarity of the two types of task, answering 'yes/no' general knowledge questions, they differed significantly in the patterns of regional cerebral blood flow they evoked: the imagery questions caused significantly greater occipital bloodflow than the nonimagery questions. The results of the covariation analysis also implicated occipital activity in the imagery condition, as well as revealing activity in the posterior temporal and parietal visual processing areas. In contrast, the nonimagery condition did not reveal visual area activation.

Electrophysiological activity during imagery Further evidence that the visual cortex participates in visual imagery comes from electrophysiological techniques: EEG (electroencephalography) and ERP (event-related potentials). In EEG techniques, supression of alpha rhythm (EEG activity in a certain range of frequencies) is associated with increased brain activity. Many authors have found that visual imagery is accompanied by alpha rhythm attenuation over the visual areas of the brain (Barratt, 1956; Brown, 1966; Davidson and Schwartz, 1977; Golla et al., 1943; Short, 1953; Slatter, 1960). A particularly well-designed study is that of Davidson and Schwartz (1977) in which the EEG alpha rhythm was measured simultaneously over the visual (occipital) and tactile (parietal) areas of the brain under three conditions: during visual imagery (imagining a flashing light), tactile imagery (imagining one's forearm being tapped) and during combined visual and tactile imagery (imagining the flashes and taps together). Whereas there was no difference in total alpha attenuation between the visual and tactile imagery conditions (i.e. the overall effects of tactile and visual imagery on general effort and arousal were the same), the site of maximum alpha attenuation in the visual imagery condition was over the visual areas, and the site of maximum alpha attenuation in the tactile imagery condition was over the tactile areas. Alpha attenuation in the combined visual and tactile imagery condition showed an intermediate balanced pattern of distribution across both visual and tactile areas.

Event-related potential techniques have also been used to examine regional brain activity during imagery. ERP differs from EEG in that it measures just the electrical activity of the brain that is synchronized with (and thus presumably 'related' to) the processing of a stimulus. Farah et al. (1989) recorded ERPs during mental imagery by presenting printed words to subjects under two different instructional conditions: In the 'reading only' condition, subjects were told to simply read the words. In the 'imagery' condition, subjects were told to read the words and image their referents (e.g. if the word is 'cat,' image a cat). ERPs were recorded from sixteen standard sites on the scalp, including occipital, parietal, temporal and frontal locations. The first 450 ms of the ERPs in both conditions were indistinguishable, reflecting their common visual and lexical processing stages. However, later components of the two conditions differed from one another: In the imagery condition there was a highly localized increase in positivity of the ERP, relative to the 'reading only' condition, at the occipital electrodes, implicating occipital activity during the process of imaging.

Farah et al. (1988) took a different approach to localizing mental imagery in the brain using event-related potential techniques, by examining the effect of imagery on the ERP to visual stimuli. Subjects were asked to image stimuli while they were presented with real stimuli, so that the effect of imagery on the ERP to stimuli could be observed. If imagery has a systematic effect on the ERP to stimuli, then there must be some common brain locus at which imagery and perceptual processing interact. More importantly, if the interaction between imagery and perception is content-specific – that is, for example, if imaging an H affects the ERP to H's more than the ERP to T's, and imaging a T affects the ERP to T's more than the ERP to H's – then that interaction must be taking place at some brain location where information about the differences between H's and T's is preserved, that is, at a representational locus. In this experiment, subjects imaged H's and T's, while performing a detection task in which an H, a T, or no stimulus was presented on each trial. The image that the subject was instructed to form on a given trial was nonpredictive of the upcoming stimulus. The ERPs to H's and T's while subjects were imaging the same letter were compared to the ERPs to H's and T's while subjects imaged the other letter. In the way, the content-specific effect of imagery on the visual ERP could be observed, while holding constant the actual stimuli to which the ERPs were recorded (equal numbers of H's and T's in both conditions) and the effort of forming and holding an image (equal numbers of H and T images in each condition). Assuming that there is a content-specific effect of imagery on the visual ERP, its scalp location will put constraints on the brain location of representations stimulated by both imagery and perception.

Imagery had a content-specific effect on the first negative component of the visual evoked potential (maximal at 187 ms), and this effect was maximal at the occipital recording sites. The occipital scalp distribution of the effect and its synchronization with the visual N1 suggest that the underlying brain location of the image-percept interaction is at least partly occipital.

The electrophysiological evidence from EEG and ERP research is thus in agreement with results from a very different methodology, regional cerebral blood flow, in implicating visual system activity during imagery. Across a variety of tasks, it has been found that imagery engages visual cortex, whereas other tasks, many of which are highly similar save for the absence of visual imagery, do not.

Functional parallels between imagery and perception after brain damage

The existence of highly selective deficits in visual abilities has contributed to our understanding of the functional architecture of visual perception by demonstrating which perceptual abilities are independent of which other abilities. If visual imagery uses the same representational machinery as visual perception, then one should expect selective deficits in the imagery abilities of patients that parallel their selective perceptual deficits. In fact, this is generally the case. The relevant studies are summarized below.

Color vision and color imagery   At early stages of cortical visual processing, color is represented separately from other visual stimulus dimensions, and brain damage affecting the cortical visual areas can therefore result in relatively isolated color vision deficits (see Cowey, 1982; Damasio et al., 1980; Meadows, 1974). A long history of the case by case study of patients with aquired cerebral color blindness has documented an association between loss of color perception and loss of color imagery (e.g. Beauvois and Saillant, case 2, 1985; Heidenhain, 1927; Humphreys and Riddoch, 1987; Jossman, 1929; Lewandowsky, 1908; Pick, 1908; Stengel, 1948). In addition to being unable to identify or discriminate among colors, these patients cannot report the colors of common objects from memory (e.g. the color of a football, cactus or German Shepherd's back), a task which most people find requires imaging the object in color. These patients are not generally impaired in their cognitive functioning; in fact, Humphreys and Riddoch (1987) documented good general imagery ability (assessed by drawings and descriptions of objects from memory) in their color-blind patient who had impaired color imagery. The implication of this association between the perception of color and imagery for color is that the two abilities depend upon the same neural substrates of color representation.

The association between impairments in color vision and color imagery has been observed in group studies as well as in case studies. In a large group study of unilaterally brain-damaged patients, DeRenzi and Spinnler (1967) found that patients who had impaired color vision also had impaired color imagery. The implication of this association between the perception of color and imagery for color is that the two abilities depend upon the same neural substrates of color representation.

Another source of evidence that color is represented by the same neural structures in imagery and perception comes from an intriguing case study by Beauvois and Saillant (case 1, 1985) of a patient whose visual areas had been neuroanatomically disconnected from her language areas by a stroke. The patient was able to perform color tasks that were purely visual, such as sorting objects on the basis of color and identifying the embedded characters in the Ishihara test of color blindness, because her visual areas had not been damaged. Her general verbal ability was also quite intact, as evidenced by a verbal IQ score of 123, because her language areas had not been damaged. However, if the task involved coordinating a visual and a verbal representation, for example naming a visually presented color or pointing to a named color, her performance was extremely poor, owing to the neuroanatomical disconnection between her language and vision

areas. The patient was able to perform a purely visual color memory task, which consisted of distinguishing between correctly and incorrectly colored drawings of objects, implying that her mental images of colored objects were not disconnected from the visual areas used in recognizing and discriminating among the colored pictures. Her performance on the verbally posed color questions depended upon the nature of the question: for questions which made use of verbal associations between objects and colors (e.g. 'What color is Paris ham?', where 'Paris ham' is also called 'white ham'; or 'What color is envy?') the patient performed normally. In contrast, for questions that appear to require mental imagery (e.g. 'What color is a gherkin?') she performed poorly. Again, this implies that whereas verbal memory associations for colors were not disconnected from the language areas of this patient with visual–verbal disconnection, imagistic representations of color were. Finally, Beauvois and Saillant directly investigated whether the patient used imagery or nonimagistic memory representations for retrieving the same information. In one condition, they asked questions such as 'You have learnt what color snow is. It is often said. What do people say when they are asked what color snow is?' or 'It is winter. Imagine a beautiful snowy landscape . . . Can you see it? Well, now tell me what color the snow is.' The patient performed normally when biased toward a verbal recall strategy, and her performance dropped significantly when biased toward an imagery recall strategy. This is again what one would expect to find if the color of mental images is represented in the same neural substrate as the color of visual percepts.

In sum, three types of evidence support the hypothesis that imaging an object in color requires some of the same neural representations necessary for color vision: individual cases of acquired central color blindness are reported to have lost their color imagery, in a group of patients with varying degrees of color vision impairment color imagery is correlated with color vision, and in a case of visual–verbal disconnection images were equivalent to visual representations in terms of their interactions with other visual and verbal task components.

'What' and 'where' in vision and imagery Patients with bilateral parieto-occipital disease often have trouble knowing *where* an object is in the visual field, without any difficulty identifying *what* the object is (DeRenzi, 1982). Thus, such a patient may quickly identify an object such as a postage stamp held somewhere in his or her visual field, but be unable to indicate its position either verbally or by pointing. Other patients, with bilateral temporo-occipital disease, may show the opposite pattern of visual abilities (Bauer and Rubens, 1985). They are impaired in their ability to recognize *what* visually presented stimuli are, despite adequate elementary visual capabilities (e.g. size of visual field, acuity), but their ability to localize *where* visual stimuli were presented is unimpaired. Thus, such a patient might fail to recognize a postage stamp by sight, but could accurately point to its location. This dissociation is evidence for a rather counter-intuitive division of labor in the visual system between the localization of stimuli and their identification, an idea which is also supported by animal experimentation (Ungerleider and Mishkin, 1982). Levine et al. (1985) studied the imagery abilities of a pair of patients, one with visual localization impairment after bilateral parieto-occipital damage and one with visual object identification impairment after bilateral temporo-occipital damage, with special attention to the distinction between spatial *location* information and single object *appearance* information in visual images. They found that the preserved and impaired aspects of vision in each patient were similarly preserved or impaired in imagery: the patient with object identification difficulties was unable to draw or describe the appearances of familiar objects, animals or faces from memory, despite being able to draw and describe in great detail the relative locations of cities and states on a map, furniture in his house, and landmarks in his city. The patient with object

localization difficulties was unable to describe the relative locations of landmarks in his neighborhood, cities in the United States, or, when blindfolded, to point to furniture in his hospital room. He was, however, able to give detailed descriptions of the appearance of a variety of objects, animals and faces. In a review of the literature for similar cases, they found that for a majority of the published cases of selective visual 'what' or 'where' deficit, when the appropriate imagery abilities were tested they showed parallel patterns of imagery deficit, and in no case was there a well-documented violation of this parallelism.

A more recent follow-up study by Farah et al. (1988) of one of the two cases described in Levine et al. (1985) suggests that the distinction between imagery for visual appearance and spatial localization observed in these patients corresponds to a distinction drawn in the cognitive psychology literature between 'visual' and 'spatial' mental imagery. 'Visual' imagery has typically been taken to be a modality-specific system for representing color, form and other aspects of objects' appearances, as they would be seen from a particular viewing perspective. This form of imagery is generally engaged by tasks that require visual information such as color or the presence of some particular detail to be retrieved from memory. 'Spatial' imagery is usually characterized as amodal, and involving a more abstract representation of the location and structure of objects in three dimensions. This form of imagery is generally engaged by tasks that require relative locations to be recalled from memory or maintained in short-term memory, and tasks that involve the transformations of mental images (e.g. mental rotation). When the patient with impaired object recognition was given a series of imagery tasks drawn from the cognitive psychology literature, he performed poorly on the 'visual' imagery tasks and performed normally on the 'spatial' imagery tasks.

Face perception and face imagery Dissociations between object recognition abilities *within* the temporo-occipital 'what' system also exist. The most selective deficit of this type consists of profoundly impaired face recognition with roughly intact recognition of other classes of visual stimuli as well as intact general intellectual and memory functioning (Bauer and Rubens, 1985). In general, the particular classes of stimuli that are hardest for such patients to recognize are also the hardest for these patients to visualize from memory, as assessed by either drawings or descriptions from memory, or by patients' introspective reports. For example, Shuttleworth et al.'s (1982, case 2) patient who had a selective face recognition deficit was also reported to 'have no voluntary visual recall (revisualization) of faces but was able to revisualize more general items such as buildings and places.' Shuttleworth et al. reviewed the literature for cases of face recognition deficit, and found that approximately 40% of 74 cases reported impairments in face imagery. They went on to caution that in many of the cases in which face imagery was not noted to be impaired 'the accuracy of the image could not be ascertained and was seriously questioned in a number of cases.' Beyn and Knyazeva (1962) compared, on an item-by-item basis, the visual imagery and visual recognition abilities of a patient with face recognition difficulties. They found a close association between the particular visual stimuli that could be recognized and imaged: the patient recognized three out of 16 objects which he was unable to image, and 13 out of 16 objects which he could image.

Visual neglect and imaginal neglect Patients with right parietal lobe damage often fail to detect stimuli presented in the left half of the visual field, even through their elementary sensory processes for stimuli on the affected side of space are intact (Heilman et al., 1985; Posner et al., 1984). This deficit is known as 'visual neglect,' and also appears to manifest itself in visual imagery. Bisiach and his colleagues (Bisiach and Luzzatti, 1978; Bisiach et al., 1979) have shown that right parietal patients with visual neglect also fail to image the left sides of objects and scenes. In Bisiach and Luzzatti's initial report, two right parietal lobe-damaged neglect patients were asked to imagine viewing a famous square in Milan (the Piazza del Duomo, with which the patients had been familiar before their brain damage) from a particular vantage point, and to describe the view. Both patients omitted from their descriptions the landmarks that would have fallen on the left side of that scene. The patients were then asked to repeat the task, this time from the opposite vantage point, from which the buildings, statues and other landmarks that fell on the left side of the previous view were visible on the right, and vice versa. The patients' descriptions of their images now included the items which had previously been omitted, and omitted the items on the left side of their current image (which had been reported before).

Bisiach et al. followed up these case studies with a group study of neglect for visual images. Right parietal-damaged patients with left-sided neglect and a control group of patients without neglect were shown abstract cloud-like shapes passing behind a screen with a narrow vertical slit in the center. Because all of the stimulus input in this task is presented centrally in the visual field, any effect of left-sided neglect in this task cannot be attributed to perceptual neglect. After viewing pairs of such shapes, the patients were to decide whether the two members of the pair were identical or different. This presumably requires mentally reconstructing images of the stimuli from the successive narrow vertical views. Patients who neglected the left halves of visual stimuli also neglected the left halves of their images, as evidenced by a greater number of errors when pairs of shapes differed on their left sides than when they differed on their right sides in the task.

The results summarized above imply that imagery shares representations with vision at multiple levels of processing. Occipital representations are implicated by the blood flow and electrophysiological data, as well as by the findings of parallel deficits in color vision and color imagery. Higher-level visual representations in the parietal and temporal lobes are also implicated by the blood flow data and by parallel imagery and vision deficits in object identity, localization and attention.

Generation of mental images

The results summarized above imply that mental images are re-activations of perceptual representations. During vision, these perceptual representations are activated automatically, triggered by the presentation of a stimulus. How are the same representations activated during imagery, when the relevant stimulus is not present? Some type of active, constructive cognitive process is needed to re-activate the appropriate visual representations on the basis of long-term visual memory information. Cognitive psychologists have called this process 'image generation,' and an influential model of the internal workings of the image generation process can be found in Kosslyn (1980).

Loss of mental image generation after focal brain damage

Recent work on the neuropsychology of mental image generation suggests that this process is dissociable from other forms of recall of nonimagistic memories, and that it is dependent upon a particular region of the posterior left hemisphere. These conclusions were initially suggested by a review of the neuropsychological literature for cases of loss of imagery after focal brain damage (Farah, 1984). Whereas most cases of loss of imagery have associated perceptual deficits as well as the imagery deficit, and are therefore most parsimoniously explained in terms of a loss of some of the representations shared by imagery and perception, a small number of cases have no accompanying visual impairments. To explain the underlying cause of the imagery deficit in these patients, it is necessary to postulate damage to some component of the imagery system other than the shared representations discussed in the previous section. The image generation process seems a likely candidate in such cases.

Fourteen of the cases reviewed by Farah (1984)

were reported to have imagery impairments with no mention of prominent visual disturbance, and were therefore classified as cases of image generation deficit. These cases can provide evidence about the modularity and localizability of image generation. Although the general neuropsychological background in many of these cases is unfortunately sketchy, image generation appears to be dissociable from other forms of recall, consistent with the modularity claim. Among these same 14 cases, there was a strong trend for left posterior lesions: most of the patients had most of their damage in this quadrant of the brain, and in no case was there evidence that the brain damage spared this area. This suggests a left posterior localization for the process of mental image generation.

Subsequent cases of impaired imagery with roughly normal vision have been consistent with the tentative localization of image generation to the posterior left hemisphere: the cases of Deleval et al. (1983), Farah et al. (1988), Grossi et al. (1986) and Pena-Casanova et al. (1985) all had CT-verified lesions in the posterior left hemisphere, affecting the occipito-temporal region. In addition, a recent group study of brain-damaged patients, carried out by Goldenberg (in press), found evidence of a special role for the left occipito-temporal region in image generation: patients who failed to benefit from an imagery mnemonic in a verbal memory task generally had damage to this region. Although Goldenberg administered several other imagery tasks to these patients, which showed differing patterns of localization, the other tasks were either not image generation tasks (e.g. mental rotation) or lacked appropriate control conditions.

When image generation is impaired following left posterior brain damage, what is the underlying nature of the impairment? There is some suggestion that patients are unable to 'assemble' mental images from their separately stored parts (Farah et al., 1988; Kosslyn, 1987). For example, the patient of Deleval et al. (1983) complained of being able to imagine only fragments of objects. Some of these patients were reported to have a subtle perceptual deficit in the simultaneous recognition of multiple objects or parts of objects, apparent mainly when reading.

Mental image generation: evidence from other neuropsychological techniques

Ehrlichman and Barrett (1983) pointed out the existence of a widespread assumption in neuropsychology that mental imagery is a function of the right hemisphere. They went on to examine and reject most of the purported evidence for this claim. The analyses of the cases of loss of imagery after focal brain damage are consistent with Ehrlichman and Barrett's conclusion that imagery is not a function of the right hemisphere, and suggest that the generation of mental images is a speciality of the left hemisphere. This conclusion is sufficiently counterintuitive that it should be subjected to further testing before we accept it. Additional studies with normal subjects and with split-brain patients have been carried out. On the whole, these studies support the lateralization of image generation to the left hemisphere, although some studies suggest that exceptions to this generalization may exist.

Studies with normal subjects   Cohen (1975) carried out a lateral tachistoscopic version of Cooper and Shepard's (1973) imagery task, in which subjects must discriminate between normal and mirror-reversed letters presented at different orientations, with or without generating mental images in advance of the stimulus presentation. She compared visual field asymmetries in three conditions: no advance information about the stimulus, the name of the stimulus known in advance, and the name and orientation of the stimulus known in advance. Subjects were told to generate images based on the advance information. Cohen found a RVF/LH advantage in the use of advance information, concluding that "the left hemisphere superiority in utilizing the name and rotation information is consistent with the internal representation (i.e. mental image) being uniquely or more

efficiently synthesized in the left hemisphere" (p. 30).

Farah (1986) used a similar paradigm to test the hypothesis of left hemisphere specialization for image generation. The basic idea of the experiment was to use the *facilitating* effect of imagery in visual discrimination tasks as a measure of the presence or quality of images. The subject's task was to decide whether a stimulus, presented briefly and to one side of a fixation point, is or is not a pre-designated 'target'. The two targets were a plus sign and a rectangular-shaped capital 'O' character. Non-targets were characters selected for being visually similar to either the plus or the 'O'. Subjects performed two versions of the lateralized discrimination task. In the 'Baseline' condition, they were pre-cued with the information about the side on which the stimulus will occur before the stimulus presentation and did not use imagery. Their task was to respond 'target' to either of the targets and 'non-target' to any of the non-targets. In the 'Imagery' condition, they were pre-cued as before with the side on which the stimulus would occur, and they were also shown one of the two targets (in central vision), which they were instructed to image in the position of the upcoming stimulus. The image should facilitate the visual discrimination between targets and non-targets, particularly when the image and stimulus are visually similar. If the left hemisphere is specialized for image generation, then the image-mediated facilitation should be greatest when the image-stimulus overlap occurs in the right hemifield/left hemisphere, where the image was generated. The results were consistent with a left hemisphere locus for image generation. Whereas performance in the baseline condition did not depend on which hemisphere initially received the stimulus, when the same task was performed using imagery as a template there was an overall left hemisphere superiority.

Kosslyn (1988) has carried out a series of experiments on the laterality of imagery processes in normal subjects using lateral tachistoscopic paradigms, in which generated images are projected onto a screen and 'probed' with stimuli on the screen falling on or near the image. Kosslyn has conjectured that the left hemisphere is specialized only for the generation of images based on what he terms 'categorical' spatial representations, in which the locations of the parts of the image are specified relative to the locations of other parts, and that the right hemisphere is superior for the generation of images based on what he terms 'metric' spatial representations, in which the precise locations of each part of the image are specified relative to a common frame. This hypothesis was tested by varying the discriminability of probes falling on versus near the image. When less spatial precision was needed, the task was performed faster in the right hemifield/left hemisphere than in the left hemifield/right hemisphere, whereas when greater precision was required the visual field asymmetries reversed, consistent with Kosslyn's prediction.

Lempert (1987) found evidence of left hemisphere specialization in two experiments measuring lateralized interference with motor activity during imagery. Her subjects listened to sentences while tapping as quickly as possible with either the left or right hand. In one experiment the use of imagery was manipulated by overt instructions to image the sentence, and in another by the nature of the sentences (e.g. 'The giant chased the jogger,' which evokes spontaneous imagery, versus 'The mood suited the moment,' which does not). Imagery use was validated by better recall for imaged than nonimaged sentences. With the exception of the male subjects in the first experiment, who did not show a recall advantage with imagery, the imagery conditions in both experiments were associated with either significant or borderline significant trends towards greater tapping decrement by the right hand (which is controlled by the left hemisphere) than by the left.

Another source of evidence on the laterality of mental image generation is the brain imaging techniques described earlier, in the section on mental imagery representation. There is a trend, in both of Goldenberg et al.'s (1987, 1988) blood flow studies, for greater left than right occipital blood flow, and Roland and Friberg's (1985) subjects showed greater left posterior temporal blood flow than right. The statistical reliability of these asymmetries is variable, but their consistency across studies is informative. In Farah et al.'s (1989) ERP study of image generation, there was a significant asymmetry in activity at the left and right occipito-temporal recording sites.

Studies with split-brain patients   The results from split-brain patients show more variability than the results from other methods, consistent with previous observations of variability in this population (Gazzaniga, 1983). In an initial study (Farah et al., 1985), the split-brain patient J.W. was given a simple imagery task adapted from one already used in imagery studies with normal subjects. The task was a letter classification task used by Weber and others (Weber and Castleman, 1970; Weber and Malmstrom, 1979). In the original version, subjects went through the alphabet from memory, classifying the lower-case forms of each letter from a to z as 'ascending' (e.g., 'd'), 'descending' (e.g., 'g'), or neither (e.g., 'a'). In the version adapted for use with the split-brain patient, a particular letter was cued by the presentation of its upper-case form. So, for example, if the stimulus was 'P,', the correct response was 'descending.' In order to cue just one hemisphere at a time with the letter to be imaged and classified, the upper case forms were presented at one and a half degrees to the left or to the right of the patient's fixation, so that only the contralateral hemisphere receives the visual input.

In order to infer that a failure in this task reflects a hemispheric image generation deficit per se, additional control tasks were developed to assess each hemisphere's ability to perform other components of the imagery task. In the *letter association* task, upper-case letters were presented to each hemisphere and the patient's task was to select the corresponding lower-case form from a nonalphabetically arranged array of letters in free vision.

Successful performance of this task shows that the hemisphere receiving the upper-case letter is capable of recognizing the upper- and lower-case letters and associating them correctly. In the *perceptual classification* task, lower-case letters were presented to each hemisphere and the patients' task was to classify the letter into the appropriate response category and respond. Unlike the imagery task, this task simply requires the patient to classify what he can actually see. Successful performance on this task shows that the hemisphere receiving the letter is capable of performing the letter height discrimination and responding. It follows that if a hemisphere can perform both control tasks, a failure in the imagery task ·cannot be attributed to a difficulty in perceptual encoding, letter recognition and association, height discrimination, or response production.

Both hemispheres were able to perform the control tasks: the right hemisphere made one error out of twenty-six trials in the *letter association* task and the left hemisphere performed errorlessly in the same number of trials. In the *perceptual classification* task, the right hemisphere was able to correctly classify 90% of the lower-case letters presented to it as 'medium' or 'not medium,' and the left hemisphere correctly classified all of the lower-case letters presented to it. A pronounced left hemisphere superiority emerged in the imagery task: the right hemisphere performed at chance level, 43% correct, whereas the left hemisphere continued to perform essentially perfectly, 97% correct.

Subsequent studies have been carried out with the same patient, J.W., as well as with patients V.P. and L.B. Kosslyn et al. (1985) found that J.W. was able to generate certain images with his right hemisphere, provided they did not involve the integration of multiple stored image parts. In this same report, V.P. was found to perform like J.W. on the letter imagery task initially, but with practice her right hemisphere became able to generate images. It should be noted that V.P.'s right hemisphere is capable of speech, and that generalizations from this particular patient to the

normal brain are therefore risky. Corballis and Sergent (1988) assessed the image generation capabilities of L.B.'s two hemispheres using the letter imagery task and a clock face imagery task. In the latter, a time was displayed digitally in one hemifield and the subject's task was to image the face of an analog clock and decide whether the two hands of the clock made an angle greater than or less than 90 degrees. In both of these tasks, the left hemisphere was significantly more accurate than the right. In the letter task, the left and right hemispheres performed 94% and 82% of the trials correctly, respectively. However, the interpretation of this difference in accuracy is complicated by the fact that the right hemisphere responded more quickly than the left. The clockface task revealed a clearer pattern of lateralization: the left and right hemispheres performed 97% and 67% of the trials correctly, respectively. The performance of the right hemisphere did not differ significantly from chance.

In summary, the results from normal subjects and split-brain subjects suggest that mental image generation is normally dependent on the left hemisphere. This generalization must be qualified by the finding that, in a patient with right hemisphere speech, and under certain task conditions, the right hemisphere may show image generation capabilities.

Relationship of mental image generation to dreaming Although dream imagery tends to be subjectively more vivid and realistic than waking imagery, there is much similarity between the two types of internal experience. This might lead one to expect that similar neural systems underlie the two processes, and the available evidence does indeed support this idea. Enduring loss of dreaming after brain injury is highly associated with loss of waking imagery, and is generally accompanied by left hemisphere damage (Farah, 1984: Greenberg and Farah 1986). The implication of the left hemisphere in dream generation runs counter to a widespread belief that the right hemisphere plays a dominant role in dreaming (Bakan, 1977; Galin,

1974; Hoppe, 1977; Stone, 1977), but is supported by the focal lesion data as well as by research with split-brain patients and an EEG study of normal subjects. Greenwood et al. (1977) found that split-brain patients do report dreaming. This implies that the left hemisphere is experiencing dreams, as it is the left hemisphere of these patients which controls speech. Ehrlichman et al. (1986) recorded EEG from sleeping subjects during REM, and periodically awakened subjects to request dream reports. EEG periods preceding the awakenings when subjects reported dreaming showed a power asymmetry indicating greater left hemisphere activity, whereas EEG periods preceding awakenings when subjects did not report dreams did not show a left-lateralized asymmetry.

In summary, the ability to generate mental images is dissociable from other forms of recall, supporting the hypothesis that mental imagery comprises a distinct module of memory. Several direct tests of the laterality of mental image generation support a left hemisphere basis for this function. Finally, there is some evidence which suggests that waking and dream imagery are the products of a single common system for image generation.

Transformations of mental images

One of the important functions of mental imagery is to allow us to mentally simulate real displacements and transformations of objects in the physical world. For example, before placing luggage in a car trunk, we visualize the different possible arrangements and decide which is the most efficient, rather than physically pushing the suitcases around until we find the best arrangement.

The ability to transform mental images appears to be doubly dissociable from the ability to generate images from memory. For example, the patient studied by Farah et al. (1988) was impaired at generating images from memory due to loss of long-term visual memory representations, but performed as well as normal subjects in various mental image transformation tasks, including mental rotation, mental size scaling and mental image

scanning. In contrast, the patient studied by Farah and Hammond (1988) was impaired at mental rotation, but performed normally on several tests of mental image generation. This implies that these abilities rely on different components of the mental imagery system.

Mental rotation is the imagery process by which we visualize what a stimulus presented at one orientation would look like at a different orientation. This process has been the focus of considerable research in both cognitive psychology and neuropsychology, primarily because it is such a clear case of a nonverbal, 'analog' cognitive process. What is meant by an 'analog' cognitive process in this context is one that is isomorphic with the physical process being represented, in this case an external, physical rotation. That is, just as a physically rotating stimulus passes through all intermediate orientations between the starting and the final orientation, so does the mental image seem to pass through representations of intermediate orientations (Shepard, 1984). The evidence for this is that increasingly greater amounts of rotation require proportionately greater amounts of time to accomplish. For example, Cooper and Shepard (1973) showed that, when asked to decide whether a misoriented letter had been printed normally or mirror-reversed, subjects' response latencies increased approximately linearly with the angular disparity of the letter from the upright position.

Studies of mental rotation in focally brain-damaged patients   Several research projects have been aimed at assessing mental rotation ability in brain-damaged patients. DeRenzi and Faglioni (1967) tested unilateral right and left hemisphere-damaged patients, further classified according to presence or absence of visual field defects. Their test of mental rotation consisted of presenting nine abstract, scrawl-like line drawings to patients, along with a single drawing that was identical to one of the nine except for a 180 degree rotation. The subjects' task was to select the identical drawing. DeRenzi and Faglioni found that both right-

and left-hemisphere-damaged patients were impaired relative to control subjects. The pattern of association between performance on their mental rotation task and presence of visual field defect differed between the right- and left-hemisphere-damaged patients, however, with only the left-hemisphere-damaged patients showing a correlation between these factors and mental rotation impairment.

Butters and Barton (1970) tested unilateral right- and left-brain-damaged patients, further classified according to the severity of various signs of parietal damage, such as constructional apraxia and left/right confusion. They used three different tests of mental rotation ability: 'the 'stick test,' in which subjects must reproduce patterns of three or four sticks either in the orientation in which the model stick pattern is shown or at a 180 degree rotation of the model orientation; the 'village scene test,' a variation of the Piagetian egocentrism task, in which subjects view a three-dimensional model of a village and select drawings which correspond to either their current view of the village or the view that they would have from a different perspective; and the 'pool reflection test,' adapted from Cattell's 'culture free' intelligence test, in which subjects match a single geometric pattern to one of four geometric patterns which is identical to a 180 degree rotation of the first pattern out of the page (equivalent to a reflection through a line in the plane of the page). Butters and Barton found that signs of severe parietal dysfunction were associated with impaired performance on the sticks task and the pool reflections task, regardless of the hemispheric side of damage, but only the right parietal patients were impaired on the village scene test. Butters et al. (1970) followed up these findings with a study of additional unilateral right-hemisphere-damaged patients on the same three tasks. They again found impairment on rotation tasks to be particularly correlated with parietal signs. In summary, on two tasks out of three, symmetrical contributions of the left and right parietal lobes were found, and on one task a right parietal deficit was found. There

was also a general correlation between degree of rotation impairment and degree of 'parietal signs,' not limited to one hemispheric group.

Ratcliff (1979) tested patients with right, left and bilateral penetrating missile wounds. His task involved viewing stick-figure men holding a black disk in one hand and a white disk in the other, and judging whether the black disk was in their right or left hand. The figures were presented in four different orientations: facing the subject upright, facing the subject upside-down, facing away from the subject upright, and facing away from the subject upside-down. Ratcliff compared subjects' performance in the upright condition to their performance in the upside-down condition, which presumably involved mental rotation. He found that, whereas there were no significant differences between patient groups in performance on the upright stimuli, the right posterior group was significantly impaired on the upside-down stimuli, compared to the other brain-damaged groups and normal control subjects.

Hadano (1984) presented unilateral right- and left-hemisphere-damaged patients with a variation of Cooper and Shepard's (1973) mental rotation task. Subjects were shown five versions of the same letter arrayed in a row, all at different orientations, and were instructed to mark the one letter that was mirror-reversed. Hadano found that both right- and left-hemisphere-damaged subjects were impaired in this task relative to normal control subjects, and that there was no significant difference between the two hemispheric groups.

Kim et al. (1984) gave two different tests of mental rotation ability to left and right, anterior and posterior brain-damaged patients. One task was borrowed from Ratcliff (1979), and the other was borrowed from Royer and Holland (1975). The latter involved viewing a 3-line pattern (e.g. H) and either a 90, 180 or 270 degree rotation of that pattern, and judging whether the second pattern was a 90 degree clockwise rotation of the first. Kim et al. did not find a significant effect of laterality per se, but they did find an interaction between laterality and caudality, such that the left anterior patients were most impaired on the Ratcliff task, and both the left anterior and the right posterior patients were most impaired on the Royer-Holland task.

There is surprisingly little agreement among the outcomes of the studies reviewed above concerning the localization of the lesions causing mental rotation impairment. One possible reason for this is that the mental rotation tasks used in the different studies may have been sensitive to cognitive and perceptual impairments other than mental rotation impairments. In some cases the tasks may have tested mental rotation and other abilities simultaneously; in other cases the tasks may not have tested mental rotation ability at all. It is not true that any task requiring identification or comparison of misoriented stimuli involves mental rotation. Corballis (1988) and Hinton and Parsons (1981) have argued that the only tasks which reliably evoke mental rotation are tasks in which misoriented stimuli must be discriminated from their mirror-images. Therefore, the only mental rotation tasks so far used with brain-damaged patients which we have reason to believe require mental rotation are Ratcliff's (1979) stick figure task, used also by Kim et al. (1984), and Hadano's (1984) letter rotation task. These investigations revealed right posterior deficits, right posterior and left anterior deficits, and right and left hemisphere deficits (with no information about caudality), respectively. On the basis of these findings with focally brain-damaged patients it is difficult to draw any firm conclusions about localization.

Studies with normal subjects: electrophysiology Electrophysiological evidence about the localization of mental rotation is similarly indecisive. Ornstein et al. (1980) measured EEG power asymmetry while subjects performed the Shepard and Metzler (1971) mental rotation task, in which pairs of complex three-dimensional block shapes are presented at different orientations and must be judged either identical or mirror images of one another. Ornstein et al. found evidence of greater left than right hemisphere involvement in this task. Using the same task, Papanicolaou et al., (1987) measured two independent indices of regional brain activity: regional cerebral blood flow, and probe evoked potentials. Both of these indices revealed greater right than left hemisphere activity, particularly right parietal activity.

Willis et al. (1979) assessed EEG power asymmetries while subjects performed the mental rotation test from the Purdue Spatial Visualization Test, and compared this asymmetry to that obtained while subjects merely matched the same stimuli without rotation. Their inclusion of a nonrotation control condition with the same stimuli is helpful in allowing us to assess the contribution of mental rotation per se to any observed asymmetry. Although Willis et al. had set out to test the hypothesis that the right hemisphere would be engaged by mental rotation, they did not find evidence to support this.

Stuss et al. (1983) recorded ERPs to stimuli in a mental rotation task and compared them to the ERPs to other stimuli in a naming task. The ERPs during mental rotation differed from the ERPs during naming symmetrically, with maximal divergence over the parietal areas. Unfortunately, the naming task is not an ideal baseline and limits the interpretability of Stuss et al.'s finding.

Peronnet and Farah (1989) recorded ERPs while subjects performed Cooper and Shepard's (1973) letter rotation task, and included a baseline measure in which all of the same processes were required except for the mental rotation. Of the three scalp electrode sites, midline occipital, parietal and vertex, the parietal lead showed the greatest effects of mental rotation. The amount by which mental rotation affected the ERP was linearly related to the number of degrees of rotation, strengthening the relation between the ERP measure and mental rotation.

Studies with normal subjects: lateralized tachistoscopic techniques Cohen (1975) presented normal subjects with a lateralized tachistoscopic version of Cooper and Shepard's (1973) mental rotation task, in which misoriented alphanumeric characters are presented and the subject must decide as quickly as possible whether the characters are normal or mirror images. She found a right hemisphere superiority for mental rotation in this task. Again, a right hemisphere was present even when the stimuli were presented upright, making it difficult to assess the amount of hemispheric specialization for mental rotation per se in this task.

Jones and Anuza (1982) presented subjects with lateralized geometric forms which were to be judged identical or mirror-images. Errors and response times increased with larger differences in orientation between the stimuli to be compared, implying that the task did elicit mental rotation. Although there was no overall asymmetry observed in either the accuracies or the response times, there was a significant interaction between visual field and angle of rotation for errors, such that the drop-off in accuracy with greater amounts of rotation was more precipitous in the left hemisphere. Jones and Anuza interpret this as support for right hemisphere specialization for mental rotation.

Many other lateralized tachistoscopic studies have been carried out in which stimuli are presented at various orientations and subjects are required to match or recognize these stimuli (e.g. Birkett, 1981; Hock et al., 1981; Simion et al., 1980), but it is unlikely that these tasks elicited mental rotation given that they did not involve discriminations between mirror-image shapes (Corballis, 1988; Hinton and Parsons, 1981).

Studies with a split-brain patient   Corballis and Sergent (1988) assessed the mental rotation capabilities of the two hemispheres of the split-brain patient L.B., using Cooper and Shepard's (1973) letter rotation task. They found that the right hemisphere of this patient was significantly better at this task than the left: overall, 92% correct versus 67% correct, respectively. Furthermore, they found that the right hemisphere showed a linear increase in response time as a function of the orientation of the stimulus, whereas the left

hemisphere's response times were not only longer, but also did not vary systematically with stimulus orientation. However, as Corballis and Sergent point out, by the last two testing sessions L.B.'s left hemisphere was performing the mental rotation task almost as well as the right: 81% correct versus 95% correct, respectively. Furthermore, the left hemisphere also showed the linear pattern of response times indicative of the mental rotation process in these last two sessions. Therefore, the two hemispheres of this patient may not differ in their potential for performing mental rotation, but rather only in their initial unpractised performance. A final reason for caution in interpreting the Corballis and Sergent findings as evidence for right hemisphere specialization for mental rotation is that the hemispheres apparently differed in their ability to perform the nonrotational components of the task, as measured by their accuracy with upright letters: the right hemisphere was able to classify 92% of the upright letters as normal or mirror-reversed, and the left hemisphere 84%.

Farah, Zaidel and Mattison (unpublished work) presented the same split-brain patient L.B. with a mental rotation task which has been validated using response-time measures in normal subjects, along with a control task involving the same stimuli in an upright orientation. The task involved judging whether two L-shapes are identical or mirror images of one another. Consistent with Corballis and Sergent's (1988) findings, both hemispheres were able to perform mental rotation, but the right hemisphere was faster and more accurate. In contrast, we did not find hemispheric differences in this patient for mental size scaling and mental image scanning.

The studies reviewed above are distressingly inconsistent regarding the localization of mental rotation. This may be due in part to the use of tasks that can be performed using strategies other than mental rotation or that require perceptual and cognitive components in addition to mental rotation which may be asymmetrically represented. A reasonable tentative conclusion might be that bilateral involvement in mental rotation seems likely, with perhaps some degree of right hemisphere superiority.

Conclusions

Let us return to the issues raised in the introduction and see how the data just reviewed bear on each of these issues. There is abundant evidence that mental imagery shares representations with visual perception, as Shepard, Finke and others have suggested. The existence of these shared representations can be inferred from findings of visual cortical activity during imagery, and from findings of parallel selective deficits between perception and imagery after brain damage.

The dissociability of mental image generation from other forms of recall after brain damage, as well as the distinct localization of this process, support the idea that the recall of images makes use of different recall processes from the recall of nonimagistic memory representations.

The internal structure of the imagery system has been illuminated in several respects by neuropsychological data: the consistency of the observed patterns of breakdown in imagery ability after brain damage with Kosslyn's (1980) conception of distinct components of imagery including long-term visual memory and an image generation process supports that componential description of the imagery system. The dissociability of 'visual' and 'spatial' imagery suggests a further functional decomposition of the imagery system. More specifically, the double dissociation of image generation from memory and mental image transformation implies that these components are functionally separate and distinct. To the extent that these abilities have been localized, their apparently distinct localizations also fit naturally with this conclusion.

Finally, the localization of mental imagery is gradually becoming clearer, as researchers have dispensed with the notion of a single 'seat' of imagery ability in the brain and begun to consider the possibility of multiple distinct localizations for different components of imagery ability. There is growing evidence that the process of generating images depends upon a region of the posterior left hemisphere, and that mental images, once generated, consist of activity in the visual cortex proper, including visual association areas in parietal and temporal cortex. There is also a suggestion that mental image rotation depends upon parietal cortex, with some degree of right hemisphere superiority for this process.

Acknowledgements

Preparation of this chapter was supported by NIH grant NS23458, ONR contract N0014-86-0094, the Alfred P. Sloan Foundation, and an NIH program project grant to the Aphasia Research Center of the Boston University School of Medicine.

References

Anderson JR: *Language, Memory and Thought.* Hillsdale, NJ: Erlbaum Associates, 1976.

Bakan P: Dreaming, REM sleep, and the right hemisphere: A theoretical integration. *J. Altered States Consciousness: 3,* 285 – 307, 1977.

Barratt PE: Use of the EEG in the study of imagery. *Br. J. Psychol.: 47,* 101 – 114, 1956.

Bauer RM, Rubens AB: Agnosia. In Heilman KM, Valenstein, E (Editors), *Clinical Neuropsychology,* 2nd Edn. New York: Oxford University Press, 1985.

Beauvois MF, Saillant B: Optic aphasia for colours and colour angosia: a distinction between visual and visuo-verbal impairments in the processing of colours. *Cognitive Neuropsychol.: 2,* 1 – 48, 1985.

Bernard M: Un cas de suppression brusque et isolée de la vision mentale des signes et des objects (formes et coleurs) *Progres Med.: 11,* 568 – 571, 1883.

Beyn ES, Knyazeva GR: The problem of prosopagnosia. *J. Neurol. Neurosurg. Psychiatry: 25,* 154 – 158, 1962.

Birkett P: Hemispheric asymmetry for classifying upright and inverted letter pairs: handedness and sex differences. *Neuropsychologia: 19,* 713 – 717, 1981.

Bisiach E, Luzzatti C: Unilateral neglect of representational space. *Cortex: 14,* 129 – 133, 1978.

Bisiach E, Luzzatti C, Perani D: Unilateral neglect, representational schema and consciousness. *Brain: 102,* 609 – 618, 1979.

Brown BB: Specificity of EEG photic flicker responses to color as related to visual imagery ability. *Psychophysiology: 2,* 197 – 207, 1966.

Brown JW: Aphasia, Apraxia and Agnosia: Clinical and

Theoretical Aspects. Springfield, IL: Charles C. Thomas, 1972.

Butters N, Barton M: Effect of parietal lobe damage on the performance of reversible operations in space. *Neuropsychology: 8,* 205 – 214, 1970.

Butters N, Barton M, Brody BA: Role of the right parietal lobe in the mediation of cross-modal associations and reversible operations in space. *Cortex: 6,* 174 – 190, 1970.

Cohen G: Hemispheric differences in the utilization of advance information. In Rabbit PAM, Dornic S (Editors), *Attention and Performance, Vol. 5.* New York: Academic Press, 1975.

Cohen R, Kelter S: Cognitive impairment of aphasics in a colour-to-picture matching task. *Cortex: 15,* 235 – 245, 1979.

Cooper LA, Shepard RN: Chronometric studies of the rotation of mental images. In Chase WG (Editor), *Visual Information Processing.* New York: Academic Press, 1973.

Corballis MC: The recognition of disoriented objects. *Psychol. Rev.: 95,* 115 – 123, 1988.

Corballis MC, Sergent J: Imagery in a commissurotomized patient. *Neuropsychologia:* 1988.

Cowey A: Sensory and non-sensory visual disorders in man and monkey. In Broadbent DE, Weiskrantz L (Editors), *The Neuropsychology of Cognitive Function.* London: The Royal Society, 1982.

Damasio AR, Yamada T, Damasio H, Corbett J, McKee J: Central achromatopsia: behavioral, anatomic and physiologic aspects. *Neurology: 30,* 1064 – 1071, 1980.

Davidson RJ, Schwartz GE: Brain mechanisms subserving self-generated imagery: electrophysiological specificity and patterning. *Psychophysiology: 14,* 598 – 601, 1977.

DeRenzi E: *Disorders of space exploration and cognition.* New York: John Wiley & Sons, 1982.

DeRenzi E, Faglioni, P: The relationship between visuo-spatial impairment and constructional apraxia. *Cortex: 3,* 327 – 342, 1967a.

DeRenzi E, Spinnler H: Impaired performance on color tasks in patients with hemispheric lesions. *Cortex: 3,* 194 – 217, 1967.

DeRenzi E, Faglioni P, Scotti G, Spinnler H. Impairment in associating colour to form concomitant with aphasia. *Brain: 95,* 293 – 304, 1972.

Ehrlichman H, Barrett J: Right hemisphere specialization for mental imagery: a review of the evidence. *Brain Cognition: 2,* 39 – 52, 1983.

Ehrlichman H, Antrobus JS, Wiener MS: EEG asymmetry and sleep mentation during REM and NREM. *Brain Cognition: 4,* 477 – 485, 1985.

Farah MJ: The neurological basis of mental imagery: a componential analysis. *Cognition: 18,* 245 – 272, 1984.

Farah MJ: The laterality of mental image generation; a test with normal subjects. *Neuropsychologia: 24,* 541 – 551, 1986.

Farah MJ: Is visual imagery really visual? Overlooked evidence from neuropsychology. *Psychol. Rev.: 95,* 307 – 317, 1988.

Farah MJ, Hammond KH: Mental rotation and orientation-invariant object recognition: dissociable processes. *Cognition: 29,* 29 – 46, 1988.

Farah MJ, Gazzaniga MS, Holtzman JD, Kosslyn SM: A left hemisphere basis for visual mental imagery? *Neuropsychologia: 23,* 115 – 118, 1985.

Farah MJ, Peronnet F, Gonon MA, Giard MH: Electrophysiological evidence for a shared representational medium for visual images and percepts. *J. Exp. Psychol. Gen.: 117,* 248 – 257, 1988.

Farah MJ, Hammond KL, Levine DN, Calvanio R: Visual and spatial mental imagery: dissociable systems of representation. *Cognitive Psychol.: 20,* 439 – 462, 1988a.

Farah MJ, Levine DN, Calvanio R: A case study of mental imagery deficit. *Brain Cognition: 8,* 147 – 164, 1988b.

Farah MJ, Peronnet F, Weisberg LL, Monheit MA: Brain activity underlying mental imagery: event-related potentials during mental image generation. *J. Cognitive Neurosci.:* in press, 1989.

Finke RA: Levels of equivalence in imagery and perception. *Psychol. Rev.: 87,* 113 – 132, 1980.

Galin D: Implications for psychiatry of left and right cerebral specialization. *Arch. Gen. Psychiatry: 31,* 572 – 583, 1974.

Goldenberg G, Podreka I, Steiner M, Willmes K: Patterns of regional cerebral blood flow related to memorizing of high and low imagery words – an emission computer tomography study. *Neuropsychologia: 25,* 473 – 486, 1987.

Goldenberg G, Podreka I, Steiner M, Willmes K: Regional cerebral blood flow patterns in imagery tasks – results of single photon emission computer tomography. In Denis M, Engelkamp J, Richardson JTE (Editors), *Cognitive and Neuropsychological Approaches to Mental Imagery.* Dordrecht: Martinus Nijhoff, 1988.

Golla FL, Hutton EL, Gray Walter WG: The objective study of mental imagery. I. Physiological concomitants. *J. Mental Sci.: 75,* 216 – 223, 1943.

Greenberg MS, Farah MJ: The laterality of dreaming. *Brain Cognition: 5,* 307 – 321, 1986.

Greenwood P, Wilson DH, Gazzaniga MS: Dream report following commissurotomy. *Cortex; 13,* 311 – 316, 1977.

Grossi D, Orsini A, Modafferi A, Liotti M: Visual imaginal constructional apraxia: On a case of selective deficit of imagery. *Brain Cognition:* 1986.

Hadano K: On block design constructional disability in right and left hemisphere brain-damaged patients. *Cortex: 20,* 391 – 401, 1984.

Hayes JR: On the function of visual imagery in elementary mathematics. in Chase W (Editor), *Visual Information Processing.* New York: Academic Press, 1973.

Hebb DO: Concerning imagery. *Psychol. Rev.: 75,* 466 – 479, 1968.

Heidenhain A: Beltrag zur kenntnis der seelenblindheit. *Monatsschr. Psychiatr. Neurol.: 65* 61 – 116, 1927.

Heilman KM, Watson RT, Valenstein E: Neglect and related disorders. In Heilman KM, Valenstein E (Editors), *Clinical Neuropsychology,* 2nd Edn. New York: Oxford University Press, 1985.

Hinton GE, Parsons LM: Frames of reference and mental imagery. In Baddeley A, Long J (Editors), *Attention and Performance, IX.* Hillsdale, NJ: Lawrence Erlbaum Associates, 1981.

Hock HS, Kronseder C, Sissons SK: Hemispheric asymmetry: the effect of orientation on same different comparison. *Neuropsychologia: 19,* 723 – 727, 1981.

Hoppe KD: Split brains and psychoanalysis. *Psychoanal. Q.:*

46, 220 – 245, 1977.

Hume D: *A Treatise in Human Nature* (1739). Baltimore: Pelican Books, 1969.

Humphreys GW, Riddoch MJ: *To See but Not to See: A Case Study of Visual Agnosia.* Hillsdale, NJ: Erlbaum Associates, 1987.

Intons-Peterson MJ: Imagery paradigms: how vulnerable are they to experimenters' expectations? *J. Exp. Psychol. Hum. Percept. Performance: 9,* 394 – 412, 1983.

Jones B, Anuza T: Effects of sex, handedness, stimulus and visual field on mental rotation. *Cortex: 18,* 501 – 514, 1982.

Jossman P; Zur psychopathologie des optisch-agnostichen storungen. *Monatsschr. Psychiatr. Neurol.: 72,* 81 – 149, 1929.

Kim Y, Morrow L, Passahume D, Boller F: Visuoperceptual and visuomotor abilities and locus of lesion. *Neuropsychologia: 22,* 177 – 185, 1984.

Kosslyn SM: *Image and Mind.* Cambridge, MA: Harvard University Press, 1980.

Kosslyn SM: Seeing and imagining in the cerebral hemispheres: a computational approach. *Psychol. Rev.: 94,* 148 – 175, 1987.

Kosslyn SM: Aspects of a cognitive neuroscience of mental imagery. *Science: 240,* 1621 – 1626, 1988.

Kosslyn SM, Holtzman JD, Farah MJ, Gazzaniga MS: A computational analysis of mental image generation: evidence from functional dissociations in split-brain patients. *J. Exp. Psychol. Gen.: 114,* 311 – 341, 1985.

Lempert H: Effect of imaging sentences on concurrent unimanual performance. *Neuropsychologia: 25,* 835 – 839, 1987.

Levine DN, Warach J, Farah MJ: Two visual systems in mental imagery: dissociation of 'What' and 'Where' in imagery disorders due to bilateral posterior cerebral lesions. *Neurology: 35,* 1010 – 1018, 1985.

Lewandowsky M: Ueber abspaltung des farbensinnes. *Monatsschr. Psychiatr. Neurol.: 23,* 488 – 510, 1908.

Mazziotta JC, Phelps ME, Halgren E: Local cerebral glucose metabolic response to audiovisual stimulation and deprivation: studies in human subjects with positron CT. *Hum. Neurobiol.: 2,* 11 – 23, 1983.

McKim RH: *Experiences in Visual Thinking.* Monterey, CA: Brooks/Cole, 1980.

Meadows JC: The anatomical basis of prosopagnosia. *J. Neurol. Neurosurg. Psychiatry: 37,* 489 – 501, 1974.

Ornstein R, Johnstone J, Herron J, Swencionis C: Differential right hemisphere engagement in visuospatial tasks. *Neuropsychologia: 18,* 49 – 64, 1980.

Paivio A: *Imagery and Verbal Processes.* New York: Holt, Rinehart, and Winston, 1971.

Papanicolaou AC, Deutsch G, Bourbon WT, Will KW, Loring DW, Eisenberg HM: Convergent evoked potential and cerebral blood flow evidence of task specific hemispheric differences. *Electroencephalogr. Clin. Neuropsychol.: 66,* 515 – 520, 1987.

Pena-Casanova J, Roig-Rovira T, Bermudez A, Tolosa-Sarro E: Optic aphasia, optic apraxia, and loss of dreaming. *Brain Lang.: 26,* 63 – 71, 1985.

Peronnet F, Farah MJ: Mental rotation: an event-related poten-

tial study with a validated mental rotation task. *Brain Cognition: 9,* 279 – 288, 1989.

Piaget J, Inhelder B: *Mental Imagery in the Child.* New York: Basic Books, 1971.

Pick A: *Arbeiten aus der deutschen psychiatrischen Universitaetsklinik in Prag.* Berlin: Karger, 1908.

Posner MI, Walker JA, Friedrich FJ, Rafal RD: Effects of parietal lobe injury on covert orienting of visual attention. *J. Neurosci.: 4,* 1863 – 1874, 1984.

Pylyshyn ZW: What the mind's eye tells the mind's brain: a critique of mental imagery. *Psychol. Bull.: 80,* 1 – 24, 1973.

Pylyshyn ZW: *Computation and Cognition.* Cambridge, MA: MIT Press, 1984.

Ratcliff G: Spatial thought, mental rotation and the right cerebral hemisphere. *Neuropsychologia: 17,* 49 – 54, 1979.

Roland PE: Cortical regulation of selective attention in man. *J. Neurophysiol.: 48,* 1059 – 1078, 1982.

Roland PE, Friberg L: Localization of cortical areas activated by thinking. *J. Neurophys.: 53,* 1219 – 1243, 1985.

Roland PE, Skinhoj E: Focal activation of the cerebral cortex during visual discrimination in man. *Brain Res.: 222,* 166 – 171, 1981.

Royer F, Holland T: Rotations of visual designs in psychopathological groups. *J. Consult. Clin. Psychol.: 43,* 546 – 556, 1975.

Shepard RN: The mental image. *Am. Psychol.: 33,* 125 – 137, 1978.

Shepard, RN: Kinematics of perceiving, imagining, thinking, and dreaming. *Psychol. Rev.: 91,* 417 – 447, 1984.

Shepard RN, Hurwitz S: Upward direction, mental rotation and discrimination of left and right turns in maps. *Cognition: 18,* 161 – 193, 1984.

Shepard RN, Metzler J: Mental rotation of three-dimensional objects. *Science: 171,* 701 – 703, 1971.

Short PL: The objective study of mental imagery. *Br. J. Psychol.: 44,* 38 – 51. 1953.

Shuttleworth EC, Syring V, Allen N: Further observations on the nature of prosopagnosia. *Brain Cognition: 1,* 302 – 332, 1982.

Simion F, Bagnara S, Bisiacchi P, Roncato S, Umilta C: Laterality effects, levels of processing, and stimulus properties. *J. Exp. Psychol. Hum. Percept. Performance: 6,* 184 – 195, 1980.

Slatter KH: Alpha rhythm and mental imagery. *Electroencephalogr. Clin. Neurophysiol.: 12,* 851 – 859, 1960.

Stengel E: The syndrome of visual alexia with colour agnosia. *J. Mental Sci.: 94,* 46 – 58, 1948.

Stone MH: Dreams, free association, and the non-dominant hemisphere: an integration of psychoanalytic, neurophysiological, and historical data. *J. Am. Acad. Psychoanal.: 5,* 255 – 284, 1977.

Stuss DT, Sarazin FF, Leech EE, Picton TW: Event-related potentials during naming and mental rotation. *Electroencephalogr. Clin. Neurophysiol.: 56,* 133 – 146, 1983.

Symonds C, Mackenzie I: Bilateral loss of vision from cerebral infarction. *Brain: 80,* 28 – 448, 1957.

Ungerleider LG, Mishkin M: Two cortical visual systems. In Ingle DJ Goodale MA, Mansfield RJW (Editors), *Analysis of Visual Behavior.* Cambridge, MA: MIT Press, 1982.

Varney NR, Digre K: Color amnesia without aphasia. *Cortex: 19,* 551 – 555, 1983.

Weber RJ, Casleman J: The time it takes to imagine. *Percep. Psychophysics: 8,* 165 – 168, 1970.

Weber RJ, Malmstrom FV: Measuring the size of mental images. *J. Exp. Psychol. Hum. Percept. Performance: 5,* 1 – 12, 1979.

Willis SG, Wheatley GH, Mitchell OR: Cerebral processing of spatial and verbal-analytic tasks: an EEG study. *Neuropsychologia: 17,* 473 – 484, 1979.

Zurif E: Neurolinguistics: some analyses of aphasic language. In Gazzaniga MS (Editor), *Handbook of Cognitive Neuropsychology.* New York: Plenum, 1984.

CHAPTER 22

Astereopsis

Matthew Rizzo

Division of Behavioral Neurology and Cognitive Neuroscience, Department of Neurology, The University of Iowa College of Medicine, Iowa City, IA, U.S.A.

Introduction to the concept of stereopsis

Information on the depth of objects in the visual environment can be successfully derived from *monocular* cues such as linear perspective, texture gradients, apparent size of familiar objects, and monocular parallax producing successive images of the same object on disparate retinal areas. By contrast, stereopsis designates the powerful process for the recovery of depth which depends on *binocular* visual interaction. Two-dimensional projections of three-dimensional objects occupy slightly different positions on corresponding portions of the right and left retinas owing to the separation of the eyes in the head. This horizontal disparity is the crucial input needed for the generation of binocular depth information.

Stereopsis is important because it contributes to our ability to localize objects accurately in the visual environment. Primates and carnivores, which have eyes located in the frontal plane and overlapping monocular inputs, benefit from this evolutionary development at the expense of a reduced visual field. As a result of stereopsis humans and non-human primates also have improved accuracy of hand movements under visual guidance. Carnivores can more easily track their prey, including animals such as rabbits, cows and horses, which have laterally placed eyes and no stereopsis (but greater panoramic vision with which to detect predators).

The study of stereopsis and of its impairment, known as astereopsis, is important for research reasons. The process is relatively 'low-level' because the neural mechanisms for the binocular extraction of depth occur early in the cortical hierarchy of visuospatial functions. Also it is 'knowledge-free' in that it does not appear to depend on visual recognition in any formal sense, and does not need to be taught. Even though stereopsis depends on the analysis of multiple interacting spatial frequency channels, the process has yielded to a computational approach as readily as other visual processes such as color vision, which similarly appears to depend on complex computations in a cerebral network for the multiplexing of inputs from three opponent cone channels. The relatively low level of complexity for stereopsis in the hierarchy of visual cognition provides an opportunity to draw parallels between cybernetic and biological systems. An integrated understanding should derive from considerations of: (1) the pertinent physiology and psychophysical performance of the normal visual system in the achievement of binocularity; (2) the processing required in any visual system to encode the information from stereoscopic images and to extract the three-dimensional configuration and distance of objects; and (3) the residual performance in animal and human visual systems following lesions affecting different cerebral levels from retina to visual association cortex.

Psychophysics

Awareness of the cues of depth perception go back to early Renaissance thinking. In order to portray a representation of the three-dimensional worlds upon two-dimensional surfaces artists and anatomists of the age explored the techniques of perspective drawing described in the preliminary insights of the English Franciscan Roger Bacon (1214–1294?) and the Italian artist/architect Leone Battiste Alberti (1404–1472). Leonardo (1452–1519), who was also interested in perspective, realized that the artistic view was a reconstruction of a scene viewed through a single eye.

Binocular cues for depth perception were convincingly demonstrated by Wheatstone (1838). He used his stereoscope to show that two drawings representing the different perspectives of the right and left eyes could be combined to give the vivid sensation of objects in depth. This first presentation of stereograms was derived from the situation in natural viewing in which each eye receives a slightly different projection from the visual panorama because of the roughly 65 mm horizontal separation of the eyes, i.e., there is horizontal spatial disparity. The method ultimately found application in the development of stereotests (discussed later) and it also prompted the development of early psychophysical frameworks to explain the process.

Geometrical considerations of disparity and distance predominated initially and permitted the determination of the *horopter*, defined as that locus of points whose images fall on corresponding retinal elements, and thus are seen as single and localized in the same direction for a given position of the eyes (Reading, 1983). The horopter is conceptualized as a curved surface in object space passing through the focal point of the eyes. Its shape changes with target distance and also varies among different species. Moreover, stereoptic visual systems tolerate a small degree of retinal non-correspondence before fusion falls and diplopia is experienced. This is reflected in the existence of an envelope in visual space surrounding the horopter, described by Panum, within which binocular fusion occurs. Points close in front of and behind Panum's space (also called Panum's fusional area) produce incomplete fusion, resulting in 'coarse' stereopsis. Diplopia occurs beyond this space, because outlying points cast strikingly disparate retinal images carried through non-corresponding visual channels.

It is useful to consider further the geometry of physical relationships which contribute to the spatial disparity needed for stereoscopic inputs. Vertical disparity does not contribute to stereopsis, and a small amount is tolerated, although large vertical disparities must be corrected prior to stereopsis by vertical vergence eye movements. Horizontal disparity is the crucial input for stereopsis. The interpretation of depth by biological and artificial systems requires the assignment of both a direction and a magnitude to the horizontal disparity of the binocular image correspondence. The direction of the horizontal disparity present in visual images is either 'crossed' or 'uncrossed'. Objects closer than the horopter are said to have a crossed disparity and convergence is necessary to fixate them, i.e., you must cross your eyes. Convergence is relaxed (the eyes are uncrossed) to view objects beyond the horopter, which are said to have uncrossed disparity. By definition, points focused at the horopter stimulate corresponding retinal elements, have zero disparity, and give rise to equivalent sensations of relative depth. The magnitude of disparity, whether crossed or uncrossed, is determined by the amount of separation between the binocular images. Good stereoacuity is the ability to resolve small separations or fine horizontal binocular disparities and is generally taken as the measure of stereoptic performance. Astereopsis is assessed clinically through measurements of stereoacuity, and the defect is not known to favor crossed versus uncrossed disparities.

Spatial disparity is not the only disparity cue for stereopsis. Temporal disparity and interocular differences in brightness may also contribute

(Pulfrich, 1922; Julesz and White, 1969; Ross, 1973). For example, the actual straight path of a swinging pendulum appears to change in depth if a neutral-density filter is used to reduce the brightness of the image to one eye, and its movement then describes an ellipse instead. The same effect is noted in patients with unilateral optic neuritis (McDonald, 1986), in whom the signal strength is reduced in one eye, and in whom transmission time to the occipital cortex is presumably increased on the basis of prolonged visual evoked potentials measured through the affected nerve (Chiappa, 1983).

Hysteresis in a non-linearity present in some biological systems and is evident in the play of animal joints, in the threshold phenomena of neurons, and in stereopsis. In stereopsis hysteresis is evident because binocular fusion for images of a given disparity is preserved as the images are separated to a considerable degree. But once fusion is broken, the original disparity must be refused. This property, which must be considered in the modeling of stereopsis, has been accounted for by Julesz (1971) by positing 'cooperative' processes deriving global information from local processes. It has also been explained by Marr (1982) on the basis of a 'memory buffer' and a '2½ D sketch'.

Theoretical accounts of stereopsis

Fusion and rivalry

Theories of stereopsis have emphasized the fusion of information from the two monocular views. The notion of a coarse type of fusion dates back to Galen. Kepler's (1571 – 1630) more modern projection theory postulated stimuli located in space at the crossings of 'mental rays' from the eyes. Contemporary interpretations have emphasized the projection of light upon corresponding retinal elements which localize that point in the same visual direction for both eyes. However, fusion theory provides an incomplete account of stereopsis because it does not incorporate the important observation that we normally fail to register con-

flicting portions of monocular projections of stereoscopic targets under direct scrutiny. This critical interaction related to binocular single vision falls under the rubric of *binocular rivalry* or *suppression,* is less understood than binocular fusion, involves different processes (Fox and Check, 1968), and is important to account for in theories of stereopsis.

When stimuli are rivalrous, one or the other may predominate in alternating fashion. The 'losing' image is said to be suppressed. Because of normal binocular suppression we are usually not aware of the discordant view of the two eyes which occurs in normal viewing when we fixate a near object. In that case, far objects are cast on disparate retinal areas. Fixating a finger at 12 inches one realizes with introspection and without refixation that single points on a distant wall are seen as double. However, in normal viewing, central processes automatically suppress the second image, usually in the non-dominant eye, averting diplopia. It is interesting to consider that covert suppression of conflicting dichotic stimuli resembles the suppression of auditory signals in dichotic listening tasks and may reflect attention-related operations. Binocular suppression might depend upon inhibitory inputs which should gate the low-level flow of visual information, possibly by neuronal feedback operations generated beyond single cortical columns in visual area V_1, whose action would thereby facilitate a more optimal conscious visual experience which is unitary. A precedent for such low-level contributions to visual attention is apparent in studies in the monkey which show changes in the firing of single neurons in prestriate but not striate cortex with changes of attention but steady fixation (Moran and Desimone, 1985; Spitzer et al., 1988).

Binocular rivalry has been documented for color, spatial frequency, motion direction and stimulus orientation (Reading, 1983). For example, when conflicting gratings or line segments differing because of orthogonality are presented to each eye, alternating gaps are seen instead of complete crossings at points of intersection. However, if the conflicting stimuli subtend only about 1.5 degrees at the fovea, the view of one eye or the other will predominate and rivalry will not occur (i.e., the image in the other eye is fully suppressed). This 1.5 degree angle is larger than would be accounted for by a single column and suggests involvement at least at the level of several orientation and ocular dominance hypercolumns. Such interactions could occur in human cytoarchitectonic area 17 (V_1) or beyond, consistent with our speculations on feedback processes above. Finally, binocular rivalry and fusion can even occur together. For example, where stereoscopic stimuli consisting of identical high spatial frequencies but conflicting low spatial frequency information are presented, the high spatial frequencies are fused and the low frequencies are seen as rivalrous (Julesz, 1971).

Neuronal basis

In the first half of the 19th century Johannes Muller suggested the possibility that neural connections from the two eyes might meet in common cells in the brain. It is now known that the inputs from each eye remain physically and functionally segregated in the six layers of the lateral geniculate body. The first opportunity for mixing comes in the striate cortex, beyond layer IV of cytoarchitectonic area 17. There, Hubel and Weisel (1968) found individual cells that responded to light in either eye. A further level of organization was identified through the discovery of ocular dominance columns consisting of vertically oriented aggregates of binocular cells which respond best to a stimulus in one eye. Direct evidence for binocular neurons which are tuned to binocular image disparity has also been obtained.

An important attempt to bridge the gulf from single cell microelectrode recordings in primates to psychophysical responses in animal and human subjects has come from studies which have identified neurons that appear to account for the processing of crossed and uncrossed disparity (Poggio and Fischer, 1977; Poggio and Talbot, 1981). One class represented by two neuronal types responds

within a selective disparity range by either excitation or inhibition of firing. Another class, also consisting of two neuronal types, has responses that correlate with the type of disparity; one type responds to objects closer than fixation and is inhibited by objects beyond, while the other type does the reverse. These properties seem sufficient to encode the crossed and uncrossed disparity present on either side of the horopter. Astereopsis might be expected to result from maldevelopment or disruption in the processing of such neurons as the result of acquired cerebral lesions.

Binocular cells are relatively ubiquitous in the primate visual system and appear to function in a distributed network. They are found not only in primary visual cortex in the region known as V_1, where they are organized into ocular dominance columns, perpendicular to the cortical surface, but also occur beyond in visual association cortical areas. Binocular neurons related to stereopsis come from the magnocellular projections of the lateral geniculate body, and belong to a system which includes cytochrome oxidase staining thick stripes, and are distributed in monkey visual association cortex in regions designated by V_2, V_3, V_4 and MT (Livingstone and Hubel, 1987; De Yoe and Van Essen, 1988). The presence of binocular cells in these regions, which also function in networks for the extraction of other basic properties of vision, e.g., spatial contrast sensitivity, form, texture and motion, provides a basis for the interaction of these properties with stereopsis. For example, a consideration of binocular cells reveals that they may be sensitive to motion. This is related to the observation that many cells in area MT, the putative motion center in primates, are binocular. These findings are compatible with the well-known close psychophysical link of stereopsis to motion in depth, and may also help explain why subjects with impaired stereopsis due to central lesions can have a symptom complex in which perceptual complaints are exacerbated by visual motion (Zihl et al., 1983).

Binocular cells also exist which respond to color. This is likely to form the basis of binocular color mixing when for example red presented to one eye, and green simultaneously to the other can give the sensation of yellow. Yet a cerebral system for color is relatively separate from a system for stereopsis. A color-dedicated system defined by Livingstone and Hubel includes parvocellular projections which proceed through a relatively ventral system located in V_1, V_2, V_3 and V_4. The magnocellular geniculate projections associated with stereopsis proceed dorsally through V_1, V_2 and V_3, have little if any projection to V_4, and project toward MT, which then directs outputs to the parieto-occipital region of monkey (Desimone et al., 1985). Binocular cells in the magnocellular stream serving stereopsis and motion are said to be 'color-blind' (De Yoe and Van Essen, 1988). Psychophysical findings also favor a relative separation of color and stereo processing. Lu and Fender (1972) reported that equiluminant heterochromatic random-dot stereograms did not give the sensation of depth, suggesting that hue contrast was not an adequate input for stereopsis. Yet consider the impression of depth conveyed at the movies by vivid colored credits set against a contrasting background, all at the same distance from the observer. This phenomenon, known as chromostereopsis, might be due to chromatic aberration through the ocular medium causing different displacements of the hue wavelengths on the two retinae causing differing disparities and differences in apparent depth. It might also be related to differences in the receptive field sizes for different-wavelength photoreceptors (Pennington, 1970). Nevertheless, the contribution of chromostereopsis is trivial except in special circumstances, and Livingstone and Hubel (1987) have concluded that color is not an important cue for stereopsis. This is consistent with our own findings that subjects with central achromatopsia can have preservation of stereopsis, while subjects with impaired stereopsis due to cerebral lesions maintain normal color vision.

Computational models
The most current theoretical approach to stereopsis goes beyond psychophysical theories of fusion and rivalry which are firmly rooted in biological observations. Marr (1982) and his collaborators explored the underlying information-processing problems of stereopsis through the implementation of a computational approach summarized below. First they defined the information-encoding tasks necessary for the representation of interacting binocular stimuli. Next they defined the processes (i.e., algorithms) which operate upon the inputs represented in the first steps, to reconstruct the depth of an object.

The fundamental problems faced by any visual system in order to achieve stereopsis are to select a location in a monocular image, to identify the same location in the other image, and to measure the disparity between those loci. The identification of corresponding points must overcome the possibility of matching 'false targets', i.e., non-corresponding points should not be matched. Possible solutions come from a consideration of the geometrical constraints of real surfaces in the physical world. Specifically: (1) a given point on a three-dimensional surface has a unique position in space at any given time and thus has a single disparity value (the 'uniqueness' constraint); (2) matter is cohesive and is separated into objects whose irregularities are small relative to the object distance; disparity thus varies continuously except for the large jumps which occur at object borders (the 'continuity' constraint); (3) the final constraint of matching is a physical consideration not related to the planar geometry of surfaces, but related to considerations of local pattern elements (the 'compatibility' constraint); it states that two descriptive elements can match if, and only if, they could have arisen from the same marking, e.g., in a random-dot stereogram, black dots can match only black dots.

From these rules obtained from consideration of physical object properties, a visual system can set about to match the monocularly available primitive features which comprise the images. Those elementary pattern features include blobs, terminations and discontinuities, from which an early visual representation of their organization known as a 'primal sketch' can be derived. Several theories of stereopsis have specified the use of zero-order crossings (relatives of edges generated from the second derivative of a low-pass-filtered intensity array from the monocular image), as the matching primitive from which a primal sketch is derived. Both the primitive features and the primal sketch are important inputs to subsequent operations. Interestingly, gray levels, which are the most elementary type of features, are not sufficient to serve as the matching primitives for stereopsis. Textons, Julesz's (1984) 'atoms' of pattern perception, are probably sufficient but may not be necessary to serve as matching primitive pattern features, and whether 'disparity textons' exist or not is unclear (De Yoe and Van Essen, 1988).

Once the matching constraints for stereopsis have been implemented and the matching primitives have been defined, stereopsis can proceed. Marr's fundamental assumption for stereopsis states that if a correspondence between stereopsis-derived primitives satisfies with sufficient detail matching constraints for objects in the physical world, then that match is geometrically correct and unique. Disparity and depth information can then be obtained. The same considerations which act as matching constraints for real images also constrain the processing for artificial psychophysical stimuli such as random-dot stereograms, which supposedly give only position information (Julesz, 1964).

Marr and Poggio (1976) developed successive algorithms for the processing of stereo information which culminated in successful machine programs for the solving of radom-dot stereograms. A generalization of their algorithm which considers compatibility, uniqueness and continuity constraints allows a similar approach to the processing of real images. Natural images can be made to resemble random stereograms by convolving them with a center-surround filter and taking the sign of the resultant values. The primitives so obtained are satisfactory inputs for stereo-algorithms which can be used to extract disparities (Poggio and Poggio,

1984). However, a successful computational model of stereopsis which achieves the processing of random stereograms does not necessarily implement the same processes used by human vision. Early computational models were based on 'cooperative' algorithms which derived global order from local operations. However, the performance of such cooperative models did not match the characteristics of the human counterpart.

Cooperative models were thought necessary to explain the properties of hysteresis and 'filling-in' in stereopsis (Fender and Julesz, 1967). The problem, however, can be approached differently by postulating the existence of a memory buffer to store the information in global matches. The second model of Marr and Poggio (1979) takes into account the existence of parallel channels matching disparity information at different spatial frequencies. These channels might correspond to monocular inputs from receptive fields of different sizes. The general idea is to match widely separated spatial features and to repeat the process over and over to achieve higher resolution. The features matched are zero-order crossings of the same sign. Vergence eye movements are brought into play, since they are driven by low spatial frequency global information to bring the image disparities closer to the range of the high spatial frequency analysers. The high-frequency analysers can then match compatible local details. All the matches are stored in an intermediate step in a memory buffer to form the '2½-dimensional sketch'. Mahew and Frisby (1981) and Baker and Binford (1981) added further constraints to the Marr-Poggio (1979) model in order to solve correspondence problems encountered for random-dot stereograms which take into account a cross-correspondence between spatial channels, figural continuity and edge continuity (Poggio and Poggio, 1984).

Astereopsis

Developmental aspects

Impairment of stereopsis can occur early in development (Kaye et al., (1981) or may be acquired in adulthood due to neurological disease. The level of impairment can be trivial from an information-processing standpoint, e.g., the mechanical limitation of fusional mechanisms in one eye due to paralysis of the III, IV or VI cranial nerves, causing the inability to achieve retinal correspondence in the face of intact sensory mechanisms. By contrast, the impairment may occur, even though the eyes have always been perfectly aligned, in adults from disruption at a high level of processing due to acquired cortical lesions (Holmes and Horrax, 1919) which should disrupt binocular neurons and their operations.

Several studies have examined the results of monocular pattern deprivation or experimentally induced strabismus in animals. In general the results have shown severe loss of binocular neurons and binocular functions such as stereopsis and binocular summation. Associated anatomical changes may result in the retina, lateral geniculate and layer IV of striate cortex involving both parvocellular and magnocellular projections. The results point to the existence of crucial periods in postnatal development of stereopsis (Hubel and Weisel, 1970; Boothe et al., 1985). Human stereopsis is evident at about 2 months of age (Bechtoldt and Hutz, 1980), and may correspond to the segregation of ocular dominance columns in layer IVc of area 17 (Held, 1984). The definition of critical periods for stereoptic ability drawn from human and animal experiments suggests relative 'windows' for corrective surgery. Children allowed to 'squint' too long may never have normal stereovision. It has been estimated that a few percent of the general population (5 – 10%) actually are stereoblind (Richards, 1970), i.e., they have astereopsis. This is often associated with uncorrected childhood strabismus or monocular deprivation comparable to animal experiments in which the developing cortex is not exposed to matching binocular disparity information during a crucial period of development.

When strabismus is long-standing and severe, a permanent abnormality in the acuity, but not of the eye itself (amblyopia), may be associated. This is presumably the result of chronic brain suppression of diplopic or rivalrous images at a critical phase causing an irreversible change (a failure of selection or maturation) in occipital neurons which process information from the amblyopic eye. Spatial contrast sensitivity may be severely reduced in an amblyopic compared to the preferred eye. However, experiments show that the eyes still behave similarly with regard to the elevation and depression of detection thresholds of a spatial grating after the presentation of masking stimuli. Those results suggest that stereoblindness in amblyopic subjects is not the result of discordant spatial frequency analysis between the two eyes. Affected individuals also may never complain of diplopia. Psychophysical evidence in stereoblind subjects demonstrates the preservation of eye-of-origin information (ultrocular discrimination) and this suggests the presence of monocular visual cortex only (Blake and Cormack, 1979).

When the strabismus is less severe, a 'microtropia' may result in which individuals fixate with the fovea of one eye and with a slightly non-corresponding region of the other retina. There are also 'monofixators' (Parks, 1969) who are inclined to look with one eye and are aware of the image in just one eye as the result of temporary cerebral suppression (but not blindness) of the information from the non-preferred eye. In this condition coarse stereopsis, indicated by the ability to fuse only large-disparity stimuli, is present. Items such as the fly on the Titmus test (3000 seconds of arc) are seen in depth, but simultaneous binocular rivalry may also result.

Impaired stereopsis may also be caused by strabismus acquired in adulthood. The condition is different from astereopsis due to developmental deprivation. Because binocular visual cortex is well established in adults, acquired strabismus precludes pointing the eyes in the appropriate direction, thus causing diplopia and binocular rivalry but not amblyopia. Correction of the ocular palsy through surgery or prisms may restore stereopsis.

Stereopsis may also be impaired in the absence of strabismus as a result of damage in visual cortices.

Such damage is most often caused by strokes (due to watershed infarctions or cerebral emboli) or by tumors, head injury or neurosurgical ablations. This latter form of astereopsis has been incompletely characterized and is discussed below.

Assessing astereopsis

1. Measurement of stereoacuity Stereoacuity is generally taken as the clinical index of stereoscopic performance (Fagin and Griffin, 1982). Stereoacuity is the measure of the visual ability to resolve a fine binocular disparity. Like fine visual (vernier) acuity in which a monocular cue such as a tiny displacement or separation in a line segment is detected, it is a powerful ability in which spatial separations in an image less than the distance between retinal cones can sometimes contribute (Julesz and Spivack, 1967). Subjects with poor stereopsis have low stereoacuity. It is important to realize, however, that the best stereoacuity for an individual varies between clinical tests. A lower stereoacuity score on one test compared to the previous performance on another is not necessarily an indication of newly impaired stereopsis.

According to Marr (1982), stereoacuity occurs late in stereoptic processing and is related to the ability to reconstruct accurately the information in convolved images. Earlier mechanisms which contribute to stereopsis and which rely on the detection of local brightness contrast, and the detection of local primitive elements remain intact. This fits well with the clinical observation that stereoacuity may be impaired in the face of relatively normal visual acuity and spatial contrast sensitivity abilities which require only the monocular identification, and localization of primitive features.

2. Stereotests Clinical tests used to diagnose stereopsis differ in the presence or absence of monocular cues and the techniques used to channel separate images into each eye. For example, each Keystone test stereopair member consists of 12 separate lines of monocularly discriminable forms. One form on each line is seen away from the plane of the others as a result of the disparity present.

The test, commonly administered in a stereoscope, gives a measure of stereoacuity determined by the line of least disparity that can be accurately read. More modern stereotests also measure stereoacuity, but they assume that the presence of monocular cues taints the assessment of stereopsis and therefore attempt to reduce superfluous cues in two ways: (1) they rely on the use of random stereograms without form (Julesz, 1971); or (2) they utilize monocularly visible form cues, but obscure the monocular contours with a background of visual 'noise' so that the target item cannot be discriminated by the naive observer in the absence of stereoscopic vision.

Many current stereotests depend on the use of hand-held cards presented at arms length (40 cm) which are specially printed in two colors or as polarized images (Reading, 1983). Anaglyphs depend on the use of red and green ink to print on the same card stereopairs which are slightly out of register by a given horizontal disparity. When viewed with spectacles composed of one red and one green lens the red lens passes the red image and the green lens the green image. The major manufacturing problems include the proper choice of inks and color filters (lenses). The vectographic technique is similar to the anaglyphic technique. Instead of different colors, it relies on superimposed but horizontally offset stimuli which reflect polarized light in orthogonal directions. The viewer wears spectacles with corresponding polarized lenses which then transmit a different image to each eye.

Orthoptists ('ortho' is Greek for straight; an 'optist' treats the eyes), who rely on commercially available stereotests for the accurate measurement of stereoacuity as an indication of stereoptic ability in patients with non-aligned eyes, have emphasized that stereoacuity depends on the particular stereotest and how it is administered (Brown and Morris, 1980; Fagin and Griffin, 1982; Patterson and Fox, 1984). Tests containing monocularly available stereocues such as the Titmus Test (Titmus Optical Co., Petersburg, VA) tend to yield higher stereoacuities; in fact the first three circles on the test are easily distinguished because they look 'different' even without the polarized spectacles. The TNO test (Alfred P. Poll Co., New York) is an anaglyph printed at relatively low contrast, and we suspect it is this feature which regularly depresses stereoacuity on this test relative to others. No matter what the test is, rivalrous appearance may provide sufficient cues for a correct response in a forced-choice test, even if there is never any fusion leading to a true appreciation of binocular depth.

3. The random-dot stereogram Before 1960, one of the greatest debates in stereopsis was to determine which cues were necessary and sufficient to produce stereopsis. Previously, stereoscopic images depended on the presence of contours, edges and intersections, as in the line drawings of Wheatstone, and in stimuli developed by taking photographs from two different camera angles. Holway and Boring (1941) showed that the progressive elimination of such monocularly recognizable cues affected the perception of depth. But the demonstration of stereopsis independent of consciously discriminable monocular cues awaited Julez's (1960, 1964) development of new psychophysical stimuli devised to eliminate those features (although, as previously mentioned, the computational derivatives used to solve them do yield zero-order crossings which are relatives of edges). Random-dot stereograms are otherwise devoid of all depth and familiarity cues except spatial disparity. The stereograms consist of a computer-generated array of local pictorial elements made of black dots. They differ in that a group of these black dots in a geometric form have been shifted by a precise amount with respect to the identical random sequence in the other member of the stereopair. When viewed stereoscopically, the geometric form is seen above or below the plane of the random background (depending on whether the disparity is crossed or uncrossed).

Julesz used his stumili to show that stereopsis was not necessarily a 'top-down' process which proceeds from the general to the specific. The determination of the 3-D configuration of a chair, for example, does not require the recognition of the monocular view from each eye with subsequent decomposition and matching of the spatial disparities of local component features. Rather, the process can be envisaged as a 'bottom-up' process proceeding from the analysis of local image elements. Whether or not the chair is recognized, its 3-D spatial configuration and distance can be appreciated. Julesz was also able to determine the level as 'retinal or cerebral' of several classical visual phenomena and illusions based on their persistence when presented in his paradigm (Julesz, 1971). Effects such as the Muller-Lyer illusion, formerly attributed to retinal processes but still appreciated in random-dot stereogram form, were now assumed to represent cortical processing which occurs at some stage beyond layer IV of area 17, where the first cortical binocular interactions are demonstrated.

The random-dot stereogram also facilitated enquiries into how binocular image matching occurs. It became apparent that the proper direction and magnitude of features did not ensure their matching even if they were points in Panum's fusional area. Experiments with filtering and masking showed that for two members of a stereopair to be fused, they have to share overlapping spatial frequencies (Frisby and Mayhew, 1976). Random-dot stereogram pair members which were low-pass and high-pass-filtered possessing no frequencies in common may be seen as rivalrous. Also, the addition of masking noise near the spatial frequencies of the RDS inhibited their fusion (Julesz and Miller, 1975). The implications are that spatial frequency analysis precedes stereopsis, and that spatial frequency selectivity, modulation transfer functions and signal-to-noise ratios are important to stereopsis (Caelli, 1981).

4. Evoked potentials In principle, the occurrence of a binocular spatial disparity in a stimulus can be time-locked to a signal-averaging device (Neill et al., 1982). The evoked potential so obtained is not the result of monocular pattern processing, but of the periodically presented binocular disparity. The electrical peaks recorded presumably reflect the activity of binocular neurons in the visual cortex and might offer the possibility of making comparisons between the behavior of single binocular neurons in animals and of binocular neuron populations in humans. Binocular rivalry associated with the presentation of conflicting spatial gratings may cause changes in the amplitude and latency of visual evoked potentials that correlate with suppression during rivalry (Cobb et al., 1967; Lawwill and Biersdorf, 1968). Evoked potential techniques, however, have not been thoroughly explored, and application to measuring human disorders of stereopsis has not progressed.

Possible mechanisms and anatomical correlates of astereopsis

In 1919 Gordon Holmes and Gilbert Horrax described the case of a soldier who suffered a gunshot wound to the head which resulted in a bilateral loss of all vision in the inferior visual fields. The lesion, which probably affected the superior visual and visual association cortices, was accompanied by a complex visual syndrome which impaired visuospatial ability. The man reported 'I cannot tell the depth of anything'. He had no evidence of dysconjugate eye position to account for this difficulty. In addition, 'drawings and photographs, which when fixed in a stereoscope appeared as tridimensional figures to normal persons, as a rule seemed to him flat when viewed in this instrument.'

Since the report of Holmes and Horrax neuropsychological studies of stereopsis have generally concentrated on a hemispheric dominance effect for the processing of stereoscopic stimuli. Carmon and Bechtoldt (1969) and Benton and Hécaen (1970) postulated that the right hemisphere was dominant. Brain-damaged subjects were asked to localize random-letter stereograms to one quadrant of a background field. Response time was prolonged in patients with damage to the right hemisphere. Unfortunately the documentation of the lesions was less than ideal because modern neuroimaging techniques such as CT and MR were

not available to assist in localization. Type, size and age of lesion were not considered. Support for the hypothesis that stereopsis could be related to right hemispheric processing also came from studies of normal individuals, in which random stereograms were presented tachistoscopically and left hemifield proved functionally superior (Durnford and Kimure, 1970; Grabowska, 1983). On the other hand, Julesz et al. (1976) found remarkably different results in normal subjects as the left and right visual fields showed equivalent stereoptic ability. Their results show that the left and right hemispheres are equally capable of stereoptic processing, assuming equal visuospatial processing by the left and right hemiretinea. However, Julesz and associates did find a difference in the upper and lower fields which was eliminated with the introduction of monocular cues. Interestingly, Gazzaniga et al. (1965) found that stereopsis was preserved after complete callosal lesions unless the chiasm was also split. This suggested little interhemispheric transfer of information regarding stereopsis, and indicated the existence of bihemispheric stereoptic ability. However, Mitchell and Blakemore (1970) found conflicting results which did suggest callosal transfer in stereopsis.

We conducted a study of the stereoptic ability in 38 subjects with verified unilateral or bilateral focal cerebral lesions (Rizzo and Damasio, 1985). The locus of the lesions was determined by CT or MR following a standard anatomical charting protocol (Damasio, H., 1983 and Chapter 1 of this volume) with the investigator blinded to clinical and experimental data. Associated deficits included visual field defects for form and luminance, with left-sided lesion disturbance of language, and with right hemispheric lesion hemineglect. Four patients had bilateral lesions of the inferior visual association cortex associated with prosopagnosia and disturbed color vision in part or all of the fields. Four others had bilateral lesions of the superior visual system. Strict criteria were used to exclude patients with strabismus and poor or nonequivalent acuity between the eyes.

Compared with normal controls, stereoacuity in

the patients was reduced by lesions of either the left or the right visual cortices. However, a unilateral lesion was never sufficient to abolish stereopsis, and we encountered several subjects with unilateral lesions in the right or left hemispheres and normal stereopsis. The highest degree of stereoptic impairment was seen when damage was bilateral and lesions were located in superior as opposed to the inferior visual cortex. Prosopagnosia and achromatopsia due to bilateral inferior lesions were associated with normal stereoacuity. Our most severely affected patients had bilateral lesions of the superior visual association cortex, above the calcarine fissures, and were reminiscent of the soldier reported by Holmes and Horrax (1919). They all suffered from complex visuospatial disturbances associated with an impairment of stereoacuity. Color vision and recognition of objects and faces were normal. The findings suggest that in humans the early operations for stereopsis occur throughout the striate cortices of both hemispheres. However, beyond that region processes are skewed toward the superior visual association cortices. A battery of neuropsychological tests revealed that none of our astereoptic subjects was demented, providing no support for the hypothesis of Lehmann and Walchli (1975) that astereopsis is caused by generalized cognitive impairment and not by localizable brain lesions.

We suggest that the impairment of stereoacuity associated with lesions of the superior visual association cortices occurs at a level of stereoptic processing beyong that which identifies local primitive elements. Interpreted in the computational framework provided by Marr (1982), the level of the superior visual association cortices is relatively specialized for stereopsis in terms of a macroscopic cortical locus involved in the computation of binocular disparities from earlier inputs, and in the operation of a memory buffer for iterative computations and storage of a 2½-D sketch. The early matching primitive features and probably the related primal sketch have already been extracted at the level of the striate cortex.

Visual acuity and spatial contrast sensitivity, which depend on the accurate localization of monocular primitives, may thus be spared by those lesions which cause reduced stereoacuity. An exception appears to occur when the lesions compromise the foveal representation in the mesial occipital lobe in the depths of the calcarine fissure, or its projections to later stages. In that case, the inputs which give the highest resolution of monocular primitives for extraction of a primal sketch are not available to operations in the superior association cortex, and stereoacuity is reduced.

The pattern of impairments which result from bilateral superior lesions leads to an association with visual disorientation (a disorder of visuospatial attention (Rizzo and Hurtig, 1987)) and in some patients with more anterior lesions to defective hand movements under visual guidance, and optic ataxia (Damasio, 1985).

Patients with impaired stereopsis and visual disorientation may have a defect in the perception of motion, as reported by Zihl et al. (1983). This is possibly due to damage in a putative human homologue of area MT. The motion defect might be worse for targets moving in depth.

It is unlikely that the concurrent impairment of stereopsis, motion vision and visuospatial attention following bilateral lesions of the superior visual system is accidental. The observation fits well with other available neurophysiological data. Using positron emission tomography, Fox et al. (1987) have provided evidence to suggest that the superior visual system, active in stereopsis, is important in tasks of visual attention. Moreover, stereopsis and motion vision both depend on magnocellular inputs that project dorsally via MT (Livingstone and Hubel, 1987; De Yoe and Van Essen, 1988) toward the occipitoparietal region of the monkey's brain which is probably homologous to the human superior visual association cortices.

It is noteworthy that bilateral damage in the superior visual association cortex in the parieto-occipital junction which impairs stereopsis may be associated with abnormal smooth pursuit eye movements (Leigh and Tusa, 1985). This could be the result of an impairment of the motor generators in pursuit-dedicated cortices, or of an impairment in the cerebral processing of a retinal error signal, or of a defect in motion detection. We do not believe that poor stereopsis affects smooth pursuit itself and have measured normal pursuit gain in astereoptic patients. However, we would not be surprised to find that impairments of stereopsis are associated with abnormal vergence eye movements which resemble pursuit in having low velocities. Vergence eye movements are used during the fusion of random stereograms, presumably to bring retinal elements into register. We have no evidence to suggest that abnormal vergence eye movements are caused by astereopsis, nor can we state that impaired stereopsis is a necessary consequence of abnormal vergence because those patients should still fuse in the distance. So far none of our patients with impaired stereopsis caused by cerebral lesions has shown an impairment of vergence eye movements.

Acknowledgement

This work was supported by NIH Program Project Grant PO NS 19632.

References

Baker H, Binford T: Depth from edge and intensity based stereo. *Proc. 7th Intern. Conf. AI,* Vancouver, B.C. pp. 631 – 636, 1981.

Bechtoldt HP, Hutz CS: De development of binocular discrimination in infants. *Bull. Psychomonic Soc.: 16,* 83 – 86, 1980.

Benton AL, Hécaen H: Stereoscopic vision in patients with unilateral cerebral disease. *Neurology: 20,* 1084 – 1088, 1970.

Blake R, Cormack R: Psychophysical evidence for monocular visual cortex in stereoblind humans. *Science: 203,* 274 – 275, 1979.

Boothe RG, Dobson V, Teller DY: Postnatal development of vision in human and nonhuman primates. *Annu. Rev. Neurosci.: 8,* 495 – 545, 1985.

Brown MH, Morris JE: Comparative analysis of current stereotests. *Am. J. Orthoptics: 30,* 93 – 96, 1980.

Caelli T: Specific issues in vision: stereopsis. In *Visual Perception: Theory and Practice.* Oxford; Pergamon Press, pp: 186 – 187, 1981.

Carmon A, Bechtoldt HP: Dominance of the right cerebral hemisphere for stereopsis. *Neuropsychologia: 7,* 23 – 39, 1969.

Chiappa K: Pattern shift visual evoked potentials: interpretation. In: *Evoked Potentials in Clinical Medicine.* New York: Raven Press, pp. 63 – 104, 1983.

Cobb WA, Morton HB, Ettlinger G: Cerebral potentials evoked by pattern reversal and their suppression in visual rivalry. *Nature: 216,* 1123 – 1125, 1967.

Damasio AR: Disorders of complex visual processing. In Mesulam M-M (Editor), *Principles of Behavioral Neurology. Contemporary Neurology Series.* Philadelphia: F.A. Davis, pp. 275 – 289, 1985.

Damasio H: A CT guide to the identification of cerebral vascular territories. *Arch. Neurol. (Chicago): 40,* 138 – 142, 1983.

De Yoe EA, Van Essen DC; Concurrent processing streams in monkey visual cortex. *Trends Neurosci.: 11,* 219 – 226, 1988.

Durnford M, Kimura D: Right hemisphere specialization for depth perception reflected in visual field differences. *Nature: 231,* 394 – 395, 1971.

Fagin FR, Griffin JR: Stereoacuity tests: comparison of mathematical equivalents. *Am. J. Optometry: 5* 427 – 435, 1982.

Fender D, Julesz B: Extension of Panum's fusional area in binocularly stabilized vision. *J. Opt. Soc. Am.: 57,* 819 – 830. 1967.

Fox P, Petersen, S, Miezin S, Raichle M, Allman J: Superior parietal cortical activation during visual and oculomotor tasks measured with averaged PET images. *Invest. Ophthalmol. Visual Sci.:* Suppl. 28, 315, 1987.

Fox R, Check R: Detection of motion during binocular suppression. *J. Exp. Psychol.: 78* 388 – 395, 1968.

Frisby JP, Mayhew JEW: Rivalrous texture stereograms. *Nature: 264,* 53 – 56, 1976.

Gazzaniga MS, Bogen JE, Sperry RW: Observations on visual perception after disconnexion of the cerebral hemispheres in man. *Brain: 88,* 221 – 236, 1965.

Grabowska A: Lateral difference in the detection of stereoscopic depth. *Neuropsychologia: 3,* 249 – 257, 1983.

Held R: Binocular vision: behavioral and neuronal development. In Mehler J, (Fox RR (Editors), *Neonate Cognition: Beyond the Blooming, Buzzing Confusion.* Hillsdale, NJ; Erlbaum, 1984.

Holmes G, Horrax G: Disturbances of spatial orientation and visual attention with loss of stereoscopic vision. *Arch. Neurol. Psychiatry: 1,* 385 – 404, 1919.

Holway AF, Boring EG: Determinants of apparent visual size with distance variant. *Am. J. Psychol.: 54,* 21 – 37, 1943.

Hubel DH, Weisel TN: Receptive fields and functional architecture of monkey striate cortex. *J. Physiol.: 195,* 215 – 243, 1968.

Hubel DH, Weisel TN: The period of susceptibility to the physiological effects of unilateral eye closure in kittens. *J. Physiol.: 206,* 419 – 436, 1970.

Julesz B: Binocular depth perception of computer generated patterns. *Bell System Tech. J.: 37,* 1125 – 62, 1960.

Julesz B: Binocular depth perception without familiarity cues. *Science; 145,* 356 – 362, 1964.

Julesz B: *Foundations of Cyclopean Perception.* Chicago: University of Chicago Press, 1971.

Julesz B: A brief outline of the texton theory of human vision. *Trends Neurosci.: 9,* 41 – 45, 1984.

Julesz B, Miller JE: Independent spatial frequency tuned channels in binocular fusion and rivalry perception. *Perception: 4,* 125 – 143, 1975.

Julesz B, Spivack GJ: Stereopsis based on vernier acuity clues alone. *Science; 157,* 563 – 565, 1967.

Julesz B, White B: Short term visual memory and Pulfrich phenomenon. *Nature; 222,* 639 – 641, 1969.

Julesz B, Breitmeyer B, Kropfl W: Binocular disparity dependent upper lower hemifield anisotropy and left right hemifield isotropy as revealed by dynamic random dot stereograms. *Perception: 5,* 128 – 141, 1976.

Kaye M, Mitchell DE, Cynader M: Depth perception, eye alignment and cortical ocular dominance of dark reared cats. *Dev. Brain Res.: 2,* 37 – 53, 1982.

Lawwill T, Biersdorf WS: Binocular rivalry and visual evoked responses. *Invest. Opthalmol.: 7,* 378 – 385, 1968.

Lehman D, Walchli: Depth perception and location of brain lesions. *J. Neurol.: 209,* 157 – 164, 1975.

Leigh J, Tusa R: Disturbances of smooth pursuit caused by infarction of occipitoparietal cortex. *Ann. Neurol.: 17,* 185 – 187, 1985.

Livingstone MS, Hubel DH: Psychophysical evidence for separate channels for the perception of form, color, movement and depth. *J. Neurosci.: 7,* 3416 – 3468, 1987.

Lu C, Fender DH: The interaction of color and luminance in stereoptic vision. *Invest. Ophthalmol.: 11,* 487 – 490, 1972.

Marr D: *Vision.* New York: WH Freeman, 1982.

Marr D, Poggio T: Cooperative computation of stereo disparity. *Science: 194,* 283 – 287, 1976.

Marr D, Poggio T: A computational theory of human stereo vision. *Proc. R. Soc. Lond. Ser. B: 204,* 301 – 328, 1979.

Mayhew JEW, Frisby JP; Psychophysical and computational studies toward a theory of human stereopsis. *Artif. Intell.: 16,* 345 – 385, 1981.

McDonald IW: Diseases of the optic nerve. In Asbury AK, McKhann G, McDonald IW (Editors), *Diseases of the Nervous System.* Philadelphia: W.S. Saunders, pp. 496 – 506. 1986.

Mitchell DE, Blakemore C: Binocular depth perception and the corpus collosum. *Vision Res.: 10,* 49 – 54, 1970.

Moran J, Desimone R: Selective attention gates visual processing in the extrastriate cortex. *Science; 229,* 782 – 784, 1985.

Neill RA, Fenelon B, Dunlop DB, Dunlop P: The visual evoked response and stereopsis. *Aust. Orthoptic J.: 19,* 25 – 29, 1982.

Parks M: The mono fixation syndrome. *Trans. Am. Ophthalmol. Soc.: 67,* 609 – 657, 1969.

Patterson R, Fox R: The effect of testing method in stereoanomaly. *Vision Res.: 24,* 403 – 408, 1984.

Pennington J: The effect of wavelength on stereoacuity. *Am. J. Optometry: 47,* 288 – 294, 1970.

Poggio GF, Fischer B: Binocular interaction and depth sensitivity in striate and prestriate cortex of behaving rhesus monkey. *J. Neurophysiol.: 40,* 1392 – 1405, 1977.

Poggio GF, Poggio T: The analysis of stereopsis. *Annu. Rev. Neurosci.: 7,* 379 – 412, 1984.

Poggio GF, Talbot WH; Mechanisms of static and dynamic stereopsis in focal cortex of the rhesus monkey. *J. Physiol.: 315,* 465 – 492, 1981.

Pulfrich C: Die stereoskopie im Dienste der isochromen und heterochromen Photometric. *Naturwissenschaften; 10,* 523 – 564; 569 – 601; 714 – 722; 735 – 743; 751 – 761.

Reading RW: *Binocular Vision.* Boston: Butterworths, pp; 21 – 42; 173 – 189; 219 – 250, 1983.

Richards W; Stereopsis and stereoblindness. *Exp. Brain Res.: 10,* 380 – 388, 1970.

Rizzo M, Damasio H: Impairment of stereopsis with focal brain lesions. *Ann. Neurol.: 18,* 147, 1985.

Rizzo M, Hurtig R: Looking but not seeing: the role of attention, perception and eye movements in simultanagnosia. *Neurology; 37,* 1642 – 1648, 1987.

Ross J: Stereopsis by binocular delay. *Nature; 248,* 363 – 364, 1973.

Spitzer H, Desimone R, Moran J: Increased attention enhances both behavioral and neuronal performance. *Science; 240,* 338 – 340, 1988.

Wheatstone C: On some remarkable and hitherto unobserved phenomena of binocular vision. *Philos. Trans., Lond. 8,* 371 – 394, 1838.

Zihl J, Von Cramon Z, Mai N: Selective disturbances of movement vision after bilateral brain damage. *Brain; 106,* 313 – 340, 1983.

Index

Subject index